# 45-Hour
# Continuing Education

## California Real Estate Salesperson & Broker

# 45-Hour
# Continuing Education

## Published by the
## Lumbleau Real Estate School
## 2016 Edition

# Table of Contents

*This is the new required CalBRE course for all salesperson and brokers that are renewing their licenses that expire in 2016 or later. This course is not required for salespersons renewing an original license for the first time.

# Real Estate
# Contracts

## Procedures and Practices

12 Hours of Continuing Education for
Salesperson and Broker License Renewal

**Lumbleau Real Estate School**
23805 Hawthorne Blvd.
Torrance, CA 90505

**DISCLAIMERS**

Although every effort has been made to provide accurate and current information in this text, the ideas, suggestions, general principles, and conclusions presented in this text are subject to local, state, and federal laws and regulations, court cases, and any revisions of same. The author and/or publisher is not engaged in rendering legal, tax, or other professional services. The reader is thus urged to consult with his or her employing broker and/or seek legal counsel regarding any points of law. This publication should not be used as a substitute for competent legal advice.

This course is approved for continuing education credit by the California Bureau of Real Estate. However, this approval does not constitute an endorsement of the views or opinions that are expressed by the course sponsor, instructor, authors, or lecturers.

## Table of Contents

## Chapter One: Contract Writing Fundamentals

**Important Terms**

arbitration
community property
condition precedent
contempt
four corners of the contract
injunction
mediation
nominal damages
punitive damages
short sale
statute of frauds

**Chapter One Learning Objectives**

After successful completion of this chapter, you should be able to complete the following:

- Understand that both spouses must sign a contract that encumbers real estate.

- Explain why it is important to be specific when writing contracts.

- Explain the phrase *time is of the essence.*

- Describe the test that determines fixtures versus real property.

## Contract Fundamentals

### What Is a Contract?

A contract is simply an arrangement between two or more people. Basically, each party gives a promise in exchange for a promise from the other party. If the promises involve the conveyance of real estate, they are put in writing, signatures are affixed, and each party's promise can be enforced.

### Modifications to the Contract

Pursuant to the California Statute of Frauds, in order to be enforceable, a contract for the sale of real property must be in writing and signed by the party to be charged. Any modifications to the contract for the sale of real property must be in writing and signed by the parties as well.

Many disputes between buyers and sellers can be avoided if all contract modifications are put in writing and signed.

### Both Spouses Must Sign

In any transaction for the acquisition, disposition or encumbrance, or an interest in real property, both married partners must sign the contract for the community property to be obligated. (This includes listings as well as purchase contracts.) Both married partners must sign all contracts and other agreements that relate to the transfer of real property, including modifications of the contract.

### Unmarried Co-Owners

The signature of both encumbering parties is also imperative for non-married buyers and sellers. A problem will inevitably arise if the non-signing buyer co-owner elects to withdraw an offer; or a non-signing seller co-owner elects to cancel a listing.

A contract signed by only one party of the community is not enforceable against the other party of the community. However, the signing party may be held liable for breach of contract if the promises made in the contract cannot be completed. In other words, the signing party is bound to the contract, and if the signing party cannot fulfill his or her promise, then he or she will have breached the contractual obligation.

## Importance of Specificity to Avoid Ambiguity

Contracts must be clear and contain specific terms. Avoid ambiguity when altering pre-printed terms or adding additional terms or conditions. A contract is ambiguous when it can be reasonably interpreted in more than one way, and the meaning of the contract cannot be interpreted between the four corners of the contract.

A court will interpret an ambiguous contract term by trying to determine the intent of the parties at the time of the contract. To avoid ambiguity, write out exactly what the parties intend.

> **Instructor Note:** Contingency clauses are a common source of ambiguity and should be drafted precisely by specifying the following:
>
> - The terms of the contingency.
> - The exact time within which the contingency must be fulfilled.
> - The rights and obligations of the parties if the contingency is not met.

## Frequently Used Terminology

Every industry has its own terminology, and the real estate industry is no different. However, some real estate terms are often misunderstood. The following are some common real estate terms and their meanings.

## REALTOR®

The term *REALTOR®* is a federally registered membership mark used by real estate professionals who are members of the NATIONAL ASSOCIATION OF REALTORS®, and agree to abide by a strict code of ethics. Not all licensed real estate professionals are REALTORS®.

**Note:** It is important to understand the pronunciation of the word *REALTOR*. It is not pronounced *rillitor*, as many real estate professionals tend to say.

## Parties

The names of the parties to be bound to the contract should be set forth with specificity. If either party is a corporation, limited liability company, or partnership, all pertinent information about the entity should be included, such as entity's exact name, address, and state of formation. In addition, if either party is an entity, the signer's authority to bind the entity should also be ascertained.

## Competence

The parties should be adults. *Adult* means a person who has attained the age of eighteen years. The parties should also be competent. Generally, in order to invalidate a contract based on incompetency, the owner must have been incompetent at the time of the execution of the contract.

## Literacy Not Necessary

The parties need not be literate or able to read the contract. Absent misinterpretation, the general rule is that an illiterate person who fails to have a contract that he or she signed read to him or her by a person available to read the contract cannot thereafter claim that he or she did not assent to its provisions.

## Time Is of the Essence

Generally, in a contract for a listing of real property or a buyer-broker employment agreement, time is usually not regarded as being *of the essence*. Time should be considered of the essence in a contract when the following apply:

- There is an express recital in the contract.

- From the nature of the subject matter, or fluctuations in the value of or from the terms of the agreement, the treatment of time as nonessential will produce a hardship, and delay by one party in completing or in complying with a term would necessarily subject the other party to serious injury or loss.

- There is an express notice that requires the contract to be performed within a stated, reasonable time given by the non-defaulting party to the defaulting party.

**Instructor Note:** Most REALTOR® pre-printed purchase contracts (although generally not buyer-broker employment agreements or listing contracts) make time of the essence, in the interest of a smooth escrow.

Many items in a real estate purchase contract either have a specific date by which they need to be completed, or are to be completed within a certain number of days after another event. The clock starts ticking and the buyers, sellers, agents, and lenders all have a limited amount of time to complete their duties and close escrow.

## Fixtures

A fixture is an item that was once personal property, but is affixed to the real estate in such a manner as to become a part of the real property. Generally, you can employ a three-part test for determining when personal property, also known as chattel, has become a fixture:

**1)** Annexation to the realty.

**2)** The chattel must have adaptability or application as affixed to the use of the real estate.

**3)** An intention of the party to make the chattel a permanent part of the realty.

The California Residential Purchase Agreement and Joint Escrow Instructions contain a list of fixtures and personal property to be conveyed (on page 3 of 8, in paragraph 8). However, any additions should be written into the contract.

## Buyer-Broker Agreement

The buyer-broker agreement is an employment agreement between a buyer and a broker. It establishes the broker as the buyer's agent, and employs the broker to locate property and negotiate terms that are acceptable to the buyer for the purchase of property. The buyer usually agrees to work exclusively with the broker and the compensation that the buyer is obligated to pay is offset by any compensation the broker receives from the listing agent.

## As-Is

In an *As-Is* contract, the seller is saying that the property will be sold in its existing physical condition and the buyer is taking the property's condition into account when making an offer. The clause does not negate a seller's common-law duty to disclose latent material defects.

## Right of First Refusal

Sometimes called *first right of refusal*, this is a provision in a contract that requires the owner of the property to give another party (usually a tenant) the first opportunity to purchase the property before it is offered for sale to another.

## Title Commitment

The *title commitment* reflects the condition of the title to the property. The commitment tells the buyer whether the taxes and assessments have been paid, whether there are deed restrictions, liens, and/or easements on the property, and what the requirements and conditions are to the issuance of title insurance on the property.

## Title Insurance

There are generally two title policies issued at close of escrow: the owner's policy and the lender's policy. The owner's policy is an insurance policy that protects a homeowner from defects in the home's title, such as a forged deed. The lender's policy protects the lender against the same sort of title defects until the loan is paid.

## Statutory Deficiency Judgment Protection

California protects homeowners against deficiency judgments during a short sale or foreclosure. With the passage of SB 458 (Corbett), signed into law by Governor Brown on July 11, 2011, it is now illegal for lenders to obtain a deficiency judgment against most homeowners after agreeing to settle their debt in a short sale. Deficiency judgment protection is extended to most borrowers on single-family homes, condominiums, and two-to-four-unit apartments in short sale transactions (although there are some exceptions).

The protection covers all parties related to or represented by the lender in the transaction. Therefore, by agreeing to a short sale, the borrower will not be pursued by the lender, the investor on the loan, or the mortgage insurer after the close of escrow.

It also specifically states that the lender cannot require the borrower to "pay any additional compensation, aside from the proceeds of the sale, in exchange for the written consent to the sale." Therefore, the lender cannot legally ask the seller to sign a promissory note or contribute cash at close of escrow.

## Contingencies

A *contingency* is a clause that requires the completion of a certain act before the parties are obligated to perform. A contingency clause is also known as a *condition precedent*. The most common contingency is a financing contingency.

When an express contingency fails, the contract will not be enforced. Contingency clauses must be drafted precisely because contingencies are a common source of ambiguity and frequently become the subject of a dispute.

At a minimum, a contingency clause should specify the terms of the contingency, the exact time within which the contingency must be fulfilled, and the rights and obligations of the parties if the contingency is not met. The following are some important considerations when drafting a contingency:

- What is the contingency?
- Who does it benefit?
- When must the contingency be satisfied? How is the contingency satisfied?
- What happens if the contingency is not satisfied?

As a rule, a party may waive any provision of a contract that is solely intended for his or her benefit. In other words, the buyer can waive a financing contingency, but the seller cannot.

## Escrow Instructions

Escrow instructions constitute a conveyance device designed to carry out the terms of a binding contract of sale that was previously entered into by the parties. Consequently, escrow instructions cannot, in any way, alter the terms of the underlying purchase contract unless the parties specifically and clearly state such alteration or modification in writing with specific reference to the fact that the alteration or modification changes the original contract.

## Boilerplate Language

*Boilerplate* is another word for *pre-printed*. Pre-printed forms are often revised or supplemented to address issues particular to a transaction. Where written provisions of the contract are inconsistent with the boilerplate provisions, the written provisions will prevail.

## Entire Agreement

When a purchase contract contains an *entire agreement* clause, it means that the contract, along with any addenda and attachments, constitute the entire agreement, and supersedes (takes precedence over) any other written or oral agreements. Furthermore, only a signed writing can modify the contract. Failure of the buyer or seller to initial any page of the contract does not affect the validity of its terms.

### Sample Entire Agreement Clause

*This contract and any attached addenda constitute the entire agreement; and it shall supersede any other written or oral agreement between the parties. It can be modified in writing only if signed by both parties. Lastly, initials (or the lack of them) on every page will not affect the validity of the contract.*

## Alternative Dispute Resolution

Alternative dispute resolution (ADR) includes dispute resolution processes and techniques that are a means for disagreeing parties to resolve their dispute outside the court system. Most real estate contracts require the parties to resort to ADR of some type, usually mediation and/or binding arbitration, before permitting the dispute to be tried in the court system.

Due to the increasing caseload of traditional courts, and the costs of litigation, ADR is gaining popularity. In addition, with ADR, the parties have greater control over the selection of the individual(s) who will decide the outcome of their dispute.

## Remedies for Breach

If the parties cannot resolve their dispute with ADR, then it may become necessary to take the matter to the next level, which would be the traditional court system. If this happens, the parties can either settle out of court (usually with the help of attorneys), and agree on a remedy to the non-breaching party, or let a court decide whether there was indeed a breach of contract, and order a remedy for the non-breaching party.

There are three basic types of judicial remedies for breach of a real estate purchase contract:

1) The remedy of damages (also called compensatory damages).

2) The remedy of restitution.

3) Coercive remedies (also called specific performance).

### The Remedy of Damages

The *remedy of damages* is generally monetary compensation to the non-breaching party for any harm he or she has suffered. Money is substituted for that which the plaintiff has lost or suffered. If the plaintiff has suffered no actual monetary harm, nominal damages are awarded.

### The Remedy of Restitution

The *remedy of restitution* is designed to restore the plaintiff to the position that he or she occupied before his or her rights were violated. It is ordinarily measured by the defendant's gains, as opposed to the plaintiff's losses, in order to prevent the defendant from being unjustly enriched by the wrong.

### Coercive Remedies

*Coercive remedies* are orders by the court to force the defendant to do, or to refrain from doing, something to the plaintiff. An injunction backed by the contempt power is one kind of coercive remedy.

This type of remedy is categorized as an equitable remedy, and is employed only if a monetary award would be an inadequate form of relief.

**Instructor Note:** Punitive damages are not generally awarded for breach of a real estate contract, unless the breach is exceptionally egregious.

## Contract Language

While it is not our intent with this course to teach you how to draft contracts from scratch, it is our intent to help you understand a few basic rules to use when you are inserting additional terms into a contract (or filling in blanks).

### Three Simple Rules from Some Experts

**Rule #1**: Never change your language unless you wish to change your meaning and always change your language if you wish to change your meaning. —*Scott J. Burnham, Drafting Contracts 228* (2d ed. 1987).

**Rule #2**: Do not use different words to denote the same things; and don't use the same word to denote different things. —*Legal Drafting Style Manual, Interim Edition, March 1978.*

**Rule #3**: Do not use "and/or." The expression is ambiguous. It has caused many lawsuits. The words "and" and "or" have quite different meanings. You might think that "and/or" means A or B, or both. Not true.

Some courts have even said "and/or" means the court can choose either "and" or "or," whichever the justice of the situation requires. Other courts have come to other conclusions. Don't use the expression. —*Robert C. Dick, Q.C., Legal Drafting* (2d).

### Using the Words *Shall*, *May*, and *Must*

As you already know, a contract includes promises. However, very often, especially when it comes to real estate contracts, a contract includes authorizations (permissions) and conditional promises (obligation only after certain conditions have occurred). Pre-printed contracts employ the words *shall*, *may*, and *must* to denote each type of action.

***Shall* is the Language of Obligation:** The word *shall* denotes a mandatory (required) action. The word can be rightfully used in two contexts:

- To indicate the inevitable: "This too shall pass," or "As you sow, so shall you reap."
- To indicate the imperative: "The buyer shall remain accessible via email or telephone during the term of the contract."

Do not use the word *shall* to express the future. When your contract requires an expression of the future, use *will* instead.

**Incorrect:** "The buyer shall qualify for financing within two weeks after contract acceptance."

**Correct:** "The buyer will qualify for financing within two weeks after contract acceptance."

**The Key to Using *Shall*:** Can you substitute *has a duty* or *is obligated* for *shall*? If so, then *shall* is being used correctly to indicate the language of obligation.

**Using *Shall* (Exercise)**

Fact Scenario: Mary has plans to visit her buyers, John and Sue, to obtain their signatures. When she called her buyers on Thursday to arrange for the visit, she learned that Sue has been ill, and has been unable to leave the house. Mary immediately promised to visit John and Sue at their home on Saturday. She intends to stop at the flower shop on her way and get Sue some get-well flowers. After the phone call, Mary called the escrow company to give the escrow officer an update.

For each of the following statements, determine whether the word *shall* is used correctly. Remember, *shall* is used to denote language of obligation.

**Statement #1:** Mary told the escrow officer not to worry. Sue shall recover in time for the scheduled close of escrow.

**Q:** Correct or Incorrect?
**A:** Incorrect. If the phrase *has a duty* is substituted for the word *shall*, it does not make sense. In this sentence, *shall* is used to indicate inevitability, which is incorrect usage.

**Statement #2:** Mary shall go to the market before going to John and Sue's home.

**Q:** Correct or Incorrect?
**A:** Incorrect. Although Mary plans to stop at the market before going to John and Sue's home, she has not promised to do so and therefore does not have a duty to do so. She is not obligated.

**Statement #3:** Mary shall visit the buyers on Saturday.

**Q:** Correct or Incorrect?
**A:** Correct. Mary made a promise, so she *has a duty* or *is obligated* to visit the buyers on Saturday.

**Statement #4:** Mary shall pay for the get-well flowers with her debit card.

**Q:** Correct or Incorrect?
**A:** Incorrect. In this sentence, *shall* is used to indicate a future event, and is not the language of obligation.

***May* is the Language of Authorization (Permitted, but not Required):** *May* indicates permission; when someone is allowed (permitted), but not obligated to do something. Just as *shall* is reserved to indicate the language of obligation, *may* is reserved to indicate the language of authorization.

**The Key to Using *May*:** Can you substitute *has permission* or *is allowed* for *may*? If so, then *may* is being used correctly to indicate the language of authorization.

**Using *May* (Exercise)**

Fact Scenario: Bob calls owner-broker Wendy at ABC Realty, and solicits the property management services of ABC Realty. Wendy, who will assign one of the certified property managers in her brokerage to be the property manager for Bob's property, has negotiated the following terms in the property management agreement: (1) Bob has the right to inspect the property management accounting records (upon written notice), and (2) Wendy has agreed to provide Bob with a monthly accounting of revenue and expenses collected from the rental property, and a monthly check made payable to Bob for the rents collected, less the property management commission.

For each of the following statements, determine whether the word *may* is used correctly. Remember, *may* is used to denote the language of authorization.

**Statement #1:** Wendy may provide Bob with monthly accounting records.

**Q:** Correct or Incorrect?
**A:** Incorrect. *May* is not used in this statement to indicate the language of authorization; instead, *may* indicates permission. Wendy does not have permission to provide monthly accounting records; she has an obligation to do so. The proper operative language for this statement is *shall*.

**Statement #2:** Bob may inspect the property management accounting records (upon written notice).

**Q:** Correct or Incorrect?
**A:** Correct. *May* is used correctly in this statement to indicate the language of authorization. Bob is permitted to inspect the property management accounting records (upon written notice).

**Must is the Language of Contingency:** *Must* is reserved to indicate a contingency or condition precedent. If an action is conditioned upon some prior action, then *must* is used to indicate the requirement. For example:

> *The seller must give written permission to the broker to place a listing sign on the seller's property, before the broker can place the sign.*

For the broker to place the sign, a condition must be fulfilled—the seller must give written permission. In this case, the seller is not contractually obligated to give the written permission, but it is a condition precedent to the broker placing a sign.

**The Key to Using *Must*:** Ask whether the party has to do A before B will happen. If so, then *must* is being used correctly to indicate the language of contingency.

**Using *Must* (Exercise)**

**Fact Scenario:** The bank has agreed to extend a loan to Glenda and Roy for the purchase of their new home. However, the bank insists that Glenda and Roy pledge their home as security. The bank may not foreclose on the property unless and until it has given Glenda and Roy written notice default and 10 days to cure the default. The loan contract provides that a default occurs if Glenda and Roy (1) fail to make a timely monthly payment; or (2) fail to keep homeowners insurance on the home.

For each of the following statements, determine whether the word *must* is used correctly. Remember, *must* is used to denote the language of contingency.

**Statement #1:** Glenda and Roy must pay in a timely manner.

**Q:** Correct or Incorrect?
**A:** Incorrect. Glenda and Roy have a duty to pay in a timely manner. This statement should use *shall*, the language of obligation, and not the language of condition precedent.

**Statement #2:** The bank must give notice of default to Glenda and Roy before foreclosing on the house.

**Q:** Correct or Incorrect?
**A:** Correct. This statement sets forth a condition precedent, so use of *must* is correct. Written notice of an event of default is a condition precedent of foreclosure. The bank is not obligated to foreclose; however, if it wishes to foreclose, it is required to give notice first.

**Statement #3:** The bank must give Glenda and Roy the loan.

**Q:** Correct or Incorrect?

**A:** Incorrect. According to the fact scenario, giving Glenda and Roy a loan is not a condition precedent to any other event. This is not the language of condition precedent. This is probably the language of authorization. The bank *may* give Glenda and Roy a loan.

**Statement #4:** The bank must give notice if Glenda and Roy fail to insure the home.

**Q:** Correct or Incorrect?

**A:** Incorrect. This one is a close call. The bank is not required to give notice unless it would like to foreclose. If the bank does not wish to foreclose, the bank is not required to give notice.

**QUIZZES ARE MANDATORY**

CalBRE regulations now require the submission of chapter quizzes before you can access the final examination. You must log in and submit the chapter quizzes online before you can access the final examination. After submitting the last chapter quiz, you will see a link to the final examination. You were issued a Personal Identification Number (PIN) and login instructions when you enrolled.

## Chapter One Quiz

1.      Any modifications to the contract for the sale of real property must be _____.

(a)     in writing
(b)     in writing and signed by the parties
(c)     backed by a fingerprint and blood sample from the parties
(d)     disregarded, because modifications automatically invalidate a real estate purchase
        contract

2.      Time should be considered *of the essence* in a contract when:

(a)     there is an express recital in the contract.
(b)     delay by one party in completing or in complying with a term would necessarily subject
        the other party to serious injury or loss.
(c)     there is an express notice that requires the contract to be performed within a stated,
        reasonable time.
(d)     Any of the above.

3.      With regard to title insurance policies, all of the following statements are true EXCEPT:

(a)     There are generally two title policies issued at close of escrow: the owner's policy and the
        lender's policy.
(b)     The lender's policy is an insurance policy that protects a homeowner from defects in the
        title to the home, such as a forged deed.
(c)     The lender's policy protects the lender until the loan is paid.
(d)     The lender's policy protects the lender from defects in the title to the home, such as a
        forged deed.

4.      All of the following are true with regard to Alternative Dispute Resolution (ADR) EXCEPT:

(a)     With ADR, the prevailing party can expect a judicial remedy.
(b)     ADR is less costly.
(c)     ADR is gaining popularity.
(d)     With ADR, the parties have greater control over the selection of the individual or
        individuals who will decide their dispute.

5.      If you can substitute the phrase *has permission* or *is allowed*, then you should use the word
        _____ to indicate the language of authorization when you are adding additional terms to a
        contract (or filling in the blanks).

        (a)      shall
        (b)      may
        (c)      must
        (d)      might

6.      A contract signed by only one party of the community property interest is:

        (a)      not enforceable against the other party of the community property.
        (b)      not real.
        (c)      not readable by humans.
        (d)      enforceable against the entire community property interest.

7.      The parties to a contract need not be:

        (a)      literate or able to read the contract.
        (b)      present when their signature is affixed to the contract.
        (c)      human.
        (d)      competent or able to understand the contract.

8.      The title commitment reflects the condition of the title to the property, and tells the buyer all of the
        following EXCEPT:

        (a)      Whether the taxes and assessments have been paid.
        (b)      Whether there are deed restrictions.
        (c)      Whether there are liens or easements on the property.
        (d)      The sales price of the property when the current owner purchased the property.

9.      _____ is designed to restore the plaintiff to the position he or she occupied before his or her
        rights were violated.

        (a)      The judicial remedy of restitution
        (b)      The judicial remedy of damages
        (c)      The coercive type of remedy
        (d)      The Alternative Dispute Resolution

10.     *May* is the language of authorization. It denotes a _____ action.

        (a)      permitted
        (b)      mandatory
        (c)      contingent
        (d)      prohibited

## Chapter Two: The Purchase Contract

**Important Terms**

comparables
disclaimer
earnest money
kickbacks
legal description
liquidated damages
quitclaim
REO properties
rescind
*time is of the essence* clause

**Chapter Two Learning Objectives**

After successful completion of this chapter, you should be able to complete the following:

- State important aspects regarding the identification of the parties to a real estate purchase contract.

- State important aspects regarding the identification of the premises that are the subject of a real estate purchase contract.

- Identify the sections of a purchase contract that measure a buyer's readiness, willingness, and ability.

- State the various regulations associated with the funds needed to close escrow.

- State the ways to describe the details associated with possession of the property, both before the close of escrow and after the close of escrow.

- Describe the various addenda associated with the purchase contract.

### The Parties and the Premises

#### Buyers

As discussed in the previous chapter, the parties to be bound to the contract should be identified with specificity.

Remember this general rule: *It takes two to sell, and one to buy.*

In most purchase contracts, the buyer and seller are identified at the beginning of the contract. Most of the time, when writing a purchase contract, you will be sitting with the buyer, so buyer identification is pretty simple.

**Use Full Names:** Identify the buyer(s) with full names, as the names appear on the buyer's driver's license, passport or 1040 tax return. Although the general rule is that with regard to a married couple, it takes two to sell and one to buy, it is recommended that you have both members of the married couple put their names on the purchase contract (unless circumstances prevent them from doing this).

For example, in the case of one spouse buying because he or she is more qualified (perhaps the other spouse has had bad credit), the spouse who is buying can always add the other spouse's name to the deed after the escrow closes.

**Unmarried Buyers:** If there is more than one buyer and the buyers are not a married couple, make sure to include the full names of all buyers (unless circumstances prevent this), because this agreement will typically become a part of the escrow instructions.

#### Sellers

Remember this general rule: *It takes two signatures to sell, and one to buy.* The signatures of all owners are required in any transaction to sell. If there is more than one seller, make sure to include all full names.

> **Instructor Note:** When you are writing the offer, you will likely be sitting with the buyer. You may not know the name of the seller or sellers. You could verify the seller's names with the listing agent, but that may not be reliable, as the listing may have been signed by only one spouse. Verify the name(s) of the seller or sellers by looking up the property at the local County Recorder's office or Assessor's office.

**Previous Owners (Former Spouses):** A spouse or other previous owner might need to consent to the sale of a home they previously quitclaimed to the current owner. A title company may not recognize the quitclaim transfer of ownership and require a new disclaimer deed to be signed by all previous owners.

Generally, this occurs in divorce cases, because the title company may not be able to warranty that there is no community interest in the property that is shared with the former spouse.

Although the real property may be in only one spouse's name, there might still be a community interest in the property. Any income earned during the course of the marriage by either spouse is community property; therefore, if any of the community income is used to make loan payments on the home, repairs on the home, etc., the community will have an interest in the property even though the property is titled in only one spouse's name.

## The Premises

**Property Description:** The property must be identified so that it can be ascertained. Ideally, property should be identified by legal description, although legal descriptions can be very lengthy and cumbersome to write.

**Assessor's Parcel Number:** Most pre-printed purchase contracts contain a space for you to insert the assessor's parcel number. It is used as another way of identifying the property in cases where there may be a typo or misspelled word in the property description.

## Outlining the Terms of the Offer

**Ready, Willing, Able, and Earnest:** When presented with an offer, the first question on the seller's mind is, "Exactly how ready, willing, able, and earnest are these prospective buyers?"

**Four very big words.** A buyer who is perfectly ready, willing, able, and earnest is one who meets the following criteria:

- The buyer wants to buy now.
- The buyer is willing to unconditionally pay exactly what the seller is asking.
- The buyer has the cash in hand.

The chances of finding a buyer who is perfectly ready, perfectly willing, perfectly able, and perfectly earnest are slim to none. What you will often find are buyers that have the potential to become ready, willing, able, and earnest. When you present an offer from a buyer, the first question on the seller's mind should be, "Exactly how ready, willing, able, and earnest is the buyer?"

## Close of Escrow Date: How Readiness Is Measured

How ready is the buyer? In other words, when can the buyer close? Tomorrow? Today? In thirty days? Obviously, if the buyer must obtain financing, the buyer is not ready. The buyer may have good potential to become ready, but is not ready in the true sense of the word.

The proposed close of escrow date is how readiness is measured. The exact date of the proposed close of escrow should be specified. Also, if the purchase contract contains a *time is of the essence* clause, then the close of escrow date is a material term, and once accepted, must be met.

## Proposed Purchase Price: How Willingness Is Measured

If you wanted to reduce the price of your property down to a dollar, you would probably find a lot of willing buyers.

**The question is not "Is the buyer willing to buy the property?"** Rather, the question is "Is the buyer willing to purchase the property for the price that the seller is asking?" The mere presentation of a bona fide purchase offer shows some measure of willingness. The proposed purchase price in the offer tells us exactly how willing the buyer is. The closer the buyer's proposed purchase is to the asking price, the more willing the buyer is. If the buyer offers exactly or more than what the seller is asking, then the buyer is perfectly willing. However, under most market conditions, the buyer will not offer exactly what the seller is asking. If the proposed purchase price is so low, in comparison to the asking price, that the seller will not accept it, we would say that the buyer is not willing.

### Method of Payment: How Ability to Buy Is Measured

If the buyer intends to pay cash, and has that cash within immediate reach, then that buyer is perfectly able to buy. If, however, the buyer must refinance another piece of real estate to obtain the cash, then that buyer is not perfectly able to buy. The buyer might very well have good potential to become able, but the buyer is not able at this time. If the purchaser intends to borrow a portion of the purchase price, and has been pre-qualified for a loan, that buyer is still not able in the true sense of the word. Instead, the buyer has good potential to become able. *Pre-qualified* does not mean *Qualified*.

**Earnest Money:** Buyers show that they are earnest in their offer to purchase by promising to deposit funds into an escrow account for the benefit of the transaction. If the buyer is promising to deposit earnest money (in California, this is referred to as the *initial deposit*) in conjunction with the offer, it must be deposited (either into a broker trust account or into an escrow depository) within a reasonable amount of time. Most states require deposit within no more than three days.

The amount of earnest money that the buyers are submitting with the offer should be a reasonable amount. What is reasonable depends on many factors, such as market conditions, length of time the property has been on the market, etc.

In most real estate purchase contracts, the amount of earnest money is also the amount of liquidated damages the seller will receive in the event of a buyer default. In California, according to the pre-printed California Association of REALTORS® residential purchase contract, the maximum liquidated damages is 3% of the purchase price. Therefore, this is generally the amount most buyers will promise to deposit to show that they are earnest in their offer.

## Close of Escrow

### Close of Escrow Date

**Note:** Look at a calendar BEFORE you choose the closing date.

Generally, the purchase contract becomes a part of the escrow instructions, since the duties of both parties are outlined in the contract. By the date of the close of escrow, the parties are required to fulfill all of their obligations and deliver to the escrow holder everything required to close escrow, which includes the following:

- The buyer delivers earnest money, down payments, and additional deposits.
- The lender delivers the loan proceeds.
- The seller delivers a clear and marketable title, along with all other required closing obligations, such as the owner's title insurance policy.

The close of escrow is often a renegotiating point, and oftentimes will be seen in a counter offer as an unacceptable part of the original contract. Either it is too soon (the sellers need more time), or it is too late (the buyers need more time), although it is usually the latter.

When writing the close of escrow date on a purchase offer, make sure to write a particular date. Do not estimate the number of days to complete the escrow. In other words, don't write *45 days*; rather, look at a calendar and see what the date will be in 45 days and list the date as specified: month, day, and year.

If the close of escrow date that you specify happens to fall on a holiday (when the escrow company or recording office is closed), the general rule is that the actual closing date will occur on the next business day. This does not make the contract voidable; however, it can still cause problems.

**Instructor Note:** Look at a calendar BEFORE you specify the date, and make sure the date you choose is a day that both the escrow office and the county recorder are open for business.

## Funds

Keep in mind that the funds should be delivered to escrow in the form of a cashier's check or money wire to the escrow holder a day or two (three days is optimum) before the scheduled close of escrow date to allow the escrow company time to prepare for the closing and complete all accounting as necessary. Seventy percent of the states in the country now have *Good Funds* laws that regulate the type of funds a title company can accept. Although independent escrow companies are not subject to this law per se, they become subject to it if they depend on the services of a title company.

### Unacceptable Forms of Payment

If funds are not received in the proper form, the close of escrow could be delayed at least one day and as many as ten days while the escrow company confirms that the funds are "good" or cleared. In most states, escrow companies cannot accept the following:

- Money orders, because stop payments can be placed on these after issuance.

- Cash, because escrow companies have no way to securely handle large sums of cash.

- Foreign currency, because an escrow company cannot be responsible for exchange rates.

- ACH transfers, because deposits into the escrow company depository must be associated with a specific escrow number and a specific branch account, and ACH transfers do not make this possible.

### Acceptable Forms of Payment

Money wire of funds is always okay, regardless of the amount. However, with regard to a cashier's check, most California escrow companies follow guidelines similar to the following:

If the buyer's deposit for closing is less than $500,000.00,

- Payment may be made in the form of a cashier's or official check drawn on a California Bank or Savings and Loan.

- These funds must be on deposit 24 hours before the escrow officer can authorize the recording of the documents to close escrow.

If the buyer's deposit for closing is for $500,000.00 or more,

- The funds MUST be deposited by wire transfer. Wired funds are not subject to the clearance procedures that can delay a closing. This form of deposit is by far the most efficient for all parties involved in the transaction.

## Details of Possession

### Possession

Typically, the seller will agree to deliver possession and keys to the buyer immediately upon close of escrow. However, if the seller needs more time in the property, any timeframe can be specified by simply handwriting the timeframe into the offer/contract. (Remember, if this is a modification of the original contract, both parties must agree in writing to the modification.)

**Note:** The terms of possession should be negotiated at the time that the original contract is created. Negotiating the terms of possession at the last minute creates undue pressure for all parties.

### Possession Agreements

Possession agreements are typically required when the date of occupancy does not coincide with the date of closing. Negotiating the terms of possession is much easier when the terms are discussed at the time that the original contract is created. Too often, when terms are discussed last minute, undue pressure is created for sellers, buyers, and their real estate brokers.

The following are some typical examples of when possession agreements may be utilized:

**Pre-Possession Agreements:** A home is vacant and the buyer would like to occupy the home prior to closing. Most brokers really frown on this, because if the buyer is in possession, and the seller is still the owner of record, the seller is liable for anything that happens to the buyer on the seller's property. However, this arrangement can reduce some of the seller's costs, mainly yard maintenance and utilities. It also can generate income for the seller in the form of rent. In the event that this is necessary or desired, the listing broker should do the following:

- Counsel the seller and buyer to seek legal advice regarding the risks associated with pre-possession.

- Advise the listing party (seller) to insist on a pre-possession agreement from the buyer. In essence, a pre-possession agreement is like a lease. While the buyer is in possession, the buyer is a tenant.

**Post-Possession Agreements:** A seller is building a new home, but the new home is not completed and ready for occupancy. In this case, the seller may choose to close on their existing home and remain in it until their new home is completed, which delays the buyer's move-in date. Another common scenario occurs when several buyers and sellers are transitioning from one house to another. It may not be feasible for everyone to move in and move out on the same day, because moving companies cannot always accommodate everyone's exact moving date. In this situation, buyers and sellers must work together to accommodate one another.

**A Caveat about Possession Agreements:** Possession agreements need to be drafted in advance of escrow closing. Thus, buyers and sellers need to properly anticipate closing and occupancy dates far enough in advance. Some issues that may arise are the following:

- The buyer may fail to close on the property.

- Once moved in, the buyer may find fault with the property, and refuse to close.

- The buyer could possibly damage the property.

**Instructor Note:** Prior to taking possession, all parties should perform a final walkthrough inspection to make sure everything is in order. It may even be a good idea to videotape the condition of the property prior to pre- or post-possession.

### Identifying the Addenda

#### Addenda Incorporated

Most Associations of REALTORS® have several pre-printed addenda that were drafted to be included in the Association of REALTORS® pre-printed purchase contract. The most common pre-printed addenda are listed and described here.

**Blank Addendum:** The blank addendum is used to add additional terms to an existing contract if there is not sufficient room on the contract. The blank addendum is essentially blank lines.

**Additional Compensation Agreement Addendum:** This addendum is used by agents who seek to disclose a fee received for services that are related to the transaction. (Compliance with RESPA.)

RESPA regulations prohibit a salesperson or broker from directly or indirectly accepting any compensation, including rebate or other consideration, for any goods or services provided to a person if the goods or services are related to or result from a real estate transaction, without that person's prior written acknowledgement of the compensation. This prohibition does not apply to compensation paid to a broker by a broker who represents a party in the transaction.

> **Instructor Note:** This rule originates from the RESPA regulations that prohibit kickbacks. The theory is that compensation given to a licensee for services that are provided to someone else will be *backcharged* to someone. Generally, the person who bears the brunt of the kickback is the client for whom the services were provided. Kickbacks to a licensee increase the cost of settlement services.

**Appraisal Contingency Notice Addendum:** There was a time when the market value was defined as the price a willing and able buyer would pay and a seller would accept in an arm's-length transaction.

Not the case anymore. It would appear that market value is now determined by underwriting requirements, which tend to be conservative and in some cases are not in synch with market realities. The Appraisal Contingency Notice addendum allows agents to help their clients to either cancel the contract and receive a refund of the earnest money (initial deposit) or waive the contingency when the appraisal comes in at a lower estimated market value than the sales price.

This addendum comes on the heels of Fannie Mae's introduction of new residential appraisal guidelines a couple of years ago (see downloadable guidelines, below). As a result of these new guidelines, there are many transactions that do not close escrow because the listing does not appraise for the price agreed upon in the purchase contract.

Typically, with REO properties, the lender does not have control over who performs the appraisal. It is very likely that the appraiser who performs the appraisal will be from out of the area and out of touch with the subtleties of the local market. When this is the case, the appraisers may choose inappropriate comparables, and the resulting estimated market value may fall below that which a knowledgeable buyer is willing to pay. As a result, the loan may not be approved.

**Example:** Broker Wayne writes an offer for Heather and Brian Buyers. The offer proposes a purchase price of $500,000. Heather and Brian need loan for 80 percent of the purchase price, or $400,000. The house appraises for $475,000. If the buyers qualify financially, the lender will give them a loan, but only for 80 percent of the appraised value, or $380,000. The buyers need to come up with an extra $20,000. If the contract includes an appraisal contingency, Heather and Brian can rescind the contract without penalty. Without an appraisal contingency, the earnest money deposit would be at risk, because canceling the contract would be construed as a buyer breach.

**Water Well Addendum:** This addendum is used when there is a domestic water well on the property.

**H.O.A./Condominium/Planned Community Addendum:** This addendum is a disclosure to the buyer, according to statutory regulations, about what information the buyer should receive, and when the buyer should receive it.

**Lead-Based Paint Disclosure:** As you know, this disclosure must be presented to the buyer for all properties built prior to 1978. For some FHA loans, the pamphlet *Protect Your Family from Lead in the Home* (downloadable below) is also required. To protect families from exposure to lead from paint, dust, and soil, Congress passed the Residential Lead-Based Paint Hazard Reduction Act of 1992, also known as Title X. Section 1018 of this law directed HUD and EPA to require the disclosure of known information on lead-based paint and lead-based paint hazards before the sale or lease of most housing built before 1978. Congress chose not to cover post-1977 housing because the Consumer Product Safety Commission banned the use of lead-based paint for residential use in 1978.

**What is lead?** Lead is a highly toxic metal that was used for many years in products found in and around our homes. Lead may cause a range of health effects, from behavioral problems and learning disabilities, to seizures and death. Children 6 years old and under are most at risk because their bodies are growing quickly. Research suggests that one of the primary sources of lead exposure for most children is deteriorating lead-based paint, lead-contaminated dust, and lead-contaminated residential soil.

**Who is vulnerable to lead exposure?** Infants, children, pregnant women, and fetuses are more vulnerable to lead exposure than others because the lead is more easily absorbed into growing bodies and their tissues are more sensitive to the damaging effects of lead. Because of a child's smaller body weight, an equal concentration of lead is more damaging to a child than it would be to an adult.

**Addendum Showing Status of Loan (Loan Status Addendum):** This addendum may accompany a purchase offer, in order to disclose to the seller and seller's agent the status of the buyer's loan application. It is a good idea to attach such an addendum to a purchase offer. This addendum should contain the name of the buyer's lender and the loan officer's contact information, and if possible, a statement that the buyers have consulted the lender and have been pre-qualified. Attaching this addendum conveys the message that the buyer is earnest in the offer, and has already taken preliminary steps necessary to purchase the property.

**Septic Tank Addendum:** This addendum is used in cases where the property is served by a septic tank or alternative waste disposal system. It is a disclosure to the buyer that an onsite wastewater treatment facility exists. Most states require this form because they recognize that undesirable history that is not revealed to the buyer may also be grounds for damages or rescission of the contract. This requirement for disclosure is balanced somewhat by the buyer's responsibility to do some due diligence. The basic rule is that if the information is readily available to the buyer, the buyer may not be able to sue the seller for misrepresentation or nondisclosure. However, the presence of a septic tank is not readily apparent to a buyer, so it is a major cause of lawsuits.

**Note:** Nondisclosure of the presence of septic tanks on residential property is one of the most popular causes of legal action.

**Assumption/Carryback Addendum:** This addendum is used when the seller is willing to carry a loan or the buyer wants to assume the seller's loan. The form includes provisions for verification of the buyer's creditworthiness by requesting such information from the buyer as a credit report, verification of employment, and verification of funds available for the down payment.

> **Instructor Note:** Most lenders incorporate into their promissory note a due-on-sale clause that may preclude the transfer of title, unless the loan is paid off. While there is the possibility of loan assumption, it is rare.

**Buyer Contingency Addendum:** This addendum is used when the contract is contingent upon the sale and closing of the buyer's property. Typically, this form will provide two options:

1) One option for the transaction in which the buyer's property is listed (buyer has not yet entered into a contract for sale).

2) Another option for the transaction in which the buyer has entered into a contract for sale, but the transaction has not yet closed escrow.

In the case of option #1, the contract is contingent on an accepted offer to purchase the buyer's property by a specified date. If the buyers accept an offer to purchase the buyer's property, the buyer is obligated to deliver specified sale documents to the seller for review. Unless the seller cancels the contract, it becomes contingent upon the successful sale and close of escrow on the buyer's property.

If the seller accepts a subsequent offer to purchase the property before the sale of the buyer's property, the seller is obligated to deliver a notice to the buyer. This notice gives the buyer a specified number of days to deliver to the seller a written agreement to remove the contingency, and written documentation from the buyer's lender that the buyer can close escrow by the agreed-upon date, even without the proceeds from the sale of the buyer's property.

In the case of option #2, the contract is contingent on the successful close of escrow on the buyer's property. The buyer is obligated to deliver specified sale documents to the seller within a specified period of time after the close of escrow on the buyer's property.

**Short Sale Addendum:** Because a short sale is contingent upon the seller's lender agreeing to accept less than the amount owed, the short sale addendum has two primary purposes:

- It clarifies the contingency.

- It sets forth the time period that the buyer is willing to wait for short sale approval.

Short sale approval typically takes from 30 days to 3–4 months or longer. Although the seller must reasonably cooperate with the lenders, the seller is not obligated to close the short sale if the lender requires a contribution from the seller. The short sale addendum has many secondary purposes:

**With Regard to Inspections and Contingencies,** the buyer should have an option about when to commence with the inspection period. The following two options should be available:

- Commencement may occur immediately upon acceptance, or

- Commencement may occur upon short-sale approval by the seller's lender or lenders.

**With Regard to Buyer's Earnest Money Deposit,** the buyer generally has a few options about how to release the earnest money deposit. The following two options should be available:

- The buyer can deposit the earnest money to the payee (escrow depository or broker trust account) upon seller's acceptance as stated in the contract, or

- The buyer can withhold the earnest money deposit until the seller's lender or lenders approves the short sale.

**With Regard to Guaranteed Approval,** the short sale addendum typically provides that there is no guarantee that the seller's bank will approve the short sale. Furthermore, the seller's bank may demand to see all of the offers and may choose a different offer.

**With Regard to the Buyer and Seller Incurring Costs and Inconvenience,** most short sale addendums explain that the buyer and seller may incur certain costs pursuant to the contract. Some of those costs may seem unfair, and may customarily be the responsibility of the buyer's lender (or seller's lender), but the lenders refuse to pay these costs.

**With Regard to the Seller Continuing to Show the Home and Send Other Offers to the Seller's Lender,** the short sale addendum will sometimes allow the seller to continue to show the home and send other offers to the bank. This means that if the seller receives a higher offer, the seller can ask the bank to accept the higher offer in lieu of the offer the seller has already signed.

**With Regard to the Short Sale Harming the Seller's Credit Rating,** every short sale addendum should contain a statement that the listing agent has advised the seller to seek professional advice about how short sales affect the seller's credit, including legal or tax consequences.

**Non-Refundable Earnest Money Addendum:** This addendum makes the buyer's earnest money (initial deposit) non-refundable, after a certain number of days. In this addendum, the buyer acknowledges that the earnest money is not refundable, regardless of the reason for cancellation of contract (even if the property fails to appraise for the sales price).

**Corporate Relocation Approval Addendum:** The seller or buyer is in the process of corporate relocation. The seller has accepted this offer contingent upon the corporate relocation happening as expected. Likewise, the buyer has presented this offer contingent upon the corporate relocation happening as expected.

**Survey Required Addendum:** This addendum provides that the parties agree to have the property surveyed, and the seller agrees to remedy any defects, or compensate the buyer for the defects.

**Tax-Deferred Exchange Addendum:** This addendum should be included if either the seller or buyer intend to enter into a tax-deferred exchange pursuant to I.R.C Code §1031. Additional costs in connection with any such tax-deferred exchange will be borne by the party who enters into the exchange.

**As-Is Addendum:** This addendum is used when the seller is selling the property in its existing condition and the seller makes no warranties to the buyer about the following:

- The condition of the property, including the operation of the appliances, and heating and cooling system.
- The fitness of the premises for any particular use or purpose.

The buyer is also advised to conduct independent inspections and investigations. The seller is not obligated to correct any defects revealed in the investigations, but the buyer retains the right to cancel the contract if the investigations or inspections reveal items that are disapproved. Typically, an as-is addendum obligates the seller to maintain the premises in substantially the same condition as on the date of contract acceptance, and remove all debris that is not a part of the sale from the premises.

**Instructor Note:** An as-is addendum, no matter how well worded, will relieve the seller or the broker of their liability to disclose known material facts or those that should be known.

**QUIZZES ARE MANDATORY**: Please log in and submit the chapter quizzes online.

## Chapter 2 Quiz

1.      Most pre-printed purchase contracts contain a space for you to insert the _____, which is another way of identifying the property in cases where there may be a typo or misspelled word in the property description.

      (a)      color and style of the home
      (b)      description of the homes in the area of the subject property
      (c)      assessor's parcel number of the subject property
      (d)      driving directions

2.      If your seller wanted to reduce the price of the property down to one dollar, there would probably be a lot of willing buyers. However, the question is not "Is the buyer willing to purchase the property?" Rather, the question is "Is the buyer willing to purchase the property for the price the seller is asking?" Which of the following is CORRECT regarding the willingness of the buyer to purchase?

      (a)      The proposed closing date tells us exactly how willing the buyer is.
      (b)      The proposed purchase price in the offer tells us exactly how willing the buyer is.
      (c)      The proposed method of payment tells us exactly how willing the buyer is.
      (d)      There is no measure of willingness.

3.      The parties are required to fulfill, by the date of the close of escrow, all of their obligations and deliver to the escrow holder everything required to close escrow. The _____ delivers earnest money, down payments, and additional deposits.

      (a)      lender
      (b)      seller
      (c)      buyer
      (d)      property

4.      By the date of the close of escrow, the parties are required to fulfill all of their obligations and deliver to the escrow holder everything required to close escrow. The _____ delivers the clear and marketable title, along with all other required closing obligations, such as the owner's title insurance policy.

      (a)      lender
      (b)      seller
      (c)      buyer
      (d)      property

5.      Which of the following types of payment might an escrow company refuse to accept and why?

      (a)      The escrow company might refuse to accept payment of closing funds in the form of a money order because stop payments can be placed on these after issuance.
      (b)      The escrow company might refuse to accept payment of closing funds in the form of cash because escrow companies have no way to securely handle large sums of cash.
      (c)      The escrow company might refuse to accept payment of closing funds in the form of an ACH transfer because deposits into the escrow company depository must be associated with a specific escrow number and a specific branch's account, and ACH transfers do not make this possible.
      (d)      All of the above are types of payments that an escrow company might refuse to accept.

6.  Possession agreements need to be drafted in advance of escrow closing. Thus, buyers and
    sellers need to properly anticipate closing and occupancy dates far enough in advance. What is a
    potential issue that may arise with regard to possession agreements?

    (a)    The buyer may fail to close on the property.
    (b)    Once moved in, the buyer may find fault with the property, and refuse to close.
    (c)    The buyer could possibly damage the property, and the seller would be liable.
    (d)    All of the above are issues that might arise.

7.  With regard to the additional compensation agreement, which federal Act prohibits a salesperson
    or broker from accepting any compensation, including rebate or other consideration, directly or
    indirectly, for any goods or services provided to a person if the goods or services are related to or
    result from a real estate transaction, without that person's prior written acknowledgement of the
    compensation?

    (a)    Fair Housing Act
    (b)    Truth in Lending Act
    (c)    Good Funds Law
    (d)    Real Estate Settlement Procedures Act (RESPA)

8.  When did Congress pass the Residential Lead-Based Paint Hazard Reduction Act?

    (a)    1992
    (b)    1978
    (c)    1977
    (d)    1982

9.  The _____ is used when the contract is contingent upon the sale and closing of the buyer's
    property.

    (a)    no-way-no-how addendum
    (b)    are-you-kidding-me addendum
    (c)    buyer contingency addendum
    (d)    short sale addendum

10. Is it possible to include an addendum that causes the earnest money (initial deposit) to be
    non-refundable after a certain number of days (if such a provision is not already written into
    the pre-printed contract)?

    (a)    Yes
    (b)    No

## Chapter Three: The Purchase Contract

### Important Terms

CLTV
conventional loan
discount points
FICO score
foreign person
LTV
PMI
REO
VA loan

### Chapter Three Learning Objectives

After successful completion of this chapter, you should be able to complete the following:

- Clearly identify the fixtures that are conveyed with the property, as well as any personal property that is conveyed with the property.

- Clearly outline the financing contingency on the real estate purchase contract.

- Clearly specify the buyer obligations with regard to financing.

- State three types of loans, and provide a brief explanation of each.

- List the steps for calculating loan costs.

- State the purpose of the commitment for title insurance, and identify the information contained therein.

- Explain the purpose of the tax prorations section of the purchase contract.

- Briefly explain FIRPTA and how it affects the real estate purchase contract and escrow instructions.

## Distinguishing Fixtures and Personal Property

### Fixtures and Personal Property

To avoid ambiguity, the contract should specifically identify all items that are to be conveyed with the property. The California Residential Purchase Agreement and Joint Escrow Instructions contain a list of fixtures to be conveyed, but any additional fixtures included in the conveyance should be added to the contract.

**Note:** Responsibility for this falls on the agent.

By definition, any existing fixtures stay with the real property. In addition, by definition, any personal property that is in the real property would not be included in the conveyance. However, many conveyances do not include fixtures, and many conveyances include personal property.

In any case, the purchase contract should clarify what is included and what is not included. If there are additional items of personal property that convey with the real property, the contract should specify that these items are of no value, and will not be considered of value by a real estate appraiser.

### Fixtures and REO Property

Missing fixtures is a common occurrence, especially in today's world of REO sales where the seller is typically a bank. Oftentimes, the defaulted promissor (person whose home was foreclosed) was bitter when they vacated the property, and took some of the smaller fixtures (such as toilets, kitchen appliances, water softeners, reverse osmosis filters) out of the property.

Generally, in a contract for the sale of REO property, the seller (who is a bank) presents lengthy addenda (sometimes as long as 30 pages), and will not accept the offer until the buyer reads and accepts all of the terms contained in the addenda. Those addenda contain very detailed descriptions about the seller NOT BEING LIABLE for missing fixtures. Furthermore, the buyer of the bank-owned property is oftentimes an investor who might not even see the property before close of escrow, and not be aware of the missing fixtures. Thus, responsibility falls on the buyer's agent to make certain that the buyer is aware of and acknowledges that the seller has made no warranties, and the property may not be readily inhabitable or marketable.

### Leased Property or Owned Property

When fixtures (such as water softeners, reverse osmosis filters, hot water heaters, etc.) are leased, they will generally be returned to the vendor (lessor). If the buyers do not know that these fixtures are leased, they expect these items to be present in the property when they take possession of the property. The buyer's agent should take the responsibility to find out which fixtures are leased, and ensure that these items are excluded from the contract.

## Specifying the Details of Financing

### Buyer's Obligation to Obtain a Loan

It is the buyer's (or buyer's agent's) obligation to note any financing contingencies in the contract. The terms of financing should be set forth very specifically.

### Buyer Qualification for the Loan

In today's market, the buyers, when presenting an offer, need to give the sellers some form of assurance that the buyers have the ability to qualify for a loan. As discussed in the previous chapter, the buyer typically conveys such a message by attaching to the purchase offer and an addendum stating the status of the buyer's loan.

**Basic Loan Status Terminology:** It is very likely that the above-mentioned addendum will contain terms such as *loan to value* (LTV) and *combined loan to value* (CLTV). In situations where more than one loan will be used (e.g., the first deed of trust note and second deed of trust note), CLTV would apply.

**Qualification Contingent on Sale of Existing Home:** If, on the above-mentioned addendum, the buyer states that the buyer is relying on the sale of an existing home to qualify for a loan and the home does not sell, then this is an unfulfilled loan contingency. The buyer is entitled to a refund of the earnest money deposit, and the contract is canceled.

## Loan Contingency

The loan contingency states that the buyer is not obligated to complete the sale unless the buyer obtains unconditional loan approval by the close of escrow. If the loan contingency is unfulfilled, then the contract is terminated.

**Unfulfilled Loan Contingency:** If the buyer, through a diligent and good faith effort, is unable to qualify for a loan, the loan contingency is unfulfilled. The contract is canceled and the earnest money (initial deposit) is returned to the buyer. The contract should state that when this situation arises, any fees for inspections or items that the buyers are responsible to pay should be deducted from the earnest money deposit before the refund is made to the buyers.

**Failure to Possess Required Closing Funds:** If the buyer fails to possess the required closing funds (down payment and closing costs), this is not an unfulfilled loan contingency. It is a breach of contract, and in most cases, the buyer will forfeit the earnest money deposit to the seller (provided that the seller agrees to accept the earnest money as liquidated damages). The down payment and closing costs have nothing to do with the loan.

**Delivery of Notice Required:** The purchase contract should specify that in the event that the buyer cannot obtain loan approval, the buyer is obligated to deliver notice to the seller or to the escrow company within a certain number of days of learning about the non-approval. Generally, the buyer's agent will use a pre-printed *non-qualify letter* to accomplish this on behalf of the buyer. The contract should state that if the buyer (or buyer's agent) fails to deliver such a notice, the buyer is in breach.

> **Instructor Note:** The buyer's notice of inability to obtain a loan must be conclusive. If the seller believes that the buyer truly did obtain loan approval or that the buyer failed to make a diligent or good faith effort to obtain loan approval, the seller should contest the notice in writing.

**Failure to Deliver Notice:** With a statement in the contract that a failure to deliver notice of an unfulfilled loan contingency puts the buyer in breach, the failure to deliver notice will result in the buyer losing the earnest money. The seller has the right to enforce the buyer's obligation to deliver the notice. If the seller agrees to accept the earnest money as liquidated damages, the earnest money is disbursed to the seller, and escrow is terminated.

## Buyer Obligations

The contract should state that the buyer agrees to work diligently to provide the lender with all of the required documentation and obtain loan approval. In addition, the contract should obligate the buyer to sign all of the required loan documents in plenty of time for the loan proceeds to fund to the escrow company and meet the requirements of the good funds laws.

**Private Mortgage Insurance:** The buyer is always responsible for paying the private mortgage insurance (PMI). All other costs of the loan (discount points, lender's title insurance policy, origination fees, and appraisal fees) are paid according to the agreement between the buyer and seller. Normally, when the loan is greater than 80% of the appraised value, the lender will require the buyer to pay discount points upfront or agree to a monthly premium for private mortgage insurance. Private mortgage insurance guarantees the lender that, in case of default, any amount of the loan that is over 80% of the appraised value of the property will be covered for the lender by the insurance.

**Discount Points:** Typically, discount points are required to be paid up front to the lender to allow the buyer (borrower) to get a lower interest rate. The cost, per point is 1% of the loan amount. The responsibility for paying the points is a matter of contract. However, in most contracts, the buyer should specify the maximum amount of points the buyer is willing to pay in order to qualify for the loan. The buyer's promise in this regard then becomes a part of the buyer's obligations, and will not be an exception in the loan contingency.

## Types of Financing

The three most common types of real estate loans available from institutional lenders are the following:

- The conventional loan (remember that the conventional loan may have a fixed rate, a variable rate, shared appreciation, graduated payments, or some combination of these variations).

- Veterans Affairs (VA) loan.

- Federal Housing Administration (FHA) loan.

### Conventional Loans

The conventional loan is the one most often used, and has several advantages over the other two. Although it may not always be assumable, it is much less hampered by federal restrictions and red tape than are the other two. Moreover, there is no set maximum amount that may be borrowed. Anyone who has a decent FICO score can qualify for a conventional loan. In addition, this type of loan takes the least amount of time to obtain.

### VA Loans

The newly originated VA loan (as opposed to one being assumed), is available to eligible armed services veterans only. This type of loan is backed by the Department of Veterans Affairs (DVA) and involves a certain amount of governmental red tape, and therefore, takes longer to obtain.

**Down Payment:** Technically, this loan does not require a down payment if the appraisal is the same as or higher than the purchase price, but since the government's appraisal (also called a certificate of reasonable value) is almost invariably lower than the purchase price, a down payment is almost always necessary, and this sum may not be borrowed commercially. The veteran may borrow from a friend or relative but not from an institutional lender.

**Note:** Not all banks, lending institutions, insurance companies, or mortgage companies offer VA-secured loans.

### FHA Loans

**Loan Limits:** FHA loans are sponsored by the Federal Housing Administration, which is a federal agency whose main purpose is to encourage home ownership. They are open to anyone with good credit. The FHA loan has a maximum limit, and this limit varies according to the average cost of a house in a particular area, and it is periodically revised upward to compensate for inflation.

The HUD website provides a search tool that allows you to look up the FHA mortgage limits for your area or several areas, and then list them by state, county, or Metropolitan Statistical Area.

**Required Home Inspection Disclosure:** If the buyer has applied for an FHA loan, HUD (Housing and Urban Development) requires that the buyer be presented with the HUD Buyer Home Inspection Notice as an addendum to the contract. Although this disclosure is required only in cases where the buyer is obtaining an FHA loan, it is a good idea to include this document as an addendum to every contract, even if the buyer is getting a conventional loan. This shows that you have advised the buyer to get a home inspection.

**General Information:** Because FHA loans are supposed to benefit buyers with moderate incomes, the loan limits are at the lower end of the housing price scale. An FHA loan is like a VA loan in the following respects:

- It can be assumable (although this is rare these days).

- It carries no prepayment penalty.

- It requires lots of paperwork to satisfy government bureaucrats.

- Its down payment may not be borrowed commercially; that is, not unless the buyer is at least 62 years old or is assuming an existing FHA loan.

## Mortgage Insurance

The FHA provides mortgage insurance as a condition of the loan and charges the borrower 0.5% of the loan balance as a premium. Because of this mortgage insurance, the FHA will lend as much as 96.5% of the purchase price. The cost of this is typically included in the monthly payment.

**Note:** The Upfront Mortgage Insurance Premium is .05% of the loan amount.

FHA mortgage insurance provides lenders with protection against losses as a result of homeowners defaulting on their mortgage loans. The lenders bear less risk because the FHA will pay a claim to the lender in the event of a homeowner's default. Loans must meet certain requirements that are established by the FHA to qualify for insurance.

In most cases, the upfront mortgage insurance cost to the borrower will drop off after five years, or when the remaining balance on the loan is 78% of the value of the property, whichever is longer.

### Eligibility Requirements

- The borrower must meet standard FHA credit qualifications.

- The borrower must be eligible for approximately 97% of the financing. (The loan will be for 97%, but will include a .05% upfront mortgage insurance premium, which is the result is a 3.5% down payment.) The borrower must be able to finance the upfront mortgage insurance premium into the loan.

- The borrower will be responsible for paying an annual premium.

- Eligible properties are one-to-four unit homes, condominium units, or manufactured housing units (provided that the manufactured housing unit is on a permanent foundation).

### FHA Does Not Set Interest Rates

FHA loans have competitive interest rates because the Federal government insures the loans. However, FHA is not the lending institution; rather, the bank is. FHA does not set the interest rates on the loans it insures; interest rates are set by the lender.

### Approved Lenders

It may be handy to have a list of approved FHA lenders in your area, so that you can obtain some literature from these lenders and educate yourself about the various lender requirements.

The HUD website provides a search tool that allows you to search for approved FHA lenders in your geographic area by using various search criteria.

## Title Commitments

### Commitment for Title Insurance

As is the custom, the purchase contract (which also serves as escrow instructions) will probably instruct the escrow agent or title company to deliver a commitment for title insurance that lists all exceptions to the title insurance policy. Copies of the report go to the buyer, seller, lender, and real estate agent(s) for their evaluation.

### What is Included in the Commitment for Title Insurance

The report compiled from the title examiner's findings provides the following information in order to show the condition of title as of a specific date:

- The vested owner's name as disclosed in public records,
- The current real estate property taxes, including whether they are paid or unpaid, and the date of the last property assessment,
- The outstanding liens, restrictions, easements, or other types of encumbrances,
- The property's legal description of record,
- The conditions under which the title company will issue title insurance, and
- A plat map (picture or drawing) that shows the location and dimensions of the property as found in recorded documents.

### No Guarantees

The commitment for title insurance makes no guarantees about insuring the title to the property. In fact, the preliminary title report does not guarantee anything regarding the property; it merely provides information regarding the contents of documents found in the public records and guarantees that the search made by the title company is complete.

## Prorations and Insurance Claims History

### Tax Prorations

The purchase contract will instruct the escrow officer to prorate the real property tax liability. The seller will be liable to pay the taxes for the portion of the year that the seller owns the home, and the buyer is liable to pay the real property taxes for the portion of the year that the buyer owns the home.

### Calculating Prorations

Taxes are prorated by the escrow officer based on a calendar month (using the exact amount of days in any month). On the settlement statement provided by the escrow officer, the sellers would have a credit to their account if they prepaid the current year's property taxes. The taxes that are prorated are based on the assessed value of the home at the time escrow closes. It is possible that the assessed value will change during the period of time between the close of escrow and the date when the taxes are due.

## Assessment Lien Prorations

If, as of the close of escrow date, the seller has already paid the assessments and fees associated with the real property, the seller is entitled to a partial reimbursement of those funds. In essence, any prepaid items, such as insurance, homeowners association fees, and other items, will be prorated and credited to the seller. Assessment liens other than homeowners association assessments would normally be prorated and assumed by the buyers, unless they are of specific benefit to the sellers and do not include the property itself.

## Insurance Claims History

In most real estate purchase contracts, the seller will agree to provide the buyer with a written five-year insurance claims history for the premises (or a claims history for the amount of time the seller has owned the property). This claims history should be in the form of a letter from the insurance company, insurance support organization (such as the Comprehensive Loss Underwriting Exchange), or a consumer report organization. The purpose of this form is to show the buyer the types of hazard insurance claims that may have been filed on behalf of the property.

## Foreign Investment in Real Property Tax Act (FIRPTA)

Every real estate purchase contract will provide escrow instructions with regard to the Foreign Investment in Real Property Tax Act (FIRPTA). FIRPTA was enacted in 1980 and provides that if the seller of real property is a foreign person, the buyer must withhold an amount equal to 10% of the gross purchase price, unless an exemption applies (26 U.S.C.A. § 1445(a)).

This process must be done through the escrow process. Rather than debiting the buyer for the full amount of the purchase price and crediting the seller with that amount, the escrow company will debit the buyer and credit the buyer in an amount equal to 90% of the purchase price, and the other 10% will be placed in a neutral escrow depository, and the escrow company will send that money, along with a report, to the appropriate government agencies.

### Exemptions

There are numerous exemptions to the FIRPTA requirements. The most common exemption is when the seller furnishes a non-foreign affidavit that states, under penalty of perjury, that the seller is not a foreign person (26 U.S.C.A. §1445(b)(2)).

Another exemption is a transaction that involves the transfer of a property acquired for use as the buyer's residence and the amount realized (purchase price) does not exceed $300,000. Under certain circumstances, a seller may obtain a *qualifying statement* from the IRS that states that no withholding is required.

### Amount Withheld

Although FIRPTA generally provides that 10% of the purchase price must be withheld, the amount withheld should not exceed the seller's maximum tax liability. The seller (or buyer) can request the IRS to determine the seller's maximum tax liability with respect to the sale.

### Brokerage Liability

A real estate broker or salesperson (broker) for either party can be held liable for the tax that should have been withheld (up to the amount of compensation received), if the broker has actual knowledge that the non-foreign affidavit is false and fails to notify the buyer and the IRS. Under certain circumstances, the broker may also be liable for civil or criminal penalties.

Any necessary withholding should be accomplished by requiring the escrow agent to withhold the required funds. The escrow company should be instructed to send the funds to the IRS at the close of escrow. The purchase contract should provide the proper escrow instructions to the escrow agent.

**Flow Chart**

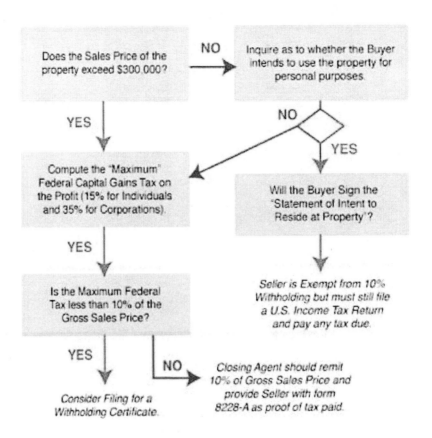

QUIZZES ARE MANDATORY: Please log in and submit the chapter quizzes online.

## Chapter 3 Quiz

1.  By definition, any existing _____ stay with the real property.

    (a)   fixtures
    (b)   personal property
    (c)   items of antique furniture
    (d)   yard working tools

2.  The _____ states that the buyer is not obligated to complete the sale unless the buyer obtains unconditional loan approval by close of escrow.

    (a)   'loan' contingency
    (b)   'fire sale' contingency
    (c)   'appraisal' contingency
    (d)   'notice to vacate' contingency

3.  The cost per discount point is _____ percent of the loan amount.

    (a)   2.5
    (b)   1
    (c)   3.5
    (d)   0.5

4.  The _____ loan is backed by the Department of Veterans Affairs (DVA) and involves a certain amount of governmental red tape.

    (a)   Federal Housing Administration
    (b)   FHA
    (c)   conventional
    (d)   VA

5.  With regard to an FHA loan, which of the following statements is FALSE?

    (a)   It carries no prepayment penalty.
    (b)   It requires little or no paperwork.
    (c)   Its down payment may not be borrowed commercially; that is, not unless the buyer is at least 62 years old or is assuming an existing FHA loan.
    (d)   It is like a VA loan in many respects.

6.  Copies of the commitment for title insurance generally go to all of the following EXCEPT:

    (a)   the buyer
    (b)   the seller
    (c)   the real estate agents
    (d)   the appraiser

7.   Taxes are prorated by the escrow officer by using a _____.

     (a)   calendar month
     (b)   30-day month
     (c)   banker's month
     (d)   quarter month

8.   With regard to tax prorations, the seller will be liable to pay taxes for the portion of the year that the seller owns the home, and the buyer is liable to pay the real property taxes for the portion of the year the buyer owns the home.

     (a)   True
     (b)   False

9.   The most common exemption to the FIRPTA requirements occurs when the seller furnishes a _____, stating under penalty of perjury that the seller is not a foreign person.

     (a)   statement of intent to reside
     (b)   non-foreign affidavit
     (c)   statement of residency
     (d)   statement of alienation

10.  An exemption to the FIRPTA requirements is a transaction that involves the transfer of a property acquired for use as the buyer's residence and the amount realized (purchase price) does not exceed _____.

     (a)   $250,000
     (b)   $500,000
     (c)   $300,000
     (d)   $100,000

## Chapter Four: Listing Duties and Clauses

**Important Terms**

bilateral contract
competitive market analysis (CMA)
duties of agency
exclusive Right to Sell
law of agency
legal description
material facts
metes and bounds description
obedience
offer
safety clause
solicitation
title search
transfer Disclosure Statement (TDS)
type of access

**Learning Objectives**

After successful completion of this chapter, you should be able to complete the following:

- State the duties of the listing agent.

- State the duties of the seller who has listed his or her property with a listing agent.

- State some of the details that should be addressed and resolved before signing a listing agreement.

- Define the standard clauses in a listing contract.

### Before the Listing is Signed

#### Your Duty to Explain

Most of the time, agents who procure listings experience such excitement at procuring the listing, that they forget to iron out relevant listing-related issues beforehand. Remember, a listing is a contract—it is an employment agreement. Successful fulfillment of the goal requires that both parties are satisfied with the details associated with the employment.

**Note:** Unless the listing terms are conducive to sale, you have acquired a liability that may never become an asset.

Understand, most sellers would rather sign the listing and "be done with it." You, as the listing agent, have a duty to make sure the seller knows that this is a legal contract, and that the seller is accountable for the way in which the details of the property are portrayed.

When you procure a signed listing, you establish an agency relationship. This means you are bound to the duties of agency, including the duty of obedience. Once the listing is signed, any new negotiation requires the agreement of both parties. Since you are bound by the duty of obedience, you MUST agree to whatever the seller proposes, as long as it is legal and not in direct conflict with the listing contract.

#### Iron Out Details

Before you list, iron out a few details. The time to resolve listing-related issues should occur before the listing is signed, and not after. In a listing contract, you (or your broker) promise to market the property to the best of your ability. In most listing contracts, the seller promises to compensate you only if the property sells. This means that a listing is a liability for you until it sells, and only then do you realize a gain. If the property does not sell, you realize no gain.

#### Dates on the Listing Contract

Most brokers prefer this type of listing agreement (we will discuss this in depth in the next chapter). Your commission could depend upon the diligence you exercise in completing this form. A listing must include the following three dates to be valid and enforceable:

- Complete commencement date (including month, day, and year).
- Complete expiration date (including month, day, and year).
- Complete signature (execution) date (including month, day, and year).

You should also make a note to periodically check all of your listings for the expiration date, because a sale of a property on which you have no current listing is no good to you or your broker. Remember, according to standard real estate law, all real estate employment agreements must meet the following requirements:

- Be written in clear and unambiguous language.
- Fully set forth all material terms, including the terms of broker compensation (if compensation is expected).
- Have a definite duration or expiration date, and show the dates of inception and expiration.
- Be signed by all parties to the agreement.

## What is Required of the Seller?

### Duties of the Seller

Understanding the duties of the seller in a listing contract seems straightforward enough, but what if the seller has different ideas than you do? First of all, the seller must be willing to sell the property! Although this statement sounds obvious, the operative word here is *sell*, and not *list*.

### Willingness to Sell Means Willingness to Complete the Following:

**Agree to Listing Compensation**: Usually, the seller must be willing to render compensation to the real estate broker when the property is sold. However, compensation is not a requirement in an employment agreement. The employment agreement establishes a relationship (agency) between the seller and the agent. The subject of compensation must be addressed in writing in the employment agreement if the agent expects the compensation to be enforceable in court.

**Disclose All Material Facts**: In the state of California, the law requires that onus of disclosure is on the seller. Generally, this entails the completion of the Transfer Disclosure Statement (TDS). This form is available at the California Association of REALTORS® website. Sellers are obligated by California law to disclose all known material facts about their property to the buyer. If a buyer requires the TDS as a condition of closing, then the seller and seller's agent are obligated to produce it. It is a good idea to take this form with you when you are obtaining a listing agreement. Have the seller fill this out at the same time. That way, when the buyer requests this form, you'll have it completely prepared, and you can produce it.

**Exceptions to Disclosure Requirements**: Sometimes, especially with REO property, the seller (who is a bank) will explicitly state in an addendum that the buyer must waive its right to a TDS as a condition of the sale. In such a case, there will be no TDS. This may also be the case with absentee homeowners, out-of-state investors, or sellers who have never seen the home, or who are not well-versed regarding the physical aspects of the home.

**Comply with Fair Housing Laws**: In order to list a property with a licensed real estate broker, the seller must be willing to offer the property to all persons without regard to race, color, national origin, familial status, age, handicap, sex, or religion. This provision should be written into the listing agreement and clarified with the seller prior to signing.

**Have Marketable Title or the Means to Obtain It**: It is a logical assumption that the seller actually owns the property being listed. However, most assumptions are dangerous and this one is particularly dangerous. The most reliable way to verify ownership is to check with the County Assessor to see who owns the property, or have a title officer perform a title search.

The official record will tell you much more than who actually owns the property. You can verify the square footage, legal description, type of construction, current year taxes, and much more.

The verification of this ownership, the current-year taxes, and a host of other items in the county records should be done before the listing agreement is signed by either party. Distance to the county seat is no longer a valid reason for not searching public records. Just about every county recorder's office provides online access to real property records.

A printout of the real property record should be added to the listing folder to show the seller that you performed diligently during the transaction.

**Agree to a Price Commensurate with Fair Market Value**: It is important to distinguish for the seller that you can list their property all day long, but the goal is not to list, but rather to sell. The features of the property are not what sell it—it is the price that sells the property. Without a realistic price, the property will not sell, no matter what the market looks like (more on this subject in the next chapter).

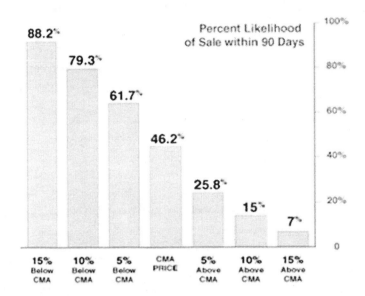

**Establish a Negotiating Position**: You have an obligation to submit all offers but the seller has the right to decline any offer that does not reflect the listing price and other conditions stated in the agreement. This means that you must establish the seller's potential for flexibility before the listing is signed.

What if the seller is absolute about the asking price, and is not willing to negotiate? If this is case, it is best to find this out before you become bound to the terms of the listing. In a declining market or a down market, there is a high probability that offers significantly lower than the asking price will be presented.

> **Instructor Note:** Powerful negotiating positions are created by the marketability of the property, and the communication skills of the listing agents who are involved in the transaction. Not only that, but the law of agency also often requires the listing agent to advise the seller about the art of negotiating. Sometimes, getting the client to understand when and how to apply negotiating strategies requires communication skills as well as patience.

**Provide Access**: The seller should be willing to provide access to the property. You, the prospective listing agent, must decide what type of access will result in a sale that is in the best interests of the seller. Generally, the access that is most convenient to the prospective buyer and the buyer's agent is most conducive to the sale, especially in a buyer's market. Take a look at the following scenario:

**Scenario: Less than Optimum Access (From Actual Case files)**

REALTOR® Deborah did a competitive market analysis (CMA) on the Smith's home in Rancho Cucamonga, California, and established that the market value of the home was $425,000.

The sellers signed the listing and agreed to pay Deborah 6% of the list price. However, after the listing was signed, they told her that she could not have a key to the home, nor could she put a lockbox on the home. They further explained that their 86-year-old grandfather who lived with them would be in the home at all times, and that they (the sellers) needed a two-day notice before each showing. As a result, when other REALTORS® wanted to show the home, there was at least a two-day delay.

Chances are, most other buyer's agents either chose not to show the home at all, or showed it last. In fact, during the first six months of the listing, there were only two showings. Consequently, the house sat on the market for a year. As a result, the sellers were forced to keep reducing the price, and were perturbed with Deborah. They felt that she was not fulfilling her promise to market the home because of the paucity of showings.

The house finally sold for $335,500, which is about $90,000 below the market value estimated in the comparative market analysis at the time the listing was signed. More likely than not, the difficulty of access was the culprit.

## What is Required of the Listing Agent?

**Diligent Marketing And Knowledgeable Advice:** Generally, a listing term consists of two phases:

- The marketing phase (before an offer is accepted).
- The escrow phase (when the seller has accepted an offer).

**Note:** The most frequent owner complaint about the service received from the listing agent is a lack of communication.

When the listing is signed by the parties, it becomes a bilateral contract—a promise for a promise. The listing agent's obligation under the agreement is to be diligent in endeavoring to find a purchaser. The indiscriminate taking by agents of long-term listings with inadequate servicing can create problems. If, at the time of entering into the listing, promises have been made to advertise the property, the owner is entitled to a reasonable amount of advertising.

The most frequent owner complaint about the service received from the listing agent is lack of communication concerning the efforts the listing agent has made on the owner's behalf to market the property. During both the marketing phase and the escrow phase, you, as the listing agent, are obligated to advise the seller with regard to the terms and nuances of the listing contract, as well as the purchase contract and all escrow-related documents. For now, let's discuss the listing contract. Purchase contracts and escrow-related documents will be discussed at a later time.

## Listing Considerations

### Standard Listing Contract Clauses

Undoubtedly, your listing contract will be tailored to the specific needs of your real estate community, and will include many other clauses than what is listed here.

### Property Description

The property description does not necessarily have to be a legal description to satisfy the Statute of Frauds. The key is that the description is unambiguous.

**Example:** Oscar contracted to convey to Ernie "... all of my (Oscar's) property in Claremont, California." If it could be shown that Oscar owned only one specific parcel of property in Claremont, California, many courts would find the legal description to be specific enough to form a contract. On the other hand, if Oscar contracted to convey to Ernie "... all of my (Oscar's) property in Orange County, the legal description most likely would be insufficient. There are at least two Orange Counties—one in California and another in Florida. So, courts are less inclined to find the legal description sufficient under these circumstances.

Most of the time, however, a legal description is best, unless the legal description of record for the property happens to be a metes-and-bounds description. In a case where the only legal description available is a metes-and bounds-description, it will suffice just to write the property description in such a way that the property cannot be confused with any other property.

> **Instructor Note:** If the only legal description available is a metes-and-bounds description, you are probably dealing with unsubdivided vacant land, in which case, the staking survey becomes particularly important. You can reference the staking survey when you are writing the property

description. For instance, in *Hill-Shafer Partnership v. Chilson Family Trust, 165 Ariz 469*, the buyer intended to purchase whatever the legal description identified, regardless of size or location. The seller did not have similar intent, but intended to convey only certain property. The legal description in the contract described property other than that which the seller intended to convey. Therefore, the court held that there was no mutual assent, and no binding contract.

### Listing Price

The listing price should be written in longhand (like a check) and then written as a numerable dollar amount.

### Compensation to the Broker

This needs your full attention. Without proper completion of this section, you have no right to a commission. The compensation is usually a percent of the selling price, but it can be a flat fee as well. Write out the listing commission in narrative form. For example, if the commission rate is 6% of the sales price, write the following:

*Six percent of sales price of property described on Line X of this contract ...*

### Broker Protection Clause

Most listing agreements include a *broker protection clause*, sometimes called an *after-expiration clause* or *safety clause*. The broker is protected if the owner sells the property, after termination of the listing, to someone to whom the property has been shown by the broker (or you, the representative of the broker) during the listing.

### Listing Signs

If a sign is placed on a property, it must comply with the municipal zoning laws. If it does not comply with the zoning laws, it is the property owner who will be cited, not the real estate broker. Furthermore, if the sign is inappropriately placed on the property and blocks road visibility, the property owner could be liable for any car accidents that occur as a result. Because the owner of the property has such liability, the owner must give written permission to the real estate agent to place the sign. In the absence of written permission to place the sign, the real estate licensee who placed it is liable for trespass.

**Note:** In the absence of written permission to place the sign, the real estate licensee who placed it is liable for trespass.

### Terms of Agency Relationship

This clause defines the terms of the agency between the listing agent and the seller. Basically, it identifies the boundaries of the relationship between the seller and the listing agent. It also specifies (among other things) the following:

- It is the listing agent who is marketing the home, not the seller. Thus, the advertising is not an offer, it is merely a solicitation for an offer.

- The seller expressly authorizes the listing agent to work under his or her control and on his or her behalf. Therefore, the agent is required to negotiate on behalf of the principal.

- Third parties may rely in good faith on the representation of the listing agent.

### Severability Clause

A severability clause is a provision in a contract that states that if parts of the contract are held to be illegal or otherwise unenforceable, the remainder of the contract should still apply. In other words, that portion of the contract is "carved out" or "severed" from the other parts of the contract. Sometimes, a severability clause states that some provisions to the contract are so essential to the central purpose of the contract that if they are illegal or unenforceable, the contract as a whole will be voided. A severability clause will not be applied if it changes the fundamental nature of the contract.

**Sample Severability Clause:** "If a provision of this Agreement is or becomes illegal, invalid or unenforceable in any jurisdiction, that shall not affect the validity or enforceability in that jurisdiction of any other provision of this Agreement; or the validity or enforceability in other jurisdictions of that or any other provision of this Agreement."

### Entire Agreement Clause

This clause declares it to be the complete and final agreement between the parties. It is often placed at or toward the end of the contract. In other words, any information that is exchanged verbally, or prior to the contract being signed, does not exist, as is not part of the arrangement. Any previous negotiations in which the parties to the contract had considered different terms will be deemed superseded by the final writing.

An *entire agreement* clause in any contract means the following:

- Failure of any party to initial any page of the contract does not affect the validity of the terms specified on that page.

- Any modification to the listing contract must be in writing and signed by both the seller and the broker.

### Multiple Listing Clause

This clause is a provision that gives the listing broker the authority and obligation to distribute the listing to other brokers in the Multiple-Listing System. As you know, the MLS is a contract among members of the MLS. When a listing is distributed to other brokers via the MLS, the listing agent makes certain representations about the property, and the listing agent is bound by contract to uphold those representations.

### Additional Terms

Usually, this section would address the length of time the seller would have to vacate, etc. Maybe the seller has a special chandelier he or she wants to keep, or perhaps the seller wants to take the custom draperies. This is also the place to state which appliances are to be included in the sale, if the contract does not enumerate this elsewhere.

### Terms of Dispute Resolution

There are three ways to handle a dispute:

1) Forget it.

2) Handle the dispute outside of court system through mediation or arbitration.

3) Utilize the court system.

In most listing contracts, both parties agree that they will attempt to handle the dispute outside the court system before utilizing the court system. The *terms of dispute resolution* clause outlines the specific methods that are available, and the details surrounding those methods.

### As-Is Clause

Frequently (especially with bank-owned property), sales of real property are made *as-is*. That is, no representation is made by the seller as to the condition of the property. The as-is clause is often used to mean that the seller will not make any needed repairs and "what the buyer sees is what the buyer gets." The clause generally means that the buyer takes the property in the condition visible to or observable by him or her.

Only rarely will such a clause or similar statement entirely relieve the seller from responsibility. Under no conditions will it shield the seller from fraudulent acts committed by his or her agent of which he or she has knowledge. If the seller wishes to invoke an as-is provision, the clause absolutely must be included in the terms of the purchase contract, but whether such a clause belongs in the listing agreement is a matter of negotiation between the listing agent and the seller at the time that the listing is written.

## Other Considerations

### Revocation Powers and Rights

What would happen if the seller wanted to terminate the listing agreement before the expiration date?

**Power to Revoke:** If, during the term of the listing, the seller no longer desires to have the agent act for him or her, and wishes to withdraw the listing, the seller has the power to revoke, but violates (breaches) his or her contract with the broker, and may become liable to the broker for payment of a commission if the property sells during the listing term specified on the listing contract.

**Right to Revoke:** The right to revoke is a right that is arranged between the seller and the broker at the time the listing is signed. The seller's right to revoke, if it is intended, should be expressly established by a definitive statement. For example:

> *Seller shall have the right to revoke this agreement providing seller furnishes to broker a written request of such intent not less than days prior to the date seller intends to withdraw from this agreement.*

### Fixtures

**Note:** Do not presume that because an item is built in, it's going to stay put.

Many printed forms do not contain standard provisions for fixtures to be included or excluded in the purchase price. It is not necessary. Fixtures are considered a part of the real estate, and are automatically included in the sale.

All too often, however, the seller finds that an item he or she intended to remove has been incorporated into the purchase price by the buyer's agent. To help avoid this problem, the listing agent should incorporate terminology that alerts any agent who reads the listing that the seller intends to remove certain fixtures. If the clause is properly prepared in the listing, the transition into the purchase contract is greatly simplified. Do not presume that because an item is built in, it's going to stay put. When a list of personal property is included in a purchase contract, a court may well find that since an attempt was made to include certain items, those not included may be excluded by implication. Use the expression "presently installed and in use on premises."

With this expression in the listing, and the purchase contract, the seller would be in violation of the agreement if he or she removed any item described. This is used in an effort to prevent the removal of an expensive item and the substitution with an inferior product.

**QUIZZES ARE MANDATORY**: Please log in and submit the chapter quizzes online.

## Chapter 4 Quiz

1.    The _____ clause is often used to mean that the seller will not make any needed repairs and what the buyer sees is what the buyer gets.

    (a)      entire agreement
    (b)      severability
    (c)      as-is
    (d)      multiple listing

2.    What should you do if your seller tells you to refrain from showing his or her property to anyone but "Nice Christian folks?"

    (a)      Write the restriction into the listing agreement.
    (b)      Advise your seller that you are not interested in listing a bigot's property.
    (c)      Call out the S.W.A.T team—the seller is breaking the law.
    (d)      Advise your seller that you are bound by all Fair Housing laws and you must offer the property to all persons without regard to religion.

3.    If a listing sign does not comply with the zoning laws, it is the property owner who will be cited, and not the real estate broker. Because the owner of the property has such liability, the owner must give to the real estate agent _____ to place the sign.

    (a)      permission
    (b)      written permission
    (c)      consideration
    (d)      irrevocable permission

4.    You have an obligation to submit all offers but the seller has the right to decline any offer that does not reflect the listing price and other conditions stated in the agreement. This means that the best time to ascertain the seller's potential for flexibility is _____.

    (a)      before the listing is signed
    (b)      after the listing is signed
    (c)      when it becomes necessary to reduce the price
    (d)      upon listing cancellation

5.    In most listing contracts, the seller promises to compensate you only if the property sells. This means that a listing is _____ for you until it sells and closes escrow—only then do you realize a gain.

    (a)      a money maker
    (b)      an asset
    (c)      a liability
    (d)      a sure-fire profit

6.    Generally, when you establish the type of access to the property, the method of access that is most convenient to the _____ is most conducive to the sale.

    (a)      prospective buyer and buyer's agent
    (b)      seller
    (c)      listing agent
    (d)      home inspector

7.    Which of the following correctly defines the *severability* clause?

      (a)    A clause that describes a condition of ownership (such as in the term *joint and severally*).
      (b)    A clause in a statute or contract that states that if any particular part of the statute or contract is found to be void or unenforceable, that part will be carved out and the balance enforced to the extent possible.
      (c)    A clause that enables one party to the contract to declare the contract void when another party to the contract breaks one of the conditions of the contract.
      (d)    A clause that allows the lender to "sever" the mortgage and declare all funds due and payable.

8.    If, after the listing has expired, the seller sells the property himself or herself to someone you have shown the property to while the listing was valid, and you are still entitled to a commission, you have probably included _____ in your listing contract.

      (a)    an entire agreement clause
      (b)    a severability clause
      (c)    a broker protection clause (or safety clause)
      (d)    a multiple listing clause

9.    _____ is present in any contractual arrangement. If the seller invokes this, he or she may violate (breach) the listing contract, and become liable to the broker for payment of a commission.

      (a)    Power to revoke
      (b)    Right to revoke

10.   Listing compensation is not a requirement to establish agency.

      (a)    True
      (b)    False

## Chapter Five: Procuring and Structuring the Listing

### Important Terms

arm's length transaction
Competitive Market Analysis (CMA)
material facts
net listing
net seller's proceeds
option
probate
value

### Chapter Five Learning Objectives

After successful completion of this chapter, you should be able to complete the following:

- Identify the three primary structures of listing agreements.

- State the attributes of a net listing.

- Define an option listing, and state some of the potential dangers behind this option.

- State the definition of *probate listing*.

- Distinguish between *price* and *value*.

- Understand the difference between *right of revocation* and *power of revocation*.

- Describe how to incorporate language about removal of fixtures into the purchase contract.

## Types of Listing Agreement Structures

Of all the instruments in real estate transactions, the most typical listing contains a real estate document that is prepared with insufficient care and skill. Even when the printed form is well composed, it is frequently used improperly. There is more to the preparation of a listing than the mechanical writing of terms and conditions. The agent must not only be able to prepare a contract with terms that are in the best interest of the client, but also tailor a listing contract to a unique situation.

### Three Primary Structures

| Structure | Description |
|---|---|
| **Exclusive Right to Sell** | Broker is compensated if the property sells during the listing term. |
| **Exclusive Agency** | Broker is compensated if broker finds the buyer; or if another broker finds the buyer. Broker is not compensated if seller finds the buyer and facilitates the sale. |
| **Open listing** | Whoever finds the buyer first is compensated (also called a hip-pocket listing.) |

### Exclusive Right-to-Sell Listing

An *exclusive right-to-sell listing* is the most commonly utilized instrument, because it is the most straightforward and least confusing. The seller pays the listing commission to the broker if the property sells during the listing term, regardless of who facilitates the sale, and regardless of who found the buyer. The owner cannot sell the property without paying a commission, unless an exception is noted in the contract.

**NOTE:** Full assurance of a commission means confident marketing.

**Why is this the preferred method?** Broker confidence, that's why. With an exclusive right-to-sell listing, the seller agrees that the named broker will be compensated if the property sells. The broker can then, confidently give his or her promise of diligence in the effort to find a buyer who is ready, willing, and able to purchase the property on the terms and conditions of the listing agreement. If there is a chance that the seller could find the buyer, facilitate the sale, and not pay the broker, the broker does not have the full assurance of a commission. This causes trepidation when it comes to marketing the property with confidence.

**What happens if the seller gives more than one exclusive listing?** The seller may not be aware that he or she should not do this. There is no specific verbiage in the listing agreement that prohibits such an act on the part of the seller. However, the onus would be on the first listing agent to explain to the seller the risks involved in doing this. If a sale does occur, the seller runs the risk of having to pay a commission to more than one broker. A second listing does not terminate the first listing.

> **Instructor Note:** If you even remotely suspect that this might happen, you must, in order to avoid a very unpleasant problem, explain to the seller the consequences of such an act. Although this sounds very academic, many sellers are unaware of the consequences and believe that it is perfectly okay to "play the field."

**What are the seller's rights with an exclusive right-to-sell listing?** The acceptance by the broker of a listing is predicated upon his or her duty to use diligence and his or her obligation to expend a reasonable amount of advertising upon each listing. Courts have held that the seller may rescind an exclusive right-to-sell listing after the broker has had a reasonable time to exercise diligence and has failed to do so.

## Exclusive Agency Listing

In an *exclusive agency listing*, the owner reserves the right to find the buyer and facilitate the sale without paying a commission.

**Note:** Less assurance of a commission means less confident marketing.

The broker is free to cooperate with another brokerage, and if the second brokerage brings an able buyer whose offer the seller accepts, then the listing broker receives a commission. The selling brokerage commission will typically be some portion of the listing commission.

## Open Listing

An *open listing* is a non-exclusive agreement, which means that the seller may execute open listings with more than one real estate broker and pay only the broker who brings an able buyer whose offer the owner accepts. With this type of listing, the seller is not hiring the broker for representation; he or she is simply hiring the broker to find a buyer.

Multiple listing services frequently discourage open listings from being marketed in the MLS, because there is potential for several simultaneous open listings. However, in 1981, in *People vs. San Diego Board of REALTORS®*, the Court of Appeal of the 4th Appellate District decided that the California Cartwright Act prohibits a MLS from limiting itself to exclusive right-to-sell listings and from declining to accept for publication both exclusive agency listings and open listings.

### Scenario: The Dangers of Open Listing (From Actual Case files)

[Marks v. Watson] Marks, a licensed real estate broker, contacted the seller regarding the sale of his property. He was informed that the seller had given an open listing to a number of brokers. Marks, believing that he too should get into the hunt, mailed a printed exclusive listing to the seller that had been altered by printing the words *open listing* at the top and crossed out the word *exclusive* from the body of the listing where it had appeared twice. The seller signed the listing and returned it to Marks.

However, the language appearing later in the listing, whereby the seller agreed to pay the agent a 5% commission whether the property was sold by the agent or someone else, including the owner, was not stricken. Thereafter, the property was sold by another broker and Marks sued the seller for his commission. The court ruled against Marks. The Real Estate Commissioner then brought disciplinary action against Marks, and Marks appealed to the court. It was held that the attempted fraudulent enforcement of such a listing constituted grounds for the revocation of the broker's license.*

*The official court document from *Marks v. Watson* is available for download from the online course.

## Other Less-Frequent Structures

### Net Listing

The words *Net Listing* are seldom printed on a standard listing form. More often than not, the title of the listing is *Exclusive Listing* or *Exclusive Right to Sell Listing*. The listing becomes a net listing due to the manner in which the agent phrases the method of compensation. For example:

   *The seller is to receive not less than a certain amount.*

The principal characteristic that sets the net listing apart from any other form of listing is the statement that "the seller is to receive not less than a certain amount" after specified costs and expenses have first been deducted from the sales price. If the amount remaining after deducting the specified expenses does not yield the net figure guaranteed to the seller, the seller may refuse to sell, even though the buyer may have met all of the terms of the listing.

The dollar amount of compensation to the broker is not stated in the listing agreement. If the property sells for more than the amount required by the seller, the broker is entitled to retain the surplus as his or her commission. If the property sells for an amount equal to or less than the net amount required by the seller, the broker may not receive any compensation (see sample net listing terminology).

> **Instructor Note:** A net listing is perfectly legitimate and perfectly legal, but it is discouraged, because a net listing may give rise to a lawsuit. If the sale results in a larger commission than would have resulted in a standard listing, the broker can be certain of an unhappy seller and charges of fraud. If the selling price is too high, it is very likely that the courts will hold the agent accountable for intentionally overvaluing the property to maximize the commission. If the selling price is too low, the agent receives a less-than-normal commission. The broker must be extra careful about his or her counseling of the property value.

### Option Listing

An option listing is not a true listing—it gives the broker an option to purchase the property. When exercising the option, the broker is in a fiduciary position and must make full disclosure of all outstanding offers and other material facts or information in his or her possession.

Among other things, the option listing can very easily become a conflict of interests. If a broker is employed to sell the property and at the same time holds an option to purchase the property himself or herself, the broker occupies the two conflicting positions of agent and purchaser. To comply with agency laws, the broker is not entitled to exercise his or her option except by divesting himself or herself of his or her obligation as agent.

When divesting himself or herself of agency status, the real estate broker is required by law to inform his or her employer in writing that he or she has decided to exercise his option. An agent has a duty, not only to make no misstatements of fact, but also to fully and completely disclose to the principal all material facts.

**Note:** The option listing can easily create a conflict of interest.

In an option situation, the disclosure must include not only the fact that the agent is acting on his or her own account, but also other facts that the agent should realize have, or are likely to have, a bearing upon the desirability of the transaction from the viewpoint of the principal.

### Probate Listing

The representative of the estate of a decedent, with court permission, may grant an open or exclusive listing on the decedent's property for a period not to exceed 90 days. Acceptance of an offer by the estate representative is subject to probate court confirmation.

### Establishing a Listing Price (Primary Objective)

Too often, listing prices are set by using emotions, rather than market analysis, as a guide. The real estate agent's primary objective is to guide the seller to a figure that is most likely obtainable for the subject property in the current market. You are obligated to provide accurate and supportable value estimates. These estimates enable buyers, sellers, lenders, and others to make intelligent decisions about what will be among the most important decisions in their lives.

**Note:** Real estate agents often take the listing at any price, hoping to beat the price down after tying up a long-term exclusive listing.

## Accurate and Supportable Value Estimates

Plainly said, sellers (by and large) do not understand the concept of fair market value. Because of the competitive nature of the business, and the lack of confidence, inexperience, and ability, some agents throw caution to the wind in their anxiety to get the seller's signature on the listing. They often take the listing at any price, hoping to beat the price down after tying them up on a long-term exclusive listing.

In a deflated market, the seller has most likely paid more for the property than the market will bear at the time of the listing. In an inflated market, sellers may have unreasonable expectations of the potential of their property, and "reach" beyond what is realistic to get the highest price. They list the property high, expecting to get offers upon which a counter offer can be made. More often than not, no offers emerge. Buyers are scared away and do not even look at the property. In addition, the price of the property might cause the electronic search facility of a typical MLS search engine to exclude the property from the search.

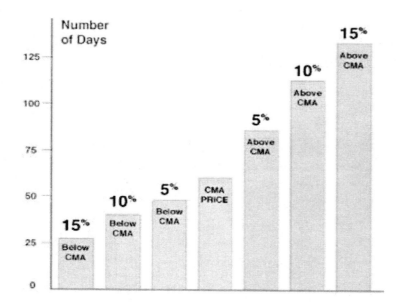

## Sellers Motive to Sell

A seller, upon listing his or her property for sale, has a motive that drives the seller's decision to acquire cash, if only for the opportunities cash makes available to him or her. The motives range from the disposal of real estate because it is no longer of use to the owner or the owner is now threatened with loss due to foreclosure, to the need for cash to accomplish a personal goal, such as acquiring a replacement home or simply putting the cash into savings.

## The Two Most Important Factors

As the listing agent, you are obligated to provide accurate and supportable value estimates. It will be these estimates that will enable buyers, sellers, lenders, and others to make intelligent decisions on what, in all probability, will be the single most important decision of their lives. The two most important factors to be considered when establishing a list price are the following:

- Market value, or the most probable price an informed buyer will pay in an arm's-length transaction.

- Seller net proceeds, or what the seller wants to obtain as a result of the sale.

### Price vs. Value

*Price* is the monetary sum paid for real property; it represents a fact. *Value* is expressed as an opinion or estimate; the market establishes value. The value is based upon competitive properties and is objective. When discussing *market value* with the seller, it is important that the agent and the seller have the same understanding of the meaning of *market value*. A good definition might be the following:

> *The estimated price, in terms of money, that a property should bring in a competitive and open market under all conditions requisite to a fair sale, with the buyer and seller acting prudently.*

### Approaches to Value

Sellers rarely understand the technical definition of market value. The real estate agent must employ a valuation technique that is simple to use and easy to understand. The simplest and probably the most reliable method is the competitive market analysis. The *competitive market analysis* is the most easily understood tool that has been developed for use by the average real estate agent. It is the most effective and simplest tool to show the seller the following:

- What has sold.
- What has expired without selling.

### Preparing the Competitive Market Analysis

1) Select three to six properties from your current listing files that are most comparable to the subject property. List the addresses, bedrooms, baths, etc. Whenever possible, you should list the exact loan balance. Do not round it off. Exact figures lend authenticity to your report. Average the listing prices of the homes. The seller will be very interested in this item.

2) Select six properties that have sold in the last 12 Months. This is what buyers paid. This is fact, not fiction. The most important information is how much they sold for and the terms under which they sold. The more recent your data, the more convincing it is. Do not select more than needed. Too much information is as harmful as too little.

3) Select six properties that have expired (unsold) during the past 12 months. This properties' prices represent what buyers would not pay. Include the date listed, the list price, and the date expired. You now (hopefully) have 18 homes that show the past and present market of the area being analyzed. You can now show the seller the market history.

**Instructor Note:** When presenting the competitive market analysis, it will help immensely if you have information on the properties the seller has seen. This is not all that difficult. Chances are, that the seller has looked fairly close to his or her home. Seldom will the seller's excursions take him or her beyond a one-mile radius.

### Seller Net Proceeds

Probably the most pressing concern sellers of real estate have about selling is the amount of money they will receive for their property on a sale. Although the amount sellers will receive is a calculable part of the purchase price, it is rarely the full amount of the purchase price.

Very often, a seller's initial belief is that the net sales proceeds will be roughly equal to the seller's equity in the property, less a brokerage fee. The costs of selling, such as retrofitting property and complying with governmental safety regulations, as well as lender payoff penalties or buyer's demands for repairs, does not occur to the seller until he or she is educated about the process.

## Unanticipated Costs

Furthermore, sellers tend not to recognize the need to fix up the property or to clear the property of structural pests and accumulated defects so that the property can be properly marketed. In other words, most sellers who have not sold real estate within the last several years are without a clue as to how to estimate their net sales proceeds.

On the other hand, real estate agents routinely sell properties and review closing statements. They have a working understanding of every expense that a seller is most likely to be confronted with to market, sell, and close escrow on a property.

## Seller's Net Sheet: The Up Side

When used properly is involved, a *seller's net sheet* can be the key to getting the listing. The estimated seller's proceeds are of vital importance to owners. Sellers who receive less than what they anticipated are not satisfied customers. When sellers are unhappy, the chances that problems will arise during escrow increase. From the standpoints of good business, agency duty, and basic fairness, you want sellers to understand what they will net from a sale if sold at the list price, and the estimated costs they will incur that will affect their net proceeds. Many agents like to estimate seller costs just a little on the high side, so any surprises are more likely to be pleasant ones.

**Note:** Owners who receive less than what they anticipated are not satisfied customers.

The seller's net sheet should first be prepared at the listing stage and again when reviewing offers or updating the figures when changes become known. It is a good idea to have the sellers initial the seller's net sheet at the time of listing. Attach a copy to the top of their listing agreement copies.

## Seller's Net Sheet: The Down Side

For the listing agent, a down side always exists when making disclosures regarding net sales proceeds. The information might cause a prospective seller to decide not to sell, or cause a seller of listed property to reject an offer and counter at a price that is unacceptable to a buyer. It is because of these pricing decisions that the net proceeds information is a material fact to the seller.

## Costs of Sale as a Material Fact

A material fact is information that, if known to a client, may affect the client's decision to sell or buy. A seller's decision to enter into a listing contract is just as important as a buyer's decision to buy. The information about sales expenses and closing costs is readily available to the listing agent, and the listing agent must disclose these costs to the seller. Sellers do not like surprises—especially surprise fees.

## Importance of Preparing the Seller's Net Sheet

Think of the seller's net sheet as insurance against surprises. Regardless of whether the seller requests a net sheet, it is best to prepare and review one with a seller. The time and effort needed to prepare a net sheet is a small premium to pay to assure that the seller is informed about fees and costs. In addition, the preparation of the seller's net sheet will be a great tool for you, the listing agent, when offers are presented. You will be able to "plug in" the new numbers on the net sheet, and properly advise the seller.

# Case Study: Preparing a Seller's Net Sheet

## Pre-Listing Research and Findings

> **Instructor Note:** For this exercise, assume that the current market is a buyer's market. (The municipal and state regulations outlined in the scenario are only for purposes of this exercise. They may not apply to your particular state or city.)

**Step One: The Call from Sellers**

On Monday morning, Paul and Cindy Seller have called their friend Lisa Broker and expressed interest in selling their two-bedroom, three-bath single-family residence, which was built in 2005 and consists of 1380 sq. feet. Lisa sets up a meeting with them on Tuesday evening at their home to discuss the possibility of accepting the listing.

**Step Two: The Drive-By**

Monday afternoon, Lisa drives by the home to take a few pictures of the exterior and get a feel for the neighborhood. Upon driving by Paul and Cindy's home on Monday afternoon, Lisa notices that the home, while only a few years old, is in disrepair. A few shingles from the roof are missing, there is virtually no landscaping, and the paint on the eves is cracked. The front yard is overrun with weeds, and the driveway has several large and unsightly oil stains. Lisa also notices that Paul and Cindy have built a makeshift carport out of metal tubing and sheet metal that is a municipal code violation. Finally, Lisa notices that the home next door, which is in foreclosure, is "tented" and is being sprayed for termites.

**Step Three: Further Research and Preliminary Competitive Market Analysis**

Lisa returns to her office and makes some calls to do some further research on the property, and learns that the property is one of the few properties in the city that is not on city sewer. The property has a septic tank.

Lisa's preliminary competitive market analysis reveals the following information:

The average price of current comparable listings is: **$362,500.00**
The average price of comparable properties that have sold recently is: **$349,000.00**
Of all the expired comparable listings, the lowest priced listing was: **$360,000.00**

**Step Four: Initial Viewing of the Home's Interior**

On Tuesday evening, Lisa arrives at Paul and Cindy's home. Cindy (who is an arts-and-crafts enthusiast), has painted several lavishly-colored murals and stenciled designs on almost every wall in the home. The murals and designs are of a nature that is completely at odds with what most buyers want. Lisa also notices a water stain on the ceiling in the living room, which undoubtedly resulted from the roof leaking water as a result of the missing shingles. Once again, Lisa takes pictures.

**The Reality of the Situation:** Lisa feels pretty sure that this home will not sell in its current shape, or at least, not in the current buyer's market. Being a conscientious real estate agent who understands that a listing is just a liability until it sells, Lisa will not accept this listing until Paul and Cindy prepare the property for sale. (Recall that this is a buyer's market.)

**Step Five: Estimate the Dollar Amount of Property Encumbrances**

During the conversation that ensues, Paul and Cindy inform Lisa that the property is encumbered by a first deed of trust note, and a second deed of trust note, as well as a mechanic's lien from the swimming pool they have recently installed:

| | |
|---|---|
| First trust deed note: | $193,000.00 |
| Second trust deed note: | $ 15,000.00 |
| Other liens: | $ 12,550.00 |
| Estimated Encumbrances: | **$220,550.00** |

## Step Six: Estimate the Cost for Property Preparation

Wednesday morning, Lisa emails the pictures of the property's exterior and interior to various home repair contractors and asks them for some *verbal quotes* (non-binding) to repair and clean up the exterior and repaint the entire interior. Finally, Lisa calls Acme Pest Control and gets a price on a termite inspection report, and an estimate on a termite fumigation. Lisa's research yields the following information:

| | |
|---|---|
| Scrape and repaint eaves: | $ 750.00 |
| Replace roof shingles and repair leak: | $ 265.00 |
| Yard cleanup and minimal landscaping: | $ 625.00 |
| **Estimated Property Preparation Expenses:** | **$1,640.00** |

**Note:** Lisa will not accept this listing until Paul and Cindy prepare the property for sale.

## Step Seven: Estimate the Cost of Property Compliance with Regulations

Additionally, Lisa must advise Paul and Cindy about certain city and state regulations that will affect their net proceeds. The city requires that all property must be in compliance with zoning ordinances, and all property owners must provide the buyer with a local compliance report prior to any transfer of ownership. Furthermore, the state requires that all sellers of property provide to the buyer a termite inspection report, termite clearance certification, septic tank functionality certification, and proof of septic tank pumping.

| | |
|---|---|
| Termite report: | $ 50.00 |
| Termite clearance (fumigation and certification): | $ 720.00 |
| Local ordinance compliance report: | $ 15.00 |
| Compliance with local ordinances: | $ 150.00 |
| Septic tank inspection report: | $ 90.00 |
| Septic tank pumping: | $ 220.00 |
| **Estimated Property Compliance:** | **$1,245.00** |

## Step Eight: Estimate the Seller's Escrow Costs and Other Closing Costs

Next, Lisa must factor the seller closing costs into the seller net sheet.

| | |
|---|---|
| Escrow fee: | $ 685.00 (max) |
| Document preparation fee: | $ 90.00 |
| Notary fees: | $ 65.00 |
| Recording fees/documentary transfer tax: | $ 125.00 |
| Title insurance premium: | $ 475.00 |
| Beneficiary statement/demand: | $ 15.00 |
| Reconveyance fees: | $ 45.00 |
| Transaction coordinator fee: | $ 150.00 |
| Miscellaneous expense (Escrow Pad): | $ 300.00 |
| Unpaid taxes: | $ 199.00 |
| **Total Estimated Seller Closing Costs:** | **$2,149.00** |

## Step Nine: Figure Broker Commission

Recall that when Lisa did her competitive market analysis on the property, she learned that the average price of comparable properties that have sold recently is $349,000.00. If Paul and Cindy were to price their property in accordance with the sales prices of comparable properties and Lisa's competitive market, Lisa's broker commission would be 6%:

Broker Commission (6% of $349,000.00): **$20,940.00**

**Step Ten: Calculate Total Estimated Debits for Seller**

Lisa can now calculate the estimated debits for the sellers:

| | |
|---|---|
| Estimated Encumbrances | $220,550.00 |
| Estimated Property Preparation Expenses: | $ 1,640.00 |
| Estimated Property Compliance Expense: | $ 1,245.00 |
| Estimated Seller Escrow and Closing Costs: | $ 2,149.00 |
| Broker Commission:* | $ 20,940.00 |
| Total Estimated Seller Debits: | **$246,524.00** |

*Based on pricing the property in accordance with competitive market analysis.

**A Note about Seller Credits:** If the information is available, seller credits (such as prepaid taxes or an impound account balance) can be credited back to the seller, which will increase the seller proceeds. However, for the purposes of this exercise, seller credits will not be applied.

**Finally: Calculating the Estimated Seller's Net**

Now Lisa is ready to calculate the seller's net sheet based on her pre-listing research and findings. Using the form below, Lisa can show Paul and Cindy approximately what their net proceeds will be if they list their property at $349,000.00.

**Seller's Net Proceeds Calculation**

**Proposed Listing Price**                                          **$349,000.00**

When Lisa did her competitive market analysis, she found that the average price of comparable sold properties in the area was $349,000.00. Assuming there were no adjustments, this would be a good proposed listing price because it is commensurate with what the market has done.

**Estimated Encumbrances**                                          **$220,550.00**

The total dollar amount of the principal balance of the first trust deed note, second trust deed note, and any other liens that encumber the property (such as mechanic's liens, judgment liens, tax liens, and improvement district bond liens, and any UCC-1 liens on any personal property that are part of the sale).

**Estimated Property Preparation Expenses**                        **$ 1,640.00**

The total estimated cost to repaint the eves, fix the roof, and install minimal landscaping.

**Estimated Property Compliance Expenses**                         **$ 1,245.00**

The total estimated cost for the termite report, termite treatment, local ordinance compliance report, septic tank inspection report, and septic tank pumping.

**Estimated Seller Escrow and Closing Costs**                      **$ 2,149.00**

The total estimated costs of half of the escrow fee, document preparation fee, notary fee, recording fee, title insurance premium, beneficiary statement, reconveyance fees, transaction coordinator fee, escrow pad, and prorations.

**Broker Commission (**Based on a 6% commission rate if the house sold at the list price) **$ 20,940.00**

**Seller Net Proceeds**                                            **$102,476.00**

**QUIZZES ARE MANDATORY:** Please log in and submit the chapter quizzes online.

## Chapter 5 Quiz

1.      In a(n) _____ listing, the listing broker is compensated if he or she finds the buyer, or if another broker finds the buyer. The listing broker is not compensated if the seller finds the buyer and facilitates the sale.

(a)      exclusive agency
(b)      exclusive right-to-sell
(c)      open
(d)      net

2.      The seller may execute _____ listings with more than one real estate broker and pay only the broker who brings an able buyer whose offer the owner accepts.

(a)      exclusive agency
(b)      exclusive right-to-sell
(c)      open
(d)      option

3.      With an _____ listing, a broker is employed to sell the property and at the same time holds an option to purchase the property himself or herself. Therefore, the broker occupies the two conflicting positions of agent and purchaser.

(a)      exclusive agency
(b)      exclusive right-to-sell
(c)      option
(d)      open

4.      Listing prices should be set using _____ as a guide, rather than emotions.

(a)      profit potential
(b)      greed
(c)      market analysis
(d)      seller desires

5.      Very often, a seller's initial belief is that the _____ will be roughly equal to his or her equity in the property, less a brokerage fee.

(a)      net proceeds
(b)      sales price
(c)      listing price
(d)      closing costs

6.      With an _____ listing, the seller pays the commission to the listing broker if the property sells during the listing term, regardless of who facilitates the sale or who found the buyer.

(a)      exclusive right-to-sell
(b)      exclusive agency
(c)      open
(d)      exclusionary

7.      With regard to a net listing, all of the following statements are true EXCEPT:

(a)     The dollar amount of compensation to the broker is generally not stated in the listing agreement.
(b)     If the property sells for more than the amount required by the seller, the broker is entitled to retain the surplus as his or her commission.
(c)     If the property sells for an amount equal to or less than the net amount required by the seller, the broker may not receive any compensation.
(d)     Net listings are strictly illegal in all states.

8.      With regard to a competitive market analysis, all of the following statements are true EXCEPT:

(a)     A competitive market analysis is an easily understood valuation tool that has been developed for use by the average real estate agent.
(b)     A competitive market analysis should show the seller what is for sale now and what has sold recently.
(c)     A competitive market analysis should never include information about properties that have expired without selling.
(d)     A competitive market analysis should include, if possible, properties that the seller will likely have seen.

9.      Many agents like to estimate seller costs just a little on the _____, so any surprises are more likely to be pleasant ones.

(a)     aggressive side
(b)     low side
(c)     high side
(d)     conservative side

10.     Price is the monetary sum paid for real property—it represents a fact. However, _____ is expressed as an opinion or estimate—it is based upon competitive properties and is objective.

(a)     Market value
(b)     Monetary editorial
(c)     Conditional price
(d)     Non-negotiable price

## Chapter Six: Buyer Agency Contracts

### Important Terms

CC&Rs
dual agency
employment agreement
errors and omissions insurance
express agency
FEMA
FHA Mortgage Insurance
Home Warranty Directory
homeowners associations
implied agency
MLS
offer
solicitation

### Chapter Six Learning Objectives

After successful completion of this chapter, you should be able to complete the following:

- Understand how an implied buyer agency can be created inadvertently.

- State the main reason to create a buyer agency.

- List a few different ways to help buyers understand their destination real estate market.

- Identify methods to counsel buyers and appropriate subject matter for such.

- Define the five types of homeowners insurance.

- State the purpose of a home warranty.

- Explain the purpose of various buyer-related documents (other than the purchase contract).

- Identify and discuss disclosure responsibilities.

### Creation of a Buyer Broker Agency

#### Creation by Accident

An agency relationship between a buyer and a real estate broker can be created by accident. In other words, even though the parties may not have consciously planned to create an agency relationship, an implied agency can be created unintentionally, inadvertently, or accidentally by their actions.

**Note:** When the buyer's and broker's intentions are in writing, the boundaries of the agency are set.

This is why the *Buyer Broker Exclusive Employment Agreement* (available from the California Association of REALTORS®) is always a good idea. When the buyer's and broker's intentions are in writing, the agency becomes an express agency, and all of the boundaries of the agency are set forth in clear language.

#### Express Agency is Always Better

In the real estate industry, an express agency is always better than an implied agency. In the performance of any service for the buyer, the listing broker runs the risk of creating an accidental dual agency. Therefore, if the conduct or representations of the broker induce the buyer to believe that he or she is the broker's principal, instead of the third-party beneficiary of the broker's efforts on behalf of the seller, then the broker may be held liable for injury suffered by the buyer as a consequence of such belief.

### Why Create a Buyer Agency?

Simple—to establish boundaries. If the buyer refuses to sign a *Buyer Broker Exclusive Employment Agreement*, the buyer is refusing representation. The buyer is refusing to create an express agency and thus, an implied agency exists. The broker is then bound by a fiduciary duty to the buyer with no boundaries and no clear-cut responsibilities to the agency, yet the buyer is not bound to "stick with" the broker. Not only that, but a buyer who refuses agency is not, in the eyes of the law, a bona fide buyer.

**Note:** A person who fails to exercise due diligence to avail himself or herself of information and assistance that is within his or her reach is not a bona fide purchaser.

A judge who issued an opinion in *Godfrey v. Navratil 411 P.2d 470* had this to say regarding buyers who refuse agency:

> *A person who fails to exercise due diligence to avail himself of information and assistance which is within his reach is not a bona fide purchaser.*

#### Sitting an Open House

In the case of a licensee "sitting" an open house, and a prospective buyer entering the home, it is the licensee's responsibility to ascertain two things:

1) Whether the buyer is currently represented by another agent, and

2) Whether the buyer wishes to be represented by the licensee who is sitting in the open house.

If the buyer has already signed a Buyer Broker Exclusive Employment Agreement with another agent, it becomes the licensee's responsibility to clearly and directly explain to the buyer, before showing the open house listing, that the licensee represents the seller and not the buyer.

## Duties of the Buyer's Agent

### Helping Buyers Understand the Real Estate Culture

With a down market, buyers are scarce, to say the least. With an up market, buyers seem to come out of the woodwork. In either market, a buyer's agent is important. A buyer's agent can make the process of relocating to a new area significantly less stressful.

Real estate markets can be vastly different from region to region. As a buyer's agent, you can help buyers understand the buying culture and the real estate market. You can clarify the differences on large items such as taxes, zoning, and other area restrictions as well as smaller items such as what items usually convey in a transaction. When buyers understand the culture in the buying market, they can make a more informed decision.

### Seven Ways You Can Help the Buyer to Relocate

There are a variety of ways that you can prepare yourself to serve relocating buyers so that you can inform them about the area they are relocating to. The more informed the buyer, the more smoothly your transaction will go. Here are seven suggestions:

**Note:** You can provide literature about schools to the buyer so that he or she can make a more informed decision.

**1. Become Informed about Schools**: Most public school systems have a contact person who is more than willing to meet with real estate agents and explain all of the options of their particular district. Your local Association may be able to have these contacts come to a meeting as a guest speaker. Generally, there are many options when it comes to public schools. As an agent, it might be valuable to visit the schools in your area and collect literature about each school. While you cannot formally request a given school, you can provide literature to the buyer so that he or she can make an informed decision about their preferred area.

**2. Coordinate the Home-Finding Experience**: Conduct research beforehand, and don't "throw" a tour together. When buyers call an agent, they generally have an idea about the style and pricing of the home they want. Don't wait until the buyers arrive at your office to conduct research. Use your MLS service to find several homes that suit the buyer's needs, then print out the listings and map out your journey.

> **Tip:** Give the buyer a map with the listings highlighted on the map. If the buyer rides with you during the tour, ask the buyer to be the navigator. This ensures that the buyer will be engaged during the entire process, and will take a more thorough notice of the different areas of town.

**3. Explain Agency to the Buyer**: When you present the buyer agency form to the buyer, help him or her to understand what it means to have a buyer agent. A buyer agency agreement is an employment agreement; it simply means that the buyer is employing you to be the agent. The form merely puts the responsibilities of both parties to the employment agreement (buyer and agent) in writing.

**4. Encourage a Home Inspection**: Are home inspections necessary? Yes, even on brand new homes. Home inspections are cheap insurance. The inspection is designed to cover the five major components of a home:

- Structural integrity
- Roof
- Electrical
- Plumbing
- Heating and air-conditioning.

New homes can have as many problems as old homes. How would the buyer know if the builder failed to use ply chips for the roof sheathing or that the gas valve on the furnace was malfunctioning? Additionally, home inspections provide valuable maintenance tips. For the best results, the buyer's agent and the buyer should be at the inspection.

The US Housing and Urban Development requires that the buyer be shown and sign the Form HUD-92564-CN: *For your Protection: Get a Home Inspection* for all transactions that will involve FHA mortgage insurance on existing property. For your reference, the HUD Form 92564 *For Your Protection: Get a Home Inspection* is available for download in the online course.

**5. Recommend that the Buyer Choose an In-State Lender**: Typically, if there is going to be a delay in the process, it will originate with the financing. Availability of the loan processor is a must. Good communication with the loan processor can be the difference between a smooth process and a not-so-smooth process.

**6. Recommend a Staking Survey**: A staking survey is not a required item to purchase a home. The lender requires only a mortgage inspection survey, which is not guaranteed for accuracy. For additional cost, it is worth it for the buyer to know where the property corners are actually located. A staking survey is particularly important when dealing with vacant land.

For instance, in *Hill-Shafer Partnership v. Chilson Family Trust, 165 Ariz 469* *, the buyer intended to purchase whatever the legal description identified, regardless of size or location. The seller did not have similar intent, but intended to convey only certain property. The legal description in the contract described property other than that which the seller intended to convey. Therefore, the court held that there was no mutual assent, and no binding contract.

*The official court document for *Hill-Shafer Partnership v. Chilson Family Trust* can be downloaded from the online course.

**7. Counsel Buyers About What They Can Afford**: There is nothing worse than showing a buyer several homes, the buyer making an offer that is accepted, and then the buyer doesn't qualify for financing, or gets scared about the new obligations of owning a home. Before the buyer begins searching for homes, have the buyer establish what he or she can afford to spend. It is a good idea to have the buyer consult with a lender. However, the lender will likely tell the buyer the maximum amount that he or she can afford—just because the buyer qualifies for a certain amount of financing does not mean that the buyer will feel comfortable about the purchase.

**Note:** In the real estate business, there are very few things worse than representing a buyer on a purchase contract just to realize that the buyer failed to qualify for financing, and therefore having to cancel the contract mid-escrow.

Remember, the loan amount isn't the only monthly payment. While it is extremely important to figure out what the buyer's monthly principle and interest payment is, the buyer also needs to factor in monthly amounts for property taxes, homeowners insurance, and homeowners association dues (if any). Also, find out what the average utility costs are in the area, and factor that in to the buyer's budget.

## Counseling the Buyer

### Home Insurance Information

There are many factors for buyers to consider when deciding what type(s) and how much insurance is needed or required on a given property. Insurance carriers have a wide variety of insurances and costs available for buyers to consider.

**Note:** Know the types of hazards unique to the area, and understand the types of hazard insurance that are available.

You should become familiar with the types of insurance required in the area, so that when a buyer makes decisions about insurance, you can provide some insight. For instance, certain parts of California are prone to earthquakes, and certain parts are prone to wildfires. It is the buyer's agent's job to know the types of hazards unique to the area, and understand the types of hazard insurance available.

> **Instructor Note:** Become familiar with the types of insurance in your area. However, be careful about calling yourself an insurance expert; or giving the buyer the impression that you are an expert.

How much insurance and which types of insurance the buyer will need depends on a number of factors, including the location of the home, home value, home construction, applicable laws, deductibles, premium costs, etc.

## Five Basic Types of Home Insurance

There are five basic types of home insurance:

**Homeowners (Hazard) Insurance**: This is the basic coverage, which includes damage or loss from hazards plus added available coverage for personal property and liability, jewelry, theft while away from home, and other such items. Factors that affect the cost are home value, age/condition, added coverage, location, and deductibles. Homeowners insurance may include wind and hail coverage, but in some areas, a separate policy will be required.

**Flood Insurance**: This indemnifies against loss by flood damage. It is required by lenders in areas that are (federally) designated as potential flood areas. This insurance is purchased through private companies, but is federally subsidized by FEMA.

**Wind and Hail Insurance**: In some locations, damage from wind and hail is not covered in the basic homeowners insurance, but insurers offer a separate policy for this coverage.

**Earthquake Insurance**: Damages resulting from earthquakes are not covered by homeowners, flood, or wind and hail insurances. This insurance is quite inexpensive and should be considered if the property is in an area where earthquakes are a possibility.

**Private Mortgage Insurance (PMI)**: This is insurance coverage for nonpayment of mortgages and foreclosure. While paid for by the homeowner, it only provides protection for the lender. Lenders usually require PMI when the mortgage amount is greater than 80% of the home value.

## Home Warranties

When a buyer purchases new construction, the builder will issue various warranties, both from the builder and from appliance manufacturers (stove, air conditioner, furnace, etc.). When buyers purchase a pre-owned home, private insurance companies have policies available that insure the buyer against defects (usually in plumbing, heating/AC, and electrical) in the home being purchased. As a buyer's agent, you can help the buyers decide on the best insurance company, coverage, and length of coverage for the buyer's specific needs.

### How Home Warranties Work

Typically, the cost of a home warranty is between $400 and $500. The common procedure is that when an owner reports an incident, the warranty company will send a contractor (generally third-party contractors) to the home. The contractor is required to check if the problem is caused by lack of maintenance or care. If so, their repair work will likely not be authorized. Counsel the buyer who buys home warranties to maintain his or her home appliances and keep maintenance records.

### Preexisting Conditions

Preexisting conditions are not covered. The home warranty company expects to start with a clean sheet and they require homeowners to fix any preexisting issues before the new policy becomes effective. This is another good reason to get a home inspection on a pre-owned home. (The home inspection will identify any faulty appliances so that they can be fixed before a home warranty contract is signed. (A link to a directory of home warranty companies by state is available in the online course.)

## Educate the Buyer about Important Documents

As a buyer's agent, you can assist your clients in becoming more informed buyers by educating them on the purpose of the documents involved in a real estate transaction. A well-informed buyer decreases your liability.

Most buyer's agents explain to their buyers the importance of reading the purchase contract and the home inspection report. However, sometimes, the other documents upon which the buyer relies are barely discussed. Although it may seem overwhelming to buyers, you should counsel buyers to review all of the documents involved in the purchase. Some documents should be reviewed as soon as they are received. In fact, a buyer may need to read certain documents even before signing a purchase contract.

### MLS Printout

Explain to the buyer that the MLS printout is similar to an advertisement. It is not an offer, because there is no power of acceptance. It is merely a solicitation for an offer.

The MLS information is usually procured from the seller, and could be inaccurate, so the buyer must verify anything important. Also, emphasize that the MLS printout is not a part of the purchase contract. Therefore, even if the printout states that the washer and dryer (or some other item) will be sold with the home, this must be written into the purchase contract, unless the item is already incorporated in the contract's pre-printed list of fixtures that are included in the sale.

**A Common Misunderstanding:** Many agents believe that the MLS listing is binding on the seller. It is not. For instance, many agents believe that if a home is listed in the MLS for a list price of $250,000, and a purchase offer for $250,000 is presented, that the seller MUST accept it. Not the case. The seller does not have to accept the purchase offer. However, if the offer is without contingencies, and it is the full price, the seller may be bound to pay a commission to the listing broker.

### Disclosure Statement

Most sellers in a traditional resale transaction provide this document, but new home sellers do not, and most REO properties do not. Sometimes, the seller will ask the buyer to waive the delivery of such a document. In cases where the seller provides this document, you, the buyer's agent, must explain to the buyer that this document is a disclosure of what the seller actually knows. It is not a representation of every possible defect in the property.

It is also important to understand that just because the buyer receives a disclosure statement, the real estate agents are not relieved from disclosing to the buyer all material facts about the property.

Generally, if the home is bank-owned, the bank will refuse to provide a disclosure statement. If a listing states that a disclosure statement is not available, or will not be provided, you, the buyer's agent, should nonetheless advise the buyer to request the disclosure statement in the offer.

### Disclosure Statement Waivers

If the seller asks the buyer to waive the disclosure statement, it is imperative that you, the buyer's agent, give the buyer a copy of the statement, so that the buyer knows and understands what he or she is waiving. The buyer should never waive the receipt of any document without first seeing a copy of the document. Even a blank disclosure statement is valuable to the buyer.

**Note:** The buyer should never waive the receipt of any document without first seeing a copy of the document.

In these circumstances, you, the buyer's agent, would be wise to obtain the buyer's written acknowledgment of receipt of the blank form. The buyer can and should utilize a blank disclosure statement as a checklist while conducting the desired inspections and investigations. The disclosure statement prompts questions that will assist the buyer in evaluating the property.

> **Instructor Note:** If the buyer consents to the waiver of the disclosure document without knowing what the document consists of, a court will hold you accountable for a breach of agency because you have allowed the buyer to make an uninformed waiver.

### Covenants, Conditions, Restrictions (CC&Rs)

A timely review of the CC&Rs is often overlooked. Inform the buyer that the CC&Rs are recorded at the county recorder's office and that they generally control certain aspects of the properties within a subdivision. By purchasing a home in such a subdivision, the buyer agrees to comply with the CC&Rs. Explain to the buyer that the CC&Rs may restrict the following:

- Certain home improvements
- How many pets can live in the home
- Where the buyer can park a car
- Whether the buyer can park an RV at his or her home, or must park it elsewhere
- Any number of other matters that may affect the buyer's daily life

Therefore, it is essential for the buyer of a new home to read and agree to these restrictions before signing a purchase contract. Most purchase contracts will not allow the buyer to cancel after the inspection period, just because the buyer does not like the restrictions.

### Other Homeowners Association Documents

In addition to the CC&Rs, homeowners associations may be governed by bylaws and architectural guidelines. Very often, if the owner of a home in the association does not comply with these guidelines, the penalty could be as severe as losing his or her home.

### Title Report or Commitment for Title Insurance

Emphasize to the buyer that the title report or commitment contains important information. The title or escrow company that provides title insurance will give the buyer a title report or title commitment listing restrictions, easements, and liens recorded against the property (in the Schedule B, Exceptions). Make sure that the buyer receives and reviews all of the listed Schedule B exceptions.

## Buyer Agency Disclosure Issues

### Statutory Duty of Disclosure

This is not a disclosure course. Therefore, it is not our intent with this course to discuss every single detail regarding disclosure in real estate, but we will try to cover the most common and most important disclosure requirements encountered from time to time.

It is the responsibility of the real estate licensee to disclose, in writing to all parties to the transaction, any information that the licensee possesses that materially and adversely affects the consideration to be paid by any party to the transaction, including the following:

- Any information that the seller or lessor is or may be unable to perform.

- Any information that the buyer or lessee is, or may be, unable to perform.

- Any material defect that exists in the property being transferred, and

- The existence of a lien or encumbrance on the property being transferred.

Failure to do so may allow the buyer to terminate the agreement and seek remedies as provided by law. Comprehensive statutory requirements for disclosure should be used by the real estate professional to establish guidelines for determining the type and class of matters that are material and that should be disclosed.

## Disclosure and Errors and Omissions Insurance

The high cost of an agent's insurance coverage has been a hot topic for a while now. Errors and omissions insurance covers errors (clerical or judgment errors) and *omissions*, which are errors of intentional or unintentional neglect. For example, if an agent misspells an owner's name, and as a result, invalidates a purchase contract, that is an error. If an agent fails to return a phone call that is crucial to the sale, this is technically called an omission. An agent might forget a required disclosure—that would also be an omission.

However, most errors and omissions insurance policies specifically exclude errors or omissions in which a law is broken.

> **Instructor Note:** In California, a failure to disclose known material facts would be a direct violation of regulatory requirements. Thus, most E&O policies would not cover such an omission. In other words, in California, the likelihood of an E&O policy covering a failure to disclose might be slim.

### FAQs About Disclosure

**Question:** What information must a seller or broker provide a prospective buyer concerning environmental hazards?

**Answer:** Sellers and brokers have a duty to disclose any known environmental conditions that affect the property.

**Question:** Will a seller or real estate licensee be liable if the disclosure statement contains inaccuracies or omissions?

**Answer:** No, as long as ordinary care was used when obtaining and transmitting the information, and the following apply:

- The errors or omissions were not personally known to the seller or the licensee, and

- The errors or omissions were based on information provided by public agencies, licensed engineers, land surveyors, geologists, structural pest control operators, contractors, or other experts who deal with matters within the scope of the license or expertise of that expert, and

- When the expert is aware that the opinion will be delivered to and relied on by the buyer, the expert will be liable to the buyer for damages suffered if the expert was negligent in rendering the opinion.

**Question:** What is the seller's responsibility when the disclosure statement states that an item is inoperable, while the purchase contract warrants that it is operable? For example, let's say the seller states in the disclosure statement that the dishwasher is not functioning. On the other hand, in the purchase contract, the seller warrants that "all built-in appliances are in working order." Is the seller responsible for fixing the dishwasher?

**Answer:** Yes. The seller is responsible for living up to his or her contractual obligations. The disclosure statement is not part of the contract; its only function is to provide information to the buyer to enable the buyer to decide whether or not to go through with the transaction. Even if the buyer decides not to cancel based on the disclosure statement, the buyer does not waive any of his or her rights under the purchase contract.

## Buyer's Agent Should Take an Active Role

Although sellers are obligated to disclose all known material facts about the property, there are likely facts about the property of which the seller is unaware. Therefore, the buyer and buyer's agent should take an active role in obtaining information about the property. The buyer and buyer's agent should do the following:

**1)** Verify all important information.

**2)** Inquire about any concerns.

**3)** Investigate the surrounding area.

### Duty to Conduct a Visual Inspection

In addition to the buyer's agent's statutory requirement to make certain disclosures to the buyer, the buyer's agent has a statutory duty to conduct a reasonably competent and diligent visual inspection and disclose to a prospective purchaser all facts that materially affect the value or desirability of the property that such an investigation would reveal.

### Responsibility for Truth and Accuracy of Statements

**Note:** Knowledge and skills beyond that of the average person.

Since the courts have held that the consumer is correct to consider a real estate licensee as a person who has knowledge and skills beyond that of the average person, the consumer can expect that the buyer's agent will not make statements without prior examination, and he or she is responsible for the truth and accuracy of any information disseminated to cooperating brokers or buyers.

**Case Law:** Court decisions have created an obligation for licensees such that the real estate licensee has a duty to disclose to the buyer all material defects in the property that are known to the licensee, as well as those that are not within the diligent observation and attention of the buyer.

**Example:** In one case, a real estate salesperson was showing a property for lease to a prospective tenant but forgot to point out that the stairs leading to the basement were defectively constructed and possibly dangerous. The lessee moved into the property and later fell down the stairs and was injured. Both the salesperson and her employing broker were liable in damages for injuries suffered by the lessee.

### Known or Should Have Known

The above-referenced case shows that the buyer's agent's duty of care is not limited to the disclosure of matters known. Because of the real estate licensee's superior knowledge and experience as well as the duty to disclose material matters, there is also a duty to discover the facts regarding the property. It is the agent's responsibility to discover any serious defects in the property that could cause an unreasonable risk or harm to the client.

**Case Law:** In one case, without verification or qualification, an agent gave information to the buyer that he had obtained from the seller regarding the capacity of the well on the property. It turned out that the well had inadequate capacity. The court held that the buyer's agent and his broker (along with the seller and listing agent) were jointly and severally liable for the buyer's damages, which were substantial.

The court recited as follows:

> *Real estate brokers and their agents hold themselves out to the public as having specialized knowledge with regard to housing, housing conditions, and related matters. The public is entitled to and does rely on the expertise of real estate brokers in the purchase and sale of its homes. Therefore, there is a duty on the part of real estate brokers to be accurate and knowledgeable concerning the product they are in the business of selling...*

QUIZZES ARE MANDATORY: Please log in and submit the chapter quizzes online.

## Chapter 6 Quiz

1.      A buyer drives by a home and sees the listing sign with the listing agent's contact information. The buyer then calls the listing agent and inquires about the price of the property. The listing agent tells the buyer the price. Even though the listing agent and buyer may have not consciously planned to create an agency relationship, they have created by their actions _____.

     (a)      an express agency
     (b)      a universal agency
     (c)      an implied agency
     (d)      an express special agency

2.      When buyers understand the culture in the buying market, they can make a more informed decision. With regard to helping buyers understand the buying market, all of the following statements are true EXCEPT:

     (a)      As a buyer's agent, you can clarify issues such as taxes, zoning, and other area restrictions.
     (b)      As a buyer's agent, you can clarify issues such as which items usually convey in a transaction.
     (c)      As a buyer's agent, you must hire the moving van and can help the buyer move.
     (d)      As a buyer's agent, you can go visit the schools in your area and collect literature from each school, so that you can provide this literature to the buyer.

3.      With regard to counseling buyers, which of the following statements is FALSE?

     (a)      Before the buyers start searching for homes, it is a good idea to have the buyer clearly establish what he or she can afford to spend.
     (b)      Before the buyer begins searching for homes, it is a good idea to have the buyer consult with a lender.
     (c)      In addition to the monthly payment on the loan, the buyer should factor into their budget the monthly amounts due for property taxes, homeowners insurance, and homeowners association dues (if any).
     (d)      If the buyer qualifies for a certain amount of financing, it's a sure bet that the buyer will feel comfortable about the purchase.

4.      Which of the following is FALSE with regard to the MLS printout on the property?

     (a)      The MLS printout is similar to an advertisement.
     (b)      The information in the MLS printout could be inaccurate.
     (c)      The MLS printout is a part of the purchase contract.
     (d)      The buyer and buyer's agent should verify information in the MLS printout if such information is material to the buyer.

5.      It is the responsibility of the real estate licensee to disclose in writing, to all parties to the transaction, any information that the licensee possesses that materially and adversely affects the consideration to be paid by any party to the transaction. Material facts include all of the following EXCEPT _____.

     (a)      any information that the seller or lessor is or may be unable to perform
     (b)      the sellers' pending divorce
     (c)      any information that the buyer or lessee is, or may be, unable to perform
     (d)      any material defect that exists in the property being transferred

6.    In the real estate industry, a written agency is _____.

      (a)    an express agency
      (b)    an implied agency
      (c)    not an agency
      (d)    the only type of agency

7.    It is important for the buyer's agent to help buyers understand the culture in the buying market because when buyers have a clear understanding, they are more apt to _____.

      (a)    dress like a local
      (b)    make a more informed decision
      (c)    learn the local hangouts
      (d)    pay a higher price for property

8.    _____ is basic insurance coverage that includes damage or loss from hazards plus added available coverage for personal property and liability, jewelry, theft while away from home, and other such items.

      (a)    Homeowners (hazard) insurance
      (b)    Wind and hail insurance
      (c)    Earthquake insurance
      (d)    Flood insurance

9.    The title or escrow company that provides title insurance will give the buyer a title report or title commitment that lists _____.

      (a)    a site plan
      (b)    all of the physical defects of the property's improvements
      (c)    restrictions, easements, and liens recorded against the property
      (d)    the elevations and structural details of the property's improvements

10.   Because of the real estate licensee's superior knowledge and experience, and the duty to disclose material matters, there is a duty to _____ the facts regarding the property.

      (a)    conceal
      (b)    shield the buyer from
      (c)    discover
      (d)    ignore

## Chapter Seven: The Promissory Note

### Important Terms

adjustable rate note
alienation clause
construction loan
convertible loans
deed of trust note
fixed rate
index rate
interest only
negotiable instrument
PMI
reconveyance deed
treasury bond

### Chapter Seven Learning Objectives

After successful completion of this chapter, you should be able to complete the following:

- Define the term *promissory note*.

- List the information that must be included on a loan agreement.

- State the three categories of promissory notes used in the real estate business.

- Describe the main aspects of an installment note, and give three examples of notes that are included in the installment note category.

- Describe the main aspects of an open-ended note, and give an example of such a note.

- Describe the main aspects of a simple note, and give an example of such a note.

- Recognize the keywords that distinguish different clauses in a promissory note.

## Promissory Note Basics

### Written Promise to Repay a Loan

A promissory note is a borrower's written promise to repay a loan. Specifically, it is a written, dated, and signed two-party instrument, which contains an unconditional promise by the maker to pay a definite sum of money to a payee on demand or at a specified future date.

The promissory note is generally not recorded. When the loan is paid, the promissory note is marked *paid in full* and returned to the borrower, along with a recorded reconveyance deed. During the term of the loan, the lender retains the promissory note (more on reconveyance deeds in the next chapter). In the United States, a promissory note secured by real property is a negotiable instrument (unless the promissory note states otherwise).

### The Loan Agreement

A typical promissory note for a loan on real property does not include all the terms and conditions of a loan. In most cases (when the loan is for real property), the terms are complex and lengthy, so the promissory note incorporates a longer, more complicated document called the *loan agreement*, which details the terms and conditions of the loan.

### The Loan Agreement is a Bilateral Agreement

**Consideration:** The loan agreement for the loan on real property is a bilateral agreement in which each party promises something to the other. The lender promises to allow the borrower to use the money for a specified period of time, conditional upon the borrower's timely repayment. The lender, in exchange for its promise, receives the benefit of interest. The borrower promises timely repayment in exchange for the use of the money.

### What must be Included in All Loan Agreements?

Depending on the specific state laws, the content and appearance of a loan agreement may differ, but all loan agreements must include the following:

- Details of both the parties entering the contract, such as name, address, contact number, and registration number (if any).
- The principal loan amount.
- The duration of the loan.
- Details about the applied interest rates.
- A formula for calculating the repayment amount.
- The repayment provisions.
- The rights secured by both the parties in relation to the loan.
- The acceleration clause, which specifies the lender's rights in case of payment default.
- The definitions and interpretations of every important term used in the contract.
- Details of the security or collateral (discussed in Chapter Nine).
- Amortization provisions, if any.
- Prepayment penalties, if applicable.
- The notary signature for legal approval.

## Loan Agreement Clauses

### Typical Clauses in a Loan Agreement Interest Rates Clause

All promissory notes must state the amount of the loan and the interest rate, which may be either fixed or adjustable. Fixed interest rates are typically set and do not change over the life of the note. Variable or adjustable interest rates move up and down based on the changes in an underlying index rate over the life of the note (more on this in a later section).

> **Instructor Note:** Even where a fixed rate loan is involved, the promissory note may provide that if the borrower fails to make the payment specified by the loan agreement, a different interest rate may be charged. Notes may also provide that if payments are delinquent, late payment charges may be incurred.

### Repayment Schedule Clause

The promissory note should set forth the repayment schedule that is adopted by the parties. It should specify the amount of each payment, when it is to be made, and where it is to be made. The buyer's agent should help the buyer-borrower understand these terms completely, since even a minor deviation may constitute a default.

### Costs of Collection Clause

Most promissory notes contain a provision that obligates the borrower to pay, in addition to all principal and interest provided in the note, all costs of collection in the event that legal action must be undertaken by the lender to collect the balance due under the note. A typical clause might read as follows:

> *The borrower shall pay all costs of collection of this promissory note including, but not limited to, attorneys' fees, paid or incurred by the lender on account of such collection, whether or not suit is filed and whether or not such costs are paid or incurred, or to be paid or incurred, prior to or after the entry of a judgment.*

### Acceleration Clause

An *acceleration clause* is a provision in a promissory note that allows a lender to demand payment of the total outstanding balance in the event of a default. This is also called the *due on default clause*. This clause is primarily invoked only upon the borrower's default, such as failure to make payments, bankruptcy, nonpayment of taxes on mortgaged property, or the breaking of loan covenants. A typical acceleration clause reads as follows:

> *If any required payment under this note is not paid when due, or if an event of default occurs, the entire outstanding principal balance hereof plus accrued interest thereon shall, at the option of the lender, be immediately due and payable without notice of demand.*

**Reinstatement and the Acceleration Clause:** Generally, lenders are not anxious to invoke the acceleration clause. The foreclosure process is time consuming and expensive. Usually, a lender would rather the borrower pay the debt, even if only through a resumption of installment payments called for under the original payment obligation. Accordingly, in many circumstances, even where the lender has invoked an acceleration clause and called the entire loan due, the lender may allow the borrower to reinstate the loan by paying the amounts in default, together with interest, penalties, and costs of collection. Reinstatement returns the defaulted borrower to the original contractual payment schedule.

A right to reinstate is mandated by statute for all real estate loans in California. According to California Civil. Code 2924c(a)(1), for a non-judicial foreclosure, reinstatement is permitted until five business days prior to the date set for the foreclosure sale. For a judicial foreclosure, reinstatement is permitted at any time prior to entry of the judicial decree of foreclosure.

### Alienation Clause

*Alienation* means the act of transferring ownership, title, interest, or estate in real property from one person to another. The alienation clause (also called a *due on sale* clause) is a provision found in most real estate promissory notes, which provides that the balance of the secured debt becomes immediately due and payable at the option of the lender upon the transfer of title to the property by the borrower.

### Prepayment Clause

Promissory notes should state whether the borrower may prepay all or any part of the loan. Some lenders do not allow prepayments or may impose a fee if prepayment is allowed. Prepayment fees typically measure the actual damage or loss to the lender that results from the prepayment, and charge the borrower an equivalent fee. To do this, a formula is used that takes into account three factors:

**1)** The amount being prepaid,

**2)** The remaining term of the loan, and

**3)** Some index of current market rates as compared with the rate on the loan.

If the index rate and the loan rate are identical, the prepayment penalty might be very small, because the lender can relend the prepaid funds in the form of a new loan at the same interest rate, and hence would suffer no loss. If the index rate is lower than the rate on the existing loan, the prepayment penalty will be a little higher.

## Types of Promissory Notes

Every real estate promissory note falls into one (or more) of three primary categories. Once the borrower's purpose is established, the promissory note is written with one of three payment structures. Each loan type is a variation of one of these primary categories: the installment note, the simple note, or the open-ended note.

### Installment Notes

For the typical buyer of a single-family residence, the installment note will be the type of note presented. An installment note provides for periodic payments of principal and interest that will reduce the loan balance to zero by the end of the time period that is specified in the note. It is either fully amortized and is paid off at the end of the term, or partially amortized and requires one or more balloon payments prior to the end of the term.

**30-Year Fixed Rate Note:** A 30-year fixed rate promissory note is one form of an installment note. Also known as a conventional loan, conventional mortgage, 30-year fixed loan, or 30-year fixed mortgage, the interest rate on this type of loan stays the same throughout the life of the loan. The interest rate is usually just a little higher than that of the 30-year Treasury Bond at the time the mortgage is issued. Each month's payment is comprised of the interest on the remaining principal, and a bit of the principal.

Since a bit of the principal is paid off, the amount of the payment the following month will be comprised of the following:

- The interest on the remaining principal, and

- A bit more of the principal than was paid the previous month.

The advantage of the fixed rate note is that the payment is the same each month. The disadvantage is that the interest is generally a little higher than an adjustable rate or interest-only loan. Adjustable rate and interest-only notes are also forms of installment notes.

## Balloon Payment Notes

A *balloon payment note* is a partially amortized installment note. It does fully amortize over the term of the note, and leaves a balance due at maturity. The final payment is called a balloon payment because of the large amount. Balloon payment notes are more common in commercial real estate than in residential real estate. A balloon payment note might have a fixed interest rate, or it may have an adjustable rate, depending on the borrower.

**Note:** Under the two-step plan, the balloon payment loan is divided into two portions.

**Two-Step Plan with Balloon Notes:** Because borrowers may not have the resources to make the balloon payment at the end of the loan term, a *two-step* plan is often used with balloon payment notes. Under the two-step plan, the loan is divided into two portions. At the end of the first portion, the balloon payment is due, and then the note "resets," using current market rates and a fully amortizing payment schedule. It's almost like having two promissory notes back to back. This option is not always available, and certain conditions apply.

## Adjustable Rate Note

This is another type of installment note. A variable or *adjustable-rate note* (ARM) has an interest rate that changes periodically according to whatever interest index rate it is tied to. The indices most commonly used are the following:

- **Six-Month Certificate of Deposit (CD) Spot Index.** This index is the weekly average of the interest rates paid by institutions on negotiable six-month certificates of deposit. Because it reflects every blip and swing of the market, it can change quickly.

- **One-Year Treasury Spot Index.** This index is the weekly average of interest paid by the U.S. Government on funds borrowed for one year. It changes more slowly than the CD index.

- **Treasury Twelve-Month Average Index.** This index is the yearly average of the monthly interest paid by the U.S. Government on actively traded securities. It changes more slowly than either of the preceding indices.

- **Eleventh District Cost-of-Funds Index.** This index is the monthly weighted average cost of what banks on the West Coast pay for their various deposits and for the advances they get through the Federal Home Loan Bank Board of San Francisco. It moves at a tortoise's pace compared to the other indices.

- **London Inter-Bank Offer Rate (LIBOR).** This index represents the rate of interest at which banks offer to lend money to one another in the wholesale money markets in London. It is a standard financial index used in U.S. Capital markets and can be found in the Wall Street Journal. In general, its changes have been smaller than changes in the prime rate.

Adjustable-rate loans come up for review periodically, sometimes every month, sometimes every six months, sometimes every year, sometimes every five years. When they do come up for review, the lender adjusts the interest rate according to the index that controls it and whatever caps the loan has.

An interest-rate cap may limit the amount the loan rate can change at each review, say 2%, or it may limit the amount the loan rate can change over the life of the loan, say 6%. A payment cap limits the amount that the payment itself can change from one review to the next.

Some adjustable-rate loans allow the borrower to convert to a fixed-rate loan beginning with the second year and extending to the fifth year. These so-called *convertible loans* relieve the borrower from worry about future interest rate increases, but they may carry a higher loan fee at the outset and another fee at the time of the conversion.

**The Foreclosure Crisis**

Unless you have been in a cave for the last few years, you are aware of the economic crisis that most prominent economists attribute in a large part to adjustable rate loans.

Cash-strapped homeowners, in an effort to pull their equity and spend it, refinanced their home loans with adjustable rate loans. These loans offered bargain rates and for the short term, cut the payments in half.

New home buyers, stretching to afford something in a super-heated market, were qualifying for loans that, in a lot of cases, were for more money than they would have been able to borrow under the terms of a 30-year fixed rate loan. In many cases, the borrowers didn't even need to produce documentation of their income. Furthermore, a lot of these buyers borrowed 100% of the value of the home, and did not produce any down payment.

**Not Fully Informed:** These borrowers were not fully informed about the terms of the loan. This may be because the disclosures and terms were contained in the promissory note, and the borrower simply did not read the promissory note, or it may be because they were misled. Whatever the reason, in mid 2006, when home prices started to level off, the loans taken out in 2004 and 2005 adjusted based on their respective index, and pretty soon, loan payments began to double. As a result of the escalating loan payments and the inability to make the payments, the lenders foreclosed on these properties.

With each foreclosure, home values declined. The economic crisis followed the decline in home values.

**Contract for Deed**

A contract for deed (sometimes called an agreement for sale) is another type of installment note, but it is not between a borrower and a traditional lender. Rather, it is between a buyer-borrower and the seller of the property. The biggest difference between this type of note and the traditional installment note is that the title to the property is not transferred to the buyer-borrower until the note is paid off. The purchase price is agreed upon at the time of the contract and the buyer repays the loan in installments. The buyer-borrower takes possession of the property for the term of the loan.

The loan payments are periodic, and there is often a balloon payment due in one, two, five, seven, or ten years. The loan may be amortized over 30 years but can be negotiated to fit the buyer's and/or the seller's needs. For this type of loan, a substantial down payment is usually required to ensure that the buyer is committed to the transaction, and each state has different regulations for this type of loan.

Obviously, for this type of loan, the seller is taking a huge risk. Therefore, the interest rate on a contract for deed is usually higher than traditional or conventional rates. Generally, each installment payment is part principal and part interest, but not always. The payment may be interest-only, with the principal due at the final payment.

Buyers are usually prohibited from incurring costs or doing remodeling that might result in encumbrances or liens on the property without permission from the contract holder (the seller).

If executed properly and with the appropriate care, a contract for deed has many positive aspects. During the period of installment payments, if the payment history is timely and documented by the seller, some lenders will consider this as creditworthiness, and approve the buyer for a new loan (at a better interest rate) so that the buyer can have title to the property.

**Closing Costs:** Closing costs on a contract for deed can be thousands of dollars less than most other financing options. Many title companies have *boilerplate* contracts that have been written and prepared by their attorneys, and the buyers and sellers can just fill in the blanks. There is usually no lender's title insurance required at this time, no mandatory appraisal or inspection costs, and no mortgage broker fees.

## Seller Carryback

Yet another type of installment note is the *seller carryback*, which is another word for seller financing. The seller carryback differs from the contract for deed (or agreement for sale) in that with a seller carryback, the seller does not retain title. Sellers can finance the entire loan with a seller carryback note, but most often, seller carryback refers to a second deed of trust note carried by the seller when the buyer is able to obtain a bank loan but does not have sufficient funds for a down payment or wants to avoid PMI.

Seller carrybacks gain popularity when interest rates from traditional banks are high or when credit is tight. In a down market, where qualified buyers are hard to find, sellers are apt to consider doing a seller carryback.

**Wraparound Loan Is a Form of Seller Carryback:** If there is a loan on the property, sellers might let the buyers "take over" the payments, although the loan remains in the seller's name. Essentially, a wraparound loan is a loan that incorporates an old, existing loan with a new loan made by the seller to the buyer. The buyer makes one payment to the seller, and the seller continues paying any old loans on their original terms. The wraparound gains popularity whenever there are high interest rates and institutional financing becomes difficult to obtain. During these times, people still have to buy and sell property so they turn to wraparounds as a means of financing.

> **Instructor Note:** When the property is not free and clear, it is important for the buyer and seller to get legal advice. The original loan might have an alienation clause, which would give the lender of the original loan the right to call the entire loan due if the seller transfers title.

## Simple Note

Not all promissory notes are standard 30-year fixed rate notes. There are many variations. Some borrowers need money only for a short term, such as a builder who is building a home on speculation. The builder wants a low interest rate, and is willing to repay the loan in a short period of time, so he or she might opt for a promissory note that specifies repayment in one lump sum at the end of the note. Such a structure is called a *simple note*.

## Construction Loan Note

A construction loan can be a simple note or an installment note. It is a temporary loan given to a borrower who is having a house built. It is payable to the building contractor, either in installments or in one lump sum at the end of construction.

## Open-Ended Note (Revolving Note)

The open-ended promissory note allows the borrower to set up a line of credit with the lender in the amount specified in the promissory note. It is, in essence, a credit card secured by real property. The borrower may obtain draws, or advances, under the promissory note up to whatever the credit limit is. After the borrower repays a portion, the borrower can make additional withdrawals not to exceed the maximum amount specified by the credit limit (which is the amount specified in the promissory note). Construction companies also find that this type of loan gives them the freedom to use borrowed funds as necessary.

**Interest Rates on Open-Ended Loans:** The interest rate on an open-ended loan is adjustable and based on an index (as listed in a previous section of this chapter). Interest paid is typically deductible under federal and many state income tax laws. This effectively reduces the cost of borrowing funds and offers an attractive tax incentive over traditional methods of borrowing (such as credit card debt).

**Home Equity Line of Credit**

A home equity line of credit (HELOC) is a loan in which the lender agrees to lend a maximum amount within an agreed period (called a term), where the collateral is the borrower's equity in his or her house. HELOC funds can be borrowed during the *draw period* (typically 5 to 25 years). Repayment is of the amount drawn plus interest. A HELOC may have a minimum monthly payment requirement (often interest-only); however, the debtor may make a repayment of any amount so long as it is greater than the minimum payment (but less than the total outstanding). The full principal amount is due at the end of the draw period, either as a lump-sum balloon payment or according to a loan amortization schedule. An open-ended note secured by real property is categorized as a second mortgage.

QUIZZES ARE MANDATORY: Please log in and submit the chapter quizzes online.

## Chapter 7 Quiz

1.  In most cases (when the loan is for real property), the terms are complex and lengthy, so the promissory note incorporates a longer, more complicated document called the _____, which details the terms and conditions of the loan.

    (a)    considerate agreement
    (b)    loan agreement
    (c)    oh-no-more-money agreement
    (d)    reinstatement of loan agreement

2.  Variable, or adjustable, interest rates move up and down based on changes in an underlying _____ over the life of the note.

    (a)    arbitrary number
    (b)    stalemate
    (c)    index rate
    (d)    loan to value ratio of the property

3.  A(n) _____ clause is a provision in a promissory note that allows a lender to demand payment of the total outstanding balance in the event of a default.

    (a)    costs of collection
    (b)    repayment schedule
    (c)    alienation
    (d)    acceleration

4.  _____ means the act of transferring ownership, title, interest, or estate in real property from one person to another.

    (a)    Alienation
    (b)    Acceleration
    (c)    Prepayment
    (d)    Repayment

5.  A 30-year fixed rate note secured by real estate is a type of _____.

    (a)    installment note
    (b)    simple note
    (c)    open-ended note
    (d)    HELOC note

6.  A(n) _____ has an interest rate that changes periodically according to whatever interest index rate it is tied to.

    (a)    fixed-rate note
    (b)    variable rate note
    (c)    adjustable rate note
    (d)    either (b) or (c)

7.      A contract for deed (sometimes called an agreement for sale) is a type of installment note, but it is not between a borrower and a traditional lender. It is between _____.

(a)     a buyer-borrower and the seller of the property
(b)     two lenders
(c)     two sellers
(d)     two buyers in a bidding war

8.      Sellers can finance the entire loan with a _____ note, but most often this term refers to a second deed of trust note carried by the seller when the buyer is able to obtain a bank loan but does not have sufficient funds for a down payment, or wants to avoid PMI.

(a)     PMI-avoidance-thingy
(b)     non sequitur
(c)     carry me home
(d)     seller carryback

9.      A home equity line of credit is a loan in which the lender agrees to lend a maximum amount within an agreed period, where the collateral is the borrower's _____.

(a)     equity in his or her house
(b)     personal property of equal or greater value
(c)     promise to pay rent
(d)     commitment to share the profits upon sale

10.     "If any required payment under a promissory note is not paid when due, or if an event of default occurs, the entire outstanding principal balance hereof plus accrued interest thereon shall, at the option of the lender, be immediately due and payable without notice of demand." This clause is an example of a typical _____ clause.

(a)     costs of collection
(b)     repayment schedule
(c)     alienation
(d)     acceleration

## Chapter Eight: Conveyance Documents

### Important Terms

equitable title
naked title
notice of default
power of sale
reconveyance deed

### Chapter Eight Learning Objectives

After successful completion of this chapter, you should be able to complete the following:

- Name and describe the elements of a deed.

- Describe the primary aspects of a standard real estate conveyance.

- Explain standard clauses that are contained in every deed of trust.

- Briefly explain the purpose of a reconveyance deed.

- Briefly explain the purpose of a trustee's deed.

- Briefly explain the purpose of a deed in lieu of foreclosure.

## Conveyance in a Nutshell

> **Instructor Note:** The signing of the documents might or might not take place in the order they are listed here. The participation of an escrow company makes it possible for the parties to complete the signings in any order. In theory, however, the signing of the documents happens in the order shown here.

### Step One: Seller Signs the Conveyance Document

The seller signs the conveyance document (warranty deed) and deposits the conveyance document with the escrow company. The deed is made payable to bearer, so the buyer is not the legal owner of the property until the deed is delivered to the buyer. The seller is the *grantor*, and the buyer (borrower) is the *grantee*.

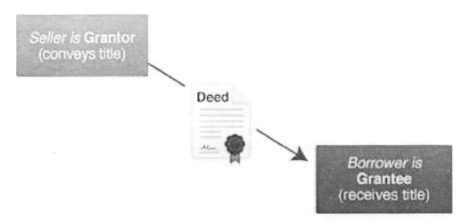

The Escrow Officer acts as an intermediary between the seller and buyer. When the seller signs the conveyance documents, the documents are held in escrow until they are recorded. Signing the conveyance documents does not transfer title. A transfer of title occurs when a conveyance document is recorded.

### The Deed Is a Contract

Whether you think of a deed as a contract or not, it is a contract. It is a unilateral contract, in which the grantor (seller) seller gives several warranties or promises to the grantee (buyer), in exchange for money. A deed requires the signature of the seller, as well as the signature of an attesting witness.

### Elements of a Deed

Just as the purchase contract, listing, lease, loan agreements, and all other real estate contracts must contain certain elements to be valid and enforceable, so must a deed. To be valid and enforceable, a deed must fulfill several requirements:

- It must state on its face that it is a deed, using wording such as "This Deed..." or "executed as a deed."

- It must indicate that the instrument itself conveys some privilege or thing to someone. This is indicated by using the word *hereby* or the phrase *by these presents* in the clause, which indicates the gift.

- The grantor must have the legal ability to grant title, and the grantee must have the contractual capacity to receive title (although the grantee does not sign the deed).

- It must be executed by the grantor, in the presence of the prescribed number of witnesses, who are known as *instrumentary witnesses* (this is known as being in solemn form).

- It must contain the signatures of the grantor and witnesses.

- It must be delivered to (delivery) and accepted by the grantee (acceptance).

- It should be, but not necessarily must be, properly acknowledged (notarized).

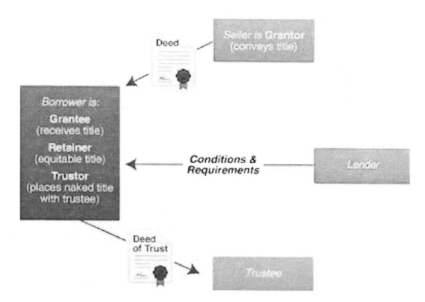

## Step Two: Buyer-Borrower Signs Promissory Note, Deed of Trust, Loan Agreement

Now that the buyer-borrower has title (from Step One), the buyer-borrower retains equitable title, and then signs a deed of trust that conveys *naked title* to a trustee.

A deed of trust deeds the naked title to the property over to a third party for that party to hold until the loan is fully paid. Naked title is not actual title. The only power transferred to the trustee in a deed of trust is the power to sell the property in the event of a default. As the illustration depicts, the buyer-borrower also receives the loan agreement and promissory note, which are the lender's written conditions and requirements for the loan.

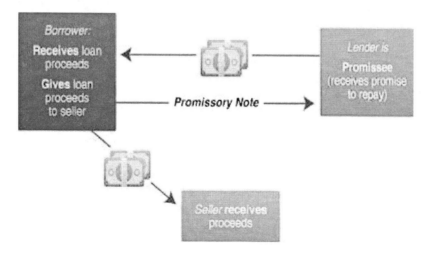

## Step Three: Lender Releases Funds

After the deed of trust is signed, and the lender has some assurance that foreclosure is possible in the event of a borrower default, the lender releases the funds to the buyer (or escrow company).

### Step Four: Recordation and Transfer of Title

Recordation of the conveyance documents transfers title officially. The escrow company will facilitate the recording of the warranty deed and deed of trust as soon as the following items are completed:

- The seller (grantor) has signed the conveyance document (warranty deed).

- The buyer (borrower, grantee, trustor) has signed the promissory note, loan agreement, and deed of trust; and has deposited all closing costs.

- The lender has deposited the loan proceeds into the escrow depository.

- The escrow company is in possession of all conveyance documents, and all applicable funds.

### Close of Escrow

Once the conveyance documents are recorded, the escrow officer will disburse the appropriate funds to the seller and close the file. As depicted in the illustration below, when everything is said and done, the buyer holds equitable title, the lender holds a promissory note, and the trustee holds naked title for the benefit of the lender.

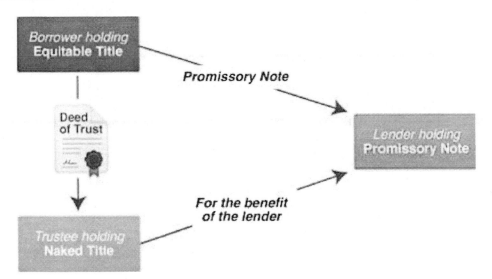

## Anatomy of a Deed of Trust

### What Is a Deed of Trust?

To secure collateral for a promissory note, the lender or escrow officer draws up a deed of trust, which describes the property against which the loan is written and, together with the acceleration clause in the loan agreement, gives the lender the power of sale, and enables the lender to foreclose on the property that is held as collateral in the event of a default.

### More Favorable than the Traditional Two-Party Mortgage

The reason that a deed of trust is generally more favorable for lenders than typical mortgage documents is that a lender, under a deed of trust, can foreclose without ever going to court. The lender is not required to file a lawsuit in order to foreclose. This power of sale is not available under a traditional two-party mortgage.

**Three Parties to a Trust Deed Arrangement**

A deed of trust contains three parties:

- The trustor, who is the buyer-borrower.
- The trustee, who is an entity that holds *bare or legal* title during the term of the loan.
- The beneficiary, who is the lender.

**Why is the Borrower Called a Trustor?** Although it may seem like the escrow company or the lender is setting up a trust and forcing the buyer-borrower to sign the paperwork, it is technically the buyer-borrower who is initiating the trust because the buyer-borrower conveys to the trustee.

**What is a Trustee?** The trustee controls the document that is in the trust. In most states, a trustee is an independent third party that does not represent the borrower or the lender. The trustee is an entity— generally a title company. The trustee also reconveys the property once the deed of trust is paid in full. The trustee responds to the lender's request to foreclose on the property, and files all of the necessary foreclosure paperwork (this course does not discuss foreclosure proceedings). Usually the lender-beneficiary selects a trustee.

**Note:** Usually the lender-beneficiary selects a trustee.

**What is a Trust?** A trust is described as a right in property, real or personal, that is held by one party for the benefit of another.

> **Instructor Note:** In California (unlike other states), the trustee and the beneficiary may be one and the same. In other words, lenders may act as trustees for their own loans and not be in jeopardy of conflict of interest. The California Attorney General's office interprets each role separately; each function has its responsibilities clearly specified.

## Covenants

Covenants in a deed of trust represent the buyer-trustor-borrower's pledge to perform or not perform specified acts with regard to property. Contained in every deed of trust are various covenants and promises. The following is a brief explanation of such covenants:

**Preservation and Maintenance:** The buyer-trustor-borrower must keep the property in good repair and neither allow any waste to accumulate nor permit deterioration of the property, such that the value of the property is diminished.

**Fire and Hazard Insurance:** The buyer-trustor-borrower will provide a fire insurance policy in an amount sufficient to protect the lender's interest and will name the lender as a party to the policy's proceeds in the event of a loss. Any surplus amount is given to the borrower.

**Legal Action:** The buyer-trustor-borrower will defend against any action or claim on the property and agrees to pay all costs and expenses in a foreclosure against the property.

**Taxes and Assessments:** The buyer-trustor-borrower will pay all taxes, assessments, encumbrances, charges, and liens against the property in a timely manner, as well as all costs, fees, and expenses of this trust.

**Beneficiary and Trustee Expenditures:** The buyer-trustor-borrower will reimburse to the beneficiary or trustee any sums expended on behalf of the borrower. This includes all expenses that the lender incurs in the event that foreclosure proceedings are necessary.

**Condemnation:** All sums secured as a result of condemnation of all or part of the property will be paid to the beneficiary to reduce the loan balance (In all states, the lender is prohibited from filing a deficiency judgment against a buyer-trustor-borrower whose property was condemned in an eminent domain action.).

**Late Payments:** Acceptance by the trustee or the beneficiary of any delinquent payments does not relieve the buyer-trustor-borrower of making subsequent payments in a timely manner. Failure of the lender to initiate foreclosure proceedings in the event of a late payment does not constitute a waiver of the lender's right to initiate foreclosure proceedings in the future.

**Reconveyance:** The trustee is required to reconvey the property to the buyer-trustor-borrower upon repayment of the loan amount, but must maintain records of the transaction for at least five years (More on this subject later in this chapter.).

**Extensions, Subordination, and Modifications:** Any changes to the agreement shall occur between the buyer-trustor-borrower and beneficiary, and the consent and joinder (joining) of the trustee shall not be required.

**Assignment of Rents:** As additional security and in the event of a default, all rents, issues, and profits that may be derived from the property shall be assigned to the beneficiary.

**Successors and Assigns:** All successors and assigns of parties to this contract are bound by its terms and conditions.

**Trustee Acceptance:** The trustee will accept this trust when the deed, properly signed and acknowledged, is recorded.

## Reconveyance Deed

### Reconveys Naked Title from the Trustee back to the Trustor

Naked title (power of sale) is transferred back to the buyer-borrower-trustor when the loan is paid off. This is done with a *reconveyance deed* (or deed of reconveyance).

A reconveyance deed's purpose is to clear the lien in the public record. In most cases, the title or escrow company will record the reconveyance deed at the time of close of escrow. It is then returned to the trustee, and held by the trustee until the loan is paid off. Once the loan is paid off and the reconveyance deed reconveys naked title back to the buyer-borrower-trustor, the trust is closed.

### What Happens if No Reconveyance Deed is Recorded?

What happens when the reconveyance deed is not prepared and recorded at the time of closing, and the borrower finds out later, sometimes years later, that an old, paid off loan still shows up as a lien against property that the borrower doesn't even own anymore? If the Seller or lender is available, a reconveyance deed can be prepared and sent to the lender for signing. The reconveyance deed is then recorded and the lien is removed.

### What Happens if the Seller or Lender Cannot be Found or Is Unwilling to Sign the Reconveyance?

In California, when a deed of reconveyance is not executed and recorded within 21 days of the trustee's receipt of all documents and money necessary to pay off the debt, a title company may prepare and record a release of the obligation within 72 calendar days from payment of the debt. This release is considered equivalent to a deed of reconveyance, which releases the borrower from any further obligation under the deed of trust.

## Trustee's Deed

### Transfers Title from Trustee to Lender

In the event of a foreclosure, the lender-beneficiary will contact the trustee, who will record a notice of default in the public record.

Once that happens, and the trustee holds the foreclosure sale, the highest bidder at the sale receives the trustee's deed. During a down market, when the asking price at a foreclosure sale is much higher than the property's value, there are usually no bidders at the sale, and the trustee simply conveys title to the lender (Foreclosure proceedings are not discussed in this course.).

### Title Insurance on a Trustee's Deed

Most title companies don't like to insure a title that was conveyed with a trustee's deed. This means that buyers who purchase property from a trustee's sale (foreclosure sale) might have problems if and when they want to sell the property to any buyer who is getting a loan to buy the property (Title insurance is required as a condition of the loan.). Some title companies will issue title insurance with some exceptions, or require a waiting period after the sale before a policy is issued.

### Trustee Sale Guarantee

The *Trustee Sale Guarantee* is a form that is issued at the beginning of foreclosure. It identifies all persons who, according to the public records, might have an interest in the property and are entitled to receive notice of the contemplated trustee's sale. It is issued by a title company to prospective bidders who wish to purchase a property at auction. The issuance of such a form does not commit the issuing company to the further issuance of a policy of title insurance after foreclosure sale, but it does entitle its recipient to a special title insurance rate accommodation if a policy of title insurance is purchased within a specified number of days from the date of sale.

## Deed in Lieu of Foreclosure

### What Is a Deed in Lieu?

A *deed-in-lieu of foreclosure* (DIL) is an instrument by which the buyer-borrower voluntarily transfers the ownership of the property to the lender-beneficiary. In theory, a deed-in-lieu of foreclosure is easier, because it saves both the borrower and the lender time and money. It saves the borrower the humiliation of having the big, fat foreclosure notice posted on the property, and it saves the lender the expense and paperwork associated with the foreclosure process.

A DIL might be an alternative for a borrower who meets the following criteria:

- Is ineligible to refinance or modify the existing loan because the property will not appraise sufficiently.
- Is facing a long-term hardship.
- Is behind on loan payments and there is no way to get caught up in time to avoid foreclosure.
- Owes more on the property than what the market will bear, and has a need to sell the property.
- Does not want to go through the effort to sell the property.
- Can no longer afford the property.

**Alternative to Foreclosure:** A deed-in-lieu of foreclosure is an alternative to foreclosure. In exchange for the DIL, the lender promises not to initiate foreclosure proceedings, and to terminate any foreclosure proceedings already underway.

**Instructor Note:** As stated earlier in this course, California protects homeowners against deficiency judgments during a short sale or foreclosure. With the passage of SB 458 (Corbett), signed into law by Governor Brown on July 11, 2011, it is now illegal for lenders to obtain a deficiency judgment against most homeowners after they agree to settle their debt in a short sale. Deficiency judgment protection is extended to most borrowers on single-family homes, condominiums, and two-to-four-unit apartments in short sale transactions (however, there are some exceptions).

**Potential Tax Liabilities:** An overlooked downside to a deed-in-lieu of foreclosure is the possible forgiveness of the deficiency balance. Even if the deficiency judgment is forgiven, a creditor is required to file a 1099C, under federal law, whenever it forgives a loan balance greater than $600. This may create a tax liability. However, the Mortgage Forgiveness Debt Relief Act of 2007 provides tax relief for some loans forgiven in 2007 through 2012.

### Typical Requirements of a Deed in Lieu

The following is a typical (although by no means exhaustive) list of requirements in order to file a deed-in-lieu of foreclosure:

- The residence must already be on the market for a specified number of days (90 days is typical).
- There can be no liens on the property (other than the deed of trust liens).
- The property cannot already be in foreclosure.
- The offer of a deed in lieu must be voluntary.

### Is a Short Sale a Better Option?

The property owner and lender may choose to do a short sale on the home. Through a short sale, the lender agrees to accept less than the balance owed on the loan. The deficiency balance is typically forgiven, although not always, and it depends on the state where the property is located. Unlike a deed-in-lieu of foreclosure, the ownership of the property is not transferred to the lender; rather, it remains with the owner.

### What Happens if the Lender Rejects the Deed-in-Lieu of Foreclosure?

If the lender will not allow a deed-in-lieu of foreclosure, then foreclosure or short sale are the only options. Most lenders will not consider accepting a DIL until the borrower is at least 90 days late on the loan payments. After the borrower has missed payments for two consecutive months, the lender will begin evaluating the property to determine the fair market value of the property. One of the primary determining factors is the market condition in the area.

Keep in mind that if a DIL benefits the lender, the lender will probably accept it. However, if the lender will gain more liability by accepting the deed, the lender will not take it.

**QUIZZES ARE MANDATORY**: Please log in and submit the chapter quizzes online.

## Chapter 8 Quiz

1.      In the warranty deed, the seller is the _____, and the buyer is the _____.

(a)     grantee, grantor
(b)     grantor, grantee
(c)     trustor, trustee
(d)     trustor, beneficiary

2.      The _____ is/are the lender's written conditions and requirements for the loan.

(a)     warranty deed
(b)     loan proceeds
(c)     money wiring instructions
(d)     loan agreement and promissory note

3.      After the conveyance documents and deed of trust are recorded, and the escrow company closes the file, all of the following are true EXCEPT:

(a)     The buyer holds equitable title.
(b)     The lender holds a promissory note.
(c)     The trustee holds naked title for the benefit of the lender.
(d)     The seller holds equitable title.

4.      A deed of trust involves three parties. The trustor, trustee, and beneficiary. The _____ is the trustor.

(a)     borrower
(b)     lender
(c)     trustee
(d)     seller

5.      On the deed of trust, the buyer-trustor-borrower pledges to _____ any sums expended on behalf of the borrower. This includes all expenses incurred in the event that foreclosure proceedings are necessary.

(a)     disregard
(b)     ignore
(c)     increase
(d)     reimburse to the beneficiary or trustee

6.      In most cases, the title or escrow company will record the reconveyance deed at the time of close of escrow. It is then returned to _____, and held there until the loan is paid off.

(a)     the borrower
(b)     the lender
(c)     the trustee
(d)     the trustor

7.      The _____ transfers title from the trustee to the highest bidder at the trustee's sale.

   (a)    warranty deed
   (b)    trustee's deed
   (c)    trustee's sale guarantee
   (d)    deed in lieu of foreclosure

8.      A _____ is an instrument by which the buyer-borrower voluntarily transfers the ownership of the property to the lender-beneficiary.

   (a)    deed of trust
   (b)    warranty deed
   (c)    deed in lieu of foreclosure
   (d)    reconveyance deed

9.      Most lenders will not consider accepting a deed-in-lieu of foreclosure until ____.

   (a)    the borrower is at least 90 days late on the loan payments
   (b)    the borrower begs shamelessly
   (c)    the borrower agrees to pay taxes on the deficiency
   (d)    they are forced to accept it

10.     With regard to a warranty deed, the _____ must have the legal ability to grant, and the _____ must have the contractual capacity to receive title.

   (a)    grantee, grantor
   (b)    grantor, grantee
   (c)    trustor, trustee
   (d)    grantor, trustee

## Chapter Nine: The Property Management Agreement

**Important Terms**

cash flow
corrective action
current rents
demographics
leverage
market rent
pro forma
profit and loss statement
return on investment
time-share project

**Chapter Nine Learning Objectives**

After successful completion of this chapter, you should be able to complete the following:

- Understand that the property manager's job is to assess owner's needs, and perform accordingly.

- Explain the aspects of a property management plan.

- Describe the purpose of a pro-forma statement.

- Define *zero-based budgeting* as distinguishable from *traditional incremental budgeting*.

- State the elements of a marketing plan.

- Describe the elements of a property management agreement.

- Describe special contractual situations, and the considerations associated therewith.

## Property Management Fundamentals

### The Property Manager Works for the Owner

When we think about developing a management plan, we must think about more than just developing it—we must think about selling it to the property owner. In order for a property management plan to be successful, it must first fulfill the owner's goals.

### What Does an Owner Want?

**Cash Flow.** *Cash flow* is the cash left over after cash expenses. It is money that the owner can spend. Cash flow takes into consideration all monies earned and spent (e.g., debt payments, operating expenses, and capital expenditures). Cash flow does not mean profit; do not confuse the two terms. Rather, cash flow means revenue collected.

### Long-Term or Short-Term Cash Flow

Some owners are concerned with immediate cash flow while other owners are more concerned with long-term cash flow benefits. Most owners who are concerned with immediate cash flow don't care what the property they are selling looks like—it's the profit and loss statement that matters. An owner who has the greatest concern for immediate cash would be reluctant to make improvements or changes in use or tenancy that could have a short-term negative effect on cash flow.

If an owner is highly leveraged (deep in debt), it usually doesn't take much to turn a positive cash flow into a negative cash flow or vice versa. Such owners may resist improvements or more-than-minimum maintenance.

On the other hand, owners who take a long-term approach are generally more secure financially. They will make improvements to the property, change the property's use and tenant type if it makes sense to do so as a long-term investment.

### Trophy Properties

On the other hand, there are some owners who are very concerned about the image that their property conveys. In fact, they consider their property a trophy, and want the prestige that goes along with being able to say they own that property. Usually, these owners are not highly leveraged, and therefore, it doesn't take too much to produce a positive cash flow. While the return on investment for such an owner might be less than for other investment properties, this type of owner will probably be happy if the property has good tenants and is well maintained.

### The Management Plan

Your property management plan is a serious document for a serious business. To the property's owner, the property is a business. The revenue generated is not just rental income, it is business revenue. The property management plan should include the following:

- Analysis of the property.
- Goals of the owner.
- Pro-forma statement.
- Reserve requirements.
- Marketing plan.

## Property Analysis

The property management plan is an analysis of the property's physical condition, the location, the nature of the tenants, the grounds, and the surrounding area.

**The Property's Physical Condition:** This includes the age of the property, as well as the quality of the construction. Your analysis should include the following:

- Recommendations for immediate maintenance: aspects of the property that need attention before the property can be rented.

- Recommendations for scheduled maintenance: aspects of the property that need routine maintenance.

- Recommendations for deferred maintenance: aspects of the property that need attention, but not immediate attention.

**Location of the Property:** Location is one factor of the property that cannot be changed. Your analysis should include the strengths and weaknesses of the property. It is important to be positive, but without sugarcoating the details. Include photos of other properties within eyeshot of the property to emphasize your points.

**The Nature of the Tenants:** If the property already has tenants, what is their status? Are they long-term renters? Short-term renters? How long have the tenants been in the property? What is the relationship of the current rents to the market rent?

> **Instructor Note:** As a rule, a down sales market makes for an up rental market. Therefore, generally, in a down sales market, short-term leases are better for the owner.

**The Surrounding Area:** Your analysis of the area should include the demographics and changes in the area, as well as the vacancy factor for similar properties in the area. New construction in the area and changes in the uses of surrounding properties will affect the subject property, too.

## Goals of the Owner

The goals should be realistic and attainable, and should be measurable and meaningful.

**Profit without Pain:** Predictably, owners want profit and they want it without pain. Most owners, especially over-leveraged owners, just care about profit, and they look to you to help them meet that goal. The problem arises when these over-leveraged owners do not consider the intermediate steps that are necessary to achieve those goals.

**Reducing the Vacancy Factor:** Vacant property definitely impedes profits. One goal must be to reduce the vacancy factor. Creating a desired rent schedule is not enough; you must include a plan to achieve that goal. The first step in reducing the vacancy factor is to analyze the following:

- Why is the property vacant?

- Is the solution within the owner's power?

- Is the property the culprit? If so, why? Is the property in disrepair? Perhaps it has a funky floor plan that causes it to be undesirable.

Your plan would include giving priority to corrective action of the condition of the property, and it would include a time table for this corrective action. Your plan might even include financing arrangements to cover the corrective action and property improvements. Finally, you should include the estimated costs for the work.

Of course, corrective action will increase expenses. Therefore, as the property manager, you might need to educate your owner on the benefits of making improvements and spending money on the property. Penny pinching by avoiding corrective action will negatively affect the owner's cash flow.

### Pro-Forma Statement

Your management plan should include a budget for the first year based on anticipated expenses and anticipated revenue. This is your pro-forma statement. Assumptions made in your pro-forma statement should be clearly explained. The owner must realize that the anticipated income will be directly related to the anticipated expenses, and that a change in net income might not be possible without a change in the budget. In some cases, a pro-forma statement can be based on a change in use.

**Zero-Based Budgeting:** Too often, managers simply add on inflationary expenses to last year's budget to establish the current year's expenses. This traditional incremental budgeting method is based on the assumption that last year's budget was wise, and all expenditures were justified. Zero-based budgeting can be used effectively to show owners what can be done.

Zero-based budgeting starts from scratch, rather than starting from last year's budget. It requires the budget expenditures to be reevaluated thoroughly, starting from the zero-base.

In zero-based budgeting, every line item of the budget must be approved, rather than only the new year's changes. During the review process, no reference is made to the previous year's budget, or whether each expenditure item has increased or decreased from the previous year.

Think of zero-based budgeting as a down-to-earth approach to budgeting. It is the same type of approach a standard family uses to establish a household budget. Advantages of zero-based budgeting are many:

- Creates more efficient planning and use of resources, because it is based on needs and benefits rather than on history.

- Encourages evaluation so that the property owners can find cost-effective ways to improve the property.

- Helps identify waste, and if desired, it can also be used for suggesting alternative courses of action.

Disadvantages of zero-based budgeting include the following:

- It is more time consuming than incremental budgeting.

- It requires specific training, due to increased complexity vs. incremental budgeting.

### Reserve Requirements

Now that you've established your budget, either with a traditional incremental method or with a zero-based method, you need to think about unbudgeted or "surprise" expenses. Your management plan should justify the amount of funds to be held as a reserve against surprise expenses. For instance, what happens if a major storm blows out several of the windows in the subject property, and it becomes necessary to replace the broken windows with upgraded energy-efficient windows? The reserve funds should be held in addition to the ordinary maintenance funds.

**How Do You Collect Funds for the Reserve?** Since a tenant is required to contribute to the reserve requirements only if the lease provides for a reserve, it is probably necessary for the property manager to either put such a provision in a lease or establish an ancillary account for the reserve, and make arrangements with the owner to make regular deposits from the rental receipts.

## Marketing Plan

The management plan should cover how you intend to market the vacant space. Most property management agreements do not provide for the owner to pay advertising costs, so the marketing plan must be prepared with frugality as well as effectiveness in mind.

**Signage:** Will you place signs on the property? If there are clear prohibitions to signage, can you present a viable alternative? Remember, if you plan to place signage on the property, you need the owner's written permission.

**Press Releases:** A press release is one of the most underutilized tools in the advertising world—it is effective advertising disguised as news. Best of all, a press release is free advertising. Your press release should include the words *For Immediate Release*. Take a look at the following example:

### Example Press Release

For Immediate Release: Downtown Commercial Building Sparks Main Street Face Lift Claremont, California - November 29, 2011 - The renovations recently completed on the Main Street 3000 building have spurred other building owners on the street to begin renovating their buildings, too, says Main Street 3000 building owner, John Murray.

In July of this year, real estate investor John Murray began a series of cosmetic and structural upgrades to his two-story commercial building, and the property has transformed from a less-than-modern office mall to a state-of-the-art retail center.

"Buildings come and go," says Mr. Murray, "but the nature of use is changing. The new business trend in this city is to hire contract employees who telecommute. The need for office space is diminishing, so we felt that transforming the building to retail space was a smart move."

According to the Chamber of Commerce statistics, the number of new retail companies opened in our city has increased in recent months. Experts believe this trend will continue, with the possibility of two or even three new retail companies coming to town before the end of next year.

Contact: Proper T. Manager
propertymanager@abc_realty.com

**Advertising Methods:** Will you use newspaper ads? Radio advertising? Brochures? Will your property have a website? Depending on the type of property, it may be necessary to hire a professional photographer to take the pictures. Is it worth it to hire an advertising company to create professional advertising materials? If so, what are the estimated costs? This section should also include how you will measure the results of the advertising.

**Open houses (or Open Commercial Spaces):** If the property is not in a high-traffic area, an open house may not be the best idea. Consumer sentiment about open houses has waxed and waned over the years, along with the ups and downs of the real estate market. In 1995, 41% of prospective tenants surveyed relied on open houses to sell their home. By 2000, that number dropped to 28%. Today, a majority of prospective tenants (especially commercial tenants) find that open houses are not useful at all.

**Providing Information to Cooperating Brokers:** Generally, you will provide information to cooperating brokers through the MLS. However, your press releases can be emailed to other brokers as well.

## The Property Management Contract

### Obligations of the Parties

The property management contract must clearly set forth the obligations of the parties.

**Contract Payment Structure**

Owners pay property managers either a rental fee, a property management service fee, or both. Sometimes, property owners pay the property manager based on a percentage of the rental.

**Length of Contract Term**

A short-term contract might require that you pay dues, but expire before your dues pay you. The term of the management contract should be directly proportionate to the amount of work that is to be expended. For instance, if the subject property is a commercial office building with a significant number of vacancies, you'll need a long-term contract. Otherwise, you will do all the hard work to market the property and place tenants, and the owner will take over when the property is fully leased.

If a contract does not allow time for you to profit from your own efforts, then you need to make sure that it allows you to profit from other people's efforts. A short-term contract (say, a one-year contract) might be appropriate if the property has a reasonable vacancy factor and is well-run at the time you become the agent. This way, you are leveraging someone else's efforts.

## Duties of the Property Manger

Obviously, the duties of the property manager will vary according to the needs of the owner and the nature of the property. However, the following are some basic duties that are included in every property management contract:

**Best Efforts to Place Tenants:** The property manager agrees to use his or her best efforts to place tenants, and generally has the authority to use other real estate brokers in whatever way is appropriate and legal to lease the space. However, the property manager must arrange for compensation to the other brokers independent of the management agreement.

**Efficient and Businesslike Management:** The property manager also agrees to manage the property in an efficient and businesslike manner, considering the age and physical condition of the property.

**Repairs:** Acting for the owner, the property manager can arrange for ordinary and necessary repairs and alterations. The owner's prior written approval is typically required for any one item of repair or alteration that exceeds a specified dollar limit. This limit should be reasonably high enough so that constant owner approval is not necessary. To lower a limit would indicate an owner's lack of trust in the property manager.

**Monthly Statement:** Most states have regulatory (or statutory) requirements that the property manager must provide to the property owner as a monthly statement of the account. Your contract should include a clause to this effect, and provide the date during the following month on which the monthly statement will be issued. The clause should also state that the amount due to the owner after the deduction of compensation to the property manager will be sent to the owner unless otherwise agreed.

## Duties of the Property Owner

**Referral:** Generally, the owner agrees to refer all rental inquiries to the property manager. Sometimes, the property owner will give power of attorney to the property manager, and the property manager will have authority to execute leases on behalf of the owner.

**Reimbursement:** The contract should provide for a procedure for the property owner to compensate the property manager for out-of-pocket expenses.

**Indemnification:** The contract should also provide that the owner agrees to hold the property manager harmless for damages or injuries to persons or property when the manager is carrying out provisions of the management contract, and to reimburse the property manager for defense costs regarding such claims.

**Insurance:** The owner must agree to carry public liability, and all other applicable liability insurances (such as elevator liability, contractual liability, etc.) agreed to be necessary to protect the owner and the manager's interests. The owner should agree to name the manager as the party insured, with the agreed-upon amount of coverage. It is also important that the insurance clause state that all insurance policies shall provide for a 10-day written notice to the property manager prior to cancellation.

## Special Contractual Situations

### Medical Office Management

Managing medical offices differs from other office management in both tenant selection and cleaning requirements. Medical office rentals usually include cleaning services. The standard of cleaning required is normally much higher than for other office spaces, because of the liability burden of the tenants. Many medical doctors want only other medical doctors in the complex because much of their clientele is found through referrals from other medical doctors. Leases frequently require that a stated percentage of the rental space will be rented to other medical doctors. Often, the most desirable medical buildings are those that are in close proximity to other medical buildings and hospitals.

### Storage Facility Management

**Mini-Storage Facilities:** Mini-storage facilities are usually the size of a garage or smaller, and rent primarily by the month. The most significant contractual consideration with mini-storage facilities is that as a property manager, you may sell unclaimed property on behalf of the owner, providing that you comply with statutory requirements.

**Storage Yards:** Storage yards are fenced and secured exterior storage areas. Some grounds may have gravel, while others may be paved. Your management contract must include provisions for extensive grounds keeping and greater-than-average pest and weed control. In addition, the management contract must provide for scheduled maintenance of the security system, and the fencing surrounding the property.

### Farm and Ranch Management

Your duties as a manager tend to focus on agricultural aspects. These duties include soil management, economic decisions regarding crops, labor management, maintenance, and other farming activities. Large farming or ranching operations are likely to involve leased land. Your management contract should provide for your authority to negotiate leases on additional land.

**New Market Lender-Owned Farms:** When lenders foreclose on a residence, they typically do not pay too much attention to the property other than to barely keep the property in compliance with health regulations. However, when a lender forecloses on a working farm operation, they generally try to keep the farm producing, since the market value of the farm is directly related to its operability.

So guess what lenders do? They hire property managers who specialize in farming. The lenders want you, the property manager, to protect the physical improvements on the property. Your management contract will provide for seeing to it that the property operability is maintained.

### Time Share Management

A time-share project is a divided interest (fractional interest) in a unit where a participating owner has exclusive use to the unit during the designated period of time. Time-shares tend to be vacation-type units in vacation-type locations. This results in a very intensive use of the units as well as the common areas.

As a property manager of a time-share property, your duties will differ from the typical property management obligations.

**Housekeeping:** As the property manager, you must supervise cleaning and preparation of a unit between occupants of that unit. Unlike hotel and motel housekeeping, all of the work is scheduled for the same turnover day. Therefore, the housekeeping requires a large crew of part-time workers or a cleaning contract. Time-share units are typically much larger than hotel rooms and contain kitchens and multiple bathrooms, so cleaning each unit is time consuming. Furthermore, there are appliances, such as a range, refrigerator, and microwave, all of which need to be cleaned so that the unit is in pristine condition for the next occupant.

**Inventory Control:** Kitchen and decorator items may disappear. This happens because many units are rented or exchanged, or owners have guests and sometimes items are broken or thrown out. At times, tenants may exchange a certain decorator item for an item of lesser value. If an item on the inventory list is missing, the previous occupant should be notified immediately.

**New Occupants:** Occupants should pick up keys at your management office. Your management contract with the owners of the unit should provide for some limitations in this regard. As a property manager, you should not be asked to stay on a property 24 hours a day to provide keys to new arrivals.

**Maintenance of Buildings and Grounds:** As the time-share manager, you are responsible for maintenance of the buildings, but you cannot be expected to perform the work yourself. Your contract should provide for hiring and firing capabilities on behalf of the timeshare organization. Pride of ownership is important to time-share owners, so units and grounds must have the look and feel of a luxury resort.

**Recreation Director:** As property manager, you or your personnel might be responsible for recreational activities. You might be tasked with scheduling tours, golf tournaments, barbecues, etc. If this is the case, you will need to have the authority to contract with many vendors to provide services for these events. Your management contract must provide for your authority in this regard, and indemnify you in case a personal injury occurs on the property as a result of such events.

**Collection of Association Fees:** Time-share owners pay a homeowner association fee to cover housekeeping, maintenance, taxes, insurance, and refurbishing of the units. Collection of these fees is always a difficult issue, due to the sheer magnitude of the task. Think about it: If you have 100 units, each of which sold in 50 separate weekly increments, you've got a total of 5000 owner statements and collections.

Another factor that causes this task to be so formidable is the fact that the owners, by and large, do not like paying it. Some resist paying it, and some will not pay it until you provide them with personal attention. As can be expected, sometimes this fee collection can become a full-time job. Your management contract should provide for procedural protocol when and if tenants or owners refuse to pay the dues.

**Mobile Home Park Management**

In California, parks with 50 or more spaces must have a resident manager. Besides renting space by the day week or month, a property manager of a recreational park might also sell utilities or cable television to the tenants. As a manager, you will probably be responsible for the enforcement of park rules, and the maintenance of common areas, including recreational facilities and a clubhouse. Your management contract needs to allow for your authority in this regard.

Some mobile home parks are owned by homeowners. Each homeowner owns his or her site, and the common areas are owned as tenants in common with the other homeowners. In such a situation, you assume a different management role. In effect, you are a condominium association manager, but the condominium units just happen to be mobile homes.

## Subsidized Housing Management

Subsidized housing offers below-market rent, based on either government ownership or government benefits to the developer. Access to subsidized housing is limited to low-income individuals and families. Managers of public or subsidized housing often take a "go with the flow" attitude, and obligate themselves to contracts that do not provide for methods to address the unique set of problems that occurs with subsidized housing.

**Unique Problems:** Statistically, subsidized housing projects tend toward higher crime rates, and higher rates of drug sales activity. Additionally, sometimes with subsidized housing, the property manager cannot evict a tenant without a large amount of justification and red tape. As a result, subsidized housing property managers have a unique set of issues that their property management contract should address.

## Possible Contractual Solutions

**Empowering the Property Manager:** Many of the subsidized or public housing problems would be solved if property managers had the authority to screen tenants, set rules and regulations, and evict tenants that fail to follow the rules and regulations. The recent trend in property management of subsidized housing is to empower managers to enforce the rules. We are beginning to see some subsidized housing projects take a tough stance against drug activity, and hold parents liable for the actions of their children. However, this tough stance is not possible unless the property management contract provides for it.

**Tenant Organizations:** The property management contract could provide for the property manager to initiate organization among the tenants. The organizations would have a charter to watch out for the safety of the residents. In addition, the property manager would meet regularly with the tenant organization and communicate their concerns to the property manager. The management personnel could provide a method for confidential reporting of criminal activity and even recommend eviction of the problem tenants.

QUIZZES ARE MANDATORY: Please log in and submit the chapter quizzes online.

## Chapter 9 Quiz

1.      A detailed statement of income and expenses of a business that reveals the operating position of the business over a period of time correctly defines which of the following terms?

(a)     Property management contract
(b)     Profit and loss statement
(c)     Zero-based budgeting evaluation
(d)     Eviction notice

2.      When you prepare a management plan, you should include an analysis of the physical condition of the property. This includes the age of the property as well as the quality of the construction. Your analysis should include all of the following EXCEPT:

(a)     recommendations for immediate maintenance.
(b)     recommendations for scheduled maintenance.
(c)     recommendations for deferred maintenance.
(d)     recommendations for neighborhood cleanup.

3.      _____ refers to aspects of the property that need attention, but not immediate attention.

(a)     Scheduled maintenance
(b)     Deferred maintenance
(c)     Catch-all maintenance
(d)     Immediate maintenance

4.      Your management plan should include a budget for the first year based on anticipated expenses and anticipated revenue. This is your _____ statement.

(a)     zero-based
(b)     corrective action
(c)     pro-forma
(d)     incremental budgeting

5.      The property manager agrees to use his or her best efforts to place tenants, and generally has the authority to use other real estate brokers in whatever way is appropriate and legal to lease the space. However, the compensation to the other brokers _____.

(a)     is independent of the management agreement
(b)     will have to be minimal
(c)     should be written into the management agreement, and is always the sole responsibility of the property owner
(d)     should be in cash only

6.      Immediate maintenance refers to _____.

(a)     aspects of the property that need attention before the property can be rented
(b)     aspects of the property that need routine maintenance
(c)     aspects of the property that need attention, but not urgent attention
(d)     aspects of the property that do not need attention

7.    Zero-based budgeting _____, rather than starting from last year's budget.

      (a)    uses a traditional incremental technique
      (b)    starts from scratch
      (c)    starts from the budget of five years ago
      (d)    repeats last year's budget


8.    With regard to time-share housekeeping, which of the following is FALSE?

      (a)    Unlike hotel and motel housekeeping, all of the work is scheduled for the same turnover day.
      (b)    The housekeeping probably requires a large crew of part-time workers or a cleaning contract.
      (c)    Units are typically much smaller than hotel rooms.
      (d)    Cleaning each unit is time consuming.


9.    A good management plan justifies an amount of funds to be held as a _____ against surprise expenses.

      (a)    guarantee
      (b)    payoff
      (c)    reserve
      (d)    satisfaction


10.   If the subject property is a commercial office building with a significant number of vacancies, you'll probably need a long-term contract.

      (a)    True
      (b)    False

## Chapter Ten: General Concepts of Leasing

### Important Terms

conspirator
lessor
lessee
meeting of the minds
reversionary
Statute of Frauds

### Chapter Ten Learning Objectives

After successful completion of this chapter, you should be able to complete the following:

- Name and describe the four essential elements that must be present in every lease.
- Explain the four types of estates.
- Explain two types of leases.
- Explain four types of rental payment structures.
- Explain the gist of a lease assignment.
- Explain the gist of a sublease.
- Explain some caveats with regard to drafting leases.
- Provide a few items of insight with regard to negotiation of lease renewals.
- State a few disclosure requirements with regard to leases.
- State a reason why recordation of a lease might be useful.

## Leases: Basic Contractual Requirements

### Lease Defined

A *lease* is a contract that transfers possession from an owner (lessor) to a tenant (lessee). While the tenant is entitled to exclusive possession during the term of the lease, the lessor retains ownership, and reversionary rights.

As you know, a lease is a contract. It is a voluntary agreement between two competent parties for consideration. The principles that apply to all contracts also apply to leases. Four basic contractual principles must be included in every lease:

**Mutuality:** This refers to a meeting of the minds. The contract must be clear and unambiguous. In the case of a lease, the terms, compensation, and property to be leased must be clearly defined.

**Capacity:** Refers to the legal ability of people or organizations to enter into a valid contract. The parties must be of legal age, and must be competent. With very few exceptions, a prospective tenant who is below the age of contractual capacity (18 years of age in most states) is as a matter of law, not competent, and has no capacity to contract.

Inability to contract can also arise when a person has been adjudicated insane or is an officer of a corporation who is not authorized to execute a contract on behalf of a corporation.

**Legal Purpose:** To be enforceable, the lease must be for a legal purpose. A lease that specifies an illegal use is not a valid contract, and therefore void.

> **Instructor Note:** This is not to say that illegal activity does not occur in leased premises, or that all lessors are unaware of such illegal activity. It simply means the contract cannot specify illegal activity. If the contract does not specify the illegal activity, and the lessee (tenant) engages in such activity unbeknownst to the lessor, this is considered to be a breach of contract, and the lessor, upon discovering the activity, must terminate the lease. If the lessor does not terminate the lease upon discovery of the activity, this is called *implied acceptance* of the activity. The lessor then becomes a co-conspirator in the criminal activity.

**Consideration:** Consideration in a contract simply means that something of value must be given by both parties to the contract. In the case of the lease, the lessor (landlord) gives exclusive possession of the premises, along with certain other promises regarding maintenance of the premises, etc., and the lessee (tenant) gives money to the landlord, along with a promise to pay the rental fee for the duration of the lease.

**Note:** Each party must realize a benefit and a detriment.

Courts are seldom concerned with the adequacy of consideration, but there must be something of value given by both sides. Each party must, as a result of the consideration, experience the benefit of having received the consideration from the other party and the detriment of having given the consideration to the other party.

### Statute of Frauds and Leases

People tend to remember verbal agreements in a way that is selectively beneficial to them. As you have no doubt been told time and again, all contracts for the sale or purchase of real estate must be in writing to be enforceable, according to the Statute of Frauds.

However, there is an exception for leases of less than a one-year duration. Technically, the requirement is that contracts must be in writing to be enforceable if, by their terms, they cannot be fully performed within one year of the date of execution. Therefore, a verbal lease for up to one year is enforceable, unless the date of its full performance is more than one year from the date of execution.

## Should All Leases Be in Writing?

Yes. People tend to remember verbal agreements in a way that is selectively beneficial to them. So, even though a certain lease might not need to be in writing to be enforceable, it certainly should be in writing, both to protect yourself as the property manager, and to protect your client, the property owner. By setting forth the lease terms as a written contract, you are protected against a situation where the lessee claims the verbal agreement was different from the agreement you claim it to be.

## Types of Leasehold Estates

A leasehold is a temporary possessory estate. This temporary estate (tenancy) can be for a fixed term and terminate, or it can be for a periodic term with an auto-renewal at the end of each period.

### Estate for Years

Leases that contract for tenancy for a fixed term and automatically terminate at the end of that term are called *leases for an estate for years*. No notice is needed by either the lessee or the lessor to terminate this type of lease upon expiration.

In fact, unless there is a breach, and one party cancels the contract, there is no termination; rather there is merely expiration. Both the lessor and lessee are entitled to the expectation that the contractual obligation ends at the expiration of the lease term, and the possessory estate reverts to the lessor. (There is notice and mutual assent required in order to change the terms of the lease within the lease period.)

### Periodic Tenancy

A lease that contracts for tenancies from period to period, such as month-to-month leases, are periodic tenancy leases. In most states, the notice to cancel a periodic tenancy would be the length of the rent-paying period, but no more than 30 days. You must keep abreast of real estate laws and regulations in your state, so that you can recognize a lawful termination with a legally compliant notice.

> **Instructor Note:** In California, the notice requirements changed from 30 days to 60 days, back to 30 days, and then back to 60 days again all in a matter of a few years. This illustrates how lobbyists and consumer advocate groups can cause laws to flip-flop.

### Estate at Will

An *estate at will* is not a type of lease. In fact, by definition, an estate at will is not in writing. It is basically a unwritten agreement between the landlord and tenant in which the landlord might say, "You may have possession as long as you and I both want you to have possession." Under an estate at will, the landlord may evict the tenant at any time, and the tenant may vacate at any time.

### Estate at Sufferance

An *estate at sufferance* is not a type of lease, either. An estate at sufferance is what happens when a tenant remains on the property in the absence of a valid current lease. It is the wrongful occupancy of property by a tenant after the lease has expired.

## Structure of Rental Payment Terms

Rental payments can be a fixed sum or a variable sum according to an agreed-upon formula. There are too many types of rental payment structures to explain all of them here, so we will explain the most common types. The most common rental payment structures are the *gross*, *net*, *triple-net*, and *percentage* structures.

## Gross Lease

A *gross lease* is simply a lease where the tenant pays a fixed amount of rent on one or more agreed-upon dates for the term of the lease. For instance, if a single family residence is leased for a six-month lease term, and the tenant pays a fixed amount of rent on a given day each month, this would be an *estate for years gross lease*.

With a gross lease, the lessor pays all of the expenses associated with ownership of the building, such as taxes and insurance on the building.

**A Special Type of Gross Lease:** A special type of gross lease that allows rent increases at various times over the duration of the lease term is called a graduated lease. Graduated leases are generally used to encourage tenants to sign long-term leases in a market of low rental activity.

## Net Lease

A *net lease* is a lease where the tenant pays a fixed amount each month as well as some of the expenses on the building. For instance, a month-to-month lease where a tenant pays a flat-fee rental payment on a given day each month, and assumes all maintenance obligations for the building, would be a periodic tenancy net lease.

## Triple-Net Lease

The lessee has to pay the net amount of three types of costs, which is how this term got its name. In a *triple-net lease*, the lessee pays a fixed amount each month as well as all of the expenses associated with the building. The lessee has to pay the net amount of the following three types of costs:

- Net real estate taxes on the leased real estate.
- Net building insurance.
- Net common area maintenance.

For instance, a five-year lease where a tenant pays a flat fee rental payment on given day each month, and is responsible for paying the building's property taxes, building insurance, and the cost of any maintenance or repairs during the term of the lease would be an *estate for years triple-net lease*.

Because the tenant is covering costs associated with the building (which would otherwise be the responsibility of the property owner), the rent charged in the triple net lease is generally lower than the rent charged in a gross or net lease agreement.

## Percentage Lease

In a *percentage lease*, the amount of rental payment in a commercial business is tied to the amount of gross income of the business. Generally, percentage leases are reserved for retail spaces. The lessee pays a flat rental fee, along with a percentage of the gross receipts.

For instance, a month-to-month lease where a tenant pays a flat fee rental payment on a given day each month, plus a percentage of gross receipts, would be a *periodic tenancy percentage lease*.

## Assignment

In a lease assignment, the lessee (assignor) transfers his or her rights to the property to another party (assignee), but retains secondary liability for the lease. The assignee becomes primarily liable to the original lessor for complying with the lease terms and the payment of rent. If the assignee defaults on the rental payments, the lessee can be held liable for the rent.

Before the assignment is valid, the original lessor must approve the assignment and agree to it. This type of arrangement is often done for prospective tenants who do not have a good credit rating. The lessee (assignor) assumes secondary liability for the assignee (i.e., acts as a guarantor or co-signer).

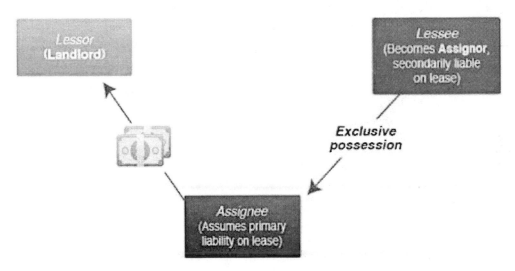

## Sublease

Under a sublease, the lessee under the lease agreement becomes a sublessor, and leases to his or her own tenant, who is the sublessee. The sublessee then pays the sublessor, who then pays the original lessor. Unlike an assignment, the lessee remains primarily liable on the lease. The sublessee is not liable on the original lease, and has no contractual obligation to the original lessor.

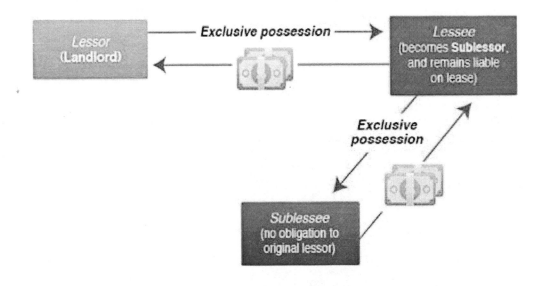

## Advantages of a Sublease

Of course, the most obvious advantage is money. It might be possible to make money on the difference between what the sublessee is paying versus what is due under the original lease.

For example, let's say that a lessee has a 10-year triple-net lease. The lessee pays a monthly rental fee of $2000, plus all expenses associated with the building. However, after five years of leasing, the lessee no longer wants to occupy the property. Over the course of the last five years, rental rates have escalated, and market rent for similar rental spaces in area is $3000 per month. The lessee could benefit financially if he or she were to sublease, rather than assign.

## Proposal to Lease

### Letters of Intent

When the lessor and lessee are serious about leasing, but many of the terms have not yet been agreed upon, one party may give the other party a letter of intent that shows the party's good faith intent to negotiate.

**Example:** Suppose developers want to build a retail mall, rent out the retail spaces, and execute percentage leases with the tenants. However, before they can break ground on the mall, they'll need financing. Before the financiers commit to investing in the retail mall, they want some reassurance that the mall space will indeed be rentable.

Before the prospective lessees (tenants) will commit to a lease, they need some reassurance that the mall spaces have attracted other prospective tenants. The proposal to lease or letter of intent to lease can be a tool to obtain financing, as well as to influence tenants to commence negotiations for leasing space.

## Drafting Leases

Lease ambiguities are generally resolved against the party who drafted the lease. Therefore, as the property manager, you must make certain that the lease is clear. Insist on the latest forms. If a problem occurs that could have been avoided by using the latest form, then you, the property manager, will face potential liability. Additionally, you should demand that any other parties to the transaction use the latest forms.

Do not attempt to modify standard clauses in a lease, or prepare new clauses; or prepare complex leases using the cut-and-paste method that utilizes clauses from other leases. These practices will expose you to liability, especially if your composition creates results that work to the detriment of the property owner. Additionally, preparing a lease using other than what is regarded as a standard-industry lease could be construed as the unauthorized practice of law (you are doing this for another and for compensation).

### Prospective Tenants Who Prepare Leases

A "take it or leave it" proposition that is oppressive and unfair will not be enforced. Be on your guard when a prospective tenant or his or her attorney has prepared a lease on an unfamiliar form. You should advise your property owner to either refuse to sign it altogether, or seek appropriate legal counsel before signing it. It is completely within your power to advise your client to sign only forms that your brokerage has endorsed.

Likewise, if your property owner (lessor) has prepared a lease or his or her attorney has prepared a lease on an unfamiliar form, it is not a good idea for you to present that lease to a prospective tenant without advising the prospective tenant to seek legal counsel before signing it—even if you do not represent the prospective tenant.

## Contract of Adhesion

A *contract of adhesion* is a biased and prejudicial contract where one party has superior bargaining ability and will not allow any modification. It is a "take it or leave it" proposition that is oppressive and unfair. A contract of adhesion that a court determines to be unconscionable (such as a lease) will not be enforced.

> **Instructor Note:** This is not to say that all "take it or leave it" propositions will not be enforced. For a court to deny enforceability, such a proposition must be oppressive and unfair, and be presented by a person who has superior bargaining power.

## Expiration Dates

For residential property, your owners will want the leases to expire when rentals are in most demand in the area. For example, in a college area, your owners will want one-bedroom rentals to expire before the beginning of the next term when there will be peak demand. This will avoid lengthy vacancy periods.

Three-bedroom units are normally rented by families with children of school age. Leases for these types of units should expire after the end of the school year, and prior to the beginning of the next school year. This will be the time of greatest demand.

In cold climates, apartment complexes with pools are desirable during the summer months, when the pool is a positive feature. In the winter months, the existence of a pool is not likely to influence prospective tenants.

When and if your property owner rents a property during a period of low rental activity, consider writing the initial lease so that it is in effect for a period other than one year. Write the lease so that the expiration date occurs at the beginning of a high rental activity or high desirability time. Then, subsequent leases can be written for one year or multiple years. The important thing is that the lease expires during a period of high rental activity.

## Length of the Lease

If you believe that rental demand will increase significantly, you should advise your client that shorter leases are in your client's best interests. In a market with a high foreclosure rate, it is likely that rental demands will increase.

**Note:** Write the lease so that the expiration date occurs at the beginning of a high rental activity time. However, if the high foreclosure rate is combined with high layoffs and a mass exodus from the area, then there will likely be a decreased demand for rental property. Don't assume that increased foreclosures mean high rental activity.

## Understanding Positions and Expectations

When negotiating, you obviously want to find the best deal for your client. You also know that the agent representing the other party wants the best deal for his or her client. Each party is bound to have an opening position advantageous to him or her as well as an idea about how low or high he or she can go. Each party is motivated by factors that are not apparent to the other party.

Powerful negotiating positions are created both by the nature of the transaction, and the communication skills of the agents involved in the transaction. Depending on the market, the client's negotiating position might be more powerful if the client treads lightly with regard to contractual demands.

Other times, the client's negotiating position is weakened if that client does not make enough demands. Getting the client to understand when and how to apply these negotiating strategies requires a salesperson not only to have negotiating skill, but also communication skill.

For instance, if your area experiences a high vacancy rate or there are competitive properties priced at lower-than-market rates, the prospective tenants have a great deal of leverage.

Some prospective tenants don't perceive this power and fail to use it, which bodes well for the property owner. Other times, they perceive that they have power, when in fact they do not, and as the property manager who represents the property owner, you must deflate the prospective tenant's perception of power by advising your property owner to stand firm on his or her requirements.

**What Options Are Available?**

With residential leases, there are usually few, if any, items to be negotiated. Prospective tenants expect to either accept the terms of the lease or look elsewhere. Property owners know that negotiating different terms for different tenants will breed ill will among the tenants. With residential leases, the market determines what options are available.

You want a quick negotiation, if possible. The longer the period of lease negotiations, the greater the chances the prospective tenant will become apprehensive.

## Rent Incentives

If, for some reason, your property owner needs to refinance the investment property or needs to borrow against the investment property, the property owner will need to show that the rental property has a good rental history with a low vacancy rate. One of the easiest and most effective ways to decrease vacancy rates is through rent incentives. Furthermore, in a market of low rental activity, rent incentives can enable your property manager to charge market rent (or even above-market rent) and reduce vacancy rates.

Rental concessions can take several forms:

**Free Rent:** Free rent is the most common concession offered; it is a great incentive. An offering of free first-month rent on a 12-month lease is greater incentive than an offering of free final-month rent on a 12-month lease.

However, an offering of free first-month rent is more likely to attract prospective tenants who tend toward defaulting on their lease obligations. In addition, tenants who receive free rent as a move-in incentive are more likely to move after their lease expires. In fact, the likelihood of tenants moving increases directly with the amount of incentives given. Tenants, especially highly mobile tenants, tend to "hunt" the market for free rent.

**Move-in Gifts:** Desirable and useful gifts, such as flat-screen TVs, or new kitchen appliances, such as a gourmet coffee pot, cost less than one month of rent, and your property owner will have greater success. Another incentive might be to provide useful items for the tenant to enjoy in the area. For instance, if the rental unit is in a golf community, why not give away a set of golf clubs in exchange for leases signed by a particular date. Other ideas include the following:

- One-year prepaid golf membership.
- One-year prepaid cable TV and high-speed internet service.
- Prepaid grocery cards.
- Prepaid gas cards.
- Prepaid biweekly housecleaning for one or two months.

## Late Renewals

When negotiating lease renewals or extensions, there are a few things to consider that will allow your property manager a better negotiating position. First, it costs money to move, especially for the commercial tenant.

Besides the time and expense of moving and the indirect expenses of acquiring new stationery, new business cards, and communicating a new location to clients, commercial tenants are likely to experience a business loss for up to six months after they move. These costs add up, and commercial clients are very willing to pay a slightly higher rent to remain at a location.

Residential tenants are far more likely to react to a rent increase by moving out than are commercial clients. With residential tenants, rather than increasing the rent upon lease renewal, you might advise your property owner to modify the structure of the lease. For instance, changing from a gross lease to a net lease will decrease the property owner's expenses, because the tenant will absorb some of the expenses.

## Other Considerations

### Recording Leases

Generally, possession is considered constructive notice to the world that a person has an interest in real estate, and recordation is just "another" constructive notice.

**Note:** Property managers for corporations or commercial outfits that lease large spaces generally record their leases.

If a lender made a loan on a property where a tenant was in possession, foreclosure of the loan would leave the lender owning the property subject to the lease tights of the tenant. However, what if the lease has been signed and the tenant has not moved in yet?

In this case, the lender would have no constructive notice of the tenant's rights. Therefore, a foreclosure of a loan could leave a tenant subject to eviction by the foreclosing lender. In such cases, the additional constructive notice (the recordation) adds strength to the tenant's case if the lender refuses to honor the tenant's lease.

Recordation is especially important if there is going to be a significant time lapse between the time the lease is executed and the time the tenant moves into the unit.

### Disclosures

Okay, okay—you have been beaten to death with the subject of disclosure. However, this course would not be complete if we did not at least a mention disclosure. Even though you are the agent of the property owner, you still have an obligation to be fair and honest to all parties to the transaction.

If, as a property manager, you know that a property is unsuitable for the tenant's intended purpose, you must disclose this information to the tenant. You must also disclose any negative information you possess that a prospective tenant would want to know.

Remember, a tenant is buying real estate. It just happens to be a leasehold estate, rather than a freehold estate. Tenants are entitled to the same disclosures as buyers.

Other disclosures are mandated by statute. These types of statutory disclosures may include the following:

- **Military Airport Disclosure:** When property is located within territory in the vicinity of a military airport, some states require that this fact is disclosed prior to the execution of a lease.

- **Military Ordnance:** Leases of residential property may require the lessor to disclose to the prospective tenant any knowledge of a former or current military ordnance location that might contain explosive materials within a stated distance of the rental.

- **Flight Path or Noise:** Property located on a busy street or in a flight path where there is a great deal of noise is a fact that is objectively material to most people, and most states would require this disclosure.

- **Flood Hazard Area:** Some states require lessors to disclose the fact that the premises is in a flood hazard area.

- **Homeowners Association Disclosure:** Many states require that lessors provide the prospective lessee with a copy of the CC&Rs prior to signing the lease.

- **Lead-Based Paint Disclosure:** To protect families from exposure to lead from paint, dust, and soil, Congress passed the Residential Lead-Based Paint Hazard Reduction Act of 1992, also known as Title X. Section 1018 of this law directed HUD and EPA to require the disclosure of known information on lead-based paint and lead-based paint hazards before the sale or lease of most housing built before 1978. Congress chose not to cover post-1977 housing because the CPSC banned the use of lead-based paint for residential use in 1978.

- **Swimming Pool Disclosure:** Drowning is a serious threat to young children. Many state legislatures have enacted statutes that require that new occupants of dwellings with pools and persons having a pool installed receive a written safety message about steps to prevent drowning and the legal responsibilities of pool ownership.

**QUIZZES ARE MANDATORY:** Please log in and submit the chapter quizzes online.

## Chapter 10 Quiz

1.  Which of the following is provable by the express provisions of a written contract, without reference to any statements or hidden thoughts outside the writing, and refers to the requirement of a contract that both parties have the same understanding of the terms of the agreement?

    (a)   Mutuality
    (b)   Capacity
    (c)   Legal purpose
    (d)   Consideration

2.  Estate for years, estate at will, periodic tenancy, and estate at sufferance are all types of tenancy. Which of the following are NOT types of leases?

    (a)   Estate for years and periodic tenancy
    (b)   Periodic tenancy and estate at will
    (c)   Estate at will and estate for years
    (d)   Estate at will and estate at sufferance

3.  An _____ is an unwritten agreement between the landlord and tenant where the landlord might say, "you may have possession as long as you and I both want you to have possession."

    (a)   estate at will
    (b)   estate for years
    (c)   estate at sufferance
    (d)   estate from period to period

4.  To avoid exposure to liability for you or your client, you should do all of the following EXCEPT _____.

    (a)   familiarize yourself with all forms
    (b)   use standard forms
    (c)   demand that any other parties to the transaction use the latest standard forms
    (d)   prepare complex leases using the cut-and-paste method, which utilizes clauses from other leases

5.  Depending on the market, the client's negotiating position might be more powerful if the client treads lightly with regard to contractual demands. Other times, the client's negotiating position is weakened if the client does not make enough demands. Getting the client to understand when and how to apply these negotiating strategies requires a property manager to not only have negotiating skill, but also _____.

    (a)   nice clothes
    (b)   a nice manicure
    (c)   good communication skills
    (d)   good command of technology

6.  An offering of free first-month rent as an incentive is more likely to attract prospective tenants who tend to _____.

    (a)   default on their lease obligations
    (b)   stay in the unit forever
    (c)   become employed by the property owner
    (d)   sign long-term leases

7.  Even though you are the agent of the property owner, you still have a legal obligation to _____.

    (a)   be fair and honest to all parties to the transaction
    (b)   protect the best interests of all parties to the transaction
    (c)   give the other parties to the transaction the benefit of the doubt
    (d)   honor all verbal promises made by all other parties to the transaction.

8.  An _____ is in effect when a tenant remains on the property in the absence of a valid current lease (i.e., after the lease expires).

    (a)   estate at will
    (b)   estate for years
    (c)   estate at sufferance
    (d)   estate from period to period

9.  In a(n) _____, the sublessee pays the sublessor, who then pays the original lessor.

    (a)   assignment
    (b)   sublease

10. If you believe that rental demand will decrease, shorter leases are probably in your client's best interest.

    (a)   True
    (b)   False

# Notes

# Disclosure
# Obligations
In Real Estate Transactions

12 Hours of Continuing Education for
Salesperson and Broker License Renewal

**Lumbleau Real Estate School**
23805 Hawthorne Blvd.
Torrance, CA 90505

## DISCLAIMERS

Although every effort has been made to provide accurate and current information in this text, the ideas, suggestions, general principles, and conclusions presented in this text are subject to local, state, and federal laws and regulations, court cases, and any revisions of same. The author and/or publisher is not engaged in rendering legal, tax, or other professional services. The reader is thus urged to consult with his or her employing broker and/or seek legal counsel regarding any points of law. This publication should not be used as a substitute for competent legal advice.

This course is approved for continuing education credit by the California Bureau of Real Estate. However, this approval does not constitute an endorsement of the views or opinions that are expressed by the course sponsor, instructor, authors, or lecturers.

## Table of Contents

## Table of Contents

## Chapter One

**Important Terms**

"as-is"
material fact
beneficiary
conservatorship
decedent's
real Estate
encroachment red flag
execution
fiduciary
power of sale
purchase money
Transfer Disclosure Statement
red flag
specific performance
writ of execution

**Learning Objectives**

Upon completion of Chapter One, you should be able to complete the following:

- Define *material fact*.

- Describe the agent's statutory duty of disclosure.

- Describe the Real Estate Transfer Disclosure Statement (TDS).

- Describe the statutory requirements for delivery of the TDS.

- Describe the agent's duty to disclose based upon his or her superior knowledge.

- Describe the agent's duty of verification.

- Describe the facts of the *Easton v. Strassburger* case.

- Define *red flag*.

**Disclosure of Material Facts**

The real estate licensee's duty to disclose is specifically related to facts that are material, and that affect the value or desirability of the property. In certain circumstances, misrepresentation of a single material fact may result in an accusation of intentional fraud.

There is no absolute standard for determining whether or not a fact is material in a particular situation. A fact may or may not be material depending upon the circumstances of each transaction.

**Material Fact:** Generally, a matter is considered material if the other party would not have entered into the contract had that party known the true facts. However, this definition is much too general and subjective to be used on a day-to-day basis by licensees who are working in the trenches.

Some facts are so obviously material that there is no doubt that prior knowledge of that fact would have affected the desirability of the property. For example, unstable soil or fill, even in small quantities, would obviously be crucial for any buyer to know. Other matters such as structural defects, building code violations, or termites and dry rot would also be considered material facts, as any reasonable seller would understand that they are of major concern to a buyer. Matters such as these can be difficult to discover by inspection, but are still material to the transaction.

The fact that the seller does not have the proper permits to operate a particular business on the premises that the buyer wants to operate, or the fact that the buyer's business use will violate city zoning ordinances, would drastically change both the value and desirability of the property to the buyer. The existence of an easement, or the lack of a proper water system for the intended use of the property, are also material facts that affect the buyer's decision to buy. Other matters that are obviously material include land that has experienced flooding, buildings that may need substantial structural repairs, and land that is not connected to the public sewer system.

The materiality of these facts is objective in nature and can be determined by examining whether the undisclosed fact had a measurable effect on the marketability, the value of the buyer's highest and best use of the property, or the buyer's or appraiser's opinion of value.

A factor can still be considered material even if it does not affect the structural or physical aspect of the property. In one case, the court held the fact that the buyer's check, in the form of a post-dated check, was a material fact that had to be disclosed to the seller. In another case, the court found that the one-year due date on a purchase-money secured obligation and the construction nearby of new competition property, were material facts.

The use of an objective or subjective standard to determine whether or not a fact is material can be key depending on the circumstances of a particular case. The test of materiality referenced by most court decisions describes a matter as material when it affects the value or desirability of the property. An objective standard would require that the matter affect either (1) the value and desirability of the property, or (2) a matter that affects the desirability of the property or the transaction where the seller knows that the particular fact is, or could be, important to the buyer.

Property located on a busy street or in a flight path where there is a great deal of noise may be a fact that is objectively material to most buyers, but a location near a school, which may be desirable to a buyer with children, may be unsatisfactory to a buyer who works a graveyard shift and sleeps during the day, when the noise of the school could be a problem. This type of fact would be material only if the seller or the seller's agent is aware of the buyer's peculiar sensitivity. As you can see, a subjective standard for determining materiality can complicate certain situations.

Recently, the courts considered this issue of subjective materiality in a case where it was not disclosed to the buyer that ten years earlier, a gruesome multiple-murder had taken place at the house. The court decided that in a case like this, where the alleged matter does not relate to the physical condition of the property, what is considered material relates to several very objective tests: (1) the gravity of the harm inflicted by nondisclosure, (2) the fairness of imposing the duty of discovery on the buyer as an alternative to disclosure by the seller, and (3) the impact on the stability of contracts if rescission is permitted. These tests were developed by the court to protect against an unreasonable rescission of the contract based on only the subjective sensitivity of the buyer.

Based on the court's analysis, the nondisclosure of these murders did produce a quantifiable effect on the market value of the property. Thus, the court determined that any time a fact would affect a provable depression in the market value of the property, the seller must disclose the fact. The court went on to clarify that its decision is not based on the very subjective personal sensitivity of the buyer and that even an insensitive buyer (one who does not care about the murders) is entitled to recourse because he or she must disclose this fact upon resale, and the market value would be less due to such a disclosure. By tying their decision to a loss in market value, the courts have kept their standard objective to protect the stability of contracts by not allowing irrational objections as a basis for rescinding a contract.

This type of objective standard still allows buyers or sellers to mention any subjective matters that are material to them, even though they might not be objectively material to a reasonable person or have a measurable effect on market value. In one case, the seller had a bad relationship with his neighbor and he made it clear that he did not want the neighbor to have the use or possession of his property. The buyer represented that he had no relationship with the neighbor when in fact he was the neighbor's nephew. The neighbor's nephew then bought the property and then resold it to the neighbor. After the property was resold to the neighbor, the court awarded the seller punitive damages. As you can see, the seller specifically mentioned his unique situation with his neighbor and established this matter as a material fact. If the seller had known that the buyer was his neighbor's nephew, he may have asked much more for the property or may not have sold to this buyer at all.

When neither party specifically mentions a unique subjective matter as being important, the objective test of materiality, which measures the effect of the undisclosed fact by its effect on the market value, should be used as a workable standard. The agent and his or her client should be able to determine, in most cases, what facts will affect the value and desirability of a particular property. In addition, although they are not comprehensive, the statutory requirements for disclosure should be used by the real estate professional to establish guidelines for determining the type and class of matters that are material and should be disclosed.

The seller also must disclose any material change in the condition of the property or the title that occurs or is discovered by the seller after the contract is executed and prior to the close of escrow. In this situation, the parties may still be obligated contractually, but the disclosure might affect the buyer's decision to complete the transaction. Nondisclosure of this type of fact may deprive the buyer of his or her right to rescind.

For example, in one case, two parties entered into an option agreement. The day before the option was exercised, the owner dedicated a public easement across the property and included in the contract an exception for utility easements. Although there was insufficient evidence of damages, the court stated that the seller had a duty to disclose this material change and by failing to do so, he deprived the buyer of the right to withdraw from the purchase.

## Agent's Statutory Duty of Disclosure

Scattered throughout the codes, there is a seemingly unlimited number of duties to disclose particular facts to one or both of the parties to a real estate transaction. Many of these duties are imposed on the seller, on the seller's agent, or on both. It is not our intent with this course to discuss every single detail regarding disclosure in real estate, but we will try to cover the most common and most important disclosure requirements encountered on a day-to-day basis.

## Real Estate Transfer Disclosure Statement (TDS)

## Introduction

As required by California Civil Code Sections 1102–1102.14, a transferee (buyer) of residential real property is entitled to a statement from the transferor (seller) that provides information regarding the physical condition of the property. This form is called the *Real Estate Transfer Disclosure Statement* and is prescribed by statute.

**Special Note:** The statutory form is provided in CC §1102.6. The disclosure statement is required in all other transactions, even if the property is being sold *as-is* or without covenant or warranty of the physical condition of the property.

This form specifically states that the disclosure statement does not constitute a warranty of the information provided. However, it states that prospective buyers may rely on the information provided by the transferor (seller) to decide whether, and on what terms, to purchase the property. The form requires the seller to (1) identify the specific fixtures, appliances, improvements and features of the property, and whether they are operable; (2) disclose any defects or malfunctions of the physical improvements; and (3) disclose (a) any features that are shared in common with adjoining owners, (b) encroachments, (c) easements, (d) additions, alterations, or modifications made without permits or that are not in compliance with building codes, (e) any fill on the property, and whether there has been any soil or flooding problems, (f) any major damage to the property, (g) zoning violations, (h) neighborhood noise problems or nuisances, (i) deed restrictions or any homeowners' association, (j) any common area facilities, and (k) notices of abatement or lawsuits that affect the property.

## Good Faith Required

The seller and the seller's agent are required to make the necessary disclosures in good faith. For the purposes of this disclosure statement, *good faith* means honesty in fact in the conduct of the transaction. If at the time the disclosure must be made, an item of information required to be disclosed is unknown or not available to the transferor, and the transferor or his or her agent has made a reasonable effort to ascertain it, the transferor may use an approximation of the information. This approximation must be clearly identified as such, be reasonable, be based on the best information available to the transferor or his or her agent, and cannot be used for the purpose of circumventing or evading the statute.

## Errors, Inaccuracies, or Omissions of Information

Neither the transferor nor any listing or selling agent shall be liable for any error, inaccuracy, or omission of any information delivered to the transferee as long as the transferor did not know of the mistake. The seller would also be relieved of responsibility for mistakes if the information in question was provided by a public agency or third-person professional. The receipt of a report from a third-person expert would not relieve the seller or the seller's agent from the common-law duty to disclose defects in the property that were known or reasonably should have been known. A written report from an engineer, surveyor, geologist, structural pest control operator, or other third-person expert, within his or her expertise, will relieve the seller and the seller's agent of the further statutory duties as to the items described in the report, if the report is given based on a specific request. In this case, the report should specify that it is provided to satisfy the statutory requirements of disclosure and should identify the specific information being furnished.

**Special Note:** When the expert is aware that the opinion will be delivered to and relied on by the buyer, the expert will be liable to the buyer for damages suffered if the expert was negligent in rendering the opinion.

## Other Items Not Included in the TDS

The Real Estate Transfer Disclosure Statement does not relieve the seller or the seller's agent of the common-law duty of disclosure, if the common-law duty is beyond the matters specified in the prescribed form. For example, if the seller or the seller's agent receives two expert's reports, he or she has a duty to disclose both reports to the buyer. Also, if there is some other unique material defect in the property that would not normally be included in the TDS, the delivery of the TDS will not relieve the seller or the seller's agent from the duty to disclose this type of material matter.

## Statutory Delivery Requirements

The seller of any real property subject to the statutory requirements for delivery of the TDS must deliver the written statement as follows:

1) In the case of a sale, as soon as practicable before transfer of title.

2) In the case of transfer by a real property sales contract, or by a lease together with an option to purchase, or on a ground lease coupled with improvements, before execution of the contract.

With respect to any transfer subject to items (a) and (b) above, the seller/transferor must indicate compliance with the statutory delivery requirements on the receipt for deposit, the real property sales contract, the lease, or any addendum attached thereto, or on a separate document. Item #11 of the standard CAR Real Estate Purchase Agreement and Receipt for Deposit (under Transfer Disclosure) is a statement that allows the parties to agree on when the disclosure statement will be delivered.

If more than one licensed real estate broker is acting as an agent in a transaction, the broker who has obtained the offer made by the transferee (buyer) is responsible to assure the delivery of the statement to the transferee (buyer), unless the seller has given other written instruction for delivery.

If the agent responsible for delivering the disclosure statement to the buyer cannot obtain the disclosure document required and does not have written assurance from the transferee that the disclosure has been received, the agent shall advise the transferee in writing of his or her right to the disclosure. The agent must maintain a record of what has been done to comply with the statutory requirements for the delivery of the statement. Any disclosure made may be amended in writing by the transferor or his or her agent. If any disclosure, or any material amendment to any disclosure, is delivered after the execution of an offer to purchase, the buyer has:

1) Three days, after delivery in person, or

2) Five days, after delivery by deposit in the mail, to terminate his or her offer by delivery of a written notice of termination to the seller or the seller's agent.

## Rescission Rights

The Real Estate Transfer Disclosure Statement contains three separate parts to be completed by the seller, listing agent, and selling agent (if any), respectively. If one of these parties fails to complete his or her part of the statement, it gives the buyer the right to rescind. For example, if the selling agent failed to execute his or her part of the disclosure statement, even though the statement was executed and delivered promptly by the seller and the listing agent, the buyer would have the right to rescind the contract.

## Exemptions

The statutory disclosure statement is not required when the transfer involves the following:

1) Transfers of a unit in a subdivision when the buyer has been given a public report.

2) Transfers required by a court order, including but not limited to transfers ordered by a probate court in administration of an estate, transfers pursuant to a writ of execution, transfers by a trustee in bankruptcy, transfers by eminent domain, and transfers that result from a decree for specific performance.

## Default and/or Foreclosure:

1) Transfers to a mortgagee by a mortgagor or successor-in-interest or a successor-in-interest who is in default.

2) Transfers by any foreclosure sale after default; transfers by any foreclosure sale after default in an obligation secured by a mortgage.

3) Transfers by a sale under a power of sale, or

4) Any foreclosure sale under a power of sale after default in an obligation secured by a deed of trust or secured by any other instrument that contains a power of sale, or

5) Transfers by a mortgagee or a beneficiary under deed of trust who has acquired the real property at a sale conducted pursuant to a power of sale under a mortgage, or

6) Deed of trust, or

7) A sale pursuant to a decree of foreclosure or has acquired the real property by a deed in lieu of foreclosure.

8) Transfers by a fiduciary in the course of the administration of a decedent's estate, guardianship, conservatorship, or trust.

9) Transfers from one co-owner to one or more other co-owners.

10) Transfers made to a spouse, or to a person or persons in the lineal blood relationship of one or more of the transferors.

11) Transfers between spouses resulting from a decree of dissolution of marriage or a decree of legal separation, or from a property settlement agreement incidental to such a decree.

12) Transfers by the State Controller pursuant to the Unclaimed Property Law.

13) Transfers as a result of failure to pay property taxes.

**14)** Transfers or exchanges to or from any government agency.

## Anatomy of the Real Estate Transfer Disclosure Statement

The Standard TDS Form used throughout this text was reproduced by the Chamberlin Real Estate School, Inc. with permission of the California Association of Realtors®.

Of all the disclosure instruments required in today's real estate transactions, the Real Estate Transfer Disclosure Statement (TDS) may be the most important. An inadequately prepared TDS can have serious implications for all the parties involved in a transaction.

Even though it is not the agent's responsibility to fill out the seller's part of the TDS, it is the agent's responsibility to advise his or her client on how to properly complete the form.

Thus far, we have discussed the different statutory requirements of disclosure. The TDS is the mandated form that is required to present these facts to a prospective buyer. Although the form itself is mandated by law, there is more to the preparation of the TDS than the mechanical aspects of filling in the blanks. The TDS must be prepared in a manner that not only looks professional but also takes into account other facts about a particular property that may not be covered by the preprinted form.

## TDS Form Introduction

### TDS Form Introduction

THIS DISCLOSURE STATEMENT CONCERNS THE REAL PROPERTY SITUATED IN THE CITY OF _____, COUNTY OF_____, STATE OF CALIFORNIA, DESCRIBED AS _____. THIS STATEMENT IS A DISCLOSURE OF THE CONDITION OF THE ABOVE DESCRIBED PROPERTY IN COMPLIANCE WITH SECTION 1102 OF THE CIVIL CODE AS OF (date) _____. IT IS NOT A WARRANTY OF ANY KIND BY THE SELLER(S) OR ANY AGENT(S) REPRESENTING ANY PRINCIPAL(S) IN THIS TRANSACTION, AND IS NOT A SUBSTITUTE FOR ANY INSPECTIONS OR WARRANTIES THE PRINCIPAL(S) MAY WISH TO OBTAIN.

### *Comments on Form Introduction*

It is important to insert the "as of" date here. Use the date on which the sellers signed the TDS to differentiate the working form from any earlier versions.

## Section I: Coordination with Other Disclosure Forms

### I. COORDINATION WITH OTHER DISCLOSURE FORMS

This Real Estate Transfer Disclosure Statement is made pursuant to Section 1102 of the Civil Code. Other statutes require disclosures, depending upon the details of the particular real estate transaction (for example: special study zone and purchase-money liens on residential property).

**Substituted Disclosures:** The following disclosures and other disclosures required by law, including the Natural Hazard Disclosure Report/Statement that may include airport annoyances, earthquake, fire, flood, or special assessment information, have or will be made in connection with this real estate transfer, and are intended to satisfy the disclosure obligations on this form, where the subject matter is the same:

☐ Inspection reports completed pursuant to the contract of sale or receipt for deposit

☐ Additional inspection reports or disclosures: _____

_____.

## *Comments on Section I*

Depending upon the details of a particular real estate transaction, there may be other disclosures required by statute to be included with the TDS. For example, the California Division of Mines and Geology has prepared maps of designated special study zones that contain potentially active earthquake faults (Pub Res C §2622). In this case, the seller or the agent of the seller must disclose to prospective buyers that the property is located within a special-studies zone of earthquake faults. On the lines provided in this section, there may be reference to a geological report. By making mention here of any additional disclosures required for a particular transaction, the seller is stating that any subsequent reports issued as a result of an additional disclosure requirement will be in connection with the TDS, and that the intent is to satisfy any disclosure obligations of the TDS that deal with this subject matter.

Any report prepared by a licensed engineer, surveyor, geologist, structural pest control operator, contractor, property inspector, government agency, or other expert, that provides information that is required to be disclosed in the TDS, should be included in this section.

The seller and the agent are then relieved of any further duty of disclosure with respect to the item(s) within that particular report. Also, any reports noted should be dated and attached to the TDS form.

### Section II: Seller's Information

### II. SELLER'S INFORMATION

The Seller discloses the following information with the knowledge that even though this is not a warranty, prospective Buyers may rely on this information in deciding whether and on what terms to purchase the subject property. Seller hereby authorizes any agent(s) representing any principal(s) in this transaction to provide a copy of this statement to any person or entity in connection with any actual or anticipated sale of the property.

**THE FOLLOWING ARE REPRESENTATIONS MADE BY THE SELLER(S) AND ARE NOT THE REPRESENTATIONS OF THE AGENT(S), IF ANY. THIS INFORMATION IS A DISCLOSURE AND IS NOT INTENDED TO BE PART OF ANY CONTRACT BETWEEN THE BUYER AND SELLER.**

Seller ☐ is ☐ is not occupying the property.

A. The subject property has the items checked below (read across):

| | | |
|---|---|---|
| ☐ Range | ☐ Wall/Window Air Conditioning | ☐ Pool: |
| ☐ Oven | ☐ Sprinklers | ☐ Child Resistant Barrier |
| ☐ Microwave | ☐ Public Sewer System | ☐ Pool/Spa Heater: |
| ☐ Dishwasher | ☐ Septic Tank | ☐ Gas ☐ Solar ☐ Electric |

| | | |
|---|---|---|
| □ Trash Compactor | □ Sump Pump | □ Water Heater: |
| □ Garbage Disposal | □ Water Softener | □ Gas □ Solar □ Electric |
| □ Washer/Dryer Hookups | □ Patio/Decking | □ Water Supply: |
| □ Rain Gutters | □ Built-in Barbecue | □ City □ Well |
| □ Burglar Alarms | □ Gazebo | □ Private Utility or |
| □ Carbon Monoxide Device(s) | □ Security Gate(s) | Other _____ |
| □ Smoke Detector(s) | □ Garage: | □ Gas Supply: |
| □ Fire Alarm | □ Attached □ Not Attached | □ Utility □ Bottled (Tank) |
| □ TV Antenna | □ Carport | □ Window Screens |
| □ Satellite Dish | □ Automatic Garage Door Opener(s) | □ Window Security Bars |
| □ Intercom | □ Number Remote Controls ____ | □ Quick Release Mechanism on |
| □ Central Heating | □ Sauna | Bedroom Windows |
| □ Central Air Conditioning | □ Hot Tub/Spa: | □ Water-Conserving Plumbing Fixtures |
| □ Evaporator Cooler(s) | □ Locking Safety Cover | |

□ Exhaust Fan(s) in _____     □ 220 Volt Wiring in _____     □ Fireplace(s) in _____

□ Gas Starter _____     □ Roof(s): Type: _____ Age: _____(approx..)

□ Other: _____

Are there, to the best of your (Seller's) knowledge, any of the above that are not in operating condition?  □ Yes  □ No  If yes, then describe. (Attach additional sheets if necessary): _____
_____

(*see note on page 2)

## *Comments on Section II*

In this section, a distinction must be made as to the relationship between the TDS and the Real Estate Purchase Contract itself. The information given in the Real Estate Transfer Disclosure Statement is only a disclosure and *Is Not Intended to Be Part of Any Contract between the Buyer and Seller.* Although the information given in the disclosure form obviously does ultimately affect the negotiations between the buyer and seller, it is incorrect to consider the Real Estate Transfer Disclosure Statement part of the purchase contract. It is a misconception by some agents and buyers that the information disclosed in the TDS constitutes a list of things to be fixed. This is not true. Such a list would normally be established at the time the buyer does a walkthrough with his or her agent. Contrary to current practice, it is a good idea to do this type of walkthrough early in the escrow, hopefully the day after the buyer receives the TDS. A thorough inspection at this time, using the TDS as a guideline, should reveal most items that potentially need to be fixed or replaced. Negotiations about these items would then take place early in the escrow, thus avoiding surprises just days before closing. The buyer can still reserve the right to do a final walkthrough just prior to close of escrow. If you find yourself regularly paying for last-minute items to save transactions, make sure the walkthrough takes place early.

## *Tips for Filling Out Section II*

1) The items listed in Section II (A) are designed to be read across; they do not make sense if read vertically.

2) This section is only asking if the subject property has the items listed below. If the property has one of the items listed below, the box next to that item should be checked.

3) **Smoke Detector(s):** In addition to checking the box, the number of smoke detectors should be penciled in as follows:

Smoke Detector(s) (#).

4) **Window Screens:** Window screens are included in the Purchase Contract and must be replaced if missing. It is a good idea to advise the seller to mark down how many screens there are and how many screens are missing, if any.

## Section II (B)

B. **Are you (Seller) aware of any significant defects/malfunctions in any of the following?**    □ Yes    □ No **If yes, check** the **appropriate spaces(s) below.**
□ Interior Walls □ Ceilings   □ Floors  □ Exterior □ Walls  □ Insulation  □ Roof(s)  □ Windows   □ Doors  □ Foundation Slab(s)
□ Driveways □ Sidewalks    □ Walls/Fences    □ Electrical Systems    □ Plumbing/Sewer/Septics □ Other Structural Components:
Describe:_____
_____
_____ If any of the above is
checked, explain. (Attach additional sheets if necessary): _____
_____

*Installation of a listed appliance, device, or amenity is not a precondition or sale or transfer of the dwelling. The carbon monoxide device, garage door opener, or child-resistant pool barrier may not be in compliance with the safety standards relating to, respectively, carbon monoxide device standards of Chapter 8 (commencing with Section 13260) of Part 2 of Division 12 of, automatic reversing device standards of Chapter 12.5 (commencing with Section 19890) of Part 3 of Division 13 of, or the pool safety standards of Article 2.5 (commencing with Section 115920) of Chapter 5 of Part 10 of Division 104 of, the Health and Safety Code. Window security bars may not have quick-release mechanisms in compliance with the 1995 edition of the California Building Standards Code. Section 1101.4 of the Civil Code requires all single-family residences built on or before January 1, 1994, to be equipped with water-conserving plumbing fixtures after January 1, 2017. Additionally, on and after January 1, 2014, a single-family residence built on or before January 1, 1994, that is altered or improved is required to be equipped with water-conserving plumbing fixtures as a condition of final approval. Fixtures in this dwelling may not comply with section 1101.4 of the Civil Code.

## Comments on Section II (B)

This section only asks the seller to disclose any significant defects or malfunctions that he or she is aware of. If the seller is not aware of the defect or malfunction, it should not be checked. By walking the inside and perimeter of the property, certain items can be brought to the attention of the seller (e.g., leaning fences, cracked driveways, or missing screens).

## Section II (C)

C. **Are you (Seller) aware of any of the following:**
1.  Substances, materials, or products that may be an environmental hazard such as, but not limited to, asbestos, formaldehyde, radon gas, lead-based paint, mold, fuel or chemical storage tanks, and contaminated soil or water on the subject property . . . . . □ Yes  □ No
2.  Features of the property shared in common with adjoining landowners, such as walls, fences, and driveways, whose use or responsibility for maintenance may have an effect on the subject property . . . . . . . . . . . . . . . . . . . . . . . . . . . □ Yes  □ No
3.  Any encroachments, easements or similar matters that may affect your interest in the subject property . . . . . . . . . . . . . . .□ Yes  □ No
4.  Room additions, structural modifications, or other alterations or repairs made without necessary permits . . . . . . . . . . . . . □ Yes  □ No
5.  Room additions, structural modifications, or other alterations or repairs not in compliance with building codes . . . . . . . . . . □ Yes  □ No
6.  Fill (compacted or otherwise) on the property or any portion thereof . . . . . . . . . . . . . . . . . . . . . . . . . . . . . . . . . . . . . . . . . . □ Yes  □ No
7.  Any settling from any cause, or slippage, sliding, or other soil problems . . . . . . . . . . . . . . . . . . . . . . . . . . . . . . . . . . . .□ Yes  □ No
8.  Flooding, drainage or grading problems . . . . . . . . . . . . . . . . . . . . . . . . . . . . . . . . . . . . . . . . . . . . . . . . . . . . . . . . . . . . . □ Yes  □ No
9.  Major damage to the property or any of the structures from fire, earthquake, floods, or landslides . . . . . . . . . . . . . . . . . . . □ Yes  □ No
10. Any zoning violations, nonconforming uses, violations of "setback" requirements . . . . . . . . . . . . . . . . . . . . . . . . . . . . . . . □ Yes  □ No
11. Neighborhood noise problems or other nuisances . . . . . . . . . . . . . . . . . . . . . . . . . . . . . . . . . . . . . . . . . . . . . . . . . . . . . . □ Yes  □ No

12. CC&R's or other deed restrictions or obligations . . . . . . . . . . . . . . . . . . . . . . . . . . . . . . . . . . . . . . . . . . . . . . . . .□ Yes  □ No
13. Homeowners' Association that has any authority over the subject property . . . . . . . . . . . . . . . . . . . . . . . . . . . . . . . . .□ Yes  □ No
14. Any "common area" facilities such as pools, tennis courts, walkways, or other areas co-owned in undivided
    interest with others . . . . . . . . . . . . . . . . . . . . . . . . . . . . . . . . . . . . . . . . . . . . . . . . . . . . . . . . . . . . . . . . . . . . . . □ Yes  □ No
15. Any notices of abatement or citations against the property . . . . . . . . . . . . . . . . . . . . . . . . . . . . . . . . . . . . . . . . . . □ Yes  □ No
16. Any lawsuits by or against the seller threatening to or affecting this real property, claims for damages by the Seller pursuant
    to Section 910 or 914 threatening to or affecting this real property, claims for breach of warranty pursuant to Section 900
    threatening to or affecting this real property, or claims for breach of an enhanced protection agreement pursuant to Section
    903 threatening to or affecting this real property, including any lawsuits or claims for damages pursuant to Section 910 or
    914 alleging a defect or deficiency in this real property or "common areas" (facilities such as pools, tennis courts, walkways,
    or other areas co-owned in undivided interest with others) . . . . . . . . . . . . . . . . . . . . . . . . . . . . . . . . . . . . . . . . . . □ Yes  □ No

If the answer to any of these is yes, explain. (Attach additional sheets if necessary): _____

_____

_____

## Comments on Section II (C)

Often, Sellers will just check "No" without giving adequate thought to the question. For example, almost every home has minor stucco cracks on exterior walls and/or small cracks over doorways. These minor cosmetic cracks can be put in the proper perspective in the explanation section, but #7 should still be marked "Yes" in this case. This rationale can also be applied to other disclosures in this section.

## Section II (D)

**D.1.** The Seller certifies that the property, as of the close of escrow, will be in compliance with Section 13113.8 of the Health and Safety Code by having operable smoke detector(s) with are approved, listed, and installed in accordance with the State Fire Marshal's regulations and applicable local standards.

**2.** The Seller certifies that the property, as of the close of escrow, will be in compliance with Section 19211 of the Health and Safety Code by having the water heater tank(s) braced, anchored, or strapped in place in accordance with applicable law.

Seller certifies that the information herein is true and correct to the best of the Seller's knowledge as of the date signed by the Seller.
Seller _____ Date _____

## Comments on Section II (D)

The agent should double-check that all smoke detectors are operable and in compliance with current law. Water heaters should also be checked to make sure they are braced, anchored, or strapped.

## Section III: Agent's Inspection Disclosure

### III. AGENT'S INSPECTION DISCLOSURE
(To be completed only if the seller is represented by an agent in this transaction.)

**THE UNDERSIGNED, BASED ON THE ABOVE INQUIRY OF THE SELLER(S) AS TO THE CONDITION OF THE PROPERTY AND BASED ON A REASONABLY COMPETENT AND DILIGENT VISUAL INSPECTION OF THE ACCESSIBLE AREAS OF THE PROPERTY IN CONJUNCTION WITH THAT INQUIRY, STATES THE FOLLOWING:**

□ See attached Agent Visual Inspection Disclosure (AVID Form)
□ Agent notes no items for disclosure.

☐ Agent notes the following items: _____

_____

_____

Agent (Broker Representing Seller) _____ By_____ Date_____
                                   (Please Print)        (Associate Licensee or Broker Signature)

## *Comments on Section III*

The agent should make specific observations regarding the subject property in this section and avoid making blanket statements such as "Per Seller's statements" or "Suggest Buyer obtain inspections to satisfy themselves that the property is as represented." These statements are not proper and can result in problems in the event of a lawsuit.

## Section IV: Agent's Inspection Disclosure

### IV.  AGENT'S INSPECTION DISCLOSURE
(To be completed only if the agent who has obtained the offer is other than the agent above.)

**THE UNDERSIGNED, BASED ON A REASONABLY COMPETENT AND DILIGENT VISUAL INSPECTION OF THE ACCESSIBLE AREAS OF THE PROPERTY, STATES THE FOLLOWING:**
☐ See attached Agent Visual Inspection Disclosure (AVID Form)
☐ Agent notes no items for disclosure.
☐ Agent notes the following items: _____

_____

_____

Agent (Broker Obtaining the Offer) _____ By_____ Date_____
                                   (Please Print)        (Associate Licensee or Broker Signature)

## *Comments on Section IV*

Our comment here would be the same basic comment that we made for Section III. We would also add that the Buyer's agent should pay special attention to specifically note any potential Red Flags or errors and/or omissions by the Seller or Seller's agent.

## Section V

V. **BUYER(S) AND SELLER(S) MAY WISH TO OBTAIN PROFESSIONAL ADVICE AND/OR INSPECTIONS OF THE PROPERTY AND TO PROVIDE FOR APPROPRIATE PROVISIONS IN A CONTRACT BETWEEN BUYER AND SELLER(S) WITH RESPECT TO ANY ADVICE/ INSPECTIONS/ DEFECTS.**

**I/WE ACKNOWLEDGE RECEIPT OF A COPY OF THIS STATEMENT.**

Seller _____ Date _____ Buyer _____ Date _____

Seller _____ Date _____ Buyer _____ Date _____

Agent (Broker Representing Seller) _____ By _____ Date _____
                                            (Please Print)                    (Associate-License or Broker Signature)

Agent (Broker Obtaining the Offer) _____ By _____ Date _____
                                            (Please Print)                    (Associate-License or Broker Signature)

**SECTION 1102.3 OF THE CIVIL CODE PROVIDES A BUYER WITH THE RIGHT TO RESCIND A PURCHASE CONTRACT FOR AT LEAST THREE DAYS AFTER THE DELIVERY OF THIS DISCLOSURE IF DELIVERY OCCURS AFTER THE SIGNING OF AN OFFER TO PURCHASE. IF YOU WISH TO RESCIND THE CONTRACT, YOU MUST ACT WITHIN THE PRESCRIBED PERIOD.**

**A REAL ESTATE BROKER IS QUALIFIED TO ADVISE ON REAL ESTATE. IF YOU DESIRE LEGAL ADVICE, CONSULT YOUR ATTORNEY.**

*Comments on Section V*

The agent must immediately deliver a copy of this document to the Buyer upon execution. Since the Seller signs this document prior to seeing any comments that might be inserted by the Buyer's agent in Section IV, the Seller should get a completely executed copy as soon as possible.

**Question & Answer Review I:**

**Complying With the Real Estate Transfer Disclosure Statement Law and the Broker's Duty to Inspect Residential Real Estate Property**

The following Q & A Memorandum has been reproduced with the permission of the California Association of Realtors® Legal and Board Services Department. These questions are not part of your homework. They are part of the reading assignment only and are designed to be a review of the preceding section.

**Question 1:** What is the Real Estate Transfer Disclosure Statement?

**Answer:** A Real Estate Transfer Disclosure Statement (TDS) is a form prescribed in Civil Code § 1102.6. Effective January 1, 1987, most sellers of residential property with 1–4 units have been required to furnish this completed form to prospective purchasers. Sellers and licensees may comply with this law by utilizing C.A.R. Form TDS, which they can obtain from most local Boards of Associations of Realtors®, or from the C.A.R. Member Products and Services Division at (800) 227-7217.

**Question 2:** What types of real estate transactions are covered by this disclosure law?

**Answer:** These disclosure requirements apply to transfers by sale, exchange, installment land contract, lease with an option to purchase, option to purchase, or ground lease coupled with improvements of real property (or a residential stock cooperative) with 1–4 dwelling units.

**Question 3:** Are there any transactions that involve property with 1–4 units, where the seller is exempt from the requirement to provide a Real Estate Transfer Disclosure Statement?

**Answer:** Yes. Certain types of transfers are specifically exempted in Civil Code § 1102.1. They are as follows:

1) Transfers that require a public report pursuant to § 11018.1 of the Business and Professions Code and transfers pursuant to § 11010.4 of the Business and Professions Code where no public report is required.

2) Transfers pursuant to court order (such as probate sales, sales by a bankruptcy trustee, etc.).

3) Transfers by foreclosure (including a deed in lieu of foreclosure and a transfer by a beneficiary who has acquired the property by foreclosure or deed in lieu of foreclosure).

4) Transfers by a fiduciary in the course of the administration of a decedent's estate, guardianship, conservatorship, or trust.

5) Transfers from one co-owner to one or more other co-owners.

6) Transfers made to a spouse or to a child, grandchild, parent, grandparent, or other direct ancestor or descendant.

7) Transfers between spouses in connection with a dissolution of marriage or similar proceeding.

8) Transfers by the State Controller pursuant to the Unclaimed Property Law.

9) Transfers or exchanges to or from any government entity.

However, it should be noted that a real estate licensee still has a duty to conduct a reasonably competent and diligent visual inspection of accessible areas in almost all of the above situations. In other words, although the seller is exempt from having to provide a disclosure statement in certain situations, a licensee must conduct this inspection, and disclose the results of the inspection, in almost all residential transactions that involve 1–4 units.

**Question 4:** Are there any situations in which a licensee does not have to conduct an inspection during a residential 1–4 unit transaction?

**Answer:** Yes. A licensed real estate broker or salesperson does not need to conduct a visual inspection of residential property that is sold as part of a subdivision in which a CalBRE public report is required (5 or more units). In addition, a broker need not conduct a visual inspection on a subdivision in which a public report is not required because it is a subdivision of improved, single-family homes, in which all improvements are complete, there are no common areas, and whose units are located entirely within the boundaries of a city.

**Question 5:** Must a Transfer Disclosure Statement be provided to a purchaser of a new residential property that is not part of a subdivision, such as a new home being built on a lot?

**Answer:** Yes. The disclosure statement must be provided to purchasers of these types of new homes.

**Question 6:** Does the Real Estate Transfer Disclosure Statement requirement apply to "For Sale by Owner" transactions?

**Answer:** The law applies even if there is no real estate licensee involved in the transaction.

**Question 7:** Who must fill out this Real Estate Transfer Disclosure Statement?

**Answer:** The seller must fill out sections I and II of the form. If any real estate licensees are involved in the transaction, the listing and selling agents usually fill out sections III and IV, respectively, based on the results of the careful visual inspections they have conducted (see Question 11 below for a discussion of whether the licensee must fill out their portion of the TDS).

**Question 8:** On 1–4 unit transactions where the seller is exempt from providing the Transfer Disclosure Statements, but where the real estate licensees involved are required to conduct an inspection, should the licensees provide the buyer with a completed TDS form?

**Answer:** No. The real estate licensees should never fill out the seller's portion of the Transfer Disclosure Statement. If they wish to, any agent involved in the transaction may disclose the results of his or her inspection on page 2 of the TDS form, or he or she can make the disclosure on a separate piece of paper.

**Question 9:** Are the real estate agents responsible for checking and commenting on the accuracy of the seller's portion of the TDS form?

**Answer:** No. The agents should simply do their own inspection and disclose their findings, on the TDS or elsewhere, whether or not their findings agree with the seller's portion.

**Question 10:** What about landlords or relocation companies who have never lived in or even seen the inside of their residential property that is 1–4 units? Are they exempt from having to fill out the disclosure statement?

**Answer:** No. A seller in this situation must fill out the disclosure statement to the best of his or her ability. In other words, unless the seller meets one of the exemptions listed in the answer to Question 3, he or she must provide a Real Estate Transfer Disclosure Statement to a buyer. The seller in this situation should probably just leave his or her portion blank, or write something to the effect of "Have never lived in or seen property," and sign it. Once again, the agents should not fill out the seller's portion. On the other hand, the buyer should also perform an inspection of the property.

**Question 11:** So, to sum up, should the licensees fill out their portion of the TDS form? Or, to put it another way, at what point is the Transfer Disclosure Statement considered complete?

**Answer:** The law is silent as to whether the real estate licensees must fill out their portion of the TDS. Therefore, the disclosure statement is probably complete after the seller finishes filling out the form. Of course, the agents should disclose the results of their inspections in writing somewhere, and the TDS is a convenient place to do so.

**Question 12:** Who is responsible for delivering the disclosure statement to the buyer?

**Answer:** If two or more real estate licensees are acting as agents in the transaction, the selling agent must deliver the statement to the buyer, unless the seller has given other written instructions for delivery. If only one licensee is involved, that licensee must deliver the statement to the buyer. If no real estate licensees are involved in the transaction, the seller is responsible.

**Question 13:** Must the disclosure statement be delivered to the buyer in person?

**Answer:** No. The law states that delivery of the disclosure statement to the buyer may be made either in person or by mail. Obviously, personal delivery is preferable.

**Question 14:** When does the disclosure statement have to be delivered to the buyer?

**Answer:** As soon as practicable before transfer of title. If possible, it would be preferable to provide the completed disclosure statement to the buyer prior to his or her signing the offer to purchase. If the buyer receives the disclosure statement after execution of his or her offer to purchase, the buyer will have a three- or five-day period to cancel the transaction (see Question 17 below for details, and Question 15 for an exception).

**Question 15:** At what time should a prospective buyer who is entering into a lease option agreement receive the Transfer Disclosure Statement?

**Answer:** The prospective purchaser should get the disclosure statement before he or she enters into the lease option agreement.

**Question 16:** When should the prospective buyer of a new home that is not exempt from the TDS requirement receive the completed form?

**Answer:** The buyer should get the TDS before he or she enters into the contract to purchase the home, even if it has not yet been built. In other words, no special rule applies.

**Question 17:** Does a buyer have a right to cancel the transaction when the disclosure statement is furnished, and after the buyer has signed the offer to purchase?

**Answer:** Yes. "If any disclosure, or any material amendment of any disclosure . . . is delivered after the execution of an offer to purchase, the transferee (buyer) shall have three days after delivery in person or five days after delivery by deposit in the mail, to terminate his or her offer by delivery of a written notice of termination to the transferor (seller) or the transferor's (seller's) agent" (Civil Code § 1102.2.).

**Question 18:** May the buyer exercise his or her right to terminate the offer for any reason, or must the buyer specifically object to a particular item on the disclosure statement?

**Answer:** The law does not address this particular point.

**Question 19:** What if, after the disclosure statement is furnished to the buyer, but before the close of escrow, an error or omission in the disclosure form is discovered?

**Answer:** The Real Estate Transfer Disclosure Statement may be amended at any time, in writing, by the seller or the seller's agent. However, if any material amendment to the disclosure statement is delivered to the buyer after he or she is already obligated under the contract, the buyer has three days, if delivered in person, or five days, if deposited in the mail, to rescind the contract. In other words, if the statement is materially amended at any time after the execution of the contract, the buyer has a right to back out of the transaction (See Question 18). More generally, any time a seller or licensee fails to disclose a material fact to a buyer, the buyer may be able to rescind, whether or not a TDS form is required or has been delivered.

**Question 20:** Is it mandatory that a Real Estate Transfer Disclosure Statement be provided to a buyer in applicable real estate transactions, or can a buyer waive his or her right to receive the form?

**Answer:** The law states that the seller must provide the disclosure statement to the buyer. It is doubtful that this requirement can be waived.

**Question 21:** What happens if the seller refuses to fill out a Real Estate Transfer Disclosure Statement?

**Answer:** The statute provides that if the seller willfully or negligently violates any of its provisions, the seller will be liable to the buyer for any actual damages that result from such a violation. If the licensee responsible for delivering the disclosure statement cannot obtain it, that licensee must advise the buyer in writing of the buyer's right to receive the statement.

**Question 22:** If a seller gives this form to the buyer, does that mean that he or she does not have to provide other disclosure statements?

**Answer:** No. Section I of the disclosure statement provides space for the seller to provide other disclosures required by law, such as a special studies zone disclosure or a purchase money lien on residential property disclosure. All other disclosures mandated by local, state, or federal law must still be provided to the buyer, in addition to the Real Estate Transfer Disclosure Statement.

**Question 23:** Are cities and counties permitted to require additional disclosures on forms mandated by California law?

**Answer:** Yes. Since July 1, 1990, a city or county has been able to require disclosures on the form described in Civil Code §1102.6a. Cities and counties may require disclosures on different forms if they act under the authority of an ordinance adopted before July 1, 1990.

**Question 24:** What information must a seller or broker provide a prospective buyer concerning environmental hazards?

**Answer:** If a seller or broker provides the consumer information booklet entitled *Environmental Hazards: A Guide for Homeowners and Buyers* to a buyer, they need not give the buyer any additional environmental information. However, sellers and brokers still have a duty to disclose any known environmental conditions that affect the property. In fact, there is a specific question on the seller's portion of the Transfer Disclosure Statement form that addresses this issue.

**Question 25:** What information must a seller or broker give a prospective buyer concerning geologic and seismic hazards?

**Answer:** If a seller or broker provides a *Homeowner's Guide to Earthquake Preparedness* booklet (now available at your local board) to a buyer, he or she need not give the buyer any additional earthquake-related information.

However, sellers and brokers still have a duty to disclose any known material seismic conditions that affect the property. Moreover, the fact that the property is in a Special Studies Zone (or a Seismic Hazard Zone, after maps are released) must always be disclosed.

**Question 26:** Must a seller of residential property disclose the existence of former federal or state ordnance locations within the neighborhood area?

**Answer:** Yes. According to Civil Code §1102.15, a seller with actual knowledge of any former federal or state ordnance locations within the neighborhood area must give written notice of that knowledge as soon as practicable before transfer of title.

An *ordnance location* is an area identified by the state or federal government as an area once used for military training purposes and that may contain explosive munitions. A neighborhood area is any area located within one mile of the residential property.

**Question 27:** Will a seller or real estate licensee be liable if the disclosure statement contains inaccuracies or omissions?

**Answer:** No, so long as the following are true:

1) The errors or omissions were not personally known to the seller or the licensee; and

2) The errors or omissions were based on information provided by public agencies, licensed engineers, land surveyors, geologists, structural pest control operators, contractors, or other experts who are dealing with matters within the scope of the license or expertise of that expert; and

3) Ordinary care was used when obtaining and transmitting the information.

**Question 28:** What is the liability under this law of a real estate licensee or seller who fails to comply with the disclosure requirements, either by making intentionally inaccurate statements or omissions, or by failing to deliver it promptly?

**Answer:** The Real Estate Transfer Disclosure law provides that anyone "who willfully or negligently violates or fails to perform any duty prescribed by . . . (this law) . . . shall be liable in the amount of actual damages suffered by a transferee (buyer)."

**Question 29:** Under this disclosure law, can a closed transaction be invalidated for failure to comply?

**Answer:** No. The Real Estate Transfer Disclosure law specifically states that a completed transaction will not be invalidated for non-compliance. However, failure to comply can result in liability.

**Question 30:** Do the listing or selling agents have to keep a copy of the Real Estate Transfer Disclosure Statement in their files?

**Answer:** Yes. Any real estate licensee involved in the transaction must keep a copy of the Real Estate Transfer Disclosure Statement for at least three years, pursuant to Business & Professions Code § 10148.

**Question 31:** Was there a law that went into effect in 1985 that required the seller to disclose structural additions or modifications?

**Answer:** Yes. Civil Code § 1134.5 went into effect on July 1, 1985. It required sellers of a 1-4 unit residential property to disclose, in writing, to any prospective buyer, if there had been any structural additions or modifications to the property and whether these additions or modifications had been done with permit. This legislation (the Real Estate Transfer Disclosure Statement law) was repealed § 1134.5, effective January 1, 1987. It should be noted, however, that the mandatory disclosure statement form requires essentially the same disclosures required under the previous law; i.e., that the seller indicate whether he/she is aware of any room additions, structural modifications or other alterations made without necessary permits or not in compliance with building codes.

**Question 32:** Does the seller have to provide a TDS if he/she sells the property "as-is"?

**Answer:** Yes. There is no exemption to providing the disclosure statement for an as-is transaction. Unless the seller meets one of the exemptions listed in the answer to Question 3, he or she must provide a Real Estate Transfer Disclosure Statement to the buyer. Remember that even in an as-is transaction, where the seller does not warrant the condition of the property, the seller is still required to disclose all known material facts that affect the value or desirability of the property to the buyer.

**Question 33:** What is the seller's responsibility when the TDS states that an item is "not working" while the purchase contract warrants that it is operable? For example, let's say the seller states in the Transfer Disclosure Statement that the dishwasher is not functioning. On the other hand, in the deposit receipt, the seller warrants that "all built-in appliances are in working order." Is the seller responsible for fixing the dishwasher?

**Answer:** Yes. The seller is responsible for living up to his or her contractual obligations. The Transfer Disclosure Statement is not part of the contract; its only function is to provide information to the buyer to enable the buyer to decide whether or not to go through with the transaction. Even if the buyer decides not to cancel based on the TDS with some negative disclosures, the buyer does not waive any of his or her rights under the purchase contract.

## Licensee's Superior Knowledge

In addition to the licensee's statutory requirement to make certain disclosures to the buyer, both the listing agent and the selling agent have a statutory duty to conduct a reasonably competent and diligent visual inspection and disclose to a prospective purchaser all facts that materially affect the value or desirability of the property that such an investigation would reveal.

The standard of care required of the licensee when making such an inspection is not the standard applicable to the average person. The courts have held that the standard is even higher than that imposed on the actual seller of the property. The licensee is subject to the highest duty of skill, care, and diligence that the real estate industry in general claims to the public and that the public has a right to expect. In the minds of the average inexperienced public, the real estate licensee has a knowledge superior to their own.

The high level of this standard has been created partially by the educational requirements imposed on both the broker and salesperson, which includes subjects such as real estate law, appraisal, financing, real estate practice, economics, and accounting. To pass the state licensing examination, the licensee must also have a good knowledge of the English language and mathematics, and as evidenced by this course, is required to complete a minimum number of hours of courses to keep his or her knowledge current. Therefore, the licensee is expected to know the law and procedures for conveyancing the legal effects of agency contracts and sales contracts, the legal effects of security liens, and the principles of business and land economics and appraisal. It is also expected that the licensee have a strong knowledge of contract law necessary to draft an enforceable contract between the buyer and seller, and to obtain assistance or advice when he or she is in doubt. If a contract is poorly drafted such that it is unenforceable, or if it is unclear or ambiguous such that litigation is necessary to clear it up, the licensee may be held liable for damages sustained by third persons.

Since the courts have held that the consumer is correct to consider the licensee to be a person with knowledge and skills beyond that of laymen, the consumer can expect that the licensee will not make statements without prior examination and that he or she is responsible for the truth and accuracy of any information disseminated to cooperating brokers or buyers.

It is clear now that the real estate licensee has a duty to disclose to the buyer all material defects in the property that are known to the licensee, and that are not within the diligent observation and attention of the buyer.

For example, in one case, a real estate salesperson was showing a property for lease to a prospective tenant but forgot to point out that the stairs leading to the basement were defectively constructed and possibly dangerous. The lessee moved into the property and later fell down the stairs and was injured. Both the salesperson and her employing broker were liable in damages for injuries suffered by the lessee.

This case shows that the licensee's duty of care is not limited to the disclosure of matters known to the licensee. Because of the real estate licensee's superior knowledge and experience as well as the duty to disclose material matters, there is also a duty on the licensee to make a reasonable investigation to discover the true facts regarding the property. It is the agent's responsibility to discover any serious defects in the property that could cause an unreasonable risk of harm to the other party.

**Duty of Verification**

The real estate licensee cannot act as a mere conduit for information from the seller. When material information from the seller is transmitted to the buyer by the licensee, the licensee has a duty to verify the accuracy of that information or disclaim knowledge of its accuracy.

For example, in one case, the listing agent gave information to the buyer that he had obtained from the seller regarding the capacity of the well on the property, but gave it without verification or qualification. It turned out that the well had inadequate capacity. The court held that the broker, his salesperson, and the seller were jointly and severally liable for the buyer's damages.

The court stated that "Real estate brokers and their agents hold themselves out to the public as having specialized knowledge with regard to housing, housing conditions, and related matters. The public is entitled to and does rely on the expertise of real estate brokers in the purchase and sale of its homes. Therefore, there is a duty on the part of real estate brokers to be accurate and knowledgeable concerning the product they are in the business of selling." Brokers and agents can protect themselves from liability by investigating the owner's statements or by disclaiming knowledge, and by requiring the seller to sign, at the time of listing, a statement that sets forth representations that will be made, and certifying that they are true and providing for indemnification if they are not.

## Easton v. Strassburger

The duty on the licensee to make a reasonable investigation of the property evolved from the case of Easton v. Strassburger (1984), 152 CA3d 90, 199 CR 383. As the leading case on this issue, the court's decision sent the message "loud and clear" to all real estate licensees that their responsibility does not stop at a mere disclosure of material facts that are known to the licensee.

## The Facts of the Case

The property was a one-acre parcel of land located in the city of Diablo. The property was improved with a 3,000 square foot home, a swimming pool, and a large guesthouse. Easton purchased the property for $170,000 from the Strassburgers in May of 1976 and escrow closed in July of that year.

Shortly after Easton purchased the property, there was a massive earth movement on the parcel. Subsequent slides destroyed a portion of the driveway in 1977 or 1978. Expert testimony indicated that the slides occurred because a portion of the property that was fill that had not been properly engineered and compacted. The slides caused the foundation of the house to settle, which in turn caused cracks in the walls and warped doorways. After the 1976 slide, damage to the property was so severe that although experts appraised the value of the property at $170,000 in an undamaged condition, the value of the damaged property was estimated to be as low as $20,000. Estimates of the cost to repair the damage caused by the slides and avoid recurrence ranged as high as $213,000.

During the time that the property was owned by the Strassburgers, there was a minor slide in 1973 that involved about 10 to 12 feet of the filled slope, and a major slide in 1975 in which the fill dropped about eight to ten feet in a circular shape that was 50 to 60 feet across. The Strassburgers did not tell the agents anything about the slides or the corrective action they had taken prior to listing the property. Easton purchased the property without being aware of the property's soil problems or its history of slides.

The listing agents had inspected the property several times during the listing period and according to the court, there was evidence that the agents "were aware of certain red flags which should have indicated to them that there were soil problems." Despite this, the agents did not request that the soil stability of the property be tested and did not inform Easton that there were potential soil problems.

The deciding factors of the case included the following:

1) At least one of the listing agents knew that the property was built on fill (red flag) and that settlement and erosion problems are commonly associated with such soil.

2) The listing agents had seen netting on a slope (red flag) that had been placed there to repair a slide that had occurred recently.

3) One of the listing agents testified that he had observed that the floor of the guesthouse was not level (red flag).

## The Results of the Legal Action

Easton filed suit against Strassburger, the real estate agency, and others. The real estate agency was charged with fraudulent concealment, intentional misrepresentation, and negligent misrepresentation. The jury found against the real estate agency only under a simple negligence theory. It returned a joint and several judgments against the defendants and apportioned comparative negligence. The jury's special verdict found all named defendants had been negligent and assessed damages of $197,000. Negligence was apportioned among the parties under the principles of comparative negligence in the following percentages:

| | |
|---|---|
| Strassburgers: | **65%** |
| Builders: | **15%** |
| Listing Agency: | **5%** |
| Cooperating Broker: | **5%** |
| Other Defendents: | **10%** |

The seller became insolvent following the sale of the property.

The real estate agency appealed the trial court judgment, relying principally upon an asserted error by the trial judge in giving the following instructions to the jury:

"A real estate broker is a licensed person or entity who holds himself out to the public as having particular skills and knowledge in the real estate field. He is under a duty to disclose facts materially affecting the value or desirability of the property that are known to him or which through reasonable diligence should be known to him."

The real estate agency contended that a broker's duty to a prospective buyer was only to disclose known facts about the property, not facts that should be known in the exercise of reasonable diligence.

Although the evidence did not establish actual knowledge of the property's history of slides and soils problems, actual knowledge was not necessary to establish liability for negligence. The jury merely had to conclude that a reasonably competent and diligent inspection of the property would have uncovered the history of soil problems.

The Court of Appeal rejected the real estate agency's contention. In its opinion, it pointed out that the law of California has long required both the seller of real property and the broker to inform a prospective buyer about material defects known to them but unknown or observable by the buyer. It further pointed out that a broker in a transaction is liable for the intentional tort of fraudulent concealment or negative fraud if he or she fails to disclose material facts about the property that are not known to, nor within the reach of the diligent observation of the prospective buyer:

> "If a broker were required to disclose only known defects, but not those that are reasonably discoverable, he would be shielded by his ignorance of that which he holds himself out to know. The rule thus narrowly construed would have results harmful to the policy upon which it is based. Such a construction would not only reward the unskilled broker or salesperson for his/her incompetence, but might provide the unscrupulous broker the unilateral ability to protect himself at the expense of the inexperienced and unwary who rely upon him. In any case, if given legal force, the theory that a seller's broker cannot be held liable for undisclosed defects would inevitably produce a disincentive for a seller's broker to make a diligent inspection. Such a disincentive would be most unfortunate, since in residential sales transactions, the seller's broker is most frequently the best situated to obtain and provide the most reliable information on the property and is ordinarily counted on to do so."

**What is a Red Flag?**

A *red flag* is a physical factor about a property that, upon seeing it, triggers a red flag in an agent's mind that says, "this is a potential material fact that may need to be investigated."

Some examples of a red flag include the following:

- Water-stained ceilings.
- Cracks in ceilings, walls, and floors.
- New additions, for whatever reason, such as new walls, rooms, garage modifications, roofs, gutters and eaves, retaining walls, wall paneling, floors, etc.

Red flags may also include defects in major appliances, such as forced-air furnaces, air conditioners, lawn sprinkler systems, swimming pools, saunas, plumbing, solar unit installations, etc.

This is obviously not an all-inclusive list of potential red flags. Possible red flags can vary depending on the particular property that is being sold. The point is that licensees must be aware of the facts and circumstances unique to each property, follow their instincts, and point out potential red flags. Licensees should also not hesitate to recommend to buyers that they should seek professional assistance when red flags appear.

**Special Note:** An as-is clause will NOT avoid Easton liability. No matter how well worded, no clause will relieve the seller or the broker of their liability to disclose known material facts or those that "should be known."

## Should the Agent Offer an Opinion?

Once the agent is aware of the red flag, and has followed a reasonably competent and diligent inspection, what should the agent do? One thing that the agent should not do is volunteer an opinion about what problem underlies the red flag. If the agent lacks the expertise and his or her opinion amounts to nothing more than a guess, the broker may give the appearance of possessing expertise that in fact he or she does not possess. Should the broker present such an impression, he or she would invite a court to judge the agent by the standard of expertise so presented.

## Can Easton Liability Be Avoided?

Is it possible to utilize a written disclaimer to avoid liability under the Easton decision? The answer is probably not. Throughout the court's opinions on the Easton decision are statements expounding on the liability of the agent due to his or her superior knowledge. The licensee might be able to reduce his or her duty to a manageable level by a written caution to the purchaser that the licensee is not trained and does not possess knowledge or skill in matters that concern soils, construction, building codes, and zoning ordinances, and that the licensee recommends that the purchaser obtain professional advice from an architect, engineer, contractor, or some other person with the education and experience in such matters. It is doubtful whether such a disclaimer will be of any value when the licensee knows that the purchaser does not obtain advice from an independent expert. It also seems most unlikely that negligence liability can be avoided by such a disclaimer.

## Easton Decision Summary

Since the original decision, the legislature has codified and modified the rules established by the courts. The following is a summary of Easton liability as it stands today:

1) It mandates only a reasonably competent inspection of the property. The decision in Easton does not clearly indicate the type of inspection required.

2) The duty to make the visual inspection is limited to residences that contain 1–4 units or manufactured homes. The duty of Easton is limited only to residential property.

3) It defines the standard of care owed by a broker to a prospective purchaser as the degree of care a reasonably prudent real estate agent would exercise, and is measured by the degree of knowledge through education, experience, and the examination required to obtain a real estate license under California law.

4) Easton liability applies to both the broker who has entered into a written contract with the seller to find or obtain a buyer, and to the broker who acts in cooperation with such a (listing) broker to find

and obtain a buyer. The Easton decision did not limit its application to brokers with written contracts.

5) It provides that the duty of inspection does not include or involve areas that are reasonably and normally inaccessible to such inspection, nor an affirmative inspection of areas off the site of the subject property or public records or permits that concern the title or use of the property, and if the property comprises a unit in a planned development, condominium, or stock cooperative, and does not include an inspection of more than the unit offered for sale, as long as the seller or the broker complies with § 1368.

6) It established a two-year statute of limitations that runs from the date of recordation, close of escrow, or occupancy—whichever occurs first.

7) It provides that the buyer or prospective buyer has a duty to exercise reasonable care to protect himself or herself, including acknowledging adverse facts that are known or within the diligent attention and observation of a buyer or prospective buyer.

   Easton stated that a buyer has a duty to make a reasonable inspection, but did not limit its application to cases where the facts were not known but determinable by a diligent inspection or observation of the buyer.

8) If certain consumer information booklets are given to the prospective buyer, a seller or broker is not required to provide additional information regarding that particular matter. These booklets include the following:

   a) The Homeowner's Guide to Earthquake Safety

   b) The Commercial Property Owner's Guide to Earthquake Safety

   c) The Environmental Hazards Guide for Homeowners and Buyers

9) It also applies to leases of such property that contain a purchase option, ground leases of such property, and the sales of such property by an installment contract of sale.

10) The rule of Easton v. Strassburger does not apply to transfers that are required to be preceded by the furnishing, to a prospective purchaser, of a copy of a public report for a subdivision.

## Question & Answer Review II:
### A Real Estate Licensee's Duty to Conduct a Visual Inspection (Civil Code Sec. 2079–2079.5)

The following Q & A Memorandum has been reproduced with the permission of the California Association of Realtors® Legal and Board Services Department. These questions are not part of your homework. They are part of the reading assignment only and are designed to be a review of the preceding section.

**Question 1:** What is the duty of the real estate licensee under this law?

**Answer:** A real estate licensee's duty under this law is defined as a duty to a prospective purchaser of residential real property comprising 1–4 dwelling units . . . "to conduct a reasonably competent and diligent visual inspection of the property offered for sale and to disclose to the prospective purchaser all facts materially affecting the value or desirability of the property that such an investigation would reveal."

**Question 2:** What type of real property is covered by this law?

**Answer:** The licensee's duty of inspection pertains to transactions that involve all residential property containing 1–4 units, including mobile homes. The only exception is for certain subdivided property.

**Question 3:** What types of transactions are covered by this law?

**Answer:** The licensee's duty of inspection applies to a typical sales transaction, as well as to a lease with an option to purchase, a ground lease of land (containing 1-4 dwelling units), and a real property sales contract (installment land sales contract).

**Question 4:** What is the legal standard of care required for a licensee's visual inspection of the property?

**Answer:** The statute defines the licensee's standard of care as the degree of care that a reasonably prudent real estate licensee would exercise. This is measured by the degree of knowledge (measured by education, experience, and examination) required to obtain a real estate license under California Law.

**Question 5:** Does a licensee's duty to inspect include inaccessible areas?

**Answer:** No. The required inspection "does not include or involve an inspection of areas that are reasonably and normally inaccessible . . ."

**Question 6:** What about transactions where the property includes common areas, such as the sale of a condominium or stock cooperative? Does Civil Code § 2079–2079.5 require a licensee to inspect all the common areas as well?

**Answer:** No. The legislation specifically states that the duty only applies to the unit offered for sale, and not to common areas or other units, as long as the buyer is provided with the information about the subdivision property that is already required by law (see CAR Deposit Receipt DLF-14 and DL-14, page 4, paragraph entitled "CONDOMINIUM/P.D.").

**Question 7:** Is a licensee required to inspect property that is partially residential and partially commercial, such as a farm with a house on it?

**Answer:** Yes, but only the residential portion of the property. That is, the licensee is required to do a reasonably diligent visual inspection of the residence, but not the commercial portion, such as farmland, or an adjoining store or restaurant.

**Question 8:** In a transaction where both a listing and a selling agent are involved, which licensee must conduct the inspection?

**Answer:** Both. If both a selling and listing agent are involved in a transaction covered by this law, both licensees must conduct an inspection. The Real Estate Transfer Disclosure Statement provides space for both the listing and selling agents to state what their inspections have revealed.

**Question 9:** What about residential transactions where the seller is not required to provide a TDS (such as probate sales, REO's, and mobile homes), but the licensee is required to visually inspect the property? What procedure should the licensee use to document this inspection?

**Answer:** Remember that the licensee's duty is to conduct a careful visual inspection of the property and disclose any red-flag indicators of potential problems to prospective buyers. Even though in such transactions the TDS is not technically required, it would be prudent for the licensee to document the results of the inspection in writing and provide this to the buyer. Generally, the report to the buyer should indicate the following:

1) When the careful visual inspection of the property was made by the licensee.
2) The results of the inspection.
3) If warranted, recommendations for further inspections by appropriate professionals that concern the condition of the property.

**Question 10:** Is there a statute of limitations for an alleged breach of this duty to inspect and disclose?

**Answer:** Yes. A lawsuit that alleges a breach of a licensee's duty under this law must be filed within two years from the date of occupancy, the date of recordation of the deed to the buyer, or the date of close of escrow—whichever occurs first.

**Question 11:** What is the buyer's responsibility?

**Answer:** The statute specifically states that nothing in this law "relieves a buyer of . . . the duty to exercise reasonable care to protect himself or herself, including those facts which are known to or are within the diligent attention and observation of the buyer . . ."

**Question 12:** Do I have to conduct an inspection on as-is sales?

**Answer:** Yes. There is no exemption in the law for this kind of transaction. Thus, while a seller may effectively limit his or her liability as far as not warranting the condition of the property, the licensee must still conduct a reasonably competent and diligent visual inspection with the appropriate disclosures to the buyer.

**QUIZZES ARE MANDATORY**

CalBRE regulations now require the submission of chapter quizzes before you can access the final examination. You must log in and submit the chapter quizzes online before you can access the final examination. After submitting the last chapter quiz, you will see a link to the final examination. You were issued a Personal Identification Number (PIN) and login instructions when you enrolled.

**Chapter One Quiz**

1.      Generally, a fact concerning a transaction is considered *material* if:

    (a)      The seller elects to disclose the fact prior to consummation of the transaction.
    (b)      Prior knowledge of the fact would have prevented the other party from entering into the contract.
    (c)      All parties to the transaction agree in advance that the fact is important.
    (d)      The seller's agent determines that the fact warrants disclosure.

2.      The seller must disclose any material change in the condition of the property or the title that occurs or is discovered by the seller:

    (a)      After close of escrow and within one year of ownership by the new buyer.
    (b)      After close of escrow and within a reasonable amount of time thereafter.
    (c)      After the contract is executed and prior to the close of escrow.
    (d)      None of the above.

3.      The Real Estate Transfer Disclosure Statement (TDS) provides information regarding the:

    (a)      Physical condition of the property.
    (b)      Property's chain of title.
    (c)      Agency's relationships among the parties to the transaction.
    (d)      Commission split among real estate agents.

4.      Neither the seller nor any listing or selling agent shall be liable for any error, inaccuracy, or omission of any information delivered to the buyer if:

    (a)      The seller or agent(s) did not know of the mistake.
    (b)      The item of information that contains the mistake was provided by a public agency or third-person professional.
    (c)      The item of information that contains the mistake was provided by a third-person expert but the mistake was known by the seller and seller's agent.
    (d)      Both (a) and (b) are correct.

5.      If more than one licensed real estate broker is acting as an agent in a transaction, who is responsible for assuring the delivery of the Real Estate Transfer Disclosure Statement (TDS) to the buyer?

(a)     The broker who represents the seller.
(b)     The broker who has obtained the offer made by the buyer.
(c)     The broker who holds a valid Listing Agreement with the seller.
(d)     The seller is ultimately responsible no matter how many agents are involved.

6.      The Real Estate Transfer Disclosure Statement (TDS) is NOT required when the transfer involves:

(a)     Transfer of a unit in a subdivision when the buyer has been given a public report.
(b)     A transfer ordered by a probate court in administration of an estate.
(c)     Transfers by foreclosure sale after default.
(d)     All of the above.

7.      The licensee's duty of care is not limited to the disclosure of matters known to the licensee, but include:

(a)     The duty to provide legal advice in situations where there is not time to consult an expert.
(b)     The duty to make minor repairs to a property when absolutely necessary.
(c)     The duty to conduct a reasonable investigation to discover the true facts regarding the property.
(d)     The duty to provide tax advice regarding the transfer of real property.

8.      The duty of the licensee to make a reasonable investigation of the property evolved from the case of Easton v. Strassburger. The facts of the case involved:

(a)     Environmental contamination.
(b)     Slide damage on the parcel.
(c)     Earthquake damage to the structure.
(d)     Flood damage.

9.      Which of the following statements is correct regarding an *as-is* clause and Easton liability?

(a)     If a property is being sold as-is, the seller and the broker are relieved of their liability to disclose material facts that "should be known."
(b)     An as-is clause will relieve the broker from his or her duty to disclose material facts that "should be known," but does not relieve the duty to disclose known material defects.

(c)     If a property is being sold as-is, the listing broker is not required to conduct a reasonably competent and diligent visual inspection of the property.

(d)     No matter how well worded, an as-is clause will not relieve the seller or the broker of their liability to disclose known material facts or those that "should be known."

10.     Is it possible to utilize a written disclaimer to avoid liability under the Easton decision?

(a)     Probably not, based on most previous court opinions.

(b)     Yes, as long as the disclaimer is properly written and signed by all parties.

(c)     Yes, because it is the buyer's responsibility to know what they are buying.

(d)     Yes, as long as negligence liability is part of the broker's errors and omissions insurance coverage.

## Chapter Two

## Important Terms·

affidavit
capacity
conservator
deeds in lieu of foreclosure
exchanges
homeowner's association
installment sales
lis pendens
partial release clause
planned unit development
safety clause
special assessments
Statute of Frauds
subdivider
subdivision
time-share
release clause
unit development

## Learning Objectives

Upon completion of Chapter Two, you should be able to complete the following:

- Describe California's disclosure law on real estate commissions.

- Describe California's condominium/common interest disclosure requirements.

- Describe California's subdivision/blanket encumbrance disclosure requirements.

- Describe California's conversion disclosure requirements.

- Describe the IRS's requirements when the seller is a foreign person (FIRPTA).

- Describe the state's tax withholding requirements on the sale of real property.

## California Disclosure Law on Real Estate Commissions

In the past, certain real estate organizations, such as real estate boards, would suggest commission schedules. These suggestions were intended to be voluntary, non-mandatory, and unenforceable. They were designed to inform the various segments of the real estate industry (i.e., judges, attorneys, lenders, etc.) of the prevailing levels of fees and commissions in the marketplace "to prevent gouging." Contrary to the intent of these suggestions, these commission schedules were abused and misused. When asked to lower the commission, a typical salesperson may have responded, "Gee, I would like to take it for five percent, but my board won't let me." Today, this practice is a specific violation of Section 10147.5 of the Business and Professions Code and Section 2785 (a) (3) of the Realtors Code of Ethics and Professional Conduct. In May of 1980, Governor Jerry Brown signed into law as an emergency measure Senate Bill 1958, which amended and clarified the law that concerns the negotiability of real estate commissions and the notice requirement for any printed form or real estate agreement.

The amended B & P Code Section 10147.5 is now operative. It reads:

10147.5 (a): Any printed or form agreement which initially establishes, or is intended to establish, or alters the terms of any agreement which previously established a right to compensation to be paid to a real estate licensee for the sale of residential real property containing not more than four (4) residential units, or the sale of a mobile home, shall contain the following statement in not less than 10-point boldface type immediately preceding any provision of such agreement relating to compensation of the licensee:

**NOTICE: THE AMOUNT OR RATE OF REAL ESTATE COMMISSIONS IS NOT FIXED BY LAW. THEY ARE SET BY EACH BROKER INDIVIDUALLY AND MAY BE NEGOTIABLE BETWEEN THE SELLER AND BROKER.**

**(b):** The amount or rate of compensation shall not be printed in any such agreement.

**Comment on (b):** This part of the code is designed to alert the seller that he or she has the right to negotiate the commission. It would be improper to print the entire agreement in 10-point bold type in an effort to conceal the disclosure that commissions are negotiable.

**(c):** Nothing in this section shall affect the validity of a transfer of title to real property.

**Comment on (c):** This means that the contract between the buyer and seller is not affected by the violation of Section 10147.5. Also, if the compensation agreement does not contain this required notice, there is no provision in the statute which would defeat the broker's right to collect his or her commission. However, violation of this section may well be interpreted by the courts as a statement of "public policy," which could defeat the broker's claim for compensation. Violation of this section would subject the broker to disciplinary action by the Real Estate Commissioner.

**(d):** As used in part (a) of this section, "alters the terms of any agreement which previously established a right of compensation," means an increase in the rate of compensation, or the amount of compensation if initially established as a flat fee, from the agreement which previously established a right of compensation.

**Comment on (d):** This appears to mean that it is permissible to lower the rate or amount of commission without inserting such a statement into the agreement.

### Question & Answer Review III: Commission Disclosures

The following Q & A Memorandum has been reproduced with the permission of the California Association of Realtors® Legal and Board Services Department. These questions are not part of your homework; they are part of the reading assignment only and are designed to be a review of the preceding section.

**Question 1:** Must a real estate broker have a written agreement with a principal to obtain a commission on the sale or purchase of real property?

**Answer:** Yes. To recover a commission in California on the purchase or sale of real property or a lease of more than one year, a real estate broker must have a signed agreement obligating a principal (seller, buyer, landlord, or tenant) to pay a commission. Civil Code § 1624(5), the Statute of Frauds provision, provides that a contract authorizing or employing a real estate licensee to act on behalf of a principal in these types of transactions is invalid, unless there is a written contract signed by *the party to be charged*; that is, the party against whom the broker will be seeking enforcement. Therefore, an oral agreement by a seller or buyer to pay a commission is not enforceable.

**Question 2:** Must a specific commission agreement form be used?

**Answer:** No. Although there are some requirements that relate to the content of commission agreements, the law does not designate a specific form for such an agreement.

The two most common types of commission agreements in residential transactions are a listing agreement and a buyer-broker agreement. These agreements create an agency relationship between a principal and a licensee and set forth the compensation to be paid for agreed services. If there is no listing or buyer-broker agreement, the "Acceptance" portion of the deposit receipt or another document may spell out the terms of the broker's employment and compensation. See Question 4.

**Question 3:** Are commissions negotiable?

**Answer:** Yes, for all types of real property. However, for probate sales, maximum commissions are set by the Superior Court in some counties (see Question 15). In addition, Business and Professions Code § 10147.5 stipulates the following:

"Any printed or form agreement which initially establishes, or is intended to establish, or alters [upward] the terms of any agreement which previously established a right to compensation to be paid to a real estate licensee for the sale of residential real property containing not more than four residential units, or for the sale of a mobile home, shall contain the following statement in not less than 10-point boldface type immediately preceding any provision of such agreement relating to compensation of the licensee:

**NOTICE: THE AMOUNT OR RATE OF REAL ESTATE COMMISSIONS IS NOT FIXED BY LAW. THEY ARE SET BY EACH BROKER INDIVIDUALLY AND MAY BE NEGOTIABLE BETWEEN THE SELLER AND BROKER.**

**Question 4:** Must a commission be tied to a percentage of the sales price?

**Answer:** No. Both the amount and manner of calculating a commission are negotiable between the broker and principal. For example, a set amount, an hourly rate, or a percentage of the sales price are all acceptable ways of establishing a commission.

**Question 5:** On the sale of 1–4 residential units, should the deposit receipt contain the commissions negotiability notice set forth in Question 3, above?

**Answer:** If there is an existing agreement and the deposit receipt does not increase the amount of commission to be paid to a broker, the negotiability notice is not required.

If, however, there is no listing or buyer-broker agreement, or the deposit receipt increases the amount of commission previously agreed upon, then the commissions negotiability notice must be set forth. For example, this may be accomplished by using C.A.R. Standard Form CA-11, Commission Agreement, as an addendum to the deposit receipt.

**Question 6:** Must an exclusive listing or buyer-broker agreement contain a termination date?

**Answer:** Yes. Any exclusive agreement engaging a broker to render services, including an exclusive agency or exclusive authorization and right to sell listing, or an exclusive authorization to locate property (buyer-broker agreement) must include a definite, fixed, and final termination date.

**Question 7:** When is the commission earned?

**Answer:** The terms of a listing or buyer-broker agreement should specify what must be done in order for a broker to earn a commission.

Unless a listing agreement provides otherwise, the listing broker is entitled to a commission upon securing a "ready, willing, and able" buyer whose offer mirrors the price and terms specified in the listing, or whose offer is otherwise acceptable to the seller. Whether an offer presented "mirrors" the terms of the listing is a question of fact, which can only be determined based on the particular facts and circumstances of each case.

An *able* buyer is someone who has both the legal capacity and financial ability to purchase the property. A person who lacks legal capacity is under a legal disability, which prevents him or her from entering into a binding contract. For example, a minor (under the age of 18) or someone under the care of a court-appointed conservator or guardian lacks the legal capacity to enter into a contract. Financial ability refers to whether a buyer has the necessary resources (e.g., cash, credit, and/or other real or personal property) to purchase the property.

It is important to note that a seller may lawfully reject any offer presented; however, if an offer meeting the terms of the listing is not accepted, the seller may be liable for the commission (note that a listing agreement may specify that the commission is not earned until the transaction is fully consummated. In this event, the listing broker has not only earned a commission upon securing a ready, willing, and able purchaser, but is also entitled to a commission after the transaction is successfully consummated).

**Question 8:** If the seller, without cause, withdraws the property from the market, may the listing broker recover a commission?

**Answer:** Yes, if the listing agreement contains a "withdrawal" provision in which the seller agrees that upon withdrawal of the property from the market without the broker's consent, the seller will pay the broker a commission. C.A.R. Standard Form listing agreements incorporate this type of provision.

**Question 9:** May a real estate broker collect a commission when the listing or buyer-broker agreement has expired?

**Answer:** Yes, under some circumstances. A broker may be entitled to collect a commission after the listing or buyer-broker agreement expires if the agreement contains a safety clause. For example, a safety clause in a listing agreement is a provision that protects the broker's claim for commission, if the property is sold within a specified period after the listing expires to a buyer with whom the broker negotiated during the listing period.

Generally, safety clauses require the broker to provide the seller with a written list of those prospects or properties with whom the broker negotiated during the term of the listing. The broker must provide that information within the time period specified in the safety clause in order to ensure a right to the commission. Many safety clauses exclude properties that are relisted with another broker after the expiration of the original listing period. Similarly, other events may obligate a seller to pay a commission under a safety clause based on the specific terms of the safety clause.

The contents of a safety clause, the period of time it will cover, and whether or not to include it in a listing agreement, are fully negotiable. If a safety clause is used in an exclusive brokerage agreement of any type, it must have a definite, fixed termination date.

**Question 10:** If a buyer or seller breaches a contract to purchase or sell real property, is the broker entitled to a commission?

**Answer:** It depends. Printed commission provisions frequently cover in detail the rights of a broker in the event of a breach by a principal. The C.A.R. buyer-broker agreement (Standard Form ABB-14) states that if a buyer's default prevents completion of any resulting transaction, the broker is entitled to the compensation provided for in the buyer-broker agreement upon the buyer's default.

**Question 11:** May a real estate broker who files a lawsuit to recover a commission record a *lis pendens* against the seller's property?

**Answer:** No. A *lis pendens* is a notice that a legal action is pending. It may be recorded as part of a pending lawsuit that concerns a right to title or possession of the real property involved.

A lawsuit for a commission is an action for *money damages* and does not generally concern a right to title or possession of the real property. If a lis pendens is recorded in these circumstances, the owner of the property will easily be able to have it removed through a procedure called *expungement*, and the plaintiff may incur liability for inappropriately "clouding" the owner's title.

**Question 12:** Is an oral agreement between real estate brokers to share a commission enforceable?

**Answer:** Yes. Real estate brokers may make and enforce an oral agreement to share a commission. However, it is a good idea to avoid misunderstandings concerning each broker's rights by having a clearly written agreement. Since there are no special rules concerning the nature or format of such an agreement, a preprinted form, a letter of agreement or any other clearly written expression of the agreed terms should be sufficient.

**Question 13:** When a real estate salesperson terminates his or her relationship with the real estate broker under whom he or she is licensed, is the salesperson entitled to any commission on pending escrows?

**Answer:** Every real estate broker is required to have a written agreement with each salesperson licensed under that broker. The agreement should cover all material aspects of the relationship between the parties, including a clear provision that explains the rights of the salesperson who was involved in pending escrows or active listings when that salesperson is no longer licensed under that broker.

For example, in the C.A.R. Broker-Salesperson Contract (Standard Form I-14), the parties agree that the salesperson will be entitled to a commission after the close of any escrow, which is pending when the licensee terminates his or her independent contractor relationship with the broker, unless the termination is "for cause." The agreement permits the broker to reduce the salesperson's share of the commission by a reasonable amount necessary to compensate another salesperson for work required on the escrow after the salesperson has been terminated. The "reasonable amount" reduction is not calculated on a statutorily prescribed formula, but is based on all the facts and circumstances involved in "winding up" the pending transaction.

A similar provision is made in Standard Form I-14 for listings that are active and that go into escrow after the salesperson has terminated.

**Question 14:** Can a real estate salesperson receive a commission directly from a principal?

**Answer:** No. A real estate salesperson can only receive a commission from the real estate broker under whom the salesperson is currently licensed, or was licensed at the time of the sale or other transaction. The real estate broker may choose either to pay the salesperson directly or to instruct escrow to pay the salesperson.

**Question 15:** Can a real estate broker share a commission with an out-of-state broker?

**Answer:** Generally, yes. The general rule is that a real estate broker may not share a commission with anyone who is not licensed to sell real property in California. However, an exception permits a real estate broker to pay a commission to a real estate broker of another state.

For further information on the laws that regulate the ability of a broker to share a commission with a non-licensee, see C.A.R.'s Question and Answer Memorandum titled *Referrals, Rebates, and Related Arrangements* under *State & Federal Laws*.

**Question 16:** How is a real estate broker's commission determined in a probate sale?

**Answer:** The determination of a real estate broker's commission on the sale of probate property depends upon whether the property is being sold pursuant to the Independent Administration of Estates Act (IAEA) or under court supervision. The IAEA outlines when an exclusive listing may be entered into without prior court approval and when real property may be sold without court confirmation. In this situation, the amount of brokerage commissions will be the amount agreed to in the listing agreement.

If the property being sold is subject to probate court confirmation, commissions are negotiable with the executor or administrator of the estate, but are subject to limits that are provided under local probate court rules. Additionally, the probate court has authority over the amount of commission provided at the time of the confirmation hearing. The court is not bound by any agreement between the broker and representative of the estate about the amount of the brokerage commission. However, the court must honor an agreement between brokers concerning the division of a commission. For additional information on brokerage commissions in probate sales, see C.A.R.'s Question and Answer Memorandum titled *Probate Sales of Real Property* and C.A.R.'s Probate Chart.

**Question 17:** Can a broker receive an advance fee or commission for services to be performed in the future?

**Answer:** There are strict regulations that concern when a real estate broker may receive a commission or other compensation in advance of performing acts that require a real estate license. The advance payment may only be made if the following requirements are met:

1) It is pursuant to a written agreement that has been submitted to the California Bureau of Real Estate for advance approval as to form, and

2) It is held by the broker in a trust account until completion of the services.

In addition, notice must be given to the principal prior to the disbursement of any funds. Additional requirements apply.

**The Subdivided Lands Act**

The *Subdivided Lands Act* applies to transactions that involve a subdivision as defined by Business & Professions Code § 11000. To subdivide means to divide a tract of land into building lots. Subdivisions can be primarily categorized as standard subdivisions and common-interest subdivisions.

A standard subdivision refers to a subdivision that does not have any commonly owned areas. A common-interest subdivision refers to a subdivision that has common areas and/or facilities that are owned and/ or operated by a homeowner's association. A standard subdivision is covered by the Act if it contains five or more improved or unimproved lots or parcels. The Act also applies to a common interest subdivision if it contains five or more undivided interests.

B & P Code § 11004.5: *Subdivided lands* and *Subdivisions* include all of the following:

1) Any planned development that contains five or more lots.

2) Any community apartment project that contains five or more apartments.

3) Any condominium project that contains five or more condominiums.

4) Any stock cooperative that has or intends to have five or more shareholders.

5) Any timeshare project that consists of 12 or more timeshare estates or timeshare uses, and that have terms of five years or more.

6) Any limited-equity housing cooperative.

The Subdivided Lands Act applies to subdivisions that are located outside the State of California, if sales are made or attempted within California.

## Who Does the Subdivided Lands Act Apply To?

The Subdivided Lands Act applies to both the owner of the subdivided property and to any subdivider who is engaged by the owner of the property. The law also applies to any real estate licensee who acts as an agent for the seller of a subdivision. If a licensee violates the subdivision laws, whether negligent or intentional, and whether the licensee is acting as a principal or as an agent for the subdivider, it is a violation of the Real Estate Law and subjects the licensee to disciplinary action by the Bureau of Real Estate.

## Subdivision/Public Report

According to the Subdivided Lands Act, the sale of any portion of a subdivision is subject to regulation by the Real Estate Commissioner. The Subdivided Lands Act is designed to prevent fraud, misrepresentation, or deceit in the public sale or lease of subdivided parcels of real property. The law accomplishes this by requiring the seller of subdivided lands to provide a prospective buyer with a disclosure of the risks that will be assumed prior to the purchase of a parcel in a subdivision. This requirement assures that the buying public can make an informed decision based on the essential facts of buying subdivided lands.

The purpose of The Subdivided Lands Act is served by requiring the subdivider to acquire a subdivision public report from the Real Estate Commissioner, who provides information regarding the subdivision. No person can sell or lease, or offer to sell or lease, any lot in a subdivision without first obtaining a public report. Once completed and approved, a copy of the report must be given to any prospective purchaser prior to the purchase of any lot, parcel, or unit in a subdivision.

## Condominium/Common-Interest Subdivision Disclosure

The seller of a separate interest (e.g., a condominium or planned unit development) is required to provide to a prospective buyer the following documents as soon as practicable before transfer of title or execution of a real property sales contract:

1) A copy of the governing documents of the common-interest development.

2) If there is a restriction in the governing documents that limits the occupancy, residency, or use of a particular interest based on age, a statement that the restriction is only enforceable to the extent permitted by Civil Code Section 51.3 and a statement specifying the applicable provisions of Section 51.3.

3) A copy of the most recent financial statement distributed pursuant to Civil Code Section 1365.

   A development's financial statement would include, but is not limited to, the following items: fiscal operating budget, estimated revenue and expenses, association reserves, and any possible special assessments.

4) A true statement in writing from an authorized representative of the association as to the amount of the association's current regular and special assessments and fees, as well as any assessments levied upon the owner's interest that are unpaid on the date of the statement. This statement must also include true information on late charges, interest, and costs of collection that, as of the date of the statement, are or may become a lien on the owner's interest.

5) Usually included in the statement required in Item 4 above, any change in the association's current and special assessments and fees that have been approved by the association's board of directors but have not become due and payable as of the date disclosure is provided.

Upon written request by the owner, an association shall, within 10 days of the mailing or delivery of the request, provide the owner with a copy of the requested items listed in Items (1), (2), (3) and (4). The association usually charges a fee for these documents but cannot charge more than a reasonable cost to prepare and reproduce them.

### Seller's Liability

If the seller fails to provide the proper disclosures, he or she may be held liable to the purchaser for actual damages, and in addition, may be required to pay civil penalties in an amount of $500.

The current C.A.R. Real Estate Purchase Contract form DR-14, Paragraph 12 can be used to make many of these disclosures by requiring them as part of the contract.

### Subdivision/Blanket Encumbrance Disclosure

If a lot, parcel, or unit of a subdivision is subject to a blanket encumbrance, the subdivider, his or her agent, or representative shall not sell or lease the lot, parcel, or unit for a term exceeding five years, until the prospective purchaser or lessee of the lot, parcel, or unit has been furnished with and has signed a true copy of the following notice:

**BUYER/LESSEE IS AWARE OF THE FACT THAT THE LOT, PARCEL, OR UNIT WHICH HE OR SHE IS PROPOSING TO PURCHASE OR LEASE IS SUBJECT TO A DEED OF TRUST, MORTGAGE, OR OTHER LIEN KNOWN AS A "BLANKET ENCUMBRANCE". IF BUYER/LESSEE PURCHASES OR LEASES THIS LOT, PARCEL, OR UNIT, HE OR SHE COULD LOSE THAT INTEREST THROUGH FORECLOSURE OF THE BLANKET ENCUMBRANCE OR OTHER LEGAL PROCESS EVEN THOUGH BUYER/LESSEE IS NOT DELINQUENT IN HIS OR HER PAYMENTS OR OTHER OBLIGATIONS UNDER THE MORTGAGE, DEED OF TRUST, OR LEASE.**

---
Signature of Buyer or Lessee Date

## Blanket Trust Deed (Mortgage)

A Blanket Trust Deed (Mortgage) is a trust deed in which two or more pieces of property are used to cover a single debt and is often used by a developer to cover more than one parcel of land under the same mortgage. For example, a developer buys a large tract of land and plans to subdivide the land into one hundred lots and then build homes on the lots. Rather than going through the expense and time of obtaining one hundred separate loans, one blanket loan covering all the lots is obtained. Since the developer will probably be developing a few lots at a time, the mortgage will include a partial release clause, which means that as the debt is repaid, individual lots will be released from the trust deed. Thus, the developer can pay off part of the obligation, have a certain number of lots released, build on the lots, and then sell them free and clear from the overall lien that still exists on the unreleased lots.

A purchaser of one lot or unit subject to a blanket encumbrance is subject to the risk that he or she may lose his or her property as a result of a default by some other lot owner subject to the same encumbrance. Therefore, the purchaser of a subdivision subject to a blanket encumbrance must be warned.

A failure of the purchaser or lessee to sign the notice does not invalidate any conveyance, lease, or encumbrance of the subdivision interest, but a violation of this requirement may subject the violator to liability for actual damages suffered, plus a fine not to exceed $500, and the attorney fees incurred by the other party in any action to recover damages.

If the blanket encumbrance does not contain a release clause, the Commissioner has provided other precautionary requirements for protection of nondefaulting lot owners (see B & P § 11013–11013.4).

## Conversions

Where a building owner intends to convert an existing building into a condominium, community apartment project, or stock cooperative, the owner must first receive approval from the local government in compliance with the provisions of the Subdivisions Map Act.

## Notice to Existing Tenants

When reviewing an approval for the conversion of an existing residential real property to a condominium, community apartment, or stock cooperative, the local government agency cannot give its approval unless each of the existing tenants is given written notice of the developer's intention to convert the building at least 180 days prior to the termination of the tenancy and 60 days prior to filing a tentative map.

The notices to existing tenants shall be as follows:

## Existing Tenants

To the occupant(s) of

_____

(Address)

The owner(s) of this building, at (address), plans to file a tentative map with the (city, county, or city and county) to convert this building to a (condominium, community apartment, or stock cooperative project). You shall be given notice of each hearing for which notice is required pursuant to Sections 66451.3 and 66452.5 of the Government Code, and you have the right to appear and the right to be heard at any such hearing.

_____
Signature of owner or owner's agent          Date

I have received this notice on _____ (Date).

_____
Signature of existing tenant                 Date

## Notice to Prospective Tenants

If a prospective tenant files an application for a rental unit within 60 days preceding the filing of the tentative map for the conversion, the prospective tenants must receive a written notice of the intention to convert the building before they pay any deposit to the landlord.

The notices to prospective tenants shall be as follows:

## Prospective Tenants

To the prospective occupant(s) of

_____

(Address)

The owner(s) of this building, at (address), has filed or plans to file a tentative map with the (city, county, or city and county) to convert this building to a (condominium, community apartment, or stock cooperative project). No units may be sold in this building unless the conversion is approved by the (city, county, or city and county) and until after a public report is issued by the California Bureau of Real Estate. If you become a tenant of this building, you shall be given notice of each hearing for which notice is required pursuant to Sections 66451.3 and 66452.5 of the Government Code, and you have the right to appear and the right to be heard at any such hearing.

_____
Signature of owner or owner's agent          Date

I have received this notice on _____ (Date).

_____
Signature of prospective tenant          Date

## Tenant's Right to Purchase the Unit

Each tenant of a proposed conversion must be given notice of an exclusive right to contract for and purchase the unit in which he or she lives. The tenant must be offered the same or better terms and conditions with which such a unit would be initially offered to the general public.

## Right to Appear at Public Hearing

At least 10 days prior to the public hearing on the tentative map that describes the conversion, each tenant must receive a written notice informing the tenant of his or her right to appear and speak at the hearing. This notice may be sent by mail and then is also usually published.

## Liability of Owner/Subdivider

Even though the local government agency cannot deny approval of the conversion just because the subdivider fails to give notice to prospective tenants, the tenant who was entitled to the notice and became a tenant of the subdivider can recover damages incurred because of the termination of the tenancy.

## Foreign Investment in Real Property (FIRPTA)

## Introduction

When the seller of real property is a foreign person, the IRS requires the transferee (buyer) to withhold a portion of the sales price under both federal law and state law.

In most situations, when real property is acquired from a foreign person, the transferee (buyer) is required to withhold from the transferor's proceeds ten percent of the gross sales price and send this sum to the Internal Revenue Service, and also to withhold one-third of the amount withheld under federal law and send this amount to the Franchise Tax Board.

The amount required to be withheld and paid to the IRS and Franchise Tax Board must be paid within 20 days after the transfer of the real property interest. The most common procedure would be to instruct the escrow agent to deliver the funds to make sure they are delivered properly. Filing and payment must be made for each transferor (seller) who is not subject to an exemption. The test of residency must be applied separately to each seller in transactions that involve more than one seller.

A *foreign person* is a nonresident alien or a foreign corporation that has not made a proper election to be treated as a domestic corporation or a foreign partnership, trust, estate, or other entity. A United States citizen is not a foreign person. A resident alien also is not a foreign person if he or she is a lawful permanent resident of the United States, which means that he or she holds a validly issued green card.

**Nonresident Alien Individual**

An individual whose residence is not within the United States and who is not a U.S. citizen, is a nonresident alien. The term includes a nonresident alien fiduciary.

An alien who is actually present in the United States, and who is not just staying temporarily (a mere transient), is a U.S. resident for income tax purposes. An alien who is considered a U.S. resident is NOT subject to withholding under FIRPTA if the alien meets either the green card test or the substantial presence test for the calendar year.

**Green Card Test:** An alien is a U.S. resident if the individual was a lawful permanent resident of the United States at any time during the calendar year.

**Substantial Presence Test:** Alternately, an alien is considered a U.S. resident if the individual meets the substantial presence test for the calendar year. Under this test, the individual must be physically present in the United States for at least:

1) 31 days during the current calendar year, and

2) 183 days during the current year and the two preceding years, counting all the days of physical presence in the current year but only 1/3 the number of days of presence in the first preceding year and only 1/6 the number of days in the second preceding year.

Days of presence in the United States: Generally, a person is treated as physically present in the United States on any day that he or she is physically present in the country at any time during the day. There are certain exceptions to this general rule; however, these details are beyond the scope of this course.

**Exemptions**

There are several exemptions available to avoid the requirement of withholding from the seller's sales proceeds.

1) Withholding by the buyer is not required when each seller delivers a non-foreign affidavit to the buyer. This affidavit must be executed by the seller under penalty of perjury that the seller is not a foreign person. The law does not require the use of a specific form, but the affidavit must include the seller's taxpayer identification number and home or office address. This affidavit will protect a

good-faith buyer from personal liability unless he or she has actual knowledge that the affidavit is false. The affidavit must be retained by the parties to the transaction for five years after the end of the year of the transfer of title.

2) Withholding by the buyer is not required when the property is being purchased as the buyer's residence and the sales price does not exceed $300,000. This exemption only applies when the transferee has the specific intention to reside in the property for at least fifty percent of the number of days the property is used. Therefore, this exemption is based upon the number of days that the property is occupied by the buyer. If the property is rented, the exemption can still apply but the buyer must occupy the property for more days than it is occupied by others.

3) Withholding is not required by the buyer when the buyer receives a withholding certificate or qualifying statement that is issued by the Internal Revenue Service, and that states that no withholding is required, or a lesser amount may be withheld.

4) The transaction is a nonrecognition transaction for the seller and the seller furnishes a notice of nonrecognition transaction.

Additional exemptions apply to certain sales of shares of stock, and to the disposition of interest in a domestic corporation. In this case, a notice is given by a seller to inform the buyer that no withholding is necessary because of a nonrecognition provision in the tax law. Examples include a like-kind exchange under Internal Revenue Code § 1031, or a seller who is covered by a U.S. tax treaty that results in nonrecognition of gain on the sale. A buyer should not close a sale in reliance on a notice of nonrecognition transaction except on the advice of a certified public accountant, attorney, or other professional tax advisor. Personal liability can result from reliance on an improper notice of nonrecognition transaction.

In addition, a buyer who relies on a notice of nonrecognition transaction must send a copy of the notice to the IRS by the 20th day after the transfer of the property.

**Transferee's (Buyer's) Liability**

**Failure to Withhold:** Failure of the buyer to withhold may result in the buyer paying a penalty equal to ten percent of the purchase price or the seller's tax liability plus interest and penalties, whichever is less, if the seller does not pay the required taxes on time.

The buyer or the agent in the transaction are not required to obtain formal verification of an exception or exemption from the withholding requirements, but if they fail to obtain written verification of the exemption, they may assume a personal liability to both the IRS and the Franchise Tax Board.

When the seller issues a nonforeign affidavit, and the buyer relies upon the affidavit in good faith, the buyer is not personally liable even if the affidavit is false. The only time the buyer assumes personal liability is when he or she has actual knowledge that the affidavit is false.

**Agent's Potential Liability**

Under California Law, if the agent knows that the seller's nonforeign affidavit is false, he or she may be held liable for fraud and may be subject to discipline by the Real Estate Commissioner based on fraud or failure to disclose material facts. To avoid personal liability and/or disciplinary action, immediately upon discovering that the seller's affidavit is false, the agent should notify the buyer, in writing, that the affidavit is false.

**Question & Answer Review IV:**
**Foreign Investment in Real Property (FIRPTA)**

The following Q & A Memorandum has been reproduced with the permission of the California Association of Realtors® Legal and Board Services Department. These questions are not part of your homework; they are part of the reading assignment only and are designed as a review of the preceding section.

**Question 1:** What is FIRPTA?

**Answer:** It is the Foreign Investment in Real Property Tax Act. Since January 1, 1985, the Act has required that a buyer withhold 10 percent of the gross sales price and send it to the Internal Revenue Service if the seller is a foreign person. The term *foreign person* has a very specific meaning and can be misleading. There are a number of exemptions and special rules.

**Question 2:** What sales are covered by FIRPTA?

**Answer:** All sales, including installment sales, exchanges, foreclosures, deeds in lieu of foreclosure, and other transactions by a foreign person of a U.S. real property interest (real property, or an interest, such as shares, in a corporation that owns real property) that closed on or after January 1,1985, unless an exemption applies.

**Question 3:** What are the exemptions to FIRPTA?

**Answer:** No withholding is required if any one of the following exemptions applies to all sellers or to the entire property:

1) The seller furnishes a *nonforeign affidavit* that states, under penalty of perjury, that the seller is not a foreign person. The affidavit must also contain the seller's taxpayer identification number. This exemption is not available if the buyer has actual knowledge that the affidavit is false, or if an agent in the transaction informs the buyer that it is false, or if the IRS requests the buyer to furnish a copy of the affidavit and the buyer fails to comply.

2) The buyer receives a *withholding certificate* (also called a *qualifying statement*) from the IRS that states that no withholding is required. A withholding certificate may also be issued that calls for a reduced amount of withholding, or

3) The property is acquired for use by the buyer as the buyer's residence and sells for no more than $300,000 (see Questions 15 through 17 for discussion of the requirements for this exemption).

4) The transaction is a *nonrecognition transaction* for the seller and the seller furnishes a notice of nonrecognition transaction.

Additional exemptions apply to certain sales of shares of stock and to dispositions of interests in a domestic corporation.

**Question 4:** Who or what is a foreign person?

**Answer:** A *foreign person* is a nonresident alien individual or a foreign corporation that has not properly made an election to be treated as a domestic corporation or a foreign partnership, trust, estate, or other entity. As a rough guideline, an individual is not a foreign person if he or she meets the following requirement(s):

- Is a United States citizen, or

- Is a resident alien (holder of a green card that has not been revoked), or

- Meets the *substantial presence* test.

Some other individuals may be U.S. persons (i.e., not foreign persons) as well. A more technical definition of "foreign person" (including the substantial presence test) appears on the reverse side of C.A.R. Standard Form AS-14.

**Nonforeign Affidavit**

**Question 5:** Is it necessary for a seller to sign a nonforeign affidavit if the seller tells the agent that he or she is not a foreign person?

**Answer:** Yes, if the buyer wants protection from potential personal liability for a tax that should be withheld. Having the seller complete and sign an affidavit of nonforeign status insulates the buyer from liability to the IRS if the seller is an individual (or multiple sellers are all individuals), unless the buyer has knowledge that the affidavit is false (see Questions 12 and 13).

Since the buyer generally has no independent way of knowing whether the seller is a foreign person, it is suggested that the following be obtained in every transaction: the seller's affidavit of nonforeign status, or the buyer's affidavit that the property will be used by the buyer as the buyer's residence for the required amount of time, or other appropriate documentation that no withholding is required.

The agent should also comply with the above for protection from potential personal liability.

**Question 6:** What form of affidavit may be used by a nonforeign seller?

**Answer:** C.A.R. Standard Form AS-14 is available for this purpose.

**Question 7:** How long should the seller's nonforeign affidavit be retained by the buyer?

**Answer:** The affidavit should be retained for five years after the end of the year of sale, and must be furnished to the IRS on request. It may be good practice to have the buyer sign a receipt for the original nonforeign affidavit.

**Question 8:** What if the seller is a foreign corporation?

**Answer:** The sale will normally require withholding unless one of the exemptions applies (see Question 3), or unless the corporation has made an election under Internal Revenue Code § 897(i) to be treated as a domestic corporation. If the corporate seller has made that election, a copy of the IRS acknowledgment of the election must be attached to the seller's nonforeign affidavit to provide full protection to the buyer and agents (see Questions 11 and 13).

**Question 9:** Must the seller's affidavit of nonforeign status (or the buyer's affidavit of intent to use property as a buyer's residence) be signed before a notary public?

**Answer:** No.

## Potential Liability

**Question 10:** What is the potential liability of the buyer for failure to withhold when required?

**Answer:** The IRS can assess the full 10 percent of the sales price that should have been withheld, or the seller's actual tax liability in the sale, whichever is less, plus interest and penalties, against the buyer. This can occur if the buyer does not obtain the seller's affidavit of nonforeign status and the seller fails to pay taxes due on the sale.

Even if the seller eventually pays taxes on the sale, the buyer can be liable for interest and penalties if the seller is a foreign person and no nonforeign affidavit was furnished.

**Question 11:** What potential liability to the IRS do the agents of the buyer and seller face?

**Answer:** An agent of the buyer or seller is potentially liable to the IRS for the 10 percent of the sales price that should have been withheld, or for the seller's actual tax liability in the sale, or for the amount of commission or other compensation received by the agent, whichever is less, plus interest and penalties, but only if the following occur:

- The seller provides a nonforeign affidavit and the agent knows the affidavit is false, or

- The interest being sold is composed of shares of stock or some other interest in a U.S. Real Property Holding Corporation and the corporation furnishes a statement that the transfer of the interest is not a transfer of a U.S. real property interest, and the agent knows the statement is false.

Additionally, the agent of the seller can be liable to the IRS for the lesser of those same three amounts, if the seller is a corporation and furnishes a false nonforeign affidavit, even if the agent does not know that the affidavit is false!

It is not clear whether an agent of the seller by subagency would be considered *the agent of the seller* for purposes of this liability.

**Question 12:** Is the buyer protected from personal liability if the seller's nonforeign affidavit is false?

**Answer:** The buyer will be protected from personal liability for the tax that should have been withheld, if the buyer relies in good faith on the seller's nonforeign affidavit. The buyer will not be protected if one of the following is true:

- The buyer has actual knowledge that the affidavit is false, or

- The buyer receives notice from an agent in the transaction that the affidavit is false.

**Question 13:** What if the buyer receives notice after a sale closes that the seller's affidavit was false?

**Answer:** Under Treasury regulations, the buyer will only be protected for consideration already paid. The regulations provide that the buyer should withhold tax from the consideration that remains to be paid, such as payments on a trust deed and note carried by the seller, up to the 10 percent that would have been withheld if not for the false affidavit. HOWEVER, the buyer's failure to make payments on the financing will expose the buyer to the possibility that the seller will commence default proceedings on the trust deed, or take other action based on nonpayment. The buyer in this circumstance should consult legal counsel immediately.

**Question 14:** Are the agents protected from liability if the seller's nonforeign affidavit is false?

**Answer:** The agents will be protected from liability to the IRS if no withholding was done due to an individual seller's nonforeign affidavit. However, if the seller is a foreign corporation that provides a false nonforeign affidavit, only the buyer and the buyer's agent will be fully protected for good faith reliance. The seller's agent can be liable for the withholding that should have occurred, even if the agent does not have knowledge that the affidavit is false. Again, it is not clear from the statute and regulations whether an agent of the seller by subagency would be considered the seller's agent for purposes of this liability.

**Residence of Buyer**

**Question 15:** When does the exemption for residential property selling for no more than $300,000 apply?

**Answer:** The exemption applies to any sale in which both of the following requirements are met:

- The total consideration (sales price) is no more than $300,000, and

- On the date of transfer, the buyer "has definite plans to reside in the property for at least 50 percent of the number of days that the property is used by any person during each of the first two twelve-month periods following the date of transfer." Days that the property will be vacant are not taken into account for this purpose. The buyer is considered to reside in the property on any day the buyer or his or her brothers, sisters, ancestors, defendants, or spouse reside in it.

**Question 16:** What if the buyer does not plan to reside in the property?

**Answer:** The exemption discussed in Question 17 will not be available. Withholding will be required if the seller is a foreign person, unless another exemption applies.

**Question 17:** Take the following example: The seller is a nonresident alien, a foreign person, and the property being sold is a single-family residence. The selling price is $225,000, and the sale is scheduled to close escrow on September 1, 1991.

The buyer intends to use the property as a residence for three months between September 1, 1991, and August 31, 1992, and for three months between September 1, 1992, and August 31, 1993. Assuming none of the other exemptions apply, is the buyer required to withhold and deduct 10 percent of the sales price?

**Answer:** It depends on what the buyer intends to do for the remainder of those two 12-month periods. Suppose the buyer has definite plans that the property will be vacant for nine months and used by the buyer as a residence for three months out of each of those 12-month periods. Based on those plans, the buyer will be using the property as a residence for at least 50 percent of the number of days the property will be in use during each of the two 12-month periods following close of escrow. As a result, no withholding will be required.

However, suppose that the buyer instead plans to use the property as a residence for three months, and has agreed to rent the property to a friend for the remaining nine months out of each of those two

12-month periods. In this case, the buyer does not plan to use the property for at least 50 percent of the number of days the property will be in use in each of the two 12- month periods. Accordingly, withholding will be required.

It is the buyer's plans on the date of transfer (normally, date of close of escrow) that will determine whether or not withholding is required.

## Handling of Funds and Reporting

**Question 18:** When withholding is required, how should the funds be handled?

**Answer:** Withholding should normally be accomplished by having the escrow agent (title company, escrow corporation, financial institution, etc.) withhold the funds required. The funds collected will normally be sent to the IRS at close of escrow, and while the law does not specify that the withholding must be done through escrow, this procedure eliminates the possibility that a buyer might withhold funds at close of escrow and then not send them to the IRS as required. Of course, withholding and transmittal of funds will require an agreement between the buyer and seller in the deposit receipt, or another sales agreement, or in the escrow instructions.

**Question 19:** When must the withheld funds be sent to the IRS?

**Answer:** Withholding must be reported and paid to the IRS by the 20th day after the close of escrow. However, the transmittal of funds should normally be made simultaneously with the close of escrow, as in the case of other disbursements of the seller's proceeds.

**Question 20:** How are the withheld amounts reported and transmitted?

**Answer:** They are reported and transmitted to the IRS on IRS Forms 8288 and 8288-A. IRS Form 8288-A will be stamped by the IRS to show receipt, and a stamped copy will be returned to the seller. The actual forms are multi-copy, and original blanks should be obtained directly from the IRS.

## State Tax Withholding on Disposition of California Real Property

Until January 1991, California's withholding law mirrored the Foreign Investment in Real Property Tax Act (FIRPTA). Current California withholding law states that in certain transactions, buyers must withhold 3 and 1/3 percent of the gross sales price on sales of California real property interests, unless an exemption applies, when the seller's proceeds will be disbursed to one of the following:

1) The seller's financial intermediary, or

2) The seller at a street address outside of California.

A financial intermediary is an agent who receives and transfers funds on behalf of a principal. The financial intermediary may be an individual, a corporation, or other business entity, and may be located within or outside of California.

This withholding must be made on any disposition of California real property interest. This includes sales, exchanges, foreclosures, installment sales, and other types of transfers.

## Exemptions

There are seven exemptions to the withholding requirement. No withholding is required if any one of the following exemptions applies:

1) The seller receives a homeowner's property tax exemption for the property conveyed for the taxable year in which the title transfers, or

2) The sales price of the property does not exceed $100,000, or

3) The buyer does not receive written notification of the withholding requirement from the escrow holder, or

4) The FTB authorizes, in writing, a reduced amount of withholding or no withholding at all, or

5) The property was reacquired by a corporate lender under a deed of trust or mortgagee through judicial or nonjudicial foreclosure, or by a deed in lieu of foreclosure, or

6) The seller is a bank acting as trustee (other than under a deed of trust), or

7) The seller is either a resident of California or a corporation that is qualified to do business in California as an individual or corporation.

## Who Is Responsible for the Withholding?

The buyer is responsible for withholding the required amount. This is typically accomplished through a written instruction to escrow. If there are two or more buyers, each is obligated to withhold. However, the obligation of all of the buyers will be met as long as at least one of them withholds and transmits to the FTB the required amount. If the buyer fails to withhold the required amount when given written notification of the withholding requirement by the escrow holder, the FTB can assess the buyer the full 3 and 1/3 percent of the sales price that should have been withheld or the seller's actual tax liability in the sale, not in excess of 3 and 1/3 percent, whichever is greater, unless the failure to withhold is due to a reasonable cause.

**QUIZZES ARE MANDATORY:** Please log in and submit the chapter quizzes online.

**Chapter Two Quiz**

1.    The amount or rate of real estate commissions is NOT fixed by law. They are set by:

   (a)    cooperating brokers from different offices.
   (b)    each broker individually and may be negotiable between the seller and broker.
   (c)    professional trade organizations.
   (d)    each area's local Board of Realtors®.


2.    The seller of a condominium is required to provide the buyer with:

   (a)    a copy of the governing documents of the development.
   (b)    an explanation of the restrictions that exist.
   (c)    a copy of the most recent financial statement.
   (d)    all of the above.


3.    Which of the following describes a *blanket trust deed*?

   (a)    A financing arrangement that does not release the borrower when the debt is repaid.
   (b)    Financing concerned with the insulating properties of the unit.
   (c)    A trust deed in which two or more pieces of property are used to cover a single debt.
   (d)    None of the above.


4.    A partial release clause included in a blanket trust deed means that as the debt is repaid by the developer,

   (a)    negative amortization accumulates and increases the loan balance.
   (b)    individual lots will be released from the trust deed.
   (c)    all lots will be released after the first payment.
   (d)    all lots remain on the overall lien.


5.    No person can sell or lease, or offer to sell or lease, any lot in a subdivision without first obtaining a:

   (a)    real estate broker.
   (b)    contractor's license.
   (c)    public report.
   (d)    certified appraisal.

6.      When a building owner intends to convert an existing building into a condominium, community apartment project, or stock cooperative, the owner must first receive approval from:

 

     (a)      the local government in compliance with the Subdivisions Map Act.

     (b)      the state legislature in compliance with federal law.

     (c)      the United States Congress in compliance with federal law.

     (d)      the board of real estate in compliance with the Code of Ethics.

7.      Each tenant of a proposed conversion must be given the right to:

     (a)      immediately move out.

     (b)      buy the unit in which he or she lives.

     (c)      file for a refund of that year's rent paid to date.

     (d)      all of the above.

8.      When real property is acquired from a *foreign person*, the IRS requires the transferee (buyer) to:

     (a)      Notify the foreign person's home country of the sale.

     (b)      Verify the foreign person's citizenship status.

     (c)      Withhold a portion of the sales price for tax purposes.

     (d)      Contact the FBI for national security purposes.

9.      Withholding under the Foreign Investment in Real Property Tax Act (FIRPTA) is NOT required when:

     (a)      each seller delivers a *nonforeign affidavit* to the buyer.

     (b)      the property is being purchased as the buyer's residence and the sales price does not exceed $300,000.

     (c)      the buyer receives a *withholding certificate* or *qualifying statement* issued by the IRS that states that no withholding is required.

     (d)      All of the above.

10.     Failure of the buyer to withhold under FIRPTA may result in:

     (a)      the buyer paying a penalty equal to 10% of the purchase price.

     (b)      the buyer paying the seller's tax liability plus interest and penalties.

     (c)      personal liability to both the IRS and the Franchise Tax Board.

     (d)      All of the above.

## Chapter Three

### Important Terms

addendum
condominium
duplex
manufactured homes
probate
townhouse
trust deed
writ of execution

### Learning Objectives

Upon completion of Chapter Three, you should be able to complete the following:

- Describe the pest control inspection and certification process.

- Describe existing California law concerning smoke detectors.

- Describe existing California law concerning water heaters.

- Describe AB 1195 and the new natural hazard disclosure.

- Describe the state's earthquake disclosure requirements.

- Describe the federal lead-based paint hazards disclosure.

## Pest Control Inspection and Certification

Although not required by law, most buyers and lenders require a structural pest control inspection report and certification that shows damage caused by existing conditions and also conditions deemed likely to lead to future infestation. If the purchase contract or the purchaser's lender requires a Structural Pest Control Report or Certification, the report and/or certification must be delivered according to statute.

If the certification or preparation of a report is a condition of the contract, or is a requirement imposed as a condition of financing, the real estate broker acting as the agent in the transaction must deliver the inspection report, certification, and the notice of work completed (certification), if any, to the buyer as soon as is practical prior to transfer of title.

If more than one real estate broker is acting as an agent in the transaction, the broker who has obtained the offer made by the buyer is responsible for delivering the required documents directly to the buyer, unless the buyer has given written directions to another broker acting as the agent in the transaction to make the delivery.

If the agent responsible for delivery cannot obtain the required documents to deliver to the buyer and does not have written assurance from the buyer that all of the proper documents have been received, the agent must advise the buyer in writing of the buyer's rights to receive those documents prior to transfer of title.

The broker responsible for delivery must maintain a record of the action taken to effect delivery to the buyer. This is usually achieved by having the buyer sign a copy of the required documents upon delivery to prove compliance. Also, the Structural Pest Control Report and Certification are usually entered into escrow and signed again at closing.

Delivery to a buyer may be in person or by mail, and delivery to the husband or wife is deemed sufficient unless the contract states otherwise.

## Smoke Detectors

Under existing law since 1986, the seller of a single-family home has been required to deliver to the buyer a written disclosure statement that indicates that the property is in compliance with current California law concerning smoke detectors.

## New Requirements from the State Fire Marshal

**Existing Dwelling Units:** According to the State Fire Marshal, effective August 14, 1992, smoke detectors must be installed in existing *dwelling units* as well as in new constructions, new additions, alterations, or repairs. A *dwelling unit* can be defined as any building or portion of a building that contains living facilities, including provisions for sleeping, eating, cooking, and sanitation. In all existing dwelling units, smoke detectors may be solely battery operated, or they may be hardwired with a battery backup.

**New Construction:** In all new construction that has occured after August 14, 1992, smoke detectors must receive their primary power from the building wiring when the wiring is served by a commercial source, and must be equipped with a battery backup. The wiring must be permanent and not contain a disconnecting switch other than that required for over-current protection. Buildings without commercial power may use battery-operated smoke detectors.

**Alterations, Repairs, or Additions:** Buildings that undergo alterations, repairs, or additions, exceeding $1,000 and for which a permit is required, or when one or more sleeping rooms are added, may install smoke detectors that are solely battery operated or hardwired with a battery backup.

For new construction, alterations, repairs, additions, or existing dwelling units, a smoke detector must be installed in each sleeping area and at a point centrally located in the corridor or area that provides access to each separate sleeping area.

## Disclosure Requirements

Existing law still requires the seller of a single-family home to deliver to the buyer a written disclosure statement that indicates that the property is in compliance with current California law concerning smoke detectors.

## Question & Answer Review V: Law & Regulations for Smoke Detectors

The following Q & A Memorandum has been reproduced with the permission of the California Association of Realtors® Legal and Board Services Department. These questions are not part of your homework; they are part of the reading assignment only and are designed to be a review for the preceding section.

**Question 1:** When is a smoke detector required for a single-family dwelling?

**Answer:** Every single-family dwelling must have an operable smoke detector approved by and installed in accordance with the State Fire Marshal's regulations. This applies to all transfers of single-family dwellings, except exemptions as provided in Question 7.

The State Fire Marshal's regulations at the time of this publication require only one smoke detector per dwelling, installed according to the manufacturer's instructions. State Fire Marshal regulations can be obtained by contacting the State Fire Marshal.

**Question 2:** Does a battery-operated smoke detector meet the requirements of the new law?

**Answer:** Generally yes. A battery-operated smoke detector satisfies the new law, unless prohibited by local rules, regulations, or ordinances. Several local ordinances require that smoke detectors be non-battery operated (such as permanently wired or electrically operated). Under state law, in such a situation, the local ordinance requirements must be met.

**Question 3:** Who is responsible for having the smoke detector installed?

**Answer:** It is the responsibility of the seller to install the smoke detector. However, there is nothing in the law that stops the buyer and seller from negotiating who will pay for the installation of the smoke detector.

**Question 4:** Must the seller make any disclosure regarding the existence of a smoke detector?

**Answer:** Yes. The seller must deliver to the buyer a written statement that indicates that the dwelling has an operable smoke detector and therefore is in compliance with the law.

The disclosure statement must be included either in the deposit receipt, as an addendum to it, or as a separate statement attached to it.

**Question 5:** When should the disclosure statement be delivered to the buyer?

**Answer:** Whenever possible, it should be delivered prior to the parties' signing a binding contract. In no event should the disclosure be made after title has been transferred from the seller to the buyer.

The disclosure statement is considered delivered by law if it is received in person or by mail by the buyer or the authorized agent of the buyer.

**Question 6:** Whose responsibility is it to complete the disclosure statement?

**Answer:** The new law specifically states that it is the duty of the seller to install an operable smoke detector and deliver a completed disclosure statement to the buyer or buyer's authorized agent.

**Question 7:** What transfers are exempt from the new law?

**Answer:** The following transfers are exempt from the requirement that an operable smoke detector be installed in the property and that a statement of compliance be given to the buyer:

- Transfers pursuant to a court order such as probate, bankruptcy, writ of execution, or decree of dissolution of marriage.

- Transfers that require a public report to be issued by the Commissioner of Real Estate pursuant to the Subdivided Lands Act.

- Transfers by judicial foreclosure, trustee's sale, or by deed in lieu of foreclosure, following default on a trust deed or mortgage.

- Transfers between co-owners or spouses.

- Transfers by will or as a result of inheritance.

- Transfers by the State Controller as unclaimed property.

- Transfers by the State for unpaid taxes.

**Question 8:** What is the penalty for non-compliance with the law?

**Answer:** Actual damages not to exceed $100.00 plus court costs and attorney fees.

## Mobile Homes

**Question 9:** Does the new law that requires smoke detectors apply to mobile homes?

**Answer:** Yes. Under Health and Safety Code Section 18029.6, all used manufactured homes, used mobile homes, and used commercial coaches that are sold on or after January 1, 1986, must have an operable smoke detector on the date of transfer. The Department of Housing and Community Development (HCD) has recently issued regulations for these types of units.

For units manufactured on or after October 7, 1973, the smoke detector must be wired to an unswitched 110-volt circuit (i.e., electrically operated). Additionally, it must be approved and listed by HCD.

If the unit was manufactured prior to October 7, 1973, a battery-operated smoke detector will comply.

Further information regarding smoke detectors in used mobile homes, manufactured homes, and commercial coaches can be obtained by contacting HCD at (916) 323-9224, or any HCD district office.

## Dwelling Units Intended for Human Occupancy

Health and Safety Code Section 13113.7 applies to all units covered by this section regardless of whether or not a transfer of title occurs. The emphasis is units. Questions 10 through 17 apply to such dwellings.

**Question 10:** What is a dwelling unit intended for human occupancy according to the new law?

**Answer:** *Dwelling units intended for human occupancy* include a duplex, lodging house, apartment complex, hotel, motel, condominium, stock cooperative, time-share project, or dwelling unit of a multiple-unit dwelling complex. For this purpose, *dwelling units intended for human occupancy* do not include manufactured homes, mobile homes, commercial coaches, or single-family residences.

**Note:** A condominium, townhouse, or stock cooperative is considered a *dwelling unit intended for human occupancy*, and therefore the discussion in this section applies, even though each one might be used as a single-family residence.

**Question 11:** When is an operable smoke detector required in such units?

**Answer:** The effective date depends:

1) On or after January 1, 1985: for all dwelling units where the owner has applied for a permit for alterations, repairs, or additions exceeding $1,000.

2) On or after January 1, 1987: for all other units.

**Question 12:** Do battery-operated smoke detectors meet the state law?

**Answer:** Yes. However, if a local rule, regulation, or ordinance requires the installation of permanently wired or electrically operated smoke detectors, the local requirements must be met.

**Question 13:** What if there are local ordinances already in effect that require smoke detectors?

**Answer:** Generally, the local ordinance will prevail, provided that the local ordinance meets the minimum requirements of the state law. If a local ordinance requires an electrically operated smoke detector, the property owner must comply.

Furthermore, if a local ordinance requires an electrically wired smoke detector but the effective date of the local ordinance occurs later than the date of the state law, the local ordinance controls.

For example, State law that requires battery-operated smoke detectors for all "dwelling units intended for human occupancy" is effective January 1, 1987. City "A" has enacted a local ordinance effective July 1, 1987, that requires all dwelling units intended for human occupancy to be equipped with electrically wired smoke detectors. The local ordinance controls and a property owner is not required to install battery-operated smoke detectors between January 1, 1987, and July 1, 1987.

**Question 14:** Is there an exception to the requirement of an operable smoke detector in a dwelling unit intended for human occupancy?

**Answer:** Yes. Dwellings that have fire sprinkler systems may be exempted by the State Fire Marshal if a determination is made that a smoke detector is not reasonably necessary for fire safety.

**Question 15:** Who is responsible for installing and maintaining the smoke detectors?

**Answer:** The owner of each unit is responsible for installing and maintaining an operable smoke detector. The owner is responsible for testing and maintaining operable smoke detectors in hotels, motels, lodging houses, and common stairwells of multi-unit dwelling complexes such as apartment buildings.

A smoke detector shall be operable at the time a tenant takes possession of a dwelling unit. An apartment complex tenant is responsible for notifying the manager or owner if the smoke detector becomes inoperable. If the owner is not notified of the existence of a deficient smoke detector, the owner is not liable for a violation of the new law.

**Question 16:** If the tenant notifies the owner of an inoperable smoke detector, what procedures must be followed?

**Answer:** The owner or owner's agent has the right to-enter the premises to install, repair, or otherwise maintain the smoke detector. Unless it is an emergency, the owner or owner's agent must give the tenant reasonable notice in writing of the intention to enter. Under the law, 24 hours is presumed to be reasonable notice. The owner or owner's agent should only enter the premises during normal business hours.

**Question 17:** What is the penalty for non-compliance with the law?

**Answer:** A maximum of $200.00 for each offense can be imposed on the owner.

Further information regarding the installation of smoke detectors can be obtained from the Department of Housing and Community Development, the Local Building and Safety Department, Planning Department, Fire Department, or other appropriate agency.

**Carbon Monoxide Detectors**

The Carbon Monoxide Poisoning Prevention Act of 2010 (Cal. Health & Safety Code §§ 13260 et seq.) was signed into law this year. It requires carbon monoxide detectors to be installed in every dwelling unit intended for human occupancy. The California legislature also modified both the Transfer Disclosure Statement (TDS) for residential one-to-four-unit real properties, and the Mobilehome Transfer Disclosure Statement (MHTDS) for manufactured homes and mobile homes, to include a reference to carbon monoxide detector devices.

Under the law, a carbon monoxide device is "designed to detect carbon monoxide and produce a distinct, audible alarm." It can be a battery-powered device, a plug-in device with battery backup, or a device installed as recommended by Standard 720 of the National Fire Protection Association that is either wired into the alternating current power line of the dwelling unit with a secondary battery backup or connected to a system via a panel.

If the carbon monoxide device is combined with a smoke detector, it must emit an alarm or voice warning in a manner that clearly differentiates between a carbon monoxide alarm warning and a smoke detector warning.

The carbon monoxide device must have been tested and certified pursuant to the requirements of the American National standards Institute (ANSI) and Underwriters Laboratories Inc. (UL) as set forth in either ANSI/UL 2034 or ANSI/UL 2075, or successor standards, by a nationally recognized testing laboratory listed in the directory of approved testing laboratories, established by the Building Materials Listing Program of the Fire Engineering Division of the Office of the State Fire Marshal of the Department of Forestry and Fire Protection (Cal. Health & Safety Code § 13262).

## How Does a Homeowner Comply with this Law?

This new law requires the owner "to install the devices in a manner consistent with building standards applicable to new construction for the relevant type of occupancy or with the manufacturer's instructions, if it is technically feasible to do so" (Cal. Health & Safety Code § 17926(b)).

The following language comes packaged with carbon monoxide (CO) detectors:

> *For minimum security, a CO Alarm should be centrally located outside of each separate sleeping area in the immediate vicinity of the bedrooms. The Alarm should be located at least 6 inches (152mm) from all exterior walls and at least 3 feet (0.9 meters) from supply or return vents.*

Building standards applicable to new construction are as follows:

Section R315 et seq. of the 2010 edition California Residential Code (CRC) [effective Jan. 1, 2011] (applicable to new one-to-two family dwellings and townhouses not more than 3 stories, and also where work requires a permit for alterations, repairs, or additions exceeding one thousand dollars in existing dwellings units):

- Installed outside of each separate sleeping area in the immediate vicinity of the bedroom(s) in dwelling units, on every level including basements within which fuel-fired appliances are installed, and in dwelling units that have attached garages.

Section 420 et seq. of the 2010 edition California Building Code (CBC) [effective Jan. 1, 2011] (applicable to other new dwelling units and also where a permit is required for alterations, repairs, or additions exceeding $1,000 in existing dwelling units):

- Installed outside of each separate sleeping area in the immediate vicinity of the bedroom(s) in dwelling units, on every level including basements within which fuel-fired appliances are installed, and in dwelling units that have attached garages.

## Penalties for Noncompliance

A violation is an infraction punishable by a maximum fine of $200 for each offense. However, a property owner must receive a 30-day notice to correct first. If an owner who receives such a notice fails to correct the problem within the 30-day period, then the owner may be assessed the fine (Cal. Health & Safety Code § 17926(c).

## Buyer's Rescission Rights

The buyer may not rescind the sale if the dwelling does not have the necessary carbon monoxide detectors. However, the buyer may be entitled to an award of actual damages not to exceed $100 plus court costs and attorney's fees (Cal. Health & Safety Code § 17926(d)).

Note the following language in the TDS and MHTDS:

Installation of a listed appliance, device, or amenity is not a precondition of sale or transfer of the dwelling. The carbon monoxide device, garage door opener, or child-resistant pool barrier may not be in compliance with the safety standards relating to, respectively, carbon monoxide device standards of Chapter 8 (commencing with Section 13260) of Part 2 of Division 12 of automatic reversing device standards of Chapter 12.5 (commencing with Section 19890) of Part 3 of Division 13 of the pool safety standards of Article 2.5 (commencing with Section 115920) of Chapter 5 of Part 10 of Division 104 of the Health and Safety Code. Window security bars may not have quick-release mechanisms in compliance with the 1995 edition of the California Building Standards Code.

## Seller's Carbon Monoxide Detector Disclosure Obligations

The Seller's disclosure obligations are satisfied when providing a buyer with the TDS or the MHTDS. If the seller is exempt from giving a TDS, the law doesn't require any specific disclosures regarding carbon monoxide detector devices (see Cal. Civ. Code §§ 1102.6, 1102.6d).

The Homeowners' Guide to Environmental Hazards also will include information regarding carbon monoxide.

**Student Note:** Local municipalities may require more stringent standards for carbon monoxide detectors.

## Landlord's Carbon Monoxide Detector Disclosure Obligations

All landlords of dwelling units must install carbon monoxide detectors. The law gives a landlord authority to enter the dwelling unit for the purpose of installing, repairing, testing, and maintaining carbon monoxide devices "pursuant to the authority and requirements of Section 1954 of the Civil Code [entry by landlord]."

The carbon monoxide device must be operable at the time that a tenant takes possession. However, the tenant has the responsibility of notifying the owner or owner's agent if the tenant becomes aware of an inoperable or deficient carbon monoxide device. The landlord is not in violation of the law for a deficient or inoperable carbon monoxide device if he or she has not received notice of the problem from the tenant (Cal. Health & Safety Code § 17926.1).

**Student Note:** If the California Building Standards Commission adopts or updates building standards that relate to carbon monoxide devices in the future, the owner is required to install the newer device if the owner makes an application for a permit for alterations, repairs, or additions to that dwelling unit with the cost exceeding $1,000 (Cal. Health & Safety Code § 17926.2(b)).

## Water Heater Bracing and Disclosure Requirements

### Introduction

Under existing law, all new and replacement water heaters sold in California on or after July 1, 1991 must be braced, anchored, or strapped to resist falling or horizontal displacement due to earthquake motion. (A new law has been signed into law that will impose additional disclosure requirements.)

The new law, effective January 1, 1996, requires an owner of any real property that contains a water heater to brace, anchor, or strap the water heater to resist falling or horizontal displacement due to earthquake motion. It is applicable to all existing water heaters, as well as new and replacement water heaters sold in California on or after July 1, 1991.

In addition, a seller of any real property must certify to a prospective purchaser that this section has been complied with, including compliance with applicable local code requirements. This certification must be in writing and may be done in existing transactional documents, including, but not limited to, the Homeowner's Guide to Earthquake Safety, a real estate purchase contract, a transfer disclosure statement, or a local option disclosure statement. C.A.R. Form SDC-14, the *Smoke Detector/Water Heater Statement of Compliance* will satisfy this requirement.

### Method of Anchoring

The new law does not specify how to anchor the appliances. Building officials say that strapping them with flexible metal plumber's tape is adequate. But the state Seismic Safety Commission's

*Homeowner's Guide to Earthquake Safety*, the definitive guide to complying with quake laws, has a diagram showing metal tubing used in addition to strapping for stabilizing the water heater. Most building inspectors think the picture in the earthquake guide will confuse people, as it may lead people to believe that the metal tubing is required along with the plumber's tape.

The Seismic Safety Commission contends that the diagram is merely an example of how to brace a water heater, not a requirement. The Office of the State Architect and most local building officials agree. Home sellers only need to follow their local building codes to comply with the law. According to our research, installation can be done with metal strapping if there is sufficient length and it is properly installed. When water heaters are not anchored, they can tip in an earthquake, spilling gallons of water, or worse, rip out a gas line that creates a fire or explosion hazard. Existing law already requires that new and replacement water heaters be installed to meet current building codes.

## Exemptions

There are no specific exemptions from this law. The legislative intent suggests this law applies only to residential properties, but the final language does not limit the requirement to residential properties.

## Penalties for Noncompliance

The law does not mention specified penalties. Noncompliance may result in imposition of damages in a civil lawsuit, but under the statute does not create a presumption of negligence or failure to exercise due care.

## AB 1195 and the Natural Hazard Disclosure Statement

### Introduction

The following information has been supplied in its entirety by JCP Geologists, Inc., 10950 N. Blaney Ave., Cupertino, CA 95014. (408) 446-4426, or reports@jcp-inc.com.

On June 1, 1998, the new disclosure requirements of AB 1195 went into effect, changing the face of natural hazard disclosure throughout California. AB 1195 mandates three new natural hazard disclosures and consolidates both new and previously required disclosures onto a new statutory form called the *Natural Hazard Disclosure Statement* (NHDS). This new form is now a legally required part of most residential property transactions.

### Three New Mandated Disclosures

AB 1195 mandates three new disclosures for the seller and/or seller's agent. Sellers are now required to disclose if their property is in a *Very High Fire Hazard Severity Zone*. Originating in response to the 1991 Oakland Hills firestorm, these zones contain a high fire risk due to topography, brush coverage, climate, etc. Properties located in a Very High Fire Hazard Severity Zone are subject to certain fire-prevention property maintenance requirements.

Another new disclosure requirement of listing agents under AB 1195 is disclosing if a property is within an area of potential flooding due to dam failure. These zones are delineated on Dam Inundation maps adopted by the California Office of Emergency Services (OES).

The Federal Emergency Management Agency issues maps through the National Flood Insurance Program (NFIP) that define flood hazard areas. If a property lies within a one-hundred-year Special Flood Hazard Area (any "A" or "V" zone), federally connected lenders are required to make sure buyers maintain flood insurance on the structure. AB 1195 mandates that the seller's agent also disclose if a property is located in a Special Flood Area (any "A" or "V" zone).

**New Disclosure Forms and Procedures**

AB 1195 also changes the way agents provide natural hazard disclosure information by creating a statutory form titled the Natural Hazards Disclosure Statement (NHDS). The NHDS consolidates the newly mandated disclosures discussed above with the existing required disclosures of State Responsibility Areas, Earthquake Fault Zones, and Seismic Hazard Mapping Act Zones. The new form lists each natural hazard disclosure and requires that the seller and their agent determine if a zone affects the property from their own "actual knowledge" or by reading the appropriate map. They must then mark either *yes* or *no* to indicate if the property is located within each of the zones. In a significant change to current disclosure practice, the seller and their agent sign the NHDS to "represent that the information herein is true and correct" in order to complete the form.

In the case of Special Flood Hazard Areas and Areas of Potential Flooding due to dam failure, there is a space provided on the NHDS for "Don't know/Information not available from local jurisdiction" in addition to the *yes* and *no* spaces. This choice is provided because these particular disclosures are triggered by either one of the following:

- *Actual knowledge* of the seller or their agent.

- The local jurisdiction has compiled a list, by parcel, of properties in the zones.

It is unclear when localities will compile such itemized parcel lists. The possibility of not knowing when your local jurisdiction has compiled the required lists could expose agents to liability by not knowing when the disclosures are "legally" triggered. However, maps are currently available that delineate both dam inundation zones and the NFIP flood zones. Last, but certainly not least, if legally challenged, it could be difficult to prove whether or not the agent or seller had *actual knowledge* that a property was in a certain zone or not. Prudent business practice suggests providing the information from the currently available map sources when possible to avoid potential liability exposure.

## Decreased Liability

The NHDS requires that the seller's agent and the seller sign the form. Requiring these signatures dramatically increases liability exposure for both agents and sellers. However, it is important to note that AB 1195 includes a provision that can protect the agent and seller from liability exposure for the disclosures. In outlining the procedures for completing the NHDS, AB 1195 references §1102.4(a) of the California Civil Code. The section of the law states that neither the transferor nor any listing or selling agent shall be liable for any error, inaccuracy, or omission of any information delivered in a report prepared pursuant to §1102.4(c):

"The delivery of a report or opinion prepared by a licensed engineer, land surveyor, geologist...or other expert, dealing with matters within the scope of the professional's license."

By referring agents to professional reports prepared pursuant to Civil Code 1102.4, the new law allows agents to avoid liability for the disclosure. This means that by using a report signed by a licensed professional, the broker, the agent, and the seller are legally shielded from the liability exposure the disclosures present.

## What This Means to Agents

AB 1195 changes the way that real estate professionals do business. It adds new disclosure requirements, consolidates existing requirements, and creates a statutory form and practice for natural hazard disclosures. Many brokers and agents may be concerned at the prospect of new rules and paperwork, or that new disclosures can only complicate a transaction. However, the new law has some serious benefits for real estate professionals. AB 1195 sets clear standards and creates a single guideline for natural hazard disclosures, making it easier to understand what is required. AB 1195 also provides one clear form for buyers, which may actually cut down on paperwork. Most importantly, AB 1195 gives real estate professionals what they want most: a clear and simple way to fulfill disclosure requirements without increasing liability exposure by using a report signed by an appropriately licensed professional, such as a geologist.

## Disclosure for Non-Residential and Traditionally "Exempt" Properties

The question has been raised as to how the recent legislation AB 1195 affects non-residential property transactions and residential transactions that are often considered exempt from disclosures. The new law primarily accomplishes two things: it introduces a Natural Hazard Disclosure Statement and mandates three new map-based disclosures. We can see how different types of transactions are affected by examining how the law applies these new mandates.

To mandate the use of the Natural Hazard Disclosure Statement (NHDS), the law adds Civil Code Section 1102.6, which statutorily defines the text of the new form and requires the use of the form when selling "any real property that is subject to this section." According to Civil Code Section 1102, properties subject to this section are "real property...improved with or consisting of not less than one or more than four dwelling units." Thus, because use of the statutory NHDS is included in Civil Code Section 1102, using the new form is only required for those transactions that are subject to Civil Code 1102.

It should be noted that there are several exemptions to Civil Code 1102. If you don't know whether or not a transaction is subject to Civil Code 1102, there is an easy "rule of thumb" that you can follow. The Transfer Disclosure Statement (TDS) is also tied to Civil Code 1102. If a transaction requires a TDS, then the statutory Natural Hazard Disclosure Statement is also needed. If a transaction is exempt from the TDS, then the NHDS is not required.

However, even when the statutory form is not required, the disclosures still are. AB 1195 addresses six map-based disclosures:

1) NFIP Special Flood Hazard Areas

2) Dam Inundation Zones

3) Very High Fire Severity Zones

4) State Responsibility Fire Areas

5) Earthquake Fault Zones

6) Seismic Hazard Zones

While these six disclosure items are listed on the Natural Hazard Disclosure Statement, they are mandated by codes that are independent of Civil Code 1102. For example, Public Resources Code 2621.9 mandates the disclosure of Earthquake Fault Zones for "all real property" transactions. Similarly, Public Resources Code 4136 mandates disclosure of State Responsibility Areas and Public Resources Code 2694 mandates Seismic Hazard Zone disclosure for all "real property" transactions.

AB 1195 also adds three new sections of independent code that mandates the new disclosures:

- Government Code 8589.3: Mandating NFIP Special Flood Zone disclosure, is added to read; "(a) A person who is acting as an agent for the seller of real property that is located within a special flood hazard area (any type Zone "A" or "V") shall disclose to any prospective purchaser..."

- Government Code 8589.4: Mandating Dam Inundation Zone Disclosure, is added to read, "(a) A person who is acting as an agent for the seller of real property that is located within an area of potential flooding shown on an inundation map shall disclose to any prospective purchaser..."

- Government Code 51183.5: Mandating Very High Fire Severity Zone disclosure, is added to read, "(a) A seller of real property that is located within a very high fire hazard severity zone shall disclose to any prospective purchaser..."

These independent codes make disclosure of the six items on the Natural Hazard Disclosure Statement mandatory for all real property transactions regardless of whether the transaction requires the actual use of the NHDS.

## Summary

To summarize, there are six natural hazard disclosure items required by California state law. Each item is addressed in its own section of the code. Each item applies to all real property transactions, including commercial and industrial property, which makes the disclosures themselves required for all transactions. When making these disclosures for most residential transactions, the Natural Hazard Disclosure Statement must be used.

## Earthquake Disclosure Requirements

## Introduction

It is well-known that California is crisscrossed with earthquake faults, both active and inactive. The potential consequences of building on land located near these faults prompted the state to pass the Alquist-Priolo Special Studies Zones Act (the Act), which was signed into law December 22, 1972. The effective date of the Act was March 7, 1973.

Under the Act, the State Geologist (Chief of the Division of Mines and Geology) is required to delineate "special studies zones" along known active faults in California. Cities and counties affected by the zones must regulate certain development projects within these zones. The Act authorizes the withholding of development permits for sites within the zones until geologic investigations demonstrate that the sites are not threatened by surface displacement from future faulting.

## Disclosure Requirements under the Public Resources Code § 2621.9

"...a person who is acting as an agent for the seller of real property which is located within a delineated special studies zone, or the seller if he or she is acting without an agent, shall disclose to any prospective purchaser the fact that the property is located within a delineated special studies zone, provided the maps prepared pursuant to this chapter, or the information contained in the maps, are reasonably available."

1) The disclosure shall be provided by one of the following means: The real estate transfer disclosure statement set out in Section 1102.6 of the Civil Code.

2) The local option real estate transfer disclosure statement set out in subdivision (a) of Section 1102.6 of the Civil Code.

3) The real estate contract and receipt for deposit.

For the purposes of this section:

*Reasonably available* means that for any county that includes areas covered by a delineated special studies map, a notice has been posted at the offices of the county recorder, county assessor, and county planning commission that identifies the location of the map and the effective date of the notice, which shall not exceed 10 days beyond the date the county received the map from the State Geologist.

Real estate contract and receipt for deposit means the document that contains the offer to sell or purchase real property, when accepted, becomes a binding contract, and that serves as an acknowledgment of a deposit, if one is received.

The seller must disclose major earthquake damage that has NOT been repaired when attempting to sell the property. For residential one-to-four unit properties, the Real Estate Transfer Disclosure Statement, Section II (Seller's Information), paragraph C(9), states the following:

"Are you (Seller) aware of any of the following: . . . 9. Major damage to the property or any of the structures from fire, earthquake, floods, or landslides? Yes/No."

For other types of property, the general legal requirements of disclosing known material facts that affect the value or desirability of property apply.

The seller must also disclose the fact of an earthquake, even when there was no major damage to the property or when major damage has been repaired. These would be considered material facts that may affect the value or desirability of the property to the buyer.

There has also been some confusion about whether the seller must give the buyer an amended Real Estate Transfer Disclosure Statement (TDS) in the event of an earthquake. According to the CAR Legal and Board Services Department, the statute is not clear on this point and no appellate court cases have interpreted this issue. A court would probably examine whether a material change in the property condition has occurred when deciding on the answer to this question. Following the 1989 Loma Prieta earthquake, most brokers were advising their agents to complete new TDS forms.

The TDS applies only to one-to-four unit family residential properties, and some sales of these types of property are exempt. If the TDS is given to the buyer after the buyer signs an offer to purchase the property, the buyer has a three- or five-day right to cancel the sale if the buyer disapproves the TDS.

Under the statute, "if any disclosure, or any material amendment of any disclosure, required to be made by this article, is delivered after the execution of an offer to purchase, the transferee shall have three days after delivery in person or five days after delivery by deposit in the mail, to terminate his or her offer by delivery of a written notice of termination to the transferor or the transferor's agent."

Therefore, if an amended TDS is required, the buyer has another three- or five-day right to cancel the sale. This was an extremely hot issue after the 1989 quake.

## The Homeowner's Guide to Earthquake Safety

In addition to the earthquake disclosure requirements contained in Civil Code Section 1102, since 1991, sellers of homes built before 1960 must deliver to the buyer, "as soon as practicable before the transfer," a copy of The Homeowner's Guide to Earthquake Safety and disclose certain earthquake deficiencies. The booklet contains a reporting form that may be used for this disclosure. The seller's real estate agent is to provide the seller of such a home with a copy of the booklet for delivery to the buyer.

The Homeowner's Guide to Earthquake Safety is developed and published by the Seismic Safety Commission. It contains information on geologic and seismic hazards, explanations of structural and nonstructural earthquake hazards, and recommendations for mitigating the hazards. It is the intention that this booklet be distributed to home sellers by real estate agents (in accordance with Section 8897.5 of the Government Code) and is also available to the buyer and the general public.

**Delivery of the Homeowner's Guide by the Broker to the Seller:** After January 1, 1993, when applicable, the broker must deliver the Homeowner's Guide to the seller. The seller is then required to deliver it to the buyer of any property built prior to January 1, 1960, with one-to-four living units of conventional light-frame construction. It must be delivered to the buyer as soon as practicable before the transfer.

It is the goal of the Legislature to ensure that all homes be anchored to their foundations, have adequately braced cripple walls, and have the water heaters braced, strapped, or anchored, and that deficiencies be disclosed by the seller to prospective buyers. This should provide prospective buyers with information on the possible vulnerability of the dwelling being purchased.

Civil Code § 2079.8 provides that if the Homeowner's Guide to Earthquake Safety is delivered to a transferee (buyer), a seller or broker is not required to provide additional information on earthquake safety, and the information from the guide shall be deemed to be adequate to inform the transferee (buyer) regarding geologic and seismic hazards. This law does not alter the broker's duty to disclose that the subject property is situated in either a Special Studies Zone or Seismic Hazard Zone.

## Exemptions

A seller is not required to deliver the Homeowner's Guide and make the additional disclosures under any of the following conditions:

1) The buyer has agreed in writing that the dwelling will be demolished within one year after the date of transfer.

2) The transfer requires the furnishing of a public report.

3) A transfer is made pursuant to a court order (e.g., bankruptcy or probate).

4) A transfer is made by foreclosure sale.

5) A transfer is made by a fiduciary in the course of administering a decedent's estate, guardianship, conservatorship, or trust.

6) A transfer is made from one co-owner to one or more other co-owners.

7) A transfer is made to a spouse, child, grandchild, or further descendant.

8) A transfer is made between spouses in connection with a divorce.

9) A transfer is made by the State Controller pursuant to the unclaimed Property Law.

10) A transfer is made as a result of a failure to pay property taxes.

## Federal Lead-Based Paint Hazards Disclosure Introduction

Sellers of homes built before 1978, and their agents, must disclose to potential purchasers the presence of any known lead-based paint hazards that affect the property. This law also applies to residential landlords and their tenants.

The new requirement that mandates disclosure of lead-based paint hazards is the Federal Residential Lead-based Paint Hazard Reduction Act of 1992. This Act directed the Department of Housing and Urban Development (HUD) and the Environmental Protection Agency (EPA) to issue regulations that required the disclosure of information on lead-based paint before the sale or lease of most housing built before 1978. Congress did not extend the law to housing built after 1978 because that year, the Consumer Product Safety Commission banned the use of lead-based paint in housing.

The act arose out of concerns about evidence that children, especially age six and under, can suffer serious health problems if they ingest or inhale lead paint chips or dust. The problems include learning disabilities, decreased growth, impaired hearing, and brain damage. Pregnant women may also carry health risks to their unborn children or may miscarry.

## When Did The Rule Take Effect?

The rule's effective date depends on the number of housing units owned.

- For owners of more than four dwelling units, the effective date was September 6, 1996.

- For owners of four or fewer dwelling units, the effective date was December 6, 1996.

## How to Comply

For covered properties, federal law requires that the seller's and lessor's agents ensure that the seller or lessor meet the following requirements:

1) Provide the federal booklet entitled *Protect Your Family from Lead in Your Home* to each buyer or lessee.

2) Use a specific addendum to each purchase contract or lease (C.A.R. Forms FLS-14 for sales and FLL-14 for leases).

3) Permit the buyer a period of 10 days before becoming obligated under the purchase contract, to allow the buyer to conduct a risk assessment or inspection for the presence of lead-based paint hazards. (The evaluation period applies only to sales, not leases. The 10-day period can be shortened or lengthened by agreement).

   **Question:** If lead is found, is the seller required to remove it?

   **Answer:** No. But the existence of lead can be used as a negotiating point in the purchase of the property, as are other problems or defects. Some buyers may negotiate with a seller to pay half the price of testing the property. Others may require the seller to put money into escrow for lead abatement.

4) Disclose to the purchaser or lessee the presence of any known lead-based paint hazards in the property and provide to the buyer or lessee any lead hazard evaluation report available to the seller or lessor.

## California Environmental Hazards Booklet

The *California's Environmental Hazards: Guide for Homeowners and Buyers* booklet has been recently revised to expand on the explanation of lead-based paint. Discussions have been underway between the California Department of Health Services, which publishes the California booklet, and HUD or the EPA, which publishes the new federal booklet, to obtain a determination that the California booklet can be used instead of the *Federal Protect Your Family from Lead in Your Home* booklet. Preliminary approval has been given. However, final approval has not yet been obtained.

When final approval for substitute use of the California booklet is obtained, C.A.R. will publish the revised *California Environmental Hazards: Guide for Homeowners and Buyers* booklet.

If the California booklet (after approval for substitute use) is not used, the federal lead booklet *must* be used. The federal booklet can currently be purchased through C.A.R. and local Associations/Boards of Realtors®.

Likewise, the revised California booklet, when approved for substitute use, will also be available.

**Special Note:** Have the buyer acknowledge in writing that he or she has been given the booklet, so that there is no question that the seller and the seller's agent have met this requirement.

## What About the Required Addendum?

When the new federal requirement takes effect, the new addendum for sales (C.A.R. Form FLS-14) will replace the HUD lead-paint disclosure statement that has been required for FHA-financed sales. Form FLS-14 will also replace the special addendum that has been required for sales of HUD-repossessed properties.

## Known Lead-Based Hazards

Federal law does not specify where the disclosure should be made. However, for sales, the Real Estate Transfer Disclosure Statement (TDS) may be used for this purpose, just as it is used to disclose other known material facts that impact a property.

Language has been added to revisions of C.A.R.'s Real Estate Purchase Agreement and Receipt for Deposit, Form DR-14, to deal with the new requirements.

## Potential Penalties

Potential penalties include the following:

- Liability of three times the amount of damages for knowingly violating this law.
- Civil penalties payable to the U.S. Government.
- An injunction if sought by HUD.
- Attorney's fees and costs, and a lawsuit brought to enforce the law.
- Criminal penalties of up to $10,000 for each violation.

**QUIZZES ARE MANDATORY**: Please log in and submit the chapter quizzes online.

**Chapter Three Quiz**

1.    Which of the following statements is INCORRECT regarding pest control inspection and certification?

      (a)    It is required by law.
      (b)    It is NOT required by law.
      (c)    Most buyers and lenders require a structural pest control inspection report and certification.
      (d)    If it is a condition of the contract, the report and certification must be delivered to the buyer.

2.    If more than one real estate broker is acting as an agent in the transaction, who is responsible to deliver the required pest control documents?

      (a)    The broker who has obtained the listing agreement from the seller.
      (b)    The broker who has obtained the offer made by the buyer.
      (c)    The seller has sole responsibility to deliver the required pest control documents.
      (d)    None of the above.

3.    Effective August 14, 1992, smoke detectors must be installed in:

      (a)    Existing dwellings.
      (b)    New construction.
      (c)    Every kind of structure whatsoever.
      (d)    Both (a) and (b) are correct.

4.    The existing smoke detector disclosure law still requires the seller to:

      (a)    Replace all smoke detectors that are working or not working.
      (b)    Inform the buyer of the manufacturer of the smoke detectors.
      (c)    Deliver to the buyer a written disclosure that indicates that the property is in compliance with current law concerning smoke detectors.
      (d)    Provide the buyer with a history of smoke detector performance.

5.    The new law regarding water heaters requires an owner of any real property containing a water heater to brace, anchor, or strap the water heater to resist falling due to:

      (a)    Flood.              (c)    Earthquake.
      (b)    Toxic waste spill.   (d)    Explosion.

6.      The new law regarding water heaters is applicable to:

        (a)     New water heaters.
        (b)     Replacement water heaters.
        (c)     Existing water heaters.
        (d)     All of the above.

7.      In addition to requiring water heaters to be properly anchored, the new law requires the seller to:

        (a)     Certify to a prospective buyer that the new law has been complied with.
        (b)     Replace the water heater if it is not properly anchored.
        (c)     Supply the buyer with an inspection receipt from a certified property inspector.
        (d)     Contact the Seismic Safety Commission on behalf of the buyer.

8.      Which of the following was passed to address the potential consequences of building on land located near earthquake faults?

        (a)     Seismic Safety Act.
        (b)     Alquist-Priolo Special Studies Zones Act.
        (c)     Tectonic Movement Disclosure Act.
        (d)     California Fault Zone Disclosure Act.

9.      Under current earthquake disclosure requirements, the seller must disclose:

        (a)     Earthquake damage that may occur in the future.
        (b)     Earthquake damage that has been repaired when attempting to sell the property.
        (c)     Earthquake damage that has NOT been repaired when attempting to sell the property.
        (d)     Earthquake damage that has occurred in the general neighborhood to similar properties.

10.     Sellers of homes built before 1960 must deliver to the buyer "as soon as practicable before the transfer," a copy of *The Homeowner's Guide to Earthquake Safety* and disclose certain:

        (a)     Toxic waste problems.
        (b)     Defects in the chain of title.
        (c)     Earthquake deficiencies.
        (d)     Flood hazard risks.

## Chapter Four

### Important Terms

closing costs
fee simple
good faith estimates
ground lease
kickback
life estate
note option
promissory note
RESPA

### Learning Objectives

Upon completion of Chapter Four, you should be able to complete the following:

- Describe the disclosure requirements under RESPA.

- Define *good faith estimates*.

- Define *kickback*.

- Describe the disclosure requirements of a Mortgage Loan Broker.

- Describe seller carry-back financing disclosure requirements.

- Define *Mello-Roos lien*.

- Describe the requirement to disclose former ordnance locations.

- Describe the state's special flood hazard area disclosure.

## Truth-in-Lending (Regulation Z)

The Truth-in-Lending Act (the Act) became effective July 1, 1969. The principal purpose of the Act is to strengthen competition among financial institutions and other firms engaged in the extension of consumer credit by making consumers aware of the costs of credit. To accomplish this goal, the Act regulates "creditors" by requiring them to make disclosures concerning the cost of credit they are extending and to regulate the various types of advertising they may use. This will hopefully prevent the average consumer from being misled as to the costs of financing. To implement the Act, the Board of Governors of the Federal Reserve System issued a regulation known as *Regulation Z*.

Since there are as many as 18 disclosures required by Regulation Z, the subsequent discussion is not intended to cover all areas in which the Act applies, but only to briefly cover certain provisions of the Act and to outline the major areas where it is most commonly applicable in the field of real estate.

## Application of the Regulations

The Truth-in-Lending Act applies to an individual or business that offers credit under the following circumstances:

1) The credit is offered or extended to consumers,

2) The offering or extension of credit is done regularly,

3) The credit is subject to a finance charge or is payable by a written agreement in more than four installments, and

4) The credit is for personal, family, or household purposes.

As far as real estate finance transactions are concerned, the Act applies to credit by a *creditor* in a residential mortgage transaction."

For purposes of the Act, a "residential mortgage transaction" is a transaction in which a mortgage, deed of trust, installment sales contract, or equivalent consensual security interest is created or retained against the consumer's dwelling to finance the acquisition or initial construction of the dwelling.

A *creditor* is a person who both (1) regularly extends consumer credit that is payable by agreement in more than four installments or for which the payment of a finance charge is, or may be, required. This also applies to consumer credit in connection with loans and sales of property or services; and (2) is the person to whom the debt is initially payable on the evidence of indebtedness, by agreement. Therefore, the Truth-in-Lending Act applies to all persons who are creditors. *Consumer credit* is defined to be the extension of credit "to a natural person" where "the money, property, or service which is the subject of the transaction is primarily for personal, family, household, or agricultural purposes." Therefore, the Act applies to a home equity loan.

Based on the above definition, a person who sells several parcels of property, such as a subdivider, is subject to the Act if the sales are financed by purchase-money notes received by the seller. Also, a real estate licensee who sells his or her own property on a regular basis more than five times in a calendar year, and who extends purchase-money credit to the buyers, is a *creditor* subject to the disclosure requirements.

## Arranger of Credit

In its definition of *creditor*, Regulation Z used to include "arranger of credit," which it defined as a person who initially arranged for the extension of credit by persons who did not meet the *creditor* definition. The Federal Reserve Board, in considering the necessity for a more specific description of the type of activity that would constitute "arranger of credit," inquired whether real estate brokers who arrange seller financing of homes should be considered "arrangers of credit." In 1982, Congress resolved the question by passing the *Garn-St. Germain Depository Institutions Act*, which amended the Truth-in-Lending law by deleting "arranger of credit" from the "creditor" definition, effective October 1, 1982. The effect of the Board's action is to release real estate brokers or other arrangers of credit from the responsibility for providing Truth-in-Lending disclosures, unless such persons otherwise come within the definition of *creditor*. Therefore, a mortgage loan broker who does not loan its own funds, but merely negotiates a loan between a homeowner and a lender, is relieved from having to comply with the Truth-in-Lending Act and Regulation Z.

In addition, the Act does not apply to a real estate licensee who prepares the deposit receipt and introduces a borrower to a lender in the usual transaction where the lender prepares its own loan documents and the licensee does not receive compensation as a result of the loan. In addition, a broker who arranges for the seller of residential property to carry back a note secured by a second deed of trust need not comply with the Act, since the seller is not a *creditor* unless he or she has made several such sales with consumer purchase-money financing. There is also no regulation imposed on the broker who arranges for the seller to carry back a note from the buyer secured by a second deed of trust on his or her personal residence and also concurrently arranges for the discounting of the note to a third party immediately upon the close of escrow. The casual seller is not a creditor in carrying back the note and thus the first transaction is exempt. The second transaction is exempt if the lender is not a *creditor* under the Act within the Act's definitions.

## Exempt Transactions

There are two basic types of transactions that are exempt from coverage under Regulation Z.

1) **Credit extended primarily for a business, commercial, or agricultural purpose.** If property is not, or is not intended to be, owner-occupied, and the creditor extends credit to acquire, improve, or maintain a rental property, regardless of the number of family units, the transaction will be considered to occur for a business.

2) **Credit over $25,000.** This dollar limitation does not apply if the loan is secured by real property, or by personal property that is used or expected to be used as the consumer's principal dwelling.

Since the Act only applies to the loan made to a natural person, it does not apply to an extension of credit to organizations or governments.

Special rules apply for the approval of credit to acquire, improve, or maintain rental property that is, or will be, owner-occupied within a year. If the property contains more than two family units and the purpose of the credit is to acquire the property, the credit is deemed to be for a business purpose. However, if the credit is extended to improve or maintain the property, it is deemed to be for a business purpose if it contains more than four housing units.

### Disclosure Requirements

Since the primary goal of the Truth-in-Lending Act is to provide consumers with information concerning the cost of credit, the main thrust of the Act is directed at requiring complete disclosure of all significant costs of the financing.

When the transaction is within the provisions of the Act, the creditor must disclose in a clear, conspicuous, and meaningful sequence the following items:

1) The amount to be financed.
2) The amount of the finance charge.
3) The annual percentage rate.
4) The method of calculating finance charges and the balance upon which a finance charge will be imposed.
5) The total payments.
6) The number and amount of payments.
7) The due dates or schedule of payments.

The disclosure statement must have simple descriptive phrases next to the most important items disclosed. Regulation Z provides suggested phrases for the required items. These phrases are not required to be used verbatim. The following is a summary of the required disclosures:

**Amount Financed.** Regulation Z requires the use of the term *amount financed* together with a brief description of the term. The suggested phrase is, "the amount of credit provided to you or on your behalf."

## Finance Charge

Regulation Z requires the use of the term *finance charge* together with a brief description such as "the dollar amount the credit will cost you." The finance charge must include any charge payable directly or indirectly by the consumer and imposed directly or indirectly by the creditor as an incident to, or a condition of, the extension of credit. Regulation Z provides examples of charges that must be included in the finance charge and examples of charges that are excluded from the finance charge. Charges of particular importance in real estate and residential mortgage transactions that Regulation Z lists among those charges included in the finance charge are the following:

1) Interest.

2) Loan fees, assumption fees, finder's fees, and buyer's points.

3) Investigation and credit report fees.

4) Premiums for mortgage-guaranty or similar insurance.

Charges that are not finance charges include seller's points, and the following fees, when occurring in a transaction secured by real property or in a residential mortgage transaction:

1) Fees for title examination, abstract of title, title insurance property survey, and similar purposes.

2) Fees for preparing deeds, mortgages, reconveyance, settlement, and similar documents.

3) Notary and appraisal fees.

4) Amounts required to be paid into escrow or trustee accounts if the amounts would not otherwise be included in the finance charge.

In addition to disclosing the amount of the finance charge, the method of calculating finance charge and the balance upon which a finance charge will be calculated must be included.

## Annual Percentage Rate

The disclosure of the *annual percentage rate* requires the use of that particular term together with a brief description such as "the cost of your credit as a yearly rate." The APR is complex and involves the use of actuarial tables, which are available from the Federal Reserve System and its member banks. The APR is usually different than the contract or nominal interest rate of interest and includes the impact on the effective rate from discount points and other finance charges.

## Total of Payments

Regulation Z requires the creditor to use the term *total of payments* as well as a brief description, such as "the amount you will have paid when you have made all scheduled payments." The total of payments (which is the sum of the payments disclosed in the payment schedule) must be disclosed for all real estate transactions under revised Regulation Z.

## The Number and Amount of Payments

The creditor must disclose the number, amounts, and timing of payments scheduled to repay the obligation including due dates. Regulation Z provides for an abbreviated disclosure of payment schedule for transactions in which a series of payments vary solely because of the application of a finance charge to the unpaid principal balance. This situation arises most frequently in graduated payment mortgages or in mortgages where mortgage insurance premiums are based on the unpaid principal balance. In these transactions, creditors need to disclose only the amount of the largest and smallest payments in the series and that the other payments may vary.

When the loan provides for a variable interest rate, the maximum permissible rate must be disclosed. The required disclosures must be made before consummation of the transaction, but may be made in escrow at the time of closing, and must be made in Spanish if the transaction was negotiated in Spanish.

**CC § 1632:** When a loan transaction is negotiated in Spanish by a real estate broker, bank, savings and loan association, or credit union, or any subsidiary or affiliate, the lender must provide a written translation of the required disclosures in Spanish before the borrower signs any document, unless the loan terms were negotiated through the borrower's interpreter. A failure to comply with this requirement is grounds for rescission of the transaction by the borrower.

## Form of Disclosure

Regulation Z requires all Truth-in-Lending disclosures that concern the credit sale or loan to be grouped together and segregated from other information. The Regulation prohibits the assumptions inclusion of any information not directly related to the disclosures required by Regulation Z. It also provides that any itemization of the amount financed be made separately from the other required disclosures. In addition, Regulation Z requires that the terms *finance charge* and *annual percentage rate* shall be more conspicuous than other required disclosures. In one case, a bank printed these words in boldface type, but it also printed several other headings and disclosures in the same type, so that one line of bolded type was not more conspicuous than the other. The court held that the lender had violated the Act, and the violation was more than technical, which entitled the borrowers to recover the statutory damages.

The disclosures may be segregated by putting them on a separate sheet of paper, or if the disclosures are on a contract or other document they may be set off from other information by outlining them in a box or by printing them in a different style, with bold-print dividing lines, or with a different color background. The portion of the sale or loan document that contains these disclosures is commonly called *the federal box*. Regulation Z contains several model forms, including forms that contain disclosures required for transactions that involve loan assumptions, variable rate mortgages, and graduated payment mortgages. Lenders may duplicate these forms or modify them by including disclosures that are required for particular transactions.

## Time of Disclosure

Regulation Z requires disclosures to be made before consummation of the credit transaction, which is usually the time of closing. *Consummation* is defined as the time that a consumer becomes contractually liable on a credit obligation as determined by law. In some situations, special variable rate and other disclosures (discussed below) must be provided at an earlier point in time.

Creditors, as a whole, have been encouraged through liberalized provision on estimates, in revised Regulation Z, to use early disclosures in order to enable consumers to have ample time to shop for credit. However, creditors involved in residential mortgage transactions subject to the Real Estate Settlement Procedures Act (RESPA) are required to make Regulation Z disclosures before consummation, or deliver or place them in the mail within three business days after receiving the consumer's written application, whichever is earlier. If the estimates turn out to be inaccurate, it may be necessary to make another disclosure at consummation.

With certain types of variable-rate transactions, earlier disclosure must be made. If the annual percentage rate may increase after consummation in a transaction secured by the consumer's principal dwelling with a term greater than one year, the following disclosures must be provided at the time an application form is provided or before the consumer pays a nonrefundable fee, whichever is earlier:

1)  The booklet titled Consumer Handbook on Adjustable Rate Mortgages published by the Federal Home Loan Bank Board, or a suitable substitute.

2)  A loan program disclosure for each variable-rate program in which the consumer expresses an interest.

## *Redisclosure*

In general, an event that occurs after delivery of the disclosures to the consumer, which renders the disclosures inaccurate, does not result in a violation of Regulation Z and does not require redisclosure. However, if disclosures are given before the date of consummation and a subsequent event makes them inaccurate prior to consummation, redisclosure is required before consummation, if the actual annual percentage rate is above or below the disclosed rate by more than 1/8 of 1 percent in a regular transaction, or more than 1/4 of 1 percent in an irregular transaction. Irregular transactions include multiple advances, irregular payment periods (other than an odd first period), or irregular payment amounts (other than an odd first or final payment).

If redisclosure is required, the creditor has the option of providing the consumer with either a complete set of new disclosures or a disclosure of only the terms that vary from those originally disclosed.

*Refinancing*

Revised Regulation Z states that a *refinancing* is a new transaction that requires new disclosures to the consumer, and that a refinancing occurs when an existing obligation is satisfied and replaced by a new one that is undertaken by the same consumer. In addition, the regulation sets forth examples of what does not constitute a refinancing, which include the following, among others: (1) a renewal of a single payment obligation with no change in the original terms, (2) a reduction in the annual percentage rate with a corresponding change in the payment schedule, and (3) a change in the payment schedule or a change in collateral requirements as a result of the consumer's default or delinquency.

*Assumption*

Revised Regulation Z states that an *assumption* is a new transaction that requires new disclosures to the consumer, and that an assumption occurs when a new party becomes obligated on an existing obligation. Whenever a creditor agrees in writing to accept a new consumer as a primary obligor on an existing residential mortgage transaction before the assumption occurs, the creditor must make new disclosures to the new obligor based on the remaining obligation. The mere addition of a guarantor to an obligation for which the original consumer remains primarily liable does not constitute an assumption.

*Variable-Rate Adjustments*

Certain new disclosures are required when an adjustment is made to the interest rate (with or without an accompanying change in the payment rate) in a variable rate transaction that is secured by the consumer's principal dwelling and with a term greater than one year. The creditor must provide the following information at least once each year during which an interest rate adjustment is implemented without an accompanying payment charge:

1) The current and prior interest rates.

2) The index values on which the current and prior interest rates are based.

3) The extent to which the creditor has foregone any interest rate increase.

4) The contractual effects of the adjustment, including the new payment amount and the loan balance.

5) The payment (if different from the payment disclosed above) that would be required to fully amortize the loan at the new interest rate over the remaining loan term.

**Consumer's Right to Rescind Under Truth-in-Lending/Regulation Z**

The right of rescission applies to most consumer credit transactions where the obligation is secured by a lien against the consumer's principal dwelling (there are a number of important exemptions). A consumer can have only one *principal dwelling* at a time. Since the definition of a dwelling is not limited to real property, transactions that involve mobile homes can be rescindable even if they are treated as personal property under state law.

## Notice of Right to Rescind

The creditor must provide each consumer who is entitled to rescind (any consumer with an *ownership interest* in the principal dwelling subject to the security interest) with two copies of the notice of the right to rescind. Creditors are not required to use any specific language when making rescission disclosures. Regulation Z contains a model rescission form that meets the requirements.

## Rescission Period

The consumer has the right to rescind until midnight of the third business day following the last of these events to occur: (1) consummation of the transaction, (2) delivery of all material Truth-in-Lending disclosures; or (3) delivery of the notice of the right to rescind. A business day is any calendar day, except Sundays and federal legal holidays. The creditor is required to give the borrower two copies of a written notice of his or her right to rescind, with a notice that explains how to exercise the right of rescission and that includes a form that the borrower can use if he or she decides to rescind.

If the creditor fails to make any material disclosure in a transaction in which a security interest is retained in the consumer's residence, or when the creditor in such a transaction attempts to circumvent the mandatory three-day rescission period, the consumer's right of rescission under the Act does not lapse until the residence is sold or three years have elapsed from the date the transaction was consummated, whichever is earlier.

In one case, a homeowner sought to make improvements to her home. The contractors presented a contract and disclosure statement to her that included a provision that the contractor would receive a deed of trust on the home to secure payment for the costs of goods and services. The contractor presented her a rescission form as required with the proper contents, but the date of the third business day after the contract was to be executed was omitted. He also gave her a blank-form deed of trust. The court held that the homeowner could rescind even though the three-day period had expired because (1) a failure to state the last day for cancellation was a material omission, and (2) the blank-form trust deed, without a property description, was a material omission because the owner testified that she did not understand that a second lien was being placed on her home. The owner was awarded the maximum statutory damages.

## Waiver of Right to Rescind

Regulation Z provides that the consumer may waive the right to rescind if the consumer determines that the extension of credit is needed to meet a bona fide personal financial emergency. To waive the right, the consumer must give the creditor a dated written statement that describes the emergency and specifically waives the right to rescind. The use of preprinted waiver forms is prohibited by the

Regulation. Prior to its revision the Regulation provided that the right to rescind could not be waived unless the consumer's welfare, health, safety, or property was jeopardized. By changing the strictness of this test, revised Regulation Z allows consumers prompt access to their money in emergency situations.

## Rescission Right Exemptions

There are a number of important exemptions applicable to residential real estate transactions. One of these exemptions concerns *residential mortgage transactions*. Under this exemption, the right of rescission does not apply to transactions made to finance acquisition or initial construction of the consumer's principal dwelling, which is secured by that dwelling, regardless of lien status. In other words, mortgages for the purpose of financing an acquisition are no longer subject to the right of rescission.

Another exemption is for a refinancing by the same creditor of a loan already secured by the principal dwelling, provided that no new money is advanced. If new money is advanced, the transaction is rescindable to the extent of the new money if the loan is secured by the consumer's principal dwelling. This exemption is most likely to arise in connection with renewals, extensions, or while refinancing balloon notes.

Since rescission rights only apply to transactions in which the secured property is currently used as the consumer's principal dwelling, Regulation Z has also exempted property that is expected to be used for something other than a principal dwelling, such as a vacant lot, vacation home, or retirement home.

## The Real Estate Settlement Procedures Act (RESPA)

### Introduction

The Federal *Real Estate Settlement Procedures Act* of 1974 (RESPA), as amended by the Real Estate Settlement Procedures Act Amendments of 1975, became law on June 30, 1976. The Act sets forth special disclosure requirements for nonexempt lenders who provide loan funds in transactions that involve the sale or transfer of one-to-four unit dwellings. The Act does not set limits on the charges lenders can levy while closing a loan; however, it does require specific procedures and forms for settlements (closing costs) that involve most home mortgage loans, including FHAs, VAs, and loans from financial institutions with federally-insured deposits. Most of the requirements are the responsibility of the lender. However, some of them directly affect the real estate licensee, title insurance companies and their agents, attorneys, and any other parties that are involved in providing settlement services.

The purposes of the Real Estate Settlement Procedures Act (RESPA) are to ensure that purchasers and sellers of residential real estate are provided with better and more timely information on the nature and costs of the settlement process, and to protect the purchaser from unnecessarily high settlement charges.

To accomplish these objectives, the Act requires advanced disclosure of settlement costs, the elimination of kickbacks or referral fees, and reduction of the amounts that buyers are required to place in escrow accounts for taxes and insurance. The Act also provides for a reform of land title record procedures, but it does not make any changes in California in this regard.

## Applicability

RESPA is applicable to the sale of residential real estate that is financed by a *federally related mortgage loan*. For the purposes of the Act, *residential real estate* is residential property for occupancy of one to four families and includes individual units in a condominium or cooperative development. Federally related mortgage loans are those that meet the following requirements:

1) The proceeds of the loan are used in whole or in part to finance the purchase by the borrower, or other transfer of legal title of the mortgaged property. Execution of an instrument that creates a security interest is not considered a transfer of legal title for purposes of this part;

2) The loan is secured by a first-lien or other first-security interest that covers real estate, including a fee simple, life estate, remainder interest, ground lease, or other long-term leasehold estate upon which the following apply:

   i) There is a structure that is designed principally for the occupancy of from one to four families, or

   ii) There is a mobile home, or

   iii) A structure designed principally for the occupancy of from one to four families is to be constructed that uses proceeds of the loan, or

   iv) There will be a mobile home purchased that uses proceeds of the loan, or

   v) A condominium unit (or a first lien covering a cooperative unit) is designed principally for the occupancy of one to four families;

3) The loan is made, insured, guaranteed, supplemented, or assisted by any federal office or agency, or in connection with any housing or urban development administered by any federal office or agency, or

4) The loan is intended to be sold by the originating lender to the Federal National Mortgage Association (FNMA), the Government National Mortgage Association (GNMA), or the Federal Home Loan Mortgage Corporation (FHLMC), and

5) The loan is made by a person defined as a *creditor* in the Truth-in-Lending Act, other than a state instrumentality, that makes loans that aggregate more than one million dollars per year.

## Exemptions

RESPA does not apply to the following situations:

1) A loan to finance the purchase or transfer of a property of 25 or more acres;

2) A home improvement loan, loan to refinance, or other loan where the proceeds are not used to finance the purchase or transfer of legal title to the property;

3) A loan to finance the purchase or transfer of a vacant lot, where no proceeds of the loan are to be used for the construction of a one-to-four-family residential structure or for the purchase of a mobile home to be placed on the lot;

4) An assumption, novation, or sale or transfer subject to a preexisting loan, except the use of or conversion of a construction loan to a permanent mortgage loan to finance the purchase by the first user;

5) A construction loan, except where the construction loan is used as or converted to a permanent loan to finance the purchase by the first user;

6) A permanent loan, the proceeds of which will be used to finance the construction of a one-to-four-family structure, where the lot is already owned by the borrower or borrowers;

7) A loan to finance the purchase of a property where the primary purpose of the purchase is for resale, or

8) Execution of a land sales contract or installment land contract where the legal title is not transferred to the purchaser upon execution. However, a loan to finance the acquisition of title pursuant to a land sales contract is a Federally Related Mortgage Loan.

**Special Information Booklet**

To accomplish the purpose of providing better and more timely information on the nature and costs of the settlement process, the Secretary of Housing and Urban Development (HUD) is required to prepare a Special Information Booklet that explains the nature and purpose of an escrow and each settlement cost, the choices available for the selection of persons who provide services incident to a settlement, and unfair practices and unreasonable charges to be avoided.

The lender must furnish a copy of the Special Information Booklet together with a Good Faith Estimate of the amount or range of closing costs to every person from whom the lender receives, or for whom it prepares a written application, an application form, or forms normally used by the lender for a federally related mortgage loan.

Where more than one person applies for a loan, the lender is in compliance with this requirement if the lender supplies a copy of the Special Information Booklet to one of the individuals applying. The lender must supply the Special Information Booklet by delivering it or placing it in the mail to the applicant on the day the application is received, or no later than three business days after the application is received.

## Lending Requirements under RESPA/Regulation X

The U.S. Department of Housing and Urban Development (HUD) has made significant revisions to the lending requirements under RESPA/Regulation X. These changes impact the Good Faith Estimate (GFE) and HUD Settlement Statements (HUD-1 and HUD-1A) and became effective with new first mortgage applications taken on or after January 1, 2010. These important regulatory changes will place new requirements on lenders to ensure that borrowers are better positioned to understand their mortgage transaction. The following is an overview of the four key changes associated with the new Regulation X requirements.

## Good Faith Estimate (GFE) and HUD Settlement Statement (HUD-1) Forms

Substantially redesigned, the GFE and HUD-1 forms will standardize how fees are disclosed, which makes it easier for borrowers to compare offers between lenders. The GFE and HUD-1 will also be aligned to provide even greater transparency for borrowers when comparing settlement charges at closing. Specific enhancements now require all lenders to disclose fees in the same manner. Loan feature information has been added to the forms so all lender fees will be combined and shown as a single amount. Lastly, a reconciliation of the GFE to the HUD-1 is now required.

For a full analysis of the new lending requirements under RESPA, visit the following web address:

*http://www.hud.gov/offices/hsg/ramh/res/respa_hm.cfm*

## One-Day Advance Inspection of Uniform Settlement Statement

Upon the request of the borrower, the person conducting the settlements must permit the borrower to inspect the Uniform Settlement Statement, completed to set forth those items that are known to such person at the time of inspection, during the business day immediately preceding the Date of Settlement.

The Uniform Settlement Statement must be delivered or mailed to the borrower and the seller, or their agents, at or before settlement, with the following exceptions:

1) The borrower may waive the right to the delivery of the completed Uniform Settlement Statement no later than at settlement by executing a written waiver at or before settlement. In such a case, the completed Uniform Settlement Statement shall be mailed or delivered to the borrower and seller as soon as practicable after settlement.

2) Where the borrower or the borrower's agent does not attend the settlement or where the person conducting the settlement does not require a meeting of the parties for that purpose, the transaction shall be exempt from the requirements of the above paragraph, except that the Uniform Settlement Statement shall be delivered as soon as practicable after settlement.

## Mailing

Mailing of settlement statements or other documents is deemed satisfied by placing the document in the mail (whether or not received by the addressee). The settlement statement should be addressed to the addresses stated in the loan application, or in other information submitted to or obtained by the lender at the time of submitting the loan application, or submitted to or obtained by the lender or person conducting the settlement. A revised address must be used where the lender or such other person has been expressly informed in writing of a change of address.

## *No Fee*

As provided in RESPA, no fee shall be imposed or charge made upon any other person, as a part of settlement costs or otherwise, by a lender in connection with, or on account of the preparation and distribution of the statement required by RESPA.

## Prohibition against Kickbacks and Unearned Fees

No person may give nor accept any fee, kickback, or thing of value pursuant to any agreement or understanding, oral or otherwise.

**Kickback:** Payment made to someone for referral of a customer or business. Unlike a commission, a kickback is made without the customer's knowledge; thus, the referral could have been made without the customer's best interest at heart. As stated above, secret kickbacks to a lender from a provider of a settlement service are specifically prohibited by RESPA.

No person may give, and no person may accept any portion, split, or percentage of any charge made or received for the rendering of a real estate settlement service in connection with a transaction that involves a federally related mortgage loan other than for services actually performed. Nothing in RESPA prohibits the payment of fees to an attorney, title company, or lender agent for services actually performed, nor do they prohibit a cooperative brokerage and referral agreement between real estate brokers.

The prohibitions in RESPA apply to any type of consideration in the form of money, services, share of profits, credits, special terms, special rates, etc. These types of payments are specifically prohibited even if there is an express or implied agreement, or a custom or practice. In addition, any prohibited payment is a violation of RESPA even though it does not result in an increase in the charge for the settlement service.

RESPA does not prohibit normal promotional and educational activities that are not conditioned on the referral of business, such as free receptions, seminars, or reports of record owners.

Thus, for example, a title company cannot rebate a portion of its insurance premium to a person who merely places an application with the company and the company does not perform services, and it cannot give any discount to a broker, attorney, or lender as a rebate for the placement of business. While a real estate broker can share his or her commission or pay a referral fee to another real estate broker, he or she cannot pay any consideration to an unlicensed finder even though such payment may be legal under state law. Since the *kickback* is prohibited even though it does not result in an increase of the cost of settlement services, a referral fee or rebate of a portion of the broker's commission to the buyer, without the knowledge of the seller, would also be prohibited. Additionally, a seller cannot require that title insurance be purchased from a specific title company as a condition of the purchase of the property.

### Limitations on Escrow Deposits

A lender within the provisions of RESPA cannot require a borrower to make an escrow deposit for the payment of taxes, insurance premiums, or other charges in excess of a sum sufficient to pay such costs for a one-month period, plus one-sixth of the amount thereof which will be incurred during the next 12-month period. Thereafter, the lender cannot require the payment of more than one-twelfth of the reasonably anticipated annual amount of such charges.

### Penalties for Violations of RESPA

Any action to recover damages under the provisions of RESPA must be brought in the District Court where the property is located, within one year of the violation.

Any person who violates RESPA by paying illegal kickbacks or unearned fees can be fined up to $10,000 and/or imprisoned for not more than one year. The person in violation may also be civilly liable to the person referred for a penalty of three times the amount of the fee paid, plus costs and attorney's fees.

If a seller requires a borrower to use a specific title company, he or she is liable to the borrower for damages equal to three times the amount of all title insurance premiums paid.

### Mortgage Loan Disclosure Statement

The Business and Professions Code describes a Mortgage Loan Broker as a person who solicits borrowers or lenders, or who negotiates for loans secured directly or collaterally by liens on real property or a business opportunity, or who performs services for borrowers or lenders in relation to such secured obligations, for others for compensation.

A person who acts as a Mortgage Loan Broker, as defined above, must be licensed as a real estate broker. Thus, a person with a salesperson license who acts in this capacity must have their license hung with a licensed real estate broker and receive compensation through that broker only. Every licensee who negotiates a loan for which a license is required, and for compensation, which is secured directly or collaterally by a lien on real property, regardless of the size of the loan, must deliver a written disclosure statement to the borrower within three business days of receipt of the borrower's written loan application, or before the borrower becomes obligated to the loan, whichever is earlier. This is true whether the loan is being processed manually or electronically.

This required statement, known as the Mortgage Loan Disclosure Statement (MLDS), must be included in a form that is approved by the Real Estate Commissioner and shall contain the following:

1) The estimated maximum expenses of making the loan to be paid by the borrower, such as appraisal, escrow, notary, recording and credit report fees, and title charges.

2) The total commission to be received by the broker who acts as an agent for the broker's services, or the total amount to be received for loan fees and other charges if the broker is the lender.

3) Any liens against the real property that will remain after the loan is made and their approximate amounts, and any liens that will be placed on the property after the loan is made, and whether any such liens will be senior or junior to the lien of the lender.

4) The estimated amounts to be paid by the borrower for fire insurance premiums, prior liens, and assumption fees.

5) The estimated balance of the loan funds to be delivered to the borrower after paying all the above amounts.

6) The principal, interest, and term of the loan, the amount and number of installments, the approximate balance due on maturity, and the following notice in 10-point bold typeface:

   **NOTICE TO BORROWER: IF YOU DO NOT HAVE THE FUNDS TO PAY THE BALLOON PAYMENT WHEN IT COMES DUE, YOU MAY HAVE TO OBTAIN A NEW LOAN AGAINST YOUR PROPERTY TO MAKE THE BALLOON PAYMENT. IN THAT CASE, YOU MAY AGAIN HAVE TO PAY COMMISSIONS, FEES, AND EXPENSES FOR THE ARRANGING OF THE NEW LOAN. IN ADDITION, IF YOU ARE UNABLE TO MAKE THE MONTHLY PAYMENTS OR THE BALLOON PAYMENT, YOU MAY LOSE THE PROPERTY AND ALL OF YOUR EQUITY THROUGH FORECLOSURE. KEEP THIS IN MIND IN DECIDING UPON THE AMOUNT AND TERMS OF THIS LOAN.**

7) The broker's name, business address, and license number.

8) A disclosure that the loan may be from broker-controlled funds, if this is the case.

9) The terms of any prepayment privileges and penalties.

10) A statement that credit or credit disability insurance is not required as a condition to the loan.

11) If the loan is within the provisions of the Mortgage Loan Brokers Act, a certification that the loan complies with the provisions of the Act. The statement must be personally signed by the borrower and by the real estate broker who are negotiating the loan or by the real estate licensee who is acting for the broker in negotiating the loan. The statement must be delivered to the borrower, and the broker must retain his or her copy for four years.

## Seller Carry-Back Financing Disclosures

### Introduction

There are specific additional duties imposed upon the licensee who negotiates a sale of real property when the seller receives a portion of the sales price in the form of a promissory note secured by the real property purchased.

In a transaction for the purchase of a dwelling for not more than four families where the purchase includes an extension of credit by the seller, and where the licensee is acting as an *arranger of credit*, a written disclosure must be made.

**Arranger of Credit:** An *arranger of credit* is any person other than a party to the transaction, who develops or negotiates credit terms or participates in the completion of the credit documents and receives compensation directly or indirectly for the arrangement of credit or the transfer of the real property facilitated by the credit.

Thus, the statute applies to a real estate broker who is acting as an agent for the sale of the property, which is the security for the note. A broker is also considered an arranger of credit when he or she is a principal in the transaction, and if neither party is represented by an agent. If an agent represents one of the parties, the licensee-principal is not subject to the statute.

An attorney who is only representing one of the parties to the transaction is not subject to the statute. When the attorney is a party to the transaction as a principal, he or she is not subject to the statute when an agent represents one of the parties. However, if an agent represents neither party to the transaction, an attorney who is a principal in the transaction is considered an "arranger of credit."

An arranger of credit does not include a person who acts in the capacity of an escrow in the transaction. However, if a broker or attorney is acting as an escrow agent in the transaction, he or she is considered an arranger of credit when acting on behalf of a party to the transaction by developing or negotiating credit terms. Neither the completion of credit documents in accordance with instructions of a party or his or her agent, nor the furnishing of information regarding credit terms to a party or his or her agent, is considered to be the development or negotiation of credit terms.

### Transactions Exempt from Disclosure Requirements of This Article

A disclosure statement must be given to the buyer in every applicable transaction by the arranger of credit. However, the disclosure need not be to the buyer when he or she is entitled to receive a Truth-in-Lending disclosure statement, or a disclosure under the Real Estate Settlement Procedure Act, or a disclosure that is required by the Mortgage Loan Brokers Act.

## Multiple Arrangers

If there is more than one arranger of credit and one of those arrangers has obtained the offer by the purchaser to purchase the property, that arranger shall make the disclosure, unless the parties designate another person in writing.

## Timing of Disclosure

The required disclosure must be made as soon as practicable, but before execution of any note or security documents. If any disclosure is made after the execution of credit documents by the purchaser, such documents shall be contingent on the purchaser's approval of the disclosures prior to execution of the security documents.

The disclosure must be signed by the arranger of credit, and the buyer and seller must sign a receipt. The arranger must retain a copy of the executed document for three years.

## Results of Non-Disclosure or Inaccurate Disclosure

Even if the required disclosure statement is not given as required, the credit document (note, deed of trust, contract of sale, or lease option) is still valid and enforceable, but the person who failed to give the notice will be liable for the actual damages suffered by the buyer or seller as the result of the omission. Even if the disclosure is not given at all, the violator will not be liable if the violation was not intentional and resulted from a bona fide error.

If any provision in the disclosure statement becomes inaccurate as a result of a subsequent event, it does not constitute a violation of this statute. Also, if any of the required information is not known or is not available at the time of the disclosure, and the arranger of credit has made a reasonable effort to obtain the information, the disclosure may refer to an approximation of the information, as long as it is reasonable, is identified as such, is based upon the best information available to the arranger, and is not given for the purpose of avoiding the statutory requirements.

## Statute of Limitations

An action rising from a violation of this article may be brought within two years from the date on which the liability arises, except that where any material disclosure under this article has been materially and willfully misrepresented, the action may be brought within two years of discovery of the misrepresentation.

## Other Miscellaneous Disclosures

## Toxic Mold Disclosure

Molds are microscopic organisms that nature uses to break down dead material and recycle nutrients back into the environment. Molds require a food source to grow and reproduce best in moist areas. As they digest organic material, they slowly destroy whatever they grow on. Molds can be identified by the presence of some sort of discoloration in a variety of different colors.

### *How Are We Exposed to Molds?*

The most common type of mold exposure is through airborne ingestion of microscopic mold spores released into the air as molds digest the organic compounds they grow on. Significant health problems usually only arise when a large number of spores are inhaled. Exposure can also occur by touching contaminated materials or surfaces or by eating contaminated food.

People vary in their sensitivity and reaction to mold exposure. Some people may react to a very small number of mold spores while others may be relatively non-allergic to mold particles. Allergic reactions (sometimes mistaken for hay fever) are the most common symptoms seen with mold exposure. These may include (alone or in combination) the following:

- Wheezing, difficulty breathing, and shortness of breath.
- Nasal and sinus congestion.
- Eye irritation (burning, watery, or reddened eyes).
- Dry, hacking cough.
- Nose or throat irritation.
- Skin rashes or irritation.

### *Toxic Mold Disclosure Requirements*

To address recent public concerns about toxic mold, the legislature in 2001 passed into law *The Toxic Mold Protection Act* (SB 732). This act is intended to study and measure permissible exposure limits of toxic mold and to establish new disclosure obligations for sellers and landlords that concern the presence of toxic mold.

A portion of the Toxic Mold Protection Act called for the creation of a taskforce to work with the California Department of Health Services (DHS) to develop permissible exposure limits for molds, adopt practical standards to assess the health threat posed by the presence of mold, adopt mold identification guidelines for the recognition of mold, and develop and disseminate remediation guidelines for molds.

Once these standards have been set by the DHS, sellers, transferors, and landlords of commercial and industrial property—but not sellers or transferors of residential property—are required to provide written disclosure of the mold conditions to potential buyers and prospective tenants, renters, landlords, or occupants.

With single-family residential properties, the Toxic Mold Protection Act changes the Transfer Disclosure Statement (TDS) to add mold to the list of natural hazards in the Sellers information, item II.C.1. In addition, there will be a new section in the Environmental Hazards Disclosure Booklet on mold. If this booklet is delivered to a transferee in connection with the transfer of real property, neither the seller nor broker is required to provide additional information that concerns the environmental hazards described in the booklet.

Licensees should note that there is no requirement imposed upon the seller, transferor, or landlord of commercial or industrial properties to conduct air or surface tests for the presence of molds. However, once a landlord is informed that mold is present in the building, heating system, ventilating system, air-conditioning system, or appurtenant structures, landlords must test for the presence of mold and take the appropriate action to eradicate the problem.

The Act also protects transferors, as well as listing and selling agents, from liability for any error, inaccuracy, or omission based upon information provided by a public agency or a report prepared by a third party expert.

**Mello-Roos Disclosure**

Based on passage of the Mello-Roos Community Facilities Act of 1982, certain housing tracts may be within what are called *community facilities districts*, where special taxes are assessed to finance designated public facilities and/or services. Mello-Roos liens are usually municipal bonds issued to fund streets, sewers, and other infrastructure needs before a housing development is built. These special assessments are paid by the seller and will be assumed by the buyer.

The Mello-Roos Community Facilities Act has become a way for developers to help finance their projects. It has also been a way for a city or governmental district to avoid the property tax limitations of Proposition 13 by including the cost and maintenance of infrastructure items in the property tax bill, as a special tax that is allowed to go above the limits of Proposition 13.

Effective July 1, 1993, the seller of a property that consists of one-to-four dwelling units or a lease (for more than five years) subject to the lien of a Mello-Roos community facilities district must make a good-faith effort to obtain from the district a disclosure notice that concerns the special tax and give the notice to the prospective buyer. Failure to give notice before the signing of the sales contract permits the buyer or tenant a three-day right of rescission after receipt of the notice.

**Disclosure of Former Ordnance Locations (Civil Code Sec. 1102.15)**

It is now well known that certain military bases in California contain live ammunition for various reasons. A seller of residential property located within one mile of such a hazard must give the buyer written notice as soon as practicable before transfer of title. For purposes of this section, *former federal or state ordnance locations* are areas identified by an agency or instrumentality of the federal or state government as areas that were once used for military training purposes, and that may contain potentially explosive munitions. This obligation may depend upon the seller having actual knowledge of the hazard. Some transactions are exempt pursuant to Civil Code Section 1102.1.

**Special Flood Hazard Area Disclosure Requirements**
**(Title 42 U.S. Code §4104 and 4106)**

A *flood hazard area* is an area designated by the federal government that is subject to flooding. The Federal Emergency Management Agency (FEMA) and the National Flood Insurance Program (NFIP) identify property that is most at risk to flooding and mandate insurance coverage. If a property is designated as being in or partially in a Special Flood Hazard Area, that property has been designated to have a 1% or greater chance of being flooded in any given year with water that is one foot or deeper. If a home loan is being sought through a federally regulated lending institution and the property is in or partially in a Special Flood Hazard Area, flood insurance will be required by the lender as a condition for the loan. The Flood Hazard Boundary Map or a Flood Insurance Rate Map, which depicts flood hazard areas, may be obtained from FEMA for a fee.

A seller of real property is required to disclose that the property is located within a flood hazard area. The law does not require that a particular form be used. However, C.A.R. Standard Form GFD-14, the *Geologic, Seismic, and Flood Hazard Disclosure*, can be used to satisfy the disclosure requirement.

**Flood Insurance:** A transferor or seller of any *affected property*, as defined, is required to notify the buyer or transferee, no later than the date of transfer, in writing, that the buyer will be required: (1) to obtain flood insurance under federal law, if such property was not insured as of the date of the transfer, and (2) maintain the insurance. The written notification must be included in documents that show the transfer of ownership. *Affected property* means any personal, commercial, or residential property where federal disaster relief assistance in a designated flood disaster area has been provided for repair, replacement, or restoration of the property, before the date the property is transferred, if the assistance was conditioned upon obtaining flood insurance for the property. Effective September 23, 1994 (H.R. 3474, § 582 (P.L. 103-325). Added 42 USC § 5154a.

**Notice Regarding the Advisability of Title Insurance**

In an escrow transaction for the purchase or simultaneous exchange of real property, where a policy of title insurance will NOT be issued to the buyer or to the parties to the exchange, the following notice shall be provided in a separate document to the buyer or parties exchanging real property, which shall be signed and acknowledged by them:

**IMPORTANT: IN A PURCHASE OR EXCHANGE OF REAL PROPERTY, IT MAY BE ADVISABLE TO OBTAIN TITLE INSURANCE IN CONNECTION WITH THE CLOSE OF ESCROW SINCE THERE MAY BE PRIOR RECORDED LIENS AND ENCUMBRANCES WHICH AFFECT YOUR INTEREST IN THE PROPERTY BEING ACQUIRED. A NEW POLICY OF TITLE INSURANCE SHOULD BE OBTAINED IN ORDER TO ENSURE YOUR INTEREST IN THE PROPERTY THAT YOU ARE ACQUIRING.**

You may have noticed that this statute does not expressly assign this duty to a specific person. We feel it is reasonable to assume that delivery of the notice is the responsibility of the escrow holder. If the broker is acting as an escrow in the transaction, that broker would be responsible for delivery of the notice.

### Disclosure of Sale Price Information (B & P Code § 10141)

Within one month after the closing of a transaction in which title to real property or in the sale of a business when real or personal property is conveyed from a seller to a purchaser through a licensed real estate agent, such agent shall inform the buyer and seller in writing of the selling price. If the transaction involves an exchange of real property or if a business opportunity is involved, the information on the sales price must include a description of the property and amount of added money consideration, if any.

If the transaction is closed through escrow and the escrow holder renders a closing statement that reveals such information, that shall constitute compliance.

**QUIZZES ARE MANDATORY:** Please log in and submit the chapter quizzes online.

**Chapter Four Quiz**

1.      The Real Estate Settlement Procedures Act (RESPA) is applicable to the sale of:

   (a)      Commercial property that is financed by a conventional lender.
   (b)      Industrial property financed by a *federally related mortgage loan*.
   (c)      Residential real estate financed by a *federally related mortgage loan*.
   (d)      Agricultural land guaranteed by the Farmers Home Administration.

2.      RESPA does NOT apply to:

   (a)      A loan to finance the purchase property of 25 or more acres.
   (b)      A loan to finance the purchase of a vacant lot where none of that loan will be used for the construction of a home on the lot.
   (c)      A loan to refinance.
   (d)      All of the above.

3.      To accomplish the purpose of providing greater and more timely information on settlement costs, RESPA requires the lender to give the borrower a(n):

   (a)      Special Information Booklet and Good Faith Estimate.
   (b)      Finance Charge Disclosure Statement.
   (c)      Annual Percentage Rate (APR) Disclosure.
   (d)      All of the above are required under RESPA.

4.      In addition to requiring disclosure of settlement costs, RESPA also prohibits:

   (a)      Payment of fees to a title company for services actually performed.
   (b)      Accepting a "kickback" for referral of a customer or business.
   (c)      Offering free receptions and seminars.
   (d)      Offering free computerized reports of record owners.

5.      If a property is designated as being in or partially in a Special Flood Hazard Area, that property has been designated to have a _____ or greater chance of being flooded in any given year with water one foot or deeper.

   (a)      1 percent
   (b)      3 percent
   (c)      5 percent
   (d)      25 percent

6.    Under *seller carryback* disclosure requirements, if there is more than one "arranger of credit," who must make the disclosure?

    (a)    The arranger who has obtained the offer by the purchaser.
    (b)    The arranger who has secured the listing from the seller.
    (c)    The arranger who helped negotiate the credit terms.
    (d)    The arranger who participated in completion of the credit documents.

7.    When must the required *seller carryback* disclosure statement be made to the purchaser?

    (a)    As soon as practicable, but before close of escrow.
    (b)    As soon as practicable, but before execution of any note or security documents.
    (c)    As soon as practicable, but before the appraisal comes in.
    (d)    As soon as practicable, but prior to recording.

8.    If the required *seller carryback* disclosure statement is not given as prescribed by law, the credit document (note, deed of trust, contract of sale, etc.) is:

    (a)    Void and unenforceable.
    (b)    Valid and enforceable.
    (c)    Voidable by the purchaser at any time.
    (d)    Voidable by the purchaser within three days.

9.    Which of the following best describes a Mello-Roos community facilities district?

    (a)    Additional taxes assessed for the privilege of living in a *quiet zone*.
    (b)    Special assessments imposed on all new construction for energy retrofitting.
    (c)    A special tax imposed on certain properties that require environmental cleanup.
    (d)    Special taxes assessed to finance designated public facilities and/or services before a housing development is built.

10.    The seller of a property subject to the lien of a Mello-Roos community facilities district must:

    (a)    Pay off the lien in full prior to transferring the property.
    (b)    Make a good faith effort to obtain from the district a disclosure notice that concerns the special tax and give the notice to the prospective buyer.
    (c)    Contact the County Assessor's Office to have the lien removed before listing the property.
    (d)    None of the above.

# Real Estate
# Red Flags

6 Hours of Continuing Education for

Salesperson and Broker License Renewal

**Lumbleau Real Estate School**
23805 Hawthorne Blvd.
Torrance, CA 90505

**DISCLAIMERS**

Although every effort has been made to provide accurate and current information in this text, the ideas, suggestions, general principles, and conclusions presented in this text are subject to local, state and federal laws and regulations, court cases, and any revisions of the same. The author and/or publisher is not engaged in rendering legal, tax, or other professional services. The reader is thus urged to consult with his or her employing broker and/or seek legal counsel regarding any points of law. This publication should not be used as a substitute for competent legal advice.

This course is approved for continuing education credit by the California Bureau of Real Estate. However, this approval does not constitute an endorsement of the views or opinions that are expressed by the course sponsor, instructor, authors, or lecturers.

## Chapter One: Red Flag Defined and Disclosure

**Important Terms**

"as-is"
community facilities tax
Foreign Investment in Real Property Tax Act
Homeowner's Guide to Earthquake Safety
industrial property
liquefaction
material fact
ordnance
Real Estate Transfer Disclosure Statement
sex offender
special studies zone
waiver

**Learning Objectives**

Upon completion of Chapter One, you should be able to complete the following:

- Define the term *red flag*.

- Define the term *material fact*.

- Describe the various disclosure requirements in the TDS.

- Describe the statutory requirements for delivery of the TDS.

- Describe the basic facts of the *Easton v. Strassburger* case.

- Describe the agent's duty of disclosure.

- Describe required geologic and seismic hazards disclosure.

- Describe the minimum standards for smoke detectors.

- Describe the *Foreign Investment in Real Property Tax Act*.

## What Is a Red Flag?

A *red flag* is a physical factor about a property that, when a broker sees it, it triggers a red flag in his or her mind that says, "This is a potential material fact that may need to be investigated."

Although this course will not provide an all-inclusive list of potential red flags, our intent is to cover the most common examples of red flags. It is very important to understand that possible red flags can vary depending on the particular property being sold. The point is that licensees must be aware of the facts and circumstances unique to each property, follow their instincts, and point out potential red flags.

Knowing which red flags to look for in a house is one thing; knowing to what extent an agent or broker is responsible for defects in a home that he or she is selling is another question altogether. Even if the law in the agent's state only requires a minimum of responsible behavior, there is always a number of things that an agent can do to improve his or her relationship with the buyer, so that the buyer is more aware of the true condition of the property. If the agent goes beyond the minimum, the use of the home after possession by the buyer will run more smoothly, the buyer will more likely consider the agent to be more responsible, and, as a result, the buyer will return to the agent for any future home purchases. In this section, we will evaluate what the agent's responsibilities are regarding disclosure and what actions can be taken to better help the buyer's purchase, whether required or not.

### Disclosure of Material Facts

In California, the landmark case of *Easton vs. Strassburger* (1984) expanded the broker's duty of disclosure. The court held that a real estate broker has an affirmative duty to conduct a reasonably competent and diligent inspection of residential property and disclose to prospective purchasers all facts revealed by the investigation that materially affect the value or desirability of the property.

Because of the Easton decision, the seller must now provide the buyer with a written *Real Estate Transfer Disclosure Statement* that details the mechanical and structural conditions of the property in a form specified by the legislature. All real estate licensees should be familiar with this form so that they can ensure that the buyer is fully informed of the property's condition.

The real estate licensee's duty to disclose is specifically related to facts that are material, and that affect the value or desirability of the property. The misrepresentation of a single material fact may result in an accusation of intentional fraud in certain circumstances.

There is no absolute standard for determining whether or not a fact is material in a particular situation. A fact may or may not be material depending upon the circumstances of each transaction.

### Material Fact Defined

Generally, a matter is considered material if the other party would not have entered into the contract had he or she known about the matter. However, this definition is much too general and subjective to be used on a day-to-day basis by licensees.

## Material Facts Described

Some facts are so obviously material that there is no doubt that prior knowledge of that fact would have affected the desirability of the property. For example, unstable soil or fill, even in small quantities, would obviously be crucial for any buyer to know. Other matters such as structural defects, building code violations, or termites and dry rot would also be considered material facts, as any reasonable seller would understand that they are of major concern to a buyer. Matters such as these can be difficult to discover by inspection, but are still material to the transaction.

The fact that the seller does not have the proper permits to operate a particular business on the premises that the buyer wants to operate, or the fact that the buyer's business use will violate city zoning ordinances, would drastically change both the value and desirability of the property to the buyer. The existence of an easement, or the lack of a proper water system for the intended use of the property, are also material facts that affect the buyer's decision to buy. Other matters that are obviously material include land that has experienced flooding, buildings that may need substantial structural repairs, and land that is not connected to the public sewer system.

The materiality of these facts is objective in nature and can be determined by examining whether the undisclosed fact had a measurable effect on the marketability, the value of the buyer's highest and best use of the property, or the buyer's or appraiser's opinion of value.

A factor can still be considered material even if it does not affect the structural or physical aspect of the property. In one case, the court held the fact that the buyer's check, in the form of a post-dated check, was a material fact that had to be disclosed to the seller. In another case, the court found that the one-year due date on a purchase-money secured obligation and also the construction nearby of new competition property, were material facts.

The use of an objective or subjective standard to determine whether or not a fact is material can be key depending on the circumstances of a particular case. The test of materiality referenced by most court decisions describes a matter as material when it affects the value or desirability of the property. An objective standard would require that the matter affect either (1) the value and desirability of the property, or (2) a matter that affects the desirability of the property or the transaction where the seller knows that the particular fact is, or could be, important to the buyer.

Property located on a busy street or in a flight path where there is a great deal of noise may be a fact that is objectively material to most buyers, but a location near a school, which may be desirable to a buyer with children, may be unsatisfactory to a buyer who works a graveyard shift and sleeps during the day, when the noise of the school could be a problem. This type of fact would be material only if the seller or the seller's agent is aware of the buyer's peculiar sensitivity. As you can see, a subjective standard for determining materiality can complicate certain situations.

## Agent's Statutory Duty of Disclosure

There is a seemingly unlimited number of duties to disclose particular facts to one or both of the parties to a real estate transaction scattered throughout the codes. Many of these duties are imposed on the seller, on the seller's agent, or on both. It is not our intent with this course to discuss every single detail regarding disclosure in real estate, but we will try to cover the most common and most important disclosure requirements encountered on a day-to-day basis.

## Disclosure Forms: TDS Review

### What is the Real Estate Transfer Disclosure Statement?

A Real Estate Transfer Disclosure Statement (TDS) is a form prescribed in Civil Code § 1102.6. Effective January 1, 1987, most sellers of residential property with one to four units have been required to furnish this completed form to prospective purchasers. Sellers and licensees may comply with this law by utilizing C.A.R. Form TDS-11, which they can obtain from most local Boards of Associations of REALTORS®, or from the C.A.R. Member Products and Services Division.

### What Types of Real Estate Transactions Are Covered?

These disclosure requirements apply to transfers by sale, exchange, installment land contract, lease with an option to purchase, option to purchase, or ground lease coupled with improvements of real property (or a residential stock cooperative) with one to four dwelling units.

### Exemptions

Certain types of transfers are specifically exempted in Civil Code §1102.1. They are as follows:

1) Transfers requiring a public report pursuant to § 11018.1 of the Business and Professions (B & P) Code and transfers pursuant to § 11010.8 of the B & P Code where no public report is required.

2) Transfers pursuant to court order (probate sales, sales by a bankruptcy trustee, etc.).

3) Transfers by foreclosure (including a deed in lieu of foreclosure and a transfer by a beneficiary who has acquired the property by foreclosure or deed in lieu of foreclosure).

4) Transfers by a fiduciary in the course of the administration of a decedent's estate, guardianship, conservatorship, or trust.

5) Transfers from one co-owner to one or more other co-owners.

6) Transfers made to a spouse, child, grandchild, parent, grandparent, or other direct ancestor or descendant.

7) Transfers between spouses in connection with a dissolution of marriage or similar proceeding.

8) Transfers by the state controller pursuant to the Unclaimed Property Law.

9) Transfers or exchanges to or from any government entity.

However, it should be noted that a real estate licensee still has a duty to conduct a reasonably competent and diligent visual inspection of accessible areas in almost all of the above situations. In other words, although the seller is exempted from having to provide a disclosure statement in certain situations, a licensee must conduct this inspection, and disclose the results of the inspection, in almost all residential transactions that involve one to four units.

**Licensee Exemption from Conducting an Inspection**

A licensed real estate broker or salesperson does not need to conduct a visual inspection of residential property that is sold as part of a subdivision in which a CalBRE public report is required (5 or more units). In addition, a broker need not conduct a visual inspection on a subdivision in which a public report is not required because it is a subdivision of improved, single-family homes, in which all improvements are complete, there are no common areas, and whose units are located entirely within the boundaries of a city.

**Delivery of the Disclosure Statement to the Buyer**

If two or more real estate licensees are acting as agents in the transaction, the selling agent must deliver the statement to the buyer, unless the seller has given other written instructions for delivery. If only one licensee is involved in the transaction, that licensee must deliver the statement to the buyer. If no real estate licensees are involved, the seller is responsible.

The law states that delivery of the disclosure statement to the buyer may be made either in person or by mail. Obviously, personal delivery is preferable.

The disclosure statement must be delivered to the buyer as soon as practicable before the transfer of title. If possible, it would be preferable to provide the completed disclosure statement to the buyer prior to the buyer's signing the offer to purchase. If the buyer receives the disclosure statement after execution of his or her offer to purchase, the buyer will have a three or five-day period to cancel the transaction.

In the case of a lease option agreement, the prospective purchaser should get the disclosure statement before he or she enters into the lease option agreement.

In the case of a new home that is exempt from the TDS requirement, the buyer should get the TDS before he or she enters into the contract to purchase the home, even if it has not yet been built. In other words, no special rule applies.

**Buyer's Right to Cancel**

"If any disclosure, or any material amendment of any disclosure ... is delivered after the execution of an offer to purchase, the transferee (buyer) shall have three days after delivery in person or five days after delivery by deposit in the mail, to terminate his or her offer by delivery of a written notice of termination to the transferor (seller) or the transferor's (seller's) agent" (Civil Code § 1102.2.).

**Structural Additions or Modifications**

Civil Code § 1134.5 went into effect on July 1, 1985, and requires sellers of a one-to-four unit residential property to disclose, in writing, to any prospective buyer, if there had been any structural additions or modifications to the property and whether these additions or modifications had been done with permit. This legislation (the Real Estate Transfer Disclosure Statement law) repealed § 1134.5, effective January 1, 1987. However, it should be noted that the mandatory disclosure statement form requires essentially the same disclosures required under the previous law; i.e., that the seller indicate whether he or she is aware of any room additions, structural modifications, or other alterations made without necessary permits or not in compliance with building codes.

## Selling Property As-Is

There is no exemption to providing the disclosure statement for an *as-is* transaction. Unless the seller meets one of the standard exemptions, he or she must provide a Real Estate Transfer Disclosure Statement to the buyer. Remember that even in an as-is transaction, where the seller does not warrant the condition of the property, the seller is still required to disclose all known material facts that affect the value or desirability of the property to the buyer.

If a seller gives the TDS form to the buyer, other disclosure statements are not required unless the parties feel they are necessary. Section I of the disclosure statement provides space for the seller to provide other disclosures required by law, such as a *special studies zone* disclosure or a *purchase money lien on residential property* disclosure. All other disclosures mandated by local, state, or federal law must still be provided to the buyer, in addition to the Real Estate Transfer Disclosure Statement.

## Other Disclosure Requirements with the TDS Form

## Natural Hazards Disclosure Form Geologic and Seismic Hazards

If the agent provides actual delivery of the proper consumer information booklet on geologic and seismic hazards, then the agent is not required to provide additional information regarding such hazards. However, this rule does not change the duty of the agent to disclose any known geologic, seismic, or other hazards to the buyer that the agent is aware of. If the agent provides actual delivery of the *Homeowner's Guide to Earthquake Safety* to the buyer, the agent is not required to provide additional information regarding such hazards to the buyer. Nevertheless, this rule does not change the duty of the agent to disclose any known geologic, seismic, or other hazards to the buyer that the agent is aware of, if:

1) A map designating the area has been provided to the city or county by the State Geologist.

2) A notice identifying the location of the map has been posted at specific county offices (county recorder, county planning department, and county assessor).

3) The map is sufficiently accurate or scaled so that a reasonable person can determine whether the property is within a delineated earthquake fault zone.

4) If the map shows that the property is located in such a zone, the agent must disclose this to the buyer. In fact, if the map does not clearly show whether or not the property is in a seismic zone, the agent must indicate "yes" on the disclosure form with regard to whether the property exists in a seismic zone. That is, unless the agent can produce a bona fide report that verifies that the property is not in the earthquake hazard zone, then the agent must mark "yes." Similar rules apply to seismic hazard zones (e.g., landslide, liquefaction), wild land areas (risk of forest fires with little, no, or questionable fire protection), special flood hazard areas (e.g., areas identified by FEMA as flood zones on the federal flood maps), potential flooding areas (e.g., dam failure inundation), and very high fire-hazard severity zones.

Nevertheless, none of these rules absolves the agent of the duty to disclose any known geologic, seismic, and other hazards.

### Home Energy Rating

If the agent provides actual delivery of the proper consumer information booklet on home energy ratings, then the agent is not required to provide additional information regarding such hazards. However, this rule does not change the duty of the agent to disclose any known home energy problems to the buyer that the agent is aware of.

### Sex Offenders

If the agent provides actual delivery of notice of the existence of a database maintained by law enforcement authorities that contains the locations of registered sex offenders, then the agent is not required to provide additional information regarding such hazards. However, this rule may not change the duty of the agent to disclose any known sex offenders in the proximity. Furthermore, a sex offender may not bring an action against a person who discloses information about any sex offenders under these circumstances.

### Industrial Properties

If a seller has knowledge of the fact that the area is zoned for industrial use, the seller must give disclosure of this to the buyer. On the other hand, the agent is not specifically covered by this rule. Nevertheless, if the California legislature has determined that such a zoning is important enough for a seller of a residence to disclose it to the buyer, it doesn't take much extrapolation to see that the agent should have known about the industrial zoning and should have disclosed it if it represents a material defect. In other words, if the legislature has determined that a seller's failure to disclose an industrial zone for a residential property is a violation, it is probably safe to assume that such a failure on the part of an agent could also represent a failure to disclose a material defect. This, of course, could vary from sale to sale, but the best philosophy is prevention through disclosure.

### Community Facilities Tax

Sellers must notify the buyer if there is a continuing lien that secures the levy of any community facilities tax. Again, although the agent is not specifically required to do this by statute, the question is, "Should the real estate agent have known about and disclosed it if it represents a material defect?"

### Ordnance Locations

A seller who has actual knowledge of any former federal or state ordnance locations within a one-mile radius of the property must give written notice of the knowledge as soon as possible before transfer of title. Examples of ordnance locations include military bases or installations, or military reserve installations. Of course, an agent is not specifically required by statute, but once again, the question is, "Should the real estate agent have known about and disclosed it if it represents a material defect?"

### Disclosure of Window Security Bars

Disclosure of window security bars and the location of the release mechanisms on those bars must be disclosed. However, this rule does not say whether the seller or the agent must disclose this information. Perhaps it is best to assume that since the legislature bothered including this provision, it is a material defect, and both the seller and agent can expect to disclose this material defect to the buyer.

## Manufactured Homes

A special form is required for manufactured homes. Agents should be sure they use this special form when applicable.

## Locally Required Disclosure Form

Local municipalities in California are allowed to establish supplemental local disclosure forms that go beyond what is required by the state law and forms. Of course, this does not mean that the local form replaces the state form; only that if the local municipality (e.g., the county or city) decides to develop such a device, it serves as a supplement for, not a replacement to, the state form.

## Waiver of Disclosure

Waiver of disclosure is prohibited. Even if persons of sound mind suggest or agree to not require a disclosure, this cannot relieve the seller or the agents of the requisite state disclosure requirement. An example of an attempted waiver would be an as-is clause in the contract. Purchasing a residential property as-is does not exempt the seller and the agents involved in the transaction from the disclosure requirements in California. This prohibition of a waiver also applies to mobile home sales.

## Miscellaneous Disclosure Requirements

## Smoke Detectors

At least with regard to single family dwellings, the seller must show in writing that the property complies with the California law regarding smoke detectors. The minimum standard for smoke detectors is to have at least one smoke detector in a central location outside each sleeping area. This means that there must be a smoke detector in each hall outside of a bedroom area. Thus, at least two smoke detectors would be required on a two-story home with bedrooms on each level.

However, if there have been additions, repairs, or alterations to the property that constitute over $1,000 in value, then regardless of age, each bedroom must have a smoke detector in addition to the hall detectors mentioned above. Furthermore, existing dwellings need only utilize a battery-operated smoke detector, while new construction must utilize hard-wired smoke detectors with battery backups. Again, question to consider here is, "If the legislature is requiring this of the seller as a significant concern, couldn't a regulator or court suggest by this that failure to do so could also represent the failure of an agent to disclose a material or significant defect to the buyer that the agent should have known about?"

## Lead-Based Paint Disclosure Requirements

Of course, existing federal law requires owners to reveal if they know that the property for sale contains lead. In addition, if the agent knows that a test has been done and that it turned out to be positive for lead, the agent must disclose this to the buyer, especially since it is likely to be considered a significant defect, given all the attention and consideration that this issue is currently receiving.

## Termite Inspections

The seller or the seller's agent must deliver a copy of any completed termite inspection as part of the obligation of the seller under the contract. Furthermore, documentation of the report and its delivery must be kept in the agent's records for three years.

## Energy Conservation Considerations

If local municipal ordinances require that any home being sold be brought up to a specific energy retrofitting requirement, the seller and the seller's agent should notify the prospective buyer of the requirements of such ordinances and who is responsible for complying with them.

## Foreign Investment in Real Property Tax Act (FIRPTA) and State Provision

This law (FIRPTA) is generally interpreted to mean that the buyer is expected to withhold 10% of the gross sales price if the seller is a "foreign person." It would probably be a good idea for any agent in the transaction to notify the buyer of the existence of this law and to recommend that he or she receive further expert consultation on how to comply so that the transaction is properly handled.

A similar law specifically requires escrow holders to notify buyers of a similar obligation on the part of buyers. However, it is recommended that any agents involved in the transaction consider doing the same.

**QUIZZES ARE MANDATORY**

CalBRE requires the submission of chapter quizzes before you can access the final examination. You must log in and submit the chapter quizzes online before you can access the final examination. After submitting the last chapter quiz, you will receive a link to the final examination. You were issued a Personal Identification Number (PIN) and login instructions when you enrolled.

**Chapter One Quiz**

1.      What is a *red flag*?

      (a)      A detrimental financing factor that may prevent the buyer from qualifying for a loan.

      (b)      A physical factor about a property that, when you see it you say to yourself, "this is a potential material fact that may need to be investigated."

      (c)      A defect in the subject property's chain of title that casts doubt on the validity of the seller's ownership.

      (d)      A questionable commission split offer that may result in the selling agent receiving less than the advertised percentage.

2.      Which of the following is considered a *material fact*?

      (a)      Unstable soil on the property.

      (b)      Evidence of dry rot.

      (c)      Lack of a proper water system.

      (d)      All of the above.

3.      A Real Estate Transfer Disclosure Statement (TDS) must be furnished to prospective purchasers of:

      (a)      apartment complexes.

      (b)      commercial buildings.

      (c)      vacant land.

      (d)      residential property with one to four units.

4.      Which of the following real estate transactions is exempt from the TDS disclosure requirement?

      (a)      Transfers from one co-owner to one or more other co-owners.

      (b)      Probate sales.

      (c)      Transfers made to a spouse or to a child.

      (d)      All of the above.

5.   If two or more real estate licensees are acting as agents in the transaction, who must deliver the statement to the buyer?

   (a)   The listing agent.

   (b)   The selling agent (the agent who obtained the offer).

   (c)   The listing agent's employing broker.

   (d)   The escrow agent.

6.   If any disclosure, or any material amendment of any disclosure is delivered in-person after the execution of an offer to purchase, the buyer has _____ after delivery of the TDS to terminate his or her offer.

   (a)   3 days          (c)   10 days
   (b)   5 days          (d)   30 days

7.   If a seller gives the TDS form to the buyer as prescribed by law, then:

   (a)   other disclosures are required as a disclosure confirmation addendum.

   (b)   other disclosures are still required to be made separately on individual disclosure statements.

   (c)   other disclosure statements are not required unless the parties feel they are necessary or if they are required by local, state, or federal law.

   (d)   other disclosures required by local, state, or federal law are not required.

8.   Which of the following statements is CORRECT in regard to the requirement to provide the TDS disclosure statement?

   (a)   Persons of sound mind may waive the required disclosure.

   (b)   An *as-is* clause in a contract waives the disclosure requirement.

   (c)   Waiver of the disclosure requirement is prohibited.

   (d)   If the sale involves a mobile home, the disclosure may be waived.

9.   How many smoke detectors are required on a two-story home with bedrooms on each level?

   (a)   At least two, in each hall outside a bedroom area.

   (b)   At least two, on the lower level only.

   (c)   At least two, on the upper level only since smoke rises.

   (d)   Only one, in the hall outside of the master bedroom.

10. Concerning the existence of lead-based paint in a home, if the agent knows that a test has been done that turned out to be positive for lead, then which of the following applies?

   (a) The agent must physically remove the lead paint, but does not need to disclose the results of the test.

   (b) The agent must disclose to the purchaser the presence of the lead-based paint hazard.

   (c) The agent should inform the party responsible for the test that they are required to remove it.

   (d) The agent may ignore the test as long as it was conducted over a year ago.

## Chapter Two: Exterior Red Flags

### Important Terms

coping
crawl space
down drain
permit
retaining wall
septic system
slab
splash block
subterranean termites
window well

### Learning Objectives

Upon completion of Chapter Two, you should be able to complete the following:

- Identify non-original construction.

- Explain the pitfalls of non-original/non-permitted construction from the buyer's perspective.

- Identify problems that may indicate inadequate drainage.

- Identify and analyze foundation cracks.

- Identify potential problems with swimming pools and spas.

- Identify exterior electrical red flags.

## Why Is an Inspection Necessary?

Buying or selling a home is one of the largest financial transactions most families will make. Buyers should know exactly what repairs and maintenance may be required in a home. Sellers should know about potential deal-killers. Uncovering potential problems will help buyers and sellers avoid unpleasant surprises.

## What Is Involved?

Most home inspections include a visual examination of the home's exterior and interior, including the roof, foundation, grading, plumbing, septic systems, heating and air-conditioning systems, appliances, visible insulation, floors, walls, windows, and doors.

## What If the Inspection Reveals Problems?

If the agent finds problems during an inspection, it does not necessarily mean the buyer should not purchase the home. The agent's inspection may uncover potential problems that will help buyers know in advance which repairs to anticipate, or the seller may be willing to make repairs in order to complete the deal.

## Exterior Red Flags

The agent's inspection for red flags should start with the exterior of the house. Look at the condition of the front and back yards. Check all of the exterior windows, doors, and outer walls. Check for the following specific exterior red flags.

## Non-Original Construction

Construction that has been added to the property since it was built is typically referred to as non-original construction. Sometimes this is minor construction (e.g., a newer or different sink than original, a new toilet, etc.), moderate construction (e.g., a new roof cover, siding, etc.), or large construction projects or renovations (e.g., finishing a basement, adding on an addition to the back or side of the house, renovating the kitchen or bathrooms, etc.).

*Figure 2.1—Non-original addition*

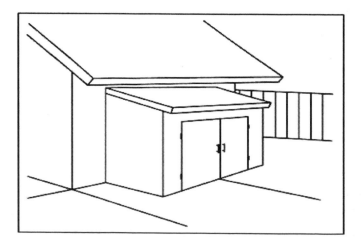

Typically, the more extensive the work, the more apparent that a non-original construction exists. For instance, agents are probably less likely to notice a three-prong outlet on one outlet in the house, while all the others are two-prong outlets as were used in most homes in built prior to 1970. It is likely the outlet is not a true three-prong outlet as it probably only has two electrical conductors from the panel box (not three) that extend to it.

On the other hand, agents are far more likely to notice an entire basement that appears to be a newer construction than the original. This is especially true if the home is older, and the basement finish is newer.

The concern with non-original construction is that building permits may not have been obtained from the local municipality. If the construction has not been permitted or not received final approval, it may be considered "illegal" or "unapproved" work. If building permits were not obtained, the seller may need to apply for a permit for the work and/or making sure it receives final approval.

In California, if building permits were not obtained or approved for non-original construction, the unapproved portion of the house must be identified as "unapproved" in the listing.

An important point to remember is that every municipality is different in the way they deal with permits, both in the type of items that need a permit and how in depth they will want to go in the inspection of already completed construction.

In many municipalities, an owner need not take out a permit on items that are not considered significant (e.g., replacing an outlet, replacing a drain pipe under a sink, etc.). Thereafter, the agent may be surprised to find which items a municipality considers significant enough to require a permit. Attempting to evaluate whether or not a municipality requires a permit for the specific non-original work is the place to start. If the municipality would have required a permit for the work, the agent should check to see if any permits were taken out at the time that the agent estimates the non-original work was done. If no permit was taken out, or a permit was taken out but not finalized, there is still work to be done.

The agent may want to notify the buyer that there may be some unpermitted, non-original construction on the property. The agent should suggest that the owner determine whether or not a permit was taken out and finalized on the property for that construction, and encourage the owner to take a permit out immediately and arrange to have the construction inspected and finalized shortly thereafter.

If the agent discovers that some unpermitted, non-original construction exists on the property, the agent should find out how far the municipality expects the owner to go in allowing for full inspection of the construction. The municipality may have the right to require at least some of the drywall be removed to check on the quality of the construction (e.g., electrical, plumbing, framing, and any other construction items that could only be checked with removal of drywall). They may decide, based on the quality of the work they can see, whether or not this is necessary. Some municipalities require full inspection with removal of drywall regardless. It is clearly up to the municipality and the inspectors to decide.

In any event, the agent does want to make sure that significant, non-original construction has been permitted and finalized.

## No Extensions on Down Drains

Down-drain extensions are an important component in helping to keep water away from the house. They reduce the risk of foundation settlement and help keep water from penetrating the basement or crawl space (if the house has one). The extensions should reach approximately two feet away from the house. Generally speaking, the extension should be made of the same material as the down drain.

*Figure 2.2: Poor drainage due to the absence of down drain extensions.*

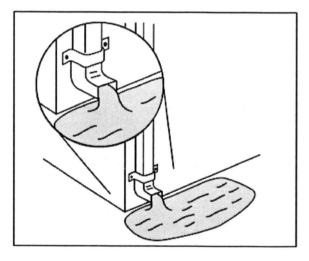

## Wood Touching Soil

Wood touching the soil at any point in a home is an "invitation to dinner" for termites. Even in areas where subterranean termites are not a significant issue, wood rot can be a major problem. Building codes typically require up to eight inches of clearance between outside wood and soil.

## Foundation Cracks

*Figure 2.3: Common foundation cracks.*

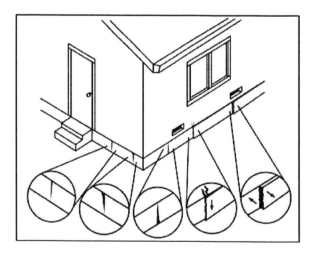

### Minor Cracks

While cracks in a home's foundation that are smaller than 1/8 inch may indicate a settlement in foundations, they are usually only a cosmetic concern. This is a general rule and should not be considered true in all cases. If other circumstances apply (e.g., there is a major cliff close to the house, or the house is brand new), the agent should consider the home to be a possible exception to this rule and recommend that the buyer contact a structural engineer for a complete evaluation.

### Medium Sized Cracks

Cracks in the foundation that are larger than 1/8 inch but less than 3/4 inch at any point along the crack could be considered large enough to indicate possible structural concerns. Even then, few homes in this category are likely to have a structural problem that represents a risk to occupants. Nevertheless, the agent should advise that the home buyer consider contacting a structural engineer.

### Medium or Large Sized Cracks

Cracks in the foundation that are larger than 3/4 inch at any point along the crack are large enough to indicate significant structural concerns in a home. While the risk of significant structural problems are possible, the defects are generally not likely to represent a risk to the occupants. Often, these cracks appear because of settlement of fill under or around the house.

### Figure 2.4: Filled building pad.

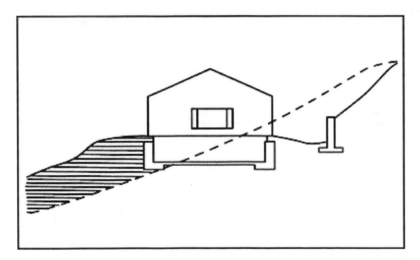

In areas where slab homes are common, it may not be unusual to find a home where the foundation and slab have been raised by a large root from a neighboring tree, thus causing a crack.

*Figure 2.5: Foundation damaged and cracked by root system.*

Generally speaking, this analysis of cracks for indication of safe habitability of homes is not intended to also evaluate for purposes of earthquake risk. The above categorization of cracks is outside of the evaluation of structural earthquake susceptibility. It should be considered a crude, red-flags indicator, outside of any considerations for earthquake resistance.

A structural defect that is less commonly found is a significantly *out of plumb* wall. As a general rule, if a wall is noticeably out of plumb, it could represent a great enough concern to contact a structural engineer for further evaluation.

## Grading

Water seepage into a home is one of the most deplored conditions by homeowners. In all but a few scenarios, down-drain extensions and grading should resolve this problem.

### *Grading around the Perimeter of the House*

The grading of the soil around the outside wall or outside perimeter of the house is very important for helping to keep the water outside, especially if the house has a crawlspace or basement. Nevertheless, perimeter grading is a concern even on slab homes, because extended water exposure next to the foundation can result in the settling of the slab.

To judge the grading, the agent should observe whether or not the ground noticeably slopes away from the house. If it appears flat or slopes toward the house, then the grading should be corrected. This also includes concrete walks that are next to house and flat, or that slope toward the house.

**Inadequate Drainage**

*Figure 2.6: Uncontrolled roof water and poor surface drainage next to structure.*

Of particular concern in homes on hillside lots is the issue of diverting the water around the house from the hillside above. As you might imagine, a great deal of water can end up being collected on the hillsides above homes—so much so that hillside homes are far more likely to end up with water in the basement than other homes are. As a result, it is important to attempt to divert this runoff away from or around the house. While there are many ways to do this, some commonly used techniques can be used to help reduce the risk of water in the basement of a home of this nature.

One of the most commonly used techniques includes simply creating a "swale" or gutter beginning near the midpoint of the yard above the house, and diagonally running the down the hill to each side such that the water that is caught in the swale will be drawn along the swale and around the house.

Another method is to create low spots in the lawn above the house and create an underground drainage system that runs the water out to the street gutter (or rear yard if applicable) as storm drainage. A more environmentally acceptable modification of this method might be to filter the water back into the ground on the downhill side of the lot.

Another concern, primarily directed at hillside homes, involves the risk of landslides. Any depressions or terrain that doesn't seem to follow the terrain around it could be considered a potential risk area. If the agent notices this in any of the areas of the lot, the agent should disclose it to the buyer. The existence of special tarps or covers over sloped soil, or erosion, could also be an indicator of some of these problems.

**Trip Hazard on Driveway due to Settling and/or Buckling**

Offsets that raise parts of the concrete higher than about 1/4 inch above or below the rest of the concrete around it are possible trip hazards.

**Driveway Slopes toward Garage without Adequate Drainage**

On some homes, the driveway may slope downhill from the street so the car can be parked in a garage on the basement or crawlspace level. The driveway will naturally collect water and direct it into the garage if there are no methods used to divert the water.

One such method is to collect the water into a drain or drywell at the base of the driveway where it meets the garage. When using this technique, the entire driveway should drain toward the drywell drain. A drywell is simply an opening to an underground space where water can run. It is not unusual for a drywell to be nothing more than a hole large enough to fit a capless, upside-down five-gallon bucket, with a hole in the bucket to serve as an access point for water draining through the drain. Thus, such a drywell has about a five-gallon capacity plus whatever the ground beneath it will absorb. Higher rainfall areas will require larger drywells.

If the house is on a hillside and there is an opportunity for the water to run around the house instead of collecting on the driveway, another such method would be to simply slope the driveway in such a way that all the water from the driveway will run off the outside edge (e.g., onto the lawn and around the house).

**Septic Systems**

A strong sewage smell indicates a malfunctioning septic system. If the agent detects any waste smell associated with the septic system, the agent should recommend to the buyer or seller that they contact a septic professional to have the system checked.

**Retaining Walls**

*Figure 2.7: Unstable retaining wall.*

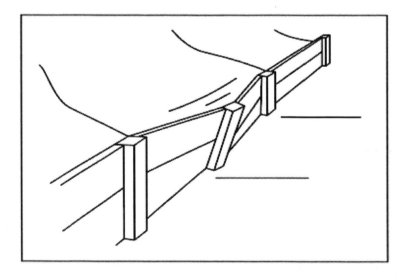

Retaining walls are usually built of wood, rock, mortared brick, or concrete. A good visual test for determining whether the retaining wall is stable is if it is noticeably out-of-plumb. The higher the retaining wall, the greater the chance that it may be out-of-plumb. In other words, an eight-foot-high retaining wall that is out of plumb to the same degree as a three-foot-high retaining wall represents a greater concern.

Retaining walls are typically very expensive to replace. The more permanent varieties (concrete, mortared brick, etc.) require much more work to demolish and rebuild. One of the easiest retaining walls to rebuild is the "railroad tie" or comparable type. Nevertheless, if a retaining wall is visibly well beyond out of plumb, the agent should recommend that the buyer contact an expert for further evaluation, especially if the wall is high.

### Inadequate Window Wells

The upper lip of the window well should be above the grade of the ground around it. In correct window wells, the lip should be above a grade that slopes away from the house. If the grade is flat or slopes toward the house, the agent should notify the seller or buyer of what changes should be made to correct grading.

To prevent water from entering the window well, the ground around it should be intact to shed water. For instance, if a crevasse exists in the ground that allows water to flow under the grade level next to the window well, the window well cannot as easily serve its intended purpose. Other compromises to the dirt or the window well itself (e.g., holes in the window well) also represent a concern.

If the eave of the roof above does not extend beyond the outer edge of the window well below, there is a very high risk that water draining off the roof will drop directly down into the window well, and potentially flood the basement or crawlspace. Use of a rain repelling cover over the window well can help prevent this from becoming a problem.

Another problem that can exist with window wells but does not relate to the function of a window well is the lack of adequate walking space that they may create when they are in a location that will be frequently walked on or around. Examples of this include window wells on the house where the driveway runs along the side of the house, and patios in the rear yard that run up against the house and involve a window well. In these cases, there is a great risk that individuals who are using the area around the window well could inadvertently step into the window well and be injured. Any type of metal grid or grate that can hold a normal adult's weight should be suitable. The agent should be sure that the grate fits over the window well in such a way that the transition from the driveway or patio to the window well does not create a trip hazard.

### Faucet Splash Blocks

Hose bibs or exterior faucets often drip, whether a hose is attached to them or not, or whether the water is on or off. Also, consider the common prank made by neighborhood kids of turning on a faucet when a homeowner is on vacation: the homeowner returns home to a flooded basement. These are just two reasons to keep splash blocks under rain gutter down drains and exterior faucets to help prevent erosion of the soil, and ultimately water infiltration around the slab into crawl spaces or the basement. More specifically, the splash block should be sloped away from the house and firmly supported so that even the backfill next to the foundation of a new home cannot settle and change the slope of the splash block.

Splash blocks are often moved accidentally (e.g., Johnny hit the splashblock while mowing the lawn and it now tips the water back toward the house). If the ground next to the house settles, the splash block could end up sending water back toward the house. The agent should check splash blocks for proper placement and orientation to ensure that water flows away from the home. If there are indications that water has been flowing back toward the home, the agent should notify the seller or buyer that a problem may exist.

**Swimming Pools and Spas**

*Figure 2.8: Swimming pool with out-of-level water surface relative to coping.*

The level of the water in a swimming pool or spa should be within 1/2 inch of the same level all the way around the pool. If it is not level, a problem may exist. Many pools get minor cracks from setting or shifting soil. The sides and bottom should be free of cracks. If a crack exists, a professional pool inspector should be called.

**Barrier Requirements**

In many states, a barrier is required between the house and pool (note: *pool* means an in-ground or above-ground swimming pool or other contained body of water that is 18 or more inches in depth, eight or more feet in width, and intended for swimming).

This law aims to impede children's access to their own pools. Likewise, all pools must have a barrier to keep out uninvited neighborhood children. Unless a local code provides otherwise, the barrier must meet the following requirements:

- Entirely enclose the pool area.

- Stand at least five feet high, measured on the outside of the barrier.

- Not contain openings, handholds, or footholds that can be used to climb the barrier. Wire mesh or chain link fences shall have a maximum horizontal mesh size of 1 and 3/4 inches.

- Contain no openings through which a sphere that is four inches in diameter can pass. Horizontal components of any barrier shall be spaced not less than 45 vertical inches apart, or shall be placed on the poolside of the barrier, which shall have no opening greater than 1 and 3/4 horizontal inches.

- Placed at least 20 inches from the water's edge.

- Prevent direct access from the house to the pool.

## Air Conditioning Unit(s) Not Level

When an air conditioning unit is not level, it could result in less efficient operation, and many times results in a shorter useful life of the unit. If an air conditioner unit is visibly out of level, then the unit should be checked and leveled.

## Exterior Electrical Red Flags

In older homes, there is a stronger likelihood that the telephone pole-to-house wire is of a cloth variety. If you see the cloth cover on this wire fraying like this, notify your buyer of this defect.

### *Exterior Outlet Not Properly Weather Stripped*

Any exterior outlet must be properly weather-stripped to reduce the risk of water infiltration when it is not in use. The most common types of weather-stripped outlets are not suitable for continuous use; they are only intended for temporary plugin (e.g., to plug in a weed whacker, lawn mower, etc.). If there is a need for a plug to be plugged in on a more permanent basis, special housing with a hinged cover must be used.

### *Exterior Switch Not Properly Weather Stripped*

Using an ordinary electrical switch in an exterior location is not acceptable. A special weatherproof switch must be used, and is usually gray in color with a side lever instead of a front lever.

**QUIZZES ARE MANDATORY**: Please log in and submit the chapter quizzes online.

**Chapter Two Quiz**

1.   Typically, non-original work is more noticeable when:

   (a)   the work is extensive.

   (b)   the work is minor.

   (c)   the work is cosmetic.

   (d)   the work is incomplete.


2.   If non-original construction has not been permitted and approved, the unapproved portion of the house must be identified in the listing as:

   (a)   partially completed.

   (b)   pending approval.

   (c)   unapproved.

   (d)   under construction.


3.   Wood touching the soil at any point in a home is a potential problem because _____ may appear.

   (a)   mold

   (b)   fire

   (c)   water damage

   (d)   subterranean termites


4.   A crack in a home's foundation of less than 1/8 inch is considered:

   (a)   minor.

   (b)   medium-sized.

   (c)   large-sized.

   (d)   catastrophic.


5.   Which of the following conditions may cause water seepage problems?

   (a)   The ground noticeably slopes away from the house.

   (b)   A concrete walk next to the house slopes away from the foundation.

   (c)   The soil is graded so the ground slopes toward the house.

   (d)   Drain extensions are used to divert water away from the house.

6.      A strong sewage smell may indicate a problem with the:

        (a)     city sewer pipes.

        (b)     septic system.

        (c)     storm drainage pipes.

        (d)     garbage disposal.

7.      Which of the following statements is TRUE regarding retaining walls?

        (a)     Retaining walls are typically very expensive to replace.

        (b)     The more permanent varieties (concrete, mortared brick, etc.) require much more work to demolish and rebuild.

        (c)     One of the easiest retaining walls to rebuild is the *railroad tie* type.

        (d)     All of the above.

8.      It is a good idea to keep a splash block under all exterior faucets to help prevent:

        (a)     erosion of the soil.

        (b)     animals from drinking.

        (c)     water waste.

        (d)     all of the above.

9.      The level of the water in a swimming pool or spa should be within _____ of the same level all the way around the pool or a problem may exist.

        (a)     1/2 inch

        (b)     5 inches

        (c)     10 inches

        (d)     24 inches

10.     To prevent water infiltration, exterior outlets must be properly:

        (a)     installed.

        (b)     painted.

        (c)     weather-stripped.

        (d)     maintained.

## Chapter Three: Roof and Garage Red Flags

**Important Terms**

combustion gases
detached garage
drywall
evaporative coolers (swamp cooler)
fire rating
junction box
masonry
rafter
rolled roofing
roof decking
shingles
solid core door
trip hazard
truss

**Learning Objectives**

Upon completion of Chapter Three, you should be able to complete the following:

- Identify the most common roof problems.

- Identify trip hazards in and around a home.

- Identify fire hazard issues between the home and garage.

- Identify power supply hazards to the house and garage.

- Test the auto-reversing mechanism on an automatic garage door.

**Roof Red Flags**

**Three or More Layers of Shingles**

The maximum number of layers of roofing material allowed on a roof may vary depending upon the regular roof loads expected in a given area and other factors. In many areas of the northeast, only two layers of roofing are allowed on the roof. In other areas of the country, it may be three. The agent should find out from the municipalities in his or her area how many layers are allowed. If there are three or more layers of shingles on the roof, it may require removal of at least one layer of shingles before applying a new layer.

Check at the eaves or lowest edge of the roof to determine how many layers of roof material are on a roof. At the eaves of roofs, roofers typically install two shingles for each full layer of shingles on the roof. Thus, the agent will expect to see four shingle edges at the eave if the roof has two layers of shingles on it, and six shingle edges if it has three layers.

**Sagging Roof Decking**

Sagging roof decks most commonly occur on homes that have a raftered structure, versus those that have the more modern trussed structure. Thus, severe sagging in roofs is most likely to be found in houses that were built before 1970. It would be unusual to find significant roof deck sag in a house with a truss roof structure, unless some trusses have been cut.

To evaluate roof deck sag, the agent should stand on the ground and line up his or her eyes with the plane of the roof deck. The agent should be oriented so that the eaves and the ridge are very close to being lined up with his or her line of vision. In general, if the agent estimates the deck sag to be more than a couple of inches, he or she should probably recommend that the buyer consider having the roof evaluated by a structural or civil engineer or framing contractor. It is not uncommon to see six or more inches of sag in raftered roofs that have split rafters beneath the deck.

**Cracked Shingles**

This usually means the shingles are beyond approximately the midpoint of their useful life (usually a watch situation.)

**Missing Shingles**

If some shingles are missing some granules, this may indicate that the shingles are approaching the end of their estimated remaining useful life. There are a number of defects on asphalt shingle roofs that deserve attention if they exist. If the shingles are cracked, even in a hairline fashion, they probably have at least passed the midpoint of their useful life; they may be older than the midpoint. Most asphalt shingles will last at least 15 years unless they are defective or of very low quality. When the agent sees the small granules on the asphalt shingles starting to detach (missing granules), then the life of the shingles is most likely less than five years. Of course, if the granules are missing in a very noticeable way (e.g., large areas of the roof look black from the extensive loss of granules), the roof is at the end of its useful life. Also, if a shingle appears to be missing here or there, then those shingles should be replaced as a partial repair.

## Rolled Roofing

If the home has any rolled roofing over the living space, the buyer should expect to replace the roof within the next five years, even if it is new rolled roofing. Rolled roofing is essentially an asphalt-shingle material on a roll. It is usually made of granuled tar paper on a roll that is about 36 inches wide. Rolled roofing generally has a useful life of 5–10 years.

## Checking Doors and Windows

A quick check of the home's doors and windows can lead to substantial energy savings. Failed weather stripping and deteriorating caulking around the framing and edges of doors and windows can allow hot air to escape and cold air to seep in. In addition, they can allow water to leak into the home, leading to wood rot and other problems. The agent should check the wood window framing and sills for damage, and point out any problems out to the principal.

## Deteriorating Chimney Masonry

It is very common to see deteriorating chimney masonry on homes, especially those without a red tile interior protection. Of course, this can be a danger to someone who is passing by the chimney and may prevent the chimney from drafting combustion gases properly.

## Evaporative Cooler Red Flags

## Combustion Vents below Evaporative Cooler Top

If the seller lives in an area that is very arid in the summer, the seller may be using evaporative/swamp coolers. These simple and less expensive window or rooftop cooling units only work in low-humidity areas. These coolers draw the air from outside into the fan compartment inside. Thus, they draw air into themselves and then into the house. If a combustion vent for a furnace or water heater is close enough to a swamp cooler, the cooler could draw low-oxygen, high-carbon-dioxide air into the house. Thus, any combustion air vents should be at least 10 feet horizontally from the swamp cooler and at least two feet above the top of the swamp cooler.

## No Evaporative Cooler Overflow Drain

This could result in significant damage to the roof below the evaporative cooler. A swamp cooler has a water reservoir in its base. Virtually every swamp cooler leaks at least some water out of this connector at some time during its life. The problem here is that the water that leaks from the swamp cooler can completely ruin the roof underneath it. Therefore, the attachment of a simple $10 hose could help avoid expensive roof damage. In fact, the water reservoir usually has a hose thread connection on it. The hose should be connected to the overflow connector on the cooler and the other end of the hose should run over the edge of the roof or into the rain gutter.

## Red Flags in the Garage

## Wood Touching Soil at the Garage Foundation, Exterior Wall, or Covering

This issue is essentially the same issue as mentioned in Chapter One in regard to wood siding on a house. Wood should be six to eight inches from the soil in order to be cost effective. This applies to attached or detached garages as well as to the exterior siding on the living space.

**Trip Hazard on the Garage Floor**

*Figure 3.1: Trip hazard test.*

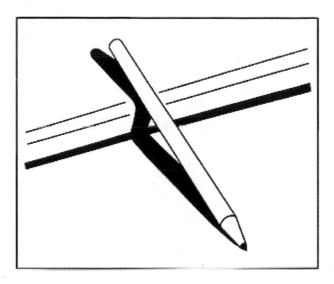

Any offsets in the floor of 1/4 inch or more are considered trip hazards and should be identified for the buyer for possible correction, and for prevention of injury while the buyer occupies the house. One way to check for trip hazards is to place a pen or pencil over the expansion joint between garage floor slabs or over a crack. If the pencil is at a noticeable angle, a trip hazard probably exists there.

**Fire Wall between the House and Garage Is Not Continuous on the Garage Side**

Garages typically must have an intact fire separation between them and the house. In most cases, this means there is drywall attached on the garage side to completely protect any walls between the house and the garage.

The common wall between the house and the garage should have a continuous drywall surface on the garage side all the way up to the bottom of the roof deck, unless the entire ceiling in the garage is covered with drywall. While this typically means that the drywall must be taped at the joints, many pre-1970s homes will not have joint compound or tape at the joints. The agent may suggest to the owner to have existing drywall taped.

**No Metal, Fire-Rated, or Solid-Core Common Door between the House and Garage**

Garages are known to be an area of high fire risk. Doorways between garages and the living spaces in homes represent one easy method for fire to reach the inside of the home from the garage. The existence of a metal or solid core wood door in the doorway between the garage and the house can create a significant block to fire spreading into the house. If the door is not a heavier wood door or a metal-type door, it is not likely to have an adequate fire rating. The agent should indicate to the buyer that the door may not have an adequate fire rating.

Any door at the garage-house doorway that does not automatically close is not providing as much fire protection for the house as it otherwise could. Thus, whether the door is a fire door or not, if the door does not completely shut automatically, the buyer should be told that this is a missing safety feature.

## Out-of-Plumb Garage Walls

In many homes that were originally built with a detached garage, the garage leans to one side or the other when viewed from the front. While this is typically due to an inadequate nonliving-space structural design from an earlier period, this can often be repaired with very little cost when compared to demolishing and building a new garage. Nevertheless, such work should be completed by a competent building contractor. The buyer should be notified if the building is noticeably out of plumb.

## Exposed Wire Connections

*Figure 3.2: A junction box without a cover is a hazard.*

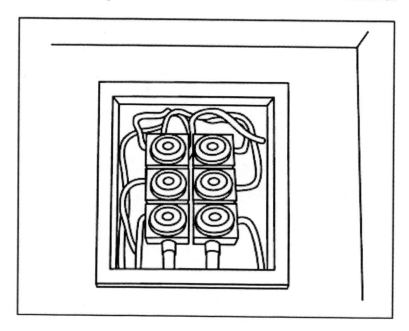

Electrical junction boxes allow for a protected wire connection within them. Often, these junction boxes do not have covers screwed onto them. Instead of protecting the wire connections, they tend to expose them. All junction boxes with wire connections in them should have a screwed-on cover that fits the box.

Detached garages were typically built in a time that did not warrant providing wiring to the garage. As time passed and people began to require electricity in their garages, many such detached garages were provided with electrical service in a less-than-professional manner. Many detached garages have a wire running to them from the house that may not be of an exterior grade. Since many of these wires have long become faded in the sun, it is nearly impossible to read any identifying marks on the wire to determine whether or not it is exterior rated. The agent should notify the buyer of the possibility that the wire may not be of an appropriate exterior grade.

**Wires to the Garage Are Too Low to the Ground**

*Figure 3.3: Wires too low to the ground.*

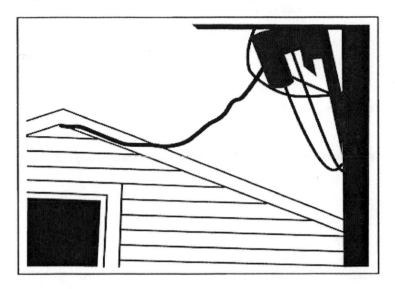

Garage-to-house wires can also represent other concerns. If the wire to the garage from the house does not clear at least 10 feet from the ground below, it would probably be considered too close to the ground for a safe clearance. Usually the best way for the agent to quickly evaluate the height is to estimate how far the wire is from the top of his or her head and then add his or her height (a height that the agent already knows) to that extra height to determine an approximate total height from the ground. If the agent finds that the clearance is less than 10 feet, he or she should disclose to the buyer that the wire from the house to the garage may be unsafe. The agent should never touch these wires with his or her hands, a tape measure, or any other object.

**Gas Water Heater in the Garage**

*Figure 3.4: Gas water heaters in the garage should be mounted on a platform that is at least 18 inches off the floor.*

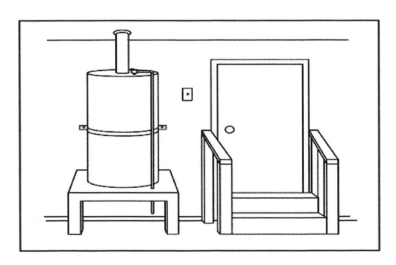

Gas water heaters that are located in the garage should be mounted on a platform that is at least 18 inches off the floor. Most building codes require that the pilot flame of a water heater in the garage be a minimum of 18 inches from the floor to minimize the chance of pilot light igniting gasoline fumes that are near the floor. Many states require a seismic safety strap to hold the water heater erect in the event of an earthquake, and energy blankets to minimize heat loss. Buyers and sellers should be informed about missing safety precautions for gas water heaters in the garage.

## Garage Door Opener Does Not Auto-Reverse

Automatic garage door openers began to be commonly used in the 1960s. When they were first manufactured, many openers did not have an important safety feature: an auto-reversing mechanism. This mechanism automatically reverses a closing garage door when adequate pressure is exerted against the closing door (e.g., a dog or small child who is caught under the door while it is closing). With the addition of an auto-reversing mechanism, automatic garage doors have become more safe.

### *Adjusting an Auto-Reversing Automatic Garage Door*

Sometimes, an automatic garage door opener does auto-reverse when a little pressure is placed upward on the closing door, but only when an exorbitant amount of pressure is used. Generally, an automatic reversing mechanism should reverse with very little pressure. Remember, we are trying to protect individuals as small as a toddler; they could potentially suffer major injury if the reversing mechanism did not reverse in time to keep from crushing their fragile bones. Thus, only if the auto-reversing safety mechanism reversed with very little pressure would the agent consider it adequately adjusted. If more pressure is required to reverse the door, the agent should tell the buyer that it needs adjustment.

**QUIZZES ARE MANDATORY**: Please log in and submit the chapter quizzes online.

**Chapter Three Quiz**

1.      Severe sagging in roofs is most likely to be found in houses that were built before:

   (a)     1950.

   (b)     1960.

   (c)     1970.

   (d)     1980.

2.      Deteriorating chimney masonry may cause a danger because:

   (a)     pieces of masonry may fall on someone passing by below.

   (b)     this may prevent the chimney from drafting combustion gases properly.

   (c)     Both (a) and (b) are correct.

   (d)     Neither (a) nor (b) are correct.

3.      Any offsets in the floor of _____ or more are considered trip hazards and should be identified for the buyer for possible correction.

   (a)     1/4 inch

   (b)     1/2 inch

   (c)     1 inch

   (d)     2 inches

4.      Which of the following represents an easy method for fire to reach the inside of a home?

   (a)     Railroad-tie retaining wall.

   (b)     Doorways between the garage and living spaces.

   (c)     Poorly designed landscaping.

   (d)     An old water heater.

5.      All electrical junction boxes should have:

   (a)     a permanent cover welded to them to protect children.

   (b)     warning labels designed to alert homeowners.

   (c)     a screwed-on cover that fits the box to protect the wires.

   (d)     clear plastic covers to allow the exterior viewing of wires.

**6.** To be considered safe, garage-to-house wires must be at least:

   (a)    8 feet from the ground.

   (b)    10 feet from the ground.

   (c)    12 feet from the ground.

   (d)    15 feet from the ground.

**7.** Gas water heaters should be elevated from the ground to:

   (a)    protect against flood waters.

   (b)    prevent animals from reaching the pilot light.

   (c)    keep the pilot light out of the reach of children.

   (d)    prevent gasoline fumes from being ignited by the pilot light.

**8.** Gas water heaters in the garage should be mounted on a platform that is at least ____ inches from the ground.

   (a)    18

   (b)    12

   (c)    10

   (d)    8

**9.** To protect pets or small children from being caught under the garage door while it is closing, garage door manufacturers now include an:

   (a)    auto-reversing mechanism.

   (b)    automatic spring detachment mechanism.

   (c)    emergency trapped alarm.

   (d)    emergency button on the remote.

**10.** An auto-reversing mechanism should reverse the garage door:

   (a)    when an exorbitant amount of upward pressure is exerted on the door.

   (b)    when very little upward pressure is exerted on the door.

   (c)    when the weather strip touches the garage floor.

   (d)    when the safety beam is broken.

## Chapter Four: Interior Red Flags

### Important Terms

three-way switch
baluster
creosote
egress point
lead-based paint
riser
shower pan
stairwell

### Learning Objectives

Upon completion of Chapter Four, you should be able to complete the following:

- Recognize potential problems with stairs and railings.

- Explain smoke detector requirements.

- Identify proper egress points in case of fire.

- Test kitchen appliances and identify potential problems.

- Recognize potential problems with fireplaces and stoves.

- Recognize bathroom red flags and hazards.

## General Interior Inspection

### Possible Peeling Lead-Based Paint

If a house was built before 1960 and has peeling paint on the inside, there is a significant risk that the paint is lead-based. If the house has peeling paint on the outside and was built before about 1980, the paint has a significant risk of being lead-based. If peeling paint exists under these circumstances, the agent should notify the buyer of the possibility that the peeling paint could contain lead and therefore represent a potential hazard. The buyer may want to order a lead-based paint test. Only a laboratory test can confirm the presence or absence of possible lead-based paint. Additionally, don't forget about the federal disclosure requirements.

### Floor Sags or Is Not Level

Floor sag or out-of-level flooring is often an indicator of settlement in the home. If the agent can noticeably tell that the flooring is sagging, the agent should inform the buyer so that the buyer can decide whether or not further evaluation is needed.

### Ceiling Stains

If stains are visible on the ceiling of a home, this could be an indicator of a leaking roof from the bathroom or kitchen above. While it is difficult to tell whether the stain was from a previous or current leak, it is still a good idea for the agent to notify the buyer of the stain.

### Inappropriate Wiring

Lamp cord should never be used in a permanent wiring system. However, lamp cord is sometimes used to add an outlet to a wall, etc., especially in pre-1960s homes. If the agent notices lamp cord being used in such a manner, the agent should disclose to the buyer that lamp cord is being used as permanent wiring in the house where it shouldn't be used.

### Stairs and Trip Hazards

Stairways represent some of the most significant risk areas in a home. Non-uniform stairs are potential trip hazards. When a person misjudges a stair, that person may potentially trip and fall. The quickest way for the agent to check stair uniformity is to begin from the top of the stairs. The agent should look down the nosings and line them up as well as possible. If they don't line up closely enough to be considered uniform, they represent a trip hazard. Building codes may allow up to a 3/8-inch difference from one step to another in riser height or tread to be considered uniform. Some experts say it should be as little as 1/4 inch. The *line-of-sight* test just explained does not definitively tell the agent whether or not the steps are truly uniform; only a careful measurement of each step can accomplish that. Nevertheless, lining up the nosings to look for deficiencies is a very cost-effective approach to identifying some of the most dangerous stairway defects in a home.

*Figure 4.1: Checking stair uniformity.*

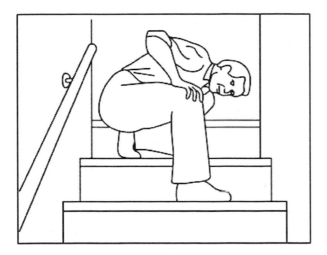

While some building codes allow as narrow a tread as 9 inches, many experts believe the safest tread depth is a minimum of 11 inches. This minimum exists so that the majority of people who use the stairs can fit all or most of their foot on the tread. If the stairs appear uniform, as per the previous test, then measuring just one or two treads per set of stairs would probably represent all of the stairs. Most experts recommend a 7-inch maximum rise and an 11-inch minimum tread.

## Railings

Stair railings serve multiple purposes. First, they help individuals safely walk up and down a set of stairs. Rails also help reduce injury if a person were to trip and begin to fall. An individual is far more likely to keep from falling and injuring themselves if that individual has a railing to grab on to.

If a rail is missing from a set of stairs, this would be considered a deficiency. Building codes require that a rail be provided on any set of stairs with as few as two steps. Other building codes and some stair experts suggest that rails should be provided on stairs that only have one step. The reason for this is that a person is less likely to expect a step up on a one-step system because there is no rail. Thus, in this case, the rail is a signal to the walker that a step lies ahead.

*Figure 4.2: Typical stairway and railings.*

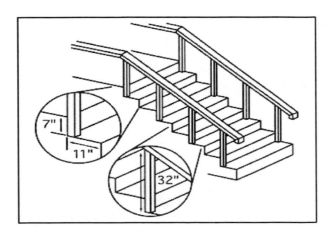

Rails should be fully graspable. If a person cannot fully grasp around a rail so that at least the tips of their fingers touch, it is likely that the rail cannot prevent a serious fall once a trip occurs. The agent should inspect each railing in the house to see whether the tips of his or her fingers touch while grasping the rail. The agent may even consider recommending child-level rails on all stairs if the buyer is likely to have smaller children in the family. Of course, the agent would want to make sure that these child-level rails are fully graspable by all the children who may use them.

A stair rail that does not provide a continuous run from the top to the bottom of the flight of stairs can also constitute a problem. If a flight of stairs has two rails—one that is along the wall where a wall exists, and another that completes the flight where the rail is in an open area (i.e., no wall to attach to) and only anchors via balusters to the steps, there will typically be a break in the continuity of the rail where the transition of the wall-attached rail to the step-attached rail occurs.

*Figure 4.3: Stair rails should provide a continuous run from the top to the bottom of a flight of stairs.*

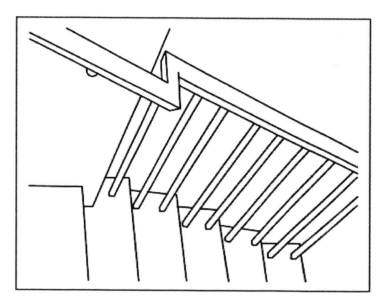

Loose rails can also constitute a risk in a number of ways. First of all, a loose rail may be on the verge of breaking. Thus, a loose rail may not be capable of handling the weight required if a person had to use it to catch themselves in the event of a fall. Furthermore, a loose rail cannot provide the accurate guide for a walker that a tight rail can, since it will move around rather than stay firm in its location.

The agent should notify the buyer if these defects with these items are present inside or outside of the house. Remember, stair-and rail-related items can be some of the most important concerns in the home.

**Stairwell Red Flags**

*Baluster Spacing*

*Balusters* are the vertical poles that typically hold up a railing. Balusters should not have a gap of more than about 4 inches. Notice that we are dealing with gaps between the balusters, not the center-to-center length between each of the balusters. The agent should use a measuring tape to check the widest gap between a few of the wider-gapped balusters. If the agent uses his or her fist (the average adult fist measures 3–4 inches in width), the agent may be able to easily estimate baluster widths if a measuring tape isn't handy.

*Figure 4.4: Baluster spacing.*

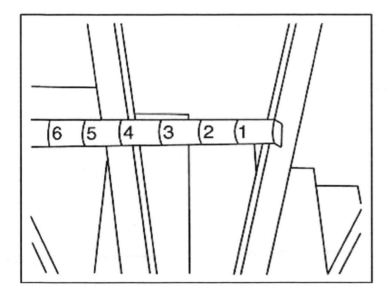

### Stairwell Lighting

Another stairway issue is inadequate lighting over stairs. Every stairwell should be well lit along its entire length. This can usually be accomplished by a single light in the middle of the stairwell on half flights, or two or three lights on longer stairwells (i.e., one full flight of stairs that rises 9 feet in elevation).

There should also be a *three-way switch* at both the top and bottom of the stairs so that no matter which direction a person is coming from, they will be able to turn on the lighting for the stairwell. A three-way switch allows the lights to be turned on or turned off at either of the two switches. If the stairs do not have a switch at both the top and bottom of the stairs that turns the lights on and/or off, the agent should disclose this to the buyer as a possible safety issue.

### Stairwell Headroom

It is not uncommon in pre-1970s homes to find that the stairs to the basement (if there is a basement) have insufficient headroom at some point along the stairway. Poor headroom is typically found at the base of the stairs. Code for new construction requires that the headroom—the measurement directly vertical from the floor or stair to the ceiling—be at least 80 inches. However, it would probably not be feasible to require all stairways to basements be 80 inches in existing homes, especially if the basement is being used as storage only. If the basement is being used as a normal living space or the stairwell has questionable headroom, a good cutoff height for minimum headroom on an existing home is probably around 74 inches to provide for most of the US population.

## Hazardous Steps

*Short steps* also represent a potential trip hazard. Many experts would define a short step as one that is 5 inches high or shorter. This step height is also called the *riser height*. Short stairs and steps are also an indication of an illegal addition.

*Figure 4.5: A hazardous step.*

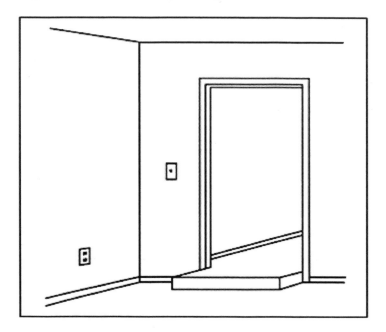

## Torn Carpet

Torn carpet represents a trip hazard on a normal, flat floor, and it represents a more significant hazard when on stairs. The agent should always be aware of deteriorating coverings on stairs, including other types of covering besides carpet. For instance, if the linoleum on a set of stairs was torn or cut on the edge of the nosing, this could also represent a trip hazard. Any tears or cuts of any material can add risk to people who walk on the set of stairs. If the cover material or the step itself is projecting above the rest of the surface of the stair, that represents an additional tripping hazard.

## Smoke Detectors

The minimum standard recommended for smoke detectors is to have at least one operating smoke detector in a central location outside of each sleeping area. This means there must be a smoke detector in each hall outside of a bedroom area. At least two smoke detectors are required in a two-story home with bedrooms on each level.

If there have been additions, repairs, or alterations to the property, each bedroom should probably have a smoke detector in addition to the hall detectors mentioned above. Furthermore, existing dwellings typically only utilize battery-operated smoke detectors, while new constructions typically utilize hard-wired smoke detectors with battery backups.

Many state laws require that smoke detectors be installed in existing *dwelling units* as well as new constructions, new additions, alterations, or repairs. The seller of a single-family home may also be required to deliver to the buyer a written disclosure statement indicating that the property is in compliance with state law concerning smoke detectors.

### Egress Points

It is important to have a method of escape from bedrooms in the event of a fire. Usually, the window offers the best opportunity for escape. However, if the sill of the window is too high above the floor, it is difficult for most people to escape through the window. Basement bedroom windows, common in homes built prior to 1970, tend be the most common culprits for this defect. If the sill or bottom of the bedroom window is more than 44 inches above the floor, the agent should notify the buyer of this defect. While it may be costly to rebuild windows to satisfy this requirement, some buyers may decide that the room in question will not be the one they use as a bedroom.

### Inspecting the Kitchen

Areas of concern in the kitchen include insects, rodents, and appliance and floor problems. The agent should open kitchen cupboard doors to look for signs of roaches or rats, and check the appliances to make sure that they all operate. Are there enough electrical outlets? Is the floor stable and level? Check for the following specific red flags:

### Sink Disposal

One of the most common kitchen-appliance problems is a food waste disposal that may be going out. Waste disposals usually sound very rough when the bearings in them are becoming worn. The agent should turn on the water to the sink that the disposal is built into before and during the test. If the disposal sounds very noisy, the agent should inform the buyer that the disposal may be on its "last leg."

### Refrigerator

The agent should check the frozen compartment of the refrigerator to see if there is frost, ice, or frozen goods in it, and check the main refrigerator compartment to see if it feels cool on the wall of the compartment.

### Range and Oven

The agent should check the range top to see if the burners or elements are operating properly. There should be no items sitting on any of the elements before the agent turns them on. The agent should also check the oven by turning on the bake or the broil option to make sure that they operate properly. There should be no items inside the oven before turning it on. The agent must remember to turn off all of the elements on the oven off before going on to other things, and check the exhaust hood above the stovetop by turning the knob or switching the settings to see that the fan and light work.

To test a microwave, the agent can place a glass of cold water inside the microwave and turn it on for a minute or two, and then check to see if the water is hot. The agent should also check to see that the light turns on when the door is opened.

## Dishwasher

It is very difficult to completely test dishwashers. If some dirty dishes are available, the agent should set them on the top shelf and run the dishwasher, and check to see if they are cleaned by the time the agent prepares to leave. Additionally, the agent should check the floor around the dishwasher for signs of leaks.

## Trash Compactor

The best way for the agent to test a waste compactor is to place some additional trash in it (e.g., a piece of newspaper). After the agent runs the cycle, he or she should check to see if the paper or trash has been crushed. The agent should then inform the buyer or seller if any problems with kitchen appliances have been identified.

## Solid Fuel Stoves and Fireplaces

## Open Cracks

Open cracks in a fireplace can be an indication of serious settling and can be a safety hazard. If there are noticeable cracks in the fireplace, the agent should suggest to the buyer or seller that they contact an expert to perform a complete inspection of the fire box and chimney. Additionally, the hearth on most wood stoves or fireplaces must extend 18 inches or more from the front of the fireplace. The absence of a hearth or one that does not extend the correct distance is a fire hazard.

*Figure 4.6: Noticeable cracks in the fireplace.*

18"

**Creosote Buildup**

Creosote buildup on fireplaces or wood stoves can cause chimney fires. If the wood stove, coal stove, etc. does not have anything burning in it at the time, the agent should open up the door and see a buildup of charcoal-like creosote on the walls or ceiling of the stove box or fireplace exists. If it is noticeable, it probably needs a cleaning. Creosote buildup that is about 1/8th inch thick or more in the fireplace is a safety hazard.

**Bathroom Red Flags and Hazards**

**Slip-Resistant Material**

The combination of water and slick tile floors can be a dangerous hazard. Bathroom floors are likely to be very slippery after a bath or shower, and may result in an increased chance of a fall. The application of textured strips or non-skid mats on the floors of tubs and showers can significantly reduce the risk of a fall. Rubber mats that secure to the floor by way of suction cups can also be effective in reducing falls.

*Figure 4.7: Tub or shower with slip-resistant material and safety handholds.*

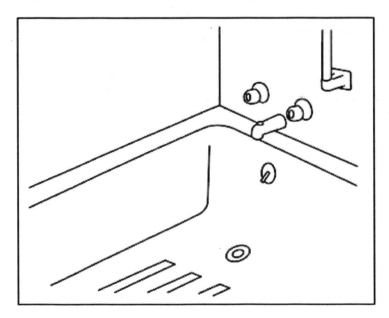

**Safety Handholds**

Safety handholds in the bathroom can significantly reduce the risk of slipping and falling in or around tubs and showers. Typically, these handholds are oriented vertically and are secured to the wall in a sturdy fashion. Since handholds are usually not required by code, they will rarely be properly installed. If the tub or shower does not have handholds, or they are not properly installed, the agent should let the buyer know about these defects.

## Tub and Tile Needs Grouting or Caulking

It is very common to find that the tile or other waterproof wall material above tubs is not well caulked where it meets the tub. This represents a concern for water seeping behind the tub, etc. If the agent notices this defect, he or she should notify the buyer.

## Shower Pan Leak

Tile or concrete floor showers need to have a special seal under the tile or concrete to drain water into the drainage system. This seal is typically referred to as a *shower pan.* If the tile or concrete shower does not have a shower pan or it has deteriorated, water can leak down to the ceiling below. To check for shower pan leaks, the agent should check for stains on the ceilings below the locations of showers. If the house was built before 1970 and has a true tile shower (not a tub/shower combination), the shower pan should be checked by a professional, and the agent should disclose this issue to the buyer.

## Tape Wrapped on Sink Drain

If tape is wrapped around the drain pipes underneath sinks in the house, this almost assuredly means that the pipes are leaking, and the agent should notify the buyer of this defect.

**QUIZZES ARE MANDATORY**: Please log in and submit the chapter quizzes online.

**Chapter Four Quiz**

1.      The quickest way to check stair uniformity is to use the:

      (a)      "plumb bob" test from the bottom of the stairs.

      (b)      "line-of-site" test from the top of the stairs.

      (c)      "vaulting test" by running up and down the stairs.

      (d)      "riser height" test by measuring each and every stair riser.

2.      Which of the following is considered a stair rail deficiency?

      (a)      A rail is missing from the set of stairs.

      (b)      A person cannot fully grasp around the rail so that at least the tips of their fingers touch.

      (c)      The stair rail does not provide a continuous run from the top to the bottom of the flight of stairs.

      (d)      All of the above.

3.      While using a measuring tape to check the widest gap between stair banisters, you notice that they are 10 inches apart. This condition is considered:

      (a)      acceptable.          (c)      borderline.

      (b)      Unacceptable.       (d)      close, but safe.

4.      Which of the following is CORRECT regarding stairway lighting?

      (a)      Every stairway should be well-lit along its entire length.

      (b)      There should be a three-way switch at both the top and bottom of stairs.

      (c)      Both (a) and (b) are correct.

      (d)      Neither (a) nor (b) are correct.

5.      Which of the following represents a potential trip hazard?

      (a)      Short steps (short riser height).

      (b)      Torn carpet at the edge of the nosing.

      (c)      Plastic carpet cover that extends above the rest of the stair surface.

      (d)      All of the above.

6.      Windows are often too high to be used as a method of escape in the event of a fire. Which room's windows tend to be the most common culprit for this defect?

        (a)     Kitchen windows.

        (b)     Upstairs bedroom windows.

        (c)     Basement bedroom windows.

        (d)     Family room windows.

7.      Which of the following should be checked on ranges and ovens?

        (a)     The burners and/or elements.

        (b)     The oven's bake and broil functions.

        (c)     The exhaust hood above the stovetop.

        (d)     All of the above.

8.      If you notice a thick buildup of charcoal-like material in a wood burning fireplace, it is probably:

        (a)     oil.

        (b)     creosote.

        (c)     tar.

        (d)     paint.

9.      While inspecting bathrooms, one should look for:

        (a)     Non-skid strips or mats on the floors of tubs or showers.

        (b)     Safety handholds in showers or tubs.

        (c)     Adequate grouting or caulking where the wall meets the tub.

        (d)     All of the above.

10.     Tile or concrete floor showers need to have a special seal under the tile or concrete to drain water into the drainage system. This is called:

        (a)     flashing.

        (b)     a "P" trap.

        (c)     a shower pan.

        (d)     sheathing.

## Chapter Five: Red Flags in the Major Mechanical Systems

**Important Terms**

breaker
breaker panel
carbon monoxide
carbon dioxide
flue
heat exchanger
HVAC
"P" trap
pressure release valve
solder

**Learning Objectives**

Upon completion of Chapter Five, you should be able to complete the following:

- Identify red flags in the major mechanical systems of a home.

- Recognize general electrical red flags.

- Examine an electrical panel and identify potential problems.

- Explain water heater bracing and disclosure requirements.

- Recognize an improperly anchored water heater.

## General Plumbing Red Flags

Another important area that the agent should check for red flags is the plumbing system. Some concerns include insufficient water pressure, clogged drains, and corroded pipes. Check all of the plumbing fixtures in the house. Do the faucets flow? Do they drip when turned off? Do the sinks drain? Do the toilets flush? Are there signs of leaks under sinks, dishwashers, or around the base of the water heater? The agent should inform the buyer if he or she locates any of these plumbing red flags.

## Lead-Based Solder on Copper Pipe

Until the early 1990s, lead-based solder could be used for joining copper to the water supply pipe. If the home in question was built before 1990 and has soldered copper supply piping on it, the agent should disclose to the buyer that lead-based solder may have been used, and that the buyer should contact Poison Control in his or her local area for further information about the use of lead-based solder.

## No "P" trap on washer drain

A "P" trap on a drain consists of the plumbing that runs down from the drain, then curves up and then back down again. Its purpose is to prevent sewer gasses from coming up into the living area. To see an example of a "P" trap, look under the sink in a bathroom. The agent should check for a "P" trap on the clothes washer drain. A missing "P" trap is more common in pre-1970s homes, when installing a washer drain was typically a retrofit.

## General Electrical Red Flags

The agent should check all of the electrical fixtures and appliances in the house. Do the lighting switches work? Do the lighting fixtures turn on and off? Do the electrical kitchen appliances, including ranges, refrigerators, and dishwashers, operate? The agent should notify the buyer if any of these electric systems are inoperative.

## Breakers and Panels

Modern building codes require that the main electrical breaker for the home is located outside. This is necessary so that firefighters or other public servants can shut off the electricity to the house, if necessary. Many pre-1970s homes do not have a main electrical shutoff, and if they do, it is often located inside the house. If this is the case, the agent should inform the buyer of this red flag. Bringing the electrical system of the house up to modern code requirements is usually cost prohibitive, and may not be required by the local municipality.

Building codes in most states prohibit exposed wiring. Besides being a safety hazard, open panel slots are a code violation and the agent should point out this defect to the buyer.

*Figure 5.1: Panel with exposed slots.*

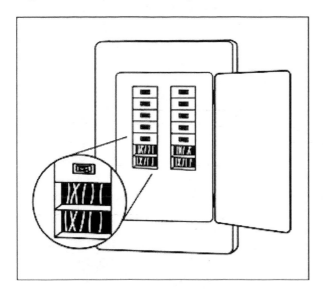

Are there any damaged plug receptacles? Are there any scorch marks? Damaged electrical outlets are a safety hazard and the agent should point out this defect to the buyer. The existence of this defect may indicate a more extensive problem with the electrical system in the home.

*Figure 5.2: Damaged electrical outlet.*

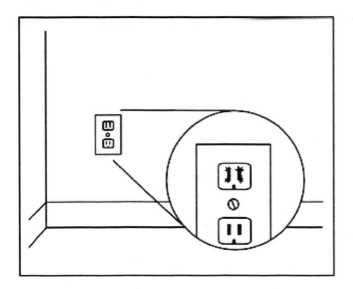

**Fuses**

Fuses with amperage ratings greater than the wiring design parameters will sometimes result in the loss of the wires' insulation value. The agent should recommend that the principal install special amperage-selective inserts to prevent the use of oversized fuses in the future.

If screw-in fuses on a panel that has an amperage rating higher than 20 amps exist, the wiring in the home is probably not adequately protected. If any of the screw-in fuses on the fuse panel are more than 20 amps, the agent should notify the buyer that the wiring may have been over-amped.

## Aluminum Wiring

Aluminum wiring is a potential fire hazard. This hazard is caused by overheating that occurs at the connections between the wire and devices such as switches and outlets, or at splices. Aluminum wiring was installed in homes in the period from the early 1960s to the early 1970s. Homes or additions built during this period may contain aluminum wiring. Aluminum wiring is still permitted for certain applications, including residential service entrance wiring and single-purpose higher amperage circuits, such as 240V air-conditioning or electric-range circuits.

The best way that the agent can check for this is to randomly select a light switch in the home or addition built during the period referenced above, and remove the cover for the switch. The agent should not reach or poke any object inside the switch area with the cover off, and should check the color of the bare portion of the wire that is connected to the switch. If the wire is a copper color, then the wire is probably copper. However, if the wire is a silver color, it is most likely aluminum. The agent should notify the buyer that there may be aluminum wire in the home. The switch cover should be replaced when the inspection is complete.

## Air Conditioner, Furnace, and Water Heater Inspection

## Smell of Gas

If the agent smells gas or suspects a gas leak, the agent should not light a match or any other open flame, should not use any electrical appliance or turn lights on or off, and should not use the telephone. Everyone in the building should leave immediately. The agent should call the gas company from another location, and notify them of the problem. The local gas company will usually respond very quickly to this type of concern—they will send a technician to the home to identify the source of the leak. The agent can then forward this information to the buyer. Additionally, the agent should notify the seller that the house gas should not be turned on until the leak is fixed. Gas shutoffs should be located for quick access and easy turnoff. Blocked or inaccessible gas valves are a red flag.

## Inadequate Combustion Air

Any gas-burning appliance needs oxygen to burn. Without oxygen, the appliance will not operate properly and it could be at risk of producing carbon monoxide. A source of air for combustion must be made available to any gas-burning appliance; oil-fired water heaters and furnaces are no exception. If there is not free communication of air throughout the house, from the basement to the upstairs area, there is probably not enough of an inside air supply to satisfy the combustion air requirements of the furnace and water heater.

One way a mechanical contractor may alleviate this problem in an existing home is to install vents at the tops and bottoms of all collapsible doors that stand in the way of the free communication of air from the furnace to the upstairs area.

## Combusted Air Backflow on the Water Heater or Heating Flue

Combusted air backflow on any gas appliance means that the air that has passed by the burners is not escaping entirely through the flue as intended, but is also escaping out into the space where the furnace and/or water heater is located. This may allow for low or no oxygen to be present, and a high amount of carbon dioxide (and possibly carbon monoxide) gas to come into the living space.

To see if this is the case, the agent should check for the feel of the hot flow of air around the uppermost lips of the mixers on water heaters or standard efficiency furnaces. The construction of medium- and high-efficiency furnaces do not allow for combusted air backflow, and therefore, they cannot be similarly checked.

Water heaters typically have a bell-shaped mixing housing that sits directly on top of the water heater with the flue rising above it. Hot air coming out from the sides of the mixing housing into the room indicates combusted air backflow. The agent should not directly touch the mixing housing or flue on gas burning appliances.

On standard-efficiency furnaces, the agent can check for hot air flow at the mixing box just below where the flue exits the furnace. The mixing box is typically a rectangular-shaped box, with an opening underneath. If hot air is coming out of the bottom of the furnace mixing box, the agent should recommend to the seller that he or she turns the furnace off until it is repaired. Disclose to the buyer the specifics of the problem.

## Water Heater Bracing and Disclosure Requirements

Effective January 1, 1996, owners of any real property that contains a water heater are required to brace, anchor, or strap the water heater to resist falling or horizontal displacement due to earthquake motion. This is applicable to all existing water heaters, as well as new and replacement water heaters sold in California on or after July 1, 1991. The law also imposes additional disclosure requirements.

Additionally, a seller of any real property must certify to a prospective purchaser that this section has been complied with, including compliance with applicable local code requirements. This certification must be in writing and may be shown in existing transactional documents, including, but not limited to, the *Homeowner's Guide to Earthquake Safety*, a real estate purchase contract, a transfer disclosure statement, or a local option disclosure statement. C.A.R. Form SDC-14, the *Smoke Detector/Water Heater Statement of Compliance*, will satisfy this requirement.

## Method of Anchoring

The new law does not specify how to anchor the appliances. One of the easiest and cheapest methods is to wrap the water heater with metal straps (known as *plumber's tape*) and to attach the ends of the straps to 2x4 wall studs with lag screws and washers. This is called the *Tape Method*.

## Pressure Relief Valve on Water Heater

All water heaters can get hot and can build up a great deal of pressure. Pressure relief valves should be installed on all water heaters, regardless of age. The pressure relief valve is typically a brass fixture located on the top of the water heater to allow for depressurization.

*Figure 5.3: Pressure relief valve.*

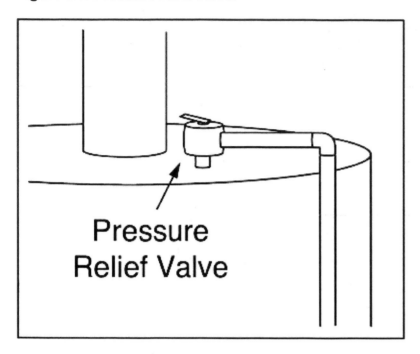

### Gas Furnace Heat Exchangers

There is a very high risk that the heat exchanger is cracked in gas furnaces that are older than 20 years. A cracked heat exchanger means that combusted air that is high in carbon dioxide and low in oxygen, and possibly high in carbon monoxide, could pass through the crack in the heat exchanger and be mixed in with ventilated air that circulates throughout the house. This is a matter of significant concern. Some utility companies will do a free inspection of the gas furnace heat exchanger. In other cases, the principal may have to pay the utility company or an HVAC specialist to conduct the inspection.

### Thermostats

One of the most important components of a home's heating and air conditioning system is the thermostat. If the home has a faulty thermostat, the HVAC system may be wasting energy dollars. To test the thermostat, the agent should turn it up to see if the heater turns on, and down to see if the air conditioner comes on. Listen for any loud noises as these systems engage.

**QUIZZES ARE MANDATORY**: Please log in and submit the chapter quizzes online.

**Chapter Five Quiz**

1.      Which of the following is considered a general plumbing red flag?

        (a)     Faucets do not flow properly.

        (b)     There are signs of leaks under sinks, dishwashers, and around the base of the water heater.

        (c)     Toilets do not flush.

        (d)     All of the above.

2.      Which of the following is considered a general electrical red flag?

        (a)     Some lighting fixtures do not turn on.

        (b)     Electrical kitchen appliances, including ranges, refrigerators, and dishwashers do not operate.

        (c)     Kitchen lighting does not work.

        (d)     All of the above.

3.      Modern building codes require the main electrical breaker for the home to be located:

        (a)     inside the house.

        (b)     outside the house.

        (c)     on the roof of the house.

        (d)     under the house.

4.      What should the agent look for when inspecting a home's electrical system?

        (a)     Damaged plug receptacles.

        (b)     Scorch marks around electrical outlets.

        (c)     Open panel slots.

        (d)     All of the above.

5.      If the agent finds screw-in fuses on a panel that has an amperage rating higher than ___ amps, the wiring in the home is probably not adequately protected.

        (a)     10        (c)     30

        (b)     20        (d)     40

6.    Aluminum wiring is a potential fire hazard that is caused by:

   (a)    flammable insulating material that may melt if the system shorts out.

   (b)    undersized wire gauge that cannot handle a typical home's power supply.

   (c)    overheating at connections between the wire and devices such as switches and outlets, or at splices.

   (d)    deterioration over time due to weather conditions.

7.    *Combusted air backflow* refers to a potential problem with:

   (a)    gas furnaces and/or water heaters.

   (b)    electrical junction boxes.

   (c)    natural gas supply lines.

   (d)    sewage pipes.

8.    The requirement to brace water heaters against falling or horizontal displacement due to earthquake motion applies to:

   (a)    replacement water heaters only.

   (b)    new water heaters only.

   (c)    new and replacement water heaters.

   (d)    damaged water heaters only.

9.    One of the easiest and cheapest methods of anchoring a water heater is with metal straps called:

   (a)    anchor tape.

   (b)    water heater tape.

   (c)    contractor's tape.

   (d)    plumber's tape.

10.   One of the most important components of a home's heating and air conditioning system is the:

   (a)    fuel supply.

   (b)    thermostat.

   (c)    insulation.

   (d)    fan.

## Chapter Six: Environmental Red Flags

### Important Terms

asbestos
Comprehensive Environmental Response, Compensation,
    and Liability Act (CERCLA)
Endangered Species Act
Environmental Impact Statement
Environmental Protection Agency (EPA)
Environmental Site Assessment
Federal Water Pollution Control Act
lead
Occupational Safety and Health Act
radon
Resource Conservation and Recovery Act
Safe Drinking Water Act
"sick building" syndrome
Toxic Substance Control Act
underground storage tank (UST)
volatile organic compounds
wetlands

### Learning Objectives

Upon completion of Chaper Six, you should be able to complete the following:

- Identify basic environmental red flags on a site.

- List the major laws that govern environmental hazards.

- Explain the value of wetlands to our environment.

- Explain the potential problems with underground storage tanks.

- Identify asbestos in a home and explain the disclosure requirements.

- Explain what radon is and understand how it forms.

- List the agent's responsibilities regarding lead in a home.

- List the most common indoor pollutants.

## Federal Environmental Laws

Real estate professionals should be aware of each of the following laws established by the United States Congress to protect the public from environmental hazards.

## The Comprehensive Environmental Response, Compensation, and Liability Act (CERCLA or Superfund)

CERCLA, enforced by the Environmental Protection Agency (EPA), created a fund to finance the remediation of environmental hazards and to compensate victims for such hazards. This act also established the duties of owners and operators of hazardous materials who handle facilities to notify state and federal governments in the event of unauthorized releases of hazardous waste into the environment. In addition, it created a National Contingency Plan and emergency response authority.

## Resource Conservation and Recovery Act

RCRA enables the EPA to regulate organizations that generate hazardous waste, hazardous waste processing facilities, and the transportation of hazardous waste.

## The Federal Water Pollution Control Act

This act directed the EPA to establish a Water Pollution Advisory Board and established a permit and licensing system to enforce pollution control standards. It addressed the release of pollutants into navigable waters and provided federal funds to assist state and local governments in the development of publicly owned water treatment facilities.

## Safe Drinking Water Act

This act required the EPA to develop and enforce national drinking water regulations in cooperation with state governments. States retain the primary enforcement responsibility for public water systems if they have adopted regulations at least as stringent as the EPA standards and have adequate enforcement capability.

## Toxic Substance Control Act

This act empowered the EPA to assess the effect of chemical substances on public health and the environment. It placed the burden of researching and testing toxic substances on the private sector, and it covers the manufacture, distribution, processing, use, and disposal of chemical substances.

## Occupational Safety and Health Act

Empowers OSHA to establish and enforce standards to ensure safe and healthy workplace environments.

## Endangered Species Act

The habitats of certain protected species under the Federal Endangered Species Act cannot be disturbed or modified. The Federal Fish and Wildlife Service is the Federal agency that deals with this issue. This agency should be contacted prior to any development or farming of land, and must be contacted if there are any federal monies that are expected to be involved in the development or use of this land (e.g., FHA, VA, FHMA, the SBA, and even the secondary mortgage market, such as Fannie Mae or Freddie Mac).

Criminal penalties exist for the violation of the Endangered Species Act. When any new developments are planned or farmland is for sale, the agent should inform the developer, commercial building buyer or seller, or farm buyer or seller, that they should contact the Fish and Wildlife Service about these issues before proceeding with development or purchase.

### Wetlands

Wetlands are areas that through surface drainage or underground water, become saturated and support vegetation typical of saturated soil conditions. In some cases, this definition could be as narrow as allowing for land that may only be wet for as few as seven days per year.

While many of the original wetlands in America have been eliminated by drainage of the water or filling with dirt, wetlands serve an important biological purpose. They help lower the Biological Oxygen Demand (BOD), which in turn helps aquatic life to survive. They also help filter out suspended solids (e.g., sediment) from the water, thus allowing the water downstream to be cleaner. Wetlands also help eliminate metals, pathogens, nitrogen, and phosphates from water. The regulation of wetlands is an attempt to reduce the loss of wetlands that promote clean water, and that provide habitats for various animal species.

Many local, regional, and state regulations limit the extent to which wetlands may be developed. However, recent US Supreme court decisions protect landowners from some development restrictions by treating onerous regulations as a "taking" under the Fifth Amendment of the Constitution. A number of Federal agencies are involved in the regulation of wetlands, including the Army Corps of Engineers and the EPA for non-agricultural uses, and the Natural Resources Conservation Service for agricultural uses.

There are potentially criminal penalties for failure to follow the laws concerning developing wetlands. An attorney that is familiar with wetlands regulations should be consulted prior to beginning development of a property or expansion of a farming use in a wetland area.

### Environmental Reports

There are two types of environmentally related reports: the Environmental Impact Statement and Environmental Site Assessment.

### Environmental Impact Statement

An *Environmental Impact Statement* is of central import in new construction. This report details the impact of a new building, development, or change in land use on the environment. This report can be quite broad, addressing the effect on the habitat of flora and fauna in the area, as well as the effect on the population, including traffic, noise, safety, and air quality. If governmental funding is involved in the project or change of use, the Environmental Impact Statement must be available to the public, and public hearings must be held, which can often criticize the results in the statement or the project as planned.

Generally, the wetlands and endangered species sections above also need to be the concern of the commercial agent who is developing new properties. Hazardous and toxic waste as well as underground storage tank issues are a common concern.

Commercial or industrial agents should consult an attorney about specific ways to deal with these issues in their state to better assure that adequate warning of the possibilities of these problems in these buildings is provided. Often, environmental site assessments will involve not only inspecting the site for evidence of problems (e.g., unexplained barren patches, unusual odors, etc.), and interviewing the sellers and the owners of neighboring properties, but also checking other resources, such as aerial photographs and title searches, to better determine what previous uses may have been made of the property. Often such an evaluation is called a *Phase I* evaluation if it satisfies the American Society of Testing Materials Standards for an environmental site assessment.

## Environmental Site Assessment

The second environmental report is the Environmental Site Assessment (ESA), which is an attempt to determine if there are any environmental hazards that could affect the use of the property and that might involve potential financial responsibility in the future.

## Underground Storage Tanks

Underground storage tanks (UST) are defined as any tank system, including its piping, that is used for the storage of hazardous substances and that has at least 10 percent of its volume underground. Federal law regulates only those tanks that are used to store petroleum or those hazardous chemicals that are regulated under CERCLA.

The agent should question the seller about past uses of the property, and ask the seller whether there is an underground tank on the property. The agent should also review the title documents to see if the property was ever used for something other than a residence. Both current and former UST owners are responsible for the maintenance of an underground storage tank. Therefore, responsibility for complying with federal UST requirements can continue even after ownership of the UST ends. If there is an underground storage tank that is located on the property, many states will require that the tank be removed if it has not been in use for six months or more.

## Asbestos

Asbestos is a carcinogenic mineral fiber. Most exposure occurs through inhalation—the inhaled asbestos fibers penetrate deep into the lungs. Fibers can also be ingested with food that is eaten in a contaminated area. The body cannot break down asbestos fibers, and there is no way to remove them once they are embedded in the lungs. A person who has been exposed to asbestos is at risk of developing a lung disease called *asbestosis* that is rarely curable.

Asbestos was used extensively in building construction from the early 1900s until the late 1970s. One of the most common exposed uses for asbestos was in ceiling texture. This texture is often referred to as *popcorn ceiling* or *cottage cheese* texture. Houses or additions that were built after 1978 are not likely to have asbestos texture.

Other common applications for asbestos include manufactured siding, roof shingles, and furnace ductwork wrap. White asbestos tape can be found at furnace ductwork junctions where the individual lengths are attached together to keep air from escaping at the joints.

Asbestos has also been used for attic or wall insulation. As attic insulation, asbestos typically has a white, flour-like look, or can appear in a more fluffy version. It can be readily distinguished from fiberglass insulation that tends to glisten when light is shone on it, where asbestos insulation does not. Asbestos insulation is typically not found in homes that were built after about 1950.

Wall and ceiling patching and joint compounds typically included asbestos until about 1977. Many flexible floor tiles and their adhesives contained asbestos as a binder for many years.

According the Federal Government, material is defined as containing asbestos if it contains more than 1% of asbestos as determined by an approved laboratory. If the seller is selling a home that he or she believes may contain asbestos, the seller should recommend that the buyer have the home tested by an asbestos abatement specialist.

Residential buildings with less than four units are exempt from having to use federal- or state-approved asbestos abatement teams to treat or remove asbestos. Nevertheless, agents are strongly discouraged from suggesting that an unqualified individual (e.g., the typical buyer) attempt to abate possible asbestos in their own home. If the agent and/or buyer suspect asbestos, they should contact the local state health department or an industrial hygienist for more information. The agent or buyer should also make that sure the testing company is not also in the business of conducting the abatement, which is a possible conflict of interest. The buyer, not the agent, should choose the testing company.

**Asbestos Abatement**

Asbestos material that has not been damaged should be left alone. If this is not the case, there are three common options for asbestos abatement: encapsulation, enclosure, or removal. Asbestos abatement should always be conducted by a licensed asbestos professional.

1) Encapsulation: A sealant is used to bind the asbestos fibers together or coat them to encapsulate the exposed asbestos.

2) Enclosure: Asbestos-insulated piping is enclosed in a protective material that prevents the release of fibers.

3) Removal: Removal of asbestos should only be done by certified asbestos professionals.

**Radon**

Radon is a naturally occurring radioactive gas that is produced by the decay of uranium and radium, and generated in the soils beneath homes. Radon is a known human carcinogen.

*Figure 6.1: Various ways radon can enter a home.*

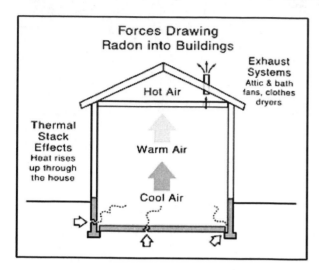

Radon can enter a home through cracks in the floor slab or foundation, or through water that runs into the house.

Generally, if the home is found to have a radon level of 4 pCi/l (picoCuries per liter of air), it is considered to be at the "action level" as determined by the EPA. This means that the house should have some type of radon mitigation equipment installed to help reduce the radon levels in the house.

Elevated radon levels have been discovered in every state. While there are factors that can predict whether or not a home is likely to have elevated radon levels, it is not possible determine whether or not a specific home has radon without a test. A radon test measures the radon level over at least a 48-hour period. Test protocol requires that doors and windows remain closed except for normal exit and entry. It is estimated that in up to half of radon tests conducted, there is tampering with the protocol requirements (e.g., a window was left open during the test, the test device was moved during the testing period, etc.). Tampering voids the results of the test.

If there are indications of radon in the seller's area, the agent should recommend to the buyer that he or she conduct a radon test after moving into the house. If a test conducted prior to the home purchase indicated a low level of radon, while a test conducted after moving in indicates elevated radon, a likely culprit could be tampering.

Mitigation of radon can be expensive (e.g., $1,000 to $3,000). If a buyer is interested in knowing about whether or not homes in the neighborhood have been found to have high radon levels, the agent should recommend that the buyer contact the radiation division of the state health department. If this division does not handle the radon issue in the buyer's state and/or there have not been any radon surveys done in the buyer's state, the department may still know whom you could contact regarding these issues. The agent should avoid suggesting that there is no need for testing, interpreting test results, or downplaying the issue.

**Lead**

Lead can have serious effects on health, especially on the health of children (e.g., brain damage can occur). People can accumulate lead in their body by inhaling or ingesting it. Remodeling efforts in a home that contains lead-based paint is one of the more significant ways lead finds its way into the human body. Additonally, toddlers tend to stick toys and other items in their mouths that may have lead on them. Children can suffer serious health problems if they ingest or inhale lead paint chips or dust. The problems include learning disabilities, decreased growth, impaired hearing, and brain damage. If pregnant women ingest lead, they may also carry health risks to their unborn children or may miscarry.

An accurate test for lead is one that bombards X-rays into the paint sample (X-ray fluorescence). If greater than 1.0 microgram of lead per square centimeter of paint is found by using this method, the paint is classified as lead-based.

Most of the federal regulations regarding lead in homes cover houses built prior to 1978. However, disclosure must be made to not only home buyers, but also to tenants by the seller or lessor and his or her agents. Oral leases are not exempted from these regulations. These disclosure requirements not only require disclosure about whether the paint in the house has been previously tested or not, but also requires that the responsible party provide copies of actual reports of the results.

Furthermore, the pamphlet entitled *Protect Your Family from Lead in the Home* must be provided, along with appropriate language in the purchase agreements or leases with regard to the disclosure, etc. For instance, the *Disclosure of Information and Acknowledgment* form must also be included along with the offer to the buyer. All agents are responsible for this unless they are buyers' agents and they are only being paid by the buyer in the transaction at hand. All agents should be sure that the buyer has received both the pamphlet and the disclosure form. In addition, the buyer has the right to have the house tested for lead within up to 10 days or another agreed-upon time limitation. However, the buyer can legally waive this opportunity.

There are some exceptions to these regulations, although they do not commonly apply except perhaps in the first case:

1) Renewals of existing leases, so long as appropriate disclosures were made at the time of the original lease (not applicable for leases that were in effect on September 6, 1996).

2) Living units that have no bedrooms or separation between the sleeping and living areas (e.g., dormitories, barracks, individual rental rooms within a residence, studios, efficiency apartments, etc.).

3) Property that involves a lease that covers 100 days or less without a lease renewal or extension.

4) Rental property certified as *lead-based paint free* by a federally certified inspector or a state-certified inspector under a federally authorized certification program.

5) Property that is being sold as a foreclosure (this exception does not apply when the home is resold).

6) Housing for the disabled or elderly, so long as children under the age of six are not expected to live in the housing.

If, after discussing these lead issues with a buyer (especially buyers with young children), the agent determines that the buyer has concerns about this issue, the agent should ask the buyer if he or she wishes to see only homes built after 1978. The agent may also want to explain that this may limit the selection of both homes and neighborhoods from which to choose.

The agent should never suggest in any way, even by implication, that there is no need to test a home built prior to 1978, and should always provide the buyer with phone numbers of the appropriate state and federal agencies. Remember, there are both civil and criminal penalties for violation of these regulations, including the possibility of treble damages.

If there are contingencies in the *Earnest Money Agreement*, it would be wise for the agent to make sure that the deadlines for testing or voiding the contract if lead is discovered are spelled out. Also, it would be wise to state in the contract how the earnest money will be handled in the event of a void by the buyer. While there is a Federal definition of how much lead must be in paint in order to be considered lead-based paint, it ultimately must be up to the buyer to decide what level he or she is willing to tolerate. Any deadlines (e.g., for testing, rescission, etc.) should be easily determinable, whether it is a specific date or a specific number of days from signing, notification, etc. to establish the deadline.

## Indoor Pollutants

## Volatile Organic Compounds

Indoor pollutants cover a large range of chemicals, including volatile organic compounds and biological- and combustion-related pollutants.

*Volatile organic compounds* is a phrase that is used to denote carbon compounds that tend to be emitted as gases into the air, whether originating from a solid or liquid compound. One of the most common culprits is pesticides. Recent evaluations have suggested that we either use or track into our house enough pesticides to make the indoor air of our house more polluted than the air outside. Careful use of pesticides and herbicides around the home is one of the best ways to reduce pesticide exposure in the home. It is a good idea for the agent to furnish a seller's questionnaire, which includes questions about the previous use of pesticides in the home.

*Formaldehyde* is another volatile organic compound that is a concern. It is often a degassed byproduct of pressed wood (e.g., *Chipboard* or OSB board) and insulation (e.g., Urea Formaldehyde Foam Insulation (UFFI)) products. After a number of years, the risk of exposure to formaldehyde is greatly reduced because any degassing of formaldehyde from the products is more likely to have completed. This issue is primarily one of sensitivity; some individuals are especially sensitive to formaldehyde exposure. The agent should ask the principal whether or not the principal knows if he or she is sensitive to formaldehyde or not. If the principal is sensitive to formaldehyde, you will want to explain to him or her that newer homes are more likely to contain formaldehyde contaminants than older homes.

**Biological Pollutants**

Biological pollutants can include mold, pollen, animal hair and excrement, bacteria, and insect parts and feces. The most common biological pollutants that may not be easily cleaned up are probably molds and bacteria. Possible moist areas in the house can create circumstances that are conducive to these growths. Sources of moisture should be eliminated and the area affected by these growths should be cleaned.

**Combustion Pollutants**

Combustion pollutants are typically gasses that are produced through heating systems that rely on fossil fuels for their energy. Having heating appliances that are in good operating condition is the best way to reduce the risk of exposure to combustion pollutants. If there are any space heaters in the home, it would be wise for the agent to forewarn the buyer that there may be some gaps in the heating system that could require supplemental heat. Fuel-burning space heaters are never considered an appropriate response to "cold pockets" in a home.

**Sick Building Syndrome**

While there are a variety of reasons for why a building is classified as *sick*, there are a few specific items that can be responsible for a sick building. Many of them are chemically related (e.g., pesticides—see *Indoor Pollutants*, above). Some are simply a matter of unsafe heating or air-conditioning systems in the building (e.g., not enough integration of fresh outside air into the system). Others are related to the building products used in construction (formaldehyde that is released from some of the pressed wood products used in construction).

Have the buyer conduct a confidential survey of the current tenants to find out whether they or any of their employees experience any unusual symptoms. If the buyer plans on significantly changing the use of the building, he or she should consider consulting an expert in heating and air conditioning to be sure that the system does not need to be modified to accommodate the new use.

Homes that are serviced with water by a well are far more likely to run into contamination problems than those that utilize a municipal source. Specific causes of well water contamination include leaking underground storage tanks, faulty septic systems, underground pipelines, hazardous and non-hazardous landfills, road de-icing, agricultural runoff of pesticides and fertilizers, surface impoundments, waste injection wells, and mining activity. Once contaminated, groundwater is difficult, if not impossible, to clean up. An individual homeowner can rarely afford to treat contaminated well water. Therefore, it is important that property owners are aware of the factors that could affect a property's drinking water supply.

Careful questioning of the seller about the history of the well and discovery of the results of any previous tests is critical. Homebuyers should also obtain their own water tests on the well water if feasible. Such a test should at least include evaluations for nitrates, coliform bacteria, pH, and dissolved solids. Tests for some of the more common metal or other contaminants should also be done (e.g., iron, sulfate, etc.).

Another level of testing can be conducted when industrial contamination of groundwater is suspected. This consists of the costly testing of water for a wide range of organic chemicals and heavy metals such as arsenic and chromium. Local, state, or federal environmental officials should be consulted about the need for such costly testing. While testing can help determine the quality of drinking water on that day, testing cannot easily predict future well-water contamination.

## Toxic Mold

### Molds: What Are They?

Molds are microscopic organisms that nature uses to break down dead material and recycle nutrients back into the environment. Molds require a food source to grow, and they reproduce best in moist areas. As they digest organic material, they slowly destroy whatever they grow on. Molds can be identified by some sort of discoloration in a variety of different colors.

### How Are We Exposed To Molds?

The most common type of mold exposure is through airborne ingestion of microscopic mold spores that are released into the air as molds digest the organic compounds they grow on. Significant health problems usually only arise when a large number of spores are inhaled. Exposure can also occur by touching contaminated materials or surfaces or by eating contaminated food.

People vary in their sensitivity and reaction to mold exposure. Some people may react to a very small number of mold spores while others may be relatively non-allergic to mold particles. Allergic reactions (sometimes mistaken for hay fever) are the most common symptoms seen with mold exposure. These may include (alone or in combination):

- Wheezing, difficulty breathing, and shortness of breath.
- Nasal and sinus congestion.
- Eye irritation (burning, watery, or reddened eyes).
- A dry, hacking cough.
- Nose or throat irritation.
- Skin rashes or irritation.

### Toxic Mold Disclosure Requirements

In 2001, to address recent public concerns about toxic mold, the legislature passed into law *The Toxic Mold Protection Act* (SB 732). This act is intended to study and measure permissible exposure limits of toxic mold and to establish new disclosure obligations for sellers and landlords concerning the presence of toxic mold.

Part of The Toxic Mold Protection Act called for the creation of a taskforce to work with the California Department of Health Services (DHS) to develop permissible exposure limits for molds, adopt practical standards to assess the health threat posed by the presence of mold, adopt mold identification guidelines for the recognition of mold, and to develop and disseminate remediation guidelines for molds.

Once these standards had been set by the DHS, sellers, transferors, and landlords of commercial and industrial property (but not sellers or transferors of residential property) were required to provide written disclosure of the mold conditions on their property to potential buyers and prospective tenants, renters, landlords, or occupants.

With single-family residential properties, The Toxic Mold Protection Act changed the Transfer Disclosure Statement (TDS), adding mold to the list of natural hazards in the Sellers information, item II.C.1. In addition, there is a section in the Environmental Hazards Disclosure Booklet on mold. If this booklet is delivered to a transferee in connection with the transfer of real property, neither the seller nor broker is required to provide additional information concerning the environmental hazards described in the booklet.

Licensees should note that there is no requirement imposed upon the seller, transferor, or landlord of commercial or industrial properties to conduct air or surface tests for the presence of molds. However, once a landlord is informed that mold is present in the building, heating system, ventilating system, air-conditioning system, or appurtenant structures, landlords must test for the presence of mold and take the appropriate action to eradicate the problem.

The act also protects transferors, as well as listing and selling agents, from liability for any error, inaccuracy, or omission based upon information that is provided by a public agency or a report prepared by a third-party expert.

**QUIZZES ARE MANDATORY**: Please log in and submit the chapter quizzes online.

**Chapter Six Quiz**

1.    Which of the following acts established a permit and licensing system to enforce pollution control standards?

    (a)    Resource Conservation and Recovery Act

    (b)    Federal Water Pollution Control Act

    (c)    Safe Drinking Water Act

    (d)    Toxic Substance Control Act

2.    Certain protected species cannot be disturbed or modified under the:

    (a)    Wetlands Act.                          (c)    Endangered Species Act.

    (b)    Environmental Protection Act.          (d)    Green Act.

3.    Wetlands serve an important biological purpose by:

    (a)    helping biological life survive.

    (b)    filtering out sediment from the water.

    (c)    eliminating metals, pathogens, nitrogen, and phosphates from the water.

    (d)    all of the above.

4.    To investigate the possible existence of an underground storage tank on the property, the agent should:

    (a)    question the seller about past uses of the property.

    (b)    ask whether there is a UST on the property.

    (c)    review title documents to see if the property was ever used for something other than a residence.

    (d)    all of the above.

5.    If you are selling a home that you believe may contain asbestos, the agent should recommend that the buyer have the home tested by:

    (a)    an asbestos abatement specialist.

    (b)    an asbestos chemist.

    (c)    a home inspection contractor.

    (d)    the seller.

6.    By using a sealant to coat exposed asbestos fibers, you are performing the asbestos
      abatement procedure called:

      (a)    enclosure.

      (b)    removal.

      (c)    encapsulation.

      (d)    overlap.

7.    Radon is a naturally occurring radioactive gas produced by:

      (a)    decay of plant and animal matter in the soil.

      (b)    decay of carbon fibers (coal) in the soil.

      (c)    decay of igneous rock in the Earth's crust.

      (d)    decay of uranium and radium in the soil.

8.    People can accumulate lead in their body by:

      (a)    inhaling it.

      (b)    ingesting it.

      (c)    both (a) and (b).

      (d)    neither (a) nor (b).

9.    One of the more significant ways lead finds its way into our bodies is through:

      (a)    illegal dumping.

      (b)    toxic spills.

      (c)    remodeling.

      (d)    repainting.

10.   Which of the following is considered a Volatile Organic Compound?

      (a)    Formaldehyde

      (b)    Pesticides

      (c)    Herbicides

      (d)    All of these.

# Agency

3 Hours of Continuing Education for
Salesperson and Broker License Renewal

**Lumbleau Real Estate School**
23805 Hawthorne Blvd.
Torrance, CA 90505

© 2015 by Mark R. Chamberlin

## DISCLAIMERS

Although every effort has been made to provide accurate and current information in this text, the ideas, suggestions, general principles, and conclusions presented in this text are subject to local, state, and federal laws and regulations, court cases, and any revisions of the same. The author and/or publisher is not engaged in rendering legal, tax, or other professional services. The reader is thus urged to consult with his or her employing broker and/or seek legal counsel regarding any points of law. This publication should not be used as a substitute for competent legal advice.

This course is approved for continuing education credit by the California Bureau of Real Estate. However, this approval does not constitute an endorsement of the views or opinions that are expressed by the course sponsor, instructor, authors, or lecturers.

# Table of Contents

## Chapter One

### Important Terms

agency
agent
beneficiary
commingling
default
divided agency
dual agency
encumbrance
escrow
fiduciary
lessee
lessor
material facts
principal
trust account
trustee

### Learning Objectives

Upon completion of Chapter One, you should be able to complete the following:

- Define *agent*.
- Define *principal*.
- Describe the various forms of agency relationships.
- Describe the duties of the principal and agent.
- Describe the difference between a dual and divided agency.

**Agency Relationship between the Broker and Principal**

**Introduction**

In a legal context, the term *agency* ordinarily describes a relationship in which two parties, the *principal* and the *agent*, agree that one will act as a representative of the other. The principal is the person who wishes to accomplish something, and the agent is the person who is employed to act on the principal's behalf to achieve that accomplishment.

**Agent Defined**

Since 1872, *California Civil Code § 2295* has provided that "An agent is one who represents another, called the principal, in dealings with third persons."

**Principal Defined**

A principal is a person who employs another to act as his or her agent in dealings with third parties, and/or who gives authority to an agent or attorney to do some act for him or her.

The word *principal* includes, when applicable to the circumstances, the seller, buyer, lessor, lessee, lender, or borrower.

**Agency Defined**

An agency is the relationship between a principal and an agent, whereby the agent represents or acts on behalf of the principal in dealings with third parties. From this simple relationship, a vast body of rules has emerged that govern the rights and duties of the principal and the agent.

The principal-agent relationship, as we define it, means a relationship in which the parties have agreed that the agent is to represent the principal while negotiating and transacting business, but only so far as the parties have authorized their agreement.

**Special Agency:** The agency relationship you will most often deal with is referred to as a special agency. The agent (broker) is a special agent, and is authorized to perform only those acts that are specifically authorized by the principal.

**General Agency:** An agency relationship in which the principal authorizes the agent to perform all acts connected with a particular trade, business, or employment. This relationship implies authority on the part of the agent to act without restriction or qualification in all matters that relate to the business of his or her principal.

**Dual Agency:** An agency relationship in which the agent acts concurrently for both of the principals in a transaction.

**Single Agency:** An agency relationship in which the agent represents only one principal.

### Duties of the Principal and Agent

The principal-agent relationship is a *fiduciary* relationship, one of trust and confidence. Each party owes to the other a duty to act with the utmost good faith. Each should be entirely open with the other, not keeping any information from the other that has any bearing on their arrangement (see this text on *dual agency*).

### Duties Owed by the Principal to the Agent

The primary duty owed by the principal to the agent is to simply comply with the terms of their employment agreement. Failure by the principal to do so will render him or her liable to the agent for damages. If the breach is material, the agent may refuse to act any further on behalf of the principal.

### Duties Owed by the Agent to the Principal

### *Obedience*

The agent is a *fiduciary* and must, at all times, act in the best interest of the principal. The agent may not do anything that could adversely affect the principal's intended purpose, whether intentional or otherwise. Thus, an error on the part of the agent, caused through ignorance, is no defense at all.

The principal-agent relationship requires all licensees to be loyal to their clients at all times. They are prohibited by law from personally profiting by virtue of their agency, except by the agreed compensation for their services. The fiduciary character that the broker assumes is the most important and outstanding aspect of the relationship. The courts regard this relationship in the same general manner and in almost the same strictness as the relationship between a *trustee* and *beneficiary*.

As a fiduciary, the agent is bound by law to exercise the utmost good faith, loyalty, and honesty while executing the duties of his or her agency. It is the duty of the agent to obey the clear instructions of the principal, so long as the instructions are legal. The instructions should be clear and unambiguous, and the involved parties can only accomplish this by executing a well-prepared contract of employment.

The agent or employee cannot compete with the principal on matters connected with the agency, and of course, cannot act as the agent for the principal's competitor.

It is the duty of the agent to obtain the best possible terms for the principal. For example, in one case, the broker was held liable to the principal, a *lessor*, for telling a prospective *tenant* that he could obtain a longer lease than the lessor wanted to provide [*Mitchell v. Gould, (1928) 90 C.A. 647*].

Another duty of the broker to the principal is to not derive secret profits at the principal's expense. Numerous cases have reiterated the rule that a broker must return to the principal any secret profit that the broker obtains, even if the property was bought or sold for what it was currently worth.

Consider the situation in which the broker pays $100,000 to purchase a property worth $100,000 from the principal, while knowing that there is a buyer who will purchase the property for $120,000. Even though the broker paid the principal for what the property was worth, the principal can still recover $20,000 from the broker.

### Reasonable Care

Unless special provisions in the agreement specify otherwise, the agent is expected to exercise the degree of care and skill that is reasonable under the circumstances. In other words, the agent has a duty to not be negligent.

**Example:** Suppose *Principal L* has funds that he wishes to lend to borrowers at current interest rates. He employs *Broker B* to act on his behalf in locating borrowers. B recommends that L lend money to *Borrower T* without investigating T's credit rating and without obtaining from T any security. T turns out to be a notoriously bad credit risk and is actually insolvent at the time of the loan. If L is later unable to collect from T, B will probably be liable to L, because she failed to exercise reasonable care while creating the loan.

Under some circumstances, the agent may be under a special duty to exercise more than an ordinary degree of care and skill. For example, if the agent undertakes to serve in a capacity that necessarily involves the possession and exercise of a special skill, such as that of a lawyer, stockbroker, or real estate broker, he or she is required to exercise the skill ordinarily possessed by competent persons who pursue that particular calling.

In the case of *Timmsen v. Forest (1970) 6 C.A. 3d 860*, a broker can be held liable to the seller for procuring and recommending a financially unsound offer. In Timmsen, the court held that a broker could be liable for misadvising a seller about the effect of a subordination provision in the seller's contract.

In the case of *Ford v. Cournale, (1973) 36 C.A. 3d 172*, it seems that the broker must obtain, explain, and critique income and expense records for the buyer of income property and act, in essence, as the buyer's investment counselor. In this case, the broker had failed to explain to the buyer of a 42-unit apartment building that the income stated in the broker's statement was based on 100% occupancy, that the list of expenses included items such as pool maintenance and management, and as a result, that the cash flow would be considerably less than the buyer anticipated. The broker had also failed to inspect the books and records of the seller.

To meet his or her duty of care, the broker may also have to know and explain the legal consequences of a transaction. In the case of *Banville v. Schmidt, (1974) 37 C.A. 3d 92*, a seller sold his property through a real estate broker and carried back a second deed of trust. The security for the obligation (the property sold) proved to be inadequate when the buyer *defaulted* on his payments to the seller-beneficiary. The broker was held liable for not recognizing and explaining to the seller what could happen when there is a default on a purchase money obligation and for not investigating the adequacy of the buyer's security.

In the case of *Wilson v. Hisey, (1957) 147 C.A. 2d 433*, the court stated that although the failure to recommend getting a title report may not, in itself, constitute negligence, a broker who affirmatively stated that there was only one encumbrance against the property thereby breached his or her duty of care.

### Duty to Account

It is the agent's duty to maintain an account of all money or property received or paid out on behalf of the principal. In this regard, an agent should never mix his or her own money or property with that of the principal. For example, the broker should set up a separate bank account or *trust account* for the principal's money. One account is usually sufficient for all principals, provided that a separate record is maintained for each principal.

**Special Note:** Many readers are of the belief that all brokers are required to maintain a trust account. This is not true. Although it is recommended, it is not required by law. A broker may deposit the trust funds into a neutral *escrow* or hold the money if properly instructed, in writing, by the person authorized to give such instructions. It is difficult for an active agency to avoid *commingling* without a neutral trust account in which the money can be deposited.

In the case of *Brown v. Gordon (1966), 240 C.A. 2d 659*, Gordon had received $1,000 from Brown as deposit on an offer to purchase a parcel of real estate. Gordon deposited the money into his trust fund but withdrew it the same day. He then commingled and converted it for his own use without the knowledge and consent of Brown. Gordon's explanation for his conduct was that he was using his trust account as his personal account to avoid possible attachment of the account as a result of a civil litigation in which he was involved. By immediately cashing the check, he felt that Brown would be less likely to renege on his offer.

Although Gordon had been a broker for 18 years without a prior disciplinary record, the court held against him, stating that "among the qualifications of a real estate broker is a full understanding of the essential duties and obligations between principal and agent, the principles of real estate practice and the canons of business ethics."

### Duty to Notify

Another important duty of the agent is to notify the principal of all relevant facts that have a bearing on the interests of the principal. The agent must do this as soon as reasonably possible after learning about such facts.

### Loyalty

Perhaps the most important duty owed by the agent to the principal is that of loyalty. Quite obviously, the agent should not compete with the principal. The agent should avoid any existing or potential conflict of interest.

For example: If *Agent B* is hired to sell goods for *Principal S*, he should not sell them to himself. If B is hired to buy goods for S, he should not buy them for himself. It is difficult, if not impossible, for the agent to completely serve in the principal's best interests when the agent's own personal interests are involved. Of course, the agent may perform such actions if the principal is fully informed and gives consent, and the consent is in writing.

A breach of fiduciary duty can subject the broker to criminal prosecution. In the case of *People v. Barker, (1960) 53 Cal. 2d 539*, a broker was convicted of grand theft for secretly profiting at the expense of his principal by covertly buying his principal's property at one price and immediately reselling it to his waiting buyer at a higher price. Furthermore, a breach of a fiduciary duty can have serious consequences in addition to civil liability to one's principal. Any such breach can result in administrative sanctions levied by the Real Estate Commissioner. In fact, a licensee may be disciplined for acts constituting a breach of fiduciary duty even if no complaint is made. In *Abell v. Watson, (1958) 155 C.A. 2d 158*, a broker's license was suspended for his failure to tell the seller that the purchaser of the seller's property was the broker's sister, even though the seller testified that he didn't care who bought the property and made no complaint against the broker.

It is considered unlawful conduct if a licensee does the following:

- Fails to disclose to the seller of real property, during a transaction in which the licensee is acting in the capacity of an agent, the nature and extent of any direct or indirect interest that the licensee expects to acquire as a result of the sale. (Although not required by law, it is wisely suggested that a licensee inform the other party of his or her license status when acting as a principal.)

- Fails to disclose to the buyer a direct or indirect interest in the property by a person related to the licensee by blood or marriage. (This includes distant relatives.)

- Fails to disclose to the buyer a direct or indirect interest by any other person with whom the licensee occupies a special relationship where there is a reasonable probability that the licensee could be indirectly acquiring an interest in the property.

- Fails to disclose to the prospective buyer, when first discussing the purchase of real property, the existence of any direct or indirect ownership interest of the licensee in the property.

If the agent, while working for the principal, acquires knowledge of any confidential information, the agent should not disclose this information to outsiders without the principal's consent. Remember, the courts have consistently equated the duty owed by an agent-to-principal with the duty owed by a trustee-to-beneficiary.

The real estate licensee who is the agent of the seller owes a duty of fair and honest dealing to the buyer. The agent must not withhold from a prospective buyer any **material facts** regarding the property which are known to the agent but unknown to the prospective buyer or otherwise unascertainable by the prospective buyer through diligent attention and observation.

**Dual Agency**

**Dual Agency Defined**

A *dual agency* is an agency relationship in which the agent acts concurrently for both of the principals in a transaction.

An agent may not act for more than one party without the consent of both parties.

The term *dual agency* does not, in itself, describe an unlawful activity. In fact, the law is reasonably clear when it states that an agent cannot legally act for two principals in negotiations with each other unless both have knowledge of, and consent to, the dual agency [B & P Code § 10176(d)]. Thus, we find that the agent can represent both parties in the same transaction.

However, such conduct is generally contrary to public policy because it places the agent in the untenable position where he or she may represent conflicting interests. For example, the agent may represent a seller who is trying to obtain the highest possible price for her property and a buyer who is trying to buy the seller's property at the lowest price possible.

The more frequently we look at the dual agency, the more we discover that the agency is almost always inevitably breached when a broker represents both the buyer and the seller. For what is the broker to do if the buyer states that he or she is willing to pay more than the seller has offered? What if the seller has told the broker that he or she would accept less than the asking price? Whatever choice the broker makes will hinder one of the principals from obtaining the best possible price, and withholding information may ensure that the duty of disclosure is breached as well. The agent who tries to act as agent for both parties is highly prone to committing fiduciary breaches. In fact, it may be impossible for an agent to avoid doing so in this situation.

### A Divided Agency Is Unlawful

Before we discuss the lawful dual agency, it is best that we explain a common unlawful dual agency, namely, the *divided agency*. As noted above, the term *dual agency* does not, in itself, denote unlawful behavior. To be unlawful, the dual nature of the agency must exist without the knowledge and consent of both parties: the buyer and seller, lessee and lessor, etc. Knowledge and consent does not limit itself to material facts. The safest rule to apply is that when the agent represents both parties in any way, the agent becomes a dual agent. When the agent becomes the agent of both parties, without the knowledge and consent of both parties, the agency is more accurately identified as a divided agency. When the agency is a divided agency, it is a violation of Section 10176(d) of the Business and Professions Code (the Real Estate Law).

In a divided agency (unlawful) the agent cannot recover commissions from either principal. Carrying this principle further, it has been held by the Supreme Court that the undisclosed dual agency is a ground for rescission by either principal without any necessity of showing injury.

The consequences of the failure to disclose a dual agency include the following:

- The right of either principal to cancel the transaction whether or not either principal incurred damages.

- The right of either principal to hold the licensee responsible for damages actually incurred.

- The right of either principal to refuse to compensate the licensee.

- The possible suspension or revocation of the licensee's real estate license.

A divided agency is always a dual agency. However, a dual agency is *not* always a divided agency. A divided agency is always a violation of law, whereas a dual agency is not necessarily a violation of law.

**There Are Two Classes of Dual Agency**

*Intentional Dual Agency*

Lawful dual agencies are difficult to create *intentionally*. Intentional dual agencies, of course, are not unknown to the law, but they are exceedingly rare and difficult to create. This is because both principals (seller and buyer) must agree to common representation by the same broker, and such an agreement must be made with the full knowledge, understanding, and acceptance of all real and potential conflicts of interest and inhibitions on performance that the dual agency may generate.

In other words, intentional dual agencies are difficult to create because of the inherent conflict between the objectives of the seller and buyer. The degree and timing of the disclosures mandated by the dual agency impose substantially impossible burdens on the dual agent in the context of the real estate marketplace.

*Accidental Dual Agency*

Some agency relationships are created by accident. This type of agency can be created by conduct or representations that reasonably induce the principal to assume that the broker is acting as his or her agent, even though no written agreement exists.

Accidental agency is nothing more than the law's way of insisting that the broker be taken at his word, whether those words are "Trust me," "I'll represent you," "I'll protect your interests," or other magic words that describe the special obligations of a fiduciary.

**Dual Agencies Are Easily Created by Accident**

Although it may be difficult or impossible to intentionally create a dual agency, it can easily be created by accident. However, accidental dual agencies are fundamentally different from intentional dual agencies. Implicit in the intentional dual agency is an agreed-upon acceptance by both principals of the broker's fiduciary duty of loyalty to both principals.

*When a broker lists and then shows to the buyer, is an accidental dual agency created?*

The accidental dual agency does not involve the acceptance that is required in the intentional dual agency and, as such, imposes on the salesperson a liability for any breach of fiduciary duty to either principal, even if such a breach is transactionally unavoidable.

The accidental agency relationship may simply be established by the parties indicating their intention that it exists. A seller, a buyer, or any other person who can establish that he or she relied on a broker may be found to be the broker's principal. The relationship can exist even when real estate is neither bought nor sold, as exemplified by the case of *Realty Projects Incorporated vs. Smith, (1973) 32 C.A. 3d 204*, in which a mortgage loan broker was held to be the agent of borrowers with whom they dealt with in the course of their business. Furthermore, a broker may be the agent of a principal from whom the agent receives no compensation. For example, a broker may be the agent of the buyer even though his or her commission is paid by the seller [Sands v. Eagle Oil and Refining Co., (1948) 83 C.A. 2d 312].

Although many real estate brokers represent buyers, the agency relationship that most commonly exists, in respect to residential properties, is one in which the broker represents the seller. It is in this relationship, the listing, that the broker has been the most effective and the most valuable. In the residential real estate transaction, the real estate broker has been proven to be the person most qualified to provide real estate marketing services for the seller.

In the performance of any service for the buyer, the listing broker runs the risk of creating an accidental dual agency. Therefore, if the conduct or representations of the broker induce the buyer to believe that the buyer is the broker's principal, instead of the third-party beneficiary of the broker's efforts on behalf of the seller, then the broker may be held liable for injury suffered by the buyer as a consequence of such belief.

### *Who does the real estate agent represent in a sales transaction?*

This question has puzzled real estate brokers, attorneys, and courts for many years. Legally, the agent represents the seller who signed the listing contract that authorizes the agent to find a buyer for the property. As mentioned earlier, this fiduciary relationship requires that the seller and the agent keep each other informed of all material facts that develop during the term of the agency. It's a two-way street of communication. Since the real estate agent is usually paid his or her sales commission by the seller rather than the buyer, agents often feel their primary (and sometimes only) loyalty is to the seller.

Since the agent works for the seller, the question arises, "Who represents the buyer?" Too frequently, the answer is "nobody."

The courts have wrestled with this dual agency problem for years without reaching a satisfactory solution. Some judges feel that the buyer is a third-party beneficiary of the seller-agent contract and is owed a duty of full disclosure by the agent. Can an agent truly be a fiduciary to both buyer and seller? The bible says, "No servant can serve two masters."

There is no easy answer to the question, "Can an agent fairly represent both the buyer and seller in the same transaction?" Probably the best solution, although not the most popular, is to not attempt this because conflicts between the best interests of the buyer and seller are sure to develop.

### In-House Sales

Because of the possibility of accidentally creating an unintentional dual agency, many real estate brokerages have a rule that an agent is not to represent both the buyer and seller in a property sale, which means that two agents must be involved in every sale. While not the perfect solution, it avoids the inherent conflict created when one agent tries to do the impossible and look out for the best interests of both the buyer and seller in the same sale.

The following case will exemplify this situation: In the case of *Ohanesian v. Watson, (1953) 118 C.A. 2d 386*, a licensed real estate broker obtained an exclusive listing on a ranch property that was advertised for sale. The prospective purchasers contacted the broker and gave him an exclusive on property they currently owned and inserted a provision that the cash proceeds from the sale of their home was to be applied to the purchase price of the ranch. Subsequently, without the knowledge of the buyer or seller, the broker acted as the agent of each, and collected a commission on the sale of the house and the ranch.

Judgment against the broker is affirmed. Notwithstanding, by acting as agent of and receiving a commission from the sellers of the ranch, he prevented the sellers from securing the full price offered by the buyers by demanding and receiving a commission from the purchasers. This specific violation is referred to as a *divided agency*.

This rule of agency is specifically mentioned in the California Real Estate Law, and its violation is cause for revocation or suspension of a real estate license. See Section 10176 (d) of the California Business and Professions Code.

**Important Note:** An In-House agency is a dual agency, even though the seller and buyer are represented by different persons.

**QUIZZES ARE MANDATORY**

CalBRE regulations now require the submission of chapter quizzes before you can access the final examination. You must log in and submit the chapter quizzes online before you can access the final examination. After submitting the last chapter quiz, you will receive a link to the final examination. You were issued a Personal Identification Number (PIN) and login instructions when you enrolled.

**Chapter One Quiz**

1.      An agent is one who represents another, called the _____, in dealings with third parties.

        (a)     customer
        (b)     principal
        (c)     master
        (d)     employer

2.      If an agent (broker) is a *special agent*, he or she is authorized to perform:

        (a)     all acts connected with a particular transaction.
        (b)     only those acts specifically authorized by the principal.
        (c)     all acts on behalf of the principal without restriction.
        (d)     only those acts that the agent feels are necessary.

3.      Which of the following would be a fiduciary duty of the agent according to the law of agency?

        (a)     Acting with the utmost good faith, integrity, loyalty, and honesty.
        (b)     Giving the principal advice about how to hold title.
        (c)     Telling the principal which escrow company to use.
        (d)     Acting as a dual agent.

4.      A dual agency is legal if:

        (a)     all parties are notified of the dual agency before close of escrow.
        (b)     the buyer and seller consent to the dual agency.
        (c)     the broker and escrow company consent to the dual agency.
        (d)     all parties are notified of the dual agency after they sign the contracts.

5.      Which of the following statements is correct?

        (a)     A dual agency is ALWAYS a divided agency.
        (b)     A divided agency is NOT always a dual agency.
        (c)     A dual agency is NOT necessarily a violation of law.
        (d)     A dual agency is ALWAYS a violation of law.

## Chapter Two

### Important Terms

age
close of escrow
common interest
disclaimer
ground lease
hold harmless clause
option
red flag
statute of limitations
subagent
vendor

### Learning Objectives

Upon completion of Chapter Two, you should be able to complete the following:

- Describe the agency law.

- Describe the duties of disclosure based upon the landmark case of Easton v. Strassburger.

- Describe the agency disclosure form.

- Explain the reasons for agency disclosure confirmation.

**Agency Disclosure Law**

**Is the Disclosure Law Really Necessary?**

Before we go into the technical details of the California Disclosure Law, we would like to introduce (or review in some cases) two areas that you should be very familiar with: (1) The *hold-harmless Clause* (found in most listings), and (2) the *Easton v. Strassburger* case.

**Hold Harmless Clause**

The following represents the contents of a typical *hold-harmless clause* found in most listing contracts (this is a statement by the seller to the broker):

"I agree to save and hold the Agent harmless from all claims, disputes, litigation, and/or judgments arising from any incorrect information supplied by me, or from any material fact known by me concerning the property which I fail to disclose."

The broker may not use the hold-harmless clause as a shield to protect the broker from his or her own negligence in securing the correct information. Additionally, the broker cannot use the clause as a defense if the broker passes along erroneous information that a reasonably competent visual inspection by the broker would have revealed.

It is well proven that it is the broker's responsibility to seek out information and ask questions. The law presumes that the broker has superior knowledge and training, and as such, assumes, at the very least, equal responsibility for passing on misinformation that could have been avoided.

To most readers, the above two paragraphs seem quite reasonable. Almost all readers agree that no one should be excused for his or her own negligence.

However, what do we do when someone comes along and says that it is the real estate agent's duty to disclose facts that should be known in the exercise of reasonable diligence? This is probably not quite as bad as it sounds. Or is it?

**Easton v. Strassburger**

The following discussion of the *Easton v. Strassburger* decision should make it clear that the agent must disclose any information to the buyer about a transaction that might remotely affect the present or future value of the property if a reasonably diligent inspection by the agent would uncover said *material facts*.

*Disclosure Responsibility of the Real Estate Agent*

On February 22, 1984, the California Court of Appeal decided the case of Easton v. Strassburger. On May 31, 1984, the California Supreme Court denied the requests of the appellant, which included the National Association of Realtors®, The California Association of Realtors, and several other organizations, and the Easton case is now judicial precedent in California. It may be cited by attorneys as authority in posing what has become known as the *Easton liability*.

## The Facts of the Case

The property in question was a one-acre parcel of land located in the City of Diablo, California. The property was improved with a 3,000 square foot home, a swimming pool, and a large guest house. Easton purchased the property for $170,000 from the Strassburgers in May of 1976 and escrow closed in July of that year.

Shortly after Easton purchased the property, there was a massive earth movement on the parcel. Subsequent slides destroyed a portion of the driveway in 1977 or 1978. Expert testimony indicated that the slides occurred because a portion of the property was made up of fill that had not been properly engineered and compacted. The slides caused the foundation of the house to settle, which in turn caused cracks in the walls and warped doorways. After the 1976 slide, damage to the property was so severe that although experts appraised the value of the property at $170,000 in an undamaged condition, the value of the damaged property was estimated to be as low as $20,000. Estimates of the cost to repair the damage caused by the slides and avoid recurrence ranged as high as $213,000.

During the time that the Strassburgers owned the property, a minor slide occurred in 1973 that removed about 10 to 12 feet of the filled slope, and a major slide occurred in 1975, in which the fill dropped about eight to ten feet in a circular shape that was 50 to 60 feet across. The Strassburgers did not tell the agents anything about the slides or the corrective action they had taken. Easton purchased the property without being aware of the soil problems on the property or the property's history of slides.

Employees of the agency inspected the property several times during the listing period and, according to the appellate court, there was evidence that the agents "were aware of certain 'red flags' which should have indicated to them that there were soils problems. Despite this, the agents did not request that the soil stability of the property be tested and did not inform [Easton] that there were potential soils problems."

The case facts included the following:

1)   At least one of the listing agents knew the property was built on fill (a red flag) and that settlement and erosion problems are commonly associated with such soil.

2)   The listing agents had seen netting on a slope (a red flag) that had been placed there to repair a slide that had occurred recently.

3)   One of the listing agents testified that he had observed that the floor of the guest house was not level (a red flag).

It does not require an expert to explain the relationship between uneven floors and the possibility of unstable soil or the relationship between past slide activity and the likelihood of future slide activity.

## Results of the Legal Action

Easton filed suit against Strassburger, the agency, and others. The agency was charged with fraudulent concealment, intentional misrepresentation, and negligent misrepresentation. The jury found against the agency only under a simple negligence theory. It returned a joint and several judgments against the defendants and apportioned comparative negligence.

The jury's special verdict found all named defendants had been negligent, and assessed damages of $197,000. Negligence was apportioned among the parties under the principles of comparative negligence in the following percentages:

| | |
|---|---|
| Strassburgers | (65%) |
| Builders | (15%) |
| Listing agency | (5%) |
| Cooperating broker | (5%) |
| Other defendants | (10%) |

The seller became insolvent following the sale of the property. The agency appealed the trial court judgment relying principally upon an asserted error by the trial judge while giving the following instructions to the jury:

"A real estate broker is a licensed person or entity who holds himself out to the public as having particular skills and knowledge in the real estate field. He is under a duty to disclose facts materially affecting the value or desirability of the property that are known to him or which through reasonable diligence should be known to him."

The agency contended that a broker's duty to a prospective buyer was only to disclose known facts about the property, not facts that should be known in the exercise of reasonable diligence.

Although the evidence did not establish actual knowledge of the property's history of slides and soils problems, actual knowledge was not necessary to establish liability for negligence. The jury merely had to conclude that a reasonably competent and diligent inspection of the property would have uncovered the property's history of soils problems.

The Court of Appeal rejected the agency's contention. In its opinion, it pointed out that the law of California has long required both the seller of real property and the broker to inform a prospective buyer concerning material defects known to them, and unknown to or unobservable by the buyer. It pointed out that a broker in a transaction is liable for the intentional tort of fraudulent concealment or negative fraud if he or she fails to disclose material facts about the property that are not known to, nor within the reach of the diligent observation of the prospective buyer. The court acknowledged the fact that no California appellate decision had expressly held that a broker is under a duty to disclose material facts about a property that the broker should have known. However, it then went on to declare that the purpose of assuring that a prospective buyer was provided with sufficient information to make an informed purchasing decision "would be seriously undermined if the rule were not seen to include a duty to disclose reasonably discoverable defects."

The court's reasoning can be summed up in the following observations:

"If a broker were required to disclose only known defects, but not also those that are reasonably discoverable, he would be shielded by his ignorance of that which he holds himself not to know. The rule thus narrowly construed would have results inimical (adverse, harmful) to the policy upon which it is based. Such a construction would not only reward the unskilled broker for his incompetence, but might provide the unscrupulous broker the unilateral ability to protect himself at the expense of the inexperienced and unwary who rely upon him. In any case, if given legal force, the theory that a seller's broker cannot be held liable for undisclosed defects would inevitably produce a disincentive for a seller's broker to make a diligent inspection. Such a disincentive would be most unfortunate, since in residential sales transactions, the seller's broker is most frequently the best situated to obtain and provide the most reliable information on the property and is ordinarily counted on to do so."

### What Is a Red Flag?

This question is impossible to answer without leaving out someone's definition of what a red flag may look like. What a red flag is to you may not be a red flag to me. Whatever the answer, it is now the law to look for red flags! Therefore, let's look at some of the more obvious red flag warnings. Some red flag examples include the following:

- Water stained ceilings.
- Cracks in ceilings, walls, and floors.
- New additions, for whatever reason, such as new walls, rooms, garage modifications, a roof, gutters and eaves, a retaining wall, wall paneling, floors, etc.

Now, consider the situation where an agent is listing an older home. Does the possibility of termites, dry rot, or other types of infestation fall within the law established by the Easton case? If so, it appears that no sale, especially the sale of an older home, can safely conclude without a structural pest control inspection.

What about major appliances, or forced-air furnaces, air conditioners, lawn sprinkler systems, swimming pools, saunas, fences, plumbing, solar unit installations, etc.?

The above is obviously not an all-inclusive list of potential red flags. Brokers must be aware of the facts and circumstances that are unique to each property, follow their instincts, and point out potential red flags. When red flags appear, the broker should not hesitate to recommend to buyers that they seek professional assistance.

### Will an "As-Is" Clause Avoid Easton Liability?

Generally, no. No matter how well worded, no clause will relieve the seller or the broker of their liability to disclose known material facts or those that "should be known."

### Should the Broker Offer an Opinion?

Once the broker is aware of the red flag, and after following a reasonably competent and diligent inspection, what should the broker do? One thing that the broker should not do is venture an opinion as to what problem underlies the red flag. If the broker lacks the expertise and his or her opinion amounts to nothing more than a guess, the broker may give the appearance of possessing the expertise that, in fact, he or she does not possess. If the broker presents such an impression, the broker would invite a court to judge him or her by the standard of expertise so represented.

**Note:** Whether the opinion is based on guesswork or expertise, all disclosures should be in writing. A written disclosure may protect the broker involved.

### A Written Disclaimer Won't Work

The question will undoubtedly arise, "Is it possible to utilize a written *disclaimer* to avoid liability under the Easton decision?" The answer is "probably not."

Throughout the court's opinions on the Easton decision are statements that expound the liability of the broker due to the broker's superior knowledge. It seems most unlikely that negligence liability can be avoided by a disclaimer. (A disclaimer is a written statement in which the broker states that he or she is not responsible or liable for his or her acts or failures to act.) There is no simple way to avoid Easton liability.

It would also be unwise for an agent to rely on the *hold-harmless clause* of the listing agreement to provide protection.

### To What Properties Does Easton Apply?

It appears that the Easton decision applies only to residential properties of one to four units, including a manufactured home as defined in Section 18007 of the Health and Safety Code, and then, probably only to personal residences. The decision referred to the fact that "a purchaser of commercial real estate is likely to be more experienced and sophisticated in his dealings in real estate and is usually represented by an agent who represents only the buyer's interests" [C.C. § 2079].

Easton applies to properties offered for sale [C.C. § 2079]. It also applies with equal force and effect to leases that include an option to purchase, ground leases of land on which one to four dwelling units have been constructed, or real property sales contracts, as defined in C.C. § 2985, for that property [C.C § 2079.1].

In a Court of Appeals case, Smith v. Rickard, the Court of Appeal ruled that the Easton duty to inspect applies only to residential properties of one to four units, and not commercial property. The mere presence of a residence on a commercial property does not transform the whole property into a residence.

In Smith vs. Rickard, two brokers (serving as dual agents) had listed a ranch that included a residence and avocado orchards that were cultivated commercially. When the buyer was inspecting the property, he noticed that some of the trees did not look well. The buyer and the brokers took the seller's word for the condition of the trees (too much water). Only after close of escrow did the buyer discover that the trees were afflicted with root rot. The buyer had to destroy hundreds of trees which resulted in a reduced cash flow, default on the loan, and eventually foreclosure and loss of the property. The buyer sued the brokers and the owner. It took the Court of Appeals to get the brokers off the hook. How easy it would have been for the brokers to call upon the expertise of an agricultural expert.

It seems obvious that preventing legal problems is preferable to solving them. The Easton case started in May of 1976, the day the agents failed to exercise their duty to both the buyer and seller, and the action was settled in 1984. The above Smith vs. Rickard case was decided in

1988. Who knows how the court will rule in the future. It may very well be decided, by a heretofore unknown and probably obscure case, that Easton applies to every transaction under 140 stories tall.

Play it safe—if something looks suspicious, disclose it. If it can't be lived in, disclose it. If the seller or the agent doesn't disclose something out of the ordinary, the buyer always sues the seller and the agent.

### What Kind of Inspection Must the Broker Conduct?

The broker (agent) must conduct a reasonably competent and diligent visual inspection of the property offered for sale [C.C. Section 2079].

### What Must the Broker Reveal from the Results of His or Her Inspection?

The broker must reveal all facts that materially affect the value or desirability of the property that such an inspection would reveal [C.C § 2079].

### To Whom Must the Broker Reveal the Results?

The broker must reveal the results of his or her inspection to the prospective purchaser of the residential property, which compromises one to four dwelling units [C.C. § 2079].

### When Must the Broker Conduct the Inspection?

The broker must conduct the inspection whenever he or she has a written contract with the seller to find or obtain a buyer. This also applies to another broker who acts in cooperation with such a broker to find and obtain a buyer [C.C § 2079].

### Scope of Inspection

The duty of inspection does not include or involve areas that are reasonably and normally inaccessible to such inspection, nor to inspection of common areas in *common interest subdivisions*, if the seller or broker supplies the prospective buyer with documents and information specified in C.C. § 1360 (Declaration of restrictions, bylaws, and articles of incorporation) [C.C. § 2079.3].

### Standard of Care of Inspection

The standard of care owed by the broker to a prospective purchaser is the degree of care a reasonably prudent real estate licensee would exercise, and is measured by the degree of knowledge through education, experience, and examination required to obtain a real estate license under California law [C.C. § 2079.2].

### Buyer's or Prospective Buyer's Duty of Reasonable Care

The law provides that a buyer or prospective buyer has the duty to exercise reasonable care to protect himself or herself, including obtaining knowledge of adverse facts that are known or within the diligent attention and observation of a buyer or prospective buyer [C.C. § 2079.5].

**Statute of Limitations**

The law provides for a two-year *statute of limitations*, which runs from the date of recordation, *close of escrow*, or occupancy—whichever occurs first [C.C. § 2079.4].

**Example:** Broker Brown called upon Mr. and Mrs. Jones to list their personal residence for sale. During the interview, broker Brown noticed water stains on the sheet rock wall in the family room. He asked the Jones' about the stains and Mr. Jones told him that the roof had leaked the previous winter and that they would have the roof repaired and the wall fixed. Therefore, the broker made no reference to this matter in the listing. Shortly thereafter, broker Brown showed the home to Mr. and Mrs. Smith. Upon entering the family room, broker Brown noticed that the water-damaged wall was now a nicely paneled wall. Presuming the repairs had been made as Mr. Jones said they would, he did not mention this to the Smiths. Several months after the Smiths had purchased the property, there was a heavy rain, and as it had done before, the water poured in, causing considerable damage to some furniture, the carpets, and the paneled wall. The seller was nowhere to be found. A discussion with the neighbors revealed to Mr. and Mrs. Smith that it was an old leak that was covered over and not repaired.

**Question:** If Mr. Smith sued broker Brown, how would the courts most likely rule?

**Answer:** Judgment would most likely fall in favor of the plaintiff, Mr. and Mrs. Smith, with damages to be paid by broker Brown. Brown should have suggested that Mr. and Mrs. Smith have the roof and wall inspected by a qualified inspector before closing escrow. Additionally, broker Brown should have been suspicious when he saw the paneled wall. A reference about the damaged wall should have appeared in the listing agreement as a warning to other brokers. Brown cannot use the hold-harmless clause as a defense.

**Easton Conclusion**

The more we think about the Easton decision, the more we wonder how real estate sales survived before the Easton decision became law. Although this is said tongue-in-cheek, there is some truth to the statement. For too many years, the buying public has had to deal with poorly prepared licensees who treated a real estate transaction like a clerk in a store. "Take the order and let the manufacturer worry about quality problems." The manufacturer in this case would be the title company, escrow company, and the buyer's lack of knowledge of his or her rights. No doubt the buyer's attorney will tell the buyer about his or her rights.

**Agency Relationships in Residential Real Property Transactions**

The California Legislature enacted the *agency legislation* in order to accomplish the following:

- Further the education of consumers about the existence of various types of agency relationships that may occur in residential real property transactions.

- Require disclosure to principals by their agents of the various types of agency relationships that may occur in transactions.

- Provide the disclosure in simple, comprehensible, and nontechnical terms.

- Require uniform disclosure to help consumers understand the agency relationship options available to them.

Since January 1, 1988, it has been required that the listing and selling agents in real estate transactions provide both buyers and sellers with specified written and oral disclosures. The listing agent *must* deliver a specified written disclosure form to the seller *prior* to the time the listing is signed by the seller, and the selling agent *must* deliver the same disclosure to the buyer as soon as practicable, but *prior* to the execution of an offer.

The law also requires the licensee (selling and listing agents) to orally inform the buyer and seller whether he or she is acting exclusively as the buyer's agent, exclusively as the seller's agent, or as a dual agent that represents both the buyer and seller.

Finally, the licensee must confirm the agency relationship in a written contract to purchase, or in a separate writing executed by the seller, the buyer, and the selling agency.

### Definitions

*The Disclosure Law* applies to the agent and associate agent. The law concerning the form of the disclosure is set forth in the following paragraphs.

The following terms have the following meanings as used in Civil Code § 2079.13:

1) **Agent:** A person acting under provisions of this title in a real property transaction, and includes a person who is licensed as a real estate broker, and under whose license a listing is executed or an offer to purchase is obtained.

2) **Associate Agent (Licensee):** A person who is licensed as a real estate broker or salesperson under Chapter 3 (commencing with Section 10130) of the B & P Code, and who is either licensed under a broker or has entered into a written contract with a broker to act as the broker's agent in connection with acts requiring a real estate license, and to function under the broker's supervision in the capacity of an associate licensee.

    The agent in the real property transaction bears responsibility for his or her associate licensees who perform as agents of the agent. When an associate licensee owes a duty to any principal or to any buyer or seller who is not a principal, in a real property transaction, that duty is equivalent to the duty owed to that party by the broker for whom the associate licensee functions.

3) **Buyer:** A transferee in a real property transaction, and includes a person who executes an offer to purchase real property from a seller through an agent, or who seeks the services of an agent in more than a casual, transitory, or preliminary manner, with the object of entering into a real property transaction. *Buyer* includes the vendee or lessee.

4) **Dual Agent:** An agent acting, either directly or through an associate licensee, as the agent for both the seller and the buyer in a real property transaction.

5) **Listing Agreement:** A contract between an owner of real property and an agent, by which the agent has been authorized to sell the real property or to find or obtain a buyer.

6) **Listing Agent:** A person who has obtained a listing of real property in order to act as an agent for compensation.

**Note:** The Civil Code does not identify nor define the term *selling agent*. Such a term merits discussion because there are usually two agents in most transactions: namely, the listing agent and the selling agent.

7)   **Selling Agent:** The selling agent is either **1)** a listing agent who acts alone (i.e., a listing agent selling his or her own listing); or **2)** an agent who acts in cooperation with a listing agent, and who sells or finds and obtains a buyer for the real property; or **3)** an agent who locates property for a buyer for which no listing exists and presents an offer to purchase to the seller. Therefore, the selling agent is the person who works with the buyer.

8)   **Listing Price:** The amount expressed in dollars specified in the listing for which the seller is willing to sell the real property through the listing agent.

9)   **Offering Price:** The amount expressed in dollars specified in an offer to purchase for which the buyer is willing to buy the real property.

10)  **Offer to Purchase:** A written contract executed by a buyer acting through a selling agent, which becomes the contract for the sale of the real property upon acceptance by the seller.

11)  **Real Property:** Any estate specified by subdivision (1) or (2) of Section 761 of the California Civil Code, in property which constitutes or is improved with one to four dwelling units, any leasehold of property exceeding one year's duration, and mobile homes, when offered for sale or sold through an agent pursuant to the authority contained in Section 10131.6 of the Business and Professions Code.

**Note:** Mixed-use commercial/industrial properties: Based upon a communication from the California Real Estate Commissioner, it appears that mixed-use commercial and industrial properties, sophisticated commercial and industrial transactions, and transactions involving unsophisticated transactions that contain one to four residential units, will be covered.

From our experiences with Easton, it appears that it would be wise to provide the *Agency Disclosures* in every transaction. There does not appear to be a reasonable reason why one should not provide the disclosures.

12)  **Real Property Transaction:** A transaction for the sale of real property in which an agent is employed by one or more of the principals to act in that transaction, and includes a listing or an offer to purchase.

13)  **Sell, Sale, or Sold:** Refers to a transaction for the transfer of real property from the seller to the buyer, and includes exchanges of real property between the seller and buyer, transactions for the creation of a real property sales contract within the meaning of Section 2985, and transactions for the creation of a leasehold exceeding one year's duration.

14)  **Seller:** The transferor in a real property transaction, and includes an owner who lists real property with an agent, whether or not a transfer results, or who receives an offer to purchase real property, of which he or she is the owner, from an agent on behalf of another. *Seller* includes both a *vendor* and a *lessor*.

15)  **Selling Agent:** A listing agent who acts alone, or an agent who acts in cooperation with a listing agent, and who sells or finds and obtains a buyer for the real property, or an agent who locates property for a buyer or who finds a buyer for a property for which no

listing exists and presents an offer to purchase to the seller.

**16)**      **Subagent:** A person to whom an agent delegates agency powers as provided in Article 5 (commencing with Section 2349) of Chapter 1. However, a *subagent* does not include an associate licensee who is acting under the supervision of an agent in a real property transaction.

Listing agents and selling agents shall provide the seller and buyer in a real property transaction with a copy of the *disclosure form* specified in Section 2079.16, and, except as provided in subdivision (c), shall obtain a signed acknowledgment of receipt from that seller or buyer, except as provided in this section or Section 2079.15, as follows:

**1)**      The listing agent, if any, shall provide the disclosure form to the seller prior to entering into the listing agreement.

**2)**      The selling agent shall provide the disclosure form to the seller as soon as practicable prior to presenting the seller with an offer to purchase, unless the selling agent previously provided the seller with a copy of the disclosure form pursuant to subdivision (a).

**3)**      Where the selling agent does not deal on a face-to-face basis with the seller, the disclosure form prepared by the selling agent may be furnished to the seller (and acknowledgment of receipt obtained for the selling agent from the seller) by the listing agent, or the selling agent may deliver the disclosure form by certified mail addressed to the seller at his or her last known address, in which case no signed *acknowledgment* of receipt is required.

**4)**      The selling agent shall provide the disclosure form to the buyer as soon as practicable prior to execution of the buyer's offer to purchase, except that if the offer to purchase is not prepared by the selling agent, the selling agent shall present the disclosure form to the buyer no later than the next business day after the selling agent receives the offer to purchase from the buyer.

## Refusal to Sign Acknowledgment of Receipt (CC § 2079.15)

In any circumstance in which the seller or buyer refuses to sign an acknowledgment of receipt pursuant to Section 2079.14, the agent, or an associate licensee acting for an agent, shall set forth, sign, and date a written declaration of the facts of the refusal.

## Disclosure Form (CC § 2079.16)

The disclosure form required by Section 2079.14 shall have this article, excluding this section, printed on the back, and on the front of the disclosure form, the following shall appear:

### Disclosure Regarding Real Estate Agency Relationship

(As Required by the Civil Code)

When you enter into a discussion with a real estate agent regarding a real estate transaction, you should, from the outset, understand what type of agency relationship or representation you wish to have with the agent in the transaction.

## Seller's Agent

A Seller's agent under a listing agreement with the Seller acts as the agent for the Seller only. A Seller's agent or a **subagent** of that agent has the following affirmative obligations:

**To the Seller:**

**a)** A **fiduciary** duty of utmost care, integrity, honesty, and loyalty in dealings with the Seller.

**To the Buyer and the Seller:**

**a)** Diligent exercise of reasonable skill and care in performance of the agent's duties.

**b)** A duty of honest and fair dealing and good faith.

**c)** A duty to disclose all facts known to the agent that materially affect the value or desirability of the property, and that are not known to, or within the diligent attention and observation of, the parties.

An agent is not obligated to reveal to either party any confidential information obtained from the other party that does not involve the affirmative duties set forth above.

## Buyer's Agent

With the Buyer's consent, a selling agent can agree to act as agent for the Buyer only. In these situations, the agent is not the Seller's agent, even if by agreement the agent may receive compensation for services rendered, either in full or in part, from the Seller. An agent acting only for a buyer has the following affirmative obligations:

**To the Buyer:**

**a)** A **fiduciary** duty of utmost care, integrity, honesty, and loyalty in dealings with the Buyer.

**To the Buyer and the Seller:**

**a)** Diligent exercise of reasonable skill and care in performance of the agent's duties.

**b)** A duty of honest and fair dealings and good faith.

**c)** A duty to disclose all facts known to the agent that materially affect the value or desirability of the property, and that are not known to, or within the diligent attention and observation of, the parties. An agent is not obligated to reveal to either party any confidential information obtained from the other party that does not involve the affirmative duties set forth above.

## Agent Representing Both Seller and Buyer

A real estate agent, acting either directly or through one or more associate licensees, can legally be the agent of both the Seller and the Buyer in a transaction, but only with the knowledge and consent of both the Seller and the Buyer.

In a dual agency situation, the agent has the following affirmative obligations to both the Seller and the Buyer:

1)       A *fiduciary* duty of utmost care, integrity, honesty, and loyalty in the dealings with either the Seller or the Buyer.

2)       Other duties to the Seller and the Buyer as stated above in their respective sections.

In representing both the Seller and Buyer, the agent may not, without the express permission of the respective party, disclose to the other party that the Seller will accept a price less than the listing price or that the Buyer will pay a price greater than the price offered.

The above duties of the agent in a real estate transaction do not relieve a Seller or Buyer from their responsibility to protect their own interests. The Seller and Buyer should carefully read all agreements to assure that they adequately express their understanding of the transaction. A real estate agent is a person who is qualified to advise about real estate. If legal or tax advice is desired, consult a competent professional.

Throughout the Seller and Buyer's real property transaction, they may receive more than one disclosure form, depending upon the number of agents assisting in the transaction. The law requires each agent with whom the Seller and Buyer have more than a casual relationship, to present them with this disclosure form. The Seller and Buyer should read its contents each time it is presented to them, considering the relationship between the Seller and Buyer and the real estate agent who is involved in their specific transaction.

This disclosure form includes the provisions of *Article 2.5* (commencing with *Section 2079.13*) of *Chapter 2 of Title 9 of Part 4 of Division 3 of Civil Code* set forth on the reverse side of the form. Read it carefully.

## Disclosure and Confirmation of Agency Relationship (CC § 2079.17)

1) As soon as practicable, the selling agent shall disclose to the buyer and seller whether the selling agent is acting in the real property transaction exclusively as the buyer's agent, exclusively as the seller's agent, or as a dual agent representing both the buyer and the seller, and this relationship shall be confirmed in the contract to purchase and sell real property or in a separate writing executed or acknowledged by the seller, the buyer, and the selling agent prior to or coincident with the execution of that contract by the buyer and the seller, respectively.

2) As soon as practicable, the listing agent shall disclose to the seller whether the listing agent is acting in the real property transaction exclusively as the seller's agent, or as a dual agent representing both the buyer and seller, and this relationship shall be confirmed in the contract to purchase and sell real property or in a separate writing executed or acknowledged by the seller and the listing agent prior to or coincident with the execution of that contract by the seller.

3) The confirmation required by subdivisions (a) and (b) shall be in the following form:

_____is the agent of (check one): (name of Listing Agent)
[ ] the seller exclusively; or
[ ] both the buyer and seller.
_____is the agent of (check one):
(Name of the Selling Agent if not
the same as the Listing Agent)
[ ] the buyer exclusively; or
[ ] the seller exclusively; or [ ] both the buyer and seller.

4) The disclosures and confirmation required by this section shall be in addition to the disclosure required by Section 2079.14.

**Listing Agents: Acting as Agent for the Buyer Only is Prohibited (CC § 2079.14)**

No selling agent in a real property transaction may act as an agent for the buyer only, when the selling agent is also acting as the listing agent in the transaction.

**Payment of Compensation: Effect on the Determination of a Relationship (CC § 2079.19)**

The *payment of compensation* or the obligation to pay compensation to an agent by the seller or buyer is not necessarily determinative of a particular agency relationship between an agent and the seller or buyer. A listing agent and a selling agent may agree to share any compensation or commission paid, or any right to any compensation or commission for which an obligation arises as the result of a real estate transaction, and the terms of any such agreement shall not necessarily be determinative of a particular relationship.

**Selecting a Specific Form of Agency Relationship: Condition of Employment (CC § 2079.20)**

Nothing in this article prevents an agent from selecting, as a condition of the agent's employment, a specific form of agency relationship not specifically prohibited by this article, if the requirements of *Section 2079.14* and *Section 2079.17* are complied with.

**Dual Agents: Disclosures Are Prohibited (CC §2079.21)**

A *dual agent* shall not disclose to the buyer that the seller is willing to sell the property at a price less than the listing price, without the express written consent of the seller. A dual agent shall not disclose to the seller that the buyer is willing to pay a price greater than the offering price, without the express written consent of the buyer.

This section does not alter in any way the duty or responsibility of a dual agent to any principal, with respect to confidential information, other than price.

**Listing Agents: Acting as Selling Agents Is Allowed (CC § 2079.22)**

Nothing in this article precludes a listing agent from also being a selling agent, and the combination of these functions in one agent does not, of itself, make that agent a dual agent.

**Modification or Alteration of Agency Contract (CC § 2079.23)**

A contract between the principal and agent may be modified or altered to change the agency relationship at any time before the performance of the act that is the object of the agency, with the written consent of the parties to the agency relationship.

**Duty of Disclosure and Fiduciary Duty: Effect of Article (CC § 2079.24)**

Nothing in this article shall be construed to either diminish the duty of disclosure owed buyers and sellers by agents and their associate licensees, subagents, and employees, or to relieve agents and their associate licensees, subagents, and employees from liability for their conduct in connection with acts governed by this article, or for any breach of a fiduciary duty or a duty of disclosure.

**QUIZZES ARE MANDATORY**: Please log in and submit the chapter quizzes online.

**Chapter Two Quiz**

1.      Which of the following statements is correct concerning hold-harmless clauses?

(a)      The clause can be used as a defense when the broker passes along erroneous information.
(b)      The clause can be used to protect the broker from his or her own negligence.
(c)      The clause may NOT be used as a shield to protect the broker from his or her own negligence in securing correct information.
(d)      It is possible to use a written disclaimer to relieve the broker of his or her liability to disclose material facts.

2.      The case of Easton v. Strassburger concerned:

(a)      massive earth movement.
(b)      fire hazard.
(c)      earthquake damage.
(d)      flood danger.

3.      Which of the following would be a *red flag*?

(a)      Water-stained ceilings.
(b)      Cracks in ceilings, walls, and floors.
(c)      New additions.
(d)      All of the above.

4.      Once the agent (broker) is aware of a red flag, and is following a reasonably competent and diligent inspection, one thing that he or she should NOT do is:

(a)      offer an opinion about what problem may underlie the red flag.
(b)      point out the red flag to his or her principal.
(c)      eventually make sure the red flag is disclosed in writing.
(d)      disclose all other material facts that are related to the red flag.

5.      While representing both the Buyer and Seller, the Seller informs the agent that she would be willing to accept a price less than the listed price if the terms were favorable. The agent's proper course of action would be to:

(a)      immediately inform the Buyer that the Seller is soft on her price.
(b)      refrain from disclosing this information to the Buyer without express permission from the Seller.
(c)      give the buyer a handwritten note that discloses this information, along with any counter offer from the Seller.
(d)      immediately step down as the agent in this transaction.

## Chapter Three

**Important Terms**

attorney-in-fact
bulk transfers
business opportunity
commercial brokers
consideration
exclusive listing
exclusive right to sell listing
executed
fixtures
goodwill
heirs
incapacity
industrial brokers
legatee
note
option
power of attorney
recording
renunciation
single agency
successors
unequivocal

**Learning Objectives**

Upon completion of Chapter Three, you should be able to complete the following:

- Describe the power of the attorney-agency relationship.

- Define *buyer brokerage*.

- Define *business opportunity*.

- Describe the various types of listing agreements.

- Explain the difference between exclusive and nonexclusive listings.

## Other Agency Relationships

### Lender/Purchaser Disclosure Statement

Scenario: You are a real estate broker, and Mr. Owner needs cash and wants you to sell a note secured by a deed of trust. You advertise (solicit through the local newspaper) for a buyer for the note and a sale is made. Or, in a different situation, you make a solicitation to a particular person to make a loan (you want him to lend $5,000 on a second D.T. to a customer) secured by real property [*B. & P. § 10232.4*].

Old Law: No disclosure was required because *B. & P. § 10232* applied only if 20 or more of the above were made during any consecutive 12 months. The 20 or more requirement was referred to as the *requirement threshold*.

Section 10232.4 requires a real estate broker who acts within the meaning of *§ 10131 (d) or (e)* to provide a lender or purchaser with a specific disclosure statement that describes the note and trust deed being funded or offered for sale, details about the borrower, and other pertinent information of value to the lender or note purchaser. Additionally, the requirement threshold has been reduced to one. This means that all brokers must provide this disclosure statement.

This is an important change because the law previously provided that only a relatively few lenders and purchasers received a disclosure statement. Now, a disclosure statement must be given to practically all non-institutional lenders and note purchasers. The information in the disclosure statement is provided to assist them in making the decision whether or not to lend money or purchase an existing note.

**Exemption:** There are several situations that do not require a disclosure statement. One of the most noteworthy is the following: *B. & P. Code, § 10232.4 (b)(2)*: "The seller of real property who agrees to take back a promissory note of the purchaser as a method of financing all or a part of the purchase price of the property."

### Single Agency

The term *single agency* denotes a relationship wherein the agent represents only one principal in a particular transaction, whether that transaction is a sale, lease, exchange, loan, or business opportunity.

### Power of Attorney

Another form of agency agreement is a *power of attorney*. This is a written instrument giving authority to an agent (not necessarily a real estate agent) to act on behalf of a principal, either as a general agent or as a limited agent. The agent acting under such a grant of authority is called an *attorney-in-fact*.

### Power of Attorney, Narrowly Interpreted

Anyone who regularly performs real estate services must be licensed and cannot evade the legal requirements by using a power of attorney.

According to a California Court of Appeal ruling (Sheetz v. Edmonds), if an individual consistently performs services for which a real estate license is required, then a power of attorney will not exempt him or her from licensing requirements.

The Court of Appeal stated that the power-of-attorney exemption is only intended to apply in cases where a property owner is compelled by personal necessity to empower another person to consummate an isolated transaction. Any other interpretation defeats the intent of the licensing requirements by allowing unlicensed persons to conduct license-required activities.

Thus, the court concluded that the power-of-attorney exemption should not be used to evade licensing requirements. Instead, it should apply in those infrequent circumstances where personal necessity impels a property owner to appoint another as his or her attorney-in-fact.

One purpose of the Real Estate Law is to ensure the integrity and competence of those engaged in the business of real estate. Consumers benefit from having only licensed professionals handle their real estate matters. (Sheetz v. Edmonds) should put any person considering a power of attorney as a means of circumventing CalBRE licensing requirements on notice that their activity may violate the law.

### Definitions

1) **Principal:** A person who authorizes another to act for him or her as his or her agent.

2) **Agent:** A person who represents and acts by authority of, and on account of, a principal.

3) **Power of Attorney:** A written instrument by which a person authorizes another to act for him or her as his or her agent.

4) **Agent:** The agent who is authorized by power of attorney to act for, and in the name of, a principal.

### Types of Power of Attorney

#### Special Power of Attorney

If the power conferred is limited or restricted in any particular way, it is a special power of attorney. It may be directed to the performance of a particular act, or acts. For example,

"To execute leases and collect rents from the tenants renting a particular parcel of real property owned by me in X County, California, on the date hereof."

#### General Power of Attorney

A general power of attorney confers a wide variety of powers upon the attorney-in-fact. In the above example, the attorney-in-fact would be granted the authority to collect the rent from all of the principal's properties, not one property only. The agent could also be granted the power to sign the principal's name and convey title.

## Who May Act Under a Power of Attorney

As a general rule, any person who is competent to contract may act under the authority of a power of attorney. However, a person may not serve as an attorney-in-fact if they have any interest adverse to those of his or her principal, unless such potential conflict is fully revealed to and understood by the principal.

## Recording of Power of Attorney

For the purpose of dealing with real property, the power of attorney must be *recorded*, and it must be acknowledged before it may be recorded.

## Execution of Instruments

When the attorney-in-fact signs the name of the principal, it is recommended that it be executed in the following manner:

/s/ Peter P. Principal (written or typed)
Peter P. Principal (typed)
By: /s/ Allen A. Agent (written signature)
Allen A. Agent, his attorney-in-fact (typed)

## Restrictions on Authority

There are several restrictions on the authority of an attorney-in-fact, based largely upon state laws. An attorney-in-fact is prohibited from making a gift deed, or making a deed, mortgage, or release without a valuable *consideration*; dealing with the principal's property for his or her own benefit; conveying the principal's property to himself or herself; mortgaging the principal's property to himself or herself; or delegating his or her authority if not expressly authorized to do so in the power of attorney.

## Termination of Power of Attorney

The acts, events, or occurrences terminating the authority of an agent to act for and bind the principal are prescribed by statute and are clear and *unequivocal*. An agency is terminated (CC Sec. 2355) by the following:

- The expiration of the term of the agency.
- The extinction of its subject.
- The death of the agent.
- The agent's *renunciation* of the agency.
- The *incapacity* of the agent to act as such.

When the principal and attorney-in-fact are married to each other, divorce, dissolution, annulment, etc., may terminate the power of attorney. Other means of termination (CC Sec. 2356) include the following:

- The revocation by the principal.
- The death of the principal.
- The incapacity of the principal to contract.

Any bona fide transaction entered into with an agent by any person without actual knowledge of the above occurrences under CC Sec. 2356, shall be binding upon the principal, his or her heirs, devisees, legatees, and other successors in interest.

**Durable Power of Attorney**

Because of the extensive legal problems involved here, we will only make mention of what is known as a *durable power of attorney*. A durable power of attorney is one under which an attorney-in-fact is authorized to continue acting for and in the name of the principal after the principal's inability to contract. Such a situation definitely needs the assistance of a qualified attorney. A durable power of attorney is essentially an estate-planning device rather than a conveyancing device.

**Buyer Brokerage**

There is an abundance of evidence present that many buyers are not aware that the broker who shows them properties or assists them in submitting offers usually does so as the *agent* or *subagent* of the seller (FTC Report). This confusion is also reflected in the decisions of a growing number of courts, and in the arguments of counsel in cases involving the nature and extent of broker liability for errors and omissions.

To fill the growing need for representation, a segment of the real estate industry is responding to the demand by buyers for agency representation by functioning primarily, or even exclusively, as *buyer's brokers*. Under such representation, a buyer's broker can investigate properties offered for sale by owners and can approach owners who have not put their properties on the market.

When seeking a listing, it is unlawful to represent to an owner of real property that the soliciting licensee has obtained a bona fide written offer to purchase the property, unless at the time of the representation, the licensee has possession of a bona fide written offer to purchase. The above violation can be avoided by creating an employment contract with the buyer.

**QUIZZES ARE MANDATORY**: Please log in and submit the chapter quizzes online.

**Chapter Three Quiz**

1.      The term *single agency* describes a relationship wherein the agent represents:

      (a)      both the buyer and seller.
      (b)      himself or herself.
      (c)      only one principal in a particular transaction.
      (d)      none of the above.

2.      Another form of agency agreement is a written instrument giving authority to an agent (not necessarily a real estate agent) to act on behalf of a principal, either as a general agent or as a limited agent. This form of agency is commonly referred to as a _____.

      (a)      power of sale
      (b)      power of attorney
      (c)      power of executor
      (d)      power of administration

3.      An attorney-in-fact can best be described as a(n):

      (a)      duly authorized person who has been granted both actual and implied powers to act as a principal for another.
      (b)      properly authorized party who is acting as a dual agent.
      (c)      attorney appointed by the court to administer the estate of a deceased person.
      (d)      legally competent person who has been given the power of attorney by another competent person.

4.      A power of attorney can be terminated by:

      (a)      the death of the attorney-in-fact.
      (b)      the revocation by the principal.
      (c)      the incapacity of the parties to the power of attorney.
      (d)      all of the above.

5.      A power of attorney that authorizes an attorney-in-fact to continue acting for and in the name of the principal after the principal's inability to contract is called:

      (a)      a general power of attorney.
      (b)      a durable power of attorney.
      (c)      a special power of attorney.
      (d)      none of the above.

# Notes

# Ethics

3 Hours of Continuing Education for
Salesperson and Broker License Renewal

**Lumbleau Real Estate School**
23805 Hawthorne Blvd.
Torrance, CA 90505

**© 2015 by Mark R. Chamberlin**

**DISCLAIMERS**

Although every effort has been made to provide accurate and current information in this text, the ideas, suggestions, general principles, and conclusions presented in this text are subject to local, state, and federal laws and regulations, court cases, and any revisions of the same. The author and/or publisher is not engaged in rendering legal, tax, or other professional services. The reader is thus urged to consult with his or her employing broker and/or seek legal counsel regarding any points of law. This publication should not be used as a substitute for competent legal advice.

This course is approved for continuing education credit by the California Bureau of Real Estate. However, this approval does not constitute an endorsement of the views or opinions which are expressed by the course sponsor, instructor, authors, or lecturers.

## Table of Contents

## Chapter One

### Important Terms

beneficiary
bona fide
caveat emptor
commingling
consideration
contract of sale
fiduciary
misrepresentation
negligence
plaintiff
puffing
recreant
rescission
Statute of Frauds
trustee
trust fund account
trust funds

### Learning Objectives

Upon completion of Chapter One, you should be able to complete the following:

- Define *professional conduct*.

- Describe unlawful conduct in sale, lease, and exchange transactions.

- Explain the difference between puffing and misrepresentation.

- Describe the California disclosure law on real estate commissions.

## Unlawful Conduct in Sale, Lease, and Exchange Transactions

In order to enhance the professionalism of the California real estate industry and maximize protection for members of the public who deal with real estate licensees (whatever their area of practice), the following standards of professional conduct and business practices have been adopted.

Unlawful conduct consists of acts that the Commissioner already considers a violation of the Real Estate Law. By placing these acts in regulation form, real estate licensees are put on notice that these acts are violations, and their licenses can be suspended or revoked for performing any act enumerated in the unlawful conduct section. Viewing these regulations in writing will prove to be very helpful to some licensees because a licensee may not realize that these acts are violations of the Real Estate Law.

### Misrepresenting Value to Acquire Interest in a Property

While performing acts within the meaning of Section 10131(a) of the Business and Professions Code, licensees shall not engage in conduct that will subject the licensee to adverse action, penalty, or discipline under Sections 10176 and 10177 of the Business and Professions Code, including, but not limited to, the following acts and omissions:

*The licensee knowingly makes a substantial misrepresentation of the likely value of real property to its owner for the purpose of securing a listing or for the purpose of acquiring an interest in the property for the licensee's own account.*

### Example #1:

*People vs. Barker (1060) 53 C 2nd 539.* The victim owned real property and asked the defendants, Mr. and Mrs. Barker, with whom he had previously dealt, for their opinion regarding an offer the victim had received. The offer was for $25.00 per acre on property owned by the victim. In their discussions, Mr. Barker stated that the property was probably worth $50.00 per acre. However, after a short time, Mr. Barker told the victim that the property was more realistically valued at not more than $35.00 to $40.00 per acre. In the meantime, Mr. Barker told Marsh that the property was valued at $50.00 per acre. Marsh offered $45.00 and gave Barker a $500 deposit. Mr. Barker then told the victim that he was unable to find anyone who would pay more than $25.00 per acre. (This, of course, was a lie.) Barker then presented an offer to the victim from Mrs. MacDonald (really Mrs. Barker, the broker's wife) at $25.00 per acre. The victim accepted the offer and a double escrow was opened for MacDonald and Marsh. Neither the victim nor Marsh knew that Mrs. MacDonald was in fact Mrs. Barker. After the escrow closed, Marsh confronted Mrs. Barker with a handwriting expert's opinion that Mrs. MacDonald and Mrs. Barker were the same person. Barker denied this, and claimed that Mrs. MacDonald was a real person living in Michigan.

The decision was that the defendants were guilty and should be convicted of grand theft. Mr. and Mrs. Barker knowingly and by false pretenses defrauded the victim of the difference between the sum they intended to pay and the amount Marsh had offered ($12,800).

*Example #2:*

Mr. Adams was about to retire and decided that the best way to sell his property was to list it with a real estate broker. One Sunday afternoon, he dropped in on broker Williams to discuss the matter and said that several brokers had told him that he should expect to receive from $85,000 to $88,000 for his property. "Oh, that sounds low to me," said broker Williams. "Property in your neighborhood has been moving well and I recall that your house is in good shape and well landscaped. Give us an exclusive on it at $93,000, and we'll make a strong effort to get what your property really is worth." Mr. Adams agreed, and Williams got the listing. Williams had salesman Brown, a newly licensed agent in his office, hold the property open the next weekend. Numerous prospective buyers saw the property, but there were no offers. When activity slowed and Mr. Adams became concerned, broker Williams reassuringly told him, "We'll just keep plugging 'till the right buyer comes along." When the 90 days had passed, Williams contacted Mr. Adams and asked for a renewal. He told him that new houses coming on the market were adversely affecting the market on resales, and recommended that Mr. Adams lower the selling price to $89,500. Adams ruefully agreed, but the lowered price did not materially increase buyer interest in the property. As the term of the 90-day extension neared its end, an agent from another office submitted an offer of $83,000, which Williams strongly recommended that Adams accept.

After a long discussion, Mr. Adams accepted the offer and charged Williams with misinforming him about the fair market value, apparently as a means of obtaining the listing of his property. During a hearing, questioning developed the following facts:

The broker had not gone through the house to make a systematic appraisal or opinion of value, his recommended offering price was not based on a systematic review of sales in the neighborhood, and there had been no indication that any property in the immediate neighborhood had been resold for as high as $93,000. When told that the circumstances tended to bear out the complainant's charge, the broker's defended himself by stating that he felt he had the right to take an optimistic view of the market.

The inevitable conclusion of the hearing was that the broker had acted in an unethical manner.

## Misrepresenting Value to Induce an Offer

*The licensee makes a substantial misrepresentation of the likely value of real property to a prospective buyer, for the purpose of inducing the buyer to make an offer to purchase the real property.*

In California, the real estate licensee is required to deal fairly and honestly with all parties and not act in a negligent manner (B. & P. Code § 10176(a), (b), (c), (d), (i); and § 10177(c), (f), (g), (h), (j), (l)). The ancient rule of *caveat emptor* (let the buyer beware) has little application in today's complicated market.

*Example #1:*

In a transaction that occurred in 1968, the broker suggested that the buyer purchase an eleven-unit apartment house. In order to induce the plaintiff to purchase, the broker made representations that the apartment would be worth $140,000 if the rents were raised. With the increased rents, the buyer would have a net spendable $500 per month.

At the close of escrow, every unit was occupied, and the new owner sent rent increase notices to each tenant. Within 60 days, 65% of the apartments were vacant, and no new tenants could be secured at the higher rent. The eventual result was a loss of the property as well as a $42,000 loss to the buyer instead of the profit the broker had represented. The result was that the buyer filed a lawsuit with verdict in favor of the buyer (plaintiff).

### *Puffing versus Misrepresentation*

Since the real estate licensee is presumed to have superior knowledge, his or her statements are more likely to be construed as a statements of fact. However, the licensee may offer his or her opinion, such as, "This is the best buy in town." The determining factor for whether or not this is an unethical act is whether or not a reasonable person would rely on the statement [*Pacesetter Homes Inc. v. Brodkin (1970) 5 C.A. 3d 206*].

Mere statements of opinion about probable potential income from property usually do not constitute fraud. However, in the above example, the broker was not stating an opinion, and therefore, it was determined that he acted in a negligent manner.

When seeking a listing, the licensee represents to an owner of real property that he or she has obtained a bona fide written offer from a buyer to purchase the property, but at the time of the representation, the licensee does not actually have possession of a bona fide written offer to purchase. This is considered *puffing*.

How many times have you heard about an agent who contacted a property owner, and in an attempt to secure a listing, told the owner that the agent had a buyer for their property, although the agent did not? The question that has to be asked is whether or not the agent has a buyer, and if the agent does, whether or not the buyer is firm. Is the agent's buyer somebody who casually told the agent that they would only be interested if the price is right?

This regulation was created to prevent such activities by penalizing the agent who claims to have buyers, usually who offer inflated prices, in order to get a listing without actually having a bona fide written offer to purchase.

### *Example #2:*

Eager for a listing, salesman Brown tells Mr. and Mrs. Jones that she has buyers looking for a house just like theirs, and that those buyers are ready to make an offer, although such buyers really do not exist. Misrepresenting the market value of the property, Brown does not quibble with Mr. and Mrs. Jones over terms, price, etc., and she sets these parameters so high that Mr. and Mrs. Jones cannot refuse to list. Brown gets a 90-day exclusive right to sell, which freezes out all of her competition.

In the meantime, because Mr. and Mrs. Jones expect a quick sale, they have started looking for a new home to purchase. Their offer on their new home is not made contingent upon the sale of their old home, as the Brown told them that she has a buyer.

A few weeks pass by, and the Jones' have not heard from Brown, and so they call her to find out what's going on. Over the phone, Brown breaks the bad news that her buyers won't pay the excessive price at which the property was listed. It is then that she begins to work on the Jones' ever increasing concern that they won't sell their home. Suddenly, Brown states that the terms are not suitable and there no longer seems to be anyone capable of paying cash to the loan. She suggests that the owners sell on a contract of sale because interest rates and points are so high. Brown also states that she may be willing to purchase the property if the Jones' substantially lower their sales price to accommodate her. The pressure becomes enormous for the Jones', who may have to forfeit their deposit on the new house if their old house does not sell quickly. Thus, Brown is able to wear down the Jones', who relist their property at the market value indicated for the property in the first place. This is the property that they may never have intended to sell and would not had it not been for the actions of saleswoman Brown.

Such a technique is unlawful and unquestionably damages the entire real estate industry. All too often, the California Bureau of Real Estate is called upon to investigate such activities. All too often, a licensee engaging in such dishonest dealings is disciplined for this conduct.

## Suggesting Commission Schedules

*During listing negotiations, the licensee states or implies to an owner of real property that the licensee is precluded by law, by regulation, or by the rules of any organization, other than the broker firm seeking the listing, from charging less than the commission or fee quoted to the owner by the licensee.*

Back when real estate boards had suggested commission schedules, the schedules were intended to be voluntary, non-mandatory, and unenforceable. They were designed to aid and inform the public, judges, attorneys, and bankers of the prevailing levels of fees and commissions in the marketplace to prevent gouging.

Yet, from time to time, these schedules, which were intended to protect the public, were abused and misused. On occasion, a salesperson would respond to a request by a client for a lower commission rate, with, "Gee, I would like to take it for 5%, but my board won't let me." Such a response is a lie and always has been. However, it is now also a violation of Section 10147.5 of the Business and Professions Code (see below). In May 1980, as an emergency measure, Governor Jerry Brown signed into law Senate Bill 1958, which clarifies and amends the measure that concerned the negotiability of real estate commissions, and the notice requirement for any printed or other form of real estate agreement.

### *California Disclosure Law on Real Estate Commissions*

The amended Section 10147.5 is now operative. It reads as following:

a) Any printed or form agreement which initially establishes, or is intended to establish, or alters the terms of any agreement which previously established a right to compensation to be paid to a real estate licensee for the sale of residential real property containing not more than four (4) residential units, or the sale of a mobile home, shall contain the following statement in not less than 10-point boldface type immediately preceding any provision of such agreement relating to compensation of the licensee:

**Notice:**

**THE AMOUNT OR RATE OF REAL ESTATE COMMISSIONS IS NOT FIXED BY LAW. THEY ARE SET BY EACH BROKER INDIVIDUALLY AND MAY BE NEGOTIABLE BETWEEN THE SELLER AND BROKER.**

**Comment:** This alerts the seller that he or she has the right to negotiate the commission. It would be improper to print the entire agreement in less than 10-point bold type in an effort to conceal the disclosure that commissions are negotiable.

b) The amount or rate of compensation shall not be printed in any such agreement.

**Comment:** When the rate is printed in the agreement, the seller may be led to believe that it cannot be changed.

c) Nothing in this section shall affect the validity of a transfer of title to real property.

**Comment:** This means that a contract between the seller and buyer is not affected by a violation of Section 10147.5. The only effect is to deny the broker the right to collect a commission and may result in their possible loss of license.

d) As used in this section, "Alters the terms of any agreement which previously established a right of compensation," means an increase in the rate of compensation, or the amount of compensation if initially established as a flat fee, from the agreement which previously established a right of compensation.

**Comment:** It is permissible to lower the rate or amount of commission without inserting such a statement into the agreement.

It should also be noted that a broker may establish, as a normal business or office practice, any commission schedule he or she wishes. However, this business privilege may not be used as a method of discriminating in a manner that would otherwise be considered unlawful.

### Misrepresenting the Relationship with an Individual Broker, Corporation, or Franchised Brokerage

*The licensee knowingly makes substantial misrepresentations regarding the licensee's relationship with an individual broker, corporate broker, or franchised brokerage company, or that entity/person's responsibility for the licensee's activities.*

Many buyers and sellers associate large corporations with safety. In certain cases this may be true, but to represent oneself as being protected by a corporate franchise organization when such is not true is considered unethical.

### Underestimating Probable Closing Costs

*The licensee knowingly underestimates the probable closing costs in a communication to the prospective buyer or seller of real property, in order to induce that person to make or to accept an offer to purchase the property.*

There's not much doubt here that knowingly underestimating closing costs is a fraud. It may be just as serious if the agent makes wild or careless guesses without supporting data or experience. Accurate closing information is not difficult to obtain, and an agent should be able to accurately estimate closing costs. Although it is not recommended, it is always preferred to overestimate closing costs and underestimate the seller's projected net. If the agent underestimates the closing costs and overestimates the seller's net, the seller is going to come after the agent for the difference.

**Making a False Statement to the Seller about the Treatment of Deposit**

*The licensee knowingly makes a false or misleading representation to the seller of real property as to the form, amount, and/or treatment of a deposit toward the purchase of the property made by an offeror.*

An earnest money deposit by a prospective purchaser of real property is considered trust funds. The deposit must be handled by the broker as prescribed by the Real Estate Law and the regulations.

Section 10145 of the Real Estate Law provides that the broker who receives trust funds must place those funds into a neutral trust fund account in a bank or other recognized depository, if the broker does not place the funds into a neutral escrow or into the hands of the broker's principal. An alternative to the preceding is that the broker's principal instructs the broker to hold the money.

In those cases where the buyer provides a down payment in the form of a check to the broker with written instructions to hold the check uncashed until acceptance of the offer, the buyer's instructions should be followed. However, the broker must inform the seller, preferably in writing, that the buyer's check is being held uncashed. The broker should provide this information to the seller no later than the actual presentation of the offer to the seller, and prior to the seller's acceptance of the offer. In the interim, the broker should enter the fact of receipt of the check into the broker's trust fund records and hold the check in a safe place (see *Commissioner's Regulation 2832*).

Although there may be a custom in real estate transactions for a broker to accept a check instead of cash as a down payment, the existence of such a custom does not justify the acceptance of a promissory note in lieu of cash, unless there is full disclosure to the seller. While checks are universally accepted as the equivalent of money in business transactions, promissory notes are not. The maker of the check represents that the maker has money in the bank to cover the check at the time the check is signed, and the failure to have such money may be a crime. The maker of a promissory note makes no such representation, and the maker's failure to pay is not a crime. It has been held under the criminal law of California that a post-dated check is, at the very best, equivalent to a promissory note.

A real estate broker, like a trustee, has the affirmative duty to disclose all material facts that may influence a principal's decision. Thus, the broker or salesperson who represents to a principal that the broker has received cash from a purchaser as a down payment, when in fact, the broker has accepted a non-negotiable promissory note, has violated the Real Estate Law.

*Example #1:*

In the case of *Dr. S. German vs. Watson (1950) 95 C.A. 2nd 862*, a real estate broker, the respondent, accepted a nonnegotiable promissory note from buyer as a deposit toward the purchase price. The broker made no mention to the seller, his client, about the nature of the deposit, and the deposit receipt (contract of purchase) merely acknowledged acceptance of a $1,000 deposit. The buyer later defaulted on the promissory note and refused to complete the sale.

The seller filed a complaint with the Real Estate Commissioner, the appellant. The respondent broker then personally made a partial payment on the promissory note to the seller, and the seller thereafter sought to withdraw the complaint he had filed with the California Bureau of Real Estate.

However, the Commissioner investigated the complaint on his own, found the broker guilty of violating the Real Estate Law, and suspended the broker's license. The broker sued the Commissioner to have the suspension set aside. The trial court reversed the suspension, finding there was no intent by the broker to defraud or act dishonestly toward the seller, and the Commissioner appealed.

Decision of the Appeals Court: Section 10176 of the Business and Profession Code (the Real Estate Law) provides that the Commissioner, on his own motion, may, and if any person files a verified complaint, shall, investigate the actions of any person engaged in the business or acting in the capacity of a real estate licensee and may temporarily or permanently revoke a real estate license where (among other provisions) the licensee has been found guilty of making any substantial misrepresentation or any other conduct, whether of the same or a different character than specified in this section, which constitutes fraud or dishonest dealing. The Commissioner found that the broker's action in failing to disclose to his principal that the $1,000 mentioned in the deposit receipt as having been received from the buyer was not cash but a nonnegotiable promissory note, executed in favor of the broker, violated the above law.

The original trial court found that the broker did not intend to, nor did mislead the sellers, and did not act in a fraudulent or dishonest manner in his dealings with the sellers. The appellant court agreed with this finding insofar as intentional fraud or dishonesty was concerned. However, in spite of the fact that the respondent acted in good faith in the matter, he still violated the spirit and letter of the Real Estate Law.

It is a well-known fact that prior to the enactment of this law, there were a considerable number of persons engaged in the real estate business who were carrying on that business in an unethical manner, and that one of the purposes of the law's enactment was to raise the standards of the profession and to require its members to act fairly and ethically with their clients. Some of the things that brokers had done theretofore, and which were not necessarily illegal or unethical, were now prohibited in the interest of protecting the public.

Thus, commingling the money (this, in effect, is what the broker did) or other property of his or her principal with his or her own is expressly prohibited. There were many brokers, prior to the enactment of the law, who placed money received from their clients in their personal accounts, but scrupulously paid their clients every cent coming to them. It was not that the commingling of a client's money necessarily meant that the client would be defrauded, but that such a practice might result in fraud or injury to the client. So it is with the undisclosed acceptance of a promissory note. In this case, the broker was able to make good on the full amount of the note because the seller insisted on it. However, the possibilities of fraud and of injury to a seller by the undisclosed acceptance of a promissory note are unlimited.

In the first place, before entering into a binding obligation to tie up his or her property by an agreement to sell, the seller is entitled to know if the buyer either cannot or will not put up cash. The seller, rather than the broker, should determine whether the reason for the buyer's not paying cash is satisfactory, and the seller should also determine whether he or she is satisfied that a promissory note is accepted as a payment, even though the broker stands ready, as in this case, to guarantee its payment.

The seller has the right to believe that if the buyer, for any reason, refused to continue with their agreement, the buyer's down payment would be forfeited and kept by the seller. But when a promissory note is accepted, the money is not there to be kept. The seller then has to deal with a lawsuit to collect on the note. The seller is at least entitled to know from his or her own agent that this situation may occur before the seller signs the agreement of sale. When the buyer provides a check, the buyer represents that he or she has the money in the bank to cover it, and that the bank will pay the amount that is called for. Moreover, if the buyer does not have the money in the bank, it may constitute a crime. A note, even one payable on demand, makes no such representation, and the failure to pay when the note is presented is not a crime. In modern business, checks are universally accepted as money; promissory notes are not.

The law of California imposed upon the real estate agent the same obligation of undivided service and loyalty that it imposes on a trustee in favor of his or her beneficiary. Violation of this trust is subject to the same punitive consequences that are provided for a disloyal, or recreant trustee. Such an agent is charged with the duty of fullest disclosure of all material facts concerning the transaction that may affect the principal's decision.

A real estate broker, like a trustee, has an affirmative duty to disclose all material facts which may influence the decision of the principal; the fact that the prospective buyer cannot or does not make the down payment on the purchase of real property in money but by a promissory note is a material fact which the seller is entitled to know before agreeing to sell; here, the agent failed to make such a disclosure and hence violated the Real Estate Law as set forth above. In the case above, the judgment was reversed and the broker's suspension was upheld.

**Misrepresenting the Buyer's Ability to Repay a Loan to Seller and Carry-Back Lender**

*The licensee knowingly makes a false or misleading representation to a seller of real property, who has agreed to finance all or part of a purchase price by carrying back a loan, about a buyer's ability to repay the loan in accordance with its terms and conditions.*

The broker must make certain disclosures concerning the buyer's credit history. He must either present the credit information provided by the buyer, or specifically state on the form that "no representation as to the credit-worthiness of the buyer is being made."

There is no requirement placed upon the broker to investigate the accuracy of the buyer's credit information. However, all parties must provide information *in good faith*. *Good faith* means *honesty in fact* (CC § 2961). If the broker is aware of false information, it is the broker's duty to inform the seller. The buyer is liable for the seller's damages caused by false credit information, even though the loan is covered by the anti-deficiency laws [*Glendale Federal S&L vs. Marina View Heights Development Co. (1977) 66 CA 3d 537*].

CC § 2963(i): A disclosure on the identity, occupation, employment, income, and credit data about the prospective purchaser, as represented to the arranger by the prospective purchaser; or specifically, that no representation as to the credit-worthiness of the specific prospective purchaser, is made by the arranger. A warning should also be expressed that Section 580b of the Code of Civil Procedure may limit any recovery by the vendor to the net proceeds of the sale of the security property in the event of foreclosure.

## Changing Terms without Permission

*The licensee makes an addition to or modification of the terms of an instrument previously signed or initialed by a party to a transaction without the knowledge and consent of the party.*

The two ideas generally incorporated in this section are the following:

- The addition of terminology.

- The modification (change) to existing terminology.

In general, a contract may be modified by the mutual consent of the parties involved, and the modification is usually supported by further consideration (C.C. 1698). A written contract may be modified by a written agreement, or by an executed oral agreement [*Coldwell Banker & Co. vs. Pepper Tree Office Center Assoc. (1980) 106 C.A. 3d 272,280*]. An executory modification must be supported by a new consideration. Errors in a contract may be corrected and omissions filled in without a new consideration. However, such changes must be made with the knowledge and consent of the parties concerned. The Statute of Frauds must be satisfied if the contract is modified within its provisions. Where one party signs a document containing blanks and the other, or the party's agent, later fills the blanks in without authority, a contract is not formed because of this unauthorized alteration.

## Representing Property Value without Reasonable Basis

*The licensee or principal represents to a prospective purchaser, with a promissory note secured by real property, the market value of the secured property without a reasonable basis for believing the truth and accuracy of the representation.*

To most licensees, it is obvious that it is a violation of law to represent that a certain loan is secured by value when in fact such value is nonexistent. However, if such a representation is a violation of an already existing law, why is it necessary to enact additional regulations that appear to be nothing more than repetitious and redundant?

The answer is relatively simple if the agent is acting in the strict capacity of an agent: the rules of agency will apply. The fiduciary obligation of the agent prevails at all times. Any breach of this duty would subject the agent to the loss of their license.

However, consider the situation where the agent is acting as a principal. Does the law of agency apply? Is the agent a fiduciary or an adversary?

Two principals occupy a relationship that is almost adversary in nature. Although the rule of Caveat Emptor does not apply in the literal sense, it does come close.

However, such is not the case between a real estate agent and his or her principal. It is reasonable to surmise (without strong evidence) that the average real estate agent is in a far superior position (more knowledgeable) than the average buyer or seller. If this is true, and it appears that it is in most cases, it would be extremely unfair to allow the real estate agent to sit on whichever side of the fence he or she wants whenever he or she wishes.

### Example #1:

In the case of *Banville vs. Schmidt 37 C.A. 3d 92; Cal. Rptr. 126*, a husband and wife brought an action for rescission of a real estate sale and for damages for negligence, fraud, and misrepresentation.

The plaintiffs had accepted an offer on their property, which they had listed with the defendant broker. The defendant broker was the purchaser of the plaintiffs' property. The accepted offer was for $2,000 cash and the assignment of a promissory note secured by a first deed of trust on another property. The offer was presented through an agent of the buyer who represented to the plaintiffs that the security was adequate and the maker of the note was financially responsible. It was found that the encumbered property was actually inadequate as security for the note, and the maker of the note was in shaky financial condition. The plaintiffs won their case because they relied upon the agent's repeated representations.

It is clear that it is not an adequate defense for an agent to claim that he or she was acting as a principal and that such transactions are "arms-length" transactions. Caveat Emptor does not apply.

## Misrepresenting the Condition of the Property to the Buyer

*The licensee knowingly makes a false or misleading representation of, or represents without a reasonable basis for believing its truth, the nature and/or condition of the interior or exterior features of a property when soliciting an offer.*

Whether the situation involving the agent and a prospect is a face-to-face confrontation or nonpersonal advertising, the agent should be careful to create an accurate picture of the product, and avoid the overuse of subjective words, particularly adjectives. Use of seemingly innocent words such as *excellent condition* or *should last for* are often interpreted by the customer more liberally than the agent intended. The line between puffing and false advertising is indeed a very thin and fragile one.

### Example #1:

Broker Anderson, acting as a management agent for owner Smith, negotiated a long-term lease. During the negotiations, Anderson stated that the house was in good condition. Shortly after moving into the house, the tenant discovered that the sewer line was badly clogged and the heater was in need of repair. Upon discovery of this, the tenant notified the broker, who responded immediately by hiring a plumber to unclog the sewer line and a repairman to fix the heater. The broker had no prior knowledge of the defects.

**Question:** Has Broker Anderson acted unethically?

**Answer:** Probably not. The fact that he acted promptly and responsibly to correct the defects, and made a sincere effort to render satisfactory service, would indicate that he had not acted in an unethical manner. However, wouldn't it have been simpler for the broker to ask the owner what defects, if any, currently exist? The odds against both a sewer and heating problem occurring spontaneously and simultaneously are great. If the owner gives the property a clean bill of health, the agent should convey to the tenant that "the owner says that the house is in good condition."

*Example #2:*

A broker was asked to list a neglected house that obviously needed a wide range of repairs. At the time of taking the listing, she strongly advised the owner that it would be to his advantage to put the house in good repair before offering it for sale, but the owner wanted it sold at once, on an as-is basis. The agent wrote a novel advertisement, offering a clunker in poor condition, as a challenge to an ambitious do-it-yourselfer.

A few days later, a retired couple who liked the location and general features, and who had been attracted to the property because of the ad, made an offer that was subsequently accepted.

During the negotiations, and while inspecting the house, the agent was careful to point out that the house was in generally poor condition. However, she did point out that since the house was constructed of concrete and stucco, it was her opinion that there would be no need for termite control since termites could not enter this type of construction.

Of course, you can imagine what occurred. While making the repairs, the buyer ripped out a sill that he intended to replace, and found it swarming with termites. There was substantial termite damage to the floors. As the old cliché goes, *if it wasn't for the fact that the termites were holding hands, the building would have fallen down.*

**Question:** Did the broker act unethically, or is this a caveat emptor sale?

**Answer:** This is definitely a violation of ethics on the part of the broker.

**Misrepresenting the Property's Size, Square Footage, Boundary Lines, Etc.**

*Knowingly making a false or misleading representation or representing, without a reasonable basis for believing its truth, the size of a parcel, square footage, improvements made, or the location of the boundary lines of real property being offered for sale, lease, or exchange.*

If a buyer asks how many square feet there are in a particular house, the broker is obligated either to say that he or she does not know (but the broker should know) or to provide the buyer with the correct square footage. If the broker tells the buyer that the house has 1,800 when he knows that it has only 1,700 square feet, or guesses about the square footage because it looks right, his actions are fraudulent. It makes no difference whether 100 square feet is significant. The same rule applies to the lot size or boundary lines [*Mills v. Hellinger (1950) 100 C.A. 2d 482; William vs. Marshall (1951) 37 C.2d 445*].

## Misrepresenting the Use of a Property

*The licensee knowingly makes a false or misleading representation, or falsely represents to a prospective buyer or lessee of real property, without a reasonable basis to believe its truth, that the property can be used for certain purposes, with the intent of inducing the prospective buyer or lessee to acquire an interest in the real property.*

## Intentional Misrepresentation

An intentional misrepresentation is an affirmative suggestion or statement of a material fact that the broker knows to be untrue [CC § 1572, Actual Fraud; 1710, Deceit]. The preceding sections of the California Civil Code apply to most unethical situations.

**QUIZZES ARE MANDATORY**

CalBRE regulations now require the submission of chapter quizzes before you can access the final examination. You must log in and submit the chapter quizzes online before you can access the final examination. After submitting the last chapter quiz, you will receive a link to the final examination. You were issued a Personal Identification Number (PIN) and login instructions when you enrolled.

**Chapter One Quiz**

1.      It is considered unlawful to misrepresent the likely value of real property to its owner for the purpose of:

   (a)    Securing a listing.
   (b)    Acquiring an interest in the property for the licensee's own account.
   (c)    Both (a) and (b).
   (d)    None of the above.

2.      In an attempt to secure a listing, salesman Jones tells Mr. and Mrs. Smith that he has buyers looking for a house just like theirs who are ready to make an offer, although such buyers do not exist. Such a technique is considered to be:

   (a)    Unlawful.
   (b)    Ethical.
   (c)    Dishonest but acceptable.
   (d)    Questionable but okay.

3.      Knowingly underestimating the probable closing costs in order to induce a person to make or accept an offer to purchase is considered to be:

   (a)    Dishonest but okay.
   (b)    Fraud.
   (c)    Standard practice.
   (d)    Preferable to overestimating closing costs.

4.      Under which of the following circumstances is it acceptable to make an addition to or modification of the terms of an instrument that was previously signed or initialed by a party to a transaction?

   (a)    One party's agent fills in some blanks without authority that were inadvertently left blank.
   (b)    One party to the transaction is out of town, and the closing of the transaction will not be delayed if the additions and/or modifications are not made.
   (c)    At least one of the two parties to the transaction authorizes the additions and/or modifications.
   (d)    The changes and/or modifications are made with the knowledge and consent of all parties concerned.

5.  When representing the nature and/or condition of the interior or exterior features of a property while soliciting an offer, the agent should:

    (a)   Use subjective words, particularly adjectives, while describing the condition of the property.
    (b)   Use particularly colorful words to entice prospective buyers.
    (c)   Avoid the overuse of subjective words, particularly adjectives, that may be misinterpreted.
    (d)   Exaggerate the condition of the property, but then back off.

## Chapter Two

### Important Terms

back-up offer
close of escrow
contingency
discount
documentary transfer stamps
escrow instructions
exchange
fraud
frivolous
material fact
secret profit
subterfuge

### Learning Objectives

Upon completion of Chapter Two, you should be able to complete the following:

- Define *material fact*.
- Explain the difference between actual and constructive fraud.
- Describe *fraudulent intent*.
- Describe the consequences of failing to explain contingencies.

## Disclosure of Material Facts

*When acting in the capacity of an agent in a transaction for the sale, lease, or exchange of real property, the licensee fails to disclose to a prospective purchaser or lessee facts known to the licensee, when the licensee has reason to believe that such facts are not known to nor readily observable by a prospective purchaser or lessee, which materially affects the value or desirability of the property.*

This section deals with *material fact*, which may be defined as a fact that would affect, or that the agent should realize would be likely to affect, the judgment of the principal while giving his or her consent to the agent to enter into a particular transaction on specified terms.

This includes the duty to make full and complete disclosure of all material facts which may influence the principal (CC § 2020). The withholding of a material fact is considered a fraud, whether intentional or not. The two categories of fraud are *actual* and *constructive*.

### Actual Fraud

CC § 1572 lists five acts that are deemed *actual fraud* when committed by a party while under contract, or by the party's connivance with intent to induce another to enter into the contract, or simply to deceive another party.

> (a)      Giving a suggestion, in the form of a fact, that is not true, by one who does not believe it to be true.
> (e)      Making a positive assertion in a manner that is not warranted by the information possessed by the person making it, and/or which is not true, even though the person making the assertion believes it to be true.
> (f)      Suppressing that which is true, by one who has knowledge or belief of the fact.
> (g)      Making a promise, by one who has no intention of performing it.
> (h)      Any other act fitted to deceive.

### Constructive Fraud

The Civil Code states that *constructive fraud* is any breach of duty that, without an actual fraudulent intent, gains an advantage for the person at fault, or anyone claiming under the person at fault, by misleading another to his or her prejudice or to the prejudice of anyone claiming under him or her. It may consist of any such act, or the omission of any such act, that the law specifically declares to be fraudulent without respect to actual fraud.

Ordinarily, misrepresentation of the law does not amount to actionable fraud, no doubt because it is presumed that everyone knows the law. Nevertheless, a fraud may be actionable when one party uses superior knowledge to gain an unconscionable advantage, or when the parties occupy some sort of confidential relationship. It appears that the agent fits this mold perfectly.

### Example #1:

In the case of *Menzel vs. Salka (1960) 179 C.A. 2nd 612*, the seller brought action against the broker to recover secret profits and commission. The seller had given the broker an exclusive listing and the broker had procured a buyer. During escrow, the buyer informed the broker that she could not complete the purchase and was willing to take $1,200 and forfeit the balance of the $6,200 deposit. The broker did not inform the seller, but instead opened up another escrow between the broker and the buyer, wherein the broker would purchase the property from the buyer for $5,000 less than the buyer was buying it from the seller. The broker testified that he told the seller about the transaction, but the seller denied such knowledge.

It was held that the broker had withheld vital information from the seller. An agent is required to exercise the highest degree of good faith toward his or her principal and may not obtain for himself or herself an advantage by misrepresentation, deceit, or concealment. In the case above, the broker was required to return the secret profit plus his commission.

An agent's duty to disclose includes the price that can be obtained, the possibility of a sale at a higher price, dealing with property in another fashion, tax consequences, and all other matters that a disinterested and skillful agent would believe are relevant [*Fisher v. Losey (1947) 78 C.A. 2nd 124; Smith vs. Zak (1971) 20 C.A. 3rd 785*].

One case even implied that if the broker had knowledge of the seller's tax situation, and the broker possessed any tax knowledge, the broker would be obligated to disclose this tax advice to the principal [*Santos vs. Wing (1961) 197 C.A. 2nd 678*].

Unless otherwise agreed, an agent is burdened with the duty to not compete with the principal concerning the subject matter of his or her agency.

**Present All Offers (Almost)**

*The willful failure of the licensee to present to, or obstruct the presentation of, any written offer to purchase that is received prior to the closing of a sale to the owner of a property, unless the owner expressly instructs the licensee not to present such an offer, or unless the offer is patently frivolous.*

It is often said that "all written offers must be presented." As we know, such a statement is not always true, such as when the offer is patently (obviously or openly) frivolous, or when the seller has set forth explicit instructions that no further offers are to be presented.

Can you think of any other circumstances under which an offer should not be presented? We can't.

It appears that the intent of this section is to make it clear to all licensees that additional written offers must be presented, even though the second offer may reduce the commission that goes to one of the brokers. Almost every listing agent has, or will, experience the time when he or she must present two offers (the second offer from a different office), knowing that there is the possibility that the second offer will be accepted and their offer will be rejected. It is tempting to pocket the other office's offer in hopes of getting the full commission. However, if the listing agent's offer is not accepted, and the agent then presents the second offer, their behavior will be grounds for their loss of license.

*A Thought to Consider:*

With the exception of selected areas (where listings are few and buyers are many, or a property is severely underpriced), it is doubtful that multiple offers will be a problem. Additionally, when there is another offer present, the agent for the buyer usually wants to accompany the offer at the time of presentation. However, we are considering the situation where the agent has two offers to present. Is it worth it to the agent to lose their license over one commission split? We don't think so. Here is a good rule to follow regarding the presentation of any offer, on any property, whether for sale or lease:

***Present all offers, unless otherwise instructed in writing.***

However, even then, the agent should tell the seller that they have an offer, even though the seller has instructed them not to present it. Consider the situation where the seller expressly instructs the agent not to show the seller any offer less than $145,000. Then, an offer comes in at $143,500 cash to the loan. This second offer will net the seller more than his or her previous conditions because there is no need for the seller to carry a second loan, which the seller had intended to sell at a discount in escrow. Should the agent tell the seller about the second offer? You bet! The agent should not be selective about which offers to present, but rather present all offers, even after the seller has accepted an offer. Who knows what's going through the seller's mind. Additionally, the second offer may serve as a back-up offer in case the first should fall through, or the seller may accept the offer with contingencies. There's no such thing as a sure thing.

**Remember:** If the seller reads, likes, and is willing to accept one offer, the seller must then be given an opportunity to read and reject all other offers.

***Example #1:***

Take the example of *Smith vs. Zak (1971) 20 C.A. 3rd 785.* The plaintiff listed real property with a broker. The property was to be condemned for a right-of-way in approximately five years, and was listed for $15,000 on the broker's advice. Thereafter, the broker opened an escrow, giving his own name as prospective purchaser of the property, and began preliminary negotiations with the prospective condemnor without the plaintiff's knowledge.

Within a few months, the broker twice submitted offers from Mr. Martin, a personal friend of the broker and a licensed real estate salesman who the broker had sponsored for licensure. The plaintiff accepted a $13,000 offer by Martin, and Martin signed escrow instructions under which the broker would take title to the property. The deal was consummated for $13,000, but the broker indicated a purchase price of $40,000 through the affixing of documentary transfer stamps. Within a year, the state commenced condemnation action and the broker asserted a fair market value of the property of $105,000. The plaintiff learned of the broker's acquisition of the property and the condemnation negotiations between the state and the broker. He brought suit against the broker.

The court held that the broker had a duty to disclose to the principal all offers to buy the property in addition to the offer accepted, and must refrain from a dual representation in a sale transaction without full disclosure to both principals. When the acts of an agent have been questioned by the principal to whom the agent has a fiduciary duty, the burden is upon the agent to prove that he or she acted in the utmost good faith toward the principal, and the agent may need to provide a full disclosure of all facts that relate to the transaction.

As a fiduciary, the broker should have undertaken on behalf of the plaintiff the acts that he undertook for his own account. Moreover, the broker was under a duty to disclose to the plaintiff his personal and professional relationship with the offeror, and the fact that the broker himself was to be the actual purchaser of the property.

Isn't it interesting that the court felt that the broker should inform the principal of his "personal relationship or friendship" with Martin (the offeror) as well as his "professional" relationship?

*Example #2:*

In the case of *Simone vs. McKee (1956) 142 C.A. 2nd 307*, judgment was obtained against a broker who did not disclose a $17,000 offer in preference for a $13,000 offer. The court stated that it is obviously a breach of a real estate broker's duty if he or she fails to disclose to the principal an offer to buy the client's property that is listed for sale with another broker.

## Present Competing Offers

*The licensee presents competing offers to the seller to purchase real property, in such a manner as to induce the seller to accept the offer that will provide the greatest compensation to the listing broker, without regard to the benefits, advantages, and/or disadvantages to the owner.*

In addition to withholding all offers, the agent may not present multiple offers in a predetermined sequence, other than those offers that are provided based on the date and/or time of the preparation of the offers, which will induce, persuade, or otherwise influence the seller's acceptance of one offer to the detriment of the others.

## Failing to Explain Contingencies That May Affect the Closing Date

*The licensee fails to explain to the parties (or prospective parties) of a real estate transaction, for whom the licensee is acting as an agent, the meaning and probable significance of a contingency in an offer or contract that the licensee knows or reasonably believes may affect the closing date of the transaction, or the timing of the vacating of the property by the seller or its occupancy by the buyer.*

There are myriad of situations that show that a late or delayed closing of a transaction can cause unbelievable problems for the buyer, seller, and agent. Some of the most common situations include the following:

- Contingencies based upon the occurrence or nonoccurrence of a specified event, such as new financing, inspections, repairs, etc.
- Possession to buyer at close of escrow.
- Possession to buyer prior to close of escrow.
- Possession to buyer after close of escrow.

*Rule A:*

The agent should never presume that either the buyer or seller is even remotely aware of the unexpected delays that almost always seem to occur. Because of this, the agent should explain to the buyer or seller that even the simplest of contingencies can cause closing delays and that the agent wants the buyer or seller to be fully informed and aware of this possibility.

### Rule B:

The agent should grant possession to the buyer at the close of escrow. Although this is not usually thought of as a contingency, it often becomes a major headache, especially if the agent does not sufficiently consider what may happen. It is not unusual for the buyer to equate possession with physical occupancy and expect to be able to move in on the day escrow closes.

### Example #1:

Escrow is scheduled to close and does close on the exact day the agent guaranteed the buyer it would. Sounds like the agent is in good shape. *Wrong!* Unbeknown to the agent, the buyer thought possession meant occupancy. On the morning after the day escrow closes, the buyer is waiting outside his new home with his family and a moving van full of furniture. To his dismay, he discovers that the seller is not the least bit prepared to move out. In fact, the seller had not planned to move out until the escrow closed on the home she is purchasing.

We could go on for an hour about this problem, but won't. The agent should always anticipate the above and try to avoid what may be a very unpleasant and expensive situation. It is truly unfortunate for the agent when he or she has to pay for furniture storage, a motel bill, and the eventual cost of a lost sale when the buyer becomes a seller. Additionally, this doesn't even take into consideration the immeasurable loss of referrals from your unhappy buyer.

### Rule C:

Real estate licensees should use caution when they recommend granting physical possession of real property to the buyer prior to close of escrow or the transfer of title.

Since 1947, Civil Code Section 1662 (commonly known as the Uniform Vendor and Purchaser Risk Act) provides for the fixing of losses for destruction of the property, unless the contract expressly provides otherwise, between the seller and the buyer. Briefly, the law states that prior to the transfer of title and/or the transfer of possession to the buyer, the responsibility for loss is on the seller. After the transfer of title or possession, the responsibility is on the buyer. In addition to the responsibility of loss due to damages, it may be necessary, in order to continue to receive insurance protection, to notify the insurance carrier.

A frequent complaint received by the Real Estate Commissioner concerns the buyer who has been given possession of the property prior to the close of escrow without an agreement or discussion as to whether there will be rental payments to the seller between the date of possession and the close of escrow. It is typical that the buyer is unaware of the demand for rent until the agent presents the escrow instructions to the buyer for his or her signature. What does a seller do when he or she has given the buyer possession prior to close of escrow, and the deal falls through?

### Rule D:

Conversely, the situation may occur where the seller is allowed to remain in the property after the close of escrow. In this case, is the seller obliged to pay rent? If the amount to be paid in rent is not stated, how much should the seller pay? Should the seller be treated as a tenant, with all of the responsibilities and benefits a tenancy agreement carries, or is the seller to be considered an occupant, as may be encountered in a hotel arrangement? How much rent per day should the seller pay if he or she overstays the close of escrow?

### There Is No Sure-Fire Solution

There is, of course, no way that the close of escrow can be guaranteed, but there are certain steps an agent can take to ensure that the involved parties are aware of what will be expected or required concerning the possession or occupancy contingency.

A broker should be certain that the buyer and seller understand what is meant by physical possession of the home and what amount of rent, if any, is to be paid. This understanding should be documented, in writing, in the deposit receipt, or in a separate rental agreement.

Insisting that the rental agreement be in writing will avoid placing the agent in the position of an arbitrator on such matters as physical possession or the amount of rental payments which the agent may be powerless to carry out.

### Failing to Disclose the Interest the Licensee-Agent Expects to Acquire

*The licensee-agent fails to disclose to the seller of real property, in a transaction in which the licensee is an agent for the seller, the nature and extent of any direct or indirect interest that the licensee expects to acquire as a result of the sale.*

The prospective purchase of the property by a person related to the licensee by blood or marriage, purchase by an entity in which the licensee has an ownership interest, or purchase by any other person with whom the licensee occupies a special relationship, where there is a reasonable probability that the licensee could be indirectly acquiring an interest in the property, shall be disclosed to the seller.

This section is not intended to prevent a real estate agent from acquiring an interest in real property, either directly, indirectly, or by way of a purchase by a relative. To the contrary, such activities are neither encouraged nor discouraged. However, concealment of such a relationship is expressly forbidden.

The courts have held that the agent's negotiation of a sale to his or her significant other, without making full disclosure to the principal, is a violation of the agent's duty to disclose all material facts. A later case concerned the failure of the real estate broker to disclose to the seller that the buyer was the broker's mother-in-law. The court stated that where the seller's real estate agent is obligated to disclose to the agent's principal the identity of the buyer, and where the buyer is not the agent, but has with the agent such blood, marital, or other relationship, which would suggest a reasonable possibility that the agent could be indirectly acquiring an interest in the property. Such a relationship is a material fact that the agent must disclose to the agent's principal. Obviously, the same disclosure requirement applies when the buyer or seller is an employee of the broker.

A good example of what can happen when there is not full disclosure is the following case where the agent lost his license. In the case of *Abell v. Watson (1957) 155 C.A. 2nd 158*, the broker breached his fiduciary duty to his client, the seller, by failing to disclose to the seller that the intended purchaser was the broker's wife or sister, and that the actual purchaser was the wife. Let us explain. The seller, Mr. Hubbard, said that he wanted to gain $17,500 net from his property. Mr. Abell, the broker, arranged an escrow, in which the purchaser named was Mr. Abell's sister or her nominee. The escrow was closed by payment of the purchase price and a deed conveying the property to Mr. Abell's wife. Mr. Abell did not tell the seller that the purchaser was to be either his sister or his wife. The Real Estate Commissioner charged Mr. Abell with fraud and dishonest dealing as defined in the Real Estate Law (B. & P. Code, Section 10176 (i)).

### Example #1:

In the case of *Baston vs. Strehlow (1968) 68 C. 2nd 662*, the broker presented to the seller an offer from a corporation for which, the broker disclosed, he was the president, and in which he was financially involved. However, the court found the broker liable for failing to reveal that he and his wife were the only shareholders and that the corporation was not the ultimate purchaser.

Generally, when listing property, one of the major items of discussion is the price at which the property will be offered for sale. If, at any time, a broker makes an offer to purchase the listed property, either at the listed price or at a lower price, prudence would suggest that the seller would already have gathered independent advice as to the market value of his or her property. If the seller does not have this information, or even if the seller does, the seller may later claim that the broker had information that the broker was required to disclose, due to being in the position of a broker. A seller may also contend that the broker's information puts the broker in a superior position over the seller to know the value of the property. This sort of transaction demands careful documentation if a broker purchases from or sells to a client.

Although there is no law (Real Estate Law) that requires a broker to disclose his or her license status when dealing as a principal, such a position is often untenable when it is discovered that the broker made a large profit.

The following illustrates how a broker can violate this section. Suppose that salesperson Anderson, working through real estate broker Johnson, obtains a listing on a home owned by Paul and Mary Sanders. Shortly thereafter, Anderson obtains an offer from buyers Paul and Donna DeSoto at a price less than what the Sanders were asking. After the sale is consummated, the sellers discover that the buyers are, in fact, closely related to the salesperson, who is secretly buying the property for himself. An interesting question always comes up when using the words *closely related*. How does a broker handle a transaction where the seller or buyer is a life-long friend? In fact, the broker's closest and dearest friend? One with whom the broker would trust his or her life?

Such *subterfuge* is patently a violation of this article. Moreover, broker Johnson, as the employer of Anderson, may also be disciplined on the ground that he is responsible for supervising the acts of his sales employees when such acts are within the scope of their business activities.

**Failing to Disclose the Ownership Interest of the Licensee-Agent**

*The licensee-agent fails to disclose to the buyer of real property, in a transaction in which the licensee is an agent for the buyer, the nature and extent of the licensee's direct or indirect ownership interest in such real property.*

*The direct or indirect ownership interest in the property by a person related to the licensee by blood or marriage, by an entity in which the licensee has an ownership interest, or by any other person with whom the licensee occupies a special relationship, shall be disclosed to the buyer.*

This section provides information that is similar to the preceding section, but differs in a significant way. The previous section refers to the licensee who expects to acquire an interest, while this section addresses the licensee who currently has an interest.

*A Common Misunderstanding*

We are going to correct a commonly encountered misunderstanding regarding a broker or salesperson who is selling his or her own personal or real property.

The Real Estate Law does not require that a licensee reveal his or her license status when selling as a principal. This means that if a licensee is selling property as a principal, without the use of the professional services available (e.g., multiple listing), the Real Estate Law does not require that the licensee reveal his or her license status. However, common sense tells us that in the event that the buyer discovered that the licensee was a seller and felt that they had been mistreated, and therefore filed suit, the first complaint the buyer (through his or her attorney) would make to the jury would be that the seller was a licensee and, as such, had superior knowledge and obviously took advantage of his or her superior position at the expense of the poor, uninformed buyer. It's not worth the trouble and expense for a licensee to withhold their license status.

A simple statement in the contract will suffice. The following is a little more formal:

> *It is clearly understood, by all parties to this transaction, that the seller (or buyer if the licensee is buying the property) is a licensed real estate broker (or salesperson).*

If you are buying the property, add the following:

> *... and is buying the property for his or her own personal use (or for investment if that is the case).*

**Failing to Disclose the Interest to the Principal in Lender, Escrow, Etc.**

*The licensee-agent fails to disclose to the principal, for whom the licensee is acting as an agent, any significant interest the licensee has in a particular entity, when the licensee recommends the use of the services or products of such entity.*

It does not appear to be legal for a licensee to recommend or guide sellers, buyers, borrowers, etc. toward a particular lender or escrow service, as long as all parties are fully informed about any fact of the transaction that may influence the principal's decision. We previously discussed this point under the subject *Material Fact*.

Also, Section 2950(h) of the Regulations of the Commissioner states that the following act by a real estate broker (which includes a salesperson) may be grounds for disciplinary action:

Failing to advise all parties in writing if he has knowledge that any licensee acting as such in the transaction has any interest as a stockholder, officer, partner or owner of the agency holding the escrow.

The selection of an escrow agent, lender, or any other of the numerous service-performing parties in a real estate transaction should be resolved by a meeting of the minds of the principals who are involved the transaction. Because the selection of an escrow holder is not usually critical to either principal in the transaction, real estate brokers have played a large role in deciding where escrow would be opened or with whom the loan would be placed. In recent years, the number of brokerage-owned companies that perform these services has increased, and they operate under entirely different names.

Although the vast majority of such activities are absolutely legal and ethical, there has been an increasing effort on the part of federal and state regulators to minimize the influence that the broker has in the selection of escrows and lenders for a transaction. The rationale underlying this effort is that buyers and sellers have the right and opportunity to compare services and charges and, if they so desire, to negotiate among themselves. One may also suspect that there is an effort to reduce the broker's temptation of concealing brokerage fees by using apparently unrelated companies.

**QUIZZES ARE MANDATORY**: Please log in and submit the chapter quizzes online.

**Chapter Two Quiz**

1.    Under which of the following circumstances could a real estate broker lawfully refuse to submit an offer to purchase to the owner of the property?

(a)    Never.
(b)    When the offer is below the fair market value of the property.
(c)    When the terms of the offer do not match the terms of the listing.
(d)    When the broker is expressly instructed not to present such an offer, or when the offer is patently frivolous.

2.    A broker should continue to present offers to the owner:

(a)    Until escrow has been opened.
(b)    Even after the seller has accepted an offer.
(c)    Until the loan has been approved.
(d)    Until an offer has been accepted.

3.    Which of the following is the proper way to present multiple offers?

(a)    In a predetermined sequence that is based on the date and/or time of the preparation of the offers.
(b)    In a predetermined sequence that will persuade the seller to accept one offer over another.
(c)    In a predetermined sequence that will provide the greatest compensation to the listing agent.
(d)    In a predetermined sequence with in-house offers presented first.

4.    If an offer to purchase contains a contingency that may affect the closing date of the transaction, what are the agent's responsibilities?

(a)    Since there is no way the close of escrow can be guaranteed, the agent has no responsibility in this area.
(b)    The agent must explain to the seller the meaning and probable significance of a contingency that may affect the closing date.
(c)    The party to the transaction that created the contingency is expected to understand the significance of that contingency without help from the agent.
(d)    The agent of the party that created the contingency is responsible for explaining to all parties that the contingency may result in an unexpected delay.

5.    Broker Johnson obtained a 90-day listing to sell Mr. Bradley's home. One week later, Broker Johnson presented a full price offer to Mr. Bradley. The prospective purchaser was Broker Johnson's wife. What are Broker Johnson's disclosure responsibilities?

(a)    Since the intended buyer is not a blood relative, Broker Johnson does not need to disclose the family relationship.

(b)     The fact that the buyer is Broker Johnson's wife need only be disclosed if a direct inquiry is made by the seller.

(c)     Broker Johnson must disclose to Mr. Bradly that the prospective purchase of the property is being made by a person who is related to him by blood or marriage.

(d)     Concealment of Broker Johnson's relationship with the buyer is not forbidden.

## Chapter Three

### Important Terms

assignor
bankruptcy
default
endorser
judgments
mechanics' lien
recording

### Learning Objectives

Upon completion of Chapter Three, you should be able to complete the following:

- Describe *unlawful conduct* as it relates to real estate financing.
- Explain the consequences of failing to disclose information about the borrower.
- Describe the consequences of knowingly underestimating probable closing costs.
- Define *advance fee*.
- List suggestions for professional conduct.

## Unlawful Conduct as Related to Real Estate Financing

The following section reviews unlawful conduct when soliciting, negotiating, or arranging a loan secured by real property or the sale of a promissory note secured by real property. Licensees, when performing acts within the meaning of subdivision (d) or (e) of Section 10131 of the Business and Professions Code, shall not violate any of the applicable provisions of subdivision (a), or act in a manner which would subject the licensee to adverse action, penalty, or discipline under Sections 10176 and 10177 of the Business and professions Code, including, but not limited to, the acts and omissions outlined below.

### Misrepresenting to a Prospective Borrower

*The licensee misrepresents to a prospective borrower of a loan, to be secured by real property or to an assignor/endorser of a promissory note secured by real property, that there is an existing lender willing to make the loan or that there is a purchaser for the note, for the purpose of inducing the borrower or assignor/endorser to utilize the services of the licensee.*

A fraud is an act intended to deceive for the purpose of inducing another to part with something of value. Fraud can be as blatant as knowingly telling a lie or making a promise with no intention of performance.

Although this section uses the word knowingly, a licensee should not represent any of the items referred to in this section unless the agent qualifies his or her statement.

The agent cannot rely on the word knowingly as a means to escape responsibility for a misstatement of fact. To say that the agent misrepresented without knowing that the statements were incorrect will not automatically get the agent off the hook. Agents are always responsible for any statement they make, and they cannot claim that they were merely passing along information or claims that were made by another.

### Failing to Disclose Information about the Prospective Borrower

*The licensee fails to disclose, to a prospective lender or note purchaser, information about the prospective borrower's identity, occupation, employment, income, and credit data as represented to the broker by the prospective borrower.*

Brokers may find it desirable to subscribe to a credit reporting agency in order to advise their clients on financing. Providing the client with credit information on which the client can base his or her decision will reduce the guesswork and "blind trust" that often characterizes these transactions.

### Failing to Disclose Information about Borrower's Ability to Meet Contractual Obligations

*The licensee fails to disclose information to the seller that is known to the licensee, and is pertinent to the ability of the borrower to meet his or her potential or existing contractual obligations under the note or contract, including information known about the borrower's payment history on an existing note, whether or not the note is in default, or whether or not the borrower is in bankruptcy.*

This section and the previous section share a common theme; namely, they relate to the borrower and his or her ability to repay the amount borrowed.

### *Effect of Recording:*

The primary importance of recording is to provide constructive notice of the recorded document to subsequent purchasers and encumbrancers (CC § 1213). Recording also establishes priorities between deeds and other recorded documents. The general rule is that an instrument obtains its priority as of the date of its recording (CC § 1214).

An agent who represents a loan as having a certain priority without first checking the record always runs the risk of giving incorrect information to the lender. Not only may there be another loan of record, but there may be other liens, such as tax liens, mechanic's liens, or judgments. The record can be checked through a title or escrow company. Often, the title company will run the check at no cost to the agent—this is a good-will gesture for future business. If the title company will not do it for free, the agent should pay for the service; this is better than losing one's license.

### Misrepresenting in Any Transaction That a Specific Service Is Free When It Is Not

*In any transaction, the licensee knowingly misrepresents that a specific service is free when the licensee knows or has a reasonable basis to know that the service is covered by a fee to be charged as part of the transaction.*

This section of the code is not entirely clear about whether it applies to the misrepresentation to the seller or the buyer, and in fact, it makes no difference.

If an agent tells a party to the transaction that a fee will not be charged, or that the agent will perform the service free, the agent cannot rely on terminology to protect him or her from acting unethically. The average principal's lack of knowledge of the multitude of real estate terms cannot be used as a means of concealing charges that the agent previously claimed would not be charged. For example, if the agent tells the buyer that there will be no points, and then submits loan origination fees, the agent will be acting unethically, and will most likely be committing fraud.

### Failure to Account to the Borrower for Disposition of the Advance Fee

The licensee acts in a transaction for the purpose of obtaining a loan, and receives an advance fee from the borrower for this purpose, yet fails to account to the borrower for the disposition of this advance fee.

### *Advance Fees:*

Some brokers may wish to collect money from loan applicants in advance to cover the cost of services to be performed while arranging the loan. Such fees are called *advance fees* (see *Business and Professions Code Section 10026*). However, advance fees may only be collected pursuant to an advance fee agreement approved by the Bureau of Real Estate prior to the use of the agreement and the collection of any such fees. Commissioner's Reg. § 2970 sets forth the basic requirements for advance fee agreements. All advertising materials used in conjunction with advance fees must also be submitted to the CalBRE for prior approval before use (see *Business and Professions Code Section 10085*).

Any real estate broker who contracts for or collects advance fees from a principal must deposit the funds into a trust account. Advance fees are trust funds and not the broker's funds. Amounts may be withdrawn for the benefit of the broker only when actually expended for the benefit of the principal, or five days after the verified accounts have been mailed to the principal. When the broker does not handle advance fees in accordance with Real Estate Law, it shall be presumed that the broker has violated Penal Code Sections 506 and 506a, and strict penalties and fines may be levied against the broker.

### Exception:

The CalBRE does not treat funds collected in advance for appraisal and credit reports as advance fees, as long as the broker collects as near as possible the exact amount(s) necessary, and refunds any excess as soon as it is identified to the principal. However, even though these funds are not treated as advance fees, they are still the principal's funds, and therefore, like advance fees, must be deposited into a trust account.

### Knowingly Making False or Misleading Representations

The following three points all begin with the word *knowingly*. Such an act on the part of the licensee concerning the items specified in each section involve material facts and constitute violations of the Real Estate Law.

The licensee does the following:

- **Knowingly** makes a false or misleading representation to a lender or assignee/endorsee of a lender of a loan that is secured directly or collaterally by a lien on real property, about the amount and treatment of loan payments, including loan payoffs, and fails to account to the lender or assignee/endorsee of a lender about the disposition of such payments.

- **Knowingly** makes false or misleading representation about the terms and conditions of a loan to be secured by a lien on real property when soliciting a borrower or negotiating the loan.

- **Knowingly** makes a false or misleading representation or represents, without a reasonable basis for believing its truth, when soliciting a lender or negotiating a loan to be secured by a lien on real property about the market value of the securing real property, the nature and/or condition of the interior or exterior features of the securing real property, its size, or the square footage of any improvements on the securing real property.

Taking these sections one step further, an agent who unknowingly passes or conveys inaccurate information, the facts of which could have been determined by reasonable diligence, may be held liable for losses to either party if such loss is based upon the negligence of the agent.

### *Disclosure Requirement (CC § 2956 - 2967)*

Many residential sales involve the seller providing the purchaser with financing for some portion of the purchase price. Seller-assisted financing arrangements were popular in the not-so-distant past when interest rates reached peak levels. Unfortunately, the process was often abused, and borrowers, sellers, lenders, and creditors never fully realized the positions they were taking. In response, the legislature enacted Civil Code Sections 2956–2967. These statutes require that both the buyer and seller be provided with a statement that discloses material information regarding the financing.

The person responsible for delivery is the arranger of credit who is, for all practical purposes, the broker arranging the sale. If there are two offices included, the selling office is responsible for providing the disclosure. The information contained in the disclosure covers such topics as credit documents, credit terms, deferred interest payments, balloon payments, buyer credit worthiness, document recording, insurance, and requests for notices in the event of defaults on senior liens. This law applies to seller financing of residential property to no more than four dwelling units.

## Suggestions for Professional Conduct

As part of the effort to promote ethical business practices of real estate licensees, the Real Estate Commissioner has issued suggestions for professional conduct in sale, lease and exchange transactions, and suggestions for professional conduct when negotiating or arranging loans secured by real property or selling a promissory note secured by real property.

The purpose of these suggestions is to encourage real estate licensees to maintain a high level of ethics and professionalism in their business practices when performing acts for which a real estate license is required.

These suggestions are not intended to be statements of duties imposed by law nor are they grounds for disciplinary action by the California Bureau of Real Estate if they are not followed. The purpose of these suggestions is to elevate the professionalism of real estate licensees.

### Professional Conduct in Sale, Lease, and Exchange Transactions

The following are suggestions for professional conduct in sale, lease, and exchange transactions. In order to maintain a high level of ethics and professionalism in their business practices, real estate licensees are encouraged to adhere to the following suggestions while conducting their business activities:

- Aspire to give a high level of competent, ethical, and quality service to buyers and sellers in real estate transactions.

- Ensure that questions are promptly answered and all significant events or problems in a transaction are conveyed in a timely manner.

- Cooperate with the California Bureau of Real Estate's enforcement of, and report to that department evident violations of, the Real Estate Law.

- Use care in the preparation of any advertisement to present an accurate picture or message to the reader, viewer, or listener.

- Keep oneself informed and current on factors affecting the real estate market in which the licensee operates as an agent.

- Make a full, open, and sincere effort to cooperate with other licensees, unless the principal has instructed the licensee to the contrary.

- Attempt to settle disputes with other licensees through mediation or arbitration.

- Advertise or claim to be an expert in an area of specialization in real estate brokerage activity, e.g., appraisal, property management, industrial siting, mortgage loan, etc., only if the licensee has had special training, preparation, or experience in such area(s).

- Strive to provide equal opportunity for quality housing and a high level of service to all persons regardless of race, color, sex, religion, ancestry, physical handicap, marital status, or national origin.

- Base opinions of value, whether for the purpose of advertising or promoting real estate brokerage business, upon documented objective data.

- Make every attempt to comply with these Suggestions for Professional Conduct and the Code of Ethics of any organized real estate industry group of which the licensee is a member.

- Obtain written instructions from both parties to a transaction prior to disbursing a purchase money deposit to a party.

**Professional Conduct When Negotiating or Arranging Loans**

The following are suggestions for professional conduct when negotiating or arranging loans secured by real property or sale of a promissory note secured by real property. In order to maintain a high level of ethics and professionalism in their business practices when performing acts within the meaning of subdivisions (d) and (e) of Section 10131 and Sections 10131.1 and 10131.2 of the Business and Professions Code, real estate licensees are encouraged to adhere to the following suggestions, in addition to any applicable provisions of subdivision (a), while conducting their business activities:

- Aspire to give a high level of competent, ethical, and quality service to borrowers and lenders in loan transactions secured by real estate.

- Stay in close communication with borrowers and lenders to ensure that reasonable questions are promptly answered and all significant events or problems in a loan transaction are conveyed in a timely manner.

- Keep oneself informed and current on factors affecting the real estate loan market in which the licensee acts as an agent.

- Advertise or claim to be an expert in an area of specialization in real estate mortgage loan transactions only if the licensee has had special training, preparation or experience in such area.

- Strive to provide equal opportunity for quality mortgage loan services and a high level of service to all borrowers or lenders regardless of race, color, sex, religion, ancestry, physical handicap, marital status, or national origin.

- Base opinions of value in a loan transaction, whether for the purpose of advertising or promoting real estate mortgage loan brokerage business, on documented, objective data.

- Respond to reasonable inquiries of a principal regarding the status or extent of efforts to negotiate the sale of an existing loan.

- Respond to reasonable inquiries of a borrower regarding the net proceeds available from a loan arranged by the licensee.

- Make every attempt to comply with the standards of professional conduct and the code of ethics of any organized mortgage loan industry group of which the licensee is a member.

**QUIZZES ARE MANDATORY:** Please log in and submit the chapter quizzes online.

**Chapter Three Quiz**

1.  To obtain business, Broker Zigler falsely represents to prospective borrowers that he has an existing lender who is willing to make an immediate loan for them. Such a technique is considered:

    (a)   Unlawful conduct.
    (b)   Acceptable in any case.
    (c)   Acceptable as long as Broker Zigler finds a lender within 30 days.
    (d)   Acceptable as long as Broker Zigler prequalifies the borrowers immediately.

2.  Broker Sampson tells prospective borrowers that he can arrange a "no points" loan when he knows that a loan origination fee will be charged that includes points. Such a practice would be:

    (a)   Acceptable since loan origination fees are charged by the lender and not by Broker Sampson.
    (b)   Acceptable since the borrower is expected to work out the fees with the lender directly.
    (c)   Unethical and most likely fraud.
    (d)   Acceptable since there are no rules that address this situation.

3.  Advance fees are:

    (a)   Trust funds.
    (b)   The broker's personal funds.
    (c)   Advance commissions.
    (d)   Lender fees.

4.  An agent who unknowingly passes or conveys inaccurate information, the fact of which could have been determined by reasonable diligence, may be held liable for losses to either party if such loss is based upon the:

    (a)   Negligence of the lender.
    (b)   Faulty work done by the termite company.
    (c)   Negligence of the agent.
    (d)   All of the above.

5.  It is recommended that disputes between licensees be settled through:

    (a)   Small claims court.
    (b)   Mediation or arbitration.
    (c)   A disciplinary proceeding initiated by the California Bureau of Real Estate.
    (d)   Civil court.

# Notes

# Fair Housing

3 Hours of Continuing Education for
Salesperson and Broker License Renewal

**Lumbleau Real Estate School**
23805 Hawthorne Blvd.
Torrance, CA 90505

**DISCLAIMERS**

Although every effort has been made to provide accurate and current information in this text, the ideas, suggestions, general principles, and conclusions presented in this text are subject to local, state, and federal laws and regulations, court cases, and any revisions of same. The author and/or publisher is not engaged in rendering legal, tax, or other professional services. The reader is thus urged to consult with his or her employing broker and/or seek legal counsel regarding any points of law. This publication should not be used as a substitute for competent legal advice.

This course is approved for continuing education credit by the California Bureau of Real Estate. However, this approval does not constitute an endorsement of the views or opinions that are expressed by the course sponsor, instructor, authors, or lecturers.

## Table of Contents

## Chapter One

### Important Terms

actual damages
aggrieved party
disability
dwellings
fiduciary
lessee
personal property
plaintiff
sublessee
trustee
unlawful detainer
Unruh Civil Rights Act

### Learning Objectives

Upon completion of Chapter One, you should be able to complete the following:

- Describe the two primary California statutes that prohibit discrimination in the sale and leasing of real property.

- Describe the California court's interpretation of a business establishment.

- Define *disability*.

- Describe the Federal Fair Housing Laws.

- Describe the Fair Housing Amendments Act of 1988.

- Define *familial status*.

- Describe the Americans With Disabilities Act.

## Discrimination

This section will discuss two acts that prohibit discrimination while leasing real property.

1.  The Unruh Civil Rights Act of 1959 (C.C. § 54 & 55)

2.  The California Fair Employment and Housing Act

## Unruh Civil Rights Act

The Unruh Civil Rights Act (C.C. § 54 & 55) provides that "all persons within the jurisdiction of this state are free and equal, and no matter what their sex, race, color, religion, ancestry, national origin, or blindness or other physical disability, are entitled to the full and equal accommodations, advantages, facilities, privileges, or services in all business establishments of every kind whatsoever." This act also prohibits discrimination against a disabled person by denying or interfering with admittance to, or enjoyment of, any public facility.

## Business Establishments

Unfortunately, the Unruh Act (the "Act") makes no attempt to define *business establishment*. However, the courts have interpreted the language of the statute to apply to "all business establishments of every kind whatsoever." *Business establishment* is not limited to a commercial establishment; it includes profit-making as well as nonprofit enterprises, and it includes public as well as private organizations. In reference to real estate activities, an owner of property is in the "business" of renting residential units and is subject to the Unruh Act, and the owner cannot discriminate when he or she offers the unit for rent. The owner also cannot evict a tenant based on the tenant's race or color. The rental of a triplex, for example, even though it is the only property owned by the owner, is enough to establish the owner in the "business," and therefore the owner is subject to the Act.

A real estate broker also operates a business establishment within the terms of the Unruh Act. The Act applies to any real estate broker in the business of acting as an agent for the rental of residential units, for the sale of homes in a tract development, and for the sale of an individual single-family residence.

## Blindness and Physical Disabilities

The Unruh Act does not intend to require a property owner to build, alter, or modify any newer existing structure to accommodate any disability by a person who may rent or use the premises, nor does the owner have to treat any blind or disabled person any differently than a person who does not have a disability.

**Special Note**: When a landlord refuses to accept tenants with dogs, he or she does not have to accept a person who has a dog, except that he or she must accept a blind or visually handicapped person, deaf person, or physically handicapped person who has a trained guide or service dog. The owner does have the right in this case to establish certain terms in the rental or lease agreement that regulate the presence of guide dogs. In addition, the landlord cannot impose an additional charge to a disabled tenant because he or she has a trained guide or service dog, but the tenant is liable for any damages caused by the dog.

Also, under the Unruh Act, a disabled person cannot be denied the opportunity to rent merely because he or she relies on the income of his or her spouse. The landlord, however, can apply normal credit standards to the combined income of the tenants.

**Enforcement of the Unruh Act**

Civil action may be brought by any aggrieved party against the persons alleged to have engaged in discriminatory conduct in violation of the Unruh Act.

The only remedy expressly provided by the Unruh Act is the recovery of actual damages suffered by the plaintiff, plus such additional amount as may be determined by a jury or a court sitting without a jury, up to a maximum of three times the amount of actual damages, but in no case less than $1,000, plus attorney's fees.

However, if the act or acts which caused the complaint include violence or intimidation by threat of violence, committed against the aggrieved parties or their property because of race, color, religion, ancestry, national origin, political affiliation, sex, sexual orientation, age, and/or disability, each person who aids or incites such conduct is liable for the aggrieved party's actual damages plus an amount equal to three times such damages, plus a civil penalty of $25,000, together with attorney's fees, for each offense.

**Age discrimination under California Law**

Since 1982, it has been unlawful to discriminate against children by refusing to provide housing either through rental or sale, except when such housing is designed to meet the needs of senior citizens. Generally, federal law preempts state law. The federal law, however, is not significantly different from California law, and in some instances, is more specific. The topic of age discrimination will be discussed more thoroughly later in this section under the Federal Fair Housing Law.

**California Fair Employment and Housing Act**

*The California Fair Employment and Housing Act* (the "Act") declares that the practice of discrimination because of race, color, religion, sex, marital status, national origin, or ancestry in *housing accommodations* is against public policy. This Act also prohibits discrimination based on physical handicap, medical condition, or age.

The predecessor of this Act, the Rumford Act, was repealed in 1980 and the current act was enacted at the same time. In order to understand the verbiage of this Act, it is necessary to define the following operational terms as follows:

The term *housing accommodation* includes any improved or unimproved real property, or portion thereof, which is used or occupied, or is intended, arranged, or designed to be used or occupied, as the home, residence, or sleeping place of one or more human beings. However, it does not include any accommodations operated by a religious, fraternal, or charitable association, or a corporation not organized or operated for private profit, provided that such accommodations are being used in furtherance of the primary purpose or purposes for which the association or corporation was formed.

The term *owner* includes the lessee, sublessee, assignee, managing agent, real estate broker or salesman, or any person having any legal or equitable right of ownership or possession or the right to rent or lease housing accommodations, and includes the state and any of its political subdivisions and any agency thereof.

The term *person* includes one or more individuals, partnerships, associations, corporations, legal representatives, trustees, trustees in bankruptcy, and receivers or other fiduciaries.
The Act states that it is unlawful to engage in the following:

1. "For any owner of any housing accommodation to discriminate against any person because of the race, color, religion, sex, marital status, national origin, or ancestry of such person.

2. "For the owner of any housing accommodation to make or to cause to make any written or oral inquiry concerning the race, color, religion, sex, marital status, national origin, or ancestry of any person seeking to purchase, rent, or lease any housing accommodation.

3. "For any person to make, print, publish, or cause to be made, printed, or published any notice, statement, or advertisement, with respect to the sale or rental of a housing accommodation that indicates any preference, limitation, or discrimination based on race, color, religion, sex, marital status, national origin, or ancestry or an intention to make any such preference, limitation, or discrimination.

4. "For any person subject to the provisions of the Unruh Act, to discriminate against any person because of race, color, religion, sex, marital status, national origin, or ancestry with reference to housing accommodations.

5. "For any person, bank, mortgage company, or other financial institution to whom application is made for financial assistance for the purchase, organization, or construction of any housing accommodation to discriminate against any person or group of persons because of the race, color, religion, sex, marital status, national origin, or ancestry of such person or persons, or privileges relating to the obtaining or use of any financial assistance.

6. "For any owner of housing accommodations to harass, evict, or otherwise discriminate against any person in the sale or rental of housing accommodations when his dominant purpose is under this section, or informed law enforcement agencies of practices believed unlawful under this section, or has testified or assisted in any proceeding under this part. This provision is intended not to cause or permit the delay of an unlawful detainer action.

7. "For any person to aid, abet, incite, compel, or coerce the doing of any of the acts or practices declared unlawful in this section, or to attempt to do so."

The provisions of the Fair Housing Act apply to the sale or rental of *all* residential dwellings or units, regardless of size or number of units in the building or how it is financed. This includes single-family residences or dwelling units, except for the rental to a single roomer or boarder who lives in the household.

There are very few exemptions to existing fair housing laws. Even when the owner's activities may be exempt under the provisions of the Fair Housing Act, they still may come within the purview of the Unruh Civil Rights Act. In addition, the discriminatory activities of the real estate licensee will almost always fall within the provisions of the Unruh Civil Rights Act in every case, regardless of any potential exemption that might exist under the Fair Housing Act.

### Enforcement

Any person claiming to be a victim of an alleged violation of the Fair Housing Act may file a verified complaint with the Department of Fair Employment and Housing, and allege a violation of the Act. The complaint must be in writing and verified, and it must include the name and address of the person who allegedly committed the violation of the Act, the particulars of the violation, and such other information as may be required by the Department.

The complaint must be filed within 60 days from the date on which the alleged violation occurred. This period may be extended for an additional period not to exceed 60 days (following the expiration of the initial 60 days) if the complainant first obtained knowledge of the facts of the alleged violation after the expiration of the initial 60 days from the date of its occurrence.

If after a verified complaint has been filed with the Department and a preliminary investigation finds that the respondent has engaged in an unlawful practice as defined in the Act, the respondent will be served with an order to cease and desist from such practice and to take one of the following affirmative actions:

1.  The sale or rental of the housing accommodation to the aggrieved person, if it is still available.

2.  The sale or rental of a like accommodation, if one is available, or the next vacancy in a like accommodation.

3.  If the Department determines that neither of the remedies under subparagraphs 1 or 2 are available, it can order the payment of actual and punitive damages not to exceed $1,000.

However, if the Department finds that the respondent has not engaged in any discriminatory practice as defined by the Act, it must state its finding of fact and serve on the complainant an order dismissing the accusation.

### Federal Fair Housing Law

Two principal federal statutes are of concern: *The Civil Rights Act of 1866* and *The Civil Rights Act of 1968*. The latter is commonly known as *Title VIII of the Federal Fair Housing Law*. The 1866 post-Civil War statute protects the rights of all persons to "inherit, purchase, lease, sell, hold, and convey real and personal property." This statute was a necessary congressional step to implement the civil rights of freed slaves. This statute prohibits discrimination based on race and national origin.

However, this statute was largely ignored and rarely enforced for the first 100 years of its existence.

**Jones v. Alfred H. Mayer Co.**

On June 17, 1968, the United States Supreme Court handed down its opinion in the case of Joseph Lee Jones, et ux., Petitioners v. Alfred H. Mayer Co. et al.

On September 2, 1965, the petitioners filed a complaint in the District court for the Eastern District of Missouri, alleging, "the respondents had refused to sell them a home in the Paddock Woods community of St. Louis County for the sole reason that the petitioner, Joseph Lee Jones, is a negro." From this landmark case, we now have a whole new all-encompassing set of rules prohibiting discrimination on the part of owners of property and their agents.

In Jones v. Mayer, the Supreme Court interpreted and applied an Act of Congress (first enacted in 1866, now U.S. Code, para 1982), and rested its constitutionality on the Thirteenth Amendment of the Constitution of the United States, the amendment prohibiting slavery. As so interpreted, Section 1982 applies everywhere, to everyone, in the United States.

To react to changing social and economic patterns in America, Congress adopted Title VIII in 1968. This law prohibits discrimination based on race, color, national origin, religion, and sex. It is the major basis for most current federal fair housing activities. The passage of this statute was a watershed in the nation's commitment to equal housing opportunity.

**Fair Housing Amendments Act of 1988**

On September 13, 1988, the *Federal Fair Housing Act of 1968* was amended by the *Fair Housing Amendments Act of 1988* (the "Act"). The most notable changes include adding (1) *familial status* (families with children) and (2) *handicap*, as protected classes and increasing penalties for violation of the Act. It is now a violation of federal law to refuse housing to anyone with children under the age of 18 or anyone who is pregnant, except when such housing is designated as housing for older persons.

**Familial Status**

*Familial status* is defined as one or more individuals who have not obtained the age of eighteen (18) years, who are domiciled with a parent or other person who has custody of them, or anyone who is pregnant. It is therefore unlawful to refuse housing to anyone with children under the age of 18 or anyone who is pregnant, except when such housing meets the definition of housing for older persons. For example, it would be unlawful for an apartment building to establish an *adults only* policy unless the complex is defined as housing for older persons as defined under the Act.

**Housing for Older Persons**

Housing providers are required to admit families with children unless the housing is categorized under the Act as housing for older persons. There are three such categories.

The first category includes all housing that is provided under state and federal programs specifically for the purpose of accommodating elderly persons.

The second category of excluded housing is housing that is "intended for, and solely occupied by persons 62 years of age or older." No conditions are attached, as long as every resident is of this age. In other words, residency by a couple, one aged 62 and the other younger than 62, would nullify that project's designation as elderly housing under this category.

The third category applies to what are familiarly known as retirement communities. The threshold age is 55, and the owner or manager must meet additional requirements in order to exclude families with children from residing in this housing. To qualify, the following criteria must be met:

1) At least 80% of the units must be occupied by one person in each unit who has attained the age of 55. The remaining units are under no restrictions. If less than 80% are occupied by persons 55 or older, the community can no longer bar families with children. And,

2) The owner or manager must, by publication of, and adherence to policies and procedures, demonstrate an intent to provide housing for persons 55 or older, and

3) Owners or managers seeking to designate housing as elderly housing must show the "existence of significant facilities and services specifically designed to meet the physical and social needs of older persons." Examples of the activities that would satisfy this requirement include congregate dining facilities, social and recreational programs, counseling and health services, education programs, emergency health care programs, transportation services, and of course, an accessible physical environment, or

4) If it is not practicable to provide significant facilities and services designed to meet the physical and social needs of older persons and the housing facility is necessary to provide an important housing opportunity for older persons, such housing facility may still be exempt from the requirements of housing children if the owner/manager who provides the housing facility can demonstrate that he or she has endeavored to provide such facilities and services, but economic factors make it prohibitive.

**Mobile Home Parks and the Federal Fair Housing Law**

There is no exception in the Federal Fair Housing Amendments Act for mobilehome parks. Therefore, mobilehome parks, unless they are designated as housing for older persons, cannot refuse housing to families with children. Unlike more traditional housing, California law has permitted mobilehome parks to establish adult-only policies. This has been based on the concept that mobilehome parks provide needed, affordable housing for senior citizens. Federal law, however, does not recognize mobilehome parks "per se" to be housing for older persons. It would appear that California Civil Code Section 798.76, which permits mobilehome parks to establish adult-only policies, would be preempted by the Federal Fair Housing Amendments Act, and mobilehome parks will have to meet the same requirements for elderly housing as other types of housing.

**Occupancy Standards**

The Federal Fair Housing Amendments Act makes it clear that local, state, or federal occupancy standards will not be affected provided that they are reasonable. The definition of *reasonable* under federal and state law has yet to be determined. However, the State Department of Fair Employment and Housing (DFEH) will not investigate any case unless the occupancy standards are more restrictive than two persons per bedroom plus one additional person. This would mean that the owner of a two-bedroom apartment should permit a minimum of five people to occupy the apartment in order to avoid investigation by the DFEH for discrimination. Neither the DFEH nor the California Fair Employment and Housing Commission define what a reasonable occupancy standard is.

## Handicapped Persons

The Federal Fair Housing Amendments Act of 1988 added physically and mentally handicapped persons to the classes of people protected under the Federal Fair Housing laws. Previously, federal law did not prohibit discrimination against handicapped persons. Since 1987, California has prohibited discrimination against persons based on blindness or physical disability.

*Handicap* is defined as a physical or mental impairment that substantially limits one or more of a person's major life activities. Such activities would include caring for one's self, performing manual tasks, walking, seeing, hearing, speaking, breathing, learning, and working. Persons with a record of such an impairment or who are regarded as having such impairments are also protected under federal fair housing laws.

Although federal fair housing laws are wide sweeping, these laws do not require that housing be made available to individuals whose tenancy would be a direct threat to the health or safety of others or would result in substantial physical damage to the property of others.

## The Americans with Disabilities Act of 1990

On July 26, 1990, President Bush signed into law the Americans with Disabilities Act of 1990 (ADA), a federal law that prohibits discrimination against individuals with disabilities. The ADA addresses discrimination in four general areas:

1) Employment (Title I);
2) Public Services (Title II);
3) Public Accommodations and Commercial Facilities (Title III); and,
4) Telecommunications (Title IV).

This section will discuss the ADA provisions and regulations that relate only to public accommodations and commercial facilities and their impact on the real estate industry.

## Purpose

The purpose of the ADA is to give individuals with disabilities civil rights protection against discrimination similar to those rights afforded to individuals on the basis of race, color, national origin, sex, and religion.

## Disability Defined

Under Title III of the Americans with Disabilities Act, the term *disability* is broadly defined. It means one or more of the following:

1) *A physical or mental impairment that substantially limits one or more of the major life activities of such individuals* (The list of examples include orthopedic, visual, speech, and hearing impairments; cerebral palsy; epilepsy; muscular dystrophy; multiple sclerosis; cancer; heart disease; diabetes; mental retardation; emotional illness; and HIV disease (AIDS), or

2) *A record of such an impairment* (This includes someone with a past history of impairment, such as an individual with a history of mental or emotional illness, and

someone who has been misclassified as having an impairment, such as someone who actually does not have mental retardation or a mental illness.), or

3) *Being regarded as having such an impairment* (The perception of the private entity is a key element of the test. For example, persons with severe burns often suffer discrimination even if they do not view themselves as impaired.).

## Exempt Categories of Behavior

The Americans with Disabilities Act specifically excludes certain *categories of behavior or disorder* from its coverage. They are listed as follows:

1) Homosexuality and bisexuality;

2) Transvestism, transsexualism, pedophilia, exhibitionism, voyeurism, gender-identity disorders not resulting from physical impairments, or other sexual behavior disorders;

3) Compulsive gambling, kleptomania, or pyromania; or,

4) Psychoactive substances-use disorders resulting from the current illegal use of drugs.

## Coverage

The ADA generally does *not* apply to residential facilities that are separately covered by the Federal Fair Housing Amendments of 1988. However, all commercial buildings are covered by Title III of ADA. Title III distinguishes between *public accommodations* and *commercial facilities*.

**Public Accommodations.** Twelve types of facilities are included within the definition of *public accommodations.* Examples include the following:

1) Places of lodging (e.g., an inn or hotel).
2) Establishments serving food or drink (e.g., a restaurant or bar).
3) Places of exhibition or entertainment (e.g., a motion picture house or theater).
4) Places of public gathering (e.g., an auditorium or convention center).
5) Sales or rental establishments (e.g., a bakery, grocery store, or shopping center).
6) Service establishments (e.g., a gas station, or an accountant's, lawyer's, or insurance office).
7) Public transportation facilities (e.g., a terminal or depot).
8) Places of public display or collection (e.g., a museum or library).
9) Places of recreation (e.g., a park or amusement park).
10) Places of education (e.g., a nursery, elementary, or undergraduate school).
11) Social service center establishments (e.g., a day care center or senior citizen center).
12) Places of exercise or recreation (e.g., a gymnasium, health spa, or golf course).

**Commercial Facilities.** *Commercial facilities* include facilities that are intended for nonresidential use and whose operations affect commerce. Some examples are factories, warehouses, and office buildings in which employment may occur.

Thus, real estate sales offices, property management companies, mortgage brokerage firms, and Boards/Associations of REALTORS®, are covered by this law. Similarly, other types of commercial buildings owned or leased by clients of REALTORS® may also have to comply with

Title III. Finally, the rules also provide that if part of a private residence is used for business purposes, that portion of the home will be covered by the Title III requirements.

As previously discussed in this section, the ADA applies *only to commercial facilities*. However, similar to the ADA, the Fair Housing Amendment Act of 1988 prohibits discriminatory housing practices based on disability. The U.S. Department of Housing and Urban Development (HUD) has issued proposed regulations to implement the law requiring that most *new multi-family residential buildings* of four or more units (including condominiums, cooperatives, and rentals), occupied after March 13, 1991, incorporate designs that are usable by physically disabled individuals. For information on the Federal Fair Housing Law of 1988, refer to page 5 of this text.

Generally speaking, the requirements of Title III that are applicable to public accommodations are the only provisions that deal with barrier removal of existing facilities and auxiliary aids and services. The requirements of Title III that are applicable to public accommodations and commercial facilities are the provisions that deal with alterations and new construction.

**Exempt Entities.** The Americans with Disabilities Act exempts the following types of entities from coverage:

1) A public entity;
2) A religious organization or an entity controlled by a religious organization; or,
3) A private club.

## Barrier Removal of Existing Facilities

A public accommodation must remove architectural and communication barriers in existing facilities where such removal is readily achievable. The phrase *readily achievable* means *easily accomplishable* and *able to be carried out without much difficulty or expense.*

The rules provide a few examples of *barrier removal*, such as installing ramps, repositioning shelves, and widening doors.

To determine whether a removal is readily achievable, a number of factors must be taken into consideration, including the nature and cost of the action needed, the overall financial resources of the affected facility, and the types of operations of the facility. Even if barrier removal is not readily achievable, other reasonable compliance actions might still be necessary.

## Auxiliary Aids and Services

A public accommodation must take steps to ensure that a disabled individual is not denied services or treated differently, unless it can demonstrate *undue burden*—i.e., significant difficulty or expense.

Examples of auxiliary aids and services include qualified interpreters, note takers, listening systems such as telecommunication devices for the deaf (TDDs), and Braille materials. In some cases, substitutes are acceptable. For example, Braille documents are not necessary if oral communications can be provided.

Title III also imposes requirements on private entities that conduct courses, seminars, and examinations for professional licensing or certification purposes. The sponsoring organizations for these activities must offer the courses or examinations at locations that are accessible to individuals with disabilities. Auxiliary aids and services, such as taped examinations or assisted hearing services, must be provided upon request, at the expense of the sponsor. In some circumstances, alternative arrangements such as at-home examinations may be acceptable.

## Alterations

Physical alterations made after January 26, 1992, that affect the usability of a place of accommodation or commercial facility, shall "to the maximum extent feasible" be conducted in a way that makes the place of accommodation or commercial facility readily accessible to disabled individuals. The definition of *alteration* does not include normal maintenance, reroofing, painting, or asbestos removal, unless these activities affect the usability of the facility. However, remodeling or reconstruction would constitute an alteration.

Special rules apply if an alteration affects access to a *primary function area*, such as a meeting room in a conference center or an office in which the facility's principal activities are carried out. In addition, the *path of travel* to bathrooms, telephones, and drinking fountains that serve the altered area must be made readily accessible and usable by individuals with disabilities, unless the cost and scope is "disproportionate to the cost of the overall alteration."

## New Construction

All new construction of a public accommodation or a commercial facility that is designed and constructed for first occupancy after January 26, 1993, must be designed and constructed to be readily accessible and usable by disabled individuals, unless it is "structurally impracticable" to meet the requirement.

For both new construction and alterations, the law does *not* require the installation of elevators in facilities of less than three stories or fewer than 3,000 square feet, unless the facility is a shopping center, shopping mall, or the professional office of a health care provider.

## Tax Credits and Deductions

The United States Internal Revenue Code has been amended to allow for the following:

1) A tax credit of up to 50 percent of *eligible access expenditures* that exceed $250 but do not exceed $10,250 is available to a small business. A *small business* is one that has annual gross receipts that do not exceed $1,000,000 or whose work force has not more than 30 full time workers. *Eligible access expenditures* include costs of removing barriers and providing auxiliary aids.

2) A tax deduction of up to $15,000 per year for qualified architectural and transportation barrier removal for businesses, regardless of size.

## Enforcement and Penalties

Disabled individuals may enforce Title III by private lawsuits. A court may award only injunctive relief. However, if the U.S. Attorney General seeks to enforce the law, the court may award (1) equitable relief, (2) monetary damages, (3) civil penalties not to exceed $50,000 for the first violation and $100,000 for subsequent violations, and (4) attorney's fees. The court is required to consider whether the facility has made a good faith effort to comply with the new law.

**QUIZZES ARE MANDATORY**

CalBRE regulations now require the submission of chapter quizzes before you can access the final examination. You must log in and submit the chapter quizzes online before you can access the final examination. After submitting the last chapter quiz, you will receive a link to the final examination. You were issued a Personal Identification Number (PIN) and login instructions when you enrolled.

**Chapter One Quiz**

1.      The Unruh Civil Rights Act prohibits discrimination in:

(a)      All business establishments of every kind.
(b)      Public establishments only.
(c)      Commercial establishments only.
(d)      For-profit enterprises only.

2.      The term *housing accommodation* DOES NOT include accommodations operated by:

(a)      Religious organizations.
(b)      Fraternal organizations.
(c)      Charitable organizations.
(d)      All of the above.

3.      The term *familial status* includes:

(a)      Families with children.
(b)      Persons 62 years of age or older.
(c)      Children 18 years of age or older.
(d)      All families.

4.      Under the Americans with Disabilities Act (ADA), the term *disability* includes which of the following?

(a)      A physical or mental impairment that substantially limits one or more of the major life activities.
(b)      Someone with a past history of impairment, such as an individual with a history of mental illness.
(c)      People who are regarded as having an impairment when they don't, such as a people with severe bums who suffer discrimination even if they do not view themselves as impaired.
(d)      All of the above.

5.      Which of the following is specifically excluded from coverage under the Americans with Disabilities Act (ADA)?

(a)      HIV disease (AIDS).
(b)      Mental illness.
(c)      Compulsive gambling.
(d)      Cancer.

## Chapter Two

### Important Terms

blockbusting
community property
creditor
Equal Credit Opportunity Act
Federal Fair Housing Law
Federal Reserve
Home Mortgage Disclosure Act
redlining

### Learning Objectives

Upon completion of Chapter Two, you should be able to complete the following:

- Describe discriminatory conduct that would lead to disciplinary action.

- Describe *panic selling*.

- Understand the Housing Financial Discrimination Act of 1977.

- Describe the monitoring and investigation of lending practices.

- Understand the Home Mortgage Disclosure Act.

- Describe the requirements of the Federal Equal Credit Opportunity Act.

**Commissioner's Regulations § 2780–2781 (Discrimination and Panic Selling)**

**§ 2780. Discriminatory Conduct as the Basis for Disciplinary Action**

Commissioner's Regulation 2780 prevents discriminatory conduct by a real estate licensee based upon race, color, sex, religion, ancestry, physical handicap, marital status, or national origin includes, but is not limited to, the following:

1)    Refusing to negotiate for the sale, rental, or financing of the purchase of real property or otherwise making unavailable or denying real property to any person because of such person's race, color, sex, religion, ancestry, physical handicap, marital status, or national origin.

2)    Refusing or failing to show, rent, sell, or finance the purchase of real property to any person, or refusing, or failing to provide or volunteer information to any person about real property, or channeling or steering any person away from real property, because of that person's race, color, sex, religion, ancestry, physical handicap, marital status, or national origin, or because of the racial, religious, or ethnic composition of any occupants of the area in which the real property is located.

It shall not constitute discrimination under this subdivision for a real estate licensee to refuse or fail to show, rent, sell, or finance the purchase of real property to any person who has a physical handicap because of the presence of hazardous conditions or architectural barriers to the physically handicapped that conform to applicable state or local building codes and regulations.

3)    Discriminating because of race, color, sex, religion, ancestry, physical handicap, marital status, or national origin against any person in the sale or purchase, or negotiation or solicitation of the sale or purchase, or the collection of payment or the performance of services in connection with contracts for the sale of real property, or in connection with loans secured directly or collaterally by liens on real property or on a business opportunity.

Prohibited discriminatory conduct by a real estate licensee under this subdivision does not include acts based on a person's marital status, which are reasonably taken in recognition of the community property laws of this state as to the acquiring, financing, holding, or transferring of real property.

4)    Discriminating because of race, color, sex, religion, ancestry, physical handicap, marital status, or national origin against any person in the terms, conditions, or privileges of sale, rental, or financing of the purchase of real property.

This subdivision does not prohibit the sale price, rent, or terms of a housing accommodation that contains facilities for the physically handicapped to reasonably differ from a housing accommodation that does not contain such facilities.

5)    Discriminating because of race, color, sex, religion, ancestry, physical handicap, marital status, or national origin against any person in providing services or facilities in connection with the sale, rental, or financing of the purchase of real property, including but not limited to processing applications differently; referring prospects to other licensees because of the prospects' race, color, sex, religion, ancestry, physical handicap, marital status, or national origin; using with discriminatory intent or effect, codes, or other means of identifying

minority prospects; or assigning real estate licensees on the basis of a prospective client's race, color, sex, religion, ancestry, physical handicap, marital status, or national origin.

Prohibited discriminatory conduct by a real estate licensee under this subdivision does not include acts based on a person's marital status, that are reasonably taken in recognition of the community property laws of this state as to the acquiring, financing, holding, or transferring of real property.

6)   Representing to any person because of his or her race, color, sex, religion, ancestry, physical handicap, marital status, or national origin that real property is not available for inspection, sale, or rental when such real property is in fact available.

7)   Processing an application more slowly or otherwise acting to delay, hinder, or avoid the sale, rental, or financing of the purchase of real property on account of the race, color, sex, religion, ancestry, physical handicap, marital status, or national origin of a potential owner or occupant.

8)   Making any effort to encourage discrimination against persons because of their race, color, sex, religion, ancestry, physical handicap, marital status, or national origin in the showing, sale, lease, or financing of the purchase of real property.

9)   Refusing or failing to cooperate with, or refusing or failing to assist another real estate licensee in negotiating the sale, rental, or financing of the purchase of real property because of the race, color, sex, religion, ancestry, physical handicap, marital status, or national origin of any prospective purchaser or tenant.

10)  Making any effort to obstruct, retard, or discourage the purchase, lease or financing, of real property by persons whose race, color, sex, religion, ancestry, physical handicap, marital status, or national origin differs from that of the majority of persons presently residing in a structural improvement to real property or in an area in which the real property is located.

11)  Performing any acts, making any notation, asking any questions, or making or circulating any written or oral statement that, when taken in context, expresses or implies a limitation, preference, or discrimination based upon race, color, sex, religion, ancestry, physical handicap, marital status, or national origin; provided, however, that nothing herein shall limit the administering of forms or the making of a notation required by a federal, state, or local agency for data collection or civil rights enforcement purposes; or in the case of a physically handicapped person, making notation, asking questions, or circulating any written or oral statement in order to serve the needs of such a person.

12)  Making any effort to coerce, intimidate, threaten, or interfere with any person in the exercise or enjoyment of, or on account of such person, or in the exercise or enjoyment of, or on account of such person's having exercised or enjoyed, or on account of such person's having aided or encouraged any other person in the exercise or enjoyment of any right granted or protected by a federal or state law, including but not limited to assisting in any effort to coerce any person because of his or her race, color, sex, religion, ancestry, physical handicap, marital status, or national origin to move from, or to not move into, a particular area; punishing or penalizing real estate licensees for their refusal to discriminate in the sale or rental of housing because of the race, color, sex, religion, ancestry, physical handicap, marital status, or national origin of a prospective purchaser or

lessee; or evicting or taking other retaliatory action against any person for having filed a fair housing complaint or for having undertaken other lawful efforts to promote fair housing.

13) Soliciting of sales, rentals, or listings of real estate from any person because of differences in the race, color, sex, religion, ancestry, physical handicap, marital status, or national origin of such persons.

14) Discriminating because of race, color, sex, religion, ancestry, physical handicap, marital status, or national origin in informing persons of the existence of waiting lists or other procedures with respect to the future availability of real property for purchase or lease.

15) Making any effort to discourage or prevent the rental, sale, or financing of the purchase of real property because of the presence or absence of occupants of a particular race, color, sex, religion, ancestry, physical handicap, marital status, or national origin, or on the basis of the future presence or absence of a particular race, color, sex, religion, ancestry, physical handicap, marital status, or national origin, whether actual, alleged, or implied.

16) Making any effort to discourage or prevent any person from renting, purchasing, or financing the purchase of real property through any representations of actual or alleged community opposition based upon race, color, sex, religion, ancestry, physical handicap, marital status, or national origin.

17) Providing information or advice to any person concerning the desirability of a particular real property or a particular residential area(s) that is different from information or advice given to any other person with respect to the same property or area because of differences in the race, color, sex, religion, ancestry, physical handicap, marital status, or national origin of such persons.

This subdivision does not limit the giving of information or advice to physically handi-capped persons for the purpose of calling to the attention of such persons the existence or absence of housing accommodation services or housing accommodations for the physically handicapped.

18) Refusing to accept a rental or sales listing or application for financing of the purchase of real property because of the owner's race, color, sex, religion, ancestry, physical handicap, marital status, or national origin, or because of the race, color, sex, religion, ancestry, physical handicap, marital status, or national origin of any of the occupants in the area in which the real property is located.

19) Entering into an agreement, or carrying out any instructions of another, explicit or understood, not to show, lease, sell, or finance the purchase of real property because of race, color, sex, religion, ancestry, physical handicap, marital status, or national origin.

20) Making, printing, or publishing, or causing to be made, printed, or published, any notice, statement, or advertisement that concerns the sale, rental, or financing of the purchase of real property that indicates any preference, limitation, or discrimination because of race, color, sex, religion, ancestry, physical handicap, marital status, or national origin, or any intention to make such preference, limitation, or discrimination.

This subdivision does not prohibit advertising directed to physically handicapped persons for the purpose of calling to the attention of such persons the existence or absence of housing accommodation services or housing accommodations for the physically handicapped.

21) Using any words, phrases, sentences, descriptions, or visual aids in any notice, statement, or advertisement describing real property, or the area in which real property is located, that indicates any preference, limitation, or discrimination because of race, color, sex, religion, ancestry, physical handicap, marital status, or national origin.

This subdivision does not prohibit advertising directed to physically handicapped persons for the purpose of calling to the attention of such persons the existence or absence of housing accommodation services or housing accommodations for the physically handicapped.

22) Selectively using, placing, or designing any notice, statement, or advertisement that has to do with the sale, rental, or financing of the purchase of real property in such a manner as to cause or increase discrimination by restricting or enhancing the exposure or appeal to persons of a particular race, color, sex, ancestry, physical handicap, marital status, or national origin.

This subdivision does not limit in any way the use of an affirmative marketing program designed to attract persons of a particular race, color sex, religion, ancestry, physical handicap, marital status, or national origin who would not otherwise be attracted to the real property or to the area.

23) Quoting or charging a price, rent, or cleaning or security deposit for a particular real property to any person, that is different from the price, rent, or cleaning or security deposit quoted or charged to any other person because of differences in the race, color, sex, religion, ancestry, physical handicap, marital status, or national origin of such person.

This subdivision does not prohibit the quoting or charging of a price, rent, or cleaning or security deposit for a housing accommodation that contains facilities for the physically handicapped to differ reasonably from a housing accommodation not containing such facilities.

24) Discriminating against any person because of race, color, sex, religion, ancestry, physical handicap, marital status or national origin in performing any acts in connection with the making of any determination of financial ability or in the processing of any application for the financing or refinancing of real property. Nothing herein shall limit the administering of forms or the making of a notation required by a federal, state, or local agency for data collection or civil rights enforcement purposes. In any evaluation or determination as to whether, and under what terms and conditions, a particular lender or lenders would be likely to grant a loan, licensees shall proceed as though the lender or lenders are in compliance with Sections 35800 through 35833 of the California Health and Safety Code (The Housing Financial Discrimination Act of 1977).

Prohibited discriminatory conduct by a real estate licensee under this subdivision does not include acts based on a person's marital status that are reasonably taken in recognition of the community property laws of this state as to the acquiring, financing, holding, or transferring of real property.

25) Advising a person of the price or value of real property on the basis of factors related to the race, color, sex, religion, ancestry, physical handicap, marital status, or national origin of residents of an area or of residents or potential residents of the area in which the property is located.

26) Discriminating in the treatment of, or services provided to, occupants of any real property in the course of providing management services for the real property because of the race, color, sex, religion, ancestry, physical handicap, marital status, or national origin of said occupants. This subdivision does not prohibit differing treatment or services to a physically handicapped person, because of the physical handicap, in the course of providing management services for a housing accommodation.

27) Discriminating against the owners or occupants of real property because of the race, color, sex, religion, ancestry, physical handicap, marital status, or national origin of their guests, visitors, or invitees.

28) Making any effort to instruct or encourage, expressly or impliedly, by either words or acts, licensees or their employees or other agents to engage in any discriminatory act in violation of a federal or state fair housing law.

29) Establishing or implementing rules that have the effect of limiting the opportunity for any person because of his or her race, color, sex, religion, ancestry, physical handicap, marital status, or national origin, to secure real property through a multiple-listing or other real estate service.

30) Assisting or aiding in any way, any person in the sale, rental, or financing of the purchase of real property where there are reasonable grounds to believe that such person intends to discriminate because of race, color, sex, religion, ancestry, physical handicap, marital status, or national origin.

## § 2781. Panic Selling as a Basis for Disciplinary Action

Commissioner's Regulation 2781 prevents discrimination based on *panic selling*, sometimes referred to as *blockbusting*. This type of prohibited discriminatory conduct includes, but is not limited to, soliciting sales or rental listings, making written or oral statements that create fear or alarm, transmitting written or oral warnings or threats, or acting in any representation, expressed or implied, regarding the present or prospective entry of one or more persons of another race, color, sex religion, ancestry, marital status, or national origin into an area or neighborhood.

A person who participates in this type of activity is hoping to benefit financially by inducing another party to enter into a real estate transaction by implying or showing that a change in the neighborhood with respect to race, color, sex, religion, or national origin may cause lowered property values, a change in the character of the neighborhood, an increase in criminal or antisocial behavior, or a decline in school quality. Panic selling or blockbusting does not occur by selling a house to a member of a minority group, but rather by attempting to drive out existing owners. Thus, the courts have construed even broad statements such as "This is a changing neighborhood" as falling under the heading of panic selling. Panic selling violates federal fair housing laws and in some states, such practice violates state fair housing laws as well as real estate licensing laws.

**Duty to Supervise**

A broker licensee shall take reasonable steps to become aware of, be familiar with, and to familiarize his or her salespersons with, the requirements of federal and state laws and regulations that relate to the prohibition of discrimination in the sale, rental, or financing of the purchase of real property. Such laws and regulations include, but are not limited to, the current provisions and any amendments thereto.

**The Housing Financial Discrimination Act of 1977 (Holden Act)**

**California Health and Safety Code § 35800–35833**

To prevent discrimination by lending institutions because of conditions, characteristics, or trends in the neighborhood or geographic area that surround the security property, California passed legislation prohibiting the practice of **redlining**, which became effective January 1, 1978.

Lending institutions include banks, savings and loan associations, or other financial institutions, including mortgage loan brokers, mortgage bankers, and public agencies.

Known as the Housing Financial Discrimination Act of 1977 (Holden Act), the law provides a unique opportunity for real estate licensees to aid in stamping out redlining, a practice that is discriminatory and which, by restricting the free flow of mortgage capital, makes it more difficult for real estate licensees to put bona fide transactions together.

The Holden Act provides a rational means of increasing the availability of housing accommodations to credit-worthy persons, and thus ensures the supply of decent, safe housing. In addition, the new law is expected to help reverse the process of abandonment and decay of certain neighborhoods, particularly in the urban centers of this state.

**Note:** Around the country, rehabilitation of neighborhoods in inner cities is on the rise, due to the joint efforts by national and city governments, lenders, appraisers, contractors and trade groups, private individuals, and investors. Newspapers, magazines, and industry spokespersons are reporting these significant events. Lenders and appraisers are detecting bargains in neighborhoods of fading property values, signaling their increased interest in the inner cities. Accepted appraisal techniques now include methodology in the recognition of these changes and those dictated by commitments to non-discriminatory conduct.

The provisions of the Holden Act cover financial assistance for financing or refinancing the purchase, construction, rehabilitation, or improvement of housing accommodations (real property used as an owner-occupied residence of not more than four dwelling units). The Holden Act also is designed to accomplish the following:

1) Encourage increased lending in neighborhoods or geographic areas in which conventional residential mortgage financing has been available.
2) Increase the availability of housing accommodations to creditworthy persons.
3) Ensure the supply of decent, safe housing.
4) Prevent the abandonment and decay of neighborhoods and geographic areas. No financial institution shall discriminate in their financial assistance wholly or partly on the basis of or consideration of race, color, religion, sex, marital status, national origin, or ancestry. Nor, will it consider the racial, ethnic, religious, or national origin composition of trends in a neighborhood or geographic area(s) surrounding a housing accommodation.

The foregoing is qualified by permitting the lender to demonstrate that such consideration in a particular case is required to avoid an unsound business practice.

The law also requires the financial institution to notify all such applicants, at the time of submitting a written application for financial assistance, of the prohibitions and right of review provided in the law. Such notice must also include the address of the Secretary and where complaints may be filed and questions asked.

## Exceptions

Lending institutions may discriminate based on the threat of health and safety of the occupant, or based on a desire to avoid an unsafe or unsound business practice. The lending institution may use fair market value as a basis of loan determination.

## Monitoring and Investigation of Lending Patterns and Practices

The Secretary of the Business, Transportation, and Housing Agency has issued rules, regulations, and guidelines for enforcement of the act, and is empowered to investigate lending patterns and practices, and to attempt to conciliate complaints. Investigation of complaints has been delegated to the state agency that regulates the particular financial institution involved.

All complaints are received by the Secretary and must be submitted in writing and verified. The Secretary will seek voluntary compliance through conference, conciliation, and/or persuasion. If these efforts are not effective, the Secretary must make a decision about the complaint and cause to have the financial institution served with an order to cease and desist with the following actions:

1) Make the loan without discrimination.

2) Make payment of damages not to exceed $1,000 to the complaintant, if the first solution cannot be effected.

The secretary shall annually report to the Legislature on the activities of the appropriate regulatory agencies and departments in complying with this part. The report shall include a description of any actions taken by the Secretary or the Secretary's designee to remedy patterns or practices the secretary determines are in violation of the Holden Act.

## The Home Mortgage Disclosure ACT (HMDA)

In the past, there has been relatively little data concerning the disposition of mortgage loan applications based on applicant characteristics. This changed with the passage of the *California Health and Safety Code §§ 35815–35816, Home Mortgage Disclosure Act (HMDA)*.

Under this act, all mortgage originators are required to report information to the Federal Reserve that relates to the income levels, racial characteristics, and gender of mortgage applicants. This data is required to be reported based on census tract characteristics. This includes loans originated as well as applications rejected. However, under ECOA, this data may not be used to discriminate.

The initial data, and that released in subsequent years, indicated substantial disparities between the approval rates of minority and non-minority applicants. Most of the federal agencies that are involved in data collection admit that disparities in HMDA data, in and of themselves, do not evidence discrimination. Nevertheless, subsequent studies concluded that a statistically significant disparity existed between minority and non-minority applicants who were only marginally eligible for loans even after examining a number of factors (including credit history) not measured under HMDA.

While most of the studies that have been performed analyze applicant characteristics, some studies are currently being performed based on census tract characteristics. A good example is a study recently released by a group associated with Ralph Nader. Using HMDA data to construct various color maps, this study concluded that lenders, particularly mortgage bankers, were affirmatively creating "effective lending territories" that exclude predominately minority areas.

As previously discussed, companies with material disparities in their HMDA data for applications and approvals must take affirmative steps to identify the reasons for the disparities. It is hoped that these lenders become sensitive to this perceived problem and aggressively take steps to address this problem.

**The Federal Equal Credit Opportunity Act (ECOA)**

The *Federal Equal Credit Opportunity Act* (ECOA) is Title VII of the Consumer Protection Act. It prohibits lenders from discriminating against credit applicants on the basis of race, color, religion, national origin, sex, marital status, age, or dependency on public assistance programs.

The Federal Equal Credit Opportunity Act prohibits lenders from asking the following:

1) The lender may not ask if the applicant is divorced or widowed. However, the lender may ask if the applicant is married, unmarried or separated. The term *unmarried* denotes a single, divorced, or widowed person and, in a community property state such as California, is of particular interest to local lenders.

2) The lender may not ask about the receipt of alimony or child support unless the applicant intends to use such income to qualify for the loan. The lender may ask the applicant about any obligations the applicant may have to pay alimony or child support.

3) The lender may not seek any information about birth control practices or the childbearing capabilities or intentions of the borrower or co-borrower.

4) The lender may not request information that concerns the spouse or former spouse of the applicant unless that person will be contractually liable for repayment or the couple lives in a community property state.

5) The lender may not discount or exclude any income because of the source of that income.

6) Lenders must report credit information on married couples separately in the name of each spouse.

7) Lenders may not ask about the race or national origin of the applicant.

## Notification of Denial and Statement of Reasons

The law also requires that a lender/creditor who denies an application for credit must provide the applicant with a *statement of reasons* or a written notification of the applicant's right to obtain a statement of reasons.

Within 30 days after receipt of a completed application for credit, the creditor shall notify the applicant of its action on the application. If an adverse action is taken, the applicant is entitled to a *statement of reasons* for such action from the creditor.

The term *adverse action* means a denial or revocation of credit, a change in the terms of an existing credit arrangement, or a refusal to grant credit in substantially the amount or on substantially the terms requested. An adverse action does not include a refusal to extend additional credit under an existing credit arrangement, where the applicant is delinquent or otherwise in default, or where such additional credit would exceed a previously established credit limit.

The statement of reasons must contain the specific reasons for the adverse action taken. A creditor satisfies the obligation of providing the applicant with a statement of reason by completing the following:

1) Provide statements of reasons in writing, as a matter of course, to applicants against whom adverse action is taken; or,

2) Give written notification of adverse action that discloses the applicant's right to a statement of reasons within 30 days and the identity of the person or office from which such a statement may be obtained.

Such a statement may be given orally if the written notification advises the applicant of his or her rights to have the statement of reasons confirmed in writing on written request. In addition to the foregoing Federal Law, state law regulates issuance of consumer credit reports, access by the consumer to such reports, and the obligations of credit reporting agencies.

## Inspection of Files

Upon the request of the consumer, every credit reporting agency must allow the consumer to visually inspect all files maintained regarding that consumer at the time of the request. The consumer may also request that the agency provide disclosure of the files in a manner selected by the consumer, chosen from among any reasonable means available to the consumer credit reporting agency.

The consumer credit reporting agency must also disclose to whom they have furnished credit reports for that consumer. The disclosure of recipients of any credit report(s) on the consumer must include the name of the recipient, or if applicable, the fictitious business name under which the recipient does business. If requested by the consumer, the identification shall also include the address of the recipient.

The consumer credit agency must also disclose a record of all inquires received by the agency in the six-month period preceding the request that identified the consumer in connection with a credit transaction that was not initiated by the consumer.

**Notification of Rights**

Any written disclosure by a consumer credit reporting agency to any consumer must include a written summary of all rights the consumer has under the law. The following written summary of rights required under the law is sufficient:

*You have a right to obtain a copy of your credit file from a consumer credit reporting agency. You may be charged a reasonable fee not exceeding eight dollars ($8). There is no fee, however, if you have been turned down for credit, employment, insurance, or a rental dwelling because of information in your credit report within the preceding 60 days. The consumer credit reporting agency must provide someone to help you interpret the information in your credit file.*

*You have the right to dispute inaccurate information by contacting the consumer credit reporting agency directly. However, neither you nor any credit repair company or credit service organization has the right to have accurate, current, and verifiable information removed from your credit report. Under the Federal Fair Credit Reporting Act, the consumer credit reporting agency must remove accurate, negative information from your report only if it is over seven years old. Bankruptcy information can be reported for ten years.*

*If you have notified a credit reporting agency in writing that you dispute the accuracy of information in your file, the consumer credit reporting agency must then, within 30 business days, reinvestigate and modify or remove inaccurate information. The consumer credit reporting agency may not charge a fee for this service. Any pertinent information and copies of all documents you have that concern an error should be given to the consumer credit reporting agency.*

*If reinvestigation does not resolve the dispute to your satisfaction, you may send a brief statement to the consumer credit reporting agency to keep in your file, that explains why you think the record is inaccurate. The consumer credit reporting agency must include your statement about disputed information in a report it issues about you.*

*You have a right to receive a record of all inquiries that relate to a credit transaction initiated in six months preceding your request. This record shall include the recipients of any consumer credit report.*

*You may request in writing that the information contained in your file not be provided to a third party for marketing purposes.*

*You have a right to bring civil action against anyone who improperly obtains access to a file or knowingly or willfully misuses file data.*

**Obligations of the Users of Consumer Credit Reports**

If any user of a consumer credit report takes any adverse action with respect to a consumer, and the adverse action is based, in whole or in part, on any information contained in a consumer credit report, that person shall do all of the following:

1) Provide written notice of the adverse action to the consumer.

2) Provide the consumer with the name, address, and telephone number of the consumer credit reporting agency that furnished the report to the person.

3) Provide a statement that the credit grantor's decision to take adverse action was based in whole or in part upon information contained in a consumer credit report.

4) Provide the consumer with a written notice of the following rights of the consumer:

   a. The right of the consumer to obtain within 60 days a free copy of the consumer's consumer credit report from the consumer credit reporting agency and from any other consumer credit reporting agency that compiles and maintains files on consumers on a nationwide basis.
   b. The right of the consumer to dispute the accuracy or completeness of any information in a consumer credit report furnished by the consumer credit reporting agency.

As long as the completeness or accuracy of any information furnished by any person to a consumer credit reporting agency is subject to a continuing dispute between the affected consumer and that person, the person may not furnish the information to any consumer credit reporting agency without also including a notice that the consumer disputes the information.

**QUIZZES ARE MANDATORY:** Please log in and submit the chapter quizzes online.

**Chapter Two Quiz**

1.    A licensee was farming a non-integrated neighborhood that was next to an integrated neighborhood by telling owners that if minority people moved into their neighborhood, their property values would go down. This is an example of:

(a)    Steering
(b)    Redlining
(c)    Blockbusting
(d)    Mainlining

2.    The Housing Financial Discrimination Act of 1977, also known as the Holden Act, has to do with which of the following?

(a)    Redlining
(b)    Rentals
(c)    Education
(d)    Subdivisions

3.    One of the main reasons for the passage of legislation that prohibited the practice of redlining was to:

(a)    Put fraudulent lending institutions out of business.
(b)    Increase the availability of housing accommodations to credit-worthy persons.
(c)    Help real estate licensees close more transactions.
(d)    Prevent discrimination regardless of public health and safety.

4.    The Federal Equal Credit Opportunity Act (ECOA) prohibits lenders from discriminating against credit applications on the basis of:

(a)    Age
(b)    Marital status
(c)    Dependency on public assistance
(d)    All of the above.

5.    Which of the following regulates issuance of consumer credit reports, the consumer's access to such reports, and the obligations of credit reporting agencies?

(a)    State law only
(b)    Federal Law only
(c)    State law and Federal Law
(d)    Bureau of Real Estate

## Chapter Three

### Important Terms

Department of Housing and Urban Development (HUD)
familial status
handicap
landlord
material fact
National Association of REALTORS® (NAR)
tenants

### Learning Objectives

Upon completion of Chapter Three, you should be able to complete the following:

- Describe the NAR/HUD Fair Housing Partnership Resolution.

- Describe HUD's Fair Housing Advertising Regulations.

- List the various words, phrases, symbols, and visual aids that may be considered discriminatory.

- Describe the disclosure requirements of AIDS-related deaths.

**NAR/HUD Fair Housing Partnership Resolution**

For over 20 years, Realtors® have actively pursued the achievement of fair housing through a Voluntary Affirmative Marketing Agreement (VAMA) with HUD. The VAMA has helped to elevate the importance of fair housing across the nation and has resulted in Realtors® leading the housing industry in its commitment to fair housing.

HUD and NAR entered into their first Voluntary Affirmative Agreement in 1975, and after several revisions and renewals, the VAMA expired in December of 1996. The VAMA sought to encourage individual real estate firms to take appropriate steps to ensure that their agents followed the fair housing law. The VAMA also encouraged Realtors® and real estate firms to support the "spirit of the fair housing law" through a variety of equal housing opportunity programs that included outreach, advertising, equal employment practices, safeguards against racial steering, and other steps that helped housing to be marketed on an equal opportunity basis.

As successful and well-intended as the VAMA was, it often placed process ahead of results and often worked against its objective of affirmatively furthering fair housing. The VAMA required endless reports and records from member Realtor® firms on their status to a degree that left many important fair housing issues unaddressed.

After 20 years, the Department of Housing and Urban Development (HUD) and the National Association of REALTORS® (NAR) decided that a new approach was needed in order to build upon the VAMA's success. The new HUD/NAR Fair Housing Partnership is results-oriented and gives far less attention to process. The new partnership focuses on the identification and eradication of housing discrimination in our communities. Because housing discrimination issues and priorities differ among communities, the new national partnership is intentionally flexible and fluid. The HUD/NAR Partnership recognizes that fair housing is a collaborative endeavor that requires shared involvement by partners in activities such as training, self-testing, public education, affirmative marketing, and the promotion of housing choice and opportunities across racial and ethnic lines.

The HUD/NAR Fair Housing Partnership is founded on the principle of supporting and focusing attention on the implementation of local community initiatives. At the national level, HUD and NAR meet regularly to identify national issues and concerns, develop joint strategies and actions to address housing discrimination, and review successes. During this ongoing, fluid, and flexible arrangement, the partnership's determinations and actions on fair housing will likely change from year to year.

Because of the varying issues and differing circumstances in local communities, HUD and NAR developed no specific model for a local partnership. NAR, local associations, and HUD field offices are encouraged to develop local fair housing partnerships based on the following principles of the national partnership:

1) Share responsibility for the achievement of fair housing;
2) Identify fair housing issues and concerns;
3) Develop measurable strategies and actions to address identified issues and concerns;
4) Evaluate the success of actions taken, and;
5) Determine future strategies and actions based on that evaluation.

**Partnership Defined**

By definition, *partnership* means that one party is cooperating with another in a joint venture or challenge, and that they are doing so through an arrangement in which each party has equal status and a high degree of independence. Partners to the arrangement also share common responsibilities and obligations.

**Why a Partnership between HUD and NAR?**

The Fair Housing Act requires HUD to work with housing industry organizations and community groups on fair housing education and voluntary programs. With offices in every state, HUD is in a position to recruit others, especially fair housing groups and government agencies that receive HUD funds. HUD also has access to a great deal of information on discrimination that occurs in the housing market. This makes HUD a perfect choice for establishing partnerships nationally with state and local Realtor® Associations.

Realtors® already work together on many fair housing issues. In fact, through their local Realtor® Associations, they have participated in partnerships that require continuing education in fair housing for license renewal. NAR includes over 1700 local associations that have participated in the VAMA and in other fair housing programs for more than 20 years. Realtors® often lead fair housing efforts in their communities, they produce and sponsor credited fair-housing training programs, and they publish and distribute helpful fair housing literature and guidance materials. Realtors® remain the public's primary source of information on home buying.

In the past, NAR has effectively worked with HUD to educate its members about fair housing laws and responsibilities, and NAR and HUD now work together to recruit other organizations for national and local partnership efforts. A few of these organizations include local fair housing advocacy groups, civil and human rights organizations, units of state and local governments (especially community development and planning offices), housing non-profits, and housing industry groups.

**Conclusion**

The HUD/NAR Fair Housing Partnership represents a significant commitment by active real-estate licensees to take an aggressive role in eliminating housing discrimination. Realtors®, in general, realize that America is becoming an increasingly multiethnic and multiracial society, and that new polices and strategies are required to foster access, mobility, and opportunity in housing for all of its people.

The new HUD/NAR Partnership represents how the organized real estate industry will seek to undo the patterns of separate and unequal housing that are widespread throughout America. Housing discrimination places a devastating burden on racial minorities. The U.S. Supreme Court has found that whites can also be harmed by housing discrimination, for it violates their right to associate with minorities.

The success of the new Partnership will depend upon the extent to which it is enthusiastically and successfully embraced in local communities, by NAR, HUD, policy makers, activists, and citizens. The vision of the Partnership is that one day, a neighborhood and community will no longer be known as the white, black, Latino, or Asian, but simply as a neighborhood and a community.

**HUD Fair Housing Advertising Regulations**

In addition to the references to advertising in the fair housing laws discussed in previous sections, this section will address the Department of Housing and Urban Development's (HUD) Fair Housing Advertising Regulations.

As discussed in previous sections, it is the policy of the United States to provide for fair housing throughout the country. The provisions of the Fair Housing Act (42 U.S.C. 3600, et seq.) make it unlawful to discriminate in the sale, rental, and financing of housing, and in the provision of brokerage and appraisal services, because of race, color, religion, sex, handicap, familial status, or national origin. Section 804(c) of the Fair Housing Act, as amended, also makes it unlawful to make, print, or publish, or cause to be made, printed, or published any notice, statement, or advertisement, with respect to the sale or rental of a dwelling that is discriminatory according to the Act.

The purpose of this part of the Fair Housing Act is to assist the advertising media, advertising agencies, and all other persons who use advertising with respect to the sale, rental, or financing of real estate. These regulations also describe the criteria HUD uses when evaluating compliance with the Fair Housing Act in connection with investigations of complaints alleging discriminatory housing practices that involve advertising.

**Use of Words, Phrases, Symbols, and Visual Aids**

The following words, phrases, symbols, and forms typify those most often used in residential real estate advertising to convey either overt or tacit discriminatory preferences or limitations. In considering a complaint under the Fair Housing Act, HUD will normally consider the use of these and comparable words, phrases, symbols, and forms to indicate a possible violation of the Act and to establish a need for further proceedings on the complaint, if it is apparent from the context of the usage that discrimination within the meaning of the Act is likely to result.

1)  Words descriptive of dwelling, landlord, and tenants: white private home, colored home, Jewish home, Hispanic residence, adult building.

2)  Words indicative of race, color, religion, sex, handicap, familial status, or national origin.
    a.  Race: Negro, Black, Caucasian, Oriental, American Indian.
    b.  Color: White, Black, Colored.
    c.  Religion: Protestant, Christian, Catholic, Jew.
    d.  Sex: The exclusive use of words in advertisements, including those involving the rental of separate units in a single or multi-family dwelling, stating or tending to imply that the advertised housing is available to persons of only one sex and not the other, except where the sharing of living areas is involved.
    e.  Handicap: crippled, blind, deaf, mentally ill, retarded, impaired, handicapped, physically fit.
    f.  Familial Status: adults, children, singles, mature persons. Nothing in this part restricts advertisements of dwellings that are intended and operated for occupancy by older persons and that constitute housing for older persons as defined in this Act. Words and phrases used in the discriminatory context should be avoided, e.g., restricted, exclusive, private, integrated, traditional, board approval, or membership approval.
    g.  National Origin: Mexican American, Puerto Rican, Philippine, Polish, Hungarian, Irish, Italian, Chicano, African, Hispanic, Chinese, Indian, Latino.

3) Symbols or Logotypes: Symbols or logotypes that imply or suggest race, color, religion, sex, handicap, familial status, or national origin.

4) Colloquialisms: Words or phrases used regionally or locally that imply or suggest race, color, religion, sex, handicap, familial status, or national origin.

5) Directions to real estate for sale or rent (use of maps or written instructions): Directions can imply a discriminatory preference, limitation, or exclusion. For example, references to real estate location made in terms of landmarks significant to a racial or national origin, such as an existing black development (signal to blacks) or an existing development known for its exclusion of minorities (signal to whites). Specific directions that reference the racial or national origin of a significant area may indicate a preference. References to a synagogue, congregation, or parish may also indicate a religious preference.

6) Area (Location) Description: Names of facilities that cater to a particular racial, national origin, or religious group, such as country club or private school designations, or names of facilities that one sex uses exclusively may indicate a preference.

## Selective Use of Advertising Media or Content

The selective use of advertising media or content, when particular combinations are used exclusively with respect to various housing developments or sites, can lead to discriminatory results and may indicate a violation of the Fair Housing Act. For example, the use of English language media alone or the exclusive use of media catering to the majority population in an area, when in such area, there are also available non-English language or other minority media, may have a discriminatory impact. Similarly, the selective use of human models in advertisements may have a discriminatory impact. The following are examples of the selective use of advertisements that may be discriminatory:

### Selective geographic advertisements.

Such selective use may involve the strategic placement of billboards; brochure advertisements that are distributed within a limited geographic area by hand or in the mail; advertising in particular geographic coverage editions of major metropolitan newspapers, or in newspapers of limited circulation that are mainly advertising vehicles for reaching a particular segment of the community; or displays or announcements that are available only in selected sales offices.

### Selective use of an equal opportunity slogan or logo.

When placing advertisements, such selective use may involve placing the equal housing opportunity slogan or logo in advertising reaching some geographic areas, but not others, or with respect to some properties, but not others.

### Selective use of human models when conducting an advertising campaign.

Selective advertising may involve an advertising campaign using human models primarily in media that cater to one racial or national origin segment of the population without a complementary advertising campaign that is directed at other groups. Another example may involve use of racially mixed models by a developer to advertise one development and not others.

Similar care must be exercised while advertising in publications or other media that is directed at one particular sex, or at persons without children. Such selective advertising may involve the use of human models of members of only one sex, or of adults only, in displays, photographs, or drawings to indicate preferences for one sex or the other, or for adults to the exclusion of children.

### Use of Equal Housing Opportunity Logotype, Statement, or Slogan

All advertising of residential real estate for sale, rent, or financing should contain an equal housing opportunity logotype, statement, or slogan as a means of educating the home-seeking public that the property is available to all persons regardless of race, color, religion, sex, handicap, familial status, or national origin. The choice of logotype, statement, or slogan will depend on the type of media used (visual or auditory), and in space advertising, on the size of the advertisement. *Table I* indicates suggested use of the logotype, statement, or slogan, as well as the size of the logotype. *Table II* contains copies of the suggested Equal Housing Opportunity logotype, statement and slogan.

### *Table I*
A simple formula can guide the real estate advertiser in using the Equal Housing Opportunity logotype, statement, or slogan. In all space advertising (advertising in regularly printed media such as newspapers or magazines), the following standards should be used:

| Size of Advertisement | Size of Logotype (in inches) |
|---|---|
| Larger than 1/2 Page | 2 x 2 |
| 1/8 page – 1/2 page | 1 x 1 |
| 4 column inches – 1/8 page | 0.5 x 0.5 |
| Smaller than 4 column inches | Do not use |

In any other advertisements, if other logotypes are used in the advertisement, then the Equal Housing Opportunity logo should be of a size at least equal to the largest of the other logotypes; if no other logotypes are used, then the type should be bold-display-face so that it is is clearly visible. Alternatively, when no other logotypes are used, 3 to 5 percent of an advertisement may be devoted to the equal housing opportunity policy statement.

In space advertising that is less than 4 column inches (one column that is 4 inches long, or two columns that are 2 inches long) of a page in size, the Equal Housing Opportunity slogan should be used. Such advertisements may be grouped with other advertisements under a caption that states that the housing is available to all without regard to race, color, religion, sex, handicap, familial status, or national origin.

**Table II**

Illustrations of Logotype, Statement, and Slogan. Equal Housing Opportunity Logotype:

**EQUAL HOUSING
OPPORTUNITY**

### Equal Housing Opportunity Statement

*We are pledged to the letter and spirit of U.S. policy for the achievement of equal housing opportunity throughout the Nation. We encourage and support an affirmative advertising and marketing program in which there are no barriers to obtaining housing because of race, color, religion, sex, handicap, familial status, or national origin.*

### Publisher's Notice

At the beginning of the real estate advertising section, all publishers should publish a notice such as that which appears in *Table III*. The notice may include a statement regarding the coverage of any local fair housing or human rights ordinance that prohibits discrimination in the sale, rental, or financing of dwellings.

**Table III**

### Illustration of Media Notice—Publisher's notice:

*All real estate advertised herein is subject to the Federal Fair Housing Act, which makes it illegal to advertise "any preference, limitation, or discrimination because of race, color, religion, sex, handicap, familial status, or national origin, or intention to make any such preference, limitation, or discrimination."*

*We will not knowingly accept any advertising for real estate that is in violation of the law. All persons are hereby informed that all dwellings advertised are available on an equal opportunity basis.*

### Fair Housing Poster

In a further attempt to promote fair housing practices throughout the real estate industry, the Department of Housing and Urban Development (HUD) requires certain persons to display an equal opportunity poster that contains the fair housing slogan and logo.

**Persons Subject**

1) Except for certain exemptions, which will be discussed later in this section, all persons subject to the Fair Housing Act shall post and maintain a fair housing poster as follows:

2) With respect to a *single-family dwelling* offered for sale or rental through a real estate broker, agent, salesperson, or person in the business of selling or renting dwellings, such person shall post and maintain a fair housing poster at any place of business where the dwelling is offered for sale or rental.

3) With respect to *all other dwellings covered* by the Act:
   a. A fair housing poster shall be posted and maintained at any place of business where the dwelling is offered for sale or rental; and,
   b. A fair housing poster shall be posted and maintained at the dwelling, except with respect to a single-family dwelling that is offered for sale or rental in conjunction with the sale or rental of other dwellings, the fair housing poster may be posted and maintained at the model dwellings instead of at each of the individual dwellings.
   c. With respect to those dwellings to which paragraph (3, b) above applies, the fair housing poster must be posted at the beginning of the construction period and maintained throughout the period of construction and sale or rental.

4) Posting and maintaining a fair housing poster is *not* required on vacant land.

**Location of Poster**

All fair housing posters shall be prominently displayed to be readily apparent to all persons seeking housing accommodations or seeking to engage in residential real-estate-related transactions or brokerage services.

Any person may obtain fair housing posters from the Department's regional and area offices. A facsimile may be used if the poster and the lettering are equivalent in size and legibility to the poster available from the Department.

## Description of Posters

The fair housing poster shall be 11 inches by 14 inches and shall bear the following legend:

**EQUAL HOUSING
OPPORTUNITY**

We do business in accordance with the
Fair Housing Act

(The Civil Rights Act of 1968, as amended
by the Fair Housing Amendments Act of 1988)

**It is Illegal to Discriminate Against
Any Person Because of Race, Color,
Religion, Sex, Handicap, Familial
Status, or National Origin**

- In the sale or rental of housing or residential lots.
- In advertising the sale or rental of housing.
- In the financing of housing.
- In the provision of real estate brokerage services.
- Blockbusting is also illegal.

Anyone who feels he or she has been discriminated against should send a complaint to:
*U.S. Department of Housing and Urban Development,*
*Assistant Secretary for Fair Housing and Equal Opportunity,*
*Washington, DC 20410*

**Disclosure of AIDS Information in Property Transfers**

Must the affliction with, or death by AIDS, of an occupant of real property be disclosed?

*No.* The California Legislature specifically declared its intention to regulate disclosures related to AIDS in situations that affect the transfer of real property or any estate or interest in real property. Civil Code G 1710.2 provides immunity from liability for failure to disclose that an *occupant* of a property was "afflicted with or died from" AIDS.

**Civil Code § 1710.2**

"No cause of action arises against an owner of real property or his or her agent, or any agent of a transferee of real property, for the failure to disclose to the transferee the occurrence of an *occupant's* death upon the real property or the manner of death where the death has occurred more than three years prior to the date the transferee offers to purchase, lease, or rent the real property, or that an occupant of that property was afflicted with or died from, ... [AIDS]."

The fact that a person has died on the premises is most likely a material fact that must be disclosed to the buyer. However, as quoted above, in particular instances, no cause of action arises against an owner of real property or his or her agent for the failure to disclose to the buyer the occurrence of an *occupant's* death or the manner of death if the following occurs:

1) The death occurred more than three years before the offer to purchase, lease, or rent the real property; or,

2) The *occupant* of the property was afflicted with or died from Acquired Immunity Deficiency Syndrome (AIDS).

Civil Code § 1710.2 states that the owner and agents are not required to disclose an *occupant's* death in certain situations. However, the death upon the property of a *non-occupant,* such as a trespasser, should be disclosed if it is a material fact that affects the value or desirability of the subject property.

**Reed v. King**

Before the legislature acted in the area of AIDS disclosure, it was unclear how to balance the conflicting issues of discrimination, invasion of privacy, confidentiality of medical information, informed consent, and civil rights concerning AIDS. The legislature acted to end confusion in this area by enacting California Civil Code §1710.2. Another bill enacted an amendment to that section to cover the troubling issue of disclosure of death on property, and was brought about by the 1983 case of Reed v. King, which involved disclosure of a multiple murder.

In Reed v. King, about two years after the purchase, a home buyer sued the broker and seller for rescission of the purchase contract and damages for failing to disclose that a multiple murder had occurred in the house 10 years earlier. The buyer did not allege either that the property had a reduced physical usefulness or lack of desirability. However, it was successfully asserted that the murders had a quantifiable effect on the market value of the property. Therefore, the California Court of Appeal held that the buyer stated a cause of action against the seller and seller's agent for their failure to disclose that the house was the site of a multiple murder.

This decision created great uncertainty as to its applicability in other death disclosure situations. For this reason, in 1987, the California Legislature specifically enacted revision to Civil Code §1710.2 to limit the Reed decision as it applies to death by AIDS.

This statute specifically states that it does not alter the law that relates to the disclosure of any other physical or mental condition or disease, and the owner or agent is not relieved of any obligation to disclose the physical condition of the premises.

Additionally, if the buyer or prospective buyer makes a direct inquiry, the owner or the owner's agent cannot make an intentional misrepresentation that concerns deaths on the property. In other words, if a potential buyer makes a direct inquiry as to whether any person died of AIDS on the premises, the disclosure must be made.

## Death That Occurs Offsite

The disclosure of a death that has occurred off the property, and was based on causes that occurred upon the property, is an unresolved question. The answer would depend on whether the combination of events constituted a material fact.

Whether information is *material* depends on all the facts of the particular case. In general, a fact would be considered material if its disclosure would affect the value or desirability of the property. Stated another way, a fact would be considered material if it would affect the decision of a reasonable buyer to buy, or the price and terms on which he or she would be willing to buy, the subject property.

## Summary

The personal nature of the AIDS disease and the uncertainty as to how it is transmitted has caused problems for the courts in this area. Certain groups have argued that there is no scientific evidence that the disease can be communicated through other than the transfer of bodily fluids, and as a result, would not be a threat to a prospective buyer.

Regardless of the different opinions on the transmission of AIDS, the general public is alarmed by the recent explosion of AIDS related deaths in the United States. Most prospective purchasers feel they should be informed of an AIDS related death on the property. The courts have decided that the privacy of the owner is also important when considering disclosure responsibility.

If there was a death on the property within three years of the offer to purchase, lease, or rent, the death *must* be disclosed. However, if the death was a result of AIDS, it *does not* have to be disclosed.

If the manner of death is an important issue to the prospective buyer, he or she can make a direct inquiry to the seller to get the facts. The statute states that if a direct inquiry is made by the buyer, the owner or the owner's agent cannot make an intentional misrepresentation concerning deaths on the property.

Additionally, the Department of Housing and Urban Development (HUD) regulations that implement the federal law state that persons who are infected with the HIV or AIDS virus are considered to be handicapped. Thus, the issue of AIDS disclosure in a real property transaction involves federal laws as well as state regulations.

**QUIZZES ARE MANDATORY:** Please log in and submit the chapter quizzes online.

**Chapter Three Quiz**

1.    The Fair Housing Partnership Resolution resulted from a collaborative endeavor between:

     (a)     The California Association of REALTORS® (CAR) and the Office of Real Estate Appraisers (OREA).
     (b)     The National Association of REALTORS® (NAR) and the Department of Housing and Urban Development (HUD).
     (c)     The National Office of Discrimination (NOD) and community development and planning offices.
     (d)     Non-profit housing organizations and public industry.

2.    The use of certain words and phrases in advertisements can lead to discriminatory results. Which of the following indicate a violation of the HUD fair housing advertising regulations?

     (a)     The use of words that state or tend to imply that housing that is advertised is available to persons of only one sex and not the other.
     (b)     Directions to real estate for sale that is presented in terms of racial- or national-origin-significant landmarks.
     (c)     The use of words that describe the dwelling, landlord, and/or tenants (e.g., white private home, colored home, Hispanic residence).
     (d)     All of the above.

3.    If the broker is selling a tract of homes, what are the requirements for displaying the fair housing poster?

     (a)     A fair housing poster must be displayed in every home in the tract.
     (b)     A fair housing poster only needs to be posted at the broker's place of business.
     (c)     A fair housing poster only needs to be posted at model homes instead of at each of the individual homes.
     (d)     A fair housing poster only needs to be posted until the first home is sold.

4.    In the course of taking a listing on a single-family dwelling, the owner informs you that his roommate died of AIDS on the property one year ago. Which of the following is correct regarding your disclosure requirements?

     (a)     If an occupant died on the property, it must always be disclosed to prospective buyers.
     (b)     If the occupant's death was a result of AIDS, it does not need to be disclosed.
     (c)     A death on the property is not a material fact in any case, and does not need to be disclosed.
     (d)     Unless the death occurred within one month of an offer to purchase, it does not need to be disclosed.

5.      If a potential buyer makes a direct inquiry about whether any person died of AIDS on the premises, what are the disclosure requirements?

   (a)      If a direct inquiry is made by the buyer or prospective buyer, the owner or the owner's agent cannot make an intentional misrepresentation concerning deaths on the property and must answer.

   (b)      Even if the buyer or prospective buyer makes a direct inquiry about deaths on the property, no cause of action arises against the owner or the owner's agent for failure to disclose.

   (c)      The owner's agent can defer the inquiry to the owner, but the owner must answer honestly.

   (d)      None of the above.

# Notes

# Risk Management

3 Hours of Continuing Education for
Salesperson and Broker License Renewal

**Lumbleau Real Estate School**
23805 Hawthorne Blvd.
Torrance, CA 90505

© 2015 by Karen Bohler

**DISCLAIMERS**

Although every effort has been made to provide accurate and current information in this text, the ideas, suggestions, general principles, and conclusions presented in this text are subject to local, state, and federal laws and regulations, court cases, and any revisions of the same. The author and/or publisher is not engaged in rendering legal, tax, or other professional services. The reader is thus urged to consult with his or her employing broker and/or seek legal counsel regarding any points of law. This publication should not be used as a substitute for competent legal advice.

This course is approved for continuing education credit by the California Bureau of Real Estate. However, this approval does not constitute an endorsement of the views or opinions that are expressed by the course sponsor, instructor, authors, or lecturers.

## Table of Contents

**Chapter One: The Nature of Risk**

**Learning Objectives**

Upon completion of Chapter One, you should be able to complete the following:

- Understand why the real estate business is susceptible to risk.
- State a few reasons why the art of negotiation is risky.
- Briefly describe why educating clients is risky.
- Briefly describe why not understanding clients is risky.
- Describe why a brokerage may experience financial difficulty even during prosperous times.
- Explain the consequences of dissatisfied clients.
- Explain the purpose of a lawsuit, and describe how to minimize the potential for a lawsuit.
- Understand the ramifications of a formal disciplinary action.
- State the necessary precautions a brokerage should take with regard to the health and safety of the licensees and employees associated with it.
- Explain the four basic strategies to manage risk.
- Explain why a brokerage should not rely on errors and omissions insurance as a primary method to manage risk.

**Why Is the Real Estate Industry So Susceptible to Risk?**

The simple answer is that real estate transactions involve large amounts of money and large amounts of anxiety.

Whenever there is money involved, especially large amounts of it, there is risk. The sale of real property is typically the biggest purchase and sale a client will ever make. Add the anxiety of the decision to the mix, and you've got high risk. When there is high stakes, there is high risk.

Management of risk is *not* the following:

**1)** *Management of risk is not crisis management.* Management of risk is crisis prevention through identifying scenarios that may precipitate a crisis, such as dissatisfied customers, lawsuits, formal complaints, or criminal charges.

**2)** *Management of risk is not damage control.* Management of risk is damage-proofing.

**3)** *Management of risk is not a task.* Management of risk is a process that is ongoing and never concludes. Sure, it is the development of procedures and policies, but it is much more than that. It is also the development of a culture in the real estate office so that the brokerage can minimize losses and maximize gains.

**The Risky Nature of Negotiating**

Powerful negotiating positions are created both by the nature of the transaction and the communication skills of the agents involved in the transaction.

Additionally, the law of agency often requires the agent to advise the client about the art of negotiating. Depending on the market, the client's negotiating position may be more powerful if the client treads lightly with regard to contractual demands.

Other times, the client's negotiating position is weakened if the client does not make enough demands. Getting the client to understand when and how to apply these negotiating strategies requires a salesperson to not only have negotiating skill, but also communication skill.

**The Tightrope Walk of Educating Clients**

The law of agency will also inevitably require that the agent educates his or her clients to protect the clients' best interests and ensure a knowledgeable negotiating position. Such a precarious position will have significant legal and professional risks. Before an agent embarks on the endeavor to educate his or her clients, the agent must be educated.

However, agents often rely on information that they receive from other uneducated parties. The risk of error and misrepresentation is significant.

**Winging It**

Too often, an agent who is caught up in the excitement of a sale has only a *cursory* understanding of the law, and advises the client while purporting to be an expert. When the client presses the agent for details, the agent *wings it*. If the client relies on such advice, and can prove such reliance was to his or her detriment when something goes wrong, the client may have grounds for a misrepresentation charge, and/or a civil lawsuit.

Agents reduce risk when they become educated, and are able to give verifiable, accurate information to their clients.

### The Danger of an Uneducated Client

Equally dangerous is an uneducated client. Agency laws require that the agent care enough about the client's needs to research the properties and terms of the transaction, and advise the client appropriately. If the client makes a harmful decision because the agent did not provide the client with enough information, the client may have grounds for a negligence charge.

### Student Notes: Risk Susceptibility

1) High money inflow and outflow means high stress in the real estate business.

2) The art of negotiating requires the agent to learn by doing and thus, learn by making mistakes.

3) The client also experiences a learning curve. If the client relies on the agent's bad advice, the client may have grounds for a lawsuit.

### Types of Risk

### Not Making a Profit (Deficit between Revenue and Expenses)

Consider why a brokerage experiences financial difficulty even in prosperous times.

Like all businesses, brokerages need income and cash flow. Many people believe that running a real estate business is an easy way to make money. Many people also believe brokerages encounter financial problems only when interest rates rise or when there is increased competition. However, this is not the case.

Brokerages are not profit centers. A brokerage is nothing more than a funnel—the medium through which commissions are paid to the salespersons and brokers who are affiliated with the brokerage. A brokerage that is poorly run will encounter financial difficulty, even in the friendliest real estate climate.

### Why Does a Brokerage Experience Financial Difficulty?

Consider why a brokerage experiences financial difficulty, even in prosperous times. What are some of the reasons why this may occur?

1) **Failure to stay abreast of the economic climate and direction of the real estate market.** Even in prosperous times, the economic climate changes daily. Brokerages need to plan expenditures based on their factual assessment of the economic climate.

2) **Failure to reduce commission levels during competition.** To compete, a brokerage may need to reduce their commission accordingly. This is a catch-twenty-two. If the brokerage does not reduce to stay competitive, the brokerage may lose income as a result. If the broker does reduce commission levels, the brokerage may lose income as a result (Even though the *Sherman Anti-Trust Act* prohibits commission fixing among brokerages, brokerages must still be

aware of the price of the competition's services, and adjust accordingly).

3) **Cash flow problems due to client defaults.** If a buyer or seller defaults on a purchase contract and the non-breaching party files suit against the breaching party, the brokerage still loses income because of the default, because the transaction did not close, and no commission was received.

4) **Poor expenditure planning.** A brokerage should plan expenditures based on realistic and factual assessments of its budget.

5) **Poor advertising planning.** Marketeers constantly approach brokerages with super-new products designed to promote real estate sales. In truth, the brokerage should be approaching the marketeers, only after the brokerage has evaluated its financial position, and has planned for the advertising costs.

6) **Failure to analyze costs vs. revenue.** Finding the time to analyze costs and revenue is challenging. From a managing risk perspective, this needs to be done for the sake of the ongoing financial viability of the brokerage.

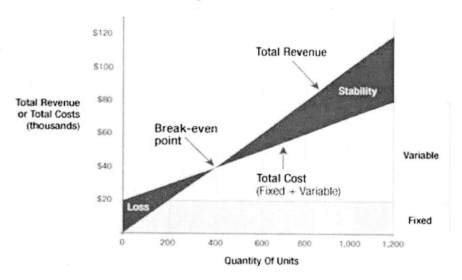

**Underlying Financial Planning Questions**

Here are some of the underlying financial planning questions that may need to be asked on a regular basis:

1) *What is the basis of the brokerage's commission splits?* If the commission splits barely meet the brokerage's costs, it is a risk to the ongoing viability of the brokerage.

2) *What kind of revenue is required for the brokerage to break even and achieve stability?*

3) *What funds are required for the growth of the company?* Company growth without the funds necessary to pay for the growth will be fatal to the brokerage.

**Dissatisfied Clients**

Most brokers and salespersons depend heavily on referrals and repeat customers. These sources of business are often the best kind because the customers already have knowledge of the brokers' or salespersons' worthiness. In other words, a broker or a salesperson picks up these types of clients because of his or her professional reputation. Hence, an injury to such reputation can affect the broker's or salesperson's future ability to pick up referrals and repeat customers.

## Lawsuits

The most obvious risk to the real estate broker is the risk of substantial financial loss (or even financial ruin) from a lawsuit. Even if the broker wins, a lawsuit is extremely difficult to deal with. Therefore, it is a significant risk to the real estate brokerage.

A lawsuit's purpose is quite simple, really. It is a procedure to determine the answers to two questions:

**1)** Did a real estate licensee violate the standard of care? (Was he or she negligent?)

**2)** Does the brokerage owe money as a result?

Thus, the easiest way to avoid a lawsuit is to comply with the law, and the easiest way to comply with the law is to understand it.

## The Easiest Way to Comply with the Law is to Understand It

A lawsuit settlement, depending on the size of the settlement, can financially cripple a brokerage. Even the threat of a lawsuit is a substantial risk, because it causes panic and anxiety within the brokerage, deflates morale, and is an impediment to the brokerage's success.

Additionally, a lawsuit or the threat of a lawsuit causes poor service, and poor service causes the threat of a lawsuit.

## Standard of Care

A real estate licensee has specialized training and should be an expert on various aspects of real estate. The courts recognize this, and thus real estate licensees are expected to have a higher standard of care than that of the average person.

Fiduciary duty requires that the standard of care commensurate with the amount of experience and education the licensee has. Courts will generally see to it that agents uphold these expectations while conducting real estate activities with the public.

## Reliance on Errors and Omissions Insurance

Even if a brokerage obtains errors and omissions insurance coverage, it cannot depend on only insurance to cover the mistakes of the licensees associated with the brokerage. *Errors and omissions insurance* covers clerical or judgment errors and omissions, which are errors of intentional or unintentional neglect. For example, if an agent misspells an owner's name, and as a result, invalidates a purchase contract, that is an error.

However, if an agent fails to return a phone call that is crucial to the sale, that act is technically an omission and covered. Additionally, an agent may forget to deliver a required disclosure—that would also be a covered omission.

However, most errors and omissions insurance specifically excludes errors or omissions in which a *law* is broken.

**Note:** In most states, a failure to disclose would be a direct violation of both statute and regulatory rules. Thus, most E&O policies would not cover such an omission. In other words, the likelihood of an E&O policy covering a failure to disclose might be slim, and the petitioner in the lawsuit will likely win.

The brokerage suffers a double dose of risk when insurance rates increase, for the following two reasons:

**1)** First, the higher the cost of insurance, the more work the brokerage must do in order to break even. Of course, this higher cost is passed on to the salesperson in the form of higher E&O premiums per transaction.

**2)** Second, the brokerage pays the price with diminished salesperson morale.

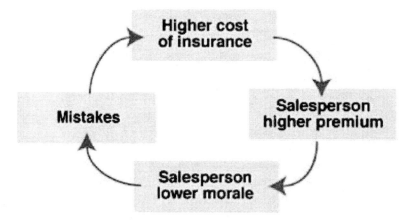

### Lawsuits as a Result of a Security Breach in Listed Property

The potential for civil suits as a result of a security breach of a listed property is too great to ignore. Agents hold keys to properties and sensitive information that, in the wrong hands, can cause extreme potential for risk with drastic consequences. Critical areas of security include the following:

**1)** Theft and burglary of personal property in a listing.

**2)** Risk of property keys being stolen, misplaced, or misused.

**3)** Tradespeople, such as home inspectors, termite inspectors, or housecleaning companies breaching their duty of care by forgetting to lock the home, losing the keys to a home, or damaging property.

### Lawsuits as a Result of an Office Security Breach

An office security breach can also result in a lawsuit. Brokerages should foster a team effort to make everyone conscious of security issues. All brokerage employees and licensees should look out for potential security vulnerabilities and contribute to the improvement of security procedures.

Security protection devices in the office that go a long way toward prevention include the following:

**1)** A fully monitored alarm system.

**2)** Top quality locks on all doors and windows.

## Formal Disciplinary Actions

The real estate regulatory authority creates rules and regulations under which agents must operate. It is the agent's responsibility to stay informed about these rules and obey them, and it is the brokerage that will be harmed if its agents do not. Generally, the punishments from the regulatory authority range from fines (penalties) to suspension of licenses. Oftentimes, the regulatory authority will require the offending licensee to take a prescribed amount of continuing education.

Truly, as with most state-sanctioned penalties, the penalty itself is the easy part. It is the damage to the brokerage's reputation that affects the brokerage most severely.

Information about an agent's history of discipline is increasingly important to the public, especially in this day and age when the slightest slip-up is posted on the internet, and readily accessible by the public, as well as other real estate professionals.

## Criminal Charges

Most regulatory authorities work very closely with the State Attorney General's office prosecutors, so criminal charges are a very real possibility.

Combine the loss of freedom as a result of jail time with the high cost of legal defense and the loss of potential income, and the broker has an extreme financial, personal, and professional loss.

Fortunately, for most agents, the offenses are not severe enough that jail time is required. Nevertheless, the risk of an agent inadvertently breaking the law is very real. Among the licensing laws, disclosure laws, mortgage brokering laws, landlord/tenant laws, and the homeowner's association laws, the number of laws affecting property transactions can be staggering. To complicate things further, some laws come from the federal level, and some from the state level.

### *The Letter of the Law is Black and White, however…*

Circumstances never are. Even the most seasoned real estate professional can inadvertently break the law. Laws are diverse, there are a lot of them, and they change all the time. Just because something is common practice, does not mean that it is legal practice.

### *Knowledge of the Law and Its Application*

A thorough knowledge of the letter of law is very valuable, but a broker must have a thorough knowledge of the application of the law as well. This means keeping up to speed on the outcomes of real estate lawsuits not only in the broker's area, but also in the entire country.

**Injury or Physical Harm to Agents or Clients**

*Duty of Care*

Quite possibly, the health and security of the agents and employees of a brokerage is the most poorly planned for and underestimated area of real estate practice, but a duty of care requires that everything reasonably practicable be done to protect the health and safety of the agents and employees.

This duty applies to all employers, employees, and independent contractors (This means all brokers, and salespersons/agents have a duty of care to protect each other).

*The Car is a Workplace*

When an agent thinks of their workplace, they probably think of an office. However, a very significant portion of a real estate agent's work is done in the car, and thus, the car is also a workplace. Many real estate agents spend a great deal of time in their cars—often in a rush, speaking on their mobile phones while searching for paperwork. Agents who work like this are accidents waiting to happen.

*Safe Driving Protocols*

Brokerage leadership should involve all staff in the development and implementation of safe driving protocols. They should encourage their agents to invest in a blue-tooth device for use during cell phone conversations that take place in the car. Accidents that occur while an agent is holding a cell phone (whether or not this is the cause of the accident) will implicate both the agent and the brokerage.

*Personal Security*

Personal safety hazards are exacerbated by casual attitudes toward personal security. Most real estate salespersons are required to conduct off-site visits. These visits may occur at strangers' homes or commercial and industrial areas.

The agent may be required to ride in a car with a person whom he or she just met. Brokerage leadership should consider a brief training and induction of all employees into various security procedures. For instance, in certain circumstances, an agent may allow the client to enter the home, while the agent waits outside.

*Agent-to-Management Alert*

An effective security procedure is the agent-to-management alert, whereby the agent calls to alert management before entering the home, and management calls the agent back after approximately ten minutes to ensure that the agent is safe.

**Student Notes: Types of Risk**

1) Not making a profit is the most common way for a real estate brokerage to go out of business.

2) Dissatisfied clients can harm a broker's reputation, and in some cases, cause legal or licensing problems.

3) Lawsuits, for which there are many causes, can almost always be avoided by applying due care.

4) Formal disciplinary actions can damage a brokerage's reputation and cause the brokerage embarrassment, as well as create a gigantic hassle and possibly loss of license.

5) Criminal charges, while not the ultimate loss, can damage the reputation of the brokerage or the broker for a long time.

6) Injury to clients or agents is the ultimate loss.

**Four Basic Strategies to Manage Risk**

**Which Type of Action Should You Employ?**

Once the broker has identified the types of risks that exist, the broker needs to analyze the likelihood of a risky event occurring, and then make a decision about which type of action he or she will employ if the risk does occur. In general, the broker have four strategies from which to choose:

1) Take preventive measures and control the likelihood of the risk's occurrence.

2) Take corrective measures and reduce the consequences of the risk.

3) Transfer a portion of the risk.

4) Do nothing (retain the risk), because the risk is so unlikely that it's not worth the time and resources necessary to address it.

*Preventive Action for Risks with High Likelihood*

This is the first strategy that most people consider. Preventive measures should be used for risks with high likelihood, with corrective measures as a backup. Common preventive strategies include the following:

- **Quality assurance.** Develop process controls to ensure the quality of risk-related activities.

- **Policies and procedures.** Create a written document that states the brokerage policies and processes that minimize the exposure to risk. Avoiding a risk may be practically impossible, but with clear office policies in place, the brokerage can reduce the likelihood of the risk. For example, no matter how carefully the brokerage's agents drive, it is impossible to completely be free of the risk of a car accident. Therefore, the brokerage may implement an office policy that each agent should avoid using a cell phone while driving, among other policies.

- **Training and development.** Ensure that the staff and the agents have the key skills and knowledge they need to conduct their jobs.

- **Contract conditions and terms.** Create contracts with staff, suppliers, agents, and clients in such a way that the brokerage is protected from risk.

- **Preventive maintenance.** Ensure that brokerage assets are maintained, and that the brokerage is well-supplied so that the agents have all of the tools they need to do their jobs.

## Corrective Action to Reduce Consequences

Even if the brokerage cannot eliminate a risk, it can minimize the impact of the risk as much as possible. Corrective measures should be in place for two reasons:

**1)** To reduce the consequences of risks that have already happened.

**2)** To address the risks that have a low likelihood of occurrence.

It does not make sense to give priority to risks that may never happen, nor does it make sense to spend time and resources implementing preventive measures to address those risks. Therefore, it is best to establish corrective measures to address those risks with low likelihood, just in case they do happen. Common corrective actions include the following:

- **Contingency planning.** This corrective measure involves drawing up plans that state exactly the methods of response if a risk arises.

- **Contract conditions.** This involves identifying the responsibilities of clients, agents, and customers in the event that a risk occurs, such as the destruction of listed property due to a fire.

- **Disaster/Information recovery.** This corrective measure involves planning for a failure in technology or a server crash that may result in the loss of records.

## Transferring a Portion of the Risk

Purchasing *errors and omissions* and *liability* insurance is the only practical method a brokerage can employ to transfer a portion of its risk.

Of course, purchasing E&O insurance, or any insurance for that matter, should almost never be the primary strategy against a risk. The brokerage should use the strategy of transferring risk concurrently with the strategies of avoiding and controlling the impact of risk. Preventive and corrective measures should always be the brokerage's primary strategy against high-occurrence risks.

A few limitations of transferring risk include the following:

**1)** The broker's E&O coverage may not be adequate. Furthermore, the broker may inadvertently do something that disqualifies him or her from coverage. Insurance policies are full of conditions and qualifications, and therefore, there is always the possibility that a loophole in the contract may cause the insurance company to not cover the broker.

**2)** If the insurance company pays a claim on behalf of the brokerage, the brokerage's premiums are sure to increase.

**3)** Most importantly, there is no way that insurance can compensate for emotional trauma or lost time. Even if the brokerage's E&O insurance pays for their monetary losses if they get sued, the litigation process is never pleasant, and it is always time-consuming. There is no way to compensate the brokerage (or the broker) for the lost time and emotional drain because of litigation.

### Doing Nothing (Retaining the Risk)

At first glance, this strategy seems akin to negligence. Not so. When a brokerage chooses this strategy, it has intentionally chosen to do nothing, rather than simply neglected to do anything.

Sometimes, the cost of preventive or corrective measures comes at too great a cost compared to the impact of the risk. For example, consider this situation:

- Is getting bombed by terrorists a risk? Yes.

- If the risk occurred, would the consequences be catastrophic? Yes.

- However, should a brokerage purchase an insurance policy to cover themselves against such a risk? Probably not.

In the above situation, the brokerage would intentionally choose to do nothing about the risk of a terrorist bombing. Even though the consequences would be catastrophic, the likelihood is so remote that the best action is no action. It is simply not practical to take action.

### Summary

None of this information should be new to you. The purpose of this chapter is to provide brokers with a refresher about the fundamentals of risk management in order to give them the foundational requirements they need to create a plan to manage their risks. Because the activities (and thus the mistakes) of the agents and employees are the responsibility of the brokerage, it is imperative that the brokerage communicates not only the risk management policies and procedures to their agents and employees, but it's also important that the brokerage communicates the reasons for such policies and procedures.

**QUIZZES ARE MANDATORY**

CalBRE regulations now require the submission of chapter quizzes before you can access the final examination. You must log in and submit the chapter quizzes online before you can access the final examination. After submitting the last chapter quiz, you will receive a link to the final examination. You were issued a Personal Identification Number (PIN) and login instructions when you enrolled.

**Chapter One Quiz**

1.      If the commission splits barely meet the brokerage's costs, _____ is directly at risk.

     (a)     the broker's reputation with the community
     (b)     the ongoing viability of the brokerage
     (c)     the broker's license
     (d)     the good standing of the agents' licenses

2.      An injury to the brokerage's professional reputation most directly affects the brokerage's future ability to:

     (a)     Get referrals and repeat clients.
     (b)     Pay the bills.
     (c)     Pay the staff.
     (d)     Buy a new computer.

3.      Most E&O insurance specifically EXCLUDES:

     (a)     Clerical errors.
     (b)     Judgment errors.
     (c)     Forgetting to return a phone call that was crucial to a sale.
     (d)     Errors or omissions in which a law is broken.

4.      Other than death or physical injury, the ultimate loss an agent can suffer professionally is:

     (a)     Injury to the agent's reputation.
     (b)     Licensing trouble for the agent.
     (c)     Criminal charges on the agent.
     (d)     Lawsuits against the agent.

5.      Which of the following is a TRUE statement?

     (a)     Preventive and corrective measures should always be a broker's primary strategy against high-impact risks.
     (b)     Errors and Omissions insurance should always be a broker's primary strategy against high-impact risks.
     (c)     Preventive measures are an absolute must for all high-impact risks, no exceptions.
     (d)     Corrective measures should be in place for all risks, whether high impact or low impact.

**Chapter Two: Brokerage Essentials**

**Learning Objectives**

After successful completion of this chapter, you should be able to complete the following:

- Briefly explain the five federal acts that regulate employment discrimination.
- State the essence of anti-trust laws, and understand common violations to these laws with regard to the real estate industry.
- State the purpose of the Do Not Call Registry, and how it relates to the policies of the real estate brokerage.
- State common violations of the Fair Housing Act, and understand the steps necessary to create a program for compliance.
- Understand how RESPA affects a real estate brokerage, and state which types of activities it regulates.
- Describe the purpose of an Affiliated Business Arrangement (ABA) disclosure.
- Differentiate among employees, statutory independent contractors, and common-law independent contractors.
- Recognize the need for a brokerage policy with regard to licensed and unlicensed real estate assistants.
- State the difference between consent and disclosure with regard to agency and dual agency.
- State the remedies to clients for an agent's breach of fiduciary duty.
- State the licensee's requirements with regard to seller and buyer representation.
- Understand the legal doctrines that apply to the drafting of contracts.
- Describe various types of conduct that may be negligent and/or fraudulent.
- Understand the need for internal dispute resolution, and describe various methods of handling internal dispute resolution.
- Explain the factors that an arbitration panel considers during an arbitration hearing.
- State the various challenges to brokerages that have arisen in recent years as a result of advances in technology.
- Understand the need for a sexual harassment policy within the brokerage.
- Understand the issues surrounding privacy, both within the brokerage and while working with clients.

**Statutory Requirements**

**Employment Discrimination**

Most of the time, real estate licensees are independent contractors, so employment discrimination and its ramifications are not hot topics in most brokerages. However, if the brokerage employs administrative staff, such as receptionists, office managers, or bookkeepers, employment discrimination might be an issue.

Whether or not the brokerage agrees with the laws regarding employment discrimination is immaterial. The broker's ability to recognize and deal with situations that most frequently cause trouble in the brokerage is the broker's best defense against risk, and the most effective tool to manage the risk of lawsuits in this regard.

Employment discrimination in the real estate industry is regulated by the following Federal Acts:

- **Civil Rights Act of 1964.** This law makes it unlawful for an employer to discriminate on the basis of race, color, religion, sex, or national origin. This Act applies to any private employer with 15 or more employees in an industry that affects interstate commerce.

- **Age Discrimination in Employment Act (ADEA).** This law prohibits discrimination against individuals aged 40 and over on the basis of age, and applies to any private employer with 20 or more employees in an industry that affects interstate commerce. When terminating an employee who is over 40, if the termination is on the basis of age, an employer may ask the employee to waive his or her rights under the ADEA, but the request must be made in writing, and the employer must provide the employee legal consideration (usually money) in exchange for agreeing to the waiver.

- **Civil Rights Act of 1991.** This law makes punitive damages and jury trials available to employees who are victims of discrimination.

- **Americans with Disabilities Act.** This law prohibits discrimination against individuals who, with reasonable accommodations, are qualified to do the job, and applies to any private employer with 15 or more full-time employees.

- **Equal Opportunity Employer Act of 1972.** A brokerage should make it very clear to all independent contractors and employees that the brokerage is an equal opportunity employer.

**Anti-Trust Compliance**

The essence of the anti-trust laws is that businesses cannot agree to restrain trade. Any statement or agreement that limits consumer choice could be construed as an anti-trust violation. The nature of a real estate practice makes a real estate brokerage particularly susceptible to anti-trust challenges.

*Price or Commission Fixing*

Price or commission fixing can result when a discussion among brokerages to fix real estate commission rates or terms or conditions of a broker-client relationship takes place. Most competing brokerages charge similar prices for the same services; however, this isn't illegal as long as each competitor sets prices independently. An antitrust violation occurs when a broker discusses and actually agrees to charge the same prices or offer exactly the same terms as one or more of the broker's competitors. A broker can avoid problems with this issue by doing the following:

- Establish the brokerage's fees, commission splits, and listing terms independently, and without any discussion with competitors.

- Refrain from informal conversations that allude to the idea of setting prices.

*Territorial Assignments*

*Territorial assignments* are agreements between competitors to divide the market geographically, by price range, type of property, or some other segmentation. These agreements are considered anti-competitive because they conspire to establish dominance in a particular market. This isn't the same thing as an individual company's practice of specializing in certain properties, such as historic buildings or custom-built housing. A broker can avoid problems with this issue by documenting his or her decisions to focus on certain property types with marketing and demographic studies.

*Association Meetings*

Associations are groups of competitors who come together to promote their common business interests. As such, they are vulnerable to allegations that during these meetings, agreements are made by members to use identical business practices, and thus, illegal conspiracies occur. Avoid problems by remaining alert to discussions at meetings that relate to commission rates, pricing structures, listing policies, or the marketing practices of other brokers.

*Boycotts*

A boycott is a concerted effort to not deal with a particular brokerage. A typical group boycott allegation in the real estate brokerage business involves a claim that two or more brokerages have agreed to refuse to cooperate, or to cooperate on less favorable terms, with a third brokerage company. The intent is to eliminate that company as a competitor, or to force it to abandon certain practices. Another form of boycott would occur if several companies collectively determined to not use a particular service provider, such as a specific newspaper.

**Do Not Call (DNC) Registry**

In 2003, the Do Not Call (DNC) Registry was put into effect. Since then, the cold-calling activities of real estate professionals have been severely hampered. Violations of the DNC rules can result in fines of up to $11,000 per phone call for lawsuits brought by the federal government, or $500 per call for lawsuits brought by consumers.

### Tools for Managing DNC Lists

*Scrub DNC Software* is a Windows-based software solution designed to remove numbers found in Do Not Call lists (National, State, and In-House DNC lists) while organizing and keeping track of your phone lists.

### DNC and the Typical Real Estate Calls

**Calling FSBO's.** A real estate professional may call a FSBO seller whose name is on the DNC on behalf of a buyer client, as long as there is no discussion about listing the property (since such discussion is a telephone solicitation).

**Calling Prior Clients with Expired Listings.** A listing broker can call prior clients with expired listings for up to 18 months after the listing has expired, even if the owner      of the expired listing is on the DNC list. However, after 18 months, the listing broker must adhere to the rules of the DNC list before making calls to expired listings.

**Calling Prior Buyers.** If the brokerage has a written buyer-representation agreement that has expired, then representatives of the brokerage can call these buyers for up to 18 months after the buyer representation agreement has expired, even if the buyer is on the DNC registry. However, after 18 months, the brokerage representatives must comply with the rules of the DNC.

**Open House Sign-in Sheets.** If the brokerage holds an open house and collects phone numbers of prospective buyers on an open house sign-in sheet, the broker should include notice on the sign-in sheet to alert these visitors that they are consenting to a follow-up call from the brokerage.

### Fair Housing

Without comprehensive education and training of all sales associates, it is highly likely that a fair housing mistake will occur.

Real estate brokerages are subject to myriad federal, state, and local fair housing laws. Fortunately, for states to adopt their own state-specific Fair Housing Act, the provisions of the act must be substantially similar to the Federal Fair Housing Act, so the state laws cannot be contrary or too different. While this may seem redundant from a legislative standpoint, it is good news for brokerages because it alleviates the need to memorize two different sets of rules.

That being said, if there is any difference at all between the state-specific Fair Housing Act and the Federal Fair Housing Act, the more protective provision will supersede. For instance, where the Federal Fair Housing Act outlines seven protected classes, state laws may include coverage for other protected classes.

### National Association of REALTORS® Fair Housing Guidelines

It may be prudent for brokerages to have a copy of the NAR Fair Housing Guidelines on hand, and use them as part of their regular fair housing compliance program.

### Specific Discriminatory Practices

The Federal Fair Housing Act specifically prohibits the following discriminatory practices:

- Refusal to sell, rent, or otherwise make available, a dwelling because of a person's membership in a protected class.

- Discrimination in the terms, conditions, or privileges of a sale or rental of housing, or in the provision of services connected with the same.

- Use of advertising that expresses a preference for or against certain persons because of their membership in a protected class.

- Representation that a dwelling is not available for sale or rent, when in fact the dwelling is available.

- Blockbusting.

- Redlining.

- Discrimination in providing access to the Associations of REALTORS®, MLS services, or other services or organizations that relate to the business of selling or renting dwellings.

### Programs for Compliance

Because there is no statutory limit on punitive damages for Fair Housing violations, non-compliance could have extreme consequences. Without comprehensive education and training of all sales associates, there is a high likelihood that somebody will make a fair housing mistake. Furthermore, fair housing mistakes are usually excluded from errors and omissions insurance policies. As a result, brokerages should adopt effective fair housing compliance programs that consist of the following:

- The brokerage's policy and public commitment to Fair Housing.

- Agent education and training with regular and systematic documentation of the training.

- Identification and correction of activities that may constitute Fair Housing violations.

**Note:** It is important for the brokerage to establish this compliance program before a plaintiff files a complaint or a lawsuit. Adoption of a Fair Housing compliance program only after a complaint is filed will be viewed as a remedial measure, but will not negate the complaint. Furthermore, showing that the brokerage has established a compliance program will not defeat a pattern or practice case, nor will it defeat a claim for punitive damages.

### The Real Estate Settlement Procedures Act (RESPA)

As all brokers are well aware, RESPA prohibits real estate licensees from accepting compensation from vendors in exchange for referring buyers or sellers to those vendors. However, consider the following question:

**Question:** Does RESPA apply to referrals to vendors whose work is done after the transaction closes, such as moving companies, gardeners, and decorating companies?

**Answer:** Not really. In fact, the payment for these services is not a violation of RESPA if it is:

- A flat fee that represents the fair market value for the service.
- Not transactionally based.

In other words, a broker cannot give a vendor (other than a settlement vendor, such as title insurance, an escrow company, or an attorney) an interest in the transaction by promising payment only if the transaction closes escrow, unless the company receiving the referral is under common ownership to the brokerage. (A copy of RESPA's *Do's and Don'ts* may be downloaded from this online course).

### Affiliated Business Arrangements (ABA's)

An exception to the RESPA regulations involves referrals among affiliated companies. If there is any degree of common ownership between the real estate brokerage and the company that is receiving the referral, then the employee or salesperson providing the referral must provide an Affiliated Business Disclosure Statement to the consumer. This disclosure statement must be on a separate piece of paper and must meet the following requirements:

- Disclose the nature of the relationship between the brokerage and the provider of the settlement service.

- Clearly state that the buyer or seller being referred to the ABA is not required to use the ABA.

- Provide an estimated charge or range of charges that are generally made by the provider of settlement services.

When referrals are made between a brokerage and an affiliated company, the referring party may not receive any compensation for the referral, nor may the brokerage for which that party works. However, if the brokerage owns the company that receives the referral, the brokerage may derive a return on its interest in the company.

### Statutory Requirements in a Nutshell

### Employment Discrimination

- **Civil Rights Acts.** Prohibit discrimination based on protected classes, and allow for punitive damages and jury trials for victims of discrimination.

- **Age Discrimination Act.** Prohibits discrimination against individuals aged 40 and over on the basis of age.

- **Americans with Disabilities Act.** Prohibits discrimination against individuals on the basis of their disability.

- **Equal Opportunity Employer.** Further promotes equal employment opportunities for American workers.

## Anti-Trust Compliance

The essence of the anti-trust laws is that businesses cannot agree to restrain trade. Violations of these laws include engaging in the following:

- Boycotting

- Establishing territorial assignments.

- Price fixing (commission fixing).

## Fair Housing Laws

Fair Housing Laws prohibit discriminatory practices based on race, religion, color, national origin, sex, familial status, or handicap.

## The Real Estate Settlement Procedures Act (RESPA)

- Prohibits real estate licensees from accepting compensation from vendors in exchange for referring buyers or sellers to those vendors.

- Applies only to transactionally based referrals.

## Employment Relationships

### Independent Contractor or Employee?

The real estate industry has always taken great pride in the idea that it is an industry comprised of self-reliant, self-motivated people. As a result, a substantial number of real estate brokerages are simply *houses* from which several self-employed salespeople run their businesses.

However, some brokerages run like typical businesses and rely exclusively on employee salespeople, and others operate with both independent contractors and an employee sales staff.

It is important that brokers understand the various types of brokerage-to-salesperson relationships, so that brokerages will be better able to establish relationships that are equitable to all parties involved. Obviously, there are advantages and disadvantages to each type of structure.

### Employer-to-Employee Relationship

In states where the broker is responsible for the actions of the licensees associated with the brokerage, the right of the broker to control the sales methods may be of utmost concern. If this is the case, and the broker wants complete control over the licensees affiliated with the brokerage, the best brokerage-to-salesperson relationship may be the relationship between an employer and the employees.

**Note:** If this applies to your brokerage, it is extremely important that you become fully knowledgeable about employment laws. You may be subject to payment of minimum wages and overtime imposed by the Fair Labor Standards Act and the provisions of the Equal Pay Act.

**Real Estate Assistants**

Hiring real estate assistants requires careful planning by the brokerage as to the duties that will be performed by the assistants. Approximately 20% of the real estate licensees (both brokers and salespersons) in the U.S. work with an assistant, according to a recent survey by the National Association of REALTORS®; and slightly over half of these real estate assistants hold a real estate license.

The responsibilities and liabilities of the brokerage mostly depend on whether the assistant is licensed or unlicensed, and whether the assistant is an independent contractor or an employee. For the most part, licensed assistants have legal status and rights that are commensurate with the license they hold, and can do any activity permitted under the licensing statutes of the state.

This type of broker-to-salesperson relationship flies in the face of statutes that require the broker to be responsible for the actions of the licensees.

**Brokerage-to-Independent Contractor Relationship**

A *common law independent contractor* is essentially an entity that is completely separate from the brokerage. The brokerage simply contracts with that entity. The brokerage cannot require the entity to perform in a directed manner, nor can it require the entity to submit to training.

Furthermore, the brokerage cannot dictate where the work is performed, nor set the hours of the independent contractor. Likewise, the independent contractor cannot expect support from the brokerage other than payment for the work completed. The cost of doing the work is absorbed by the independent contractor. However, this method flies in face of statutes that require the broker to be responsible for the actions of the licensees who are affiliated with the brokerage. In other words, how can the statutes require the broker to be responsible for the actions of the licensees if the broker cannot control the methods by which the licensees accomplish their objective?

Therein lies the dilemma. So, the category of *statutory independent contractor* was established.

**Special Category for Real Estate Licensees: Statutory Independent Contractor**

As a result of the confusion that frequently arose (both with the IRS and the state regulatory commissions) because of the dilemma described above, Congress (and the IRS), under the Tax Equity and Fiscal Responsibility Act (TEFRA), established the statutory independent contractor classification, especially for real estate licensees, in 1982.

The provisions of this classification are contained in Section 3508 of the Internal Revenue Code, which lists three criteria that qualify real estate licensees for this classification:

- The licensee's license must be active and in good standing.

- Substantially all of the licensee's compensation for the activities requiring a license must be directly related to sales or other output, rather than to number of hours worked.

- A written agreement must exist between the licensee and the brokerage that must provide that for federal tax purposes, the licensee will not be treated as an employee with respect to activities that require a license.

Note, however, that the statutory independent contractor classification applies only for federal tax purposes. If the licensee is a statutory independent contractor for federal tax purposes, and the state regulatory agency classifies the licensee as an employee, the standards of the more restrictive type of classification will supersede the three classifications of broker-salesperson relationships.

### License Monitoring by the Brokerage

In states that provide that the broker is responsible for the actions of the licensees affiliated with the brokerage, the brokerage will be liable for unlicensed activity. This means that if a licensee allows his or her license to expire, and conducts activity that requires a license, the broker will be liable for such license violation. Furthermore, if such activity is the subject of a lawsuit, the brokerage will have absolutely no defense, and will likely be the losing party in the lawsuit.

Therefore, in such states, it is wise for the brokerage to have a policy that states the following:

- The licensee is to keep his or her license current and on active status.

- The licensee is responsible for costs associated with continuing education and license renewal.

### Address Changes for Real Estate Licensees

Most state regulatory agencies require that all licensees have a current mailing and/or residence address on file, just in case there is a complaint about the licensee's conduct. Along these lines, the regulatory agencies will require that in the event of a change of address, the licensee and/or broker must notify the agency within a certain number of days of the address change.

Thus, if a broker is in a state where the broker is required to notify the agency of an address change, then the broker will need to establish a policy for the licensees to notify the broker of such change.

### Agency Requirements

### Disclosure of Agency

The law of agency requires that both parties to the agency (the principal and the agent) know about the agency, and elect to move forward in their relationship. The reasoning here is that the parties need to know what their role will be during their relationship, and the agent needs to establish the boundaries of the job description. Without this understanding, the consumer's expectations for a particular relationship may be different from what the licensee intends. The principal's confusion about the role of the agent may breed mistrust, and eventually lead to lawsuits and liability for the brokerage.

An agency disclosure form is required in many states for all residential transactions, and is probably advisable whether or not it's required by law. Disclosure of agency must be timely; this disclosure should be made to the seller at the time that the listing agreement is signed. This disclosure should also be made to the buyer at the earliest practical opportunity. It should be meaningful, and in the form of a clearly written explanation of what the agency relationship means.

### Consent or Disclosure: What's the difference?

There is a misconception among real estate licensees that just because certain methods of conduct are disclosed to the client, the client has consented to those methods. This is not true.

Disclosure is keeping the principal informed during the process, while consent to the conduct means the client has given his or her informed permission before the conduct. Most states require that the client give his or her permission in writing.

### With Dual Agency, Consent is Necessary

As most brokers know, the concept of informed consent is central to the legality of the dual agency. Both the buyer and the seller must consent to be a party in a dual agency relationship. The primary implication with dual agency is that the agent's duty of loyalty is limited—the agent's loyalty cannot extend to one party to the detriment of the other.

**Note:** In most cases, buyers and sellers are not legally required to sign a consent to dual agency. If a seller refuses to sign, the broker must make it clear to the licensees within his or her brokerage that they should not show the home to prospective buyers without disclosing to the buyer that the brokerage cannot represent the buyer. In the case of buyer(s) who are working with licensee(s) within the brokerage and purchasing a property that is listed with the brokerage, licensees should indicate on the form the date the property was presented and that the buyer refused to sign. Full disclosure should be made to the buyer that the buyer will be unrepresented in the purchase.

### With Dual Agency, Win-Win is the Goal

When the role of a dual agent is compared to the role of an attorney, it seems that the dual agent's job is more difficult because the dual agent must promote a win-win situation, while an attorney simply focuses on the best interests of his or her own client. It has been said that anyone can promote a win-lose situation—that's nothing but a game, but promoting and accomplishing a win-win situation takes patience and integrity.

Although a dual agency relationship is an extremely difficult relationship to maintain, it can be done. If done correctly, dual agency can be extremely advantageous to the principals because the lines of communication have been streamlined, and the control of the transaction lies with only one brokerage, rather than two.

### Fiduciary Duty

A broker owes certain fiduciary duties to a principal. These fiduciary duties come in addition to the other duties or obligations set forth in the real estate employment agreement.

For the sake of review, the traditional fiduciary duties include the following:

- Reasonable care
- Obedience
- Accounting
- Loyalty
- Disclosure

### *Remedies for Breach of Fiduciary Duty*

From a management-of-risk standpoint, these remedies, if invoked, will have an extreme impact on a brokerage. In other words, when any one of these remedies is invoked, the brokerage will lose money—probably a lot of money. There are three primary remedies available to the principal:

1) **Rescission.** A principal has a right to rescind any transaction that involves an agent's breach of agency. A breach in agency gives rise to the presumption that the transaction was unfair to the principal(s). This presumption entitles the principal to rescind such a transaction without even showing that the transaction was in fact unfair! When a real estate transaction is rescinded, the purchaser of the property deeds the property back to the seller and the seller refunds the purchase price. In the case of undisclosed dual agency, the principal need only prove that the dual agency was undisclosed, and it will entitle the principal to rescind the transaction.

2) **Forfeiture of commission.** Breach of fiduciary duty is considered to be a breach of an employment contract. Consequently, when an agent breaches fiduciary duty, the agent is technically not entitled to payment, and the brokerage can be ordered to return any compensation received.

3) **Damages.** An agent's breach can also cause the agent to be liable for damages. For example, if the agent breached its duty of reasonable care to research market value, and the buyer principal paid too high of a price for the property, the brokerage may be liable to compensate the buyer for the difference.

### Seller Representation

Although many real estate brokers represent buyers with residential property transactions, the agency relationship with the seller generally precedes the agency relationship with the buyer. Historically, real estate brokers have proven to be more effective in the listing relationship than attorneys, because a listing requires not just agency, but marketing skill. In the residential real estate transaction, the real estate broker is most qualified to provide real estate marketing services for the seller.

A listing agreement with a seller creates an express agency relationship between the seller and the brokerage. A listing agreement is an employment agreement and an agency agreement. Therefore, to be enforceable, listing agreements must meet the following requirements:

- Contain clear, unambiguous language.

- Contain a beginning and ending date.

- Fully set forth all material terms.

- Contain signatures of all parties to the agreement.

### Disclosure Requirements: Seller Representation

The laws of agency require that the licensee notify the principal of all material facts that have a bearing on the interests of the principal, as soon as reasonably possible after learning of them. Yet, the laws of agency also require that all non-material facts be kept confidential. Therefore, the following dilemma becomes clear: which facts are material, and which are not?

Generally speaking, if an agent can answer *yes* to *any one* of the following questions, the fact is material. If the answers to *all three* questions are *no*, then fiduciary responsibility requires that the fact be kept confidential:

1) If you were the buyer, would the fact affect your decision to purchase the property? (Note the words *affect your decision*, not *change your decision*.)

2) Does the fact pertain to any physical aspect of the property?

3) Does the fact pertain to the client's ability to perform his or her contractual obligations?

### Known or Should Have Known

The words *should have known* are particularly important to real estate licensees. Because of the fiduciary duties of agency, ignorance can be a prosecutable offense.

If a licensee were required to disclose only known defects, but not those that are reasonably discoverable, the licensee would be shielded by his or her own ignorance of that which he or she professes to know. Such a construction would not only reward the unskilled broker or salesperson for his or her incompetence, but would provide the unscrupulous licensee the unilateral ability to protect himself or herself at the expense of the inexperienced and unwary who rely upon the licensee.

The theory that a seller's broker is only liable for disclosed defects would inevitably produce a disincentive for a seller's broker to make a diligent inspection. Such a disincentive would be most unfortunate since in residential sales in particular, the seller's broker is most frequently the best person to obtain and provide the most reliable information on the property, and is ordinarily counted on to do so.

### Are Written Disclaimers a Safety Net?

Is it possible to utilize a written disclaimer to avoid liability for misrepresentation of material facts or non-disclosure of material facts?

Probably not. Courts have held that there is a duty on the part of real estate brokers to be accurate and knowledgeable about the product they are in the business of selling. A written disclaimer may relieve the seller from disclosure duties, but it will not relieve the agent.

## Case Law

In one case, a real estate salesperson was showing a property for lease to a prospective tenant but forgot to point out that the stairs leading to the basement were defectively constructed and possibly dangerous. The lessee moved into the property and later fell down the stairs and was injured. Both the salesperson and her employing broker were liable in damages for injuries suffered by the lessee.

This case shows that the licensee's duty of care is not limited to the disclosure of matters known to the licensee. Because of the real estate licensee's superior knowledge and experience, and his or her duty to disclose material matters, it is also their duty to discover the facts regarding the property. It is the agent's responsibility to discover any serious defects in the property that could cause an unreasonable risk or harm to the client.

### Secret Profits: Seller Representation

In a California case, a broker was convicted of grand theft (that's right—grand theft) for secretly profiting at the expense of his seller by covertly buying the seller's property at one price and immediately reselling it to his waiting buyer at a higher price [*People vs. Barker, 53 Cal. 2d 539*].

## Buyer Representation

While the requirements of seller representation are fairly clear-cut, an agency relationship between a buyer and a real estate broker is not quite as straightforward, because it can be created by accident.

In other words, even though the parties may not have consciously planned to create an agency relationship, an implied agency can be created unintentionally, inadvertently, or accidentally by the actions of the parties. This is why a written agreement for buyer representation is always a good idea.

When the buyer and broker's intentions are in writing, the agency becomes an *express* agency, and all of the boundaries of the agency are set forth in clear language. In the real estate industry, an express agency is always better than an implied agency.

### What if the Buyer Refuses to Sign an Agency Agreement?

If the Buyer refuses to sign an agreement, the buyer is refusing representation. In other words, the buyer is refusing to create an express agency and thus, an implied agency exists. The broker is then bound by fiduciary duty to the buyer with no limitations to the agency, yet the buyer is not bound to any duty except the duty to be reasonable.

### Disclosure Requirements

When representing buyers, the duty of disclosure usually boils down to a disclosure with regard to the buyer's ability to uphold a promise to purchase a property.

### Case Law

The landmark case of *Lombardo v. Albu* [4 P.3d 395] involved an action in tort in which Lombardo, the seller of real property, sought damages from the buyer's real estate agent for failing to inform the seller that the buyer was or might have been unable to perform because of financial difficulties (The official case law document for *Lombardo v. Albu* may be downloaded from the online course).

**Judicial History.** The Lombardos filed an action against their agent, the buyers, and the buyer's agent, Albu. Fairly construed, the count against Albu alleges the tort of negligent misrepresentation. It alleges that Albu failed to disclose material facts about the buyer's ability to perform that were relevant to the Lombardos' decision to agree to reschedule closing dates and to refrain from terminating the contract. The trial Court granted Summary Judgment in favor of the buyer's agent on the basis that the buyer's agent (Albu) had no legal duty to the seller. The Arizona Court of Appeals affirmed the trial court decision and the Lombardos appealed.

The case went on for several years, and the most relevant outcome of this case for real estate licensees are the changes that were made to the disclosure laws with regard to buyers.

Facts of the Case:

- The Lombardos were the sellers. They were behind in their payments. One of the lien holders extended the payment period in order to give the Lombardos an opportunity to sell the house.

- In February 1994, the Lombardos listed the property for sale.

- Elaine Albu, a buyer's representative, presented an offer in the name of one buyer, who was married, except the offer was not in the name of the married couple, it was in the wife's name only.

- The sellers and the buyer reached an agreement with a closing date of June 30, 1994.

- In April 1994, the buyer told the agent Albu that her husband had filed for bankruptcy and was subject to IRS tax liens. The buyer also told Albu that the reason she was making the offer to purchase in her name only was because she hoped that lenders would not make the connection or would extend credit to her only. She told Albu that she and her husband were going to be a special financing case.

- At the time (1994), many people felt that disclosing the bankruptcy would have been a violation of agency. Albu did not tell the Lombardos that her client was not an *able buyer* or might be unable to perform to the agreement made in the contract. Had the Lombardos been told, they would have sought other conditions in the purchase contract—for example, the right to keep the property on the market.

- Despite several extensions of the closing date, the buyer was never able to close and the Lombardos lost the equity in the property at a trustee's (foreclosure) sale.

**Contract Creation by Agents**

In states where real estate licensees are given the privilege to write contracts, these licensees are given both a privilege and a burden. The legal risk to a brokerage where the licensees are permitted to write contracts is substantial.

However, it is not nearly as substantial as the financial burden to a brokerage in states where an attorney is required if there is a proposed change to a contract. In those *attorney* states, clients must pay for (and wait for) the attorney service each time either of the parties to any contract makes the slightest change to the terms.

### *The Burden of Contract Creation*

With the privilege of contract writing comes its burden, and the necessity for training and supervision. Let's take a look at three legal doctrines:

1) **Ambiguity in contract terms.** It is a legal doctrine that courts will generally interpret any ambiguity in the language of a contract against the person who wrote (or whose agent wrote) the language. For example, if the buyer's agent writes a term in the contract on behalf of the buyers, and that term is disputed in a lawsuit, then the court may interpret the term in a way that least favors the buyers.

2) **Statute of Frauds.** The Statute of Frauds is a legal doctrine (written into the laws of nearly every state) that requires all contracts for real property to be in writing. Nothing that is exchanged verbally between the buyer and seller can be considered part of the contract according to the Statute of Frauds. For example, consider the following scenario (taken from an actual lawsuit):

   i) The close-of-escrow date was June 15, and the buyers were to take possession on June 16.
   ii) On June 12, the sellers had an emergency (one of the sellers went into labor two months early), and as a result, they were unable to sign the conveyance documents, and were also unable to move out of the property by the agreed-upon possession date.
   iii) The listing agent did not procure a written extension of the closing date, because the sellers had given explicit, verbal instructions to their agent to *not* bother them while they were dealing with complications from the delivery.
   iv) Therefore, the listing agent provided written disclosures to the buyers about the situation, but because the seller did not sign those disclosures, they did not serve to amend the contract.
   v) The listing agent and the listing agent's broker felt that the disclosure should have been adequate to properly amend the contract, given the circumstances.
   vi) The buyers became angry about the delay in moving into the home, and were not sympathetic to the seller's situation.
   vii) The sale did not close on June 15. The buyers cancelled the contract, and demanded the return of their earnest money, claiming that the sellers breached.
   viii) A civil court action found the sellers in breach of contract, and the buyers were given back their earnest money. The judge cited the Statute of Frauds as the basis for the decision, because in the sale of real estate, written contracts are enforceable, and any amendments must be in writing, and signed by both parties.
   ix) The sellers then filed a complaint against the listing agent, stating that the agent was negligent, and should have written a *plan b* that would accommodate an emergency situation into the contract.
   x) In this case, no disciplinary action was initiated against the agent, but the agent was forced to pay damages to the buyer for neglecting to write the contract to accommodate for an emergency.

3) **Improper terminations.** Too often, when a transaction goes wrong, the sellers and the buyers are only concerned about who gets the earnest money held in escrow. Once that determination is made, they sign instructions to release the funds to one party or another, and each side simply walks away. The parties end up walking away with a legally valid contract still on the table.

This is not the proper way to terminate a contract. Agents typically do not have the incentive to properly wrap up the loose ends of a contract, because when a transaction falls through, commissions fall through, also.

However, once it is decided who gets the earnest money, the parties should sign a termination to the purchase contract. The words *Rescission of Purchase Contract* or *Cancellation of Purchase Contract* should be clearly written at the top of the document, and the document should contain the following:

    i)    The names of the parties and the date of the contract.
    ii)   The reason for termination, as well as the provisions in the purchase contract that specify the conditions under which termination is allowed.
    iii)  Whether the termination is a rescission or a cancellation.
    iv)  The terms of the termination, specifically the terms that state to whom the earnest money deposit will be released.
    v)   The parties' agreement not to file suit against each other.

The instructions to release the earnest money should be given to the holder of the earnest money only after the parties sign the termination.

## Misrepresentation and Fraud

### Negligent Misrepresentation

Misrepresentation is the number one reason why civil suits are filed against real estate agents. These civil suits are brought by dissatisfied buyers who discover material defects in the physical condition of the property after closing. This represents the number one financial risk for brokers. Therefore, it is wise for a brokerage to develop policies regarding misrepresentation. However, in order to do so, the broker must have a clear understanding of the legal basis from which claims are brought.

### *Case Law*

According to case law that arose from the case of *Coleman v. Watts* [87 F. Supp. 2d 944], the rules regarding liability for negligent misrepresentations in business transactions are as follows:

- One who, in the course of his or her business, profession, or employment, or in any other transaction in which he or she has a pecuniary interest, supplies false information for the guidance of others in their business transactions, is subject to liability for pecuniary loss caused to them by their justifiable reliance upon the information, if he or she fails to exercise reasonable care or competence in obtaining or communicating the information.

- There must be a duty owed and a breach of that duty before one may be charged with the negligent violation of that duty.

- One who fraudulently misrepresents fact, opinion, intention, or law for the purpose of inducing another to act or to refrain from action in reliance upon it, is subject to liability to the other in deceit for pecuniary loss caused to him or her by his or her justifiable reliance upon the misrepresentation.

### Other Court Decisions

In the California case of *Timmsen v. Forest* [6 CA. 3d 860], the Court held that a broker can be held liable to the seller for procuring and recommending a financially unsound offer. Additionally, the Court held that a broker could be liable for misadvising a seller of the effect of a subordination provision in his or her contract.

In the case of *Wilson v. Hisey* [147 CA. 2d 433], the court stated that although the failure to recommend getting a preliminary title report might not, in itself, constitute negligence, a broker who affirmatively stated that there was only one encumbrance against the property thereby breached his or her duty of care. Agents are required to exercise reasonable skill and ordinary diligence and not to act negligently.

In a third California case, a broker was found to have breached his duty of loyalty and was held liable to his principal (a lessor), for telling a prospective tenant that he could obtain a longer lease than the lessor wanted to give [*Mitchell vs. Gould, 90 CA. 647*].

### Fraudulent Misrepresentation

A real estate licensee's actions constitute fraudulent misrepresentation if the licensee engages in the following scenarios:

- Makes an affirmative statement with knowledge of its falsity (such as stating that an undesirable condition does not exist when it does, or that a desirable condition exists when it does not).

- Makes an affirmative statement with reckless disregard for the accuracy of the statement.

- Fails to disclose information about the property or the transaction.

### Fraudulent Concealment

According to the head notes of the Coleman v. Watts (supra) case, fraudulent concealment occurs under the following circumstances:

- Concealment of an existing material fact that, in equity and good conscience, should be disclosed.

- Knowledge on the part of the party against whom the claim is asserted that such a fact is being concealed.

- Ignorance of that fact on the part of the one from whom the fact is concealed.

- The intention that the concealment be acted upon.

- Action on the concealment that results in damages.

## Disputes and Litigation

### Internal Dispute Resolution

Every brokerage should have, as a part of its management of risk, an internal complaint-handling procedure. The purpose of this procedure is to focus on client complaints and respond to them before they escalate. Powerful communication is the most effective weapon against lawsuits.

### *Appointment of Brokerage Ombudsman*

The risk management committee of the National Association of REALTORS® recommends that each office designate an individual to serve as a point person for handling client complaints (ombudsman). Because most dissatisfied clients expect a response to their complaints within a reasonable time, ignoring the client would be unwise. If one individual is responsible for fielding and responding to complaints, then the brokerage can establish a systematic approach to resolution, and avoid a lawsuit.

### *Diffusing Angry Clients*

**Learning expectations.** Generally, clients are angry because they expected one manner of service, and got another. The first rule of managing an angry client is to learn about what the client expected. A surprising number of angry clients, when allowed to speak their piece, will diffuse on their own.

When the client speaks, remember that the client based his or her expectations on what he or she believed to be good information. Most angry clients never intended to be dissatisfied.

**Acknowledging the anger.** When clients become stuck in an unreasonable pattern of behavior, it is generally because their feelings are not validated. When the clients' feelings are validated, there is a certain rapport that develops. However, caution must be taken here: There is a fine line between validating clients' feelings and taking the blame.

**Solutions.** What does the client need or want to resolve the situation? It may be something simple, such as an apology. Again, in this case, an apology is an expression that the brokerage regrets the client's dissatisfaction. It is not an expression that the brokerage accepts the blame.

### Alternative Dispute Resolution

The word *alternative*, when it refers to dispute resolution, means "an alternative to traditional civil (court) proceedings." There are two types of alternative dispute resolution:

1) Mediation
2) Arbitration

## Mediation

During mediation, each party to the dispute tells his or her side of the story, and a mediator helps them reach a compromise. In mediation, who is "right" and who is "wrong" is immaterial. The primary concern is whether the parties can come to an equitable compromise.

If the parties resolve their dispute through mediation, they sign an agreement that spells out the terms of their settlement. Their agreement is binding, and acts as an enforceable contract between them.

## Arbitration

In an arbitration due process hearing, the prevailing party must prove they are entitled to the disputed funds by a preponderance of the evidence. This is the same standard used by courts in civil cases. The word *preponderance* translates to *greater weight*. Once a hearing panel makes an arbitration award, that award becomes the legal basis for a court to enter judgment against the non-prevailing party. If a non-prevailing party fails to pay the award, the award can be enforced by the courts. The arbitration process is bona fide in most states that enforce state Arbitration Acts.

### Procuring Cause Arbitration

The majority of arbitration claims involve a dispute between REALTOR® about which REALTOR® is entitled to cooperative compensation in a transaction. Most disputes ordinarily involve the selling portion of a commission. In the REALTOR® arbitration system, procuring cause arbitration is generally used to decide these disputes.

The National Association of REALTORS® has established procuring cause guidelines for use in resolving arbitrable disputes. These procuring cause guidelines were developed to assist arbitration hearing panels while determining procuring cause during arbitration hearings. A copy of the National Association of REALTORS® Procuring Cause Guidelines may be downloaded from the online course.

### Factors for Consideration by Arbitration Hearing Panels

**Factor #1: No predetermined rule of entitlement.** Every arbitration hearing is considered in light of all of the relevant facts and circumstances as presented by the parties and their witnesses. 'Rules of thumb', prior decisions by other panels in other matters, and other predeterminants are disregarded.

**Factor #2: Arbitrability and appropriate parties.** Is the case arbitrable? Arbitration Hearing Panels may consider questions of whether an arbitrable issue actually exists and whether the parties named are appropriate to arbitration.

**Factor #3: Relevance and admissibility.** Frequently, hearing panels are asked to rule on questions of admissibility and relevancy. While state law (if applicable) controls, the general rule is that anything the hearing panel believes may assist it in reaching a fair, equitable, and knowledgeable decision is admissible.

**Factor #4: Communication and contact.** Many arbitrable disputes will turn on the relationship (or lack thereof) between a broker (often a cooperating broker) and a prospective purchaser. Panels will consider whether, under the circumstances and in accord with local custom and practice, the broker made reasonable efforts to develop and maintain an ongoing relationship with the purchaser. Panels will want to determine, in cases where two cooperating brokers have competing claims against a listing broker, whether the first cooperating broker actively maintained ongoing contact with the purchaser or, alternatively, whether the broker's inactivity, or perceived inactivity, may have caused the purchaser to reasonably conclude that the broker had lost interest or disengaged from the transaction (abandonment).

**Factor #5: Conformity with state law.** The procedures by which arbitration requests are received, hearings are conducted, and awards are made must be in strict conformity with the law. In such matters, the advice of the Association legal counsel should be followed.

**Factor #6: Totality of the circumstances.** The standard of proof in board-conducted arbitration is a preponderance of the evidence, and the initial burden of proof rests with the party that requests arbitration. The objective of a panel is to carefully and impartially weigh and analyze the parties' whole course of conduct and render a reasoned peer judgment with respect to the issues and questions presented, and to the request for award. Arbitration panels consider the following:

- The nature and status of the transaction or the listing agreement.
- The roles of and relationships among the parties.
- Which broker had initial contact with the purchaser.
- The conduct of the parties up to the arbitration.
- The continuity of the parties' actions and breaks in continuity.
- The conduct of the buyer and/or seller.

### *Litigation*

Unfortunately, not all disputes can be handled outside of the court system. To manage those disputes that end up in court, it is important for a broker to have at least a basic knowledge of the legal process. Knowledge of the legal process will give a broker confidence and coping skills. Below are the basic steps in the litigation process after an unsuccessful alternative dispute resolution:

1) **Summons.** Summons and complaint will be served upon the brokerage. At this point, the broker should immediately forward this summons to his or her attorney. The broker should not attempt to negotiate a settlement with the complainant at this point, because whatever the broker says may be held against him or her.

2) **Brokerage response.** After the broker meets with his or her attorney to discuss the issue, the broker should prepare a responsive pleading. This is a formal document that is filed with the court system and is the means by which a party to a legal proceeding responds to allegations or claims.

3) **Discovery.** Both parties now go through the process of discovery to elicit the facts of the case. Discovery can be accomplished through interrogatories, deposition, or a combination of the two.

4) **Pretrial motions.** Any time prior to the trial, pretrial motions may be filed. If any of these motions are filed and granted, it will put an end to the proceedings. Such motions may include the following:

    i)   A motion for voluntary dismissal by the plaintiff (complainant).
    ii)  A motion to dismiss.
    iii) A motion for summary judgment by the defendant.

Once one of these motions is granted and the proceedings end (unless granted *without prejudice*), the issues cannot be brought up again in the future.

5) **Trial.** If the pretrial motions did not stop the proceedings and the case goes to trial, the trial will be structured as follows:

    i)   Plaintiff's opening statement.
    ii)  Defendant's opening statement.
    iii) Presentation of plaintiff's evidence.
    iv) Presentation of defendant's evidence.
    v)  Plaintiff's closing arguments.
    vi) Defendant's closing arguments.
    vii) Court ruling (verdict).

## Technology

The real estate industry has changed more rapidly over the last 15 years than it has in the last 100 years. The onset of the internet has changed not only the way that real estate business is conducted, but has also changed the real estate market. Plainly stated, with new technology comes new opportunity. With new opportunity comes new risk (i.e., new ways to be sued).

The risks associated with the use of technology are not the types of risks brokerages have traditionally encountered. The issues that dominate the discussion are *copyright law* and *trademark law*.

## Copyright Law

The author's creativity is protected, but not the ideas or facts behind the expression.

Authors of certain works, such as websites, are entitled to certain rights with regard to their works. These rights extend only to the author's expression of his or her ideas, and not the ideas or facts behind the expression. In other words, it is the author's creativity that is protected, and without that creativity, there is nothing to protect under copyright laws.

### *Photographs of Properties*

Copyright issues can arise during the normal course of the real estate business, such as when using photographs of properties that are offered for sale. If the real estate licensee uses photographs that are taken by another person, and does not obtain permission to use those photographs, then the reproduction and distribution of the photographs by the licensee will be regarded as copyright infringement. Courts will award both monetary and injunctive relief if they find such an infringement.

### *Internet Copyright Issues*

Several lawsuits have occurred that involve copyright infringement on the internet. In each case, if the plaintiff was able to establish a valid copyright and unauthorized use of the plaintiff's copyrighted material, the plaintiff was able to enforce the copyright. Two important factors with regard to the real estate industry have come about as a result of these recent lawsuits:

- The factual compilations of real property information that relate to properties being offered for sale by an MLS are eligible for copyright protection. Internet-based usage of the databases must be done with permission. Brokerages or licensees who *frame* the contents of the MLS into their personal websites without permission may be liable for copyright infringement.

- Photographs of properties are separately copyrightable works. Photographs of properties may not be used by brokers or licensees without the permission of the person who took the photograph.

### *Sharing Software*

Software is protected by copyright. It may be tempting for real estate licensees and/or employees of a brokerage to share the cost of a single package and then load copies of the software onto multiple computers. Brokers should be aware that this activity is a violation of the license agreement granted by the software developer.

### Trademark Law

In the real estate industry, icon value is very important. Many big-name real estate companies, such as REMAX®, Coldwell Banker®, and Century 21® have registered trademarks. The internet has caused such trademarks to become very valuable to their owners as trademark names. Internet users will use a search engine to type in a trademarked name.

However, many times, real estate licensees will include these trademarked names in the metadata of their websites. The result is that users who type in the trademarked real estate name will be shown the website of the licensee's real estate company!

These practices have resulted in a multitude of lawsuits, and of course, multitudes of new legislation. Trademark owners now have a right to sue for bad-faith regeneration of their trademark. This new legislation is commonly referred to as the *Anticybersquatting Act*.

### Emails and Defamation

Agents, when sending email messages, must be particularly conscious about what is in their messages. Email messages can reach audiences for which they are never intended, and it is no place for off-the-cuff statements. Brokerages are liable for the statements made by their agents because of the potential for defamation lawsuits that stem from the contents of email messages. Here are a few important facts to remember:

- Most email messages are never really deleted; they are archived, and they can be retrieved.

- Emails are discoverable in litigation.

- Emails can be sent to others by accident.

- Some communications are too sensitive to be sent via email.

**Sexual Harassment and Privacy**

**Sexual Harassment**

Sexual harassment is any verbal or physical conduct of a harassing nature, requests for sexual acts or favors, unwelcome sexual advances, or any other conduct, of which the purpose or effect unreasonably interferes with an individual's work performance or creates a hostile, intimidating, or offensive work environment. Sexual harassment is illegal.

Because harassment is a serious offense, your brokerage should have strict policies in place with regard to harassment. Furthermore, your brokerage should develop and enforce a written sexual harassment policy to reduce the liability just in case there is a sexual harassment suit filed.

**Privacy Issues**

**Within the Office**

Most larger real estate brokerages are set up to have an email function that enables licensees and employees to communicate with one another and with the broker. Regulations of these intra-office networks is governed by the Electronic Communications Privacy Act, which prohibits arbitrary monitoring of messages, but allows employers to monitor the email messages exchanged over their system. Case law has established that an employee has no reasonable expectation of privacy with regard to messages sent over an office system.

However, there is no case law that establishes whether the same will hold true for independent contractors, but conventional wisdom tells us that if a broker is held responsible for the actions of the licensees within the brokerage, then the broker should have a right to monitor the email messages that are sent over the brokerage network.

**Client Privacy**

Twenty years ago, the term *identity theft* was not commonplace. Today, it is. Virtually all agents develop lists of clients and prospects, and use databases to store information about those clients and prospects. In response to the continuing reports of the careless handling of sensitive personal information that belongs to clients and prospects, not only are there new laws regulating such storage of information, there are many more laws that are proposed.

At this point, no single standard has emerged, but brokerages should have a policy in place to protect any sensitive data they collect against unauthorized access or use. Privacy policies should address what information is collected, how that information will be used, and how it is protected.

**QUIZZES ARE MANDATORY**: Please log in and submit the chapter quizzes online.

**Chapter Two Quiz**

1.      Which of the following Acts applies to private employers with 15 or more employees, and makes it unlawful for an employer to discriminate on the basis of race, color, religion, sex, or national origin?

     (a)      Civil Rights Act of 1964.
     (b)      Age Discrimination in Employment Act.
     (c)      Civil Rights Act of 1991.
     (d)      Americans with Disabilities Act.

2.      The essence of the anti-trust laws is that businesses cannot agree to:

     (a)      Discriminate on the basis of one of the protected classes.
     (b)      Split commissions.
     (c)      Terminate an employee because of his or her age.
     (d)      Restrain trade.

3.      Approximately _____ of the real estate licensees (both brokers and salespersons) in the U.S. work with an assistant, according to a recent survey by the National Association of REALTORS®.

     (a)      10%
     (b)      50%
     (c)      20%
     (d)      5%

4.      Which of the following is a TRUE statement?

     (a)      In an arbitration hearing, there must be a predetermined rule of entitlement.
     (b)      All citizens of the U.S. have a right to arbitration before the REALTOR® arbitration board.
     (c)      All cases are arbitrable.
     (d)      The factual compilations of real property information that relate to properties that are offered for sale in an MLS are eligible for copyright protection.

5.      Which of the following correctly defines the term *responsive pleading*?

     (a)      A formal document that is filed with the court system and is the means by which a party to a legal proceeding responds to allegations or claims.
     (b)      A writ or process that commences the plaintiff's (complainant's) action and requires the defendant to appear and answer.
     (c)      A formal set of written questions that are required to be answered in order to clarify matters of evidence and help to determine in advance what facts will be presented during any trial in the case.
     (d)      A judgment that is issued without a court hearing.

**Chapter Three: Creating and Implementing a Plan**

**Learning Objectives**

After successful completion of this chapter, you should be able to complete the following:

- Write the objectives for your brokerage.
- Analyze reasons why your brokerage may not achieve its objectives.
- Create and implement a personalized risk management plan.
- Understand the importance of communication and develop a training module to teach licensees the art of communication.
- State the types of things that cause advertising risk, and explain possible remedies.
- Describe the most common reasons for lawsuits, and take preventive measures.

## Creating a Plan to Manage Risk

In any business, some risk is necessary. However, some risk is unnecessary because it is not in line with the brokerage's objectives. Such activities are called *impediments* to the brokerage objectives.

For instance, if a brokerage objective is to develop a long-term and loyal client base, then client satisfaction is important. It follows, then, that the agents must be accessible and approachable. Thus, have agents who don't understand the use and utility of email may be an impediment to the brokerage objective.

As another example, suppose the brokerage objective is to specialize in vacant land sales. If that's the case, then a property management contract would be an impediment to the brokerage objective because it usurps time and energy that is not in line with the brokerage objectives.

In the next two sections, you will see example brokerage objectives and have the chance to write the objectives of your brokerage, as well as impediments to those objectives. Then, you can use those objectives and impediments to modify your brokerage policies manual.

### Step One: Identify Brokerage Objectives and Impediments

| Objective | Impediments |
|---|---|
| *To conduct an ethical and successful real estate brokerage and uphold our reputation for excellence and integrity.* | • Misconduct and misrepresentation<br>• Inefficient or outdated processes<br>• Uneducated sales staff |
| *To maintain a financially stable brokerage, in light of the brokerage's special requirements.* | • Ineffective financial systems<br>• Non-motivated sales force<br>• Ineffective cost management<br>• Too much expenditure for office staff<br>• Overpaid sales force<br>• Ineffective marketing materials |
| *To conduct the brokerage as an integral component of the community, and be recognized for our contributions to the community.* | • Poor community involvement<br>• Brokerage disciplinary actions<br>• Publicized complaints about the brokerage<br>• Tainted brokerage reputation |
| *To provide a high level of care to our clients.* | • Outdated technology<br>• Disorganized transaction management<br>• Poorly supervised sales force<br>• Incompetence<br>• Mismanaged transactions |
| *To use real estate marketing technology to generate new clientele.* | • Computer or internet illiteracy<br>• Ill-equipped office spaces |
| *To conduct an ethical and successful property management division.* | • Inefficient or outdated processes<br>• Overworked property management staff<br>• Untrained accounting staff |

**Exercise 1.1: Identify Brokerage Objectives and Impediments**

Use a piece of scratch paper and write the objectives for your brokerage on the left and the impediments to those objectives on the right. You will use the information in the form to modify your brokerage policies manual.

**Step Two: Write the Brokerage Policies**

If your brokerage has more than five salespersons, you want the brokerage policies as well as the reasoning behind each policy to be well-documented. In the event of a lawsuit or disciplinary action, a well-written brokerage office policies manual will go a long way toward proving your intent to reasonably supervise those for whom you have vicarious liability.

If your brokerage does not already have a policies manual, use this downloadable manual to give you the beginnings of one. As you learn more about the processes to manage risk, you can update your manual. The policies manual is central to the communication of your brokerage's plan to manage risk. Using your brokerage objectives as a guide, modify your brokerage policies manual to suit your brokerage's needs. This is where your managerial experience comes into play. There are many aspects to running a brokerage. Your policies should address all aspects as well as all relevant details thereof.

**Step Three: Develop a Culture**

**Broker Communication to Licensees**

Since the activities and mistakes of the agents are the legal responsibility of the broker, and the activities and mistakes of the non-agents are the financial responsibility of the brokerage, it is imperative that the broker communicate not only the preventive procedures to the agents and staff, but the reasons for such policies and procedures.

**Communication in General**

Brokers should train the licensees of the brokerage in the art of communication. In many cases, conflicts can arise because of a simple case of miscommunication. Some helpful tips for training sessions include the following:

**The art of questioning.** Licensees should understand that letting a misunderstanding go unclarified is likely to cause problems for the brokerage. Communication should be a two-way street. Licensees should practice role playing where they paraphrase what another party says. This will help the brokerage licensees grasp a clear understanding of client objectives.

**The art of giving opinions.** An opinion can cause problems if the person listening to the opinion does not know that it is an opinion. Opinions stated as facts cause problems. Licensees should practice stating opinions and then making it clear that their opinions are not fact.

**The art of written follow-up.** Oral statements, when misinterpreted or misremembered, will give rise to misguided assumptions, which will give rise to dissatisfaction when reality differs from what was perceived when the assumption was made. Licensees should be counseled and trained in the art of email follow-up to phone calls and in-person conversations.

**Using care when using jargon.** Even though it's difficult to get through a conversation with a client without using jargon, it is always necessary to make sure that the client understands what the licensee is saying. Licensees should be trained in the art of defining terms as they speak, so as to avoid confusion.

### Risk-Free Advertising

The toughest aspect of writing advertising copy is to keep it truthful, while still making it exciting to read for the prospective buyers. There is a fine line between exciting ad copy and inaccurate or misleading ad copy. Advertising the features of a home and neighborhood can entice buyers, but if a buyer later disputes the accuracy or fairness of those ads, the brokerage could end up with a complaint or a lawsuit. Here are some tips to consider when reviewing draft ad copy:

- Superlatives, such as *totally* or *completely*, when combined with descriptive words such as *remodeled* or *upgraded*, can mislead. The phrase "totally remodeled master bathroom," for example, can mean many things. Is everything in the bathroom new? What about the pipes or lighting fixtures? If the listing agent doesn't know for sure (and it's not enough to rely on the seller's word), it's safer to replace *totally* with a neutral characterization such as *beautifully* or *impeccably*.

- Brand names, such as *Sub-zero* or *travertine* should be replaced with generic product descriptions unless the listing agent knows that the feature is a product made by the specified brand name. For example, instead of advertising a *Jacuzzi* tub, call it a jetted tub. If the tub isn't the *Jacuzzi* brand, the buyer could later claim that the listing agent misrepresented the feature.

- Consider what expectations may be built into property descriptions. Common ad language such as "the backyard is ready for a pool" may imply to a prospective buyer that a pool can be easily installed for a standard price. If the area's soil is known for difficulty in excavating, or if the lot is at a significant slope, such ad language could be challenged later. Similarly, "a perfect opportunity for room additions" might imply that it won't be difficult to obtain building permits, yet in some communities, building permits can be impossible to obtain.

- Avoid vague language. "All appliances are brand-new" could be interpreted in a variety of ways. Does *all appliances* include the heater and air conditioner, or just the kitchen appliances? Does *brand-new* mean the appliances have never been used? Clarify the ad by removing potential arguments and substituting words such as "newer kitchen and appliances."

### Avoid Slip-Ups

Every real estate transaction presents potential legal slip-ups. Combine the stress of the real estate buying and selling experience with the propensity for lawsuits, and brokers will either receive lawsuits or threats of lawsuits. However, did you know that despite the growing number of suits, licensees are found not liable in almost 75 percent of the cases, according to a new report by the National Association of REALTORS® Legal Affairs?

Let's take a look at the most common types of suits and how to avoid them:

- Misrepresentation is by far the most popular reason to sue a real estate brokerage. Nearly two-thirds of the lawsuits brought against real estate brokerages are for misrepresentation or failure to disclose. About one-third of the misrepresentation suits are associated with misrepresented foundational and structural features. Other misrepresentations involve property boundaries, the roof, and termite problems. Common subjects for a failure to disclose lawsuit are easements, renovating without a permit, environmental problems, and title problems.

  If a broker receives property information from a third-party source, the broker should attribute the information to that source, saying, for example, "According to the seller, the roof is three years old." The courts have told us that brokers may rely on statements that the seller makes, unless the broker has reason to doubt that what the seller says is true.

- Use seller disclosure forms (and be sure that the seller fills out the form).

- Avoid making predictions, such as "This well will never run dry" or "The value of this house is sure to appreciate." (Stating opinions as fact.)

- A Breach of Fiduciary Duty accounts for about 10 percent of suits against brokerages. Many of the suits involve claims of undisclosed dual agency.

- Fair Housing violations account for only 1 to 2 percent of litigation. However, because of the absence of a statutory limit on punitive damages, the judgments and penalties can result in financial ruin. In recent years, some suits have been brought against MLS's because their members included remarks in internet listings that violated the fair housing law, such as "no children" or "perfect for empty nesters." Publishing such information on the internet carries the same liability as publishing it in print.

- The unauthorized practice of law spawns lawsuits whenever brokers or salespeople provide advice outside their scope of authority or expertise.

  Exactly what actions would constitute unauthorized practice of law? The courts have tried to strike a balance in their definition and take public policy into consideration. They don't want the public damaged by unskilled practitioners, but they'll look at whether it's in the public's interest to allow brokers to engage in certain activities, such as drafting clauses in legal documents. To be safe, urge clients to hire a lawyer if they have legal questions.

**QUIZZES ARE MANDATORY**: Please log in and submit the chapter quizzes online.

**Chapter Three Quiz**

1.      Publicized complaints and a poorly supervised sales force will directly affect the brokerage's:

        (a)      commission splits.
        (b)      community reputation.
        (c)      cost of office space.
        (d)      desk fees.

2.      The phrase "all appliances are brand new" should be replaced with a phrase such as:

        (a)      newer kitchen appliances.
        (b)      all appliances are decent.
        (c)      all appliances are like new.
        (d)      all appliances are state of the art.

3.      The courts have told us that agents may rely on statements that the seller makes, unless the agent:

        (a)      has reason to doubt that what the seller says is true.
        (b)      has a better way to spin the advertising.
        (c)      has more college education than the seller.
        (d)      is in the construction business.

4.      About one-third of the misrepresentation suits are associated with misrepresented _____.
        Other misrepresentations involve property boundaries, the roof, and termite problems.

        (a)      marketability of title
        (b)      roof repair
        (c)      property boundaries
        (d)      foundational and structural features

5.      Some states, such as California and Arizona, require that the agent not only disclose known material facts, but that the agent also:

        (a)      pay for a home inspection.
        (b)      pay for a termite inspection.
        (c)      conduct a reasonable visual inspection of the property and disclose what that inspection reveals.
        (d)      dissect the home to find latent defects.

# Notes

# Trust Fund Handling

3 Hours of Continuing Education for
Salesperson and Broker License Renewal

**Lumbleau Real Estate School**
23805 Hawthorne Blvd.
Torrance, CA 90505

**DISCLAIMERS**

Although every effort has been made to provide accurate and current information in this text, the ideas, suggestions, general principles, and conclusions presented in this text are subject to local, state, and federal laws and regulations, court cases, and any revisions of the same. The author and/or publisher is not engaged in rendering legal, tax, or other professional services. The reader is thus urged to consult with his or her employing broker and/or seek legal counsel regarding any points of law. This publication should not be used as a substitute for competent legal advice.

This course is approved for continuing education credit by the California Bureau of Real Estate. However, this approval does not constitute an endorsement of the views or opinions that are expressed by the course sponsor, instructor, authors, or lecturers.

# Table of Contents

## Chapter One

## Important Terms

advance fee
beneficiary
commingling
escrow
impound account
inure
obligor
principal
security deposits
trust fund
trustee
trust fund bank accounting

## Learning Objectives

Upon completion of Chapter One, you should be able to complete the following:

- Define *commingling*.

- Describe how commingling occurs.

- Distinguish between trust funds and non-trust funds.

- Describe the requirements for handling advance fees.

- Identify shortages and overages in a trust fund bank account.

## I. General Information

In the normal course of doing business, real estate brokers and salespersons receive trust funds on behalf of others. Brokers and salespersons must handle, control, and account for these trust funds according to current law. This section discusses the legal requirements for receiving and handling trust funds in real estate transactions as set forth in the Real Estate Law and the Commissioner's Regulations. The discussions in this section will pertain to real estate trust funds received by licensees, and to non-trust funds such as real estate commissions, or general operating funds. It will cover the requisites for maintaining a trust fund bank account and the precautions a licensee should take to ensure the integrity of such an account. It will also explain and illustrate the trust fund record keeping requirements under the Business and Professions Code.

## Trust Funds Defined

Trust funds are money or other things of value that are received by a broker or salesperson on behalf of a principal or any other person, and which are held for the benefit of others in the performance of any act(s) for which a real estate license is required.

Trust funds may be cash or non-cash items. A few examples include cash, a check used as a deposit (whether made payable to the broker or to an escrow or title company), a personal note made payable to the seller, or even a pink slip to a car that is given as a deposit.

## Trust Fund Handling Requirements

It is a fact that trust funds belong to others and are only entrusted to the care and handling of a real estate licensee for a limited period of time. Therefore, the licensee has a fiduciary responsibility to the owner of the funds. This duty requires that the licensee handle the funds according to the law and use them only for the purpose authorized by the fund's owner(s).

A typical trust fund transaction begins with the broker or salesperson receiving trust funds from a principal in connection with the purchase or lease of real property.

A real estate licensee who accepts funds from others in connection with any transaction for which a license is required must place them in one of the following:

1) A neutral escrow depository.
2) The hands of the offeree or owner.
3) A trust account that is maintained by the licensee.

Current law mandates that trust funds must be handled in a specific manner. For this reason, a licensee must be able to distinguish trust funds from non-trust funds.

If the broker (or broker's salesperson) fails to place the funds into one of these three authorized places within three business days following receipt of the funds by the broker or by the broker's salesperson, he or she is liable for *commingling* the funds.

If the funds are placed into a trust account in a bank or recognized depository, they must remain there until he or she makes a disbursement pursuant to instructions from the person(s) entitled to the funds.

**Commingling:** Mixing deposits or monies belonging to a client (trust funds) with one's personal money.

An exception to this rule is when a check is received from an offeror in connection with an offer to purchase or lease. In this case, the deposit check may be held uncashed by the broker until acceptance of the offer if the following conditions are met:

1) The check by its terms expressly provides that it is not to be negotiated by the broker, or the offeror has given written instructions to the broker that the check shall not be deposited or cashed until acceptance of the offer.

2) The offeree is informed either before or at the time the offer is presented for acceptance, that the check is being so held.

If the offer is later accepted, the broker may continue to hold the check undeposited only if the broker receives written authorization from the offeree to do so. Otherwise, within three business days following receipt, the check must be placed into a neutral escrow depository, into the trust fund bank account, or into the hands of the offeree if both the offeror and offeree expressly agree to this option in writing.

If a real estate salesperson accepts trust funds on behalf of the broker under whom he or she is licensed, the salesperson must immediately deliver the funds to the broker or, if directed by the broker, place the funds into the hands of the broker's principal, into a neutral escrow depository, or deposit the funds into the broker's trust fund bank account.

**Identifying the Owner(s) of the Trust Funds**

A broker must be able to identify which of the parties in a transaction owns the trust funds and is entitled to receive them, since these funds can be dispersed only upon the authorization of that person. The person who is entitled to the funds may or may not be the person who originally gave the funds to the broker or the salesperson. In some instances, the party that is entitled to the funds will change upon the occurrence of certain events in the transactions. For example, in a transaction that involves an offer to buy or lease real property or a business opportunity, the party entitled to the funds that are received from the offeror (prospective buyer or lessor) will depend upon whether or not the offer has been accepted by the offeree (seller or landlord).

Prior to the acceptance of the offer, the funds received from the offeror belong to that person and must be handled according to his or her instructions. If the funds are deposited in a trust fund bank account, they must be maintained there for the benefit of the offeror until acceptance of the offer. Or, as discussed in the previous section, if the offeror wishes, the offeror's check may be held uncashed by the broker as long as he or she gives written instructions to the broker

to do so, and the offeree is informed before or at the time the offer is presented for acceptance that the check is being so held.

**Special Note: Broker Acting as Principal**

A real estate broker who is acting as a principal in the business of buying, selling, or exchanging real property sales contracts or promissory notes that are secured directly or collaterally by liens on real property, must place all funds received by himself or herself in a neutral escrow depository unless delivery of the note or contract is made simultaneously with receipt of the funds.

**II. Advance-Fee Trust Funds**

An *advance fee* is any fee which is claimed, demanded, charged, received, collected, or contracted as consideration for a listing, advertisement, or offer to sell or lease property or for a business opportunity (other than a newspaper advertisement), or for the referral to a real estate licensee, or for soliciting borrowers or lenders, or for negotiating a loan that regards real estate or a business opportunity.

Some brokers may wish to collect a fee before they render any services. Specifically, it is a practice of some brokers to obtain a nonrefundable fee from the seller in advance to cover the advertising of properties or businesses for sale (while giving no guarantee that a buyer will be found). Such fees are called *advance fees*.

**Approval of Advance-Fee Agreements**

All materials used by the broker for obtaining an advance fee, including all advertising, letters, cards used to solicit prospective sellers, and all contract forms to be used for obtaining an advance fee, must be submitted to the commissioner at least ten days before they are used. The commissioner also must approve the form of all advance-fee agreements that the broker intends to use. The commissioner will disapprove of any such materials if they are misleading, false, or deceptive.

All such materials must accurately and clearly describe (1) the services to be rendered, (2) the fee to be earned and when it will be earned, and (3) the date when performance of the services will be completed. The materials cannot exonerate the broker from liability for oral representations by himself or herself or his or her agents, nor can they contain any guarantee of the results of the broker's services, or a representation that a buyer will be available immediately. A failure to seek the commissioner's approval prior to the use of such materials justifies an injunction by the commissioner or disciplinary action against the licensee. Use of materials that the commissioner has disapproved is a misdemeanor.

**Advance Fee Trust Fund Handling**

All advance fees received by the broker are trust funds and not the broker's funds. The broker must place them in a trust account until they are expended for the benefit of the principal. If they are not placed into a trust account, it is presumed that the agent has embezzled the funds, and the principal can recover treble damages and the attorney's fees incurred while prosecuting the suit for collection.

Once the advance fee has been placed in the trust account, the funds cannot be withdrawn except for the benefit of the principal. The funds cannot be withdrawn for the benefit of the agent until the agent's services are completed, the agent has prepared an accounting, and five days have expired after the accounting has been mailed to the principal.

## Advance Fee Accounting and Record Keeping Requirements

The licensee must render an accounting to the principal at the end of each calendar quarter and when the agent's services are completed. The accounting must be verified and describe the services rendered, the amount of the advance fee, the identity of the trust account, where the fee has been deposited, and an itemization of the purpose of each withdrawal. If the withdrawal was for the payment of advertising, the accounting must also include a copy of the advertisement and a statement that states when and where the advertisement was published. If the advance fee was for arranging a loan, the accounting must identify the name and address of the prospective lenders solicited.

Upon request, a copy of the accounting must be furnished to the commissioner, and in any event, the advance fees are subject to the general regulations applicable to trust funds.

## III. Trust Fund Bank Accounts

## General Requirements

Trust funds received by a licensee that are not forwarded directly to the broker's principal or to a neutral escrow depository, or for which the broker does not have authorization to hold uncashed, must be deposited to a trust fund bank account.

*Business and Professions Code Section 10145* requires that a trust account meet the following criteria:

1) It must be designated as a trust account in the name of the broker as trustee.

2) It must be maintained with a bank or recognized depository located in California.

3) It cannot be an interest-bearing account for which prior written notice can, by law or regulation, be required by the financial institution as a condition to withdraw the funds, except as noted in the following discussion of *interest bearing accounts*.

## Interest Bearing Accounts

The broker has no obligation to place trust funds into an interest bearing account. Trust fund bank accounts normally may *not* be interest bearing. However, a broker may, at the request of the owner of the trust funds, or of the principals to a transaction or series of transactions from whom the broker has received trust funds, deposit the funds into an interest bearing account in a bank or savings and loan association if all of the following requirements are met:

1) The account is in the name of the broker as trustee for a specified beneficiary or specified principal of a transaction (or series of transactions).

2) All of the funds in the account are covered by insurance that is provided by an agency of the federal government.

3) The funds in the account are kept separate, distinct, and apart from funds belonging to the broker or to any other person for whom the broker holds funds in trust.

4) The broker discloses the following information to the person from whom the trust funds are received and to any beneficiary whose identity is known to the broker at the time of establishing the account:
   i) How the interest will be calculated and paid under various circumstances.
   ii) Whether or not service charges will be paid to the depository, and by whom.
   iii) Possible notice requirements or penalties for withdrawal from the account.

5) No interest earned on funds in the account shall inure directly or indirectly to the benefit of the broker or to any person licensed to the broker. Not even authorization by the fund's owners shall legally permit the broker to collect the earned interest on trust funds.

6) In an executory sale, lease, or loan transaction in which the broker accepts funds in trust to be applied to the purchase, lease, or loan, the parties to the contract shall have specified, either in the contract or by a collateral written agreement, the person to whom interest earned on the funds is to be paid or credited.

The only other situation where a real estate broker is allowed to deposit funds into an interest bearing account is when the broker is acting as an agent for a financial institution that is the beneficiary of a loan. In this case, the broker may deposit funds into an interest bearing account and maintain those funds, that are received from or for the account of an obligor (borrower), in order to pay interest on an impound account to the obligor, as long as the following are met:

1) The account is in the name of the broker as the trustee.

2) All of the funds in the account are covered by insurance that is provided by an agency of the federal government.

3) All of the funds in the account are funds held in trust by the broker for others.

4) The broker discloses to the obligor how interest will be calculated and paid.

5) No interest that is earned on the funds shall inure directly or indirectly to the benefit of the broker nor to any person licensed to the broker.

### Commingling of Trust Funds Is Prohibited

The licensee's personal funds may not be commingled with trust funds. Commingling is strictly prohibited by the Real Estate Law, and violation may result in revocation or suspension of a real estate license.

The following situations are examples of commingling:

- Personal or company funds are deposited into the trust fund bank account. This is a violation of the law, even if separate records are kept.

- Trust funds are deposited into the licensee's general or personal bank account rather than into the trust fund account. In this case, the violation is not only commingling, but also handling trust funds contrary to *Business and Professions Code Section 10145*. It may also be grounds for suspension or revocation of the licensee's license.

- Commissions, fees, or other income that is earned by the broker and collectible from the trust account is left in the trust account for more than 25 days from the date they were earned.

A common example of commingling occurs when rents and security deposits on broker-owned properties are deposited into the trust account. These funds relate to the broker's own property and are not trust funds, and therefore, may not be deposited into the trust fund bank account. Additionally, mortgage payments and other payments on broker-owned properties may not be made from the trust account even if the broker reimburses the account for such payments. Any personal business that is conducted through the trust account is specifically prohibited by the Real Estate Law.

### *Exceptions*

A real estate broker's personal funds may be commingled in the trust account in the following two specific instances:

1) Since banks sometimes have service charges out of necessity, the broker is allowed to maintain up to $200 of personal funds in a trust account to cover these types of bank charges. Trust funds may not be used to pay for these expenses. However, the better practice is to have the bank charge the broker's office or general account for the trust account fees and charges.

2) Commissions, fees, and other incomes that are earned by a broker and are collectible from trust funds that are deposited into the broker's trust account may remain there for a period not to exceed 25 days. As long as the broker disburses the fee from the trust account within 25 days after it is earned, there is not a commingling violation. Income earned shall not be taken from trust funds that are received before depositing such funds into the trust fund bank account. Also, under no circumstances may the broker pay personal obligations from the trust fund bank account even if such payments are a draw against commissions or other income. The broker must first issue a trust account check to himself or herself for the total amount of the income earned, adequately document such payments, and then pay personal obligations from the proceeds of that check.

### Trust Fund Liability

Trust fund liability arises when funds are received from or for the benefit of a principal, and decreases when funds are disbursed according to instructions from that principal. The aggregate trust fund liability at any one time for a trust account with multiple beneficiaries is equal to the total positive balances due to all beneficiaries of the account at the time. Note that beneficiary accounts with negative balances are not deducted from other accounts when calculating the aggregate trust fund liability.

Funds on deposit in the trust account must always equal the broker's aggregate trust fund liability. If the trust account balance is *less than* the total liability, a trust fund shortage results. Such a shortage is in violation of *Commissioner's Regulation 2832.1*, which states that the written consent of every principal who is an owner of the funds in the account shall be obtained by a real estate broker prior to each disbursement, if such a disbursement will reduce the balance of funds in the account to an amount less than the existing aggregate trust fund liability of the broker to all owners of the funds. Conversely, if the trust account balance is *greater than* the total liability, there is a trust fund overage. An overage is also a violation of the Real Estate Law since non-trust funds may not be commingled in the trust account.

### Maintaining Trust Fund Integrity

A trust fund discrepancy of any kind is a serious violation of the Real Estate Law. Many broker and salesperson licenses have been revoked after a California Bureau of Real Estate (CalBRE) audit disclosed a trust account shortage, even in those cases where the shortage had been corrected prior to the audit. To ensure that the balance of the trust account at all times equals the trust fund liabilities, a broker should take the following precautionary measures:

1) Deposit intact, and in a timely manner, to the trust account all funds that are not forwarded to escrow or to the funds' owner(s), or which are not held uncashed as authorized. This practice, required under *Commissioner's Regulation 2832*, lessens the risk of the funds being lost, misplaced, or otherwise not deposited into the trust account. A licensee is accountable for all trust funds received, whether or not they are deposited. Bureau auditors have seen numerous cases where trust funds received were properly recorded on the books, but were never deposited to the bank.

2) Maintain adequate supporting papers for any disbursement from the trust account, and accurately record the disbursement both in the Bank Account Record and in the Separate Beneficiary Record. The broker must be able to account for all disbursements of trust funds. Any unidentified disbursement will cause a shortage.

3) Disburse funds against a beneficiary's account only when the disbursement will not result in a negative or deficit balance to the account. Many trust fund shortages are caused because the broker makes disbursements for a beneficiary in excess of funds received from or for account of that beneficiary. In effect, the over-disbursements are paid out of funds that belong to other beneficiaries with positive balances. A shortage occurs because the balance of the trust fund bank account, even if it is a positive balance, is less than the broker's liability to those other beneficiaries.

4) Ensure that a check deposited to the trust fund account has cleared before disbursing funds against that check. For example, this applies when a broker, after depositing an earnest money deposit or check for a purchase transaction, has to return the funds to the buyer because the offer is rejected by the seller. A trust fund shortage will result if the broker issues the buyer a trust account check and the buyer's deposit check bounces or for some

reason fails to clear the bank.

5) Keep accurate, current, and complete records of the trust account and the corresponding beneficiary accounts. They are essential to ensure that disbursements are correct.

6) On a monthly basis, reconcile the cash record with the bank statement and with the separate record for each beneficiary or transaction.

**Trust Funds Cannot Be Used as Offset**

Even if a licensee thinks that he or she has money due to himself or herself, either from the licensee's broker or from a third party, the licensee cannot attempt to withhold trust funds as an offset against the alleged debt. Even if the claim by the licensee is valid, trust funds may not be used.

**Example:** The owner of property owed the broker $1,000 and had signed a personal note for this amount. The note was overdue. The owner listed her property with the broker and the broker obtained an offer with a $1,000 deposit which he placed in his trust account. The escrow instructions called for a portion of the $1,000 in order to close. The broker refused to release the money on the grounds that the owner owed him this money and he could use it as an offset. This is not correct. Even though the owner did owe the money and there was no dispute about this indebtedness, it was separate and apart from the trust funds involved in the transaction. The broker should have turned the entire $1,000 over to the escrow as instructed by the seller. To collect on the note, the broker's recourse should be action in the civil courts.

**QUIZZES ARE MANDATORY**

CalBRE regulations now require the submission of chapter quizzes before you can access the final examination. You must log in and submit the chapter quizzes online before you can access the final examination. After submitting the last chapter quiz, you will receive a link to the final examination. You were issued a Personal Identification Number (PIN) and login instructions when you enrolled.

**Chapter One Quiz**

1.     Which of the following is considered trust funds?

       (a)     Cash.
       (b)     A check used as a deposit.
       (c)     A personal note made payable to the seller.
       (d)     All of the above.

2.     A real estate licensee who accepts funds from others in connection with any transaction for which a license is required must place them in:

       (a)     A neutral escrow depository.
       (b)     The hands of the offeree or owner.
       (c)     A trust account maintained by the licensee.
       (d)     Any of the above.

3.     When a real estate licensee accepts trust funds from his or her client in connection with the purchase of real property, the licensee must place these funds into the proper place:

       (a)     By the next working day following receipt.
       (b)     Within three business days following receipt.
       (c)     By midnight of the current business day.
       (d)     By midnight of the third business day following receipt.

4.     Commingling is one of the greatest single causes for loss of license. Which of the following is NOT considered commingling?

       (a)     Holding an uncashed deposit check after acceptance of an offer when directed to do so by the seller.
       (b)     Cashing a deposit check (made out to the broker) and placing the money in the broker's safe, properly identified as being the deposit received from the buyer.
       (c)     Depositing either cash or a check received as a deposit in the broker's personal account to be held until called for by the escrow officer.
       (d)     Depositing money received by the broker's client into the broker's personal account to pay miscellaneous expenses.

5.    Owner Armstrong gave Broker Weeks an exclusive authorization to sell Armstrong's ranch. As part of the agreement, Broker Weeks agreed to advertise the ranch in a catalog that Weeks publishes and distributes to other real estate brokers. For this added service, Armstrong paid Broker Weeks a $ 1,000 fee at the time the listing was signed. Under current real estate law, this payment:

(a)    May be forfeited by owner Armstrong if the owner breaches the listing agreement.
(b)    May be cashed or deposited by Broker Weeks without records that reflect the disposition of such funds.
(c)    May be retained by Broker Weeks in any manner he wishes.
(d)    Must be deposited into a trust account and disbursed only to pay advertising expenditures that are incurred by Broker Weeks in advertising the ranch property.

## Chapter Two

### Important Terms

credits
debits
escrow
payee
payor
reconciliation

### Learning Objectives

Upon completion of Chapter Two, you should be able to complete the following:

- Describe the various types of record keeping systems.
- Define *reconciliation*.
- Describe the reconciliation process.
- Describe trust account withdrawal requirements.

## IV. Trust Fund Accounting Records

A broker cannot manage a trust fund properly without maintaining adequate records to account for trust funds received and disbursed. This is true whether the funds are deposited to the trust fund bank account, sent to escrow, held uncashed, or released to the owner(s) of the funds.

### Record Keeping Systems

There are two types of accounting records that may be used for trust funds: columnar records in the formats prescribed by *Commissioner's Regulations 2831 and 2831.1*, and records other than columnar records that are in accordance with generally accepted accounting practices.

Certain basic characteristics must be present in an accounting system to be acceptable under the Commissioner's Regulations, regardless of the type of system used. To be an acceptable system, the records must show the following:

- All trust fund receipts and disbursements contain pertinent details that are presented in chronological sequence.

- The balance of each trust fund account is calculated based on recorded transactions.

- All receipts and disbursements exclusively reflect each beneficiary's account, and are presented in chronological sequence.

- The balance owed to each beneficiary or for each transaction is present and is based on recorded transactions.

Either manually produced or computerized accounting records are acceptable. The type and form of records that are appropriate to a particular real estate operation as well as the means of processing transactions will depend on factors such as the nature of the business, the number of clients, the volume of transactions, and the types of reports needed. For example, manual recording on columnar records may be satisfactory for a broker who handles a small number of transactions, while a computerized system may be more appropriate and practical for a large property management operation.

### Types of Accounting Records

### Columnar Records

If the broker elects to use a columnar record system, the form of these records are prescribed by *Commissioner's Regulations 2831 and 2831.1*. The necessary forms are published by the California Bureau of Real Estate and can be ordered over the phone. Which form to use depends on whether the trust funds received are deposited to the trust account, forwarded to an escrow depository, or sent directly to the owner of the funds. The following CalBRE forms are available:

1) Columnar Record of All Trust Funds Received and Paid Out (CalBRE form RE 4522).

2) Separate Record for Each Beneficiary or Transaction (CalBRE form RE 4523).

3) Record of All Trust Funds Received—Not Placed in Broker's Trust Account (CalBRE form RE 4524).

4) Separate Record for Each Property Managed (CalBRE form RE 4525).

The first two CalBRE forms (above) are required when trust funds are received and deposited, or supposed to be deposited, to the trust fund bank account. The third form is required when trust funds received are not deposited to the bank account, but are forwarded to escrow or to the owner of the funds. The fourth form involves clients' funds from rental properties that are managed by the broker and may be used instead of CalBRE form RE 4523.

**Columnar Record of All Trust Funds Received and Paid Out (CalBRE Form RE 4522):** This record is used to journalize all trust funds deposited to and disbursed from the trust fund bank account. At a minimum, it must show the following information in columnar form:

- Date that the funds were received.
- Name of payee or payor.
- Amount received.
- Date of deposit.
- Amount paid out.
- Check number and date.
- The daily balance of the bank account.

All transactions that affect the bank account are entered in chronological sequence on this record regardless of payee, payor, or beneficiary. If there is more than one trust fund bank account, a separate record must be maintained for each account, pursuant to *Commissioner's Regulation 2831*.

**Separate Record for Each Beneficiary or Transaction (CalBRE Form RE 4523):** This record is maintained to account for the funds received from, or for the account of, each beneficiary or for each transaction, and deposited to the bank account. With this record, the broker can ascertain which funds are owed to each beneficiary or for each transaction. The record must show in chronological sequence the following information in columnar form:

- Date of deposit.
- Amount of deposit.
- Name of payee or payor.
- Check number.
- Date and amount.
- Balance of the individual account after posting transactions on any date.

A separate record must be maintained for each beneficiary from whom the broker received funds that were deposited to the trust fund bank account. If the broker has more than one trust fund account, each account must have its own set of separate beneficiary records so that they can be reconciled with the individual trust fund bank account record as required under *Commissioner's Regulation 2831.*

**Record of All Trust Funds Received—Not Placed in Broker's Trust Account (CalBRE Form RE 4524)**: This record is used to keep track of funds received and not deposited to a trust fund bank account. A broker is not required to keep records of checks made payable to service providers, including but not limited to escrow, credit and appraisal services, or when the total amount of such checks does not exceed $1,000. However, upon request of the California Bureau of Real Estate or the maker of such checks, a broker shall account for the receipt and distribution of such checks. A broker shall retain, for three years, copies of receipts issued or obtained in connection with the receipt and distribution of such checks. This record must show:

- The date that funds were received.
- The form of payment (check, note, etc.).
- Amount received.
- Description of the property.
- Identity of the person to whom funds were forwarded.
- Date of disposition.

Trust fund receipts are recorded in chronological sequence, while their disposition is recorded in the same line where the corresponding receipt is recorded. Transaction folders that are usually maintained by a broker for each real estate sales transaction, and that show the receipt and disposition of undeposited checks, are not acceptable alternatives to the *Record of Trust Funds Received but Not Deposited to the Trust Fund Bank Account* form.

**Separate Record for Each Property Managed (CalBRE Form RE 4525)**: This record is similar to and serves the same purpose as the *Separate Record for Each Beneficiary or Transaction* form. It does not have to be maintained if the separate record is already used for a property owner's account. The *Separate Record for Each Property Managed* form is useful when the broker wants to show some detailed information about a specific property that the broker is managing.

## DOCUMENTATION REQUIREMENTS
(Source: CalBRE: Trust Funds—A Guide for Real Estate Brokers and Salespersons)

In addition to accounting records, the Bureau of Real Estate requires that the broker maintain copies of all documents prepared or obtained in connection with any real estate transaction handled. The following Table, which is not intended to be all-inclusive, lists the various types of transactions normally handled by a licensee and the corresponding documents necessary to evidence that type of transaction;

| Type of Transaction | Documents Needed |
|---|---|
| 1. Receiving trust funds in the form of:<br>  1. Purchase deposits from buyers<br>  2. Rents and security deposits from tenants<br>  3. Other receipts | Real estate purchase contract and receipt for deposit, signed by the Buyer.<br><br>Collection receipts |
| 2. Depositing trust funds | Bank deposit slips |
| 3. Forwarding buyers' checks to escrow | Receipt from title/escrow company and copy of check |
| 4. Returning buyers' checks | Copy of buyer's check signed and dated by buyer, signifying buyer's receipt of check |
| 5. Disbursing trust funds | Checks issued*<br>Supporting papers for the checks, such as invoices, escrow statements, billings, receipts, etc. |
| 6. Receiving offers and counteroffers from buyers and sellers | Real estate purchase contract and receipt for deposit, signed by respective parties |
| 7. Collecting management fees from the trust fund bank account | Property management agreements between broker and property owners. (Note: If only one trust fund check is issued for management fees charged to various property owners, there should be a schedule or listing on file showing each property and amount charged, and the total amount, which should agree with the check amount.)<br><br>Cancelled checks* |
| 8. Reconciling bank account record with separate beneficiary records<br><br>* Copies of cancelled checks must include | Record of reconciliation |

## Non-Columnar Records

A broker may use trust fund records that are not in the columnar form as prescribed by *Commissioner's Regulations 2831 and 2831.1.* However, such records must be in accordance with generally accepted accounting practices. Whether the records are prepared manually or by computer, they must include at least the following records:

- *Journals* to record, in chronological sequence, the details of all trust fund transactions.

- *Cash ledger* to show the bank balance as affected by the transactions recorded on the journals. The ledger is posted in the form of debits and credits.

- *Beneficiary ledger for each of the beneficiary accounts* to show, in chronological sequence, the transactions that affect each beneficiary's account, as well as the balance of the account.

**Journals:** The journals are a daily chronological record of trust fund receipts and disbursements. A single journal may be used to record both the receipts and the disbursements, or a separate journal may be used for each. To meet minimum record keeping requirements, a journal must show the following:

- Records of all trust fund transactions in chronological sequence.

- Sufficient information to identify the transaction, such as the date, amount received or disbursed, name of or reference to payee or payor, check number or reference to another source document of the transaction, and identification of the beneficiary account that is affected by the transaction.

- Correlation with ledgers. For example, it must show the same figures that are posted, individually or in total, in the cash ledger and in the beneficiary ledgers. The details in the journals must be the basis for posting transactions on the ledgers and arriving at the account balances.

- Total receipts and total disbursements regularly; at least once a month.

**Cash ledger:** The cash ledger shows, usually in summary form, the periodic increases and decreases (credits and debits) in the trust fund bank account and the resulting account balance. It can either be incorporated in the journals or it can stand as a separate record—for example, it can stand as a general ledger account. If a separate record is used, the postings must be based on the transactions that are recorded in the journals. The amounts posted on the ledger must reflect those shown in the journals.

## Recording Process

Keeping complete and accurate trust fund records is easier when the broker regularly follows specific procedures. The following procedures may be useful for developing a record keeping routine:

1.  Record transactions daily in the trust fund bank account and in the separate beneficiary records.

2.  Consistently use the same specific source documents as a basis for recording trust fund receipts and disbursements. (For example, receipts should always be recorded based on the *Real Estate Contract and Receipt for Deposit* form, and disbursements should always be recorded based on the checks issued from the trust account.)

3.  At the time entries are made, calculate the account balances on all applicable records.

4.  Reconcile the records monthly to ensure that transactions are properly recorded on both the bank account record and the applicable subsidiary records.

5.  If more than one trust fund bank account is maintained, keep a separate set of properly labeled columnar records (cash record and beneficiary record) for each account.

## V. Reconciliation of Trust Fund Accounting Records

There is an interrelation among the trust fund bank account record, the separate beneficiary or transaction record, and the bank statement. If there is an entry made on one record, there must also be a corresponding entry on the other records.

To assure the accuracy of the records, they must be reconciled at least once a month. The balance of all separate beneficiary or transaction records that are maintained must be reconciled with the *Record of All Trust Funds Received* form and disbursed at least once a month, except in those months when the bank account did not have any activities. A record of the reconciliation must be maintained, and it must identify the bank account name and number, the date of the reconciliation, the account number or name of the principals or beneficiaries or transactions, and the trust fund liabilities of the broker to each of the principals, beneficiaries, or transactions.

Similar to balancing a check book, *reconciliation* is the process of comparing two or more sets of records to determine whether their balances agree. This process should reveal if the records are completed accurately.

Two reconciliations must be made at the end of each month:

1)  Reconciliation of the bank account record with the separate beneficiary or transaction records.

2)  Reconciliation of the bank account record with the bank statement.

### Reconciling a Bank Account Record with Separate Beneficiary or Transaction Records

This reconciliation, which is required by *Commissioner's Regulation 2831.2*, will substantiate that all transactions entered on the bank account record were posted on the separate beneficiary or transaction records. The balance on the bank account record should equal the total of all beneficiary record balances. Any difference should be located and the records corrected to reflect the correct bank and liabilities balances. *Commissioner's Regulation 2831.2* requires that this reconciliation process be performed monthly, except in those months when there is no activity in the trust fund bank account, and that a record of each reconciliation be maintained. This record should identify the bank account name and number, the date of the reconciliation, the account number or name of the principals or beneficiaries or transactions, and the trust fund liabilities of the broker to each of the principals, beneficiaries, or transactions.

## Reconciling the Bank Account Record with the Bank Statement

The reconciliation of the bank account record with the bank statement will disclose any recording errors by the broker or by the bank. If the balance on the bank account record agrees with the bank statement balance as adjusted for outstanding checks, deposits in transit, and other transactions not yet included in the bank statement, there is more assurance that the balance on the bank account record is correct. Although this reconciliation is not required by the Real Estate Law or the Commissioner's Regulations, it is an essential part of any good accounting system.

## Suggestions for Reconciling Records

Later in this course, there will be a detailed example on how to perform the reconciliation process. However, the following are a few general suggestions:

1) Before performing the reconciliations, record all transactions up to the cut-off date in both the bank account record and the separate beneficiary or transaction records.

2) Use balances as of the same cut-off date for the two records and the bank statement.

3) For the bank account reconciliation, calculate the adjusted bank balance both from the bank statement and from the bank account record. (Trust account audits made by the California Bureau of Real Estate have revealed that licensees commonly make errors by calculating the adjusted bank balance based solely on the bank statement but not on the bank account record. While they may know the correct account balances, they may not realize their records are incomplete or erroneous.)

4) Keep a record of the two reconciliations performed at the end of each month, along with the supporting schedules.

5) Locate any difference among the three sets of accounting records in a timely manner. A difference can be caused by any of the following: Not recording a transaction, recording an incorrect figure, erroneous calculations of entries used to arrive at account balances, missing beneficiary records, and bank errors.

## Trust Account Withdrawals

Withdrawals may be made from a trust fund account of an individual broker only upon the signature of the broker or one or more of the following persons, if specifically authorized in writing by the broker:

1) A salesperson licensed to the broker.

2) A person licensed as a broker who has entered into a written employment agreement, pursuant to Section 2726, with the broker.

3) An unlicensed employee of the broker with fidelity bond coverage at least equal to the maximum amount of the trust funds to which the employee has access at any time.

Withdrawals may be made from the trust fund account of a corporate broker only upon the signature of one of the following:

- An officer through whom the corporation is licensed pursuant to Section 10158 or 10211 of the Code.

- One of the persons enumerated in paragraphs **1)**, **2)**, or **3)**, above, provided that specific authorization in writing is given by the officer through whom the corporation is licensed, and that the officer is an authorized signatory of the trust fund account.

### Contract Copy Required for All Signatories

Under Business and Professions Code Section 10142, any time a licensee prepares or has prepared an agreement that authorizes or employs that licensee to perform any acts for which a real estate license is required, or when the licensee obtains the signature of any person to any contract that pertains to such services or transaction, the licensee must deliver a copy of the agreement to the person signing it at the time the signature is obtained. Examples of such documents are listing agreements, real estate purchase contracts and receipts for deposit forms, addendums to contracts, and property management agreements.

### Broker Supervision

A broker shall exercise reasonable supervision over the activities of his or her salespersons. Reasonable supervision includes, as appropriate, the establishment of policies, rules, and procedures; and systems to review, oversee, inspect, and manage the following:

1) Transactions that require a real estate license.

2) Documents that may have a material effect upon the rights or obligations of a party to the transaction.

3) Filing, storage, and maintenance of such documents.

4) The handling of trust funds.

5) Advertising of any service for which a licensee is required.

6) Familiarizing salespersons with the requirements of federal and state laws regarding the prohibition of discrimination.

**7)** Regular and consistent reports of the licensed activities of a salesperson.

The form and extent of such policies, rules, procedures, and systems shall take into consideration the number of salespersons employed and the number and location of branch offices.

A broker shall establish a system for monitoring compliance with such policies, rules, procedures, and systems. A broker may use the services of brokers and salespersons to assist in administering the provisions of this section, so long as the broker does not relinquish overall responsibility for the supervision of licensed activities, duties, and compensation.

**QUIZZES ARE MANDATORY:** Please log in and submit the chapter quizzes online.

**Chapter Two Quiz**

1.      Which of the following is TRUE regarding trust fund accounting records?

(a)     Only manually produced accounting records are acceptable.
(b)     Only computerized accounting records are acceptable.
(c)     Either manually produced or computerized accounting records are acceptable.
(d)     Only professionally produced accounting records are acceptable.

2.      When broker Smith accepts a deposit check from a client, she forwards the check directly to escrow. According to trust fund record keeping requirements, which of the following is CORRECT?

(a)     It is NOT necessary to keep a record of trust funds received and forwarded to escrow.
(b)     It is NOT necessary to keep a record of trust funds that are not deposited into the trust account.
(c)     A record of trust funds that are received but not deposited to the trust fund bank account must be maintained.
(d)     Transaction folders that are maintained by a broker for each transaction, which shows the receipt and disposition of undeposited checks, are acceptable alternatives to formal records.

3.      To assure the accuracy of trust fund accounting records, they must be reconciled at least:

(a)     Once a month.
(b)     Once every six months.
(c)     Once a year.
(d)     Once every two years.

4.      Which of the following defines the term *reconciliation*?

(a)     Comparing two or more sets of records to determine whether their balances agree.
(b)     Periodically emptying an account to obtain a zero balance.
(c)     Ensuring that debits always equal credits.
(d)     Checking the chronological sequence of trust fund receipts and disbursements.

5.    Funds may be withdrawn from a real estate broker's trust account by an unlicensed
      employee for the following reason:

      (a)    For the payment of miscellaneous expenses.
      (b)    For the payment of general operation expenses, provided that a proper account
             is created and the money is returned.
      (c)    Only for the payment of advertising.
      (d)    When the unlicensed employee has written authorization from the broker and has
             fidelity bond coverage.

## Chapter Three

### Important Terms

administrator
advance fee
commingling
conversion
enjoin
executor
receiver
trustee

### Learning Objectives

Upon completion of Chapter Three, you should be able to complete the following:

- List the most common types of trust fund violations.
- Describe the state's audit & examination process.
- Describe the consequences of trust fund violations.
- Describe the process by which disciplinary action is taken.
- Understand the reasons for which the CalBRE will investigate a licensee.

## VI. Trust Fund Audits and Examinations

The Real Estate Commissioner continuously audits and examines brokers' trust fund records on a state-wide basis. If an audit or examination uncovers trust fund imbalances or if accounting procedures look like they may cause a potential monetary loss situation, even if a loss has not yet occurred, the commissioner can initiate disciplinary proceedings against the licensee.

After giving notice that an audit will take place, the broker must make all books, accounts, and records available for examination by the commissioner or his or her designated representative during regular business hours, and shall, upon the appearance of sufficient cause, be subject to audit without further notice (except that such audit shall not be harassing in nature).

## VII. Consequences of Trust Fund Violations

The potential penalties for a licensee's violation of the laws concerning the handling of trust funds are diverse and may be very costly in terms of money, reputation, and the ability to continue licensed real estate activities. Potential penalties range from possible violations of the Realtors® Code of Ethics and Professional Conduct, to injunctions, receivership, suspension, or revocation of the licensee's real estate license.

Substantial monetary costs to and criminal penalties against the violator, in addition to the loss of the violator's ability to earn income, may also occur. Potential monetary costs may include the costs of audits, court fees, attorney fees, and treble damages. In addition, a violator of trust fund rules may be criminally liable for embezzlement under *California Penal Code Sections 506 and 506(a)*. Needless to say, the improper handling and/or accountability of trust funds could destroy a licensee's real estate career.

## Ethics and Professional Conduct

In order to enhance the professionalism of the California real estate industry, and maximize protection for members of the public who deal with real estate licensees, whatever their area of practice, the following standards of professional conduct and business practices are adopted:

### *Unlawful Conduct in Sale, Lease, and Exchange Transactions*

Knowingly making a false or misleading representation to the seller of real property as to the form, amount, and/or treatment of a deposit toward the purchase of the property made by an offeror.

### *Unlawful Conduct when Soliciting, Negotiating, or Arranging a Loan Secured by Real Property or the Sale of a Promissory Note Secured by Real Property*

Knowingly making a false or misleading representation to a lender or assignee/endorsee of a lender of a loan, that is secured directly or collaterally by a lien on real property, about the amount and treatment of loan payments, including loan payoffs, and the failure to account to the lender or assignee/endorsee of a lender as to the disposition of such payments. When acting as a licensee in a transaction for the purpose of obtaining a loan, and in receipt of an advance fee from the borrower for this purpose, the failure to account to the borrower for the disposition of the *advance fee*.

### *Business and Professions Code Sections*

**B&P Code Section 10081.5: Trust Fund Account Violations; Injunctive Relief; Receiver:**

Whenever the commissioner believes (from evidence) that any real estate licensee has violated or is about to violate the provisions of Section 10145, the commissioner may bring an action in the name of the people of the State of California, in the superior court of the State of California, to enjoin the licensee from continuing the violation or engaging herein or doing any act or acts in furtherance thereof.

In the event that the commissioner has conducted an audit which reflects commingling or conversion of trust funds in excess of ten thousand dollars ($10,000), the court may enter an order that restrains the licensee from doing any act or acts in furtherance thereof, and from further exercising the privileges of his or her license pending further order of the court, provided that a hearing shall be held on the order within five days after the date thereof.

After such hearing in the manner provided by law, an order may be entered to appoint a receiver, or such other order as the court may deem proper. The order to appoint the receiver shall specify the source of the funds from which the fees of the receiver and the costs of administering the receivership are to be paid. Unless provided for in the order, the commissioner shall not be liable for payment of the fees or costs.

A receiver who is appointed by the court pursuant to this section may, with the approval of the court, exercise all of the powers of the licensee or its officers, directors, partners, trustees, or persons who exercise similar powers, and perform similar duties, including the filing of a petition for bankruptcy of the licensee.

**B&P Code Section 10148: Retention of Documents; Inspection and Audit; Costs of Audit; Recovery; and Determination of Cost:**

1) A licensed real estate broker shall retain, for three years, copies of all listings, deposit receipts, cancelled checks, trust records, and other documents executed by the broker or obtained by the broker in connection with any transactions for which a real estate broker license is required. The retention period shall run from the date of the closing of the transaction, or from the date of the listing if the transaction is not consummated. After notice is made, the books, accounts, and records shall be made available for examination, inspection, and copying by the commissioner or his or her designated representative during regular business hours, and shall, upon the appearance of sufficient cause, be subject to an audit without further notice, except that the audit shall not be harassing in nature.

2) The commissioner shall charge the real estate broker for the cost of an audit, if prior to the audit the commissioner has found, in a final desist and refrain order issued under Section 10086 or in a final decision following a disciplinary hearing, that the broker has violated the law.

3) If the broker fails to pay for the cost of an audit as described in subdivision (b) within 60 days of mailing a notice of billing, the commissioner may suspend or revoke the broker's license or deny the renewal of the broker's license. The suspension or denial shall remain in effect until the cost is paid or until the broker's right to renew his or her license has expired.

The commissioner may maintain an action for the recovery of the cost in any court of competent jurisdiction. In determining the cost incurred by the commissioner for an audit, the commissioner may use the estimated average hourly cost for all persons performing audits of real estate brokers.

### *Penal Code Sections*

### Section 506: Persons Controlling or Entrusted With Property of Another:

Every trustee, banker, merchant, broker, attorney, agent, assignee in trust, executor, administrator, collector, or person otherwise entrusted with or having in his or her control property for the use of any other person, who fraudulently appropriates it to any use or purpose not in the due and lawful execution of his or her trust, or secretes it with a fraudulent intent to appropriate it to such use or purpose, and any contractor who appropriates money paid to him or her for any use or purpose, other than for that which the contractor received it, is guilty of embezzlement.

### Section 506(a): Collector of Accounts or Debts; Definition; Prosecution and Punishment:

Any person who acts as a collector, or who acts in any capacity in or about a business that is conducted for the collection of accounts or debts owing by another person, and who violates Section 506 of the Penal Code, shall be deemed to be an agent or person as defined in Section 506, and subject for a violation of Section 506, to be prosecuted, tried, and punished in accordance therewith and within the law. *Collector* means every person who collects, or who has in his or her possession, or under his or her control, property or money for the use of any other person, and who fraudulently misappropriates that property or money.

### Knowing How to Lose Your License May Help You Keep It

Over the last several years, the California Bureau of Real Estate has disciplined large numbers of licensees for violation of the Real Estate Law. The most common violation of the Commissioner's Regulations involves trust fund accounts and trust fund records.

The first step in avoiding disciplinary action by the California Bureau of Real Estate is to understand its disciplinary procedures when an action is necessary.

### *Basis for Investigation*

The CalBRE may investigate a licensee based upon a complaint filed with the CalBRE or upon its own motion, if it receives information that an investigation is warranted. In addition, the CalBRE audits real estate brokers who are selected randomly under the Bureau's routine audit program.

The basic process through which disciplinary action is taken by the CalBRE is as follows:

1) **The CalBRE conducts an audit or an investigation of the licensee's activities or alleged misconduct.** During this first step, the CalBRE staff obtains statements from the complaining party/parties, if any, and witnesses, if any.

2) **If warranted, an accusation is filed against the licensee.** An accusation is a written statement of charges that sets forth the acts or omissions with which the licensee is being charged. The licensee is referred to as the *respondent* in an accusation. The accusation will usually be accompanied by a form entitled *Notice of Defense*. Additionally, the CalBRE may include any other information it deems relevant. A Notice of Defense is a document that the respondent files with the CalBRE if the respondent wishes to do one of the following:
   a) Request a hearing.
   b) Challenge the jurisdiction of the CalBRE to proceed upon the charges.
   c) Object to the accusation on the grounds that it is indefinite or uncertain.
   d) Admit to the accusation in whole or in part.
   e) Present a defense.
   f) Object to the accusation on the grounds that compliance with the cited regulation would result in the material violation of another regulation. Service of the accusation documents may be by any means. However, no adverse action may be taken against a licensee unless the licensee was either personally served or served by registered mail to the latest address on file with the CalBRE, or if the licensee returned a Notice of Defense.

Filing a Notice of Defense, within 15 days after service of the accusation, entitles the licensee to a hearing on the merits of the charges. Further, the Notice of Defense acts as a specific denial of all parts of the accusation that are not specifically admitted. A licensee who fails to file a Notice of Defense within 15 days after service of the accusation waives his or her right to a hearing. The Notice of Defense shall be in writing, signed by or on behalf of the respondent, and contain the respondent's mailing address.

3) **A hearing is held before an Administrative Law Judge (ALJ), in which testimony is presented under oath and evidence is presented.** Prior to the hearing, the parties have the right to gather information by requesting and obtaining the names and addresses of all witnesses, whether or not they are intended to be called to testify. Further, the parties are entitled to inspect and copy any of the following:
   a) Statements of complaining persons.
   b) Statements of parties to the proceeding or witnesses.
   c) All writings that are relevant and admissible as evidence.
   d) Investigative reports.

Depending upon the residence of the respondent, the hearing will generally be conducted in the county where the transaction took place. The hearing may also be conducted at any other place within the state, upon the consent of all parties.

All parties will receive a notice of hearing at least 10 days prior to the hearing date. The hearing date cannot be held prior to the expiration of the time within which the respondent is entitled to file a Notice of Defense.

Although formal rules of evidence need not be strictly adhered to by the parties or the ALJ, subpoenas may be issued for witnesses to appear or documents to be produced during the hearing.

Also, the licensee is entitled to be represented by counsel at the hearing.

4) **A proposed decision is made by the ALJ.** The ALJ must prepare a proposed decision within 30 days after the case has been submitted.

5) **The commissioner either adopts the proposed decision, reduces the penalty imposed by the proposed decision, or rejects the proposed decision.** If rejected, the commissioner decides the case upon the record, including the hearing transcript, and then issues a decision. The proposed decision becomes effective 30 days after it is delivered or mailed to the respondent, or sooner if the CalBRE orders an earlier effective date.

6) **The licensee either accepts the decision or seeks a reconsideration or judicial review of the decision.** The licensee must file a petition for reconsideration before the effective date of the proposed decision.

7) **The charges are either dismissed or the licensee's license is revoked, suspended, or restricted.** One year after the revocation, the licensee may petition for reinstatement.

## VIII. Sample Transactions to Explain the Use of Records

In order to demonstrate the trust fund record keeping requirements discussed in this course, we present simulated trust fund transactions for a typical real estate office over a 30-day period. The following sample transactions illustrate a system that uses columnar records. However, as previously discussed, the broker may use other types of records as long as they meet generally accepted accounting standards of practice.

**Situation:** James Adams, a real estate broker, owns and operates a small one-man real estate office that specializes in residential sales and property management. Broker Adams has one trust fund bank account. This example reflects the trust account activity for this office, for the month of September 1998.

| 1998 | Transactions |
|------|--------------|
| September 1 | Opened a trust account with First County Bank, and deposited $100 of the broker's own money to cover bank service charges. |
| September 1 | Entered into agreements to manage the following rental properties: |

| Address | Owner's Name | Number of Units |
|---------|--------------|-----------------|
| 1538 South Ave. Anycity, CA | T. Eddie | 1 |
| 3490 Tower St. Anycity, CA | L. Stewart | 4 |
| 9152 High Way Anycity, CA | W. Allen | 4 |
| 2351-2353 Kingston Wy. Anycity, CA | S. Manly | 2 |
| 7365 Meadow Cir. Anycity, CA | J. Bird | 1 |

| 1998 | Transactions |
|------|--------------|
| September 2 | Received a $2,000 check payable to the broker from Mr. and Mrs. Dennis White as deposit for their offer to buy a house on 625 Lake Drive, Anycity, CA, which is owned by Mr. and Mrs. Richard J. Jensen. Buyer's offer instructed broker to hold the check uncashed until their offer is accepted by the Jensens. |
| September 3 | Deposited the following rents received from tenants of managed properties: |

| Property | Tenant's Name | Rent Received |
|----------|---------------|---------------|
| 1538 South Ave. | B. Hamms | $600 |
| 3490 Tower St., Unit 1 | R. Robertson | $350 |
| 2351 Kingston Way | I. Warren | $450 |
| | **TOTAL:** | **$1,400** |

| 1998 | Transactions |
|------|--------------|
| September 4 | Received $750 from T. Sundance, which represents rent of $500 for September 5 to 30, and a $250 security deposit, for 7365 Meadow Circle. |
| September 5 | Was notified by the Jensens that they accepted the offer from the Whites on their property. |
| September 7 | Deposited the $2,000 check from Mr. and Mrs. White. |
| September 8 | Obtained an exclusive listing to sell a six-plex on 915 Galaxy St., Anycity, CA, owned by R. Jays. |
| September 9 | Received $1,000 from W. Allen, owner of 9152 High Way, to cover anticipated expenses for the property. Amount was deposited the same day. |

| September 10 | Issued the following checks to pay for various expenses connected with the managed properties: | | | |
|---|---|---|---|---|
| | Check No. | Payee | Purpose | Amount |
| | 1001 | ABC Mortgage Co. | Mortgage pymt. for 1538 South Ave. | $450 |
| | 1002 | Anycity Treasury | Utilities for 1538 South Ave. | 35 |
| | 1003 | Professional Cleaners | Cleaning for 3490 Tower St., Unit 1 | 55 |
| | 1004 | Mr. Handyman | Minor Repairs on 2351 Kingston Way | 25 |
| | | | **TOTAL:** | **$565** |
| September 14 | Received a $4,000 check from B. Sun, payable to Title Escrow Company, with an offer to buy the 915 Galaxy St. property. | | | |
| September 15 | Received R. Jays' acceptance of the buyer's offer on 915 Galaxy Street. | | | |
| September 16 | Delivered the $4,000 check from B. Sun to Title Escrow Company. | | | |
| September 18 | Issued check number 1005 for $2,000 to First Title Co. for account of Mr. and Mrs. White, buyers of the 625 Lake Drive property. | | | |
| September 23 | Received an offer and a $3,000 check as deposit from R. Olive to buy a single family house on 31009 Technology Street, owned by T. Evans. | | | |
| September 25 | Returned R. Olive's check after T. Evans rejected the offer. | | | |

| September 26 | Charged property management fees to the following accounts and issued check number 1006 for $330 payable to the broker: | |
|---|---|---|
| | Property Owner | Management Fee |
| | T. Eddie | $45 |
| | L. Stewart | 100 |
| | W. Allen | 80 |
| | S. Manly | 60 |
| | J. Bird | 45 |
| | **TOTAL:** | **$330** |

| September 30 | Sent statement of account to each owner of the managed properties. |
|---|---|

## Background Information

James Adams keeps four types of columnar records:

1) **Record of All Trust Funds Received and Paid Out:** Trust Fund Bank Account (hereinafter referred to as *Bank Account Record*). This record is required under *Commissioner's Regulation 2831* for each bank account.

2) **Record of All Trust Funds Received—Not Placed in Broker's Trust Account** (hereinafter referred to as *Record of Undeposited Receipts*): This is required under *Commissioner's Regulations 2831*.

3) **Separate Record for Each Beneficiary or Transaction** (hereinafter referred to as *Separate Beneficiary Record*). This is required under *Commissioner's Regulation 2831.1*.

4) **Separate Record for Each Property Managed** (hereinafter referred to as *Separate Property Record*). This serves the same purpose as the Separate Beneficiary Record.

To explain the recording process, listed below are the entries made on the books by James Adams as well as the documents prepared or obtained as support for each transaction.

**Note:** Each entry to any record shows all the pertinent information of the transaction such as the date, name of payee, name of payor, amount, check number, etc. The daily bank balance is computed and posted on the Bank Account Record after recording transactions. The balance owing to the client is computed and posted on the Beneficiary Record or Separate Property Record, after posting transactions. Any entry made on the Bank Account Record has a corresponding entry on a Beneficiary Record or Separate Property Record, after posting transactions. Any entry made on the Bank Account Record has a corresponding entry on a Beneficiary Record or a Separate Property Record, and vice versa. All records, except the Record of Undeposited Receipts, show entries in chronological sequence regardless of transaction type. The Record of Undeposited Receipts shows the disposition of a trust fund in the same line in which the receipt is entered, rather than in chronological sequence.

*Step-By-Step Trust Account Entries*

| Transaction Date | Documentation | Entries |
|---|---|---|
| September 1 | Deposit slip prepared by broker. | Record the deposit on the following:<br><br>1) The Bank Account Record. Balance is $100.<br><br>2) A newly prepared Separate Beneficiary Record for James Adams. Balance is $100. |
| September 1 | Management agreements signed by property owners and broker. | No entries are needed since there was no receipt nor disbursement of trust funds. |
| September 2 | Real Estate Purchase Contract and Receipt for Deposit signed by Mr. and Mrs. White.<br>Collection receipt No. 1 issued to the Whites. | Entered transaction on the Record of Undeposited Receipts.<br><br>Necessary since the check was deposited. |
| September 3 | Collection receipts nos. 2, 3, and 4 issued to B. Hamms, R. Robertson, and I. Warren, respectively. | Record the $1,400 receipt on:<br><br>1) The Bank Account Record. New balance is $1,500.<br><br>2) Newly prepared Separate Beneficiary Records for:<br><br>• T. Eddie: balance is $600<br><br>• L. Stewart: balance is $350<br><br>• S. Manly: balance is $450 |

| September 4 | Collection receipt No. 5 issued to T. Sundance.<br><br>Receipt showed that $500 of the $750 was for rent and the other $250 was for security deposit. | Record the $750 receipt on:<br><br>1) The Bank Account Record. New balance is $2,250.<br><br>2) Separate Beneficiary Records:<br><br>• J. Bird: Sundance's Security Deposit, balance is $250.<br><br>• J. Bird: Balance is $500.<br><br>(Since security deposits will be accounted to the tenant in the future, James Adams keeps a separate record for deposits. Total liability to the owner is the sum of the two records—one for security deposits, and the other for rents and other transactions.) |
| --- | --- | --- |
| September 5 | Real Estate Purchase contract and Receipt for Deposit signed by Mr. White. | No entries were made since no trust funds were received or disbursed. |
| September 7 | Deposit receipt prepared by broker. | Record $2,000 deposit on:<br><br>1) The Bank Account Record. New balance is $4,250.<br><br>2) A newly prepared Separate Beneficiary Record—Mr. And Mrs. White, and Mr. and Mrs. Jensen. Account balance is $2,000.<br><br>3) Record of Undeposited Receipts. (Show the disposition of check previously entered on record.) |
| September 8 | Exclusive Listing Agreement signed by sellers and broker. | No entries needed. |
| September 9 | Collection receipt No. 6 issued to W. Allen. | Record receipt on:<br><br>1) The Bank Account Record. New balance is $5,250.<br><br>2) A newly prepared Separate Beneficiary Record—W. Allen. Balance is $1,000. |

| September 10 | Checks issued by broker. Supporting papers for each check. | Record disbursements on: <br> 1) The Bank Account Record. New balance is $4,685. <br> 2) Separate Beneficiary Records: <br> • T. Eddie: New balance is $115. <br> • L. Stewart: New balance is $295. <br> • S. Manly: New balance is $425. |
| --- | --- | --- |
| September 14 | Real Estate Purchase Contract and Receipt for Deposit signed by B. Sun. | Record receipt on the Record of Undeposited Receipts. |
| September 15 | Real Estate Purchase Contract and Receipt for Deposit. | No entry is needed since there was no receipt or disbursement of funds. |
| September 16 | Receipt issued by Title Escrow Company. | Note disposition of check on the Record of Undeposited Receipts. |
| September 18 | Check issued by broker. Receipt issued by First Title Company. | Record disbursements on the: <br> 1) Bank Account Record. New balance is $2,685. <br> 2) Separate Beneficiary Record. Mr. and Mrs. White/Mr. and Mrs. Jensen. New balance is $0. |
| September 23 | Real Estate Purchase Contract and receipt for Deposit signed by R. Olive. | Record details of receipt on the Record of Undeposited Receipts. |
| September 25 | Real Estate Purchase Contract and Receipt for Deposit rejected by T. Evans. | Post the return of check to R. Olive on the Record of Undeposited Receipts. |
| September 30 | List showing the breakdown of the check amount showing the charge to each. <br> (NOTE: A list is necessary as support for a check disbursement chargeable to a number of beneficiaries; posting the entries on the separate records without such a list is not sufficient.) | Record disbursement on the: <br> 1) Bank Account record owner. New Balance is $2,355. <br> 2) Separate Beneficiary Records for: <br><br> Owners     New Balance <br> T. Eddie     $70 <br> L. Stewart    $195 <br> W. Allen     $920 <br> S. Manly    $365 <br> J. Bird      $455 |

After recording the daily transactions, the next step in the trust fund accounting process is to reconcile the records at the end of the month. James Adams will now prepare a reconciliation schedule. Adams will compare the bank balance on the Bank Account Record with the bank statement balance from the bank statement (this is the bank reconciliation), and also with the total of the Separate Beneficiary Records balances (this is the control account reconciliation).

**QUIZZES ARE MANDATORY:** Please log in and submit the chapter quizzes online.

**Chapter Three Quiz**

1.    In an effort to enforce trust fund handling requirements, the real estate commissioner continuously:

    (a)    Sponsors lectures on trust fund handling throughout the state.
    (b)    Audits and examines brokers' trust fund records on a statewide basis.
    (c)    Calls brokers to keep them up to date on trust fund handling requirements.
    (d)    Continuously changes the trust fund handling laws to keep brokers on their toes.

2.    The potential penalties for a licensee's violation of the laws that concern the handling of trust funds include:

    (a)    Injunctions.
    (b)    Suspension of license.
    (c)    Revocation of license.
    (d)    All of the above.

3.    In the event that the commissioner has conducted an audit that reflects commingling or conversion of trust funds in excess of ten thousand dollars, the court may:

    (a)    Imprison the licensee for not more than thirty (30) days.
    (b)    Automatically revoke the violator's license without a formal hearing.
    (c)    Restrain the licensee from doing business pending a formal hearing.
    (d)    Confiscate any and all commissions earned by that licensee during the preceding calendar year.

4.    The most common violation of the Commissioner's Regulations concern:

    (a)    Fair housing violations.
    (b)    Trust fund accounts and records.
    (c)    Ethics and professional conduct.
    (d)    Agency disclosure.

5.    The process through which disciplinary action is taken by the California Bureau of Real Estate starts with a complaint, followed by a(n):

    (a)    Formal hearing to examine evidence and hear testimony.
    (b)    Decision to impose a penalty or dismiss the charges.
    (c)    Appeal by the accused licensee to have the charges dropped.
    (d)    Investigation of the licensee's activities or alleged misconduct.

# Notes

# Management & Supervision

by Karen Bohler

3 Hours of Continuing Education in Real Estate for
Salesperson and Broker License Renewal

**LUMBLEAU REAL ESTATE SCHOOL**

23805 Hawthorne Blvd.
Torrance, CA 90505

**DISCLAIMERS**

Although every effort has been made to provide accurate and current information in this text, the ideas, suggestions, general principles, and conclusions presented in this text are subject to local, state, and federal laws and regulations, court cases, and any revisions of the same. The author and/or publisher is not engaged in rendering legal, tax, or other professional services. The reader is thus urged to consult with his or her employing broker and/or seek legal counsel regarding any points of law. This publication should not be used as a substitute for competent legal advice.

This course is approved for continuing education credit by the California Bureau of Real Estate. However, this approval does not constitute an endorsement of the views or opinions that are expressed by the course sponsor, instructor, authors, or lecturers.

# Table of Contents

## Chapter One:  Broker Compliance

### Learning Objectives

Upon completion of Chapter One, you should be able to complete the following:

- Explain the administrative requirement for the broker to establish brokerage policies.
- Describe why a broker must monitor compliance with the brokerage policies.
- Explain the necessity to provide the rationale for the brokerage policies when the brokerage policies are established.
- Establish policies and procedures for your brokerage, using the sample policies as a guide.
- Understand the purpose of the Broker Compliance Evaluation Manual.
- Explain the legal reasons for each of the questions in the General Business Practices section of the Broker Compliance Evaluation Manual.
- Explain each question in the Broker Self-Evaluation Compliance Checklist.

**The Administrative Requirement for the Broker to Monitor Compliance with Policies**

According to the Regulations of the Real Estate Commissioner[1], a broker is required to establish a system for monitoring compliance with such policies, rules, procedures and systems. A broker may use the services of brokers and salespersons to assist in administering the provisions of [the policies] so long as the broker does not relinquish overall responsibility for supervision of the acts of salespersons licensed to the broker.

**Policies and Procedures**

The Brokerage Policies and Procedures documentation (whether electronically delivered or delivered in hard copy form) is the broker's best and most useful tool for complying with brokerage personnel. Getting the personnel to read the policies might be prove to be difficult, but training the brokerage personnel about the contents of the documentation, and holding the agents accountable for violating the policies is very possible.

Regular, structured (but short) training sessions regarding brokerage policies are the key. Also, the broker should have a means of procuring from all brokerage personnel, a commitment to adhere to the policies.

> **NOTE:** The commitment from the brokerage personnel could be part of the Broker-Salesman Relationship Agreement, which is required by the Regulations of the Real Estate Commissioner, Title 10, Chapter 6, Article 4, Regulation 2726.

The Policies and Procedures documentation provides uniformity and continuity in all brokerage business related matters. If exceptional circumstances arise, all licensees and employees of the brokerage should first refer to the documentation. This is especially important in large real estate firms, when the broker is very busy with supervisory duties. If the documentation does not provide a satisfactory answer, the licensee or employee should confer with the broker for appropriate guidance.

**Document the Policy and the Reason for the Policy**

When the broker prepares the Policies and Procedures documentation, he/she should make certain that the brokerage policies as well as the reasoning behind each policy are well-documented. In the event of a lawsuit or disciplinary action, well-documented policies will go a long way toward proving the broker's intent to reasonably supervise those for whom he/she is responsible.

**A Living Document**

The Policies and Procedures documentation is a living document, which means it is never complete; and it is never finished. It should regularly be revised to accommodate new relevant issues. Maintenance and updates to the documentation are the responsibility of the broker, as is the communication of the updates to all brokerage personnel.

---

[1] Regulations of the Real Estate Commissioner (As Contained in the California Real Estate Code): Title 10, Chapter 6, Article 4, Regulation 2725. http://www.bre.ca.gov/files/pdf/relaw/2015/regs.pdf

## Broker Compliance Evaluation Manual

In August of 2010, the California Bureau of Real Estate (CalBRE) created and published the Broker Compliance Evaluation Manual, which is downloadable from the CalBRE website: http://www.calbre.ca.gov/files/pdf/brkrcomp.pdf. The manual was not designed to encompass all of the broker's obligations and responsibilities. It was designed to assist the real estate broker in ascertaining the brokerage compliance with real estate regulations. It contains many of the questions that a broker would be asked if he/she were visited by a Bureau of Real Estate representative. This manual can also be used in conjunction with CalBRE form RE540.[2]

The manual is comprised of several evaluative questions, and is divided into two sections:

- Section 1: General Business Practices; and
- Section 2: Trust Fund Handling (discussed in section titled Trust Fund Handling on page 38).

## The General Practices Section

### Are the broker's salespersons properly licensed?

All persons performing activities requiring a real estate license for compensation must hold a valid real estate license. It is unlawful for any broker to employ or compensate, directly or indirectly, any person for performing licensed activity unless that person is a licensed broker, or a salesperson licensed to the broker. A salesperson may not accept compensation for licensed activity nor pay compensation for licensed activity except through the broker under whom he/she is at the time licensed.[3]

#### Broker Should Monitor Licenses

The broker should have some procedure in place to monitor the expiration dates of the licenses of his/her salespersons. Real Estate broker and salesperson licenses expire four years after issuance. However, under certain conditions, licensees may be suspended during the license term for back child support payments, recovery fund payouts, or be barred from holding any position of employment in the real estate industry.

With this in mind, brokers should periodically check the license status of their salespersons and broker associates on the Bureau of Real Estate's website. The broker must also retain possession of the licenses of his/her salespersons while in the broker's employ.

#### Hiring (or Employing) Disbarred Licensees[4]

Disbarred licensees cannot be hired in any real estate capacity. CalBRE maintains a list of licensees; for whom a Notice of Intention and Bar Order or a Decision to disbar has been filed. Therefore, before hiring any real estate licensee, the broker should check the CalBRE list at

---

[2] Downloadable from CalBRE website at http://www.calbre.ca.gov/files/pdf/forms/re540.pdf.
[3] *California Business and Professions Code* Section 10137.
[4] *California Business and Professions Code* Section 10087.

http://www.dre.ca.gov/Licensees/BarOrders.asp.  The persons or entities on the list are barred from:

- Holding any position of employment, management, or control in a real estate business,
- Participating in any business activity of a real estate salesperson or a real estate broker,
- Engaging in any real estate related business activity on the premises where a real estate salesperson or real estate broker is conducting business, and
- Participating in any real estate related business activity of a finance lender, residential mortgage lender, bank credit union, escrow company, Title Company, or underwritten title company for a period of thirty-six (36) months from the effective date of the Bar Order.

### Expired Licenses

Once the license has expired, no licensed activity can be performed by the licensee until the license has been renewed. The late renewal period (often referred to as the "grace" period) simply allows the licensee to renew on a late basis without retaking the examination; it does not allow the licensee to conduct licensed activity during the late renewal period.

### Unlicensed Activity Violations (A word from CalBRE)

The real estate licensing requirement is the cornerstone to providing consumer protection to the purchasers of real property and those persons dealing with real estate licensees. Therefore, the enforcement of these requirements must be vigorous. Real estate brokers who pay unlicensed individuals for performing acts that require a real estate license will be disciplined and held accountable to pay appropriate fines and penalties.

Real estate brokers should establish systems within their offices to ensure that salespersons working for them complete their continuing education, renew their licenses on time, and do not continue to work while holding an expired license.

### Salesperson Accepting Compensation for Licensed Activity

A salesperson may not accept compensation for licensed activity nor pay compensation for licensed activity except through the broker under whom he/she is at the time licensed.[5]

### Delivering Compensation for Licensed Activity to Unlicensed Person

It is a **misdemeanor**, punishable by a fine of $100 for each offense, for any person, whether **obligor**, escrow holder or otherwise, to pay or deliver to compensation to any person other than

---

[5] *California Business and Professions Code* Section 10137.

a person who holds a valid broker's license. If the broker has issued written instructions to direct or deliver payment to a licensed individual, such payment or delivery is not a violation.[6]

> **NOTE:** The above paragraph is extremely important, because escrow companies who write and deliver commission checks to the brokerage might be liable for misdemeanor charges if the checks happen to be written to a person with an expired or suspended license.

### Does the broker notify the Bureau of Real Estate upon the hiring and termination?

Whenever a real estate salesperson enters the employ of a broker, the broker shall notify the commissioner of that fact within five days.[7] This notification can be given to the commissioner on a Salesperson Change Application (form RE214[8]), or entered into the CalBRE public information system through the *eLicensing* system at http://calbre.ca.gov.

A broker may give notice to the commissioner of the termination of a broker/salesperson relationship using the same form (RE214) or through the eLicensing system. The notice to the commissioner of the termination must be given within ten days[9] of the termination.

### Does the broker have a written broker-salesperson agreement with each salesperson?

Every broker must have a written agreement with each of his/her salespersons, whether licensed as a salesperson or as a broker under a broker-salesperson arrangement. The agreement shall be dated and signed by the parties and shall cover material aspects of the relationship between the parties, including supervision of licensed activities, duties and **compensation**.[10]

### Is the broker properly supervising?

A broker shall exercise reasonable supervision over the activities of his or her salespersons. Reasonable supervision includes, as appropriate, the establishment of policies, rules, procedures and systems to review, oversee, inspect and manage:

- Transactions requiring a real estate license.
- Documents which may have a material effect upon the rights or obligations of a party to the transaction.
- Filing, storage and maintenance of such documents.
- The handling of trust funds.
- Advertising of any service for which a license is required.
- Familiarizing salespersons with the requirements of federal and state laws relating to the prohibition of discrimination.

---

[6] *California Business and Professions Code* Section 10137.

[7] Regulations of the Real Estate Commissioner (As Contained in the California Real Estate Code): Title 10, Chapter 6, Article 4, Regulation 2710. http://www.calbre.ca.gov/files/pdf/relaw/2015/regs.pdf

[8] Downloadable from CalBRE website at http://www.calbre.ca.gov/files/pdf/forms/re214.pdf.

[9] Regulations of the Real Estate Commissioner (As Contained in the California Real Estate Code): Title 10, Chapter 6, Article 4, Regulation 2752.

[10] Regulations of the Real Estate Commissioner (As Contained in the California Real Estate Code): Title 10, Chapter 6, Article 4, Regulation 2726.

- Regular and consistent reports of licensed activities of salespersons.

The form and extent of the broker's policies, rules, procedures and systems must take into consideration the number of salespersons employed and the number and location of branch offices.[11] A broker shall establish a system for monitoring compliance with such policies, rules, procedures and systems.

> **NOTE:** The broker's primary concern when inspecting documents is ensure that the items, terms and warranties listed in the contract are legitimate and true.

### The Broker must not Relinquish Overall Responsibility for Supervision

A broker may use the services of brokers and salespersons to assist in administering the policies so long as the broker does not relinquish overall responsibility for supervision of the acts of salespersons licensed to the broker.[12] (More on this topic in *Supervision of all transactions involving a real estate licensee* on page 17)

## Does the broker retain copies of all documents?

A licensed broker must retain for three years, copies of all listings, deposit receipts, canceled checks, trust account records, and other documents executed by him or her or obtained by him or her in connection with any transaction for which a broker's license is required. (More on this topic in *Chapter Three: Records Management and Trust Fund Handling,* on page 35.) The retention period runs from the date of the closing of the transaction or from the date of the listing if the transaction is not consummated.

### Documents must be Available upon CalBRE Request

After reasonable notice, the books, accounts and records shall be made available for audit, examination, inspection and copying by a CalBRE representative during regular business hours.[13]

## Do the documents disclose the negotiability of commissions?

The broker must make certain that his/her agreements and forms are not preprinted with any amount or rate of compensation.[14] To pre-print the commission rate is to effectively state that the commission rate is fixed and not negotiable.

Any printed or form agreement which initially establishes, or is intended to establish, or alters the terms of any agreement which previously established a right to compensation to be paid to a licensee for the sale of residential real property containing not more than four residential units, or for the sale

---

[11] Regulations of the Real Estate Commissioner (As Contained in the California Real Estate Code): Title 10, Chapter 6, Article 4, Regulation 2725.  http://www.calbre.ca.gov/files/pdf/relaw/2015/regs.pdf

[12] Regulations of the Real Estate Commissioner (As Contained in the California Real Estate Code): Title 10, Chapter 6, Article 4, Regulation 2725(g).

[13] *California Business and Professions Code* Section 10148.

[14] *California Business and Professions Code* Section 10147.

of a mobile home, must contain the following statement in not less than 10-point boldface type immediately preceding any provision of such agreement relating to compensation of the licensee:

> **NOTICE: The amount or rate of real estate commissions is not fixed by law. They are set by each broker individually and may be negotiable between the seller and broker.**

> **NOTE:** As used above, "alters the terms of any agreement which previously established a right to compensation" means an increase in the rate of compensation, or the amount of compensation if initially established as a flat fee, from the agreement which previously established a right to compensation.

### Does the broker have a license for each business location?

A broker is authorized to conduct business only at the address listed on his/her license. If the broker maintains more than one place of business within the State, he/she must apply for and procure an additional license for each **branch office** so maintained. The application for a branch office license must state the name of the person and the location of the place or places of business for which the license is desired.[15]

### Is the broker using an unlicensed fictitious name?

A broker must not use a fictitious name in the conduct of any activity requiring a real estate license unless the broker first obtains a license bearing the fictitious name. (A fictitious business name is frequently referred to as a "dba" - doing business as.)

> **NICKNAMES:** Where a licensee is a natural person, the use of a nickname in place of his or her legal given name (first name) shall not constitute a fictitious name for purposes of this section, provided that where the nickname is used, the licensee also uses his or her surname (last name) as it appears on their real estate license, and includes their real estate license identification number as required by Section 10140.6 of the Code.

To obtain a license bearing a fictitious name,[16] the broker must apply to the Department and attach a certified copy of the fictitious business name statement filed with the county clerk.

The Real Estate Commissioner may refuse to issue a license bearing a fictitious name to a broker if the fictitious name:

- Is misleading or would constitute false advertising

---

[15] California Business and Professions Code Section 10163.

[16] According to CalBRE regulations, a name is fictitious when it does not contain the surname of the individual conducting the business, or when it implies that there is more than one owner. A name that suggests the existence of additional owners is one that includes such words as "Company," "& Company," "& Son," "& Sons," "& Associates," "Brothers," "Team," and the like. A name is not fictitious if it sets forth an individual's surname and the words merely describe the business being conducted, such as "Realty," "Loans," "Property Management," and other words relating to the type of business an individual is engaged in.

- Implies a partnership or corporation when a partnership or corporation does not exist
- Includes the name of a real estate salesperson
- Constitutes a violation of the provisions of Sections 17910, 17910.5, 17915 or 17917 of the Code (these Sections provide the procedures for issuance of a fictitious business name)
- Is the name formerly used by a licensee whose license has since been revoked

> **NOTE:** The general statute governing fictitious business names is contained in Section 17900 of the Business and Professions Code.

### Is the broker providing the Real Estate Transfer Disclosure Statement?

The obligation to prepare and deliver the **Real Estate Transfer Disclosure Statement** (TDS) to the prospective buyer is imposed upon the seller and the seller's broker and any broker acting in cooperation with the seller's broker. If more than one broker is involved in the transaction, the broker obtaining the offer is required to deliver the TDS to the prospective buyer, unless instructed otherwise by the seller.[17]

The TDS must be given to the prospective buyer as soon as practicable before the transfer of title, or, in the case of a **lease option**, sales contract, or **ground lease**, before the execution of the contract. If the TDS or amended TDS is delivered after the execution of an offer to purchase, the buyer has three days after delivery in person, or five days after delivery by deposit in the mail, to terminate the offer by delivering a written notice of termination to the seller or to the seller's broker.

In addition, the listing broker and the selling broker each have the duty to conduct a reasonably competent and diligent visual inspection of the property and to disclose to a prospective buyer all material facts affecting the value or desirability of the property that an investigation would reveal.

### Is the broker conducting escrows?

Section 17403.4 of the Financial Code[18] requires all written escrow instructions executed by a buyer or seller to contain a statement in not less than 10-point type which includes the license name and the name of the department issuing the license or authority under which the person is operating. Section 17403.4 does not apply to supplemental escrow instructions or modifications to escrow instructions. (For further information, see Real Estate Commissioner's Regulation 2950,[19] which sets forth prohibitive conduct associated with conducting escrows.)

### *Exemptions to the Escrow Law*

Section 17006(a) (4) of the Financial Code[20] exempts a licensed broker from the Escrow Law when:

- The broker is performing acts in the course of or incidental to a real estate transaction; and

---

[17] *California Business and Professions Code* Section 10176.5.

[18] California Financial Code Section 17403.4: http://www.leginfo.ca.gov/cgi-bin/displaycode?section=fin&group=17001-18000&file=17400-17425

[19] Regulations of the Real Estate Commissioner (As Contained in the California Real Estate Code): Title 10, Chapter 6, Article 19, Regulation 2950. http://www.calbre.ca.gov/files/pdf/relaw/2015/regs.pdf (See page 361.)

[20] California Financial Code Section 17006: http://www.calbre.ca.gov/files/pdf/refbook/ref08.pdf

- The broker is an agent or a party to the transaction; and
- The broker is performing an act for which a real estate license is required.

The exemption is personal to the broker and the broker must not delegate any duties other than duties performed under the direct supervision of the broker.

> **NOTE:** The broker's exemption provided for above is not available for any arrangement entered into for the purpose of performing escrows for more than one business.

## Broker Self-Evaluation Compliance Checklist

The Broker Self-Evaluation Compliance Checklist[21] is designed to assist you in conducting a self-evaluation of your residential real estate business activities. The checklist covers the most common violations found during CalBRE broker office surveys.

> **NOTE:** The questions on the Compliance Checklist mirror the concepts in the Broker Compliance Evaluation Manual.

The checklist is comprised of five sections:
- Licensing Compliance
- Trust Account Compliance
- Supervision
- Required Disclosures
- Record Keeping[22]

Each question in the checklist has a citation of an applicable regulation. For your reference, copies of the cited code sections are included in the checklist document.

### Questions in the LICENSING Section

1. YES/NO: Do you have a branch office license for each location from which you conduct business? (California Business and Professions Code Section 10163).
2. YES/NO: Are you operating with an unlawful fictitious business name? (Regulations of the Real Estate Commissioner Section 2731)
3. YES/NO: Are you employing salespersons without CalBRE notification? (Regulations of the Real Estate Commissioner Section 2752)
4. YES/NO: Are you employing expired/unlicensed salespersons? (California Business and Professions Code Section 10137)
5. YES/NO: Are you employing salespersons without contracts? (Regulations of the Real Estate Commissioner Section 2726)

---

[21] Downloadable from CalBRE website at http://www.calbre.ca.gov/files/pdf/forms/re540.pdf.
[22] Discussed in the *Trust Account Compliance and Record Keeping* sections in Chapter Three: Records Management and Trust Fund Handling on page 24.

### Questions in the SUPERVISION Section

1. YES/NO: Do you exercise reasonable supervision over the activities of your salespersons? (Regulations of the Real Estate Commissioner Section 2725)
2. YES/NO: Can you describe your system to monitor compliance with established policies and procedures?(Regulations of the Real Estate Commissioner Section 2725)

### Questions in the REQUIRED DISCLOSURES Section

1. YES/NO: Do you keep receipts for delivery of pest control documents? (Regulations of the Real Estate Commissioner Section 2905)
2. YES/NO: Are definite termination dates included in exclusive listings? (California Business and Professions Code Section 10176(f))
3. YES/NO: Are negotiability of commission disclosures provided? (California Business and Professions Code Section 10147.5)
4. YES/NO: Are Real Estate Transfer Disclosure Statements provided? (California Business and Professions Code Section 10176.5)

**QUIZZES ARE MANDATORY**

CalBRE regulations now require the submission of chapter quizzes before you can access the final examination. You must log in and submit the chapter quizzes online before you can access the final examination. After submitting the last chapter quiz, you will receive a link to the final examination. You were issued a Personal Identification Number (PIN) and login instructions when you enrolled.

**Chapter One Quiz**

1.    If the TDS or amended TDS is delivered after the execution of an offer to purchase, the buyer has _____, to terminate the offer by delivering a written notice of termination to the seller or to the seller's broker.

    (a)    ten days after delivery in person, or eleven days after delivery by deposit in the mail
    (b)    three days after delivery in person, or five days after delivery by deposit in the mail
    (c)    one day after delivery in person, or two days after delivery by deposit in the mail
    (d)    five days after delivery (regardless of delivery method)

2.    Which of the following statements is FALSE?

    (a)    The Real Estate Commissioner may refuse to issue a license bearing a fictitious name to a broker if the fictitious name is the name formerly used by a licensee whose license has since been revoked.
    (b)    The Real Estate Commissioner may refuse to issue a license bearing a fictitious name to a broker if the fictitious name includes the name of a real estate salesperson.
    (c)    A fictitious business name is not the same as a "dba" – (doing business as) name. It is entirely different.
    (d)    Where a licensee is a natural person, the use of a nickname in place of his or her legal given name (first name) shall not constitute a fictitious name, provided that where the nickname is used, the licensee also uses his or her surname (last name) as it appears on their real estate license, and includes their real estate license identification number.

3.    The broker must make certain that his/her agreements and forms are _____.

    (a)    not preprinted with any amount or rate of compensation
    (b)    preprinted with the amount of compensation
    (c)    preprinted in such a way that the salespeople do not need to fill in any variable information
    (d)    never used to establish the commission rate

4.      Broker Dan employs three licensees:  Two have salesperson's licenses, and one has been issued a broker's license. Which of the following statements correctly describes Dan's overall responsibility for the agents who work for him?

(a)      Dan is responsible for the activities of the salesperson licensee, but not responsible for the activities of the broker licensee.

(b)      Dan must supervise the activities of all his employees; but Dan is not responsible to ensure that the employees follow the law.

(c)      Dan's only responsibilities to his employees is to assist them if they ask for assistance.

(d)      Dan may not relinquish overall responsibility for supervision of the acts of his employees.

5.      Whenever a real estate salesperson enters the employ of a broker, the broker shall notify the commissioner of that fact within _____.

(a)      five days
(b)      24 hours
(c)      ten days
(d)      seven days

## Chapter Two: Supervision, Procedures, and Training

### Learning Objectives

Upon completion of Chapter Two, you should be able to complete the following:

- Explain the requirements for a broker to supervise all transactions involving a real estate licensee.
- Summarize the court conclusions of relevant case law concerning broker supervision.
- Summarize the court conclusions of relevant case law concerning broker's failure to supervise.
- State the requirements for supervision of restricted licensees.
- State the definition of "close supervision", and provide examples of how a broker might supervise in this manner.
- State the requirements for appointing branch or division managers, and recognize the forms that must be used for the appointment and assignment of supervisory responsibility.
- State the compliance requirements for team names and team marketing.
- Identify the Federal laws that prohibit discrimination in the workplace.
- Identify the Federal and state laws that prohibit discrimination based on race, religion, color, national origin, sex, familial status, or handicap.
- Recognize the rules of advertising, according to California Business and Professions Code sections 10140.6, 10159.5, 10235, 10235.5 and 10236.4.
- Explain the requirement for a broker to regularly and consistently report on the licensed activities of salespersons.

**Supervision of all transactions involving a real estate licensee**

In California, the broker is responsible for the actions of the licensees associated with the brokerage, so the right of the broker to control the sales methods is of utmost concern. Even though real estate salespersons are considered independent contractors when it comes to tax law and the I.R.S., for liability purposes, they are considered employees of the employing broker, because the broker is liable for their conduct.

Therefore, the broker is required to review and initial all of the contracts and documents that are associated with all transactions, and take responsibility for all of the contents of the documents.

**(Case Law) Employee or Independent Contractor?**

**[Payne v. White House Properties Inc. (1980) 112 Cal App 3d 465][23]**

Verna Lee Payne was a salesperson at White House Properties, Inc. (Brokerage). Ms. Payne and the Brokerage had a Broker-Salesperson contract whereby Ms. Payne received 100 percent commissions earned by her and paid a monthly desk rental fee and expenses incurred by her on her own behalf. This contract, along with respondent's procedures manual, set forth the terms and conditions of Ms. Payne's contractual agreement with the Brokerage. Under California law, the Brokerage was required to exercise reasonable supervision over its salespersons.

When Ms. Payne terminated her relationship with the Brokerage, she wanted to collect worker's compensation, so she filed a claim against the Brokerage to collect, contending that because she was required to conduct her business under the supervision of a Brokerage, she was technically an employee. The issues at bar were:

> (1) Was Ms. Payne an employee or an independent contractor for purposes of workers compensation?

> (2) Was Ms. Payne an employee or an independent contractor for purposes of Brokerage exercise of supervision?

***Court Conclusion #1: Eligibility for Worker's Compensation Determined Case by Case***

In most instances the real estate salesperson would be an employee for the purposes of worker's compensation, but that determination remains a question of fact, and should be determined on a case by case basis. (In this case, Ms. Payne did not present sufficient evidence to support her claim that she was an employee for purposes of worker's compensation.)

***Court Conclusion #2: Exercise of Supervision Precludes an Independent Contractor Relationship***

The court concluded that because a broker is required by law to supervise a salesperson, insofar as his/her relationship with his broker is concerned, the salesperson cannot be classified as an independent contractor. It further concluded that any contract which purports to change that relationship is invalid as being contrary to the law.

---

[23] Read the entire case from here: http://law.justia.com/cases/california/court-of-appeal/3d/112/465.html

Section 10177(h)[24] of the California Business and Professions Code requires that brokers supervise their salespeople. Exercise of supervision precludes an independent contractor relationship. Therefore, a salesperson is an employee of his or her broker regardless of what the contract with the broker claims the relationship to be.

**Violations for Failure to Supervise When Brokerage is a Corporation**

Lack of supervision on the part of a broker is a recurring problem. In case after case, CalBRE has to address the problem of real estate brokers becoming designated officers of corporations owned by salespersons or unlicensed individuals and then not properly supervising the operations.

While it is legal for brokers to become designated officers of corporations they do not own, they must remain mindful of their duty to supervise the licensed activities of the corporation. All too often, real estate brokers do not take this responsibility seriously and the public suffers as a result.

California Business and Professions Code 10159.2(a), makes the designated broker of a corporation responsible for the supervision and control of the activities conducted on behalf of the corporation by its officers and employees as necessary to secure full compliance with the provisions of [the law], including the supervision of salespersons licensed to the corporation in the performance of acts for which a real estate license is required.

### Remedy

Brokers must understand the responsibility that they take on when they become the designated officer of a corporation or allow a group of salespersons to work under their individual broker license. The absentee broker may find himself/herself not only the subject of a CalBRE disciplinary action, but also the subject of a civil lawsuit. In the end, the costs greatly outweigh any benefit received in the income that is usually paid for the use of a license.

**(Case Law) Failure to Supervise: [Holley v. Crank (9th Circuit 2004) 258 F3d 1127][25]**
*Court Conclusion: Designated broker of corporation is charged with responsibility to ensure compliance*

The designated officer/broker, not the corporate entity itself, is charged with the responsibility to assure corporate compliance with the real estate law. The conclusion that the designated officer/broker is personally responsible for supervising the salesperson's compliance with the law is supported by the legislative history of the California Business and Professions Code section 10159.2.[26]

---

[24] Section 10177 (h) of the California Business and Professions Code states in part: "The commissioner may suspend or revoke the license of any real estate licensee, or may deny the issuance of a license to an applicant, who has [violated license laws] if, as a broker licensee, failed to exercise reasonable supervision over the activities of his salesmen."

[25] Download full case here: http://caselaw.findlaw.com/us-9th-circuit/1081230.html

[26] California Business and Professions Code section 10159.2 makes the designated makes the officer designated by a corporate broker licensee responsible for the supervision and control of the activities conducted on behalf of the corporation by its officers and employees as necessary to secure full compliance. This includes the supervision of salespersons licensed to the corporation in the performance of acts for which a real estate license is required.

**(Case Law) Failure to Supervise: [Norman v. Dep't. of Real Estate, 93 Cal.App.3d 768, 776-77]**

Court Conclusion: A real estate broker must reasonably be charged with responsibility for the corporate compliance with the Real Estate Law

The California Business and Professions Code section 10211 stipulates that a person or persons applying for a corporate license to practice real estate must designate in the application an officer of the proposed corporation who holds a valid real estate broker's license. That person becomes the "designated officer" of the corporation. The purpose of this provision is to provide the public, in its dealings with real estate corporations, the same licensing protections afforded it in dealing with non-corporate real estate concerns.

### Real Estate Assistants

The responsibilities and liabilities of the brokerage mostly depend on whether the assistant is licensed or unlicensed, and whether the assistant is an independent contractor or an employee. Licensed assistants have legal status and rights commensurate with the license they hold (broker license or salespersons license); and can do any activity permitted under the California licensing statutes.

### Supervision over restricted licensees

A Restricted Real Estate Salesperson (RRES) license is issued to a person who has a history of prohibited conduct, but whose *current* conduct is lawful. The RRES license is issued only upon the condition that a broker will accept responsibility for close supervision of the licensee. When a person is issued a RRES, their real estate license is revoked,[27] and a new license (the restricted license) is issued.

> **NOTE:** Think of a restricted license like a probationary license to allow that salesperson to redeem him/herself under the auspices of a real estate broker.

The broker who accepts responsibility for the person applying for the RRES license is required to complete Form RE 552[28] or Form RE 214A[29] and certify that:

- The broker has read the decision of the Real Estate Commissioner outlining the basis under which the RRES licensee was disciplined.

- The broker will ensure that all transactional documents that the RRES licensee prepares will be reviewed and you will otherwise exercise close supervision over the licensed activity of that applicant.

### Close Supervision and Greater Burden of Responsibility for the Broker

With the greater burden of responsibility, the broker is extending the opportunity for the restricted licensee to exhibit evidence of rehabilitation which will be required at a later date should the

---

[27] Regulations of the Real Estate Commissioner (As Contained in the California Real Estate Code): Title 10, Chapter 6, Article 18.7, Regulation 2930 (3). http://www.calbre.ca.gov/files/pdf/relaw/2015/regs.pdf

[28] Downloadable from CalBRE website at http://www.calbre.ca.gov/files/pdf/forms/re552.pdf.

[29] Downloadable from CalBRE website at http://www.calbre.ca.gov/files/pdf/forms/re214a.pdf.

individual seek to petition for a license. You must ensure that your current supervising rules, policies, and procedures, are modified and amended to comply with the close supervision conditions of employment for the RRES licensee. Additional steps that the broker takes to closely supervise will be recognized as *efforts* on the part of the employing broker to exercise "close supervision".

> **NOTE:** These measures should align with the basis of the disciplinary action brought against the RRES, so it is essential that you become thoroughly familiar with the disciplinary action that brought about the license revocation.

### Examples of Close Supervision Efforts

*TRUST FUND JOURNAL*—If the RRES licensee has a history of trust fund violations, perhaps the broker can require the RRES licensee to not only complete the office trust-fund log, but complete an additional transactional and trust fund journal that is exclusive to the office manager and the broker.

*PRE-APPROVAL OF CONTRACT*—For the RRES licensee with a history of not procuring earnest money deposit checks prior to opening escrow, perhaps the broker could require that the allow the broker to pre-approved first page of the purchase contract along with a copy of the deposit check before the licensee presents the offer.

*CALL-UP SYSTEM*—If an RRES license is issued because the salesperson forgot to renew his/her license on time and continued to perform acts that require a license, the broker could institute a call-up system to ensure that the RRES has completed the continuing education courses on schedule and has filed the renewal application on time (see *Required Proof of Continuing Education* on page 20). The call-up date should be well before the expiration of RRES's license; and the broker could ensure that the continuing education is completed by prohibiting the licensee from facilitating purchase contracts or denying that licensee access to the MLS.

## Required Proof of Continuing Education for RRES Licensee

Within nine months after the effective date of the decision regarding the disciplinary action, the RRES licensee must present evidence to the Real Estate Commissioner that the licensee has, since the most recent issuance of an original or renewal real estate license, taken and successfully completed 45 hours of continuing education[30] as required for renewal of a real estate license. If the RRES licensee fails to satisfy this condition, the Commissioner may order the suspension of the restricted license until the RRES licensee presents such evidence.

## Professional Responsibility Examination Condition for RRES Licensee

Within six months after the effective date of the decision regarding the disciplinary action, the RRES must take and pass the CalBRE Professional Responsibility Examination[31] including the payment of

---

[30] California Business and Professions Code Section 10170.5 for specific education requirements.
[31] CalBRE Prof Responsibility Exam: http://www.calbre.ca.gov/files/pdf/ProfessionalResponsibilityOverview.pdf

the appropriate examination fee. If Respondent fails to satisfy this condition, the Commissioner may order suspension of the restricted license until RRES licensee passes the examination.[32]

### Roles and Responsibilities of Branch or Division managers
### (Including salespersons acting as branch or division managers)[33]

It is permissible, for a broker to appoint a real estate licensee as a branch office or division manager ("branch manager") to oversee and supervise the day-to-day operations of licensed activities in a branch or division real estate office. However, the person that the broker appoints must agree to be subject to potential sanctions and discipline from CalBRE for failure to properly supervise the activities of licensees which require a real estate license.

A real estate licensee cannot qualify to be a branch manager if he or she:

- Holds a restricted license; or
- Is or has been subject to a bar order; or
- Is a salesperson with less than two years of full-time real estate experience within five years preceding the appointment.

### What is required for the appointment?

If such an appointment is made under the terms of the new law, it must be in writing and CalBRE must be notified at the time the appointment is made and terminated.

> *Is a broker required to appoint a branch manager as allowed under section 10164 of the Business and Professions Code?*
>
> No. Such an appointment is entirely optional under the new law.

> *Is a broker allowed to appoint a branch manager in the same manner and method that he/she has always done so and not be bound by the terms of the new law?*
>
> Yes. The broker continues to have the authority to appoint a branch manager under CalBRE Regulations 2724 and 2725. However, if there is not an appointment and delegation under the new law, the broker is solely liable for failure to supervise all licensed activities conducted by the brokerage. Thus, the broker must establish policies, rules, procedures and systems that establish how the broker will personally review, oversee, inspect and manage all licensed activities of the brokerage.

---

[32] Regulations of the Real Estate Commissioner (As Contained in the California Real Estate Code): Title 10, Chapter 6, Article 18.7, Regulation 2930 (5). http://www.calbre.ca.gov/files/pdf/relaw/2015/regs.pdf (See page 354.)

[33] Advisory and Guidance to Licensees Regarding Senate Bill 510 (2011), Effective July 1, 2012, Pertaining to the Appointment by Real Estate Brokers of Branch Office or Division Managers

*If the broker appoints a branch manager, and the appointment is made in writing, will the appointment be subject to sections 10164 and 10165 of the Business and Professions Code?*

It depends on the mutual intent and understanding of the broker and the appointed branch manager. A branch manager's appointment will fall under the provisions of the newly enacted Code sections if both you and branch manager agree.

In order to make the appointment subject to the new Code sections, the appointment must be in writing, and the branch manager must agree to accept the delegated responsibility in a written contract; and CalBRE must be notified using forms RE242[34] and RE210.[35]

> **NOTE:** Even though there was and is no such requirement under CalBRE Regulations 2724 and 2725, it is arguably a prudent practice to use a written agreement for any appointment of a branch manager, whether under the new law or not.

*If the broker appoints a branch manager subject to the provisions of sections 10164 and 10165 of the Code, May CalBRE impose discipline on the branch manager's real estate license for the failure to properly supervise?*

Yes. Conversely, if a branch manager is not appointed pursuant to the new law, he or she would not be subject to CalBRE discipline for failure to supervise, and the broker would remain exclusively liable for the supervision of all licensed activities conducted by the brokerage operation.

*If the broker appoints a branch manager subject to the provisions of sections 10164 and 10165 of the Code, May CalBRE impose discipline on the broker's license for the activity or activities of salespersons or broker-associates that the branch manager was supposed to supervise?*

Yes. The broker is not relieved of his or her ultimate responsibility to supervise all licensed activities conducted under the broker's name by appointing a branch manager under sections 10164 and 10165 of the Code. However, in assessing whether the broker's license should be disciplined, CalBRE will consider whether the broker has established adequate policies, rules, procedures and systems to review, oversee, supervise, inspect and manage licensed activities for a brokerage of the size, geographic reach and scope of licensed activities.

> **NOTE:** The appointment of a branch manager subject to sections 10164 and 10165 is a relevant factor that CalBRE will consider in evaluating the sufficiency of the rules, procedures and systems.

---

[34] Downloadable from CalBRE website at http://www.calbre.ca.gov/files/pdf/forms/re242.pdf.
[35] Downloadable from CalBRE website at http://www.calbre.ca.gov/files/pdf/forms/re210.pdf.

### Why is the new law beneficial?

The new law is intended and expected to result in better supervision and more accountability to the public. If there are license disciplinary consequences to the branch manager, then an appointment of branch managers under the new law will better enable the broker to *manage the branch managers* while allowing the branch managers to manage the line level sales agents who report to him or her at the branches or division offices. When a branch manager is accountable, the branch manager tends to be more diligent with supervisory duties.

## Compliance for Salespersons working as Teams

## The Team Name[36]

AB 2018 defines a "team name" as a professional identity or brand name used by a salesperson, and one or more other real estate licensees, for the provision of real estate licensed services. AB 2018 specifies that the use of a team name does not constitute a fictitious business name and would not require a separate license if (1) the name is used by two or more real estate licensees who work together to provide licensed real estate services, or who represent themselves to the public as being a part of a team, group, or association to provide those services, (2) the name includes the *surname* (last name) of at least one of the licensee members of the team, group, or association in conjunction with the term "associates," "group," or "team," and (3) the name does not include any term or terms, such as "real estate broker," "real estate brokerage," "broker," or "brokerage" or any other term that would lead a member of the public to believe that the team is offering real estate brokerage services, or imply or suggest the existence of a real estate entity independent of a responsible broker.

### When a Team Name is used in advertising...

When a "team name" is used in advertising and solicitation materials, including print or electronic media and "for sale" signage, it must include, and display in a conspicuous and prominent manner:

- The "team name" and the name and license number of at least one of the licensed members of the team;
- The responsible broker's identity.

### The Team Name Must <u>NOT</u>

The team name must not include any term or terms, such as broker or brokerage that would lead a member of the public to believe that the team is offering real estate brokerage services, or that implies the team is operating independent of the real estate brokerage of which it is a part.

### Does CalBRE have to approve the team name?

No. Effective January 1, 2015, as long the team name is in compliance, a broker may permit salespersons to use a team name without having to submit the name to be approved as a fictitious name by CalBRE.[37]

---

[36] See  Advisory and Guidance to Licensees Regarding Senate Bill 146, Effective July 16, 2015, Pertaining to Fictitious Business Names & "Team Names"  http://www.dre.ca.gov/files/pdf/AdvisoryAB2018.pdf
[37] California Business and Professions Code Sections 10159.7

### *May a broker prohibit his/her salespersons from using a team name?*

Yes. The broker retains the right to prohibit her or his salespersons from using team names.

### *Are there special requirements when using a team name in advertising?*

Yes. If a team name is used in advertising, all the following rules apply:

- All advertising that includes the team name including print or electronic media and "for sale" signs, must include the licensee's name and license number. The name and license number must be displayed in a conspicuous manner.
- The name of the brokerage under which the members of the team are a part, must be displayed as prominently and conspicuously as the team name in all advertising.
- The advertising material must not contain any terms that imply the team is a real estate entity independent of the responsible broker.[38]

### *Does a team name still need to be registered as a fictitious name with the county?*

The cautious answer is yes. A team name appears to constitute a fictitious business name under California Business and Professions Code § 17900 (5) (c). Therefore, to avoid possible claims that the name is misleading or should have been registered, it would be advisable to register the name with the county even if it is not required to be registered with the CalBRE. However, an argument can be made that because the team name is never to be used independently of the brokerage that it may not properly constitute a fictitious name.

## Employment Discrimination

Most of the time, real estate licensees are independent contractors, so employment discrimination and its ramifications are not hot topics in most brokerages. However, if the brokerage employs administrative staff, such as receptionists, office managers or bookkeepers, employment discrimination might be an issue. Whether you agree or disagree with the laws regarding employment discrimination is immaterial. Your ability to recognize and deal with situations that most frequently cause trouble in a brokerage is your best tool for compliance.

### *Case Study*

SCENARIO: Eighty-five year-old Doris is a licensed salesperson who works for Brokerage X under Broker Vic Timis. Doris has not facilitated a sale in over a year, and Broker Vic has a written policy that all agents in the firm must facilitate at least one sale per year. After several attempts to counsel Doris and encourage more productivity, Broker Vic decides that he must sever Doris's license from the brokerage. Broker Vic calls Doris into his office and explains that he must sever her; and tells her why. He completes the severance action via the CalBRE website while Doris is sitting there. He cites her lack of productivity as his reason for severance. As Doris is leaving the office, Vic makes the statement,

> *"You are getting older now. You've earned the right to retire, and enjoy your golden years without the burden of work."*

---

[38] California Business and Professions Code Sections 10159.6

Doris's attorney tells her that her Broker Vic's conduct is out of line, and she should file a civil suit against Vic for violation of the **'Age Discrimination in Employment Act'**.

***If Doris files a civil lawsuit against Broker Vic, what is Vic's best defense?***

Vic's best defense is that he cited her lack of productivity as his reason for severance, and because Doris had not facilitated a sale in over a year, she was not in compliance with the Brokerage policy that all agents in the firm must facilitate at least one sale per year. Also, Vic should assert that his statement that she has earned the right to retire was merely an incidental statement that was made in the name of friendship after the severance had taken place. At the time the statement was made, Vic was no longer Doris's employer.

## Federal Laws that Prohibit Employment Discrimination

*CIVIL RIGHTS ACT OF 1964*—This law makes it unlawful for an employer to discriminate on the basis of race, color, religion, sex or national origin. This Act applies to any private employer with 15 or more employees in an industry affecting interstate commerce.

*AGE DISCRIMINATION IN EMPLOYMENT ACT (ADEA)*—This law prohibits discrimination against individuals aged 40 and over on the basis of age, and applies to any private employer with 20 or more employees in an industry affecting interstate commerce. When terminating an employee who is over 40, if the termination is on the basis of age, an employer may ask the employee to waive his/her rights under the ADEA, but the request must be made in writing, and the employer must provide the employee legal consideration (usually money) in exchange for agreeing to the waiver.

*CIVIL RIGHTS ACT OF 1991*—This law makes punitive damages and jury trials available to employees who are victims of discrimination.

*AMERICANS WITH DISABILITIES ACT*—This law prohibits discrimination against individuals who, with reasonable accommodations, are qualified to do the job and applies to any private employer with 15 or more full time employees.

*EQUAL OPPORTUNITY EMPLOYER ACT OF 1972*—A brokerage should make it very clear to all independent contractors and employees that the brokerage is an equal opportunity employer.

## Fair Housing Discrimination

*BROKERAGE COMPLIANCE PROGRAM AND TRAINING*—Because there is no statutory limit on punitive damages for a Fair Housing violations, non-compliance could have extreme consequences. Without comprehensive education and training of all sales associates, there is a high likelihood of a fair housing mistake. Furthermore, fair housing mistakes are almost always excluded from errors and omissions insurance policies. As a result, brokerages should adopt effective fair housing compliance programs that consist of:

- the brokerage's policy and public commitment to fair housing,
- agent education and training with regular and systematic documentation of the training,
- identification and correction of activities that might constitute fair housing violations.

**NOTE:** It is important for the brokerage to establish this compliance program before a plaintiff files a complaint or a lawsuit. Adoption of a fair housing compliance program only after a complaint is filed will be viewed as a remedial measure, but will not negate the complaint. Furthermore, a showing that the brokerage has established a compliance program will not defeat a **pattern or practice** case, nor will it defeat a claim for **punitive damages**.

### State Vs. Federal: Which Law Prevails?

As a general rule, the law that places the greatest burden or provides the greatest protection against discrimination will prevail.

*SUBSTANTIALLY SIMILAR*—If the U. S. Department of Housing and Urban Development (HUD)[39] has certified that the state or local law is substantially equivalent to the Fair Housing Act, HUD must refer complaints it receives to the appropriate state or local enforcement agency for handling.

**NOTE:** Even though the coverage of state and local fair housing laws is often different than that provided by the federal law. The protection offered by the Fair Housing Act applies across the nation, regardless of state and local laws.

### California Department of Fair Employment and Housing (DFEH)

In California, Fair Housing complaints are referred to the California Department of Fair Employment and Housing (DFEH)[40], and the majority of the complaints are handled under the purview of the that department. As a substantially equivalent agency, DFEH's findings are usually accepted by HUD.

*WHO CAN FILE A FAIR HOUSING COMPLAINT?* Complaints can be filed by individuals, the Director of DFEH, or a community organization.

### Fair Housing Complaints with the California DFEH

When a client perceives that he/she has been a victim of fair housing discrimination, that client might file a complaint with the DFEH. It is important that all real estate licensees understand the complaint process. See *DFEH Complaint Process Flowchart* on page 28 for an easy to understand flowchart of the process. Understanding practical applications of the Fair Housing Act will help ensure that the associates of the brokerage do not inadvertently violate the Fair Housing Act.

**REMEMBER:** courts have determined that a violation may be proven even if there was no intent to discriminate, as long as there is evidence of a discriminatory effect. Plus, you never know when your fair housing practices are being tested; testers from government or private groups can pose as home seekers, and their evidence is fully admissible in court.

---

[39] See: http://portal.hud.gov/hudportal/HUD
[40] California Department of Fair Employment and Housing URL: http://www.dfeh.ca.gov/.

**The Complaint Process**

*INTAKE*—Complainants are first interviewed to collect facts about possible discrimination. Interviews are normally conducted by telephone. Prior to the interview, a Pre-Complaint Questionnaire, (DFEH-700-01[41]) English or (DFEH-700-01S) Spanish, must be filled out and mailed to the Department. After the Department has received the completed questionnaire, the Department contacts the complainant to arrange the telephone interview.

*FILING AND OPPORTUNITY FOR RESOLUTION*—If the complaint is accepted for investigation, the interviewing Consultant drafts a formal complaint on the DFEH's standard form. It is signed and served on the Respondent. (For purposes of this course, the respondent would be a real estate licensee or employee of a brokerage.) If applicable, the complaint is also filed with HUD. The Respondent is required to answer the complaint and is given the opportunity to voluntarily resolve it. A **no-fault resolution** can be negotiated at any time during the complaint process.

*INVESTIGATION*—DFEH investigates every case in a standard, timely manner. DFEH has the authority to take **depositions**, issue **subpoenas** and **interrogatories** and seek **Temporary Restraining Orders** when appropriate. If the investigative findings do not show a violation of the law, DFEH will close the case.

*CONCILIATION*—Formal **conciliation** conferences are scheduled when the investigative findings show a violation of the law. During the conciliation conference, the Department presents information supporting its belief that there has been a violation and explores options to resolve the complaint. If formal conciliation fails, the Housing Administrator may recommend litigation.

*LITIGATION*—After issuing an accusation, DFEH legal staff litigates the case. Based on the option of the parties, the case may be heard before the Fair Employment and Housing Commission (FEHC) or in civil court.

*REMEDIES*—The FEHC may order remedies for:
- out-of-pocket losses
- injunctive relief
- access to the housing previously denied
- additional damages for emotional distress
- civil penalties up to $10,000 for the first violation[42]

---

[41] Download DFEH-700-01 here:
http://www.dfeh.ca.gov/res/docs/PCI/PreComplaintInquiry_Housing_fillable_2015npp.pdf.
[42] Instead of civil penalties, a court may award unlimited punitive damages.

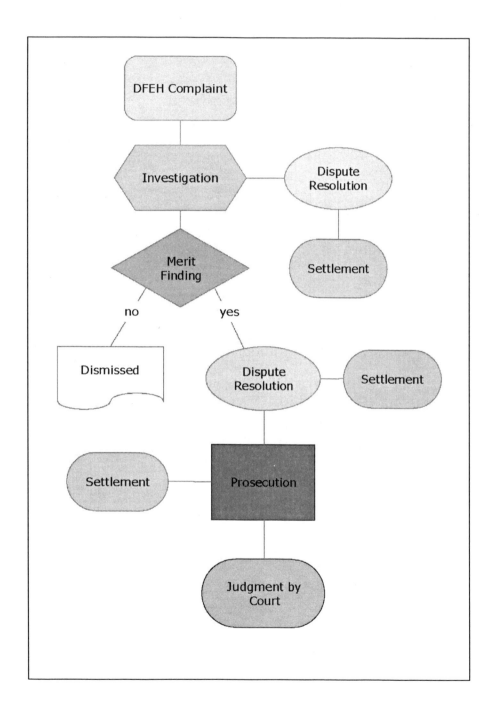

**Fair Housing Case Law: [Meyer v. Holley, 537 U.S. 280 (2003)]**[43]

In light of an opinion of the Supreme Court of the United States, the United States Court of Appeals for the Ninth Circuit has considered once again whether a broker can be liable for violations of the Fair Housing Act ("Act") based on the actions of his salespeople.

*FACTS OF THE CASE*—Mary Ellen and David Holley ("Buyers"), a mixed race couple, were looking to purchase property in Twenty-Nine Palms, California. The Buyers visited Triad, Inc., d/b/a Triad Realtor ("Brokerage") to help them with their search and spoke with Grove Crank, a Triad representative. The Broker had turned the day-to-day operation of the Brokerage over to Crank. During the Buyers' home search, Crank allegedly prevented the Buyers from purchasing a home for racially discriminatory reasons. The Buyers eventually built their own house in the town, and the home they intended to bid on sold for less than the Buyers' proposed offering price. The Buyers filed lawsuits against both the Brokerage and the Broker personally, alleging violations of the Fair Housing Act.

### Court Conclusion: Broker Can Be Liable for Salesperson's Violations of Fair Housing Act

*LIABILITY BECAUSE DUTY TO COMPLY WITH FAIR HOUSING ACT IS NON-DELEGABLE*— Broker Meyer had potential liability in his capacity as owner, president, or designated officer/broker for Crank's actions because the Broker's duty to comply with the Fair Housing Act was non-delegable.

*PERSONAL AND INDIVIDUAL LIABILITY FOR ACTIONS OF SALESPEOPLE (CRANK)*— Because a designated real estate broker in California is legally responsible for the actions of the salespeople, then the broker can be held personally liable for the actions of the salespeople. Therefore, the Broker is individually liable for the violations of the Fair Housing Act by his salespeople. Since the Broker had delegated the operation of the Brokerage to Crank, an agency relationship existed between the two and Crank had a responsibility to assure that the Brokerage was in compliance with the Act as well as state housing laws. Due to the agency relationship between the parties, the Broker could be individually liable for the actions of Crank.

**Advertising of Any Service for which a License is Required (California Business and Professions Code sections 10140.6, 10159.5, 10235, 10235.5, and 10236.4)**

**Advertising Must Disclose that Licensee is Performing Licensed Activity (Section 10140.6(a))**

A real estate licensee shall not publish, circulate, distribute, or cause to be published, circulated, or distributed in any newspaper or periodical, or by mail, any matter pertaining to any activity for which a real estate license is required that does not contain a designation disclosing that he/she is performing acts for which a real estate license is required.

**Advertising Must Contain License Identification Number (Section 10140.6(b))**

A real estate licensee shall disclose his or her license identification number and, if that licensee is a **mortgage loan originator**, the unique identifier assigned to that licensee by the Nationwide Mortgage Licensing System and Registry, on all **solicitation materials** intended to be the first point

---

[43] Download full case at:  https://www.law.cornell.edu/supct/pdf/01-1120P.ZO

of contact with consumers and on real property purchase agreements when acting as an agent in those transactions. This regulation does not apply to classified rental advertisements reciting the telephone number at the premises of the property offered for rent or the address of the property offered for rent.

### Advertising with a Fictitious Name Must Comply with Regulations

Marketing and solicitation materials, including business cards, print or electronic media and "for sale" signage, using a fictitious business name[44] shall include the responsible broker's identity in a manner equally as prominent as the fictitious business name. (See *Is the broker using an unlicensed fictitious name?* on page 10.)

Advertising, including print or electronic media and "for sale" signage, containing a fictitious business name shall include the salesperson's name and license number.

### Misleading Advertising is prohibited

No real estate licensee shall knowingly advertise, print, display, publish, distribute, telecast or broadcast, or cause or permit to be advertised, printed, displayed, published, distributed, televised or broadcast, in any manner any statement or representation with regard to the rates, terms, or conditions for making, purchasing or negotiating loans or real property sales contracts which is false, misleading or deceptive.

Indicating or otherwise implying any specific yield or return on any note other than the interest rate specified in said note shall be prima facie evidence that such advertisement is misleading or deceptive unless the advertisement sets forth the actual interest rate specified in the note and the discount from the outstanding principal balance at which it is being offered for sale.

### Advertising of Loan Must Contain License Disclosure

No real estate licensee or mortgage loan originator shall place an advertisement disseminated primarily in this state for a loan unless there is disclosed within the printed text of that advertisement, or the oral text in the case of a radio or television advertisement, the Bureau of Real Estate number and the unique identifier assigned to that licensee by the Nationwide Mortgage Licensing System and Registry under which the loan would be made or arranged.

### Regular and consistent reports of licensed activities of salespersons.

### Annual Mortgage Loan Business Activity Reports

A real estate broker who makes, arranges, or services one or more loans in a calendar year that are secured by real property containing one to four residential units, shall annually file a business activities report, within 90 days after the end of the broker's fiscal year or within any additional time as the commissioner may allow for filing for good cause. The report shall contain within its scope all of the following information for the fiscal year, relative to the business activities of the broker and those of any other brokers and real estate salespersons acting under that broker's supervision:

---

[44] In accordance with California Business and Professions Code section 10159.5. (a).

- Name and license number of the supervising broker and names and license numbers of the real estate brokers and salespersons under that broker's supervision. The report shall include brokers and salespersons who were under the supervising broker's supervision for all or part of the year.
- A list of the real estate-related activities in which the supervising broker and the brokers and salespersons under his or her supervision engaged during the prior year. This listing shall identify all of the following:

  - Activities relating to mortgages, including arranging, making, or servicing
  - Other activities performed under the real estate broker's or salesperson's license
  - Activities performed under related licenses, including, but not limited to, a license to engage as a finance lender or a finance broker or a license to engage as a residential mortgage lender or residential mortgage loan servicer.

- A list of the forms of media used by the broker and those under his or her supervision to advertise to the public, including print, radio, television, the Internet, or other means.
- For fixed rate loans made, brokered, or serviced, all of the following:

  - The total number, aggregate principal amount, lowest interest rate, highest interest rate, and a list of the institutional lenders of record. If the loan was funded by any lender other than an institutional lender, the broker shall categorize the loan as privately funded
  - (B) The total number and aggregate principal amount of covered loans

## Termination and Reporting

A real estate broker shall notify CalBRE when he/she is no longer subject to this requirement. If a broker has already made reports required by Sections 10166.07 and 10166.08 within the year, he/she shall continue reports for that year, but shall notify the department prior to the expiration of that year that he/she will no longer be subject to this requirement in the succeeding year.

## Reporting of Violations to NMLS & R 10166.15. (a)

The commissioner shall regularly report violations of this article, as well as enforcement actions taken against any mortgage loan originator to whom an endorsement has been issued, and enforcement actions taken against any individual for failure to obtain an endorsement as a mortgage loan originator, to the Nationwide Mortgage Licensing System and Registry.[45]

## Confidentiality of Reports

Except as otherwise provided in Section 1512 of the SAFE Act, the requirements under any federal or state law regarding the privacy or confidentiality of any information or material provided to the Nationwide Mortgage Licensing System and Registry, and any privilege arising under federal or state law, including the rules of any federal or state court, with respect to that information or material, shall continue to apply to the information or material after the information or material has been disclosed to the Nationwide Mortgage Licensing System and Registry. The information and material may be shared with all state and federal regulatory officials with mortgage industry oversight

---

[45] See: http://mortgage.nationwidelicensingsystem.org

authority without the loss of privilege or the loss of confidentiality protections provided by federal or state law.

(b) For these purposes, the commissioner is authorized to enter agreements or sharing arrangements with other governmental agencies, the Conference of State Bank Supervisors, the American Association of Residential Mortgage Regulators, or other associations representing governmental agencies as established by rule, regulation or order of the commissioner.

(c) Information or material that is subject to a privilege or confidentiality under subdivision (a) shall not be subject to either of the following:

- Disclosure under any federal or state law governing the disclosure to the public of information held by an officer or an agency of the federal government or the state.
- Subpoena or discovery, or admission into evidence, in any private civil action or administrative process, unless with respect to any privilege held by the Nationwide Mortgage Licensing System and Registry with respect to the information or material, the person to whom the information or material pertains waives, in whole or in part, in the discretion of the person, that privilege.

## Reporting Activities or Restricted Licensees

Respondent shall report in writing to the Bureau of Real Estate as the Real Estate Commissioner shall direct by his Decision herein or by separate written order issued while the restricted license is in effect such information concerning Respondent's activities for which a real estate license is required as the Commissioner shall deem to be appropriate to protect the public interest.

Such reports may include, but shall not be limited to, periodic independent accountings of trust funds in the custody and control of Respondent and periodic summaries of salient information concerning each real estate transaction in which the Respondent engaged during the period covered by the report.

**QUIZZES ARE MANDATORY:** Please log in and submit the chapter quizzes online.

**Chapter Two Quiz**

1.  It is permissible, for a broker to appoint _____ as a branch office or division manager ("branch manager") to oversee and supervise the day-to-day operations of licensed activities in a branch or division real estate office.

    (a)    any real estate licensee
    (b)    a licensee who holds a restricted license
    (c)    a salesperson who holds a license and has two years of full-time real estate experience within the previous five years
    (d)    any licensed or unlicensed person who is a bona fide employee of the broker

2.  Broker Hal has an office policy that prohibits the use of team names and team marketing. If Broker Hal's office policy is challenged, will the law force him to retract his policy and allow team names and team marketing?

    (a)    Yes, because CalBRE has regulations in place that govern the use of team names. Thus, it is not proper for a broker to prohibit the use of teams and team names.
    (b)    No. Broker Hal is well within his right to prohibit his salespersons from using team names and team marketing.
    (c)    Yes, because under the Regulations of the Real Estate Commissioner, a Broker cannot restrict marketing in this way.
    (d)    No, because the Regulations of the Real Estate Commissioner do not apply to teams and team marketing.

3.  If Fair Housing complaint against a real estate licensee goes through litigation, and it is determined that the real estate licensee is at fault, that real estate licensee is liable for civil penalties up to _____ if it is his/her first violation.

    (a)    $10,000
    (b)    $20,000
    (c)    $11,000
    (d)    $1,000

4.  Which of the following Federal laws applies only if the employer has 15 or more full-time employees?

    (a)    The Equal Opportunity Employer Act.
    (b)    The Americans with Disabilities Act.
    (c)    The Age Discrimination in Employment Act.
    (d)    The Civil Rights Act of 1991.

5.      According to California Business and Professions Code section 10140.6(b), a real estate
        licensee (who is not a mortgage loan originator) must disclose _____.

        (a)     his/her or her license name on real property purchase agreements when acting as
                an agent in those transactions
        (b)     his/her or her license identification number on real property purchase agreements
                when acting as an agent in those transactions
        (c)     his/her or her license identification number on all solicitation materials intended to
                be the first point of contact with consumers
        (d)     his/her or her license identification number on all solicitation materials intended to
                be the first point of contact with consumers and on real property purchase
                agreements when acting as an agent in those transactions

**Chapter Three: Records Management and Trust Fund Handling**

**Learning Objectives**

Upon completion of Chapter Three, you should be able to complete the following:

- State the statutory time frames for the retention of all transaction records.
- State the penalty for altering or destroying records.
- State the requirements for electronic record storage.
- Describe the statutory requirements form placement and handling of trust funds.
- State the penalties for mismanagement of trust funds.
- Identify the requirements for reconciling trust funds.

## Records Management

The Commissioner has an ongoing program of examining brokers' records. As necessary, audited licensees are made aware of deficiencies in record keeping and records management. If an audit discloses improper records management practice, appropriate disciplinary proceedings may be initiated.

## Transactional Documents must be retained for Three Years

According to California Business and Professions Code section 10148, a licensed real estate broker shall retain for three years copies of:

- all listings
- deposit receipts
- canceled checks
- trust records
- other documents executed by him/her or obtained by him/her in connection with any transactions for which a real estate broker license is required

The retention period shall run from the date of the closing of the transaction or from the date of the listing if the transaction is not consummated.

## Documents to be Made Available for CalBRE Audit

After notice, the books, accounts, and records shall be made available for examination, inspection, and copying by the commissioner or his or her designated representative during regular business hours; and shall, upon the appearance of sufficient cause, be subject to audit without further notice, except that the audit shall not be harassing in nature. This subdivision shall not be construed to require a licensed real estate broker to retain electronic messages of an ephemeral nature.[46]

## Possible Charge for the Audit (If the Audit Reveals a Violation)

The commissioner shall charge a real estate broker for the cost of any audit, if the commissioner has found … that the broker has violated California Business and Professions Code Section 10145[47] or a regulation or rule of the commissioner interpreting Section 10145.

## If a Broker Fails to Pay for the Cost of an Audit…

If a broker fails to pay for the cost of an audit as described in within 60 days of mailing a notice of billing, the commissioner may suspend or revoke the broker's license or deny renewal of the broker's license. The suspension or denial shall remain in effect until the cost is paid or until the broker's right to renew a license has expired.

The commissioner may maintain an action for the recovery of the cost of an audit in any court of competent jurisdiction. In determining the cost incurred by the commissioner for an audit, the

---

[46] 'Electronic messages of ephemeral nature' is defined in California Civil Code Section 1624(d).
[47] California Business and Professions Code Section 10145 pertains to handling of trust funds, interest-bearing accounts, and the statutory definition of neutral escrow.

commissioner may use the estimated average hourly cost for all persons performing audits of real estate brokers.

## Destroying, Altering, Concealing, Mutilating, or Falsifying Documents

The bureau may suspend or revoke the license of any real estate broker, real estate salesperson, or corporation licensed as a real estate broker, if the real estate broker, real estate salesperson, or any director, officer, employee, or agent of the corporation licensed as a real estate broker knowingly destroys, alters, conceals, mutilates, or falsifies any of the books, papers, writings, documents, or tangible objects that are required to be maintained by this section or that have been sought in connection with an investigation, audit, or examination of a real estate licensee by the commissioner.

## Electronic Record Storage[48]

A real estate broker may use electronic image storage media to retain and store copies of all listings, deposit receipts, canceled checks, trust records and other documents executed by him or her or obtained by him or her in connection with any transaction for which a real estate broker license is required, provided the following requirements are satisfied:

- The electronic image storage shall be nonerasable "write once, read many" ("WORM") that does not allow changes to the stored document or record.
- The stored document or record is made or preserved as part of and in the regular course of business.
- The original record from which the stored document or record was copied was made or prepared by the broker or the broker's employees at or near the time of the act, condition or event reflected in the record.
- The custodian of the record is able to identify the stored document or record, the mode of its preparation, and the mode of storing it on the electronic image storage.
- The electronic image storage system contains a reliable indexing system that provides ready access to a desired document or record, appropriate quality control of the storage process to ensure the quality of imaged documents or records, and date ordered arrangement of stored documents or records to assure a consistent and logical flow of paperwork to preclude unnecessary search time.

> **NOTE:** Records stored in electronic format are subject to the three-year retention requirement, and Section 10148 of the California Business and Professions Code.

## Means of Viewing Records that are Stored Electronically
### (Paper Copies of Documents on Request)

A broker will maintain at the broker's office a means of viewing copies of documents or records stored electronically. After notice, such documents or records shall be made available for examination, inspection, and copying by the Commissioner or his or her designated representative during regular business hours. A broker shall provide, at the broker's expense, a paper copy of any document or record requested by CalBRE.

---

[48] Regulations of the Real Estate Commissioner (As Contained in the California Real Estate Code): Title 10, Chapter 6, Article 4, Regulation 2729. http://www.calbre.ca.gov/files/pdf/relaw/2015/regs.pdf

## Retention of Documents that Contain Electronic Signatures

A real estate broker who obtains documents in connection with any transaction for which a real estate broker license is required when such documents contain an electronic signature pursuant to the Uniform Electronic Transactions Act (Section 1633.1 et seq. of the Civil Code) or the Electronic Signatures in Global and National Commerce Act shall retain a copy of such documents, including the electronic signatures. The broker shall retain a copy of such documents by:

- Causing a paper copy of the document to be made; or
- Using electronic image storage media.[49]

The broker may retain copies of such documents at a location other than the broker's place of business.

## Trust Fund Handling

Real estate brokers and salespersons receive trust funds in the normal course of doing business. They receive these funds on behalf of others, thereby creating a fiduciary responsibility to the funds' owners. Brokers and salespersons must handle, control and account for these trust funds according to established legal standards. California real estate law is very specific about how trust funds are to be handled and how records are to be maintained. While compliance with these standards may not necessarily have a direct bearing on the financial success of a real estate business, non-compliance can result in unfavorable business consequences.

## Required Placement of Trust Funds

Within three business days of brokerage receipt of the trust funds, the broker must place the funds:

- into the hands of the owner of the funds,
- into a neutral escrow depository, or
- into a trust fund account[50]

### Restriction on Interest-Bearing Trust Accounts

Except as expressly provided [by law][51], the account into which the trust funds are deposited shall not be an interest-bearing account for which prior written notice can by law or regulation be required by the financial institution as a condition to the withdrawal of funds.

### Uncashed Check Held by the Broker until Acceptance

A check received from the offeror may be held uncashed by the broker until acceptance of the offer if

---

[49] Regulations of the Real Estate Commissioner (As Contained in the California Real Estate Code): Title 10, Chapter 6, Article 4, Regulation 2729. http://www.calbre.ca.gov/files/pdf/relaw/2015/regs.pdf

[50] A trust account must be in the name of the broker or in a fictitious name if the broker is the holder of a license bearing such fictitious name, as trustee at a bank or other financial institution.

[51] By provision in California Business and Professions Code Section 10145 or by Regulations of the Real Estate Commissioner 2832.

- the check by its terms is not negotiable by the broker or if the offeror has given written instructions that the check shall not be deposited nor cashed until acceptance of the offer, and
- the offeree is informed that the check is being so held before or at the time the offer is presented for acceptance

### *Deposited within three business days of Acceptance*

If the broker holds the offeror's check until acceptance, the broker must place the check in a neutral escrow depository or the trust fund account, or into the hands of the offeree if offeror and offeree expressly so provide in writing, not later than three business days following acceptance of the offer unless the broker receives written authorization from the offeree to continue to hold the check.

### Trust Fund Handling for Multiple Beneficiaries.

The written consent of every principal who is an owner of the funds in the account shall be obtained by a real estate broker prior to each disbursement if such a disbursement will reduce the balance of funds in the account to an amount less than the existing aggregate trust fund liability of the broker to all owners of the funds.

### Trust Account Withdrawals

Withdrawals may be made from a trust fund account of an individual broker only upon the signature of the broker or one or more of the following persons if specifically authorized in writing by the broker:

(1)  A salesperson licensed to the broker;

(2)  A person licensed as a broker who has entered into a written agreement pursuant to Section 2726 with the broker;

(3)  An unlicensed employee of the broker with fidelity bond coverage at least equal to the maximum amount of the trust funds to which the employee has access at any time;

(4)  Withdrawals may be made from the trust fund account of a corporate broker only upon the signature of:

- An officer through whom the corporation is licensed pursuant to Section 10158 or 10211 of the Code; or
- One of the persons enumerated in paragraph (1), (2) or (3) above, provided that specific authorization in writing is given by the officer through whom the corporation is licensed and that the officer is an authorized signatory of the trust fund account.

> **IMPORTANT:** An arrangement under which a person enumerated in paragraph (1), (2) or (3) above is authorized to make withdrawals from a trust fund account of a broker shall not relieve an individual broker, nor the broker-officer of a corporate broker licensee, from responsibility or liability as provided by law in handling trust funds in the broker's custody.

## Trust Fund Records

Every broker must keep a record of all trust funds received, including uncashed checks held pursuant to instructions of his or her principal. The broker must maintain a record of all trust funds received and disbursed for *each account* that contains trust funds.

### Information Required for the Records

The record shall set forth in chronological sequence the following information in columnar form:

- date trust funds received
- from whom trust funds received
- amount received
- with respect to funds deposited in an account, date of said deposit
- with respect to trust funds previously deposited to an account, check number and date of related disbursement
- with respect to trust funds not deposited in an account, identity of other depository and date funds were forwarded
- daily balance of said account

### Generally Accepted Accounting Principles

Maintenance of journals of account cash receipts and disbursements, or similar records, or automated data processing systems, including computer systems and electronic storage and manipulation of information and documents, in accordance with generally accepted accounting principles, shall constitute compliance [with the law] provided that such journals, records, or systems contain the [legally required] elements and that such elements are maintained in a format that will readily enable tracing and reconciliation in accordance with Section 2831.2 (see *Trust Account Reconciliation* page 43).

### No Records Required for Checks Less than $1000 Made Payable to Third Parties

A broker is not required to keep records pursuant to this section of checks which are written by a principal, given to the broker and made payable to third parties for the provision of services, including but not limited to escrow, credit and appraisal services, when the total amount of such checks for any transaction from that principal does not exceed $1,000. Upon request of CalBRE or the maker of such checks, a broker shall account for the receipt and distribution of such checks. A broker shall retain for three years copies of receipts issued or obtained in connection with the receipt and distribution of such checks.

### Separate Record Required for Each Beneficiary or Transaction

A broker shall keep a separate record for each beneficiary or transaction, accounting for all funds which have been deposited to the broker's trust bank account and interest, if any, earned on the funds on deposit.[52]

---

[52] Regulations of the Real Estate Commissioner Title 10, Chapter 6, Article 15, Section 2831.1

## Improper Handling of Trust Funds

Improper handling of trust funds is cause for revocation or suspension of a real estate license, not to mention the possibility of being held financially liable for damages incurred by clients.

## CalBRE Comprehensive Publication about Handling Trust Funds – Great Resource!

CalBRE has created a comprehensive publication[53] that discusses the legal requirements for receiving and handling trust funds in real estate transactions as set forth in the Real Estate Law and the Regulations of the Real Estate Commissioner. It describes the requisites for maintaining a trust fund bank account and the precautions a licensee should take to ensure the integrity of the account. It is a great resource to become knowledgeable about the trust fund requirements.

### *How should a brokerage handle an earnest money check which is to be deposited into escrow upon acceptance of the offer?*

A brokerage may hold the check until the offer is accepted and then deposit the funds into escrow, but only when directed to do so by the buyer. Also, if this is the practice, the broker must disclose to the seller that the check is being held in uncashed form. In such cases, it is good practice to include such a disclosure in the purchase contract. The brokerage must keep a columnar record of:

- the receipt of the check,
- the name of the escrow company, and
- the date the check was forwarded to the escrow depository

### *Must a broker-owner of rental properties place security deposits in a trust account?*

No. Money the broker-owner receives on his/her own property is received as funds payed to a principal, not funds paid to an agent. As such, these are not trust funds and should not be placed in the trust account.

### *Must a brokerage keep a deposit receipt signed only by the buyer at the time of the offer, and rejected by the seller?*

Yes. Records of rejected offers must be retained for three years.

### *Must a brokerage maintain separate trust fund accounts for property management collections and earnest money deposits?*

Since property management funds usually involve multiple receipt of funds and several monthly disbursements, CalBRE suggests that separate trust fund accounts be maintained for property management funds and earnest money deposits. However, all trust funds can be placed in the same trust fund account as long as separate records for each trust fund deposit and disbursement are maintained properly and the account is not an interest-bearing account.

---

[53] Downloadable from CalBRE website: http://www.calbre.ca.gov/files/pdf/re13.pdf.

*If the buyer and seller decide to go directly to escrow and the buyer makes out a check to the escrow company and hands it directly to the escrow clerk, must the brokerage maintain any records of this check?*

No. A brokerage must maintain records only of trust funds which pass through the hands of employees or agents of the brokerage for the benefit of a third party.

*How long must a brokerage keep deposit receipts?*

Deposit receipts must be maintained for three years.

## Trust Fund Record Keeping Violations

Trust fund handling and record keeping is one of the most common problem areas. We see case after case in which brokers handle trust monies on behalf of others and either convert the monies to their own use, or do not have the expertise to maintain proper accounting records and end up with shortages in their trust accounts. To avoid problems in this area, all real estate brokers should be familiar with the laws and regulations that govern the handling of trust funds by real estate brokers.[54]

### Two Common Reason for Deficiencies in Trust Fund Records

*LACK OF KNOWLEDGE*—The most common problem found among brokers who maintain poor trust fund records is a lack of knowledge of what the law requires in the area of trust fund record keeping and a lack of basic bookkeeping or accounting skills. Brokers often attempt to handle large amounts of trust funds without any specific training in the area. This often results in a trust fund disaster. Brokers should understand that simply because they are able to handle large amounts of trust funds by virtue of their license, it doesn't necessarily follow that they should. Before accepting any trust funds, brokers should make sure that they have the proper knowledge and skills necessary to handle and account for the trust funds that are received in their business operations. The level of knowledge and skill that is necessary will vary with the type of operation and the amount of trust funds that are handled. Brokers must be able to recognize the limitations of their knowledge and skills as their business operations expand and either get further training or hire professionals with appropriate training.

*LACK OF SUPERVISION*—A second common problem found among brokers who maintain poor trust fund records is a general lack of supervision over their trust fund operations. It is common to find brokerage operations where the responsible broker has simply turned this aspect of the operation over to office personnel. A broker must always exercise vigilant and consistent oversight of the trust fund operation to ensure that there is compliance with the law.

## Trust Fund Conversion and the Potential for Criminal Prosecution

Of even more concern than poor record keeping, are trust fund shortages resulting from the deliberate conversion of trust funds for personal use by the broker or by employees of the broker. When this occurs, it is taken very seriously. Real estate brokers who are found to have converted

---

[54] California Business and Professions Code, Section 10145, General statute governing the handing of trusts funds and Regulations of the Real Estate Commissioner.
Regulation 2831.1 - Maintaining separate records for each beneficiary.
Regulation 2831.2 - Performing monthly reconciliation of trust fund accounts.
Regulation 2834 - Allowing unlicensed and unbonded signatories on a trust account.

trust funds can be assured that disciplinary action will be taken against their license. Also, the potential for criminal prosecution exists.

**Trust Account Reconciliation at Least Once per Month**

The balance of all separate beneficiary or transaction records must be reconciled with the record of all trust funds received and disbursed at least once a month, except in those months when the bank account did not have any activities. A record of the reconciliation must be maintained, and it must identify the bank account name and number, the date of the reconciliation, the account number or name of the principals or beneficiaries or transactions, and the trust fund liabilities of the broker to each of the principals, beneficiaries or transactions.

**QUIZZES ARE MANDATORY:** Please log in and submit the chapter quizzes online.

**Chapter Three Quiz**

1. A real estate broker can store records electronically as long as _____.

    (a)    electronic records are backed up on a monthly basis
    (b)    the broker is able to provide a paper copy of any document or record requested by the CalBRE
    (c)    the electronic image storage media is an erasable, "read-write" file that allows changes to the stored document or record
    (d)    records copied and stored in electronic format are retained for one year

2. When a broker keeps records electronically, the program he would use for record retrieval is a _____ program.

    (a)    RAM
    (b)    SCORE
    (c)    WORM
    (d)    DOS

3. A broker is not required to keep trust fund records of checks written by a principal, and made payable to third parties for the provision of services, when the total amount of such checks for any transaction from that principal does not exceed _____.

    (a)    $5000
    (b)    $100
    (c)    $1000
    (d)    $500

4. If the broker holds the offeror's earnest money check until acceptance, the broker must place the check in a neutral escrow depository or the trust fund account, or into the hands of the offeree within _____ following acceptance of the offer, unless the broker receives written authorization from the offeree to continue to hold the check

    (a)    three business days
    (b)    five calendar days
    (c)    one business day
    (d)    36 hours

5. Broker Shawn owns several rental properties which are managed by the property management division of Shawn's brokerage; and the tenants pay their rent directly to Shawn. The funds should **NOT** be _____.

    (a)    deposited to an account that Shawn holds jointly with her husband
    (b)    deposited to Shawn's personal account
    (c)    spend on personal purchases
    (d)    deposited to the broker trust account

# Notes